CONFLICTING MEMORIES
ON THE "RIVER OF DEATH"

Conflicting Memories
on the
"River of Death"

The Chickamauga Battlefield and the
Spanish-American War, 1863–1933

Bradley S. Keefer

The Kent State University Press
KENT, OHIO

© 2013 by The Kent State University Press, Kent, Ohio 44242

All rights reserved

Library of Congress Catalog Card Number 2012013525

ISBN 978-1-60635-126-0

Manufactured in the United States of America

Library of Congress Cataloging-in-Publication Data

Keefer, Bradley S.

Conflicting memories on the "river of death" : the Chickamauga Battlefield and the Spanish-American War, 1863–1933 / Bradley S. Keefer.

p. cm.

Includes bibliographical references and index.

ISBN 978-1-60635-126-0 (hardcover : alk. paper) ∞

1. Chickamauga and Chattanooga National Military Park (Ga. and Tenn.)—History.

2. Chickamauga, Battle of, Ga., 1863.

3. Chattanooga, Battle of, Chattanooga, Tenn., 1863.

4. Battlefields—Conservation and restoration—United States—Case studies.

5. Historic preservation—United States—Case studies. I. Title.

E475.81.K44 2012

973.7'359—dc23

2012013525

British Library Cataloging-in-Publication data are available.

17 16 15 14 13   5 4 3 2 1

Dedicated to the memory of
Mom, Dad, Grandma Fay, and all the "Old Boys"
who still stand guard over their battlefields

Contents

Illustrations

Preface and Acknowledgments

When I started this project ten years ago I was interested in getting to the bottom of one burning question: Why is Chickamauga not like Gettysburg? Offhand, the answer seemed simple. Gettysburg is one of the most well-known, and certainly one of the more important, events in American history; therefore its battleground could reasonably be considered one of the most sacred places in the country. President Abraham Lincoln suggested as much in his famous speech in November, 1863. If we accept that reasoning as valid (which we will do, in spite of much evidence to the contrary), then two further questions arise. First, how did Gettysburg acquire that sacredness? Second, why didn't this other important 1863 battle and its blood-stained ground achieve this same status? In other words, was there something about Gettysburg that was lacking on the battlefield at Chickamauga that made it special? Or, did something happen to the Chickamauga landscape that made it less likely to be remembered and venerated? Numerous other scholars have tackled the first part of this dilemma by carefully studying and analyzing the creation of the Gettysburg National Military Park and the larger-than-life myths that make it a shrine to thousands of historians, buffs, reenactors, and tourists. This study grapples with the second question by looking at the history of the Chickamauga and Chattanooga National Military Park from the time of the battle in 1863 through the twentieth-century aftermath of the War Department's intensive military use of the landscape as a training ground in 1898.

In the course of my research, I have discovered that making sacred ground out of a Civil War battlefield was not that difficult, particularly when the veterans of the battle had the means and desire to carry out the task. The tricky, and often controversial part, was imbuing the landscape with meaning and preserving those meanings in the face of outside forces, unforeseen threats, and the passage of time. The Chickamauga battlefield has endured more than a century and a half of use—and occasional abuse—at the hands of soldiers, farmers, the forces of nature, technology, and the general public. Throughout it all, the landscape has retained many of the characteristics that the battle's veterans bestowed on it at the turn of the century. The monuments, markers, cannons, woods, and fields are restored and maintained much as they were in 1895. Although there is urban sprawl nearby, the Chickamauga battlefield is surprisingly devoid of modern development; the garish double-decker tour buses, licensed guides, and NPS-approved reenactors that are so prevalent at Gettysburg are mostly absent at Chickamauga. In short, there seems to be nothing about this battlefield that would suggest why it has failed to maintain the same hold on the imagination as Gettysburg.

As is often the case, what I discovered in the process of trying to answer the initial question became the main focus of the story. The use of the Chickamauga battlefield during the Spanish-American War (and its subsequent uses during the World Wars) may or may not explain why it is not as revered as Gettysburg. What is apparent is that its Civil War meanings and memories kept reemerging after each disruptive use and continue to dominate the landscape today. It is also clear that although mentioning the Battle of Chickamauga often draws blank looks from anyone outside the Civil War community, trying to explain Camp George H. Thomas to most people requires an even more elaborate back story. Even though the Battle of Chickamauga is no Gettysburg, it still holds a place in the nation's historical consciousness that probably surpasses our memories of the entire War with Spain and the Philippine Insurrection put together.

There are dozens of conflicts around the "River of Death." Some of them, like the battle of Chickamauga, were physical encounters; many more were differing memories between armies, generals, soldiers, and civilians who had a stake in the events that took place on that landscape. The comparisons between Gettysburg and Chickamauga make up one of those conflicting memories, but in spite of the deeply rooted origins of that rivalry, it is not the most important. What emerges from this study is a deeper set of questions about the construction and preservation of collective memories and what happens when contradictory memories collide over differing interpretations of a specific geographic environment. Places have meaning; whether those meanings are derived from nature, bestowed upon them by people, or created by events, they are in flux and changeable due to time, place, and perspective. Chickamauga Creek may have been a sacred place to the Cherokee, but the land around it was also sanctified by the blood and sacrifice of the soldiers who fought there in 1863. The memories carved in stone by the veterans on that battlefield have persevered over time and withstood numerous challenges over the ground's appropriate uses and meaning. Several of these challenges make up the focus of this book.

I have been fortunate that so many people kept pushing me to finish this project in spite of my well-known tendency to procrastinate. My first set of thanks goes to the group of Kent State Stark Campus friends and colleagues who encouraged me to pick something "big" that would make an impact in the field. Led by my Shawnee brother Miyaa8we and Leslie Heaphy, they have never wavered in their support and encouragement. They, along with my "sister" Mary Beth (a Keefer by choice, rather than birth), provided valuable input during the revision of the manuscript. I must also thank Tom Sosnowski and the assistant deans at both the Stark and Ashtabula Campuses for giving me schedules and load lifts that allowed me to maintain the balance between teaching, work, and play for the past fifteen years. I would be remiss if I did not acknowledge the Ohio Academy of History for its 2006 Outstanding Dissertation Award, which brought this project to the attention of Kent State University Press; and Dr. Timothy Smith, whose encouragement and recent work on National Military Parks confirmed the importance and uniqueness of my topic. I owe a big thanks to the staff at the Press, particularly Joyce Harrison, for seeing me through the process of getting it into print. I am especially grateful to James Ogden III and the staff at the Chickamauga and Chattanooga National Military Park for giving me access to their archives and to the folks at the Chattanooga-Hamilton County Bicentennial Library for tolerating the trail of debris I left from their clipping files to the copy machine and being so generous in reproducing photos from their collection. The folks at the East Tennessee Historical Society in Knoxville, Marie at the Chattanooga History Center, and Dave at Eastern National also contributed to the research and publication of this book.

Finally, it is regrettable that the culmination of this project comes after the passing of those who would have taken the most pride in it. To Dad, Mom, Granny, Auntie, and too many others who have left this earthly plane before I was ready to see them go, I can only say "thanks" and add, "I'm sorry it took so long."

BSK

INTRODUCTION

"The Battlefields are the Memories"

T his is a book about a battle, three armies, two wars, and one battlefield. It is a story of heroism and despair, victory and defeat, reconciliation and rejection. It spans nearly seventy years and includes four U.S. presidents, several secretaries of war, a host of generals, and thousands of regular Americans from all walks of life who found themselves, for better or worse, in the service of their country. It touches on themes like reunion, duty, manhood, loyalty, and courage. It deals with memories and the values, images, and meanings that go with those memories, and examines the actual, physical landscapes associated with them. Most of all, it tells the story of what happens when one group of soldiers disagrees with another on the meaning and importance of the same piece of sacred ground.

The Battle of Chickamauga was one of several large, bloody battles fought during America's Civil War. It was the key event in a military campaign involving the Union Army of the Cumberland, led by Maj. Gen. William S. Rosecrans and the Confederate Army of Tennessee under Gen. Braxton Bragg, that began in July and ended in late November, 1863. While there was other fighting near Chattanooga, Tennessee, during this important series of events, the monumental struggle along Chickamauga Creek—the "River of Death"—on September 19 and 20 is the focus of this story. After the skillful capture and occupation of Chattanooga in early September, Rosecrans pushed his army of 60,000 men into northern Georgia in pursuit of Bragg's retreating forces. Taking advantage of strong reinforcements, including elements from Robert E. Lee's Army of Northern Virginia, Bragg's larger, veteran army unexpectedly attacked Rosecrans as he frantically reassembled his scattered divisions on the road back to Chattanooga.

The resulting two-day battle was filled with incredible carnage, intense drama, unforeseen disaster, and memorable heroics. After a bloody stalemate in the woods and creek bottoms on the first day, Bragg's army launched relentless but futile attacks against the Union lines on the second morning. Just before noon, an error by Rosecrans allowed the Confederates to achieve a massive breakthrough that routed half the Union army, including its commanding general. However, the remaining Federal forces, led by Maj. Gen. George H. Thomas, occupied high ground on Snodgrass Hill, where they repulsed repeated Confederate attacks and managed to withdraw in good order back to the defenses of Chattanooga. Bragg's victory was incomplete and his subsequent attempt to lay siege to Chattanooga was a dismal failure. His army was routed by the Army of the Cumberland—with help from reinforcements led by generals Joseph Hooker, Ulysses S. Grant, and William T. Sherman—at the Battles of Lookout Mountain and Missionary Ridge in late November, 1863.

In terms of the numbers of troops involved and the casualties suffered by both armies, the battles of Chickamauga and Chattanooga were among the largest of the war. In addition to the luminaries mentioned above, this campaign also included famous characters like Lee's "War Horse" James Longstreet; the hero of Cedar Creek, Philip Sheridan; future President of the United States James Garfield, and Gen. John Bell Hood, who led the Army of Tennessee to its destruction late in the war. The outcome of this campaign cost both Rosecrans and Bragg their commands and propelled Grant to even higher rank as the commander of all Union armies for the rest of the war. There are numerous published accounts and historical works on this battle that testify to its importance among both the veterans and modern historians who study the Civil War. Yet, somehow, this campaign and these battles don't really resonate in our broad understanding of the war. Sandwiched between Gettysburg and Vicksburg in 1863 and the Atlanta and Overland Campaigns during 1864, the actions around Chattanooga are easily relegated to a secondary level in the popular memory of the war. It is the memory, not the history, of this campaign that is the focus of much of this study.[1]

A growing number of scholars identify collective memories as one of the ways that societies give meaning in the present to events from the past. The origins of memory studies are rooted in the work of sociologists and anthropologists, who use the concept of collective memory to analyze class, ethnicity, and other types of group identities within the context of the social sciences.[2] Groups of people construct collective memories by combining the documented, recorded events of the past with the often selective recollections of the event's participants and other members of their particular community. As the participants grow older and their ability to recall the actual events becomes increasingly less effective, the rituals and ceremonies that commemorate those past events become more important in determining *if* and *how* they are remembered. Eventually, the group's memories and recollections become intertwined with the documented facts as part of the "imagined" history of the community. Although the formal study and preservation of history often depends on memory, some collective memories become more a part of a community's heritage (its mythical, imagined past) than its actual history (the documented, researchable past). As is often seen in both postwar and modern accounts of the American Civil War, the terms "heritage" and "tradition" are often used interchangeably to promote specific interpretations of the war and reinforce the values they represent.[3]

In recent years, a significant number of American historians have added their perspectives to the topic of collective memory in the United States, particularly as it applies to conflicting cultural values such as patriotism, loyalty, and ethnic, regional, or national identity.[4] One of the striking elements contained within the range of memory theories is the role that contradictory and conflicting perspectives play in the overall process of memory construction. There is often a clear distinction between official/civic memories and the more vernacular/popular memories held by specific groups within a society. Since memory is often tied to identity, the more diverse and heterogeneous a society, the more potential exists for conflicting memories. Thus, official memories attempt to create homogeneity by focusing on events, myths, and values that are common to the majority; while vernacular memories uphold unique or contrary views held by a subgroup or minority. John Bodnar defines public memory as "the intersection of official and vernacular cultural expression" that "help[s] a . . . society understand both its past, present, and, by implication, its future." Unlike historical facts, memories of past events can be altered, manipulated, or forgotten by one or more segments in a community in response to the needs of a changing, dynamic present.[5]

This study focuses on several sets of conflicts over the construction and maintenance of memories surrounding the Battle of Chickamauga and the military park its veterans created on the battlefield landscape. The first disagreements have to do with the battle itself, its results and significance, and the "heroes" and "villains" from both of the primary armies involved. The meaning of the Battle of Chickamauga was clouded almost immediately by controversies on both sides. Although half of the Union force was driven from the field, the inspiring stand on Snodgrass Hill saved the Army of the Cumberland from annihilation and prevented an immediate Confederate thrust toward Chattanooga. However, when the Union forces achieved final victory two months later on Missionary Ridge, the Army of the Cumberland's role in the successful rout of the enemy was overshadowed by the presence of Grant, Sherman, and elements from other Union armies. The crushing failure of the Confederate Army of Tennessee to make the most of its win at Chickamauga left a lasting stain on the record of that troubled army. The mixed results of this campaign make both the historical record and the construction of memory even more complicated.

The most important participants involved in the construction of Civil War memories were the veterans of both the Union and Confederate armies. After a period of readjustment to civilian life, they were motivated by the need to bond with former comrades and preserve the record of their own deeds, along with those of their commanders and the units in which they served. By the last decades of the nineteenth century, the veterans sought to solidify their role as community leaders in a rapidly changing industrial society beset by new and alarming problems. By exploiting their status as the "greatest generation," the veterans of the Civil War worked to preserve the memories of their accomplishments and place them into a context that promoted the values that they (and many others) believed were in the nation's best interests.

As David Blight has shown in his excellent 2001 work *Race and Reunion,* these veterans led a movement toward sectional reconciliation that, by the 1890s, had largely succeeded in healing the nation and reuniting the white populations of the North and South. Although this reconciliation came at the expense of African-Americans, who remained a marginalized and exploited minority, it helped construct a lasting national (official) memory of the war that softened decades of bitter sectional controversy. By the time the United States entered the War with Spain in 1898, many white Northerners and Southerners had found common ground in their heroic, sentimentalized memories of the conflict. This view of the sectional conflict influenced historians and the public to such an extent that it still dictates some of the ways present-day Americans remember the war.[6]

On the eve of its sesquicentennial, hundreds of thousands of Americans are actively engaged in reenacting the battles, studying the documents, collecting the artifacts, and preserving the battlefields of the Civil War. In many ways, society's current efforts to uphold the legacy of the War Between the States still closely reflect the memories and perspectives of the war's active and influential veterans. Intensely partisan Civil War reenactors join forces to recreate the lifestyles and battles of both Union and Confederate soldiers without making specific references to slavery as the war's primary cause or the consequences of the war and Reconstruction on African-Americans. Civil War roundtables, popular periodicals, television programs, documentaries, and commercial films often emphasize the importance of famous leaders and battles—like Lee at Gettysburg—over others. Those who defend the use of Confederate flags, slogans, and emblems echo the rhetoric of the war's veterans with terms like "honor," "courage," and "heritage," while stubbornly denying the ugly realities of racism and sectionalism that continue to surround those symbols.[7]

An important component of the ongoing construction of memory is the association between significant events and the locations where they occurred. These physical landscapes provide a focal point for the rituals and commemorative activities that people perform to reinforce memories of the past. The most obvious commemorative landscapes are cemeteries and battlefields; but historic birthplaces, homes, bridges, or the sites of violence or tragedy are often used as the focal point for ongoing memory construction. Geographer Kenneth Foote describes the gradual process of sanctification through which sites of violence or tragedy are made "sacred" by members of the community. Foote explains that the ways people modify and sanctify a specific landscape are important for "symbolizing and sustaining collective values over long periods of time." These "help sustain memory and cultural traditions" that might otherwise be lost or forgotten.[8]

Part of the process of sanctification that separates truly sacred ground from other types of landscape is the emphasis on commemorative uses and the corresponding exclusion of other activities on the ground. Whereas cemeteries automatically imply a dominant and solemn commemorative purpose, restored houses, historic birthplaces, and even battlefields are often used for education, entertainment, recreation, relaxation, office space, or to store and display artifacts. Public access to sacred ground via roads, pathways, trams, tour buses, and the like, combined with the various ways that historians and staff interpret the site, can combine to compromise its sacred status. The story of the Chattanooga and Chickamauga National Military Park during the War with Spain illustrates how the construction of powerful collective memories, the sanctification of a site by one group of veterans, and the introduction of disruptive, non-commemorative activities related to another war can produce some contradictory and conflicting images of the landscape, the soldiers involved, and the wars themselves.

At a 2002 conference in Chattanooga, Tennessee, conducted by the Civil War Preservation Trust (CWPT), the featured speaker, National Park Service (NPS) historian Dennis Frye, used the issues surrounding battlefield preservation to frame a discussion of memory and its importance to American history. After establishing that the "past provokes [the] present," he went on to remind the audience that "the battlefields ARE the memories."[9] Throughout the long process of memory construction, one of the most traditional, effective, and ongoing ways to construct and enhance national memories of the Civil War has been through the preservation of its battlefields as "sacred landscapes." By the 1890s, Civil War veterans had recognized that by building monuments documenting their accomplishments on the actual battlefields, they could permanently share their memories of comradeship and combat with fellow veterans and the public. To help gain control of the land on which these battles were fought, the veterans constructed collective memories that passionately invoked images of duty, heroic bloodshed, and selfless sacrifice. Having established their claim to both the memories and the landscape, the veterans then created partnerships with local and state governments, community business interests, and the U.S. Congress to obtain support, funding, and official recognition for their newly created battlefield parks.

The preservation of this sacred ground and the memories of heroism that went with it seemed particularly important within the rapidly changing society of the late nineteenth century. Many Americans, disturbed by industrialism, immigration, populism, labor unrest, urbanism, and other social problems, looked to the Civil War generation to find examples of leadership, sacrifice, and truly admirable "American" values. Not only did Civil War battlefields represent sites of past courage and sacrifice by American fighting men (often with little real distinction between Union and Confederate "heroes"), but they served as symbolic bastions against the scourge of immigration and commercialism that threatened to overwhelm Americans' heritage as a distinct people with a clearly identifiable past. Thus, the study of the creation, development, and preservation of sacred landscapes is not only relevant for understanding the Civil War generation's efforts to construct its own memories, but explains why American society often continues to use many of the same methods, rhetoric, and images to uphold both the history and heritage of important events and ideas in the face of disruptive social change.[10]

The veterans of Chickamauga and Chattanooga responded to the ambiguous and controversial outcome of their campaign by identifying, preserving, and sanctifying their own sacred landscape. Due in large part to the efforts of former Confederates, local civic leaders, and members of the Society of the Army of the Cumberland, the battlefield became the first National Military Park authorized by the Congress in 1890. It was officially dedicated by veterans from both sides on the anniversary of the battle in September of 1895. The Chickamauga and Chattanooga National Military Park was primarily conceived, planned, and sanctified by surviving members and reunion groups from both armies. In spite of controversies surrounding the battle (not only between the Union and Confederate veterans, but among the former commanders and participants within both armies), the battlefield park ultimately reflected a spirit of reconciliation and mutual respect. In the minds of both Union and Confederate veterans, the landscape itself had been set aside as "sacred" ground in recognition of their sacrifices, which made it off-limits to most commercial development and non-related uses. More importantly, the battlefield landscape at Chickamauga acted as the central point for the preservation of memory, where both veterans and civilians could "experience" history and draw inspiration from the patriotism, heroism, and sacrifice of their countrymen.

An additional element that influenced the carefully constructed merger of landscape and remembrance at Chickamauga was an 1896 codicil added to the original enabling legislation that allowed the use of the battlefield park as a site for military study and training. In the context of Civil War memory in the 1890s, this was a perfectly reasonable idea. Since the major battles of the Civil War were the largest ever fought on the North American continent and had been planned and executed by some of America's most storied commanders, it seemed logical that they be the objects of study for future generations of military leaders. For the veterans of the Union Army of the Cumberland, it gave them a chance to highlight the accomplishments of their most successful, but often underappreciated commander, George Thomas—the "Rock of Chickamauga." In addition to the tactical lessons offered by studying the battle, the popular belief that Civil War soldiers provided ideal models of patriotism and courage in a changing society also provided a reason for allowing a new generation of officers, cadets, and soldiers to prowl the battlefields of their grandfathers and fathers. This non-commemorative activity might have been only a minor disruption if use of the park had been limited to a Regular Army or National Guard unit once or twice a year. However, in 1898, bigger events overwhelmed the Chickamauga battlefield, threatened its status as sacred ground, and challenged the Civil War veterans for control over the memories associated with its landscape.

At its outset, the Spanish-American War provided a perfect opportunity for aging Civil War veterans to uphold and manipulate public memories of their own war. The racial, gender, and patriotic rhetoric that surrounded the United States' long dispute with Spain over Cuba played nicely into the reconciliatory spirit of the Civil War reunions that white veterans were regularly holding on or near mostly southern battlefields. The outbreak of war in April 1898 and President William McKinley's call for 125,000 state volunteers conjured up echoes of the "Spirit of '61" for the Civil War generation, and many of them enthusiastically raised their voices in support of the war effort. Thus, the veterans generally applauded the War Department's plan to use Chickamauga Park as a major camp of rendezvous and instruction for dozens of volunteer regiments preparing for the invasion of Cuba. After all, by exposing thousands of young men to their own sacred ground, Civil War veterans could reinforce their own patriotic role and make an important contribution to the current war effort. At this point, the interests of the Civil War veterans (many of whom were serving at all levels of government and in the military) and the government agencies (which considered the Civil War generation a valuable political and economic constituency) were fairly well aligned.

After a promising start in May, the situation at the training camp went from bad to worse; by August, nearly 700 men had died in a typhoid fever epidemic. On top of that, only a small percentage of the 60,000 troops that made up this volunteer army got out of Georgia before the war abruptly ended in an American victory. Tracing the disruption and subsequent fallout caused by the War

Department's alleged mismanagement of Camp George H. Thomas allows us to analyze the impact of this dirty, disease-ridden installation on the "sacred" landscape created by Civil War veterans. Once it was clear that the soldiers in Camp Thomas did not treat the memorial park with enough respect, the Civil War veterans worked tirelessly to defend its positive qualities and restore the physical and symbolic integrity of their commemorative landscape. Conversely, thousands of Spanish-American War soldiers saw Chickamauga in a completely different, and largely negative, light. Their memories of the battlefield landscape revolved around the tedium and suffering of a military experience that produced no opportunities for heroism and a large number of useless and non-glorious deaths.

Ultimately, the ability of the Civil War veterans to denounce the recent occupants of the park as complainers and regain control of their commemorative landscape illustrates the contrasts between groups of veterans over the memory of "popular" and "unpopular" wars in the twentieth century. Since Camp Thomas was a negative experience for many of its veterans, the memories surrounding it became decidedly ambiguous and unclear. Likewise, the controversies and political fallout stemming from the health problems among the troops in Cuba, the controversial treaty with Spain, and the ongoing conflict in the Philippines influenced the construction of memories for the entire Spanish-American War. This resulted in a one-sided restoration and reinterpretation of the park that reflected only the landscape's Civil War associations. In the long run, Spanish-American War veterans found themselves unable to establish a lasting set of national memories beyond those associated with the battleship *Maine* and Teddy Roosevelt's Rough Riders at San Juan Hill. The inefficient and disease-riddled camp at Chickamauga and the short, messy little war that spawned it were easily forgotten by a nation moving rapidly into the new century.

Until recently most of the studies looking at the creation of battlefield parks focused on Gettysburg as the best representation of the Civil War's most "sacred ground." Carol Reardon's 1997 study, which explored the ongoing process of memory construction that created the legend of Pickett's Charge and the "High Water Mark," opened the door for a flurry of books and articles on the subject. Edward Linenthal includes Gettysburg in his 1993 review of America's most important landscapes, while numerous other historians have devoted book-length studies to the creation of the battlefield park and its role as one of the nation's primary shrines to American heroism.[11] The scholarship of battlefield studies has grown since Timothy Smith added to his impressive body of work on the Shiloh battlefield with a study that recounts the creation of the first five National Military Parks during the 1890s, and *A Chickamauga Memorial* in 2009, which goes into considerable detail on the founding and history of the Chickamauga and Chattanooga National Military Park.[12]

It is no coincidence that Gettysburg and Chickamauga both bear mentioning in the context of this and other studies. There is ample reason to believe that Chickamauga's veterans felt compelled to respond to the public fascination with the eastern theater and the great battle that dominated both Northern and Southern memories of the war from the summer of 1863 and beyond. Archibald Gracie wrote in his book's preface that "There were other great battles besides Gettysburg, each of which has claims to historical recognition." He goes on to say that "the most pretentious and inaccurate of Gettysburg's claims is that it was a decisive battle and the most important one of the war" and he makes it clear that "the highwater [sic] mark of this issue, Southern Independence, was reached on the 20th of September, 1863." During the early efforts to rally support for the creation of the park at Chickamauga, Army of the Cumberland veteran Henry Van Ness Boynton frequently referred to the Battle of Chickamauga as "the Gettysburg of the West" and challenged his comrades to build a better, more inclusive park that would recognize both sides equally.[13]

There are a handful of articles specifically dealing with the establishment of Camp George H. Thomas during the Spanish-American War. Chattanooga historian Jerry Desmond, Gregory D. Chapman, and Pennsylvanian Richard Sauers all tell the story of the military's 1898 occupation of the park. These articles tend to be somewhat repetitive, since Sauers and Desmond both cite Chapman's work, while all three depend heavily on John Paige and Jerome Greene's 1983 administrative history of the park and Graham Cosmas's excellent, 1971 book-length assessment of the War Department's efforts in the Spanish-American War. While all of these do an adequate job of describing the camp, the soldiers, and the problems that led to the outbreak of typhoid fever, none of them connect or contrast the military use of the park with the commemorative goals of the Civil War veterans or the park commissioners.[14]

This study will fill that gap by tying together the controversies surrounding the battle in 1863, the creation of the park in the 1890s, and its use as a military training ground in 1898 with the connecting thread of collective memory. The first five chapters trace the construction of Civil War memories among the veterans of the Army of the Cumberland and Army of Tennessee from the onset of the Chickamauga Campaign through the 1870s and 1880s. These include the controversies surrounding the battles of Chickamauga and Chattanooga and the ways the veterans attempted to sort out those issues, defend the reputations of their leaders, and strengthen their place in the national memory of the war. This carries us into the creation of the park in chapters six and seven, where the work of Henry Boynton to design, build, and protect the Army of the Cumberland's primary commemorative landscape were as impressive as his Medal of Honor–winning heroics in the battle itself. Boynton became the voice of the

Army of the Cumberland, unflinchingly and eloquently promoting the identity, memory, and the soldierly virtues of his comrades. When those things were threatened by dissent at any point, he led the counterattack.

The next four chapters (eight through ten) discuss the use of memory, manhood, and reunion imagery during the buildup to the War with Spain and trace the use of the park as a training ground during the summer of 1898. The resulting disease scandal, the Civil War veterans' defense and restoration of the park, and the creation of Fort Oglethorpe are the subject of chapters eleven through fourteen, while chapter fifteen looks at the both the legacy and continued use of the park after the death of its Civil War–era commissioners. It also discusses the plight of the Spanish-American War veterans in the aftermath of World War I. Although the memories that surround the 1863 Chickamauga campaign and the battle are partially dependent on the outcome of the fighting around Chattanooga, the focus of this story increasingly narrows to the Chickamauga portion of the National Military Park. There are two reasons for this: first, the physical characteristics of the two portions of the park are quite different. The Chattanooga portion consists of small "reservations" separated from one another by private property, while the Chickamauga battlefield is one huge, unbroken piece of land. Therefore, nearly all of the large-scale military uses of the park, including Camp Thomas, were relegated to the Chickamauga landscape. Secondly, and more importantly, because of the participation of other armies and commanders in the battles around Chattanooga, Thomas's stand on Snodgrass Hill at Chickamauga represents the Army of the Cumberland's crowning moment and serves as the main focus of its unique identity.

Although it is not the "shrine" that Gettysburg has become, the Chickamauga Battlefield is a unique example of a sacred site that was used for non-commemorative activities, yet retained its ability to promote the collective memories of its founders. Given the current atmosphere surrounding historic preservation, which identifies nearly every Civil War battle site as sacred ground, the juxtaposition of practical—but clearly intrusive—public and military uses of this major battlefield park makes it unique. What is even more intriguing is that even after this controversial episode, the Civil War veterans, park commissioners, and the Chattanooga community continued to promote these non-commemorative uses of their valuable landscape to gain a practical outcome (a permanent army installation). Ultimately, they found a way to banish the negative associations created by Camp Thomas, champion the park's practicality, protect the memories of the Army of the Cumberland and its erstwhile Southern opponents, and still uphold the primary meaning of the battlefield's "River of Death."

ONE

"The Consequences Will Be Momentous"

In the fall of 1863, two huge armies engaged in a bloody, titanic struggle near a meandering creek in northern Georgia known to some by its Cherokee name as the "River of Death." For the Union and Confederate soldiers who experienced this pivotal Civil War battle, the "River of Death" accurately described the mayhem and human destruction that characterized the Battle of Chickamauga. Whereas in many cases, Union and Confederate accounts often disagreed on the significance and intensity of certain battles, there was no such debate concerning the brutal two-day encounter along Chickamauga Creek. As the veterans of the Union Army of the Cumberland and Confederate Army of Tennessee told and retold the stories of their services in the "late war," their accounts of Chickamauga consistently focused on the sinister images and memories conjured up by this otherwise inconspicuous trickle of water and the tangled landscape that surrounded it.[1]

The Battle of Chickamauga, with its swirling confusion and close-quarters combat, had been the common soldier's fight. Although Confederate Gen. James Longstreet's crushing attack, Union commander William S. Rosecrans's abandonment of the field, and George H. Thomas's epic stand on Snodgrass Hill loom large in virtually all accounts of the battle, it was the heroic determination among the infantrymen, dismounted cavalry, and artillery batteries that ultimately determined the outcome of this struggle. In spite of the failure of many of their commanders at the army and corps levels, the small units of both the Army of the Cumberland and the Army of Tennessee made the question of victory or defeat a matter of yards and inches, hours and minutes, bullets and bayonets. In doing so, they left a powerful legacy of courage and determination of which they were understandably proud.

The horrifying, brutal, and sanguinary nature of the combat that took place during those two days in September dramatically fulfilled the area's dark and ominous Cherokee legacy. As Chickamauga's veterans forged their postwar recollections, they understandably appropriated the "River of Death" as one of the key symbols of this battle's ferocity and its importance to the war's grow-ing legacy of courage and valor. As the battlefield became the focal point for the veterans and their memories, the creek "that ran red with human blood" and the "dark primeval woods" surrounding it became sacred places belonging almost exclusively to the men from the two armies who had fought, suffered, and died there.[2]

Appropriately, the fields and woods around the "River of Death" changed very little in the decades after the battle. The landscape had absorbed many of the scars, leaving the ground virtually untouched, save for the efforts of a few hardscrabble farmers to plant crops or graze livestock. At first glance, the battlefield seemed devoid of lofty heights or prominent landmarks; its pow-er resonated quietly and subtly among the rocks, trees, open meadows, and stately monuments that gradually dotted the fields. By 1895, with the Cherokee culture long since driven from the area, the Civil War veterans were able to lay primary claim to the landscape by placing their statues, cannons, and de-scriptive markers on a carefully preserved and recreated battlefield. Although some conflicts existed between the Union and Confederate interpretations of the battle and its outcome, its memory as the war's bloodiest two days and the corresponding meaning of "River of Death" seemed securely in the hands of its participants.[3]

Just a few years later, in the summer of 1898, a soldier drafted a letter to the governor of Iowa from his regiment's "Camp on the River of Death" that in-troduced a whole new meaning to this phrase and the landscape it described. The soldier was one of thousands assigned to Camp George H. Thomas. Like many of the troops at Camp Thomas, he and his comrades in the 52nd Iowa Infantry had volunteered to fight the Spanish in Cuba and were "willing to die, if need be" in the service of their country. Yet for them, Chickamauga Creek, the military park that bore its name, and the camp established by the War Department within its boundaries had become synonymous with "death and sickness," rather than courage and valor. For these Iowans and many other veterans of the Spanish-American War, Chickamauga was the scene of suffering and misery that they hoped to leave as quickly as possible. It was a place sooner forgotten than remembered. As those veterans reflected on the Spanish-American War's uncertain place in the nation's collective memory, they referred to Chickamauga as their "River of Death" in a different and far more ambiguous context than either the Cherokee or the stalwart veterans of the great Civil War battle.[4]

The contrast between these two sets of experiences on the same piece of ground illustrates the influence that time and perception have on the construction of memory. The Union and Confederate veterans who fought and suffered in the Battle of Chickamauga had thirty years to place their ordeal in a heroic context, which allowed the creation and dedication of the National Military Park to become a celebration of mutual valor and sectional reconciliation for the entire nation. The young men who found themselves at Chickamauga in 1898 went there with equally heroic expectations, only to have them dashed by boredom, disappointment, and sickness in a matter of a few short weeks. The 60,000 Spanish-American War volunteers not only physically damaged the park landscape during their short stay, but their complaints about the food, water, and tedium of camp life seemingly contradicted the Civil War standards of duty and manhood. In the conflict that ensued, the memories corresponding with the intended use of the ground as a sacred landscape triumphed over those that recalled it as a place of hardship and misery.

The differences between the soldiers who fought at Chickamauga and built a park on the battlefield and the men who occupied it in 1898 are at the center of this divergence of memory. The construction of lasting collective memories often begins with the original experience and evolves over time through the performance of rituals that enhance the significance of the past and give those events meaning. The veterans of the Battle of Chickamauga had at least three years of involvement in a huge, important, and historically significant war on which to construct their initial memories of the battle. They were part of a large army during a massive national calamity that mobilized millions of men and involved a substantial portion of the public. In the decades after the war, issues of Reconstruction and race complicated, but did not inhibit, the construction of memories among the men who fought for the Union and the Confederacy. The celebrations of Memorial Day, regular reunions at the local and regimental level, and the creation of army-specific and national veterans' organizations helped keep the threads of memory alive.

For the Union and Confederate soldiers who fought in the fierce battle of the Chickamauga, the distinctive character of that struggle became one of the key elements in the construction of their memories. During the three decades leading up to the creation of the Chattanooga and Chickamauga National Military Park, the former soldiers of the Army of the Cumberland and Army of Tennessee revisited the events of September 1863 in their memoirs, articles, and in private and public discussions of the battle and its outcome. Their collective desire to preserve the landscape and uphold the memories associated with it required a great deal of cooperation and communication between former comrades and their old enemies. By the time their commemorative landscape was created, sanctified, and dedicated, the Civil War image of the "River of Death" was clearly accepted and understood by the men who fought there.

The volunteers who found themselves on this landscape in 1898 had comparably little on which to build their memories. With the exception of the Regular Army troops who passed through the park, most of the volunteers were inexperienced soldiers. Although their patriotism and enthusiasm may have been similar to that of the Northerners and Southerners who had answered the call back in 1861, much of the rest of their experience took an entirely different direction. Unlike the Civil War units that had months and years to mature and become veterans, most of the regiments that assembled in the summer of 1898 were brand new. Although a few had been state National Guard units, the bulk of these troops had been recruited, organized, and briefly trained in a matter of weeks before being sent to Camp Thomas. Aside from the local send-offs and generally pleasant trips from their home states to Georgia, the rest of their experience became a short but increasingly intense ordeal. Many unexpected hardships—boredom, disease, disappointment, confusion, and frustration—were packed into less than half a year. Not only were the actual experiences relatively brief, but the overall impact of their sacrifice turned out to be unclear and unsatisfying.

For all of its buildup, the War with Spain turned out to be a tainted victory. Although the American army and navy triumphed over the weaker and overrated Spanish in a scant three months, many factors conspired to blur the war's outcome and make it difficult for its veterans to construct meaningful and lasting memories. There were only a handful of national heroes to counter the disease and health scandals that began even before the war ended. The public debate over the treaty with Spain went on for some time while U.S. forces were engaged in a bloody conflict with Filipino rebels in the most distant of its new possessions. For the thousands of men who had trained at Camp Thomas, the war's rapid conclusion cut short their military experience and left them with conflicting and ambiguous memories. The unit cohesion enjoyed by Civil War veterans had barely had time to gel before many of the regiments found themselves either back at home or engaged in tedious and often frustrating occupation duties in the Caribbean. What memories they did carry from their time in the army were tinged with bitterness and reflected the new set of horrors that became associated with the "River of Death."

To trace the paths of memory that converged in the summer of 1898, we need to start near the beginning, when the collective identities of the Civil War armies that fought at Chickamauga were forged. What made the Battle of Chickamauga special to the veterans of the Army of the Cumberland and the Army of Tennessee was the way that this particular fight contributed to the evolution of both armies from organizations consisting mostly of raw recruits in 1861 to seasoned fighting units by the summer of 1863. The operations and battles prior to the Chickamauga-Chattanooga campaign had put both armies in a position to help determine the outcome of the war. However, each had something to prove to themselves; particularly since both felt that they unfairly operated in the shadows of their more famous eastern and western counterparts. The identities these Union and Confederate officers and men carried into the battle would endure long after it ended and provide the framework for their memories and the park they built to preserve them.

From the perspective of many participants and a significant number of historians, the year 1863 determined the outcome of the War Between the States. During that tumultuous twelve months, the Union Army of the Potomac suffered a catastrophic defeat at Chancellorsville in May only to recover and win its greatest victory at Gettysburg in July. Its opponent, the Army of Northern Virginia, not only lost its first major battle that summer but suffered the loss of General Thomas "Stonewall" Jackson, whose untimely death deprived the Confederates of both a great commander and a symbol of their rightness with the Almighty. In the West, Ulysses S. Grant and his armies lay siege to the city of Vicksburg, Mississippi, and captured it and its 29,000 defenders on Independence Day, cutting the "Father of Waters" in half and isolating the western Confederacy. Grant's triumph signaled his rise from the ignominy of his shaky performance at Shiloh to being a major leader in the Union war effort in the West. The Army of the Cumberland and its rebel counterpart the Army of the Tennessee had begun 1863 by mauling one another in the bloody carnage of Stones River, near Murfreesboro, leaving the fate of eastern Tennessee hanging in the balance.

Along with the dramatic strategic implications of this pivotal year, these battles had a profound effect on the men in the ranks of both armies. At the core of the major forces engaged were a large number of veterans in their second full year of service. Although whittled down by combat, sickness, and other forms of attrition, the fighting regiments in blue and gray consisted of hardened, experienced, disciplined, and coldly efficient soldiers. Bolstered by the volunteers from the summer of 1862 and a growing trickle of conscripts, draftees, and bounty men, the veteran soldiers of the armies of the Potomac, Northern Virginia, and those in the Tennessee and Mississippi valleys must have certainly sensed that winning the war was largely up to them. The starry-eyed idealism and romantic notions of war that had motivated them as recruits in 1861 were long gone. They had been shattered in the gore, confusion, and horror on dozens of battlefields in Tennessee, Virginia, Kentucky, Maryland, and Mississippi. Whether bound by personal honor, loyalty to their comrades, or devotion to their causes, the soldiers of '63 were generally committed to serving their terms, winning the war, and with luck going home in one piece.[5]

Once it was abundantly clear to the men in the ranks that their ability to control victory and defeat depended on what happened on the battlefield, they rarely shied away from going into combat. This is not to be confused with the bravado of the early war and the oft-stated concerns that the war might end before the unit saw action. Veteran soldiers realized that to fight well was the key to victory; with enough victories, the war would end and they could go home. Thus, the reputation and identity of the company, regiment, brigade, division, corps, or army ultimately depended on its performance on the battlefield and its contributions to the outcome of the campaign and the war. Combat was not the by-product of military service; it was the primary purpose of that service and the tangible measure by which the soldiers' contributions would be weighed. Although many men hated and feared the confusion and carnage of combat, they understood its meaning in the larger picture of the war and its subsequent role in the construction of their war memories.[6]

Even while they were still engaged in the grim business of combat, the soldiers were already constructing the memories that would define their service and embed their accomplishments into the collective memory of the nation. As Carol Reardon points out in her insightful work on Pickett's Charge at Gettysburg, the soldiers engaged in that bloody hour's work came away believing that something truly remarkable had just happened. Their letters to loved ones and newspapers, journal entries, and eyewitness accounts passed down by word of mouth all reinforced the notion that what happened at Gettysburg on July 3, 1863, was perhaps the most important moment of the war. The compelling images of "the flower of Lee's army"—his Virginians—advancing in unbroken ranks across the open field was indelibly sealed into the minds of those who witnessed it. To stop such a force took an equally Herculean effort by the members of Winfield Hancock's II Corps and thus solidified their reputation as the finest fighters in the Union army. Eventually, these memories were passed down by the veterans and etched in stone on the monuments that dot the great battlefield park at Gettysburg. Regardless of the color of uniform or theater of war, the soldiers felt the burden of history around them as they fought and worked toward creating and maintaining lasting memories of their contributions.[7]

The Civil War battlefield experience, particularly as it related to fierce fighting in huge encounters like those at Gettysburg and Chickamauga, forged a specific set of images and memories that had a long-term effect on the soldiers and leaders who fought there. Not only did these giant conflagrations have important tactical and strategic implications that affected the outcome of the war, but they left powerful impressions on the soldiers and commanders who experienced them. For the men in the ranks of the armies of Cumberland and Tennessee, the battle on the banks of Chickamauga Creek represented yet another level of vicious and horrific combat in a war that had already propelled many of them through the brutal fights of 1862 at Shiloh, Perryville, and Stones River. With all of the questions surrounding the larger issues of victory and defeat at the Battle of Chickamauga, both Union and Confederate veterans focused on the combat experience as the key element in their memories of the fight. What distinguished them from soldiers in other theaters of the war (and to some extent, those in other wars) was the intensity of their battle experiences.

The Civil War soldiers' gradual development toward a collective identity rooted in battle included three elements that helped define and construct lasting images and memories. These revolved around comrades, units, and leaders. At any level, this war was a monumental occurrence that affected both the nation as a whole and many of its citizens. Since the soldiers who made up the combat regiments on both sides were mostly volunteers recruited from their own communities and counties, their first orientation tended to be toward the locally raised company and the men in it. The natural loyalties of family, friends, and neighbors made these companies remarkably homogenous and created a strong bond that carried them through the unevenly divided periods of training, tedium, and terror that characterized the soldier experience. As they became veterans, these bonds were enhanced by the comradeship of men who had endured the trials of the battlefield together. While it could be argued that a larger sense of duty to cause and country motivated these men to fight and die on the battlefield, their devotion to their comrades certainly weighed heavily as the war grew longer and more destructive. Since the people back home also held a great deal of affection for "the boys" in the service, it is not surprising that many of the memories that emerged from the war were focused on the men who shared blankets, rations, and hardships for three years or more as members of the same unit.[8]

The sense of belonging that bound the men of volunteer companies to one another was frequently extended to include the larger units of the army as well. The soldiers in Civil War regiments wore their numbers and state identities on their equipment and proudly emblazoned them onto their flags. The performance of the regiment in drill was not only a source of pride, but was the key to survival in the chaotic swirl of the battlefield. Official battle reports often singled out individual regiments for praise or blame and were seen as a measure of the unit's courage, morale, and efficiency. Although a few larger organizations, like Wilder's Lightning Brigade in the Army of the Cumberland; the Irish, Iron, and Gibraltar Brigades in the Army of the Potomac; or the Stonewall and Texas brigades in the Army of Northern Virginia, gained fame and identities of their own, the main expressions of memory and pride for most soldiers were reserved for the boys of "the brave old regiment." Not surprisingly, the process of memory construction also began with the regiments and the communities that supplied them with their soldiers. Members of the 9th Ohio Infantry hoped that documenting their regiment's wartime experiences would " . . . commemorate the dead . . . inspire the living . . . enrich prosperity . . . [and] foster the highest ideals." After the war, burials, reunions, monument dedications, memorial days, and patriotic holidays all provided opportunities for remembering the regiment and recognizing the local heroes.[9]

By the third year of the war, the armies themselves became a source of identity for the men who served in them. Spurred by the press and public attention given to the eastern Union Army of the Potomac and its opponent, the Army of Northern Virginia, forces in the western theater of the war sought to develop their own sense of importance to the war effort. This tended to be more difficult in the West than in the East. The odd department arrangement favored by the Confederacy early in the war created numerous separate commands that merged and separated as the situation dictated. The loss of John C. Pemberton's Confederate army at Vicksburg in July 1863 left the Army of Tennessee as the largest and most coherent Southern force in the field west of the Alleghenies. This army's lack of success and its divisive command situation had already affected its image and identity before the events around Chattanooga in the fall of 1863. The arrival of troops from other departments, including two divisions of the Army of Northern Virginia during the Chickamauga campaign further complicated this organization's already tarnished self-image and affected its abilities to construct a clearly defined set of memories in the years after the war.[10]

For the Army of the Cumberland, the situation was even more complicated. Not only did it have an equally uneven record of success, but up until October 1862 it had been commanded by Gen. Don Carlos Buell and known as the Army of the Ohio. In addition to operating in the shadow of the high-profile eastern theater, its rival in the West by mid-1863 was primarily Ulysses S. Grant's (later William T. Sherman's) Army of the Tennessee, whose veterans of the successful siege and conquest of Vicksburg were rapidly developing into a clearly identifiable, effective fighting unit. Yet, with these other Union forces in the region tied up on the Mississippi, the responsibility for securing control of central Tennessee in the summer of 1863 fell directly into the hands of the Army of the Cumberland and its commander, William S. Rosecrans. Having stood up to their Confederate counterparts most recently at the bloody, but indecisive battle of Stones River, the veterans of the Army of the Cumberland could claim a modest record of victory, but no dramatic successes on the level of Vicksburg or Gettysburg. For this army and its commander, the Battle of Chickamauga would further complicate, rather than clarify, its search for recognition and identity among the other Union armies in the West.[11]

In both of these western armies, the ability of the soldiers to develop a sense of their collective identity was compromised by the realities of the war in that part of the country. Individual regiments, brigades, and divisions were shifted from one army or department to the other, depending on the situation. Differences in recruiting, training, tactics, logistics, geography, and the selection of officers separated western troops from their eastern counterparts and influenced the development of both armies. Many of the newer regiments in the Union army had spent frustrating months guarding towns and bridges or chasing Confederate irregulars before being assigned to newly organized brigades or divisions in major army units. Periodic reshuffling of troops and commanders within the army hampered unit cohesion all the way to the corps level.[12]

For the Confederates, similar bureaucratic issues, along with ineffective support from the states, an inferior pool of officers, and flawed tactical thinking contributed to the Army of Tennessee's "unenviable record" of "inglorious failure." Like their Yankee counterparts, the common soldiers in the Confederate army lacked nothing in the way of spirit, courage, and resolve. However, circumstances beyond their control, often in spite of their best efforts, had conspired to deprive them of victory. Although both armies had pounded one another at Shiloh in April, 1862; Perryville in October; and Stones River on the cusp of the New Year, neither the Army of the Cumberland nor the Army of Tennessee had experienced a complete and decisive victory that could change the course of the war and give the men a source of pride and confidence in themselves as a cohesive military organization. The lack of this unity meant that to the soldiers, press, and public, the personality of each army was heavily influenced by the character and accomplishments of its commanding generals, who brought their own strengths and weaknesses to the 1863 summer campaign.[13]

Energetic, talkative, and excitable, Maj. Gen. William Starke Rosecrans seemed to have brought the Army of the Cumberland to the verge of greatness by the summer of 1863. He had gained command of the army based on his early success in western Virginia under George McClellan and his solid performance at the battles of Iuka and Corinth, Mississippi, in late 1862. His hard-earned, yet inconclusive repulse of Bragg's offensive at Stones River had earned him President Abraham Lincoln's personal thanks for providing the victory-starved nation with something like a success during the dark, discouraging winter of 1862–63. Since then, however, Lincoln had expressed some impatience with the general's meticulous, seemingly endless planning throughout the early part of 1863. As the spring's good weather rolled into early summer, the President and his chief advisor Henry Halleck chafed at the general's failure to move quickly or aggressively against either the Confederate army or the important rail center at Chattanooga.[14]

FIG. 1: Gen. William S. Rosecrans was a hero after the Army of the Cumberland's victory at Stones River, but his defeat at Chickamauga and dismissal afterward destroyed his promising career. Library of Congress.

On the eve of the campaign, General Rosecrans had an experienced, but uneven, set of subordinates, led by his ambitious new chief of staff, James A. Garfield. His infantry corps commanders included the reliable George H. Thomas, an egotistical and overrated Alexander McCook, a mediocre Thomas C. Crittenden, and Gordon Granger, who led a two-division reserve. With the exception of the stolid Thomas, whose modesty and Virginia upbringing may have inhibited his opportunity for promotion to the army's commander, Rosecrans, his staff, and the army's leading generals were a confident, ambitious, occasionally profane group who were fond of spirits and not reluctant to brag about their accomplishments. In spite of its bumpy track record thus far, the Army of the Cumberland's was clearly "Old Rosy's" army; his gregarious nature, concern for his soldiers, and commanding personality made him popular with his men, the press, and the northern public.[15]

On the other side, Braxton Bragg's tenure with the Army of Tennessee had pushed that organization to the verge of anarchy. In the latter half of 1862 he took his army north into Kentucky, where the offensive stalled at the Battle of Perryville. He withdrew into middle Tennessee only to pull back further south after the bloody New Year's fight at Stones River. Bragg's reputation for being courageous, yet stubborn and inflexible dated back to his peacetime Regular Army career, service in the Mexican War, and his mediocre performance as a corps commander at Shiloh, where he was unable to overcome the Union defenses at the "Hornet's Nest" for several critical hours. Where Rosecrans was sociable and reasonably diplomatic with his subordinates, Bragg was secretive, blunt, and uncommunicative. Having endured several open attempts by generals William Hardee, Leonidas Polk, John C. Breckinridge, and Benjamin Cheatham to have him dismissed, Bragg kept his plans and feelings to himself. Yet, once the campaign began, he stubbornly expected obedience and efficiency from corps and division commanders who often distrusted and despised him. On top of his personality flaws, Bragg was often physically ill and may have suffered from bouts of depression, paranoia, and what might be described by modern therapists as an anxiety disorder. Although the men in the ranks may not have shared their corps and division commanders' high level of hatred for Bragg, his "tyrannical" policies toward deserters, failure to provide adequate supplies, and the constant bickering among the army's key leaders could not have done much for morale. Following the fall of Vicksburg in July, the pressure on the Army of Tennessee to reverse the Confederacy's fortunes and live up to its own heroic potential increased considerably.[16]

In many ways, the summer and fall of 1863 represented the most critical period in the most critical year of the war. After the shocking Union successes in the East at Gettysburg and on the Mississippi at Vicksburg, the tide of

FIG. 2: Gen. Braxton Bragg commanded the Army of Tennessee at Perryville and Stones River but was unable to follow up the decisive victory at Chickamauga that would have turned the tide in the western theater. Library of Congress.

Confederate victory that had peaked at Chancellorsville was beginning to recede. For the two armies in central Tennessee, the stakes could not have been higher. The men of the Army of the Cumberland sought the one great victory that could raise them and their commander to the heroic heights occupied by George G. Meade, Ulysses S. Grant, and their respective armies. For the Army of Tennessee, the situation was more dire and foreboding. While a decisive victory could liberate much of the state from Union control and blunt the North's momentum, a defeat could ruin the army and threaten the cause of Southern independence. Richmond diarist John Jones insightfully summarized the issues at stake upon hearing the first reports from Chickamauga: "If Bragg beats Rosecrans utterly, the consequences will be momentous. If beaten by him, he sinks to rise no more. Both generals are aware of the consequences of failure."[17]

Jones's observation was more than mere hyperbole. Given the outcome of the Gettysburg and Vicksburg campaigns, it is not a stretch to say that one more defeat might have brought the Confederacy to its knees. If ever an army carried the weight of the nation on its shoulders, the Army of Tennessee can be said to have hoisted that burden by mid-July, 1863. For the Army of the Cumberland, the pressure was nearly as intense to finish the job that its counterparts had initiated quite spectacularly in Pennsylvania and Mississippi. It had an opportunity to deliver a knockout punch to a rebellion that was weaker than it had been since the beginning of the war. With little exaggeration, one could argue that the fates of two nations were potentially at stake. Although the campaign did not produce either of these decisive outcomes, the ensuing battles near Chickamauga Creek and on the heights surrounding Chattanooga provided ample context for the construction of lasting memories once the fighting ended.

In contrast, the men and boys who arrived in the Chattanooga area in 1898 did not carry the fate of their nation on their shoulders. The Spanish enemy had challenged America's pride and insulted its manhood, but posed no real threat to the sovereignty of the United States. Nor did these volunteers have the benefit of the deep and lasting experiences of previous battles and campaigns or the memories that grew from them. Instead, they inherited a set of heroic expectations from the previous generation that reflected an ongoing conflict between the nation's past and its present values. Hoping to emulate their forefathers, rescue an allegedly oppressed people, and complete the reconciliation of the North and South, they marched blithely off to war, filled with martial spirit but lacking the supplies, support, and experience necessary to fill the shoes that preceded them. Instead of combat and glory, which provide the key building blocks of memory, many found only sickness, disappointment, and frustration. While they occupied the same physical landscape that had helped define the Chickamauga veterans' sense of accomplishment, they absorbed little of that landscape's sacred qualities. Although their ordeal lasted only a few months and lacked much of the drama and scope that the Civil War provided, it is their story that generates many of the conflicting memories surrounding the "River of Death."

TWO

"The Fate of the Army Depended on This Charge"

If the reputation and identity of armies was based on their combat experiences, then both the Army of the Cumberland and the Army of Tennessee should have gone into the summer of 1863 fully confident in themselves. Both had been in serious battles the previous year, but neither had achieved decisive results. Not only did great strategic issues hinge on the operations around Chattanooga, but the eyes of both nations were on these two armies and their commanders. With the other key armies either resting or eliminated (as in the case of Pemberton's captured garrison) after grueling summer campaigns in Pennsylvania and along the Mississippi, the contending forces in Tennessee took center stage. By the end of 1863, both armies emerged battered and bloodied, with both commanders fired, after causing both governments to funnel thousands of additional reinforcements into the fray.

Nearly everything leading up to the Battle of Chickamauga portended great things for the Union Army of the Cumberland. Between 24 June and 4 July 1863, in what became known as the Tullahoma campaign, Rosecrans outguessed and outflanked Bragg while skillfully maneuvering his army from Murfreesboro to the gates of Chattanooga. In spite of this stunning success, Rosecrans spent nearly six weeks of additional planning before finally chasing the Confederates out of the city and into the hills to the south at the beginning of September. For Rosecrans and his postwar defenders, the Tullahoma campaign and capture of Chattanooga should have earned the general and his army many well-deserved accolades, but the absence of a major battle and the accompanying outpouring of blood kept this success out of the public's eye.

Indeed, if the object of the campaign had simply been to seize and occupy Chattanooga, then this argument would have been a valid one. However, one historian of the Army of the Cumberland observed that "brilliant campaigns . . . without battles, do not accomplish the destruction of an army." Bragg's forces seemed to be in disordered retreat somewhere in northern Georgia, and Rosecrans, who was still being pressured by officials in Washington, felt obligated to go after them. The Tullahoma campaign had been a model of both planning and execution, but no one was entirely satisfied with its outcome. Rosecrans had finally initiated the campaign against Chattanooga in response to Henry Halleck's direct orders and was miffed because General Ambrose E. Burnside had not moved his small army into eastern Tennessee to protect his northeastern (left) flank. His uncharacteristically aggressive pursuit reflected his frustration at not being allowed to conduct the campaign at his own discretion and his desire to bring it to a spectacular and successful conclusion.[1]

Thus, after securing Chattanooga in the first week of September, Rosecrans overruled a more cautious Thomas and immediately ordered his army to pursue Bragg's scattered divisions. Stoked by false reports of Confederate demoralization and unaware that Bragg had been strongly reinforced, the energized Union commander divided his army and sent his infantry corps forward on several roads that passed through different gaps and openings in the ridges south of the city. At this point, the initiative shifted to Bragg, who recognized the opportunity to strike and possibly destroy the individual parts of the Union army while they were too far apart to support one another. It was here that Bragg's horrible command style and miserable relationship with his subordinates served to completely undermine this great tactical opportunity. Twice, he ordered his corps commanders D. H. Hill and Leonidas Polk to attack vulnerable elements of Rosecrans's army at McLemore's Cove and near Lafayette, and twice, they and several of their division commanders failed to respond with anything resembling energy and efficiency.[2]

The resulting near misses not only failed to do any damage to significant portions of the Union army, they served to warn Rosecrans that something had gone terribly wrong with his triumphant pursuit and convinced him to order a re-concentration of the army's divided corps somewhere on the roads leading to Chattanooga. The Union commander's alarm was matched by equal amounts of frustration throughout the Confederate army. As its high command increasingly deteriorated in a divisive fog of uncertainty and distrust, the army's veterans openly cursed the blundering, finger-pointing, and lost opportunities that deprived them of a rare chance for an easy and decisive victory.[3]

In many ways, these initial encounters foretold one of the unique characteristics of the engagement at Chickamauga. For the most part, the conduct and outcome of this monumental battle reflected the fighting abilities of the troops and unveiled the shortcomings of both armies' commanders. Throughout the two days that the battle unfolded, both Rosecrans and Bragg frequently operated on mistaken assumptions, failed to adjust to changing circumstances, and gave orders from the rear that did not reflect the realities of the front lines. For Rosecrans, the primary goal in the days and hours leading up to the battle's climax was to reunite his four infantry corps, which were often separated from one another by terrain, distance, or the fog of war. His success in doing so propelled the contest into its second day and gave his army a chance to win the battle.

In spite of all his previous setbacks and frequent timidity, Braxton Bragg was the aggressor throughout the two-day engagement. He had received reinforcements from both the Trans-Mississippi, the Deep South, and Virginia, and actually outnumbered his Union counterpart. Unfortunately, Bragg underestimated the amount of ground that the Union army could cover and made a battle plan that was almost immediately outdated by the time the two armies clashed on the west side of Chickamauga Creek on the morning of the nineteenth. Throughout the day, he stubbornly assumed that the bulk of the Union force was still at Lee and Gordon's Mills, when in fact most of it had pushed well north of that point. His plan was for most of his infantry to get beyond the Union left and block the route to Chattanooga. Instead, he ran into Rosecrans's brigades and divisions as they came onto the battlefield and never gained the position, numerical advantage, or control of the action that he desperately needed.[4]

Although Chickamauga Creek itself was important during the first day-and-a-half of the fighting, the key feature to understanding the whole battle is Lafayette Road, which ran north and south and served as the main route into Chattanooga. By the eighteenth, Rosecrans had much of his army marching north on this road and several smaller parallel roads in the direction of Chattanooga. Bragg's army was also coming from the south and angling gradually northwest, putting it on a collision course with the Union force. The creek, which meandered between the two armies in a roughly northeastern path, was a significant obstacle to Bragg's original plan of attack, which had his forces turning west to strike at the Yankees on or near Lafayette Road. Since the banks of the creek were steep, wooded, and slippery, his troops had to cross the creek at a series of bridges and fords scattered from near Lee and Gordon's Mills in the south to the northernmost Ringgold Bridge, some six or seven miles distant. To destroy the Union army and/or prevent its return to Chattanooga, Bragg's troops needed to use the northern crossings and get ahead of the Union main body. This meant that the most important approaches were the furthest away from the objective, so if they were defended—or if Confederate commanders did not get their men to the right places at the right times—it would throw the plan into disarray.

Thanks to some stubborn Union resistance on the part of Col. Robert Minty's cavalry at Reed's Bridge and of Gen. John Wilder's mounted infantry at Alexander's Bridge, the Confederate offensive never really got started on the eighteenth. However, there were enough Confederate forces showing their strength along the creek by evening to threaten Rosecrans's marching route and force him to instinctively deploy his forces parallel to Lafayette Road, facing east during the night. Bragg, who had his headquarters far in the rear of the action, still assumed that the bulk of the Union army was concentrated well to the south and accordingly massed his troops to strike what he believed to be its exposed left flank. However, Rosecrans had ordered Thomas to move his XIV Corps behind and to the left (north) of Thomas Crittenden's XXI Corps position, which placed most of his veterans directly in the path of Bragg's proposed attack.

What began on the morning of the nineteenth was a fluid, chaotic slugfest, in which opposing brigades and divisions hustled onto the battlefield and recklessly crashed into one another in the woods and fields east of Lafayette Road. Since elements of both armies were still in the process of arriving by various meandering country paths, there was no set pattern to the way they entered the fighting. As the morning battle heated up between Thomas's men and parts of Gen. William Walker's Reserve Corps, other Confederate units from both Polk's and Simon Bolivar Buckner's two corps flowed toward the sound of the guns and into the fight.[5]

Ironically, it was Thomas who initiated the battle by overreacting to the 69th Ohio's mistaken claim that it had burned Reed's bridge and isolated a single Confederate brigade on the west side of the creek. Not only had the bridge not burned completely, but enough rebels had crossed the creek to seriously outnumber and outflank the three brigades of John Brannan's division that he sent to investigate. Throughout the morning, as units from the north end of Thomas's line advanced eastward into the growing fire fight without coordinated support, they were smashed in the flank by Confederate units pushing from the east, who in turn were hit in the flank by more Union brigades advancing from the south via Lafayette Road.

By noon, nearly all of the brigades in Brannan and Absalom Baird's Union divisions had been badly mangled by this combat and had inflicted a significant amount of damage on parts of Walker's Corps and Nathan Bedford Forrest's cavalry, which had fought largely without much help from the rest of the Confederate forces in the vicinity. Several units found themselves flanked and nearly routed during this melee, so that a soldier in the 105th Ohio thought that he outran his colonel's horse and that "every leap I made would beat the celebrated leap of Brady over Cuyahoga Falls." From late morning on, fighting on this end of the line died down as these units rested and refitted from their early morning ordeal. At the same time, the continued flow of troops from the south fed the growing roar of battle in the area around the Brotherton family's farmhouse, where forces of Crittenden's XXI Corps and more advancing Confederates from Polk and Buckner's Corps converged toward the fields bordering both sides of Lafayette Road.[6]

The first of these units to enter the fray was Cheatham's division of Polk's Corps, which formed on the left of John Liddell's men (from Walker's Corps) and advanced against the right of Thomas's line. His men crashed into two fresh brigades of Brig. Gen. Richard Johnson's division, which Rosecrans had detached from Maj. Gen. Alexander McCook's XX Corps and given to Thomas to strengthen his battered battalions. Johnson's men were soon reinforced by Maj. Gen. John Palmer's XXI Corps division, which quickly tipped the fighting in this part of the field in the Federals' favor. As Cheatham's Confederates were being pushed out of the woods east of Lafayette Road, they took fire on the flank from two brigades of Horatio Van Cleve's XXI Corps division that were advancing from the southwest.

With additional Union units filing in to this line, the momentum of the battle clearly belonged to the Federal forces, as Cheatham's shattered brigades fell back to the southeast. But more Confederate manpower was entering the field at about this time, as generals Alexander Stewart, Bushrod Johnson, and John Bell Hood brought their troops into the melee along the critical roadway. Stewart's division attacked in a column of brigades, rather than in the usual formation of two or three brigades abreast, which gave his assault more power along a narrower front. This massive column smashed into Van Cleve's worn regiments and drove them back across the road and into the Dyer farm's fields.[7]

The arrival of Hood's division on the field represented one of the unique elements of the Battle of Chickamauga, which was the presence of James Longstreet's Corps from the Army of Northern Virginia in the western theater.[8] Hood's men were the first to arrive from the Ringgold Station depot and found themselves in battle early on the nineteenth before Longstreet himself reached the field. As a result, Hood was not under the direct command of any of Bragg's corps commanders and was able to react to whatever opportunities the battle offered. His division was the third blow of a one-two-three punch delivered by his men, Stewart's division, and the troops of Bushrod Johnson, who had attacked on Stewart's left and collided with additional Union troops from the XXI Corps. Just as Johnson's troops swept across Lafayette Road, they were hit in the flank by Gen. Thomas Wood's two brigades and sent reeling in disorder. Before they could consolidate their position, these Federal units were flanked in turn by two brigades of Evander Law's brigade of Hood's corps.

At this point late in the afternoon, the Confederates seemed to have briefly seized the momentum. It would not last. Stewart's troops had penetrated the

Federal center near the Brotherton house and nearly reached Rosecrans's head-quarters, but their attack stalled when Johnson's support got sidetracked. By the time Hood's troops attempted to exploit their success, Wilder's Lightning Brigade and fresh Union units commanded by Phillip Sheridan had launched a counterattack to regain control of the road and nearby Viniard farm. According to one participant, a Union brigade commander who noticed that the 93rd Ohio had lost its colonel, "took the old flag and said 'come on 93' and we rallied to a man and made a charge and captured two pieces of artillery [and] fell back again behind some logs." Similar fierce encounters raged at this end of the line until it was nearly dark and the continuity of the Union line was nominally restored.[9]

As if to demonstrate the inflexible decision making within the Confederate high command, the last action of the day took place at the northern end of the line and involved Gen. Patrick Cleburne's division of Hill's Corps. In spite of the way the battle had evolved to the south during the day, Bragg still attempted to implement his plan to drive the Union forces from north to south by attacking Thomas's line in the woods east of the Lafayette Road. As Baird, Brannan, and Johnson's battered Union troops withdrew to a more consolidated position, Cleburne's brigades came screaming out of the smoky twilight three abreast and crashed into the remaining Federal units near the Winfrey field. During the ensuing melee, Confederate general Preston Smith was shot dead along with most of the mounted officers on his staff when they rode into Union lines in the darkness. Hundreds of additional soldiers from both sides were killed and wounded in a nighttime collision that one participant thought was "one of the most furious that has occurred during the war." Aside from forcing a few Union regiments back from their advanced positions, the attack failed to shake Thomas's line and fizzled out in the darkness.[10]

Both armies were bruised but intact at the end of the brutal first day. In spite of some fierce fighting, neither had been able to seize the initiative or make any significant break in the enemy's line. The nature of the combat on the nineteenth contributed to the soldiers' memories of Chickamauga as a confused, chaotic, close-quarters struggle in a tangled, wooded environment. Because units for both armies arrived on the field and pitched into the fighting without a great deal of direction, there was no clear sense of being on the offensive or defensive, so the fighting swirled wildly through the woods and fields. Michael Fitch, a veteran of the 21st Wisconsin, recalled "the charging and falling back of both sides; the difficulty in keeping alignments; the impossibility of officers recognizing friend or foe; the losing [sic] of batteries and single pieces; their recapture; and the awful slaughter" during the fighting on the nineteenth. Fitch also observed correctly that "when troops are outflanked

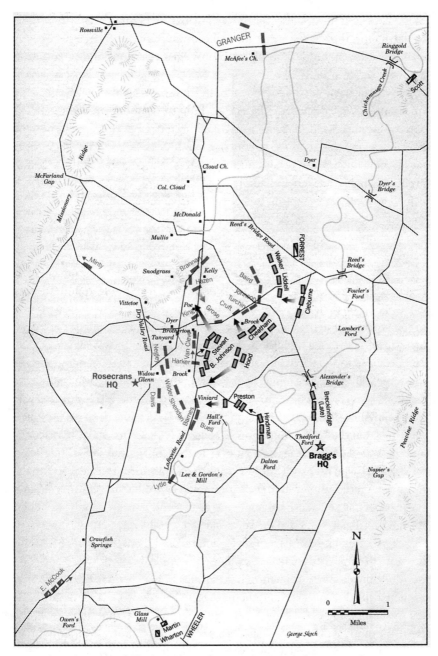

FIG. 3 (MAP): Battle of Chickamauga, afternoon, 19 September 1863. After a morning of confused fighting, the battle lines stabilized along the Lafayette Road, where they would remain until the next day. Courtesy of Eastern National.

or attacked in the rear, however brave they may be in other positions relative to the enemy, they will as a rule go to pieces [and] that the veteran troops as well as the new regiments, would become disheartened and confused in such a position."

On the first day at Chickamauga, both Union and Confederate units were frequently knocked blindly from one position to another by repeated attacks and counterattacks from enemy units that they did not even know were on the field. Norman Smith of the 105th Ohio recalls his company performing "Right face double quick march Halt Front Right dress" three different times before eventually being flanked and nearly routed. In many such cases, ground was gained and lost for no reason except that the enemy was there and shooting, so men instinctively fired back into the smoke and gloom. The bloody combat on the nineteenth was indecisive, but in many ways helped solidify Chickamauga's reputation as a particularly brutal confrontation.[11]

These memories were enhanced by the soldiers' experiences during their night on the battlefield. With a few exceptions, units had simply stopped fighting and established their lines among the dead and wounded. The close proximity of the enemy made fires inadvisable, so "it was a night of pinching cold and little sleep" as the men huddled in the darkness. Parts of the woods caught fire, and the usual sounds of wounded men groaning, with "heart-rending appeals for water and help," were joined by the screams of men being burned alive. The smoke-shrouded creek bottom took on a sinister atmosphere as nervous pickets fired at anything that moved, including stragglers and troops consolidating their positions. On the Union left, Thomas ordered his men to build breastworks, and the sound of their axes echoed over to the Confederates in Walker's and Polk's corps, who realized that they would have to confront those works in the morning. Everyone knew that the battle would continue the following day and the prospect of more carnage unnerved even veteran troops along both lines. At the creek itself, wounded men crawled and stumbled among the thickets in search of water, and as many of them suffered and died, the "River of Death" began to live up to its ancient Cherokee name.[12]

While the common soldiers of both armies were encountering the horrors of the battlefield and dreading the next day's bloody work, their commanders were initiating events that would also become an important part of the memories and myths surrounding the battle of Chickamauga. Whereas neither army commander played a decisive role in the first day's fighting, they both would figure prominently in the decisions and actions that subsequently determined the outcome of the conflict. In addition, several subordinate officers who contributed to the controversial results of the battle made their presence known during that restive night. Had it not been for the massive loss of life on the battlefield the following day, some of the stories from the night of the nineteenth—particularly in the Confederate camp—would border on the unbelievable.

On the Union side, one cannot help but compare accounts of the "council of war" at the Widow Glenn house with Rosecrans's conference at Stones River and a similar council held in a small farmhouse by General Meade and his subordinates on the second night at Gettysburg. In all three cases, the army commander was faced with clear choices of action following a day or more of bloody combat: retreat, attack, or hold. The very reason for the Chickamauga council invites scrutiny under the spotlight of memory. For Rosecrans and his supporters, the meeting was a logical way for him to assess the condition of his army and relay the following day's plans directly to his subordinates. According to his critics, however, Rosecrans was rattled and uncertain after the mighty carnage of the first day and needed reassurance and direction from more stable and confident minds. If the goal of the campaign was to protect Chattanooga, then there may have been reason to consider that the army withdraw in that direction, but to do so in the face of the enemy was a dangerous prospect and thus highly unlikely to be successful. In spite of the fluid nature of the first day's fighting, there seemed to be little inclination on Rosecrans's part to attack Bragg's army the next day. Perhaps the experience at Stones River, where the Army of the Cumberland allowed Bragg to wear out his army attacking it in a strong position on the second day, convinced the Union commanders that it was best to take a defensive posture and let the Confederates make the first move.

The decision to maintain a defensive stance also favors the role of George Thomas in the battle and in memory. According to one of the legends of Chickamauga, Thomas spent most of the meeting at the Widow Glenn's asleep in the corner, only to awaken occasionally and admonish Rosecrans to "strengthen the left" in preparation for the next day's action (this is likely an apocryphal story and bears a remarkable resemblance to the account of General G. K. Warren sleeping during the meeting at Gettysburg). This incident serves to enhance Thomas's reputation by portraying him as unruffled by the day's fighting and crediting him as the author of a defensive strategy that would have been successful had it been orchestrated correctly by the commanding general during the battle. Predicting what turned out to be Bragg's actual plan revealed Thomas's keen grasp of the situation and, according to his supporters, illustrated his confidence in the XIV Corps to hold the critical ground. Since many of Rosecrans's decisions the next day would reflect his desire to hold and strengthen his left flank, those who championed Thomas's role in the battle could point to the importance of his contribution to the "council of war" the night before.[13]

Meanwhile, in the Confederate camp, the command situation took a bizarre turn and set the stage for a great deal of future controversy. Bragg, apparently frustrated by the haphazard way that the battle had unfolded, decided to reorganize the command structure of his army prior to the next day's fighting. He created two wings. The Right Wing, commanded by General Polk, was made up of Cheatham's division of his own corps, plus Cleburne and Breckinridge's divisions from Hill's Corps, and the two divisions of Walker's Reserve Corps. The Left Wing was commanded by General Longstreet and consisted of T. C. Hindeman's division from Polk's Corps, Buckner's Corps (Stewart, William Preston, and Bushrod Johnson's divisions), and his own two divisions under Hood and Lafayette McLaws. Aside from the obvious confusion initiated by splitting up Polk's Corps and placing many of the Army of Tennessee's divisions under an unfamiliar commander, this restructuring also caused a ripple effect throughout the whole army as regimental, brigade, and division commanders were "bumped" upward to fill vacancies caused by combat losses and sudden promotions. Rather than simplify the chain of command, this midnight organizational shift served to further muddy it. Bragg had found yet a new way to undermine the effectiveness of his army, and the dubious results would be seen even before the dawning of the new day.

In a logical world, a general who had just rearranged the structure of his army's chain of command would spend the rest of the night communicating with his new wing commanders and familiarizing them with each other and their new subordinates. But Braxton Bragg did not operate in a logical world. When James Longstreet stepped off of the train with his staff in northern Georgia, there was no one from the Army of Tennessee there to meet him. The man who was to command a wing of an unfamiliar army in combat within a few hours was allowed to wander in the darkness looking for his headquarters, the commanding general, or any of his own divisions, without any directions or assistance. Whether from neglect, incompetence, misunderstanding, or a combination of one or more of these, Bragg had gotten off to a terrible start with the prickly Longstreet, which would lead to devastating consequences later in the campaign. In addition, the creation of the wing commands left D. H. Hill with a reduced corps under the command of an officer who had just recently been his equal in rank. Not only did this seem like a demotion to the already miffed Hill, but it virtually removed him from the chain of command that passed to and from his former divisions. Thus, Bragg's orders to Polk for an early-morning attack on the Union left failed to reach either Hill or John C. Breckinridge, whose fresh division of Kentuckians was to lead the assault. The situation in Longstreet's wing was not much better, as he struggled to work with his new command on the verge of a great battle.[14]

The climactic fight on 20 September had a tardy beginning but quickly devolved into chaos during the late morning. Bragg's planned attack at dawn against Thomas's XIV Corps did not get rolling until about 9:30 A.M. Led by Breckinridge's division, Polk's infantry repeatedly hurled itself against Thomas's breastworks without cracking the line. Two of Breckinridge's brigades got across the Lafayette Road and threatened Thomas's flank, but Thomas's reserves and part of James Negley's division beat them back. In spite of their overall lack of success, these attacks had one important result that affected the progress of the battle as the morning wore on. Rosecrans was acutely aware that the attacks on the left threatened his safest route back to Chattanooga. As the pressure on Thomas mounted and he called to the commanding general for support, Rosecrans responded by shifting brigades to the left as he sent reinforcements to Thomas.

The result was a continual process of "dressing to the left" at the divisional and brigade level. Over the course of the morning, as the roar of battle contin-ued on his left, Rosecrans meticulously shifted brigades and ordered those to their right to "dress left" and close up on the regiments to their left. This was a simple process on the parade ground, but in the uneven terrain and mix of woods and field at Chickamauga, it was not always clear where one brigade line began and another ended. Although there had been sporadic pressure against the Union right by Stewart's division during the morning, Rosecrans knew that a substantial portion of Bragg's army was somewhere to his front and ordered all of his troops to be ready to respond to any threat that might emerge in the vicinity of the Brotherton farm.[15]

The crisis came late in the morning and, depending on the version of the story being told, it was caused by a combination of factors. Uneven terrain, the usual fog of battle, Rosecrans's anxiety for the integrity of his line, the time be-tween the issuance and delivery of orders, and a clash of bruised egos between the commanding general and a subordinate all contributed to the catastrophe that befell the Union right flank. In the standard account, staff officer Sanford Kellogg was riding along the line west of the Brotherton field when he thought he spotted a gap between Wood's division and Reynolds's division in Rose-crans's constantly shifting line. Without checking carefully, he returned to the Glenn house and reported this gap to the excitable Rosecrans, who promptly gave orders to have Wood's brigade dress left to cover this hole and "support" Reynolds's line. The report of such a gap seemed credible to Rosecrans based on his belief that Brannan had already pulled his division out of the line to support Thomas, thus creating the break in the line.

In any case, General Wood was puzzled when he received this order, since he was already in contact with the unit on his left (neither Kellogg nor Rosecrans realized that Brannan's two brigades were still in place) and could see there was no gap. But Woods had been the target of Rosecrans's profanity-laced criticism the day before for moving too tentatively and was not inclined to send a message back asking for clarification. The commanding general's order clearly directed him to connect with Reynolds's troops, so he dutifully pulled his regiments out of line, marched in column behind Brannan's "invisible" division, and headed further to his left. Although he had been assured by one of McCook's staff officers that the troops to his right would "dress left" to cover the hole this shift created, these movements were not coordinated, and for a short time, Rosecrans's carefully maintained battle line was dangerously disconnected. It was at precisely this moment that Confederate Wing Commander Longstreet launched a thundering assault against that exact point in the line.[16]

The attack could not have come at a worse time for the Union troops west of the Brotherton farm. Since Longstreet was sending nearly three divisions into a fairly narrow area, he had arrayed his brigades in a massive column that was two brigades across and nearly six brigades deep. As they rolled into the gap, they struck the tail end of Wood's brigades moving in column across their front. These units were caught unprepared, out of formation, and unable to resist the wave of Confederates that smashed into them. When they routed, they exposed Brannan's right to enfilading fire, which caused the eventual collapse of parts of that line as well. Within minutes, a battle that had been a virtual stalemate for nearly thirty-six hours turned into a chaotic Union rout and triumphant Confederate pursuit, with two corps commanders and nearly half of the Union army streaming back toward Chattanooga. Longstreet's troops surged into the gap and brushed aside the isolated remnants of the Union right wing. This included Wilder's Lightning Brigade, whose veterans claimed that it was ordered to escort Assistant Secretary of War Charles Dana to Chattanooga just as it had repulsed a Confederate charge and was about to launch a counterattack against Longstreet's exposed flank. With little opposition, the rebel column began to right wheel slowly toward the vulnerable right flank of Thomas's line. At this moment, with the complete destruction of an entire Union army a real possibility, the course of the war could have been significantly altered and the Confederacy might have been able to counter the summer's defeats at Gettysburg and Vicksburg.[17]

But this was the Army of Tennessee, operating under an unwieldy command structure with Braxton Bragg as its commander and facing an unknown and unprecedented tactical situation. As quickly as the Confederate attack succeeded, it began to flounder as it penetrated the soft underbelly of the Union line. During the course of the morning, Union forces had massed a considerable number of guns on a ridge just beyond the Dyer field, and these began to hammer at the gray brigades in the open fields below. Confederate troops eventually overran some of these unsupported guns, but the delay allowed some Union infantry units to organize a defense and launch some limited counter-attacks. A bullet fired during one of these counterattacks critically wounded General Hood, leaving one of Longstreet's divisions without its principal com-mander at a critical moment. Neither Longstreet nor Bragg was present at the point of the breakthrough, so neither was immediately aware of the extent of his advantage. Instead of swinging to the right, some of the Confederate units continued forward and essentially lost contact with the battle, while others maneuvered cautiously under sporadic Union fire. Thus, in spite of its spec-tacular charge and the stunning route of its opponent, the Confederate Left Wing had to spend some critical time reorganizing and untangling its assault-ing units before it could fully exploit its advantage.[18]

On the Union side, the situation was at just as confused and even more critical. In spite of his efforts to rally them, Rosecrans was unable to stem his panicked troops' momentum toward the rear and the perceived safety of Chat-tanooga. When he reached McFarland's Gap and the road back to the city, he found himself torn between his desire to ride toward Thomas and his duty to protect Chattanooga. Rosecrans's chief of staff, James Garfield, persuaded his commander to accompany the fleeing portion of his army, which included corps commanders McCook and Crittenden, back to Chattanooga to organize an effective defense of the city. Garfield himself would ride to Thomas and ap-prise him of the extent of the disaster that had befallen the rest of the army and help determine the best course of action for those who remained in position. Had the whole army retreated during the early afternoon, Rosecrans's personal withdrawal from the field would have looked like the correct decision and his reputation might have overcome his tactical blunders. Unfortunately for both Rosecrans and Bragg, many of the soldiers of the Army of the Cumberland were not willing to give up the field without a fight. In spite of the tremendous carnage and high drama of the battle thus far, the conflict's most remembered (and perhaps most controversial) moments were about to take place on a piece of high ground known as Snodgrass Hill.[19]

At the heart of what would be recorded by both historians and veterans as one of the Army of the Cumberland's greatest moments were the troops of George Thomas's XIV Corps, who had been holding their ground around the Kelly farm all day against constant Confederate pressure from Breckinridge, Cleburne, and other units of Polk's wing. Aided by rough breastworks and supported throughout the day by troops that Rosecrans had shuffled from the right, Thomas's veterans had managed to inflict heavy casualties on the attacking Confederates, including a mortal wound to Confederate general

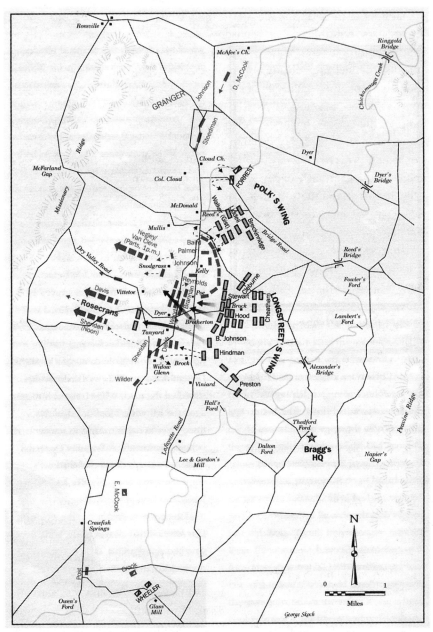

FIG. 4 (MAP): Battle of Chickamauga, afternoon, 20 September 1863. Longstreet's breakthrough on the Union right flank forced Thomas to defend the left with his own corps and the remnants of other units. Courtesy of Eastern National.

Benjamin Helms, President Lincoln's brother-in-law. However, Thomas's men would have been completely flanked after Longstreet's breakthrough had it not been for the troops who rallied on Horseshoe Ridge during the early afternoon following the rout of the army's center and right wing. These troops consisted of fragments from Van Cleve's, Brannan's, Wood's, Reynolds's, and Negley's commands, who had escaped the initial panic and made their way to a line of guns that General Negley had amassed on the ridge by late in the morning. Although Negley eventually pulled out with much of this artillery and abandoned the battle, "this isolated line . . . repeatedly repulsed the most furious assaults of Longstreet's massive lines." This patchwork defense, along with Thomas's breastworks, was enough to slow down the momentum of the Confederate juggernaut until late afternoon, when Bragg and Longstreet finally decided to send their battalions in for the kill.[20]

The "stertorous breathing of a terrible battle" had been going on continuously since Breckinridge's men had first hit Thomas's line at 9:30 that morning and was about to reach a new level of intensity on the darkening slopes of Snodgrass Hill. Unlike the climax at Gettysburg, where the outcome of the great charge on the last day was determined by less than an hour of fighting, the troops who held the high ground at Chickamauga had endured hours of intense combat leading up to the last desperate hour. The Union soldiers under Thomas's command were exhausted, thirsty, low on ammunition, and decimated by casualties when they were called upon to hold off wave after wave of advancing Confederates in the late afternoon of 20 September. Upon hearing that there was no more ammunition, one soldier from the 79th Pennsylvania wrote, "well, I thought 'that looks pretty blue,'" before he joined his unit's retreat.

Many of the Confederates were equally frazzled as they negotiated the woods and rocks at the base of the ridge where the Union forces continued to fire down on them. Both sides sensed the importance of the last hours of daylight. For the Army of the Cumberland, it was a matter of survival. One man wrote "it would seem as though every man realized that the fate of the army depended on this charge." Everything that it had done in the past could be swept away if Thomas's wing was overrun and destroyed. The Army of Tennessee had its greatest victory in its grasp; to let it slip away would be a crushing blow to its collective morale. With everything at stake and the battle hanging in the balance, fresh troops arrived and raised the intensity to another level.[21]

Gordon Granger had been posted north of the main line at McAfee's Church with James B. Steedman's division of the Reserve Corps throughout the whole battle. As the afternoon wore on, he and Steedman listened to the sounds of combat surging in their direction and realized that they were needed on the field. Both Granger and Steedman claimed credit for making the decision to go into the fight without orders from Rosecrans, but regardless of who came up with the idea, it was up to Granger to approve the forced march toward the sound of the guns. Thomas's ability to hold the line east of the Lafayette Road allowed Steedman and his men to enter the left of the Union perimeter, double-quick across the rear of the defensive horseshoe, and hurl themselves at Bushrod Johnson's Confederates, who were flanking the far right of the Union line. The already fierce fighting escalated; "seized as if with frenzy both friend and foe struggled with a determination almost superhuman." As if there was not enough drama in the moment, Steedman himself led the charge that saved the flank. Much less spectacular, but just as important, was the arrival of the reserve ammunition train, which Granger had thought to bring along when arriving a short time later with the rest of the reinforcements. The most dramatic memories of Granger's relief also included accounts of a Napoleon-like Thomas gazing with anxiety at the approaching cloud of dust, wondering whether it signaled the approach of friend or foe, and emotionally thanking Granger (or Steedman) for his timely arrival, stating, "you have saved my army."[22]

Granger's arrival bought Thomas more time, but the situation was still critical as the Confederates began to increase the pressure on the makeshift Union line. Up until the late afternoon, the Southerners had not been able to coordinate the two wings of their army against the remaining Yankee regiments. Polk's rebels continued to put pressure on Thomas's left by assaulting the troops behind the breastworks, but other than some of Forrest's cavalry, only a few Confederates had crossed the Lafayette Road beyond Thomas's left, and none of these had put any real pressure on that exposed flank. On Longstreet's wing, the pursuit of the fleeing Union troops and the lack of command and control among the rest of his brigades had prevented them from making coordinated attacks or finding the gap between the two legs of the Yankee defense salient. After an unsatisfactory meeting with a seemingly depressed and uncertain Bragg, Longstreet committed his reserve division under William Preston and attempted to crush Thomas's line once and for all. By around 4:00 P.M., Polk had gotten his men organized and began to push them harder against the weary XIV Corps soldiers still crouched behind their breastworks.[23]

Thomas eventually realized that he could not hold the entire line against this pressure, so he ordered the divisions that had been holding the line in the Kelly field since morning to pull back toward the higher ground on Snodgrass Hill. There was considerable debate among postwar participants about the reasons for and timing of this decision. Garfield arrived on the field at about this time and claimed that his was the first clear information that Thomas had on the disaster that had befallen the army's right wing, information that prompted Thomas's decision to withdraw from his most advanced positions. Garfield

FIG. 5: Gen. James B. Steedman's arrival with part of the Reserve Corps helped stabilize Thomas's line on Snodgrass Hill late in the afternoon on 20 September. Library of Congress.

also carried an order for a general withdrawal to Rossville Gap to reunite with other elements of the army that had rallied there and to better protect Chatta-nooga. Thomas's most vehement defenders (who were also likely to be critical of Rosecrans) claim that this order was followed reluctantly and contradicted Thomas's earlier vow to "hold his position until darkness." This decision also may have been influenced by the sound of the Confederates cheering from one end of their line to the other, which left the Yankees under the impression that they were close to being surrounded.[24]

The act of withdrawing under fire was a tricky and costly procedure for many of the weary troops involved. As the frontline troops withdrew, the Confederate veterans smelled blood and renewed their attacks, capturing both men and guns. There was close-range, hand-to-hand fighting "with charge and countercharge" all along the line between Confederates going for the kill and Yankees struggling for survival. As Thomas began his general retreat in the late afternoon, the regiments left behind had to fend for themselves, often fighting with little or no ammunition. In the confusion, several, including the 21st Ohio, which, according to one historian, "fought one of the most historic defensive battles of the war," missed the command to retreat (or were given contradictory orders by unknown officers) and were captured en masse. Some accounts have "night finding Thomas's command . . . still holding the ridge," but most historians agree that there was still daylight left when Thomas got his beleaguered men off of the hill and on the road toward Rossville. Delaying the retreat until nightfall would certainly make Thomas's stand more heroic and uphold his alleged pledge to hold this place until dark. It would also give the Confederates some excuse for not attempting to pursue the fleeing Federals and complete the victory that many of them knew they had won.[25]

Like much of the rest of the battle, Bragg's failure to order an aggressive pursuit is clouded in controversy. His critics, who included Nathan Bedford Forrest and James Longstreet, claimed that Bragg was so out of touch with the battle that he failed to realize the extent of his army's victory. Instead, he fussed about Polk and Hill's poor performance earlier that morning and lamented the failure of his original plan to drive the enemy back to McLemore's Gap. There are also accounts that claim that even the troops on the front line did not realize that all of Thomas's men had retreated and thus did not take up a pursuit because they expected to continue the fight in the morning. The most likely explanation had far more to do with the condition of the Confederate forces than the mentality of their generals.

The two-day battle had inflicted horrific casualties on the officers and enlisted men of the Army of Tennessee. The troops who held the field on the evening of the twentieth were suffering from exhaustion, thirst, hunger, a shortage of ammunition, and were badly disorganized after a day of nearly constant combat. There were few rebels who had not been heavily engaged, and the army possessed no well-rested reserves to take up an energetic pursuit. Forrest, who had been dogging the Yankees and had seen the extent of their distress, howled in protest at the lack of action, but it did no good. The victorious rebels had to be content with their battlefield celebration and the capture of large numbers of prisoners, guns, small arms, and flags from their erstwhile opponents.[26]

For the numbers engaged, Chickamauga was one of the bloodiest battles of the war. Nearly 17,000 Confederates and 16,000 Union soldiers had been killed, wounded, or captured. The loss of officers, including Union brigade commanders William Lytle and Hans C. Heg and Confederates Preston Smith and Benjamin H. Helms, had been staggering at all levels. Both armies experienced disturbing breakdowns at the upper levels of command. Rosecrans and two of his corps commanders were completely driven from the field. Normally reliable division commanders like James Negley and Philip Sheridan seemingly lost their will to fight and only reluctantly stopped short of fleeing the entire twelve miles to Chattanooga by the end of the day. Bragg's chain of command had nearly completely broken down in the middle of a great victory, which added to the growing hostility between the commanding general and his chief subordinates.[27]

At some point, memories of the battle differed among the soldiers, the armies, and the leaders, depending on what they saw and how they interpreted the relative importance of the events they participated in. One Union veteran thought that the Battle of Chickamauga "was lost by defective tactics, like many another [sic] good fights." Another expressed a more cynical view, describing Chickamauga as "a useless, disastrous battle." Oddly, one could argue that this veteran was on to something, since the significance of this titanic struggle was still very much up in the air in the weeks after the battle. The Union force was bloodied but intact; the Confederates had been equally damaged and were in only slightly better shape than the Yankees in Chattanooga. Unlike Gettysburg, where the participants could sense a clear outcome in the hours and days after the battle, the final assessment of victory or defeat could only come after another series of dramatic events.[28]

If the object of the Union Army of the Cumberland was to defend Chattanooga, as Rosecrans would later claim, then the Battle of Chickamauga was a costly but successful Union effort to keep Bragg from recapturing the city. However, the Confederates saw the battle as a bungled Federal effort to win a decisive victory over Bragg's army, thus making the outcome of the battle a Confederate success by crippling and demoralizing a substantial part of the Union Army. Ultimately, the interpretation of this campaign's goals would have a significant impact on how its participants constructed their memories of the battle and explained their meaning. Although the outcome of the fighting on 19 and 20 September seemed to signify that a decisive Confederate triumph had taken place, subsequent debates over the actual purpose of the campaign have clouded and confused the significance of this Confederate battlefield victory. This is compounded by the correspondingly interwoven and overlapping images of Rosecrans's apparent panic, Thomas's resolute determination, and Bragg's failure to finish the job.[29]

If there was one thing the soldiers who fought at Chickamauga could agree on, it was that the two-day battle in the woods and clearings around the creek was one of the fiercest of the war. Whether veterans of the horrific fighting at Shiloh or Perryville or inexperienced troops from the garrisons of Kentucky or posts along the Mississippi, the soldiers who participated in the fighting at Chickamauga knew that they had been in an enormous conflict unlike anything they had ever seen. One postwar writer summed up the feelings of many when he wrote: "No battle in the Civil War was more stubbornly fought on both sides than was that of Chickamauga. Considering the number of men engaged, it was by far the bloodiest, and was characterized from first to last by exhibitions of bravery on both sides not surpassed in any battle in history. No writer of fiction ever portrayed anything equal to the reality. The monuments . . . that stand there now remind those who participated . . . of the dreadful carnage, but cannot convey to one that did not witness it the faintest conception of the battle."[30]

After citing eyewitness accounts of severed heads placed on stumps and dead soldiers with ears and limbs cut off, historian John Bowers concluded that contrary to the war's earlier sense of civility, "now the beast had popped out." He further postulates that "the canker that held every lust, hate, and demonic urge . . . in the human soul had been lanced" and that "whatever was darkest in the American psyche came out" at Chickamauga. While the evidence left by participants and historians may only partially bear this out, the bloodshed and courage on the "River of Death" provided the clearest foundation on which combatants of both sides, of all ranks, could begin to build their memories. However, before anyone could put this battle into perspective, the rest of the campaign had to play itself out in the trenches and on the hills surrounding Chattanooga, where the wounded, but still scrappy, Army of the Cumberland had taken refuge.[31]

Several specific events and actions around Chattanooga had a direct effect on the meaning and memory of the Battle of Chickamauga. Along with the inevitable sack of the hapless Rosecrans, the War Department attempted to reorganize the Army of the Cumberland by replacing some of its principal officers, restructuring two infantry corps, and augmenting the army with troops from other theaters. The arrival of Ulysses S. Grant and troops from the Union Army of the Tennessee also challenged the Army of the Cumberland's pride and identity by forcing them to share credit for lifting the siege and eventually defeating the enemy. For the Confederates, another uprising among the Army of Tennessee's high command led to the detachment of Longstreet's troops to an obscure operation elsewhere, a change in commanders in several infantry corps, and the gradual decline in morale among the officers and men at all levels. Ultimately, the fate of the two armies culminated spectacularly on

Missionary Ridge when the Army of the Cumberland's veterans routed the Confederates from a seemingly impregnable, but ultimately flawed, position.

It is safe to say that Rosecrans sealed his fate when he followed Garfield's advice to leave the field in the late morning at Chickamauga. The fact that half his army stood and fought for hours after he fled magnified his error in judgment and transformed it into an unforgivable blot on his professional reputation. Rosecrans did an admirable job of preparing the defenses around Chattanooga in the weeks after the defeat at Chickamauga, but many observers (including Garfield) felt that Rosecrans was a broken and shattered commander who did not have the heart to raise his army's morale or break the siege of the city. Among the general's most vocal critics was Assistant Secretary of War Charles Dana, who peppered Washington with reports indicating Rosecrans's increasing depression and lack of will. Dana was a "Thomas man" (or at least claimed to be after the war) and lobbied openly to have Rosecrans replaced with the "Rock of Chickamauga."[32]

However, the debacle at Chickamauga had unnerved Gen. Henry Halleck and President Lincoln to such an extent that they felt that more dramatic changes were needed. They not only fired Rosecrans, they also relieved generals McCook and Crittenden and disbanded the two army corps (XX and XXI) that they had formerly commanded. The troops in those corps were placed in the newly created IV Corps and put under the command of Gen. Gordon Granger, whose reputation had survived (and perhaps been enhanced by) the mess at Chickamauga. Thomas was appointed to command the Army of the Cumberland, but the War Department took the dramatic extra step of ordering General Ulysses S. Grant to take charge in Chattanooga.[33]

Grant's arrival as the new "savior" of Chattanooga was just one of the things that left a bad taste in the mouths of the Army of the Cumberland's veterans. Along with Grant came thousands of troops from the Army of the Tennessee led by William T. Sherman, two infantry corps from the east (the XI and XII Corps) commanded by Joseph Hooker, and a whole bevy of staff officers, observers, and other personnel who could potentially steal credit for the army's accomplishments. For most of the Army of the Cumberland's soldiers and veterans, their memories of the siege of Chattanooga—and the whole Chickamauga/Chattanooga campaign—were influenced by the dramatic charge up Missionary Ridge on 25 November 1863. Up until that point, the army had watched other troops and commanders gain the glory for opening the supply lines, seizing Lookout Mountain, and pressuring the Confederates at Tunnel Hill. When they were ordered to seize the rifle pits at the base of the ridge, the Army of the Cumberland's infantry soldiers took the opportunity to play their part with great enthusiasm. After taking the first line and receiving enemy fire

FIG. 6: Gen. Thomas Crittenden lost his command and saw his former corps disbanded after most of it was routed at Chickamauga. Library of Congress.

from above, the troops advanced without orders and clambered up the uneven slopes of the ridge. What could have been a reckless mistake turned out to be "the most prominent feature of the engagement" and the army's greatest triumph when the enemy unexpectedly broke and ran, leaving the crest and the victory to the cheering veterans of Chickamauga.[34]

While the losers at Chickamauga were at least partially redeemed by their performance at Missionary Ridge, the winning Confederate army suffered a humiliating and crushing defeat. Not surprisingly, the psychological collapse of the Army of Tennessee began not long after the firing had stopped in the gloomy woods around Snodgrass Hill. Bragg's failure to order a pursuit, his obsessive complaints about Hill and Polk, and his miserable relationship with Longstreet all served to knock the glow off the army's victory in the days after Chickamauga. Both Longstreet and cavalry commander Nathan B. Forrest believed that a vigorous pursuit of the fleeing Union army would have resulted in an even greater victory and openly criticized Bragg's handling of the battle in their reports and public comments. By the time the army settled into its positions around Chattanooga, the animosity between these forceful officers and their commander had grown out of control. Bragg sent Forrest on a raid into central Tennessee and ordered Longstreet to take his corps toward Knoxville to threaten Ambrose E. Burnside's Union forces, who were feeling their way toward Bragg's rear. By sending Forrest and Longstreet away, Bragg silenced two of his critics, but he deprived his army of its mounted reconnaissance arm and nearly 15,000 veteran infantry.

Within the rest of the army, the ongoing disputes between Bragg and his corps commanders led to the replacement of Polk and Hill with Breckinridge and the reluctant William Hardee, whose previous run-ins with Bragg had caused his absence from the fight at Chickamauga. At first, the situation around Chattanooga favored Bragg's plan to invest and starve out the Union garrison. The Yankees were disorganized and discouraged, their commander rattled and uncertain, and their supply line thin and vulnerable. By this time, Bragg had not only accepted the outcome of Chickamauga as a great victory but was certain that the Union forces in Chattanooga were near collapse and incapable of breaking out of his trap. As a result, he never ordered his army to significantly strengthen its positions on Lookout Mountain and Missionary Ridge during the months that they occupied them. Although the positions were visually impressive, they were flawed by poor engineering, lack of access from one end to the other, and some serious line-of-sight impairments at various key points. Not only that, but their lofty perch provided the Confederate soldiers with a bird's-eye view of the growing strength of their opponents. By the time the Union forces struck, the southern army was bored, demoralized,

FIG. 7: Gen. Gordon Granger's timely arrival with the Reserve Corps on 20 September at Chickamauga earned him command of the newly created IV Corps after the battle. Library of Congress.

undersupplied, and lacked confidence in its commanding general. In many ways, the army that fled from the crest of the ridge on that November day had been beaten by its own flaws before the Yankees ever fired a shot.[35]

The aftermath of the Battle of Chickamauga and the struggle for Chattanooga paved the way for the construction of unique and contradictory memories by the battle's veterans, historians, and the public in the years after the war. Both armies had experienced extraordinary highs and lows during the course of the campaign, and both had suffered from dramatic shifts in the fortunes of battle that determined victory or defeat. Each army had seen its commanding generals fail miserably; each had a subordinate commander rise to the occasion and make a significant contribution to the outcome of the campaign. Both the Army of the Cumberland and the Army of Tennessee would fight on for another year and a half after Chickamauga. What happened in that period also influenced the construction of memory for the veterans of both armies and contributed to the controversial status that each occupied in the national history of the war.

THREE

"The Grandest [Cause] That Ever Rose, the Purest That Ever Fell"

It would take several decades after the cessation of hostilities before the veterans of the battles around Chattanooga could fully construct memories of the war and define its meaning. However, the construction of memories that began in the woods, fields, and hills surrounding the "River of Death" continued even as the fighting raged for another eighteen months. Just as the identities of the Army of the Cumberland and Army of Tennessee had been forged by their experiences leading up to the autumn of 1863, the outcome and aftermath of this campaign continued to influence both the commanders and men in the ranks. Once the war ended, the soldiers from both sides returned home to a nation and a region wracked by four years of trauma, death, and destruction. After a period of readjustment and reconstruction, the veterans began to reassess their experiences and share them with former comrades at reunions and meetings. The challenges they, along with the rest of the nation, faced helped give the war meaning and fit it into the larger context of American history and society.

To place the Battle of Chickamauga and its veterans in a larger perspective, we need to take a moment to examine how Americans remembered the wars leading up to the Civil War. From the time of the Revolution, Americans have grappled with the powerful emotions and memories generated by conflicts against both foreign and domestic foes. The forms of commemoration used and the memories they generated evolved over time as the fledgling nation sought to develop, strengthen, and preserve its collective identity. The process of remembering war often became entangled with nationalism, politics, economics, race, class, regionalism, and other cultural factors. These elements, combined with war's heroes and villains, glories and tragedies, and winners and losers, made the construction of war memories a complicated undertaking. Needless to say, the unique circumstances of the Civil War created a new set of challenges in the construction of America's war memories.

As social concepts, war and memory go together extremely well. Warfare produces several things that memory thrives on, namely drama, controversy, heroism, and death. In turn, these heroic images bring forth the types of values—courage, sacrifice, duty, patriotism, loyalty, and manhood—that are important to the maintenance of community and national identities. Collective memories, and their accompanying rituals and commemorations, play a critical role in giving meaning to wars and the hardships that they entail. According to Kurt Piehler, the process of remembering war is an exercise in both vernacular and civic memory that demonstrates how "rituals, holidays, monuments, . . . cemeteries, and . . . veterans organizations . . . have been used to advance the agendas of dominant, if often competing, elites" within American society. This array of competing views, methods, and interpretations frequently raises questions about which war memories society will preserve and who is responsible for undertaking the commemorative rituals necessary for that preservation.

Even more revealing is how the carefully constructed civic and public memories from previous wars have often been used by national leaders to rally support for the next armed conflict. By invoking the "sacred" memories of the nation's heroes, both living and dead, those who influence public culture attempt to motivate the current generation to live up to the accomplishments and sacrifices made by previous ones. In other cases, memories can serve the interests of other segments of the community and act as a catalyst for peace and a deterrent to future wars. As demonstrated by the American Revolution, the War of 1812, the Mexican War, and by the Civil War and the Spanish-American War, this process can be complicated if the memories of previous wars are clouded by defeat, controversy, dramatic social change, or contrasting vernacular memories.[1]

Before the Civil War, much of war's drama and heroic memory focused on great leaders and great deeds. During the first half of the nineteenth century, the nation turned several of its great warriors into presidents and occasionally remembered the victories that secured independence and forged its early identity. However, in spite of their familiarity to many people, these famous leaders (with the exception of George Washington) did not serve particularly well as the focal point for constructing either vernacular or official memories of the new nation's early struggles. The problem was mostly caused by politics. As the country's political factions and parties evolved and battled for power, they attempted to put their respective ideological stamps on the legacies of the armed conflicts that established the nation. Since most of the aforementioned leaders were eventually associated with one political faction or another, their ability to serve as central figures in a single national narrative was severely compromised. In addition, many people felt that the veneration of individuals was elitist and non-democratic and therefore contrary to the widely held revolutionary ideals of individualism and equality.[2]

In spite of the conflicts over these initial constructions of memory, one set of early local commemorations held a possible key to forging some sort of national military narrative. In the towns of Lexington and Concord, ritual commemorations of the war's first shots focused on the image of the minuteman, the prototypical citizen-soldier. Unlike the exclusive image of the Society of Cincinnati (a group of veterans whose membership was limited to Continental Army officers), the veterans of the revolution's first bloody encounters were average citizens who simply rose to the historic moment. Although the two communities sparred over the memories of the engagements that took place on 19 April 1775, they both agreed that the courageous spirit of the citizen-soldiers and the sacrifice made by those who were killed and injured were important enough to be included in the identity of the new nation. This thread of constructed memory corresponded with the creation of two commemorative landscapes, one at Lexington Green and the other around Concord's North Bridge, which provided locations for anniversary celebrations, monument dedications, and patriotic rhetoric.[3]

America's next two wars did little to help the nation construct a clear, official narrative that could be adopted by a wide cross-section of its citizenry. The War of 1812 was a controversial, politically divisive conflict that produced a narrow victory over Great Britain. Although it resulted in few tangible territorial, diplomatic, or economic gains, it did establish the United States as a nation willing to stand up to European powers. Aside from Andrew Jackson, whose subsequent political career made him a controversial hero at best, the most persistent national memory of the war was of the unsuccessful British bombardment of Fort McHenry and the resulting veneration of the flag in Francis Scott Key's "Star Spangled Banner." Not only had many of the citizen-soldiers failed to live up to the legacy of their revolutionary forefathers, but a fair number of Federalists from New England, where the minuteman memory was born, had opposed the war and supported the enemy.[4]

The War with Mexico took place nearly thirty-five years after the War of 1812, and could not draw much inspiration from the memory of those early events. Rather than a righteous struggle for liberty, the war against Mexico was seen by many Americans as part of a program of expansion that was favored by one political party and bitterly opposed by the other. Although the nation generally rallied around the volunteers from the various states, the most visible heroes of this war were graduates of the United States Military Academy at West Point. These were trained soldiers whose professionalism contradicted the "plowshares into swords" minuteman image. Most commemorative activities connected with these earlier conflicts tended to be on a vernacular level, as communities remembered the local boys who died and honored the ones who came home with the occasional statue, monument, or burial at a local cemetery.[5]

It is not hard to imagine the difficulty faced by civic leaders in constructing a coherent national memory when one considers the regional and political divisions that plagued the country during the first half of the nineteenth century. As the sectional differences between the North and South escalated, each side tried to appropriate the symbols and memories of previous generations to uphold their own political positions. As the crisis over slavery and states' rights became more bitterly debated following the Mexican War, constructed memories of the past polarized along sectional lines. Southerners saw themselves as the heirs to the revolutionary patriots and claimed George Washington as the prototypical American and champion of Southern liberty. Northerners wrapped themselves in the "Star-Spangled Banner" and called upon the memory of the minutemen of Lexington and Concord to protect the sacred Union of their forefathers. When war broke out in 1861, both sides invoked the memories of the revolution to justify their efforts to "save the Union" or "protect states' (Southern) rights." Ironically, it is from this fratricidal conflict and its contentious aftermath that Americans were finally able to construct their most enduring, albeit contentious, collective memories of the meaning of war.[6]

Like all memory building, this process took time. Constructing a set of national memories out of the chaos and carnage of the Civil War was an extremely difficult task. Former Confederates coped with defeat by almost immediately constructing what became known as the "Myth of the Lost Cause." The North, politically torn over the issue of the freed slaves and devastated by Abraham Lincoln's shocking murder, was divided between those who wanted to "wave the bloody shirt" and punish the South and others who hoped to reunite the nation as quickly as possible. It had been a war fought not just by armies, but by machines, factories, railroads, and civilians. It had provided glory enough for those who sought it, but also unimaginable amounts of hardship, misery, and destruction for many.[7]

If there was a common denominator that bound a large segment of the American public to a common memory of the Civil War, it was death. Not only had astounding numbers of men been killed on the battlefield, but thousands more had died of disease in camps, hospitals, and both northern and southern prisoner-of-war compounds. Civilians, most notably those in the South, had increasingly suffered from sickness, malnourishment, and deprivation, particularly as the realities of defeat closed in on them. The citizens of the North experienced death by reading the growing casualty lists in their newspapers, living among the multitudes of grieving parents and widows, and gazing in horror at the stunning photographs of battlefield carnage taken by Matthew Brady, Tim O'Sullivan, and others. The dramatic loss of so many lives, particularly among the young men of both sections, demanded that society construct some sort of context that would help place these losses into perspective. Since more cohesive memories were still under construction, both Northerners and Southerners embraced the symbols and rituals surrounding "heroic" death as the first chapter in a larger narrative of the war.[8]

By focusing on death and the suffering surrounding it, Americans could utilize and modify rituals and ceremonies that were already in place. The war had accelerated the frequency of death and perhaps numbed the intensity of feelings surrounding it, but it had not altered people's need to give meaning to the loss of their loved ones. Even before the war, Victorian Americans placed a considerable amount of importance on the notion of "dying well" and constructed a clear set of standards to separate a "good" death from a bad one. By possessing an unshakable faith in Christian salvation, demonstrating unwavering devotion to family, and displaying an unselfish concern for the living, an individual could claim to have approached death in an honorable and dignified way. Noting the style and manner of his or her death was an important way that loved ones attempted to construct a positive and lasting memory of that person.

The wartime deaths of large numbers of men in the prime of life triggered modifications to the "good death" paradigm by adding heroism, duty, and sacrifice to the list of elements required to give death a positive meaning. Throughout the war, letters, reports, newspaper accounts, and funeral eulogies reinforced the idea that the men killed in the war should be remembered for their noble sacrifice and sense of duty. The general idea was that the loss of a son or husband was somehow offset by the gain to the nation or the cause that their sacrifice entailed. The "mass suffering" shared by those in the field and on the home front served as a common experience that strengthened widely held values of faith, resilience, and humility in the face of adversity. Whatever private expressions of bitterness may have come out during the war, the postwar period gradually saw notions of wasted lives and useless slaughter replaced with idealized memories of heroic sacrifice in both the North and the South.[9]

Interestingly, much of the momentum for the veneration of the dead in the years immediately following the war came from women, particularly southern women. There was an urgent need in the defeated South to find a meaning for all those deaths, and it was very much left to women to provide that meaning. When the Federal government began re-interring the bodies of Union dead in the years after the war, Southerners responded by seeking to pay homage to their own slain and missing. Many of the Confederate dead had been buried in mass graves on fields that had been in the possession of Union forces at the end of the battle. This not only made it nearly impossible to identify individual bodies, but it was often difficult to pinpoint the locations of the burials. Confederate ladies memorial associations, led mostly by local women throughout the South, made the effort to find the soldiers' graves from their home states and create proper memorials to the missing and unidentified Confederate dead. By raising funds, arranging burials, and dedicating monuments, the ladies memorial associations constructed and preserved the memory of the Southern cause and venerated the men who fell defending it. In the process, they constructed a powerful set of images and vernacular memories that were "dedicated to the Confederate Soldier and all who loved, lost, or suffered, in that Cause, the grandest that ever rose, the purest that ever fell." By invoking the powerful commemorative rhetoric of a civic religion, the virtues of duty, sacrifice, and valor that had once been a shared memory for all Americans from the time of Lexington and Concord now came under the constructed memory umbrella of the Lost Cause.[10]

In many ways, defeat united Southerners more effectively than victory motivated those in the North. While individual states, communities, and families sought to recover their dead from often remote battlefield graves in the South, the North lacked the level of coordination that characterized the southern women's efforts. Rather than try to exhume thousands of Union bodies from hundreds of locations for shipment to local cemeteries in their home states, the Federal government created military cemeteries at Arlington and on several of the major battlefields where the men had fallen. Not only would re-interment be less costly, but more importantly the process created effective commemorative landscapes in the South that recognized the sanctity of the Union dead.

The precedent for the use of battlefield cemeteries as commemorative landscapes had already been established by the creation and dedication of the military cemetery at Gettysburg in November 1863. Lincoln's address that day not only defined the purpose of the war, it reinforced the virtues of sacrifice and devotion and sanctified the ground on which Union soldiers had fought and died. The dedication ceremonies at the newly created cemeteries, including the one at Arlington, would echo this language and reinforce the idea that Northern soldiers had died for a more noble cause and deserved equal, if not greater, veneration than the fallen Confederates. Eventually, both North and South created their own regional "memorial days" that used the language of commemoration and the ritual veneration of the war's dead to construct separate, but similar, collective memories of the recent conflict.[11]

The Civil War set a standard for remembering war that shifted much of the attention away from national issues toward a focus on the duty and sacrifice of the common soldier. The source of this vernacular memory stems from the veterans themselves and the communities where they lived before and after the war. The narrative theme of this "myth of the war experience" is the transition from civilian to soldier, with a particular emphasis on the personal sacrifices made to achieve that transition. It is in many ways a natural extension of the veneration of the dead; in fact, it draws on the some of the same imagery and similar commemorative language. In the context of this construction, the war experience is a journey. It takes the soldier from the warmth and security of civilian life, through a hardening and training period, and into the transcendental test of battle. Thus, war is not just a physical experience; it is a spiritual rite of manhood for those who participate. The experience of war creates a sense of belonging and accomplishment among veterans that is not limited to generals, officers, or those who win awards for distinguished service or extraordinary valor. This interpretation narrows the gap between those who were killed and those who risked being killed and allows the commemorative rhetoric of "sacrifice" to extend to the living, as well as the dead.[12]

The focus on the common soldier and the gradual acceptance of the myth of the war experience meant that the initial responsibility for commemorating war fell largely on local communities rather than governments. Soldiers could be remembered by their fellow citizens without making reference to the success or failure of causes for which they died, thus eliminating the need to rationalize victory or explain defeat during the process of commemoration. In the absence of an existing national memory, the symbolic image of the common soldier constructed localized, vernacular memories of the war that did not require any official rituals to legitimize them. It was a pattern learned during the country's earlier wars and applied soon after the Civil War on a much larger scale.

During the postwar years, larger sectional and regional memorial associations and veterans groups erected and dedicated statues to the conflict's soldiers and heroes in urban public spaces. Smaller towns and communities created their own memorial landscapes honoring the common soldier. Large numbers of remarkably similar statues of soldiers appeared in town squares, on village greens, and in cemeteries and other public spaces throughout both the North and South. These were usually commissioned by civic leaders, purchased with funds raised in the community, and dedicated with the blessing and participation of local veterans. When custom-made statues became too expensive, many communities purchased one of the "generic" soldier statues that were being aggressively manufactured and marketed by several companies. The quality and appearance of these mail-order statues ranged from exquisite to poor, with corresponding incidents of fraud, manufacturing defects, and carelessness not uncommon. However, regardless of the outcome of these efforts, many communities purchased, erected, and dedicated such statues as a means of remembering their particular contributions to the great national struggle.[13]

The veneration of the common soldier has a profound effect on the way Americans remember war. Although the statues in all those town squares fit into a larger narrative framework of duty and sacrifice, they are also vernacular tributes to local men who went off to war and either died heroically or came back to become productive citizens and models for future generations. Thus, the construction of war memory is a complex, and sometimes contradictory, mix of vernacular and official memories that involves veterans, widows, civic organizations, local and state governments, businesses, churches, and regular citizens. While most of these monuments were dedicated with a great deal of official commemorative rhetoric, there are also strong expressions of vernacular autonomy, as communities sought to give meaning to their keenly felt sense of loss. By the 1880s, an increasing number of veterans and their communities sought to construct memories of their own contributions to the war. Rather than simply plugging into the vague, fractured, and yet undefined official memory of the "late unpleasantness," the veterans constructed a more personalized and exclusive set of memories of their participation in the conflict.[14]

As American society entered into the volatile and rapidly changing "gilded age," the earlier veneration of the war's veterans evolved into an even more important model for a set of nationally acknowledged civic virtues. Aging veterans held reunions and reminisced among themselves, while published recollections and unit histories filled with commemorative language flooded the book market. Labor agitation, immigration, industrial expansion, and technological innovation led many Americans to search for the values and principles that seemed to be missing from the current era. The images of heroism, the collective memories of the veterans, and the public's need for an official narrative would lead to the construction of a common and enduring collective memory of the war. The war's theme would increasingly be reunion; its symbol, the heroic common soldier; and its primary commemorative landscape would occupy the hallowed ground of its greatest battlefields.

The construction of the veterans' battlefield memories took place in a wide variety of forums. Reunion proceedings, newspaper articles, published journals, memoirs, speeches, and works by self-proclaimed "historians" all strove to recount the story of the cataclysmic experience that had affected so many people across the United States. Prior to the publication of all the volumes of *The War of the Rebellion: Official Records of the Union and Confederate Armies* by the War Department in the late 1890s, much of the information on the events of the war came directly from the veterans themselves. These eyewitness accounts, including many of the reports in the *Official Records*, were inconsistent and unreliable.[15]

As the number of years since the end of the war increased, so did the veterans' desire to be remembered. In addition, political issues, pending pension legislation, and the struggles surrounding reconstruction led many veterans to create organizations that allowed them to share common memories and exercise their considerable strength in numbers. Many veterans had been taking part in regimental reunions since the end of the war, and these existing groups provided the foundation for many of the larger organizations that emerged in the 1870s and 1880s. In the South, the United Confederate Veterans, along with a host of women's commemorative groups, worked to keep the Lost Cause alive and uphold the values of the Confederacy during and after the dark days of Reconstruction. Northern groups like the Grand Army of the Republic (GAR) and the Military Order of the Loyal Legion of the United States (MOLLUS) drew numerous members from the Union army, including many of its prominent officers. In addition, the Society of the Army of the Cumberland and its counterpart representing the Union Army of the Tennessee formed organizations that briefly attempted to combine forces as a single entity before controversies split them into separate and distinct groups. Whether individually or collectively, the veterans on both sides worked to construct and preserve the memories of their service as they matured into the nation's leading citizens.[16]

For both the Union and Confederate participants in the battles of Chickamauga and Chattanooga, the process of remembering and preserving a record of their accomplishments was complicated by the controversies left over from the events of 1863 and beyond. As the veterans formed their organizations and societies and began the process of memory construction, they encountered challenges to their accomplishments and collective identities stemming from the heroism, mistakes, and disagreements among their commanders and comrades. While the aging veterans sorted through the issues, defended their fellow combatants, and repudiated their critics, they built the framework for their collective memories and laid the groundwork for the creation of unique and ultimately sacred battlefield landscapes by the last two decades of the nineteenth century.

The Civil War left the nation devastated. Over 600,000 men were dead, thousands of families lost their loved ones, and millions of dollars worth of property had been destroyed. For the men returning from the front after years of service, the first impulse must have been an attempt to return to some sense of normality. After marching in the Grand Review and basking in the glow of victory, most Union volunteer regiments mustered out and returned to the towns and counties where they had been recruited many months and years before. The southern veterans returned to shattered homes and communities and attempted to come to grips with the loss of both their cause and many of their comrades. Many of the men on both sides nursed physical and psychological injuries that healed slowly, if at all. Before the process of memory building could begin, the horrors of war needed to be forgotten.

The Grand Review that took place in Washington, D.C., in May 1865 was an important moment for many Union veterans and the victorious North. It gave the soldiers who had served in the Army of the Potomac, Army of Georgia, and Army of the Tennessee a chance to display the manly, martial qualities that had helped them prevail in the recent struggle. The Army of the Potomac marched first in the two-day parade and was notable for its disciplined style, newly issued uniforms, and the confidence that came from having bested the Army of Northern Virginia. In the eyes of many observers, however, the western armies stole the show. Lacking the spit and polish of the Easterners, they made up for it in the colorful, cocky, and professional way they marched down the main street of the nation's capital. Sporting a multitude of uniforms, headgear, and accouterments and accompanied by loot, farm animals, and "contraband" Negroes, the "bummers" of Sherman's army reminded the spectators that only through invasion, devastation, and conquest had victory over the South been assured.

Although certainly a fitting catharsis for the public after the shocking death of Lincoln and an inspiring spectacle to all who witnessed it, the review was not entirely the inclusive display of national unity that it was meant to be. As Stuart McConnell points out, the contrast between the eastern and western armies served to highlight the regional and cultural differences among people in the North that can be easily overlooked when discussing reunion and reconciliation. Some soldiers openly expressed their disdain for the soldiers of other armies, and incidents of confrontation and conflict were not unusual. Gen. William T. Sherman's public feud with Secretary of War Edwin Stanton also came to a head when the fiery commander refused to shake hands with Stanton on the reviewing stand. The absence of black Union troops from the review, in spite of their important contribution to victory, portended the eventual exclusion of former slaves from the reunification narrative. For members of military organizations in marginal theaters of the war or those in smaller, defunct, or auxiliary forces like the Army of the Ohio, the Army of the James, and Army of the Cumberland, the Grand Review was a reminder of collective identities lost or forgotten. Finally, it seems that the very spectacle of a "victory parade" by northern forces was a slap in the face to a defeated South, whose own fragmented armies staggered home as individuals to a devastated society.[17]

If the Grand Review signaled the symbolic beginning of the North's reaction to the war's conclusion, adherence to the Lost Cause was the central catalyst for the Southern process of coping, healing, and rationalizing its defeat. Spurred by women's memorial groups, a cadre of prominent veterans, and a mix of journalists, amateur historians, and clergy, many Southerners continued to embrace this ideology and the accompanying commemorative images. Southern "virtues" were represented by Stonewall Jackson, Robert E. Lee, and the noble Confederate foot soldiers, both living and dead. The worship of Confederate patriots was carried out in memorial ceremonies, funerals (or reburials), and on a regular basis in churches and schools throughout the South. Charles R. Wilson characterized these rituals as symbols of a "civic religion" that literally portrayed the South as a region experiencing some sort of biblical jeremiad from which it would emerge both stronger and more virtuous. In this context, the qualities demonstrated by the Confederate cause and its soldiers became the measuring stick for the next generation of white, Protestant, southern youth.[18]

Unlike the victorious North, where many people wanted to forget the war and get back to some degree of peacetime normality, the defeated South incorporated the war into its daily social and cultural life. Reminders of the recent conflict, such as devastated cities, ravaged landscapes, and numerous temporary burials and permanent cemeteries littered the region. Although Gaines Foster does not see the Lost Cause as a religion, he agrees that many secular institutions—schools, social clubs, and local governments—utilized wartime imagery on a regular basis as a motivational tool and means of keeping order in disrupted communities. The formation of memorial associations and veteran's organizations gave both men and women the opportunity to actively participate in the creation of the Lost Cause and the construction of regional memories. In many ways, the South was far more successful in giving the war a permanent place in its collective memory during the first ten years after Appomattox. Once the Radical Republicans took charge of Reconstruction in 1867, the former Confederates made even more use of the Lost Cause imagery to cope with the temporary loss of political, social, and economic power during this tumultuous period.[19]

The elevation of the common soldier to sacred status by both the North and South led to a number of important developments in the construction of war memories. It spurred the creation of cemeteries and memorials throughout the nation that allowed both civilians and veterans the opportunity to engage in commemorative rituals and ceremonies. These events initially centered on local soldiers from individual communities but often drew attention, support, or representation from veterans who may have belonged to the same regiment but lived in different towns. This common interest prompted many veterans to suggest that company or regimental reunions be held on a more regular basis so that the celebration of their accomplishments, the commemoration of fallen comrades, and the preservation of memories could be carried out more systematically. However, in the midst of joyful reunions and solemn celebrations, the returning soldiers had to deal with the trauma and horror of what they had seen and experienced on the battlefield.

In spite of the image of the stoic Civil War veteran that emerged from the war and continues to this day, there is certainly some evidence that many veterans suffered from a variety of postwar problems. Obviously, the numbers of physically disabled former soldiers returning to society served as a constant reminder of the war's cost. The years after the war saw increasing numbers of Union veterans filing pension claims for a variety of disabilities related to their service. As much as most veterans clung to the primary memory of the war as a positive, heroic experience, they also went into great detail to explain the physical problems that resulted from it. For a few soldiers, the horrific sights and sounds of combat left permanent psychological damage that went largely unacknowledged and untreated. Eric Dean points out that the stress of maintaining the heroic façade may have contributed to a few of the emotional problems that veterans experienced after the war, while others were directly related to the horrors that the men had endured in combat, prison camps, and hospitals. In spite of the evidence that indicates that numerous Civil War veterans may have suffered from post-traumatic stress disorder, the generally accurate perception was that the Union soldiers' return "was like beginning life all over again" with a focus on "not so much of what was past as of what was to come."[20]

In spite of the veneration heaped on the Confederate veterans by proponents of the Lost Cause, the pressure on Southern soldiers to suppress the traumatic effects of war was even greater than on their northern counterparts. After reburying its dead, the South turned to its living heroes for inspiration in the dark decades after the war. Robert E. Lee, who one admirer described as "the embodiment of a Lost Cause and the realized King Arthur," was virtually worshipped by adoring southern crowds wherever he went, which eventually forced the ailing general to take elaborate measures to avoid the stress and bustle of these public demonstrations. Often reviled by his critics during the conflict, former Confederate President Jefferson Davis experienced similar accolades following his confinement at Fortress Monroe after the war. Elaborate funerals and memorials celebrated the lives of great men like Thomas "Stonewall" Jackson, while the heroic mantle passed to their offspring, wartime subordinates, and the common soldiers. During the era of Reconstruction, the burden of upholding southern honor fell to the Confederate veterans, some of whom responded by forming organizations like the Ku Klux Klan, which embraced the mystical past and encouraged the preservation of its virtues. Far less extreme, but just as effective, were the memorial associations and veterans organizations that emerged after the war to convey the memory of the Confederacy to the next generation.[21]

While the purpose of the memorial associations was largely commemorative, the veterans' organizations that formed in both the North and South served a multitude of purposes. The early postwar groups in the South tended to focus on explanations for the loss of the war and dished out praise and blame accordingly to whomever would listen. Led by former general Jubal Early and a cabal of Virginians, the Southern Historical Society elevated the memory of Lee and vilified those who suggested that anything of importance took place outside the eastern theater and the Army of Northern Virginia. On the other hand, the United Confederate Veterans (UCV), formed in 1889 and led by John B. Gordon, extended its interests beyond the mere preservation of wartime controversies and took an active role in the creation of the so-called New South in the years following reconstruction. Although they remained dedicated to the preservation of Confederate memory and the maintenance of white supremacy, the UCV urged Southerners to adopt a more reconciliatory position toward the North to bring northern tourists, businessmen, and industry into the region. Encouraged by the UCV, southern veterans began to attend commemorative events on the sites of Union victories and invite Union veterans to commemorative activities in the South.[22]

Likewise, the Grand Army of the Republic (GAR) had its origins in the desire to uphold the Union victory and counter the growing Lost Cause propaganda emanating from the South. The Soldier's Clubs that made up the early posts were more political in nature and were not able to create or sustain a workable national framework. However, in 1866, Maj. Benjamin F. Stephenson formed a more permanent national organization consisting of posts, districts, and departments that became the Grand Army of the Republic. After its third commander-in-chief John Logan declared a northern Memorial Day that allowed the nation to recognize the war dead from the winning side, the GAR vowed to promote "the establishment and defense of the late soldiery of the United States, morally, socially, and politically."

The creation of individual chapters gave the GAR both a local and national influence, and one writer observed that "the Posts themselves . . . are monuments to heroes." While generally non-partisan in its politics after 1870, the Grand Army's support for Reconstruction stemmed from its desire to see the former Confederacy humbled and suppressed as a consequence of its defeat. In addition, the GAR also emerged as a powerful political mechanism for the creation and administration of a pension system that eventually encompassed veterans of all of America's wars. As time went on, the Union veterans, much like their southern counterparts, developed a grudging respect for their former foes and eventually succumbed to the reconciliation impulses of the 1880s and 1890s by occasionally attending joint reunions and ceremonial events.[23]

Time was certainly a factor in determining the amount of influence and cooperation that these groups had on each other and society at large. As Paul Buck recounts, the nation's 100th birthday in 1876 was unevenly celebrated in the South and brought forth expressions of bitterness and frustration on both sides. Gerald Linderman refers to the period from 1865 to 1880 as one of "hibernation," during which both veterans and the public avoided confronting "the late war" openly or directly. The process of national healing did not really begin until at least the early 1880s, when President Garfield's assassination and a yellow fever epidemic in the South brought many Americans together for the first time without regard for sectional affiliation. By the late 1880s, the role of the veterans in American society was more prominent, and membership in the GAR climbed steadily to several hundred thousand by 1890.

For many veterans, however, national politics and pension debates shared a less than equal status with the important process of memory construction and preservation. Writing in 1912, a member of MOLLUS wrote that a "large number of our companions . . . have interesting recollections . . . and . . . may be willing to recount them in a way that will teach the present and future generations what their ancestors did to preserve the Union." As the veterans aged, they sought the company of their comrades in the regiments, brigades, and armies in which they had served. By reconnecting with those men and reliving their common memories, the veterans could establish their place in the national memory of the late war. One of the most active and influential of these organizations was the Society of the Army of the Cumberland, which, together with its tireless leader Henry Van Ness Boynton, would forge a new level of reconciliation with the South and separate his army's identity from those of its rivals and critics.[24]

FOUR

"Stamp Out Venerable Falsehoods"

The process of memory construction in the decades after the end of the Civil War was often uneven and inconsistent due to the differences between northern and southern perspectives and unresolved social and political issues. The focus on death and the common soldier helped generate the first waves of commemoration via the construction of national cemeteries and the ritual activities surrounding the reburial of soldiers and the erection of local monuments in communities around the country. For the veterans, the need to reconnect with their former comrades led to the creation of unit-specific and local organizations that eventually merged to form national groups like the Grand Army of the Republic (GAR) and United Confederate Veterans. The next steps introduced the formation of organizations that consisted of members of individual armies who served in particular units and/or specific theaters of the war.

The creation and growth of the Grand Army of the Republic gave Union veterans a focal point for their collective identity as "saviors of the nation" and provided political clout in the debate over pensions. However, the GAR could not meet all the needs of all the Union veterans. Since many of their wartime experiences revolved around specific military units—regiments, brigades, divisions, corps, and armies—and specific campaigns involving those units, it was natural for the veterans to want to maintain those identities while preserving and constructing their memories of the great conflict. The creation of army-specific reunion organizations during the postwar era helped direct the veterans' collective memories toward the events that they had personally participated in. While most Union veterans could celebrate the significance of the victory at Gettysburg or the fall of Vicksburg, those events were particularly important to the men of the armies that had made them possible. The recognition given to certain battles by the press and public at the time carried over into the postwar years and kept old rivalries, resentments, and jealousies alive.

As the veterans published their memoirs and engaged in heated wars of words in periodicals and newspapers like the *National Tribune,* the need for individual units to construct, preserve, and promote their own specific memories increased. Each of the major Union armies spawned societies specifically geared toward upholding the memory, reputation, and accomplishments of that particular organization, occasionally at the expense of other armies and their respective societies. Like its contemporaries, the Society of the Army of the Cumberland became an active participant in this process of memory construction from early in its history and played an active role in upholding the reputation of its leaders and soldiers until well into the twentieth century.

The main Union armies began to create specific societies near the end of the 1860s and during the early 1870s. The Society of the Army of the Potomac formed in 1869 and included members of the wartime Third Corps Union. The Society of the Army of the Tennessee, which originally consisted only of its officers, came into being a year later as a way to "keep alive that kindly and cordial feeling which has been one of the characteristics of this army during its career in the service . . . and contributed . . . to its glorious achievements in our country's cause." Both of these organizations intended to uphold the exclusive identities of their specific armies by promoting the continued comradeship among the organization's veterans.[1]

Despite its less prominent role in the history of the war, the Society of the Army of the Cumberland predated both of these when it met in Cincinnati for its initial meeting in 1868. In his welcoming address, Col. Stanley Mathews noted that "We have not formed a new association. We are gathered together to put into form the terms of the old one." In its original charter, the Society repeated sentiments similar to those found in the Army of the Tennessee bylaws, but specified that "the object of the Society will be to perpetuate the memory of the fortunes and achievements of the Army of the Cumberland." Although the original meeting was open to "every officer or soldier who at any time served with honor in that army," it consisted of specific officers who had responded to a circular sent out earlier in the year. As the Army of the Cumberland led the way in attempting to preserve its collective identity during the postwar era, it encountered some interesting and peculiar obstacles in the process.[2]

Ironically, it was the Army of the Cumberland's own history that made its quest for identity so challenging. Technically, the Army of the Cumberland did not even exist until William S. Rosecrans designated it as such in the fall of 1862. Yet, in its previous incarnation as the Army of the Ohio, many of its men and officers had experienced their first combat, won their initial victories, and gained experience in an army "whose marches and battles had veteranized [them] in the best arts of war." In addition, both of the Army of the Cumberland's most prominent commanders endured controversies during their tenures that extended after the war and followed them to their graves. Rosecrans's dismissal after Chickamauga was a humiliating end to what had been a solid career and proved to be a stigma that was difficult to overcome, even after the passage of many years.

In spite of his success as commander of the Army of the Cumberland from Chattanooga to the end of the Atlanta campaign, George Thomas never overcame the label of slowness bestowed on him by Grant, Sherman, and others, including President Lincoln. In spite of the claim that "all jealousies, and envyings [sic], and rivalries died away in the face of a common enemy" during the war, the Society of the Army of the Cumberland still had to deal with postwar threats to its identity due to its inclusion in the other western armies. From the time of its reorganization after Chickamauga through the Atlanta campaign and beyond, the army was subdivided as part of Sherman's mammoth force and rarely operated as a single entity. In addition, several of its former officers, most notably Philip Sheridan, went on to win fame with other armies. For members of the Society of the Army of the Cumberland, the quest for ownership of its identity and memory would be complicated by some of the controversies surrounding specific events that took place during the battles of Chickamauga and Chattanooga.[3]

Any discussion of Rosecrans's precipitous fall from grace has to begin with the fatal order he gave in the late morning of 20 September 1863 that changed the course of the Battle of Chickamauga. Although there were some debates over who was responsible for the breakthrough that shattered the right wing of the army, it was awkward even for the loyal veterans of the Army of the Cumberland to defend Rosecrans's disastrous decision to leave the field after making such a horrendous mistake. General Wood, whose movement triggered the debacle, blamed Rosecrans for issuing the faulty order and openly resented the implication that he had done anything wrong by obeying it. In his report, he makes sure to note that McCook was present when he received it and that Thomas saw it later and confirmed that "Reynolds did not need any help" before agreeing to lead his division further to the left. Clearly, Rosecrans had misunderstood the situation on the field and conveyed vague instructions based on flawed information, but Henry Cist argues that Woods stubbornly failed to seek clarification of Rosecrans's message "*and to this extent he is responsible*" for the rout of the right wing.[4]

Regardless of who was fully at fault, the events that took place after the breakthrough served to seal Rosecrans's fate. There is little doubt that the general displayed personal courage as he attempted to rally his broken flank and make contact with Thomas on the left. However, as he sat on his horse under fire in the midst of fugitives who "were as deaf to reason in their mad panic as would be a drove of stampeding cattle," he succumbed to the reasonable belief that the battle was essentially lost and that his duty lay in the defense of Chattanooga. Some postwar writers saw it differently. Veteran J. T. Woods lamented that "in the exercise of unexplainable wisdom [Rosecrans] retired with his staff to Chattanooga . . . at the head of gay escorts, with fluttering battle flags." The image of Rosecrans "in bed at Chattanooga, snug and safe, when the gallant Thomas . . . was stemming the furious onslaught of the rebel army," would haunt Rosecrans's legacy, in spite of its lack of veracity. By sending the ambitious and duplicitous Garfield to contact the resolute Thomas, Rosecrans compounded this negative image and inadvertently sowed the seeds of his own downfall.[5]

Several stories of Rosecrans's apparent loss of nerve during the latter stages of the battle could be traced to Garfield, who allegedly told Jacob D. Cox, author of an account of the battle critical of Rosecrans, that the commander was "abstracted" [sic] and responded "listlessly and mechanically" to his staff. Cox claims that the conversation he had with Garfield after the battle confirmed his belief that Rosecrans "lacked poise . . . and the steadiness of will necessary to handle great affairs successfully." In perhaps the most damning assessment, Cox describes "the fatal defect of the liability to be swept away by excitement and to lose all efficient control of himself and others in the very crisis" that required self-control. Even Henry Cist, a Rosecrans supporter, stated that after arriving in Chattanooga, the general "had the appearance of one broken in spirit" and that the apparent rout of half his army was a "blow so strong it staggered him." Rosecrans defended himself by pointing out that he issued clear and coherent orders to defend the approaches to Chattanooga at the time he was supposed to be so confused and that he based his decision to go back to the city on the long-held claim that holding it was the overall object of the campaign. Even if his choice to go back to Chattanooga was rational, Rosecrans's detractors found a way to justify his dismissal a few weeks after the battle because "the confidence of the army in him had been broken, if not destroyed."[6]

In spite of Rosecrans's failings, the Army of the Cumberland's veterans felt that the way he had been treated by the War Department both before and after the battle had insulted their collective honor and identity. There had been an ongoing struggle between Rosecrans and Henry Halleck during the entire summer leading up to the Battle of Chickamauga, much of it spawned by Halleck's impatience with the general's deliberate, self-serving style during the campaign and Rosecrans's equally stubborn refusal to be coerced into action. Even one of the men who eulogized Rosecrans admitted that "while he was considerate and regardful of his inferiors and his equals, there was something in his temperament that put discord and sometimes enmity between him and his superiors in rank."

In addition to identifying Halleck and Secretary of War Edwin Stanton as culprits, the veterans who wrote histories of the Army of the Cumberland were quick to blame Gen. Ambrose Burnside for his "inexcusable" and "criminal" failure to support Rosecrans's movement from his base in Knoxville. They insisted that had the army commander received less pressure and more cooperation, the whole campaign would have been more successful. Although few contemporaries believed that Rosecrans fought the Battle of Chickamauga "from no other motive than a vain wish to win greater victories than Grant," there were questions over his state of mind after the battle. Charles Dana questioned the general's ability to lead the army and suggested that he was "dazed and mazy" and "insensible to the impending danger" that faced him in Chattanooga. In his opinion, "[the army's] respect for Rosecrans as a commanding general had received an irreparable blow."[7]

Much to the relief of most men in the Army of the Cumberland, the War Department gave the job to George Thomas, who predictably hesitated to take it at the expense of his former commander.[8] While no one doubted Thomas's capabilities, there were justifiable concerns in Washington that the forces in Chattanooga were inadequate for the defense of the city and defeat of Bragg's army. Halleck ordered Burnside to the relief of Chattanooga and dispensed a large portion of Grant's army from Mississippi toward the city as well. Within weeks, it was clear that the Army of the Cumberland was not going to get the chance to redeem itself alone. The bulk of the Army of the Potomac's old XI and XII corps was coming from Virginia, along with the eastern army's former commander, Joseph Hooker. There was a plethora of brass headed for Chattanooga, including Ulysses S. Grant, William T. Sherman, William "Baldy" Smith, and a host of other luminaries who were sent by the War Department to make things happen in the beleaguered city. There would be a considerable amount of postwar discussion regarding the supposedly "demoralized" condition of the Army of the Cumberland in Chattanooga during this period, including General Grant's concern "that they would not get out of their trenches to assume the offensive" and lift the rebel investment of the city.[9]

The Army of the Cumberland veterans led by Henry Cist claimed that Rosecrans and Thomas had already begun to take steps to reopen the supply lines when other members of Grant's staff arrived to put things in motion. Baldy Smith claimed that he planned the Brown's Ferry operation, which began the process of re-establishing a supply line, prior to Grant's arrival. Later, during the creation of a campaign map in the 1890s, his claim triggered a series of debates and Congressional hearings over who should take credit for the movement's success in mid-October. One historian notes the "awkward" clashes between Grant and Thomas's respective chiefs of staff and observes that "Thomas . . . probably wondered why Grant, a man he outperformed at West Point and

arguably outperformed on the battlefield, was in charge instead of himself."
This was only one of several lingering issues stemming from the inclusion of
Grant, Sherman, and others into the life of the Army of the Cumberland.[10]

For the veterans of the Army of the Cumberland, the siege of Chattanooga
and its aftermath provided mixed and often bitter memories. During the first
few weeks of their investment, the Army of the Cumberland's veterans dug
extensive entrenchments, endured a temporary but intense food crisis, created
an unofficial truce with the enemy to prevent the needless "murder" of men
who were merely occupying the lines, and took comfort in the fact that help
was on the way. The men got paid, gambled, wandered around the city, buried their dead, and enjoyed the music of both Union and Confederate bands.
Shortly after the reinforcements arrived and the supplies began to flow, the
rain commenced, turning the trenches to mud. Years later, General Grant reflected positively on the merger of the three armies:

> In the battle of Chattanooga, troops from the Army of the Potomac,
> from the Army of the Tennessee, and from the Army of the Cumber-
> land participated. In fact, the accidents growing out of the heavy rains
> and the sudden rise in the Tennessee River so mingled the troops that
> the organizations were not kept together, under their respective com-
> manders during the battle. There was no jealousy—hardly rivalry. In-
> deed, I doubt whether the officers or men took any note at the time . . .
> of this intermingling of commands. All saw a defiant foe surrounding
> them, and took for granted that every move was intended to dislodge
> him, and so it made no difference where the troops came from so that
> the end was accomplished.

While Grant may have been sincere when he expressed this memory years later,
the role he assigned to Thomas and the bulk of the Army of the Cumberland
could be interpreted otherwise as the veterans reflected on the campaign.[11]

Although the hero of Snodgrass Hill had been elevated to command of the
army, it was clear that Thomas was not making the key decisions regarding the
liberation of the city. In the operations that opened the "cracker line," drove the
enemy off of Lookout Mountain, and took steps to force Bragg's army off the
ridges, the Army of the Cumberland served as the holding force while Hooker
and Sherman's troops did the heavy work. While playing second fiddle was
preferable to starvation and capture, the veterans of Chickamauga eventually
chafed at their supporting role while other units gained the glory. When given
the chance, the Army of the Cumberland rose above and beyond the occasion
by taking Orchard Knob on November 23, then storming Missionary Ridge
and crushing the rebel army two days later. Years afterward, Thomas noted

FIG. 8: Federal camps near Chattanooga. The presence of winter huts and leaves on the trees indicates that the photo was probably taken in the spring of 1864. Library of Congress.

that "we would have starved before we gave up that place" and joked that the army's efforts that culminated in the charge on Missionary Ridge had all been motivated by the desire to finally get fed. However, the most likely interpretation for the reckless charge up the rugged slopes was that "the brave men of Thomas's army . . . were burning to wipe out the defeat at Chickamauga."

In his memoirs, Grant seemed to downplay the accomplishment when he told Sherman that "by attracting the attention of so many of the enemy" in attacking Bragg's flanks, Sherman and Hooker made "Thomas's part certain of success." One historian writes that Grant's "reluctance to use Thomas's troops in major fighting had strangely backfired" and that "the Army of the Cumberland was no longer an ugly orphan . . . [it] had been redeemed." Ultimately, the Army of the Cumberland veterans knew that the success on Missionary Ridge had saved their army's reputation and ensured that they and their commander would achieve some measure of immortality. For Thomas, however, the successes on Snodgrass Hill and Missionary Ridge served to cloud rather than clarify his place in history and memory.[12]

Thomas had been with the Army of the Ohio early in the war and had risen to corps command in the Army of the Cumberland by being reliable, loyal, and popular with his men. The XIV Corps was clearly Thomas's corps, and its performance at Chickamauga had validated both its commander and the rank and file. Ironically, the well-earned sobriquet, "Rock of Chickamauga," associated with Thomas and his men would serve as a point of controversy rather than validation. The major complaint against George Thomas was that he was too deliberate, too slow, and too inclined toward defensive warfare to be considered among the great commanders. While his defensive stand on Snodgrass Hill was truly heroic, Thomas can be criticized for several things relating to the Battle of Chickamauga. For one thing, his constant demand for troops to strengthen his left was one of the reasons that the right was so weak by late morning on the twentieth.

The fact that he controlled much of the XX and XXI Corps by the time of the breakthrough partially exonerates McCook and Crittenden, who only led fragments of their corps off the field in the afternoon. Many of the troops from other units who remained to fight with Thomas faced an uphill struggle to get their own participation and memories recognized in the face of some XIV Corps claims to having held the ground all by itself. There are also a few critics, among them Sheridan and Garfield, who claimed that Thomas missed the opportunity to counterattack the exhausted Confederates late in the afternoon and "that there was no necessity for an immediate retreat on Rossville." At the very least, Thomas's voluntary withdrawal (orders from Rosecrans notwithstanding) from the position he had fought so hard to hold seemed less glorious than holding out until darkness or victory.[13]

Likewise, the unexpectedly successful charge up Missionary Ridge is remembered as having taken place in spite of Thomas's orders rather than because of them. According to many accounts, questioning words were exchanged between Thomas and Grant as they watched the troops go beyond the rifle pits at the base of the hill, without reforming, and toward the crest. Until it was clear that the Confederate line was broken, Thomas was hard pressed to defend the decision to go up the ridge. In the long run, the success of the attack clearly belonged to the men of the Army of the Cumberland, not its commander. Writing in *Battles and Leaders of the Civil War*, Gen. Joseph Fullerton claims that angry words were exchanged between Thomas and Grant as the troops exceeded their orders to advance to the rifle pits. However, in his account, Grant claims that he had authorized an attack after the troops carried the rifle pits and "reformed." His recollection gave division commander Sheridan the lion's

FIG. 9: Gen. George H. Thomas, whose heroics as the "Rock of Chickamauga" earned him command of the Army of the Cumberland and a special place in the hearts of its veterans. Library of Congress.

share of praise for making the rout of Bragg's army complete. Just as recognition for the overall liberation of Chattanooga is often attributed to Grant and others, credit for the destruction of Bragg's army on the crest of Missionary Ridge could not be assigned to Thomas beyond his role as inspiration for his loyal men. While celebrating the accomplishments of his men, Thomas "quietly" noted in his report that "the original plan of operations was somewhat modified to meet and best take advantage of emergencies which necessitated ... [such] modifications."[14]

The implication that Thomas was slow and reluctant to take offensive action followed him out of Chattanooga, throughout the rest of the war, and beyond. In many ways, the incorporation of Thomas's army into Sherman's force for the next campaign and his performance as an independent commander at Nashville late in 1864 served to seal his reputation as a competent but passive leader. General Sherman noted that even while serving under other commanders, Thomas's old XIV Corps had "imbibed somewhat his personal character [of] steadiness, good order, and deliberation ... always safe, slow, and sure." When Sherman created the Army of Georgia from the XIV and XX Corps, he noted that "Thomas was not pleased with these changes" since these units "have technically been part of his Army of the Cumberland." Thus, one of the main tasks for the Society of the Army of the Cumberland was to rescue its army's collective identity from the blur of its 1864 dispersion to other armies and uphold the reputation of its beloved commander.[15]

When Sherman left Atlanta for the March to the Sea, he took the XIV Corps and left behind the XXIII and IV Corps, along with units scattered all over north Georgia and Tennessee. Thomas and this makeshift force played a key role in achieving final victory in the West by crippling, then destroying, Hood's depleted Army of Tennessee at Franklin and Nashville as Sherman pressed on to Savannah. The December 1864 victory at Nashville was tainted by reports that Grant had ordered Thomas's dismissal if he did not move quickly to attack Hood in the first two weeks of December. This incident and the opinion that he was "slow beyond excuse" plagued Thomas for the rest of his life. One obituary observed that "his patience before the battle [of Nashville] when the wiseacres at Washington were clamoring for an immediate advance ... was no less remarkable than his tactics on the battlefield." His death in California occurred as he was drafting a reply to yet another series of letters accusing him of being tentative, slow, and indecisive at Nashville.[16]

The "slowness" stigma against Thomas cut deeply into the collective pride of the Army of the Cumberland's veterans and led to a widening gap between their organization and the societies representing the armies of the Tennessee and Georgia. When it was first organized, the Society acknowledged its connection to the Army of the Tennessee and included tributes and toasts to its officers and men at its meetings and banquets. The final break with the Army of the Tennessee came when Sherman published his memoirs in 1875 and made reference to Thomas's "seemingly passive" approach to defeating Hood and asserting that he was "slow in mind and action." A negative review of Sherman's book in one periodical asserted that he was "inferior to Thomas in steadiness and resolution" and that his memoirs "will neither reward him for the trouble they will bring, nor increase his reputation for fairness and prudence."

Meanwhile, former members of the Army of the Cumberland felt compelled to write rebuttals that would set the record straight and protect the reputation of the army's most successful commander. When Grant's memoirs failed to correct the negative impression of Thomas, some Army of the Cumberland veterans, including H. V. Boynton, retaliated by questioning both Sherman and Grant's judgment and motives. When Boynton, among others, raised the specter of Grant's drinking in several public forums, Sherman responded by calling Boynton "a coyote, a hyena, scratching up old forgotten scandals, publishing them as something new." The feud between Sherman and Boynton went on for many years until at one point Sherman exclaimed that "for a thousand dollars [Boynton] would slander his own mother."[17]

Whether they were malicious and intentional or simply the misunderstood recollections of former comrades, the slights against Thomas's reputation cut deeply into the collective identity of the veterans of the Army of the Cumberland. Referring obliquely to Grant and Sherman's memoirs in an 1892 speech, Henry Boynton stated that the veterans of the Army of the Cumberland should "stamp out venerable falsehoods which have been given currency in history and install truth in their place." Proclaiming that since others had taken shots at the Army of the Cumberland's achievements, "it is but fair to make comparisons" between the respective commanders and their armies, pointing out the casualties and mishaps surrounding key battles in the careers of both Grant and Sherman. Although he conceded that "the fame of these great captains is assured beyond the power of pen and word to destroy it" Boynton made it clear that the Army of the Cumberland would not play second fiddle to other commanders or armies, including those in the eastern theater.[18]

The wartime rivalry between the eastern and western armies carried over to many of the veterans on both sides. In the same 1892 speech, Boynton exclaimed that in "the East . . . the magnitude of the operations . . . in which the Army of the Cumberland engaged has not been fully comprehended." This disconnect extended beyond the commanders to the common soldiers in the respective armies. One postwar writer observed that "it is evident that the Eastern soldier was not fortified with the same serene and immovable belief in

FIG. 10: The "Big Four" western generals: Ulysses Grant, William Sherman, James McPherson, and George Thomas. In spite of his unblemished record of success, Grant and Sherman both described Thomas as a commander who was often slow to take action. Library of Congress.

victory that supported his Western comrade." He speculated that the eastern soldiers' "fastidious" need for order and cleanliness would have been severely tested during the siege of Chattanooga. For the Army of the Cumberland the east/west dichotomy was compounded not only by its association with other corps and armies from both theaters before and after the war, but also because of the defection of a few prominent western officers to the east. Most notable among these were Philip Sheridan and James A. Garfield.[19]

Sheridan had been a popular and effective infantry officer before Chickamauga who managed to distance himself from Rosecrans, McCook, and Crittenden after that battle by making much of his belated attempt to return to Thomas late in the day on the twentieth. In spite of his tardy arrival on the battlefield, he claimed that "had General Thomas held on and attacked the Confederate right and rear from where I made the junction with him on the Lafayette road, the field of Chickamauga would have been relinquished to us." After impressing Grant at Chattanooga and following him east in the spring of 1864, he made himself a household name after rallying his defeated army at the battle of Cedar Creek in October of that year. He was present at Appomattox and parlayed his association with the eastern high command into a long career in the Regular Army and federal government. All of this was not lost on his former comrades. In one postwar speech, a former Army of the Cumberland comrade remarked that Sheridan's ride from the field at Chickamauga had not been as glamorous as the one immortalized in the poem.[20]

After serving Rosecrans as chief of staff, James Garfield left the army shortly after Chattanooga to rejoin the U.S. Senate, where he used his heroic exploits at Chickamauga to advance his political career. During the 1880 presidential campaign, a flowery biography insisted that Garfield had "procured permission" from a reluctant Rosecrans to "ride to the sound of the guns" and "be where there was danger." The author describes Garfield, after a harrowing ride to reach Thomas, sitting coolly under a tree with a white dove perched above his head. Such accounts subtly condemned Rosecrans for leaving the field at Chickamauga and reminded readers that Garfield "refused to believe that Thomas was routed or the battle lost." His arrival at the same time as Granger's reinforcement also helped him claim that he had actively helped save Thomas's hide. Ambrose Bierce was less impressed and wrote "A good deal of nonsense used to be talked about the heroism of General Garfield . . . there was no great heroism" in joining Thomas. After all, he had found his way to Thomas himself and "never felt that it ought to make me President."

Garfield had also supported Dana's dispatches to Washington that implied that the general was not in full control during the early siege of Chattanooga and conveniently left the service—and the beleaguered Rosecrans—during this critical time. Garfield's duplicity came to full light when his dispatches criticizing Rosecrans were published—along with rebuttals from Rosecrans himself—in the Society's account of its former commander's 1902 burial at Arlington National Cemetery. Garfield's "glowing and truthful eulogy" of Rosecrans in the House of Representatives shortly after the battle and his sudden assassination a few months after being elected President made him difficult to criticize in his own right, but his abandonment of both Rosecrans and the army left a bitter taste in the mouths of his former comrades.[21]

In many ways the postwar controversies on the losing side were no less complicated than those that engulfed the Army of the Cumberland. Because of the dismal track record of the Army of Tennessee under his command, Braxton Bragg was a convenient scapegoat for the disaster that befell his army and the Confederacy in the late fall of 1863. For the most part, the anti-Bragg argument centers on his failure to finish off Thomas at Chickamauga and his careless investment of Chattanooga afterward. On the other hand, there was plenty of blame to go around for the failures that plagued the Army of Tennessee. As the evidence has consistently revealed, corps commanders Polk and Hill both failed to execute orders during the Chickamauga campaign that could have given the Confederates great advantages and perhaps decisive victories.

While there is no doubt that the addition of General James Longstreet and two divisions of the Army of Northern Virginia helped win the Battle of Chickamauga, the South Carolinian's disgust with Bragg and his general criticisms of the Army of Tennessee cast both the army and its commander in a negative light. When another eastern transplant, John Bell Hood, took over in July 1864, he tried to regenerate the army's offensive instincts by hurling it at Thomas and James "Birdseye" McPherson in a series of desperate and unsuccessful attacks on the outskirts of Atlanta. Hood succeeded in wasting the rest of the army's men in the futile assault at Franklin in late November and was finally dismissed after his army's total collapse at Nashville. Ultimately, the emphasis on Lee and the Army of Northern Virginia that dominated early Lost Cause propaganda tended to obscure and marginalize the veterans of the West and kept them from actively taking control of their collective memories. As a result of all of these factors, they struggled to create a strong postwar army organization that could control the tricky process of memory construction.[22]

Braxton Bragg was as hard a man to defend as he was to like. Unlike many of his contemporaries, Bragg did not publish his version of the war before his death in 1876, thus leaving his memory in the hands of others. Captain William Snow, who wrote about southern commanders shortly after the war, conceded that "he was not very popular" but generously speculated that since he was supported by President Jefferson Davis, "he must have been deemed well fitted for his post." Bragg's post-battle report from Chickamauga reveals the negative tone that marked his character and memory. After pointing out that his army was "exhausted by two days of battle," he went on to say that "any immediate pursuit by our infantry and artillery would have been fruitless." He continued: "though we had defeated him and driven him from the field . . . it had only been done by heavy sacrifices, in repeated, persistent, and gallant assaults upon superior numbers strongly posted and protected." Such language seems to support Longstreet's contention that Bragg did not even know the extent of his victory and makes it difficult to support the commander's version of events. As one southern historian tallied up Confederate casualties from the gory battle, he concluded simply that, "such sacrifice in battle was fruitless without adequate pursuit, which was not made" after Chickamauga.[23]

One of the more damaging accounts of the Chickamauga campaign came from D. H. Hill, who wrote a lengthy, oft-quoted piece in *Battles and Leaders of the Civil War* that blamed Bragg for much that went wrong. Hill not only proclaimed that "another hour of daylight would have insured [Thomas's] capture" on September 20, but that "the great blunder of them all was not pursuing the enemy on the 21st." The other critical voice came from Longstreet, who pulled no punches in his dislike of Bragg's handling of the campaign. In his report to Secretary of War Seddon after Chickamauga, James Longstreet not only expressed the belief that the failure to pursue Rosecrans was a great error, but went further in criticizing Bragg on the record. His exasperation is revealed in his letter: "it seems that he cannot adopt and adhere to any plan or course, whether of his own or of someone else" and that "nothing but the hand of God can save us or help us as long as we have our present commander." The publication of this letter (minus the identity of its author) in Richmond after the battle stunned war clerk diarist John Jones who wrote, "while others are exulting in the conviction that Rosecrans will be speedily destroyed, I am filled with alarm for the fate of Bragg's army, and for the cause!"[24]

In his memoirs, Longstreet bitterly noted that Bragg's report "failed to note the conduct of his officers," and he summarized his feelings toward the army commander in a couple of short sentences: "A peculiar feature of the battle was the early ride of both commanders from the field, leaving the battle to their troops. General Rosecrans was generous enough to acknowledge that he left the battle in other hands. General Bragg claimed everything for himself, failing to mention that other hands were there." Since both Hill and Longstreet's accounts were widely published and the outcome of the campaign was well-known, Bragg's reputation as the man who frittered away a great victory remained soundly in place.[25]

The same memoirs that vilified Bragg served to deflect the blame from others who bore some responsibility for the army's failure during the campaign. Although Hill conceded that "blunders by each of us in authority committed before the battles of the 19th and 20th" may have affected the outcome, Bragg still bears responsibility for letting the victory get away. Longstreet successfully justified his own errors in his memoirs, focusing on Bragg's ill-fated decision to send him and his troops to Knoxville as proof of the commander's poor decision making. If there was any hope of putting a positive spin on the memory of Bragg at Chickamauga from the Confederate point of view, it disappeared after the general replaced most of his detractors in the weeks after the battle, only to spectacularly lose everything that had been gained at Chattanooga.

Perhaps no army in the war, with the possible exception of the Army of the Potomac during 1861–62, suffered more from the failings of its commanders than the Army of Tennessee. The unfortunate outcome of the Chattanooga campaign came as little surprise when considering the two-year-long relationship between the army and General Bragg that led up to it. From Shiloh to Perryville, Stones River to Tullahoma, and finally to Chickamauga and Chattanooga, the officers and men of the Army of Tennessee had followed Braxton Bragg from one disappointment to another. In each of these battles, the soldiers fought courageously, only to be deprived of victory by some failure in their commander's plans or in the execution of them. The infighting among the army's general officers was not lost on the men either. As the letters, reports, circulars, and rumors swirled around the army, morale suffered accordingly.

In spite of his biases, D. H. Hill was correct about Bragg when he stated that "his many retreats, too, had alienated the rank and file from him." No matter how it is won, "the one thing a soldier never fails to understand is victory." Bragg could not supply victories or overcome the flaws in his personality that made him grouchy, narrow-minded, and tentative under pressure. Although one southern veteran claimed that the collapse of the Army of Tennessee on Missionary Ridge "was nothing more than a stampede of our army [based] . . . on a flying report that the enemy were getting in our rear," most of the observers, both Union and Confederate, agreed that it was a breakdown in morale caused by a lack of faith in the commander that led to the rout of the army. Hill observed that "it seems to me that the élan of the southern soldier was never seen again after Chickamauga," and although the men of the Army of Tennessee "fought stoutly to the last," they did so " . . . with the sullenness of despair and without enthusiasm of hope."[26]

One of the great ironies for the Army of Tennessee was that it won the Battle of Chickamauga with the help of outside units and lost the struggle for

FIG. 11: Gen. James Longstreet's two divisions from the Army of Northern Virginia helped win the Battle of Chickamauga, but his inability to work with Bragg led to Confederate defeats at both Knoxville and Chattanooga. Library of Congress.

Chattanooga when most of those units went elsewhere. Just as the Army of the Cumberland had to share credit for victory at Chattanooga with the Union Army of the Tennessee and the XI and XII Corps, the Confederate force was compelled to acknowledge that it owed part of its success at Chickamauga to others. The addition of Simon Buckner's troops from the Army of Mississippi and the two divisions from the Army of Northern Virginia were key factors that gave the Confederates numerical superiority on 19 and 20 September. General Hill, who had come from the East to take command of a corps in the Army of Tennessee after the shake-up that followed Stone's River, was barely a part of the army before being replaced by wing commander Longstreet in the middle of the battle. The wing structure helped avoid a sharp division between the core of the Army of Tennessee and the newcomers, but it also prevented effective cooperation between commanders at all levels who barely knew one another. Bragg's failure to coordinate the two wings during the critical hours in the afternoon of the twentieth is partly his fault and partly the result of unfamiliarity between officers, staffs, and soldiers. When all was said and done, the Union veterans who defended Snodgrass Hill could correctly say that "a vast army, representing a large fraction of the military strength of the Confederacy, had only gained a barren victory, if a victory at all."[27]

By the same token, just as the Army of the Cumberland had to share the credit for the victory at Chattanooga, the Army of Tennessee had to bear the onus of defeat all by itself. Generals Polk and Hill, who bore the brunt of Bragg's anger for their failure before and during the Battle of Chickamauga, both lost their commands, while Gen. Simon B. Buckner left the Army of Tennessee on his own. Gen. William Hardee was persuaded by President Davis to return to the army as a corps commander and John C. Breckinridge, whose division had been badly mauled at both Stones River and Chickamauga, was given command of Hill's former corps. Longstreet's open criticism of Bragg in the aforementioned letter and directly to President Davis made cooperation between the two next to impossible by the end of October. Having abandoned plans to move the entire army from in front of Chattanooga, Bragg settled on sending Longstreet's 15,000 men to confront Burnside at Knoxville.

This poorly planned, badly executed, and ultimately unsuccessful expedition not only soiled Longstreet's record as an independent commander, but deprived Bragg of badly needed troops as he faced the Union build-up at Chattanooga. While U. S. Grant could say with some accuracy that there was "no jealousy" resulting from the "intermingling of commands" in the Union army during the operations against Bragg, the Confederate commander could not say the same about his own army. After he had banished his detractors and scapegoats, Bragg could blame no one for the disaster except his men, himself, and the president who sustained him when all the evidence indicated that he should not have. For all intents and purposes, the Army of Tennessee entered the last year of the war so badly damaged that neither Joseph E. Johnston nor John Bell Hood could save it.[28]

Joseph Johnston's tenure as commander of the Army of Tennessee continued the unfortunate pattern that plagued it throughout its history. Although he succeeded in reorganizing, re-supplying, and raising the morale of the army during its winter in Dalton, Georgia, he faced the imposing task of stopping Sherman's relentless drive to Atlanta in the spring of 1864. Operating on good ground from entrenched positions, the army gave a solid accounting of itself over the summer as it countered Sherman's flanking moves. Although Johnston was holding his own in this giant chess game, his army continued to retreat and yield ground to the Union advance. This displeased Jefferson Davis, whose personal dislike for Johnston was matched only by the general's disdain for the wishes of his commander-in-chief. Again, it was personalities and politics that undermined the army, not its fighting ability. The veterans remembered Johnston fondly partly because his tactics kept casualties down and partly because of who succeeded him. Unfortunately, while Johnston was keeping his plans to himself and frustrating the president, a disgruntled subordinate was sending negative reports to that same chief executive. The ubiquitous outsider, John Bell Hood, was plotting his own ascension to power at the expense of both Johnston and the army. He succeeded by suggesting that defensive warfare had made the Army of Tennessee soft and that taking the offensive would save both Atlanta and the honor of the men.[29]

Hood's tenure as commander virtually destroyed the Army of Tennessee. As much as his memoirs tried to pass the blame on to others, the veterans of both armies recognized that Hood's aggressive tactics sacrificed his men. The foul-up at Spring Hill, Tennessee, where Hood's subordinates failed to act and allowed John Schofield's retreating army to pass them in the night, showed the continuing dysfunction in the army's command structure. The crippled, overmedicated, short-tempered Hood performed more like Bragg instead of his former mentors, Lee and Jackson. When confronted with formidable defenses at Franklin, and convinced that "the army ... [was] unwilling to give battle unless under the protection of breastworks," he threw his infantry at the works without artillery support and sacrificed the flower of the Army of Tennessee in the resulting bloodbath.

Hood's investment of Nashville was even more ineffective than Bragg's had been at Chattanooga. The Army of Tennessee was outnumbered, undersupplied, and incapable of sealing off the Union forces from food and supplies.

FIG. 12: This photo of Confederate prisoners in Chattanooga, probably taken early in 1864, is one of the few known images of soldiers from the ill-fated Army of the Tennessee in the field. Library of Congress.

The winter siege became a death watch for the army. When Thomas finally moved, his army crushed Hood's weakened defensive positions and routed his army. Even for a beaten army in a lost war, it was an incredible collapse by such experienced troops. Unlike Missionary Ridge, where the rout was unexpected, the defeat at Nashville seemed inevitable. Once again the army had been misused by its commanders and sacrificed needlessly. That the damage was inflicted by its old adversaries from the Army of the Cumberland provided little comfort at the time but eventually united its veterans as they remembered this climatic battle's many controversies.[30]

The fate of the two armies remained tied to the very end. In the spring of 1865 the skeleton of the Army of Tennessee ended up in the Carolinas under William Hardee as the last-ditch defense against Sherman's triumphant army. In the process, they fell in with Joseph Johnston again and tangled with the XIV Corps at Bentonville, North Carolina, and in numerous skirmishes along the way. By all accounts, the men fought well in the final encounters and surrendered with honor.[31] The two armies that had shared victory and defeat, overcome adversity, and slaughtered one another on many battlefields were forever united by common memories of combat, hardship, and duty. These memories would be constructed during the processes of reminiscence, debate, and recollection. The veterans did not just remember the past; they re-fought it and reconstructed it to fit the present.

However, the need to construct and consolidate the collective memories of the veterans of the Union Army of the Cumberland and Confederate Army of Tennessee was far more important than simply refighting old battles. To that end, the former foes needed leadership, clearly defined goals, and an identifiable commemorative landscape. All three would be provided in the person of Henry Boynton, the dynamic newspaperman, former commander of the 35th Ohio Volunteer Infantry, and relentless champion of the Army of the Cumberland, who would bring the two armies together on their greatest battlefields.

FIVE

"Offering Your Lives . . . in Vindication of Your Manhood"

The veterans of the Army of the Cumberland and the Army of Tennessee faced daunting challenges in the preservation of their organizational identities and the construction of postwar memories. Having been the victim of reorganization and the dispersal of its key units, the Army of the Cumberland barely existed as a single entity at the end of the war. As a result, it lost the opportunity to take its place in the Grand Review and struggled to separate its accomplishments from those credited to other armies and commanders. For the Confederates, the legacy of failure that followed their disputed victory at Chickamauga tainted the identity and collective memory of the Army of Tennessee's veterans. The remaining units of the Army of Tennessee surrendered in North Carolina in April 1865 as part of a makeshift force operating hundreds of miles from the state that had given the army its name. As individuals, the veterans of both armies had done their part to keep their accomplishments and memories alive in memoirs, letters, articles, and commemorative ceremonies that honored both the living and the dead. The next step in the construction and preservation of the collective memories of these two armies would lead them back to the savage battle on the banks of the "River of Death."

As the 1880s ushered in a growing sense of sectional reconciliation, it also brought an increased amount of commemorative activities in the form of statue dedications, the maintenance of national cemeteries, and the funerals of prominent military leaders. Amid this flurry of public recognition of the war's importance, the veterans of some of its greatest battles were drawn back to the battlefields as they sought to create permanent venues for memory construction. Union veterans of the Army of the Potomac and some enterprising local citizens had already begun creating a park on the Gettysburg battlefield utilizing its sanctification by President Abraham Lincoln's 1863 speech, public identification as the "high tide of the Confederacy," and its close proximity to northern population centers to establish a sacred public site. Since most of the war's major battles were fought in the South, however, it seemed inevitable that veterans of battles in Virginia, Georgia, Tennessee, Mississippi, and the Carolinas would claim some of these landscapes as their own. During the late 1880s, members of the Society of the Army of the Cumberland joined with some of their former foes and identified the fields and woods around Chickamauga Creek as the place where they would establish their primary commemorative site. Using a combination of perseverance, political muscle, local support, and their connections in the War Department, the veterans created a site that was alternately sacred, historical, and educational, thus providing a model for other commemorative parks.

The creation of the parks also perpetuated the ongoing conflicts among the participants over the times, places, and significance of the events on the battlefields. Old rivalries came back to life, memories were tested, and disagreements between former foes and comrades turned the design and placement of monuments into major controversies. By the time the Chickamauga Military Park was partially completed, it became clear that the collective memories of the Society of the Army of the Cumberland and its influential spokesman Henry V. N. Boynton would dominate the interpretation of the battlefield. Those internal conflicts, along with other social and economic issues, spurred a flurry of memory construction by the veterans and a public hoping to connect the uncertain present to a more glorious and satisfying past.

The process of reconciliation was not an easy one, nor did it come to all Americans at once. A study by John R. Neff in 2005 argues that the constant and ongoing commemorative activity in both the North and South delayed and inhibited the process of sectional reunion. Neff points out that the northern "Cause Victorious" myth and the use of the "bloody shirt" countered the Lost Cause and kept the bitterness of the conflict alive well into the twentieth century. His analysis of commemorative practices "explores the role of death in condensing, and occasionally defying, American nationality." There is certainly some support for this thesis. For example, in spite of the role that Confederate veterans played in perpetuating the mythology of Pickett's Charge at Gettysburg, it was not until after the turn of the century that Confederate veterans began to place monuments on the battlefield.

Controversies over Confederate symbols and the racial violence surrounding the Civil Rights era and the end of Jim Crow reignited sectional hostility during the war's centennial in the 1960s. Renewed debates over the Confederate flag's presence on public flagpoles and logos in South Carolina, Georgia, and Mississippi reached a fever pitch in the late 1990s, nearly a century after the commonly accepted era of reconciliation, and brought out long-simmering emotions over the meanings and symbolism of the Old South. If nothing else, the sheer numbers of Confederate-themed books, articles, artwork, slogans, images, and rhetoric, along with thousands of "rebel" reenactors who can be found in the modern Civil War community seem to suggest that there is still a tangible sense of sectional separation.[1]

Yet there is far more support among modern historians for the idea that the American public's inclination toward reconciliation during the last two decades of the nineteenth century was extremely widespread and played an important role in the construction of lasting memories of the Civil War. It is also clear that this process would not have taken place without the participation of the veterans from both sides and their respective organizations. By coming to a consensus that the war was an unfortunate bloodletting between equally brave members of the same "family," the veterans opened the door for the reunion of the sections under a single, national flag: the rejuvenated Stars and Stripes. Finally, as David Blight points out in his influential works on Frederick Douglass and the issue of race, "those who remembered the war as a rebirth of the republic in the name of racial equality would continue to do battle with the growing number who would remember it as the nation's test of manhood and the South's struggle to sustain white supremacy." Thus, in welcoming the return of its rebel prodigal sons and brothers, the nation gradually turned its back on its colored brethren.[2]

There were a number of reasons that Americans from the North and South decided to overcome their postwar hostility and move forward. Politically, it was in the interest of both southern and northern Democrats to put aside their sectional differences and unite to break the long Republican hold on both Congress and the White House. To accomplish this, the South had to neutralize black Republican voters, which it did through intimidation, occasional violence, and the eventual enactment of Jim Crow laws that restricted African American voting rights. With the cooperation of northern Democrats, white Southerners isolated and excluded their political opponents and constructed a functional social order based on racial separation. For Republicans, the split in the party prior to the election of 1872 and the corruption and embarrassment of President Ulysses S. Grant's second administration served to take the steam out of Radical Reconstruction and shifted much of the party's attention to other pressing issues. In spite of the restoration of heavy-handed white rule in much of the South by the middle of the 1880s, moderate Northerners could rightly claim that they had fulfilled the purpose of the war by saving the Union, ending slavery, and promoting political, if not social, equality between the races.

There were also economic opportunities that pushed northern investors and southern businessmen closer together to find ways to develop the south's economy. For the South to recover from the catastrophic results of the war it had to tear itself away from its dependence on cotton and the antiquated plantation system. Many poor Southerners, both white and black, were trapped as tenants or sharecroppers on unproductive land owned by absentee landowners. For the region to recover, it needed an influx of people, capital, and industry from the more developed and prosperous North. The collapse of reconstruction and the promise of Federal aid that followed the Compromise of 1877 spurred the construction of railroads and industry in numerous parts of the south. By the 1890s, the "New South" was regaining a measure of prosperity on its own terms, with both legal and de facto white supremacy and racial segregation firmly in place. To make this merger of northern capital and southern development work, the issues of race and the lingering resentments from the "late war" had to be at least overlooked, if not completely eliminated.[3]

In some ways, the success of sectional reconciliation represented a broader national acceptance of the South's "Lost Cause" version of the war. This was only possible after the South had modified the framework of its memories to fit a changing American society. As the United States underwent a shift from being a nation of farmers to one of entrepreneurs, corporations, and industrial workers, there was a longing for the traditional images and values of the previous generation. What the South had to offer was a mythologized version of its antebellum past, complete with docile slaves, a languid gentility, and charming hospitality. Through a combination of popular literature, minstrel shows, and subtle but effective marketing, the South was seen by many urban Northerners as an exotic, appealing region where life was simple and blacks were a happy and subordinate working class. Thus, the loss that should be truly remembered and lamented as a result of Southern defeat was not that of slavery or Confederate independence, but rather the region's attractive, idealized, traditional way of life. Even former Union soldiers who had seen the real South during their service in the war were charmed by its climate, geography, and spirit. In the decades after the war, a parade of veterans, ranging from former Army of the Cumberland commander William S. Rosecrans to the simplest Yankee private, visited southern towns, spas, and resorts to enjoy both the weather and the hospitality.[4]

One of the more compelling theories regarding reconciliation comes from historian Nina Silber, who suggests that the process of national reunion can be seen by examining late nineteenth-century northern male attitudes toward southern women. Using popular literature and copious anecdotal evidence, she argues convincingly that as the images of southern women shifted from antebellum belles, to wartime secessionist harpies, to postwar fallen angels, they became objects to be alternately idealized, conquered, and redeemed by northern men. It was a process of parallel memory construction and collective forgetting; as Southerners idealized and internalized idyllic images of the Old South's virtuous womanhood, Northerners hoped to "rescue" the widows and daughters of the Confederacy by instilling an appreciation for the American—rather than southern—way of life.

Conversely, the spunky girls in these popular novels taught Yankees that the sacrifices, heroism, and determination of the South's soldiers and civilians were evidence of shared American—not just southern—values and qualities. She writes that "Yankees sought to recreate the Victorian ideal through the reconciliation process. Their image of the South conformed to the image of the ideal feminine sphere; in northern eyes, the South became a region of refined domestic comfort, and the reunion of North and South restored the sense of domestic harmony that northern society no longer possessed." Even if the "romance of reunion" was not as widespread as Silber suggests, it is clear that to successfully reunite the nation, the veterans, politicians, and public had to create common ground on which to construct common memories.[5]

That ground, both literally and figuratively, consisted of the images and descriptions of the heroic sacrifices of the soldiers from both armies on the battlefields of the war. As noted in an earlier chapter, the burial and reburials of the war's dead and the erection of monuments to the individual states' and communities' fighting men consumed much public energy in the decades after the war and reinforced a "cult of the common soldier" that carried on well into the twentieth century. The rituals of Decoration Day in the South and Memorial Day in the North not only kept the focus on the dead, but provided a platform on which living veterans could express their feelings toward fallen comrades and remind listeners of the importance of their efforts. The involvement of southern women in the process of memorialization and commemoration thrust women into the spotlight, on the one hand, but tended to reinforce traditional notions of manly duty, honor, and sacrifice, on the other. These mothers and daughters of the Confederacy kept the "Lost Cause" alive by reminding men that it was their duty to protect southern values and virtues, whatever the risk. Having endured the humiliation of defeat and failure in the war itself, southern society sought to restore its manhood by combining both Union and Confederate veterans in a mutually appreciated cult of honor. Ironically, during the height of Jim Crow, this impulse toward the preservation of virtue often led white men to commit murder and lynch black men whom they suspected of violating the purity of southern womanhood.[6]

Society's perception of white manhood weighed heavily on the trend toward the veneration of the Civil War's veterans and the reunion of North and South. For aging veterans in the South, the "Lost Cause" "emerged . . . as a southern narrative of racial victory . . . [that] had to be defended at all costs."

With this myth in place, Reconstruction could be seen as a continuation of the same struggle, with the potential equality of the Black man an omniscient reminder of what was at stake. As the southern states were redeemed and restored to white rule, manhood was regained at the expense of the former slaves. The virtues of the Confederacy were taught in schools, academies, and churches throughout the South as a means by which the region could restore its collective identity and males could reinvigorate their lost manhood. One consequence of this was the continued oppression of black men, who represented both the consequence of southern defeat and a threat to both white manhood and womanhood. The second result of this search for manhood is a focus on the veterans of the war who were the ideal symbols of all that was desirable in the American male. This, of course, was the key to the reconciliation movement; it portrayed southern values as distinctly American at their core and thus shared by their veteran counterparts in the North.[7]

For the North, the perceived threats to manhood that spurred a reinvigoration of interest in the war and reconciliation came from several sources. First, the growing industrial and urban orientation of much of American society seemed to threaten the traditional values and standards of manhood from the previous generations. Along with this came the flow of immigrants, the creation of a working class, and active labor unions, all signs of changing times. Even the West was slowly being conquered, taking away the excitement, danger, opportunity, and exotic native appeal of the frontier. The response to this rapidly changing society was an attempt to reorient to a purer, more genuine sense of community. Nina Silber notes that "confronted with the haunting specters of class conflict, ethnic strife and the alienation that their own industrialized society had produced, many northerners remained unconvinced about [the need to] . . . obliterate what remained of the old southern legacy."[8]

With the Civil War veterans providing the ideal example of manhood, many Americans hoped to instill the values of this heroic generation on what appeared to be a physically soft, morally weak, overly materialistic society. This was exemplified by the notion of "vigorous manhood" promoted by the likes of Theodore Roosevelt, which encouraged Americans to pursue an active, rugged, and strenuous lifestyle to counter the tendencies toward passivism and complacency. The trend that Kristen Hoganson describes as the "manly ideal of politics" emphasized the aggressiveness of the political arena and the need to draw upon the masculine qualities of the Civil War veterans who made up much of the leadership of the late nineteenth century. In this context, "sectional union . . . could offer a bridge . . . between a modern and pre-modern world" and the strengthened hope for a truly reunited United States.[9]

It would not have been possible to reconnect the two sections without the approval and participation of the war's veterans and their organizations. During the period of hibernation and throughout Reconstruction, veterans on both sides clung to their respective positions in victory and defeat and correspondingly denounced their enemies. During the 1870s and '80s, separate Memorial Day and Decoration Day celebrations in northern and southern states were platforms for the respective causes, with few compliments reserved for the enemy soldiers and politicians who had been the cause of all the death and suffering. Even as those activities became more secular, veterans' reunions began to reflect the increasing perception that the war had been about heroism and sacrifice that was shared by soldiers on both sides.

The growing number of "Blue and Gray" reunions and mutual appearances at funerals, monument dedications, and other commemorative events represented a merger of two sets of vernacular memories into a powerful and dominant one. While not universally accepted, the emphasis on the heroic commonality of the combat experience won many aging veterans over to the camp of sectional reconciliation. As time passed, the debates surrounding the definition of manhood increasingly made reference to the Civil War battlefield ordeal as the symbol of duty, courage, and devotion to the American way of life. Historian John Pettegrew writes that "widespread respect and appreciation for the courage and sacrifice of Union and Confederate soldiers contributed to American nationalism" and that "memory of the war became an historical overlay to turn-of-the century conceptions of citizenship" and the corresponding definition of manhood.[10]

According to Michael Kammen, the mobilization of veterans' organizations during the gradual but steady process of reconciliation was aided by several factors. Given the large numbers of potential members and overall economic prosperity, especially among Northerners in postwar America, it was inevitable that political, fraternal, and veterans' groups would emerge, multiply, and prosper. In addition, the growth of cities concentrated diverse groups of people and made organizations more accessible to one another. Finally, the rapid expansion of a national railroad system "made it convenient for veterans and their families to attend encampments and meetings." This use of railroads "marked the first in a series of transformations in American transportation extremely conducive to curiosity about tradition and national heritage." Gatherings of veterans took place in both the North and the South with increasing frequency. The cities of Baltimore, Richmond, Chicago, Annapolis, Boston, Fredericksburg, and New Orleans hosted reunions and ceremonies that drew large numbers of both Union and Confederate participants and demonstrated the "lasting sentiments of good will" among former foes.[11]

Ultimately, as the men who faced one another in the Civil War came together to reminisce, they found more in common with one another than with the materialistic new generation that seemed to be challenging the values they had fought to preserve. Speeches given by veterans and political figures from both sides praised the spirit of brotherhood and predicted that healing the wounds of the war would assure the nation's greatness. Echoing a popular notion that the war itself was a necessary national growing pain, Gen. John H. Palmer, an Army of the Cumberland veteran, speaking in 1895 at the dedication of Chickamauga Military Park, noted that "the Civil War was caused by a sectional challenge to American manhood, and that challenge was accepted by years of bloody and desolating war. In that war, the American people learned to properly estimate each other, which is the only foundation for harmonious, national unity." He went on to praise the former Confederates' "gallantry and courage" and proclaimed that "I never allowed myself to forget that you were Americans, freely offering your lives in the defense in what you believed to be your rights and in vindication of your manhood." Given this trend toward forgiveness and a growing desire among white, Protestant Americans to reconnect with their shared heritage, the locations most likely to pull together former foes from all regions of the country were the battlefields on which they had met and fought.[12]

The reunions and ceremonies that drew veterans together served as the rituals of memory construction; thus, the themes of reconciliation and reunion made up the central focus of those collective memories. There were other elements present in American society that played a role in the creation of battlefield parks as the focus of memory and reunion. One was the sense of nostalgia for what many white Americans felt was a purer, more genuine past. This helped enhance the attractive image of the Old South as a place where the older generation of Americans, not just Southerners, would feel comfortable among familiar, rural, and genteel surroundings. The rapid emergence of a modern industrial society with all of its uncertainties, challenges, and threats to the traditional order of things left white Americans longing for some connection to what seemed to be a better past. In this context, and aided by the passage of time, memories of the great sectional conflict became valuable tools in the creation of a common heritage that needed to be strengthened against the threats posed by modernity.

This nostalgic search for the past extended beyond the Civil War period. The centennial of the nation's independence rekindled an interest in the revolutionary period and stimulated the construction and rededication of monuments to the heroes and events of that period. At the same time, Washington D.C. became the central point for the erection of a flood of monuments honoring the nation's great men, including many from the Civil War. The desire among many Americans to rekindle the flame of national pride and patriotism naturally led them to see war, and particularly the Civil War, as the symbol of the nation's struggle. In light of this viewpoint, reconciliation became the crowning climax of that struggle. Their new importance in this frenzy of memory-building was not lost on the veterans, who found new ways to connect the public to their experiences by preserving the battlefields on which they had fought and died.[13]

The ongoing process of memory construction taking place during the 1880s and 1890s provided an ideal context for the creation of commemorative landscapes and the establishment of sacred sites around which American values could be reenergized. The renewed focus on manhood, sacrifice, and reconciliation by many Northerners and Southerners spurred an interest in the creation of monuments, memorials, and other physical symbols of the nation's strength under duress and its perseverance during times of social and economic change. The importance of sacred ground to the construction of memory allows us to reexamine the process by which Civil War veterans actively utilized battlefields as "prime examples of sacred patriotic space where memories of the transformative powers of war and the sacrificial heroism of the warrior are preserved."

The process of constructing memories on battlefield landscapes is far from simple. Edward Linenthal observes that battlefields ". . . are ceremonial centers where various forms of veneration reflect the belief that the contemporary power and relevance of the 'lessons' of the battle are crucial for the continued life of the nation. [And] that the patriotic inspiration to be extracted from these places depends not only on proper ceremony but on a memorialized, preserved, restored, and purified environment." He goes on to note that they are also "civil spaces" that can be used by a variety of secular groups of "various ideological persuasions" to "argue about the nature of heroism, the meaning of war, [and] the efficacy of martial sacrifice." In addition to their sacred and ideological importance, battlefields are frequently the objects of scholarly study or military activities, destinations for vacationers, aesthetically pleasing pastoral parks, and sources of both public and private revenue for the communities nearby. The battlefield at Gettysburg represents the confluence of all these elements better than any other. In identifying Gettysburg as one of the nation's primary sacred places, Linenthal observes that "the processes of veneration, defilement, and redefinition that have taken place at Gettysburg . . . have created . . . a rich cultural archive of various modes of remembrance." As a result, the Gettysburg Park serves as a comparative reference point for the discussion of the Chickamauga battlefield that is the subject of this study.[14]

The facts surrounding the creation of the Gettysburg battlefield are well-documented in a variety of sources. However, what makes the historiography of this park's development so important to the study of other Civil War sites are the debates surrounding the meanings and appropriate uses of the sacred battlefield landscape. The origin of the park essentially began within weeks after the battle, when two local attorneys lobbied for the creation of a national cemetery for the Union dead near the climactic point of the battle on Cemetery Ridge. This led to the creation of the Gettysburg Battlefield Memorial Association (GBMA) in September 1863 and resulted in the memorable dedication of the cemetery and battlefield by President Lincoln on 19 November of that year. With the sacredness of the landscape thus established, the GBMA continued the process of burying the dead and working to preserve both the historical integrity and the "golden mist" of memory that surrounded this significant Union victory.

Under the leadership of John B. Bachelder, the postwar "expert" on the battle and a longtime director of the GBMA, the commemorative landscape gradually took form with the purchase of land, construction of markers, placement of cannon, and the dedication of monuments by the battle's veterans. His isometric drawing of the battlefield, which gave early visitors a bird's-eye view of the entire landscape, and the self-guided tour booklet he wrote facilitated the design of the park's roads and interpretive signs. Beginning in 1878, Union veterans began meeting on or near the battlefield and constructed the first unit monument on the grounds outside of the National Cemetery. To keep the placement of monuments from becoming too random, the association required that regiments mark the flanks of their positions and place their monuments within this regimental front. Only two Confederate monuments were in place before 1888. As noted previously, despite the reconciliatory spirit, there were not many others erected (including one featuring a grand statue of Robert E. Lee) until after the turn of the century. When the GBMA finally approved the placement of Confederate markers and monuments, they limited them to the positions that the units or states held before advancing, which served to separate most of them from the most frequently visited parts of the battlefield.

In addition to the controversies surrounding the participation of the Confederates, many veterans from both sides had mixed reactions to Bachelder's long-standing dominance and authority over nearly every aspect of the park. Based primarily on his suggestions, the GBMA promoted the "High Water Mark" as the battle's key point, enacted regulations governing monument design, and worked to keep the battlefield in as much of its original state as possible. In 1893, several years after the creation of the Chickamauga and Chattanooga National Military Park, the GBMA shifted some of the responsibility for managing the park to the newly created Gettysburg Battlefield Commission, which shared authority with the War Department until Congress authorized the creation of the Gettysburg National Military Park in 1895.[15]

The history of Gettysburg Park is replete with controversies over collective memory, monument placement, and the relative importance of some events over others. A large number of both popular and scholarly articles and books have debated, analyzed, and rehashed the events of 1–3 July 1863, with an increasing interest in the memories surrounding key issues in the battle. The defense of Little Round Top on 2 July and the Confederate assault known as Pickett's Charge on the third day still dominate the literature on the battle, despite the growing realization among many historians that a handful of individuals like Bachelder, Joshua Chamberlain, and Dan Sickles deliberately directed public focus toward particular events.[16]

There are similar studies on lesser-known elements of the battle that show the depth and variety of the veterans' memory construction. However, it has often been the battlefield itself that has drawn the attention of photographers, historians, the preservation community, and the public over the years. In 1975, William Frassanito published a book of photographs taken by Matthew Brady, Timothy O'Sullivan, and others in the days and weeks after the battle and offered his readers modern photographs recreating the exact camera positions that corresponded with the nineteenth-century views. Photographs also play a role in several books documenting the great Blue and Gray reunions commemorating the fiftieth and seventy-fifth anniversaries of the battle in 1913 and 1938, respectively. These gigantic reunions became the primary national symbols of reconciliation and solidified the physical and spiritual connection between the veterans and the battlefields that they had fought on. Well-publicized and oft-reproduced photographs of aging veterans shaking hands over the wall at "the angle" have come to represent the sentimentalized and nostalgic view of the war that still dominates American popular memory.[17]

Most of the recent scholarly histories of the battlefield include references to the early creation of the park, Bachelder's role, the controversies over monuments, and the big reunions. However, the more compelling issues dominating these works are those surrounding the various interpretations of the park and its multiple uses as a sacred site, commemorative landscape, tourist attraction, and commercial enterprise. Several of these historians highlight the conflict between the battlefield's status as "holy ground" and "American shrine" and the public, commercial, and heritage-based interests that have been present since its earliest days. At least one historian concludes that the struggles between the sacred and secular at Gettysburg have created a dangerous ambiguity when it comes to giving meaning to the site.[18]

What nearly all of these writers have concluded is that the history, myths, and memories of the battle are explicitly linked to the battlefield itself. The soldiers were aware of it and exercised their control over those elements in their placement of markers and monuments. Abraham Lincoln knew it when he gave his famous address; Franklin Roosevelt knew it when he dedicated the Peace Light Memorial on the battle's seventy-fifth anniversary. The other message that comes through in the work of these scholars is that the Gettysburg battlefield has been subjected to numerous and often conflicting social, economic, political, and cultural forces as it developed into one of the nation's most visible sacred sites. The battlefield that is seen today is not so much a snapshot in time as the product of those conflicting forces. Much of the public's continued interest in the battlefield is generated by the desire to somehow make a connection with the men and events that took place there.[19]

This yearning to reconnect to the past is one of the characteristics of collective memory that most historical and heritage sites try to enhance and exploit. The degree to which they are successful often determines whether they are considered historically significant, culturally uplifting, or commercially successful. The creation of the Gettysburg battlefield illustrated some of the difficulties inherent in the construction of a commemorative landscape. Some of those same challenges, along with more unique ones, faced the veterans of the Army of the Cumberland and Army of Tennessee as they set out to create and preserve their own sacred ground on the site of their greatest battle.

Unlike the Gettysburg battlefield, the landscape around Chickamauga Creek did not draw a great deal of attention after the battle. Following the Union victory in November 1863, the Union dead were buried in a cemetery on the outskirts of Chattanooga with relatively little public fanfare. The armies marched away, leaving nature and the local citizens behind to heal the wounds of battle that scarred the landscape. For all intents and purposes, the site of the great and bloody battle of Chickamauga lay unrecognized, unmarked, and unsanctified for nearly thirty years after the events of September 1863. During this time, the Society of the Army of the Cumberland continued to draw on its members and former commanders to continue promoting the army's place in the memory of the war. Eventually, Confederate veterans, the forces of reconciliation, collective memory, a receptive local community, a cooperative national government, and the driving leadership of several key individuals all combined to produce America's first official National Military Park.

The great battles of 1863 and the subsequent military occupation "had brought general disaster and dislocation" to the city of Chattanooga and the surrounding area. At the end of the war, Chattanooga was swamped with both black and white refugees, vulnerable to disease epidemics, and beset by a "large number of vicious, outbreaking [sic] persons, and thefts." Although some businesses and industry, like the iron foundries established by the Union army for its railroads, had arrived during the war, the demobilization of troops

FIG. 13: This 1864 view of Chattanooga looking from 5th Street and Walnut toward Cameron Hill shows the wartime impact on the city and the strong military presence on the surrounding landscape. From the Paul A. Hiener Collection, Chattanooga–Hamilton County Bicentennial Library.

and the end of the occupation left the city's postwar recovery up to its citizens. Compared to some areas of the South, the area around Chattanooga suffered somewhat less under the pressures of Reconstruction.[20]

One of the individuals who aided substantially in Chattanooga's recovery was John T. Wilder, the former commander of the Army of the Cumberland's famed "Lightning Brigade." While stationed in Chattanooga during the war, Wilder recognized its economic potential, and after returning to Indiana for a short time, he moved back to Chattanooga to help establish the Roane Iron Company in 1867. As a former ironworker, Wilder not only brought with him a great deal of enthusiasm and business experience, he also succeeded in raising nearly $1 million in capital to get the operation started. Wilder became an important citizen in Chattanooga and served as an excellent ambassador for Northerners in general and the Society of the Army of the Cumberland in particular. He held several elected offices in the city and served on the Chickamauga Park Commission before his death in 1917.

The other important character in Chattanooga's postwar growth was Adolph Ochs, a northern-born Jew who arrived in Chattanooga from Knoxville in 1877 and bought the *Chattanooga Times*, a struggling paper in a still-struggling town. Within a few years, he had turned it into a successful, nonpartisan,

community paper and was one of the city's leading proponents of moderniza-
tion and progress. He gained even greater fame and fortune when he became
the editor of the *New York Times,* where he used his influence to promote the
economic development of the South and the city of Chattanooga. Ultimately,
both of these men would have direct, positive, and active roles in the creation
of the Chickamauga and Chattanooga National Military Park.[21]

Whereas the battlefield at Gettysburg surrounds the town, the distance
between Chattanooga and the scene of fighting at Chickamauga was nearly
a dozen miles and straddled the Georgia-Tennessee state line. As a result of
this inconvenient geographic situation, the Chickamauga battlefield was rural,
isolated, and slow to recover from the ravages of battle. While riding over the
Chickamauga field in December 1863, General Grant and his staff observed "a
grisly scene, with leering skulls stuck on poles and body parts laid on stumps
and logs. Wild hogs had rooted up the shallowly buried carcasses and fed on
the rotting remains." Grant was said to have observed during this tour that
"these trees would make a good lead mine." The intervening years allowed the
land to heal, in spite of the presence of bullet holes, lead balls, and the ever-
present artifacts in the woods and fields.

What did not happen at Chickamauga, however, was the kind of public attention given to the Gettysburg battlefield in the months and years after the fight.
After declaring Chickamauga "the greatest battle fought during the war," Army
of the Cumberland veteran and society officer Joseph Fullerton observed that

> For more than a quarter of a century after the battle, these fields and
> woods, under the ownership of the unprogressive natives, remained
> practically unchanged. Not as many as fifty acres of woodland have
> been cleared, hardly a field has been changed either in shape or manner
> of cultivation, and but one house has been built on the seven thousand
> acres, owned by two hundred persons. . . . Even the rail fences used for
> fuel by the opposing armies at the time of the battle have not yet been
> fully replaced. Fortunately for us, this great field remains practically as
> it was when the battle was fought.

General Fullerton had put his finger on the contradictory disadvantages and
benefits of having the Army of the Cumberland's key battlefield in such a remote place. On one hand, there was very little infrastructure to work with; on
the other, the veterans had a nearly blank canvas on which to construct their
park and their memories.[22]

Even the topography of the Chickamauga field conspired to mire it in ob-
scurity. Not only did it lack the Round Tops and sweeping fields of Gettysburg,
but its landscape paled in comparison to the area around Chattanooga where

the final chapters of the campaign had played out. Army of Cumberland historian Thomas Van Horne waxed eloquent about the site of one of his army's greatest accomplishments:

> Battlefields become a part of history equally with the story of the conflicts enacted upon them. They are mapped on stone and steel, and delineated in pen pictures, appear in historic narration in intimate association with the deeds of heroes. Not alone do the topographical features which suggest plans of battle . . . become historic, but those also of mere grandeur and beauty, whenever the hosts of war commingle in deadly strife, where nature has been lavish of her gifts . . . and in all that is grandly concomitant with grandest battle, Chattanooga is pre-eminent.

Although he was referring to the stunning views from and of Lookout Mountain and the dramatic heights of Missionary Ridge, he could just as well have been talking about the two battles themselves. There are few contemporary photographs of the Chickamauga battlefield; yet dozens of images taken by George Barnard, Robert Linn, and others in and around Chattanooga filled volumes and captured imaginations then and now. Just as the dramatic landscape surrounding the city dominated the countryside, the "battle above the clouds" fought on those hills stubbornly served to overshadow the carnage in the thickets, briars, and hardscrabble fields around the "River of Death."[23]

Not only did the landscape lack development and drama, it had gone undedicated and unsanctified by the men whose comrades had shed their blood on it. The War Department had authorized the creation of the National Cemetery to hold the Union dead from Chickamauga, but it was located on the southeastern outskirts of Chattanooga, far from where many of the Army of the Cumberland's soldiers had fallen. Following a practice that he had begun with the Army of the Ohio on the Mill Springs battlefield, Gen. George Thomas issued the order creating the cemetery on 25 December 1863, with the internment of bodies from both the Chickamauga and Chattanooga battlefields beginning immediately. Unlike Gettysburg, where a professional designer laid out the cemetery, the Army of the Cumberland's own chaplain, and later historian, Thomas A. Van Horne, used little more than the lay of the land to arrange the burials. On top of that, the burials were random; there was no arrangement by either state or unit. According to popular accounts, the unpretentious General Thomas characteristically told the burial details to "Mix them up; I am tired of states [sic] rights."

Although the Confederates had established a cemetery for their fallen soldiers in Chattanooga following the Battle of Stones River, it was 1877 before a local women's Confederate memorial association raised the first commemorative monument to its southern heroes. The dedication ceremony was reported to have included both Union and Confederate veterans, but neither it nor the National Cemetery came close to providing the dramatic public rituals that had sanctified both the dead and the field on which they fell at Gettysburg.[24]

The commemorative process that began with the formation of the armies, the campaigns, and the construction of national cemeteries spanned nearly thirty years prior to the creation of the Chickamauga and Chattanooga National Military Park. Before they had a battleground to focus on, the members of the Society of the Army of the Cumberland contributed to the process of memory construction by debating issues surrounding battles, defending themselves and their leaders from criticism, and glorifying the accomplishments of their army. The attacks leveled at both Rosecrans and Thomas by more famous generals like Sherman and Grant motivated the army's veterans to remember their own leaders and enhance their accomplishments. Although Grant's fame and status as victorious general and president of the United States kept him in the forefront of public memory, the former commanders of the Army of the Cumberland were not idle during this period. Their postwar lives and eventual deaths generated a host of memories and commemorative rituals that carried the army's veterans through the decades leading up the creation of the battlefield park.[25]

After resigning from the Regular Army in 1867, William Starke Rosecrans served five months as Ambassador to Mexico near the end of President Andrew Johnson's administration. He made an impact on national politics in 1868 when he solicited the help of Robert E. Lee in drafting the White Sulphur Letter, which tried to reestablish southern loyalty, denounce racism, and win Democratic voters. Not only did it fail to produce a victory for Horatio Seymour over Grant in the election, but it elicited some hostile responses from many people in the North. While Rosecrans's motives may have been true, this effort at reconciliation was too soon and obviously politically motivated; it did nothing to enhance the general's clouded reputation. In his letter to the first meeting of the Society of the Army of the Cumberland, he wrote "let us live true to our great record and we shall live a band of brothers, honored and beloved; and dying, leave names hallowed in the grateful remembrance of coming generations."[26]

George H. Thomas, who was belatedly promoted to the rank of major general in the Regular Army near the end of the war, faithfully remained in the service of his country. He skillfully managed the volatile postwar situation in a huge military district encompassing six southern states but was shocked and frustrated by the pervasive racism and violence in the region. In 1866, he was presented with a gold medal from the state of Tennessee as "a token of regard and appreciation" for his decisive victories at Chattanooga and Nashville. In contrast to

FIG. 14: A veteran of the Army of the Cumberland holds General Thomas's headquarters flag with a banner describing it as a "relic." The veterans honored Thomas with a statue in Washington, D.C., and a large funeral upon his death in 1870. Library of Congress.

many of his contemporaries in both armies, he avoided politics and accepted an assignment to the far-off Military Department of the Pacific, where he died in 1870 at the age of fifty-three. Listing him among the four top generals in the war, *Harper's Weekly* noted that "Thomas has been more fortunate than our other great generals. He has never suffered a defeat in the field." The respected periodical described his death a few years later as "a national calamity."[27]

By some accounts, the Virginian may have been the mostly widely respected officer in the Union military but his modesty, reluctance to play politics, and the possible enmity of a powerful block of his contemporaries worked against his legacy. Thomas responded to few of his critics, left no memoirs, and apparently destroyed nearly all of his personal papers before his death. Part of his family in Virginia never forgave him for remaining with the Union. When called upon to address the inaugural meeting of the Society of the Army of the

Cumberland, he spoke very briefly, saying "we have assembled here from all parts of the country; showing an earnestness and an interest in the work we have done, and a willingness to do whatever may be required of us by our country, which is gratifying to every patriotic heart." The veterans of the Army of the Cumberland defended him endlessly before and after his death; his stand on Snodgrass Hill on 20 September 1863, became the symbol of the army's spirit and determination and the centerpiece of its collective memories.[28]

Thomas's untimely death galvanized the members of the Society of the Army of the Cumberland into action, and they began to raise funds for the commission of a mounted statue of the general in Washington, D.C. After raising $10,000 on its own and getting an appropriation from Congress, they hired sculptor John Quincy Adams Ward to create the statue for a total cost of $35,000. It was completed on time to the great satisfaction of everyone involved and dedicated on 19 November 1879, at an event described as "the grandest ever witnessed at the capital . . . since the Grand Review of troops in May 1865." The mounted figure captured the general's "power, strength, and action" and honored Thomas's "conspicuous and unselfish devotion to public duty." Thomas was not the last member of the Army of the Cumberland to get a statue, but he was certainly the most deserving.[29]

The members of the Society also raised funds for a statue honoring James Garfield following his assassination in 1881. Garfield died on 19 September which happened to be the anniversary of the battle and the day that the Society of the Army of the Cumberland was holding its annual meeting in Chattanooga. The Society formed a memorial committee on the spot, but fundraising for the monument proved to be more difficult than it had been for the popular Thomas. Only a Garfield Memorial Fair, run by the wives of the memorial committee, allowed them to raise $15,000 of the $25,000 needed to commission the statue. Once again, the society turned to John Quincy Adams Ward, who had created the popular Thomas statue, as their sculptor of choice. His ambitious design portrayed Garfield as a standing, rather than mounted, figure surrounded by three figures representing his careers as a scholar, statesman, and general. The dedication on 12 May 1887, was impressive, but did not reach the level that Thomas's unveiling had reached less than a decade earlier. The usual array of generals, congressmen, and Army of the Cumberland veterans joined President Grover Cleveland in honoring Garfield. Michael Kammen writes that "interest on the part of Washingtonians was minimal, and even among survivors of the Army of the Cumberland, it was nominal." He attributes this to an overall public lethargy about the war, but one cannot help but believe that Garfield's alleged duplicity toward Rosecrans back in 1863 had something to do with it.[30]

FIG. 15: James A. Garfield's version of the Battle of Chickamauga undermined Rosecrans, mildly praised Thomas, elevated the Ohioan to the presidency in 1880, and earned him an elaborate monument to his service following his assassination in 1881. Library of Congress.

FIG. 16: Gen. Phillip Sheridan and his staff, including George Custer, photographed while serving under Grant in the eastern theater. The public overlooked Sheridan's mediocre performance with the Army of the Cumberland after his heroics at the Battle of Cedar Creek in October 1864. Library of Congress.

The Society's third attempt to honor one of its former commanders after his death was a frustrating experience that began around the time of Philip Sheridan's death in 1888 and did not produce a statue until 1908. As it had before, the Society raised money and commissioned Ward as the sculptor. This time, however, the design he came up with after a six-year delay portrayed the general in his old age; this did not please Sheridan's widow, his son, or the veterans, who ended up rejecting it and firing Ward in 1905. He sued the Society for $35,000, and it took an appeal to Secretary of War William Howard Taft to help the suit go in its favor. Eventually, Gutzon Borglum, who had also designed several other high-profile monuments, created a stirring statue that showed the general on his horse Rienzi, rallying his men at Cedar Creek. The dedication on 25 November 1908, the anniversary of his division's triumph at Missionary Ridge, was reported to have been well-attended and included a speech by President Theodore Roosevelt. It seems ironic that the statue's design recognized Sheridan for his accomplishments after his service with the Army of the Cumberland had ended; this was just another symbol of that army's continuing struggle for recognition.[31]

Perhaps no one was busier in the years leading up to the creation of the park than Henry Van Ness Boynton, recording secretary of the Society of the Army of the Cumberland, Medal of Honor recipient, and Washington correspondent for the *Cincinnati Commercial Gazette*. In addition to his role as both Sherman's chief critic and George Thomas's great defender, Boynton used his influential position as a correspondent and Washington insider to get involved in several high-profile political controversies. In 1872, his testimony in front of a House investigating committee helped distance Vice President Henry Wilson from the Credit Mobilier scandal, in spite of continued speculation by some people that Wilson had been less than honest during his interview with Boynton. He appeared again as a behind-the-scenes player in the disputed presidential election of 1876 by suggesting that promoting southern railroad interests might supply some of the votes needed to break the deadlock in favor of Rutherford Hayes. After that, he emerged as a lukewarm advocate for Kentucky Republican John Harlan's appointment to the Supreme Court in 1877.[32]

Boynton took on the role of defender of the Union and its veterans by successfully leading the public outcry protesting Democratic President Grover Cleveland's plan to return captured Confederate battle flags to the southern states. However, he emerged as a firm advocate for reunion by the time the idea for a battlefield park was conceived. One contemporary historian described him as "one of the most noted, loved, feared, and respected of journalists" and went on to describe his qualities thus: "His distinguishing characteristic as a journalist is his sterling sense of integrity, inspired by a sense of justice, that can be appealed to at all times. He is feared by knaves of all sorts, for his singularly incisive style, backed by his courage, makes him terrible in his assaults on wrong." In short, Henry Boynton was a confident, pugnacious bulldog; a man who finished what he started and rolled over those who got in his way. He put all of these qualities to good use in defending the honor of the Army of the Cumberland, vilifying its detractors, and creating a commemorative landscape with the Chickamauga and Chattanooga National Military Park, which stands as his most notable achievement.[33]

The decades preceding the creation of the park saw a gradual evolution of national memories about the war. The passage of time, along with dynamic social forces, had softened the sectional bitterness from the war and led to an increasing movement toward reconciliation between old enemies. Common themes centering on heroism and sacrifice gave white veterans a place to focus their collective memories and stimulated mixed reunions and commemorations. The Gettysburg experiment set a precedent for constructing sacred ground, while the funerals of Thomas, Garfield, and Sheridan gave the veterans a chance to literally place their heroes on a pedestal. The next step was to create another set of commemorative landscapes that would highlight the accomplishments of the western armies in similar ways as Gettysburg honored those in the East.

SIX

"No Place for Lovers to Bide Tryst"

There can be little doubt that Henry Boynton was the right man in the right place at the perfect time for the creation of the Chickamauga and Chattanooga National Military Park. He possessed the incentive, the connections, the hard-headed determination, and the driving self-interest to take a good idea and turn it into a 7,000-acre reality in the span of seven years. The process began with a carriage ride on the Chickamauga battlefield in the summer of 1888. It culminated in Congressional legislation, significant expenditures of public money, and a giant dedication ceremony in 1895 that celebrated both the Army of the Cumberland and the theme of national reconciliation. In the midst of this process, veterans from several northern and southern states revisited the battlefield, retraced their steps, and relived the terrifying, stimulating, life-changing moments of their youth. They occasionally argued over the details of the battle and the interpretation of the landscape, but ultimately created a park that could be used by all Americans for a variety of purposes.

The genesis of the plan unfolded during the Society of the Army of the Cumberland's first visit to Chattanooga in 1881. As they toured the surrounding area many veterans expressed alarm at their inability to identify some key points of interest on their old battlefield. The planning continued in May 1888 when Boynton and his former brigade commander, Ferdinand Van Derveer, rented a carriage and took a tour of the neglected battlefield. Noting how badly the undergrowth had obscured many familiar landmarks, they discussed the need to reconstruct the landscape in the manner of the Gettysburg park to preserve its historical integrity. Since the Chickamauga and Chattanooga battlefields were located in two southern states, Boynton and Van Derveer correctly surmised that they would need the help and support of Confederate veterans to build their park. So in the second major departure from the Gettysburg model (the first being the lack of a cemetery on the battlefield itself) they decided to invite Confederate participation in the project and include Confederate monuments on the landscape.[1]

First, however, they would have to drum up support from fellow members of the Army of the Cumberland. During the summer leading up to the Society's September meeting in Chicago, Boynton published a series of letters in the *Commercial Gazette* touting the need for a park and soliciting support for the army's veterans. He reminded readers that:

> History has not done justice to Chickamauga, but its verdict is sure. Many of the misconceptions of the days following the battle still exist in the popular mind. It may be years before they are cleared away; but eventually the Chickamauga campaign will stand in the history of our war as unequaled in its strategy by any other movement of the contest, and as unsurpassed, and probably not equaled, for the stubbornness and deadliness which marked the fighting of Unionist and rebel alike; and furthermore, it will stand as a substantial Union victory.

As usual, Boynton left little doubt as to his feelings and motives for the park and pressed on with a single-minded determination that produced quick results.[2]

The initial committee created to investigate the park idea was formed during the Society of the Army of the Cumberland's annual meeting in September 1888; it included Boynton and former Union officers Henry Cist, Absalom Baird, Russell Alger, and Charles Masterson. They chose governors from the states that had supplied troops in the battle to make up a board of directors. Society members began mapping the park in November, and on 13 February 1889, the committee of the Chickamauga Memorial Association met with General Rosecrans, Union veteran Sanford C. Kellogg, and former Confederates William Bate, Joseph Wheeler, Alfred Colquitt, Edward Walthall, and Marcus Wright to approve the creation of a joint memorial battlefield association. Although lacking the needed charter, this unofficial association could begin soliciting support from both private incorporators and the Federal government for the eventual creation of the park. Just as importantly, the Society of the Army of the Cumberland had secured southern support and participation, thus freeing it from the appearance that the park was largely its "pet" project.[3]

The culmination of this initial planning stage came on 19 and 20 September 1889, during a larger than usual meeting of the Society of the Army of the Cumberland at Crawfish Springs, which had once served as Rosecrans's headquarters and was located at the southeastern edge of the proposed park. At this time, the various associations were combined to create the Chickamauga Memorial Association, which included a local contingent led by the venerable Adolph Ochs and John Wilder, who became its president. It was during this gathering that Boynton elaborated on the scope of the project, which at-

FIG. 17: Henry V. Boynton, Army of the Cumberland veteran, Medal of Honor recipient, Thomas's stalwart defender, and the driving force behind the creation of the Chickamauga and Chattanooga National Military Park. Brady-Handy Collection, Library of Congress.

tempted to acquire "the entire field from Rossville Gap to Crawfish Springs" and included the key sites in and around the city of Chattanooga. In the spirit of optimism that prevailed regarding this expansion of the park, Boynton exclaimed that "the natural features, which for all time will clearly mark the lines of battle, are such that scarcely anything is needed but tablets to mark the positions of forts and headquarters." While this may have been true of Lookout Mountain, Orchard Knob, and Missionary Ridge, it was not the case for the main battlefield. In fact, as the veterans led their families around the field on that anniversary weekend, they realized how difficult it would be to find and identify the locations of individual units and actions.

These details were in the near future, however, and the rest of this inaugural weekend was given over to speeches, celebrations, and a giant "Blue and Gray" barbeque for over 12,000 people. The themes at this event shifted alternately between recognition and reconciliation. It is here that Boynton referred to the proposed Chickamauga Park as a "western Gettysburg" that would recognize both sides, while Rosecrans stated that "It took great men to win that battle, but it takes greater men still, I will say morally greater, to wipe away all the ill feeling which naturally grows out of such a contest." The presence of such large numbers of veterans from both armies was a significant symbol—just as the much smaller 1888 gathering at Gettysburg had been—that the process of healing and reunion was an unstoppable force. Boynton repeated the case he had made in the previous year to Chickamauga veterans when he asked "why should it not, as well as Eastern fields, be marked by monuments and the lines accurately preserved for history?" After all, "there was no more magnificent fighting during the war than both armies did there. Both sides might well unite in preserving the field where both, in a military sense, won such renown." By making this vision a reality, Boynton put Chickamauga, the Army of the Cumberland, and its stalwart Confederate counterparts back into the public eye, at least for a while.[4]

The next phase of the plan was to obtain recognition from the state of Georgia, in which most of the Chickamauga battlefield lay. The Chickamauga Memorial Association received a twenty-year charter from the state of Georgia on 4 December 1890, which allowed it to solicit members, raise funds, and develop the park grounds. Boynton also recognized that the presence of numerous U. S. Regular Army troops and batteries in the battle would be the ideal catalyst for the acquisition of Federal funds to support the park. By putting the park under the jurisdiction of the War Department, the veterans would not only get financial help, but would find it easier to buy land, road easements, and develop other infrastructure. By comparing Chickamauga's numbers, casualties, and results to the great battles of history, Boynton successfully pushed a bill through Congress that brought his vision of one great park encompassing both the Chickamauga and Chattanooga battlefields to full fruition. Sponsored by Ohio Congressman and veteran Charles H. Grosvenor, the resulting House Bill 6454 made its way quickly through the Military Affairs Committee, passed the House in twenty-three minutes, and was approved by the Senate shortly afterward. President Harrison, himself a Civil War veteran, signed the bill into law on 18 August 1890. The bill essentially ceded the designated lands, roads, and rights of way belonging to Georgia and Tennessee to the Federal Government to create the park and the twenty-two-mile-long Military Road that would connect the two ends of it with each other. Congress also authorized an initial budget of $125,000 to get the project up and running.

Upon passage of the bill, the secretary of war created a park commission under his authority to oversee the development and operation of the new park. Union veteran Joseph Fullerton and Confederate veteran Alexander P. Stewart were the "civilian" members of the commission, while Captain Kellogg (who happened to be George Thomas's nephew) was the military representative serving as secretary. Boynton's position as "assistant in historical work" essentially meant that, like John Bachelder at Gettysburg, much of the responsibility for marking the field and battle lines would be his. In addition to the physical labor of clearing brush, cutting trees, and improving access, three main tasks consumed the time and energy of this first batch of commissioners. One was the purchase of the private land on which the proposed park lay; the second was physically developing the park's grounds. The third was the tedious process of "preserving and suitably marking for historical and professional military study the fields of some of the most remarkable maneuvers and most brilliant fighting of the War of the Rebellion." The former would trigger battles with local landowners over the government's right to take the land and the price they expected for it. The second would be accomplished without much fanfare. The latter brought hundreds of veterans from the respective states to the park "for the purpose of ascertaining and marking the lines of battle of the troops engaged therein," which turned out to be much more difficult than anyone imagined.[5]

The purchase of land was the responsibility of Commissioner Fullerton, who had the advantage of Federal "condemnation" laws that gave the government the right to purchase land in order to fulfill a Congressional mandate. Since the primary goal was to enclose the main Chickamauga battlefield, the land in that region received the most attention from the commission and its agents. Interestingly, a Grand Army of the Republic post in Chicago held some purchase rights at twenty-five dollars per acre for a project that had not come to fruition. The land was good for fruit and vegetable farms, and there were deposits of coal and iron in the region; also, a railroad spur had been built along the edge of the battlefield area. All of these factors, along with the knowledge among the more than 200 owners that the government really wanted the land, led to an escalation in land values that approached seventy dollars per acre. After purchasing only 1,400 acres in the first few months and following a visit by Secretary of War Redfield Proctor in May, the government instituted condemnation proceedings. It took three rounds of condemnations and a protracted court battle to finally acquire over 5,300 acres at about thirty dollars per acre for a total cost of around $154,000. By the time the commission added some of the land on Missionary Ridge, Orchard Knob, and other small tracts around Chattanooga, it had spent roughly $400,000 of the $575,000 that Congress had appropriated.

Some land simply could not be acquired, particularly on Missionary Ridge and Lookout Mountain, where the park boundaries were not clearly established. Without the condemnation option, the government could not (or would not) deal with the "exaggerated ideas of values" and the "exorbitant prices" that influenced some landowners to hold out for the best deal. By 1894, in spite of Boynton's best efforts, the government gave up completely on some of these parcels. Debates within the commission over the amount of money being spent on land and court cases caused a rift between Fullerton, Alexander Stewart, and Kellogg that was not resolved until Kellogg was reassigned to Paris by the War Department in 1893. Critics of the park project thought that the property acquisitions benefited "land syndicates" and questioned the government's condemnation process. Nonetheless, the commission continued to acquire land well into the twentieth century in its attempt to meet the mandated 7,600-acre size for the park.[6]

Alexander Stewart was the commissioner in charge of building the park's infrastructure, which involved clearing brush, cutting trees, constructing roads, and developing facilities for staff and visitors. His job was somewhat more complicated by the constant stream of veterans, state commissioners, government bureaucrats, and sightseers who visited the battlefield while the work was going on. Stewart, who lived near the park and often used a bicycle to get around, had an able group of assistants, including topographical and civil engineers, to implement the physical creation of the landscape. These professionals, along with many of the workers hired by the commission, were themselves veterans of both the Union and Confederate armies. Congress appropriated various sums of money to pay for the removal of trees, stumps, and non-period buildings, along with providing funds for the task of mapping and paving the roads that corresponded to wartime routes.

Several non-period farm buildings in the park were demolished, while others, like the Brotherton, Kelly, and Cravens houses, had to be rebuilt or restored to something like their 1863 appearances. Stewart made a favorable impression on the communities when he ordered gun carriages from a Chattanooga foundry, even though they were a bit more expensive. The first "interpretive facilities" built on the newly acquired land were five seventy-foot-high iron and steel towers placed at key locations on both the Chickamauga and Chattanooga portions of the battlefield. These were intended to "afford visitors and students unobstructed views of the terrain in all directions" and directly addressed the commission's desire to make the park more educational and instructional rather than recreational.[7]

It is here that the Chickamauga and Chattanooga Park made a sharp departure from the Gettysburg model. Instead of evolving outward from the National

FIG. 18: Joseph Fullerton, an Army of the Cumberland veteran who served as one of the first commissioners of the Chickamauga and Chattanooga National Military Park. Courtesy of the Chattanooga–Hamilton County Bicentennial Library.

Cemetery, which had been built according to fairly modern ideas regarding memorial park design, the style of the Chickamauga battlefield sprang from a grassroots effort on the part of its veterans to tell their story in very specific ways. Commissioner Fullerton spelled this idea out at the Society of the Army of the Cumberland's 1892 meeting:

> An idea has gone out that we propose to lay out the grounds in grace-ful plats, to make beautiful walks, to plant flower beds and to set up fountains. This is a rather tame, indeed, a low view to take of the Park. Those who started the project had a far grander and nobler conception of the work. A park for health-seekers, for esthetics or pleasure seek-ers, with fine drives, shady walks, and flowing fountains, can be made anywhere with money. But there is the one and only place in the world where there can be a "Chickamauga." There will be no place here for the gaudy display of rich equipages and show of wealth; no place for lovers to bide tryst; no place for pleasure seekers or loungers. The hosts that in the future come to this grand park will come rather with feelings of awe and reverence. Here their better natures will be aroused; here they will be imbued with grand and lofty ideas; with courage and patriotism; with devotion to duty and love of country.

Clearly, this was not to be mistaken for a city park or simple tourist attraction. Nor was it a Gettysburg, where genteel visitors could make a short trip from Washington or Philadelphia to have a picnic and take in the sights. Chicka-mauga Park was sacred ground imbued with a practical purpose, to tell the story of this important and bloody battle from the perspective of the men who fought in it. The process of marking the lines would give those veterans a chance to relive and refight the battle and in the process sanctify the field for its proper commemorative and historical purposes.[8]

The whole process of marking the battlefield would be immensely compli-cated by several unavoidable factors. On one hand, the sheer logistics involved in identifying all of the brigade-, division-, and corps-level units engaged; their positions and movements during two days of fighting; and the outcome of their participation on each day were imposing to say the least. For the most part, the park commission was prepared to provide the cannons, tablets, and maps necessary to accomplish this task. On the other hand, each state was re-sponsible for providing granite markers for individual units at the battery and regimental level, as well as more elaborate unit and state monuments as de-sired. That there would be arguments over the interpretation of events and the exact positioning of all of these markers and monuments seemed pretty likely and could therefore be safely deemed "unavoidable." The same could not be said for the clash of personalities, egos, and opinions that swirled around the park's historical consultant and those who both supported and disagreed with him. Tim Smith observes that the strong-willed Boynton "became involved in many historical quarrels . . . and won most of those quarrels."[9]

The process of "marking the lines" began with maps and accounts supplied by the War Department, including the *Official Records*, which were being published at about the same time the field was being laid out. Knowing how unreliable some of those reports could be led the commissioners to occasionally request input from the officers and men of the units that had engaged in the battle. For the Confederates, much of this feedback came during the first gathering of the United Confederate Veterans on the battlefield in 1890. The former Confederates made themselves available to the park commissioners and gave them a great deal of useful information on their positions at Chickamauga, Missionary Ridge, and Lookout Mountain. In general, the biggest obstacle to accuracy was still the natural terrain, thick foliage, and "destructive farming practices" that kept the veterans from recognizing the exact spots that they had occupied during the fighting. For example, one of the controversies that caused a rift between Captain Kellogg and the other commissioners involved asking members of several U.S. Regular Infantry regiments to clarify and correct the positions that Kellogg had erroneously assigned to them. Once the lines were finalized, cast-iron tablets describing the action were placed in the appropriate spots, along with surplus artillery pieces representing supporting batteries.[10]

The placement, selection, and construction of unit memorials and markers were complicated by the fact that twenty-eight states had troops engaged at Chickamauga and Chattanooga. Each unit from each state was entitled to mark its participation in the battle, which meant that there were potentially hundreds of individual monuments to be located, designed, placed, and dedicated over the next few years. To further confound the process, the park commissioners had final approval over where the monuments could be placed and what they could say in regard to the unit's participation in the battle. To expedite this process, a number of states created their own battlefield commissions to coordinate the placement of monuments on behalf of the state's regiments. For the most part, these state commissions worked reasonably well with the park commissioners in getting most of the monuments in place. At times, however, individual units contested their own state commission's findings or protested the park's handling of their monument's placement. Not surprisingly, these issues spurred another round of arguments between veterans over incidents in the battle; some of these got even more complicated because they involved members of the park commission in their previous roles as participants in the battle.

Ohio had been one of the states that had provided a large number of troops to the battles around Chattanooga; thus it would have a great deal of work to do in the new park. Rather than try to document the activities of all of the state commissions that worked to mark the battlefield, the Ohio Commission can serve as a model to illustrate the trials and tribulations facing the veterans, the state commissions, and the park commissioners during this laborious process. The first step was passage of an act by the Ohio General Assembly in May 1891 "to provide for the erection of monuments and tablets to mark the positions of Ohio troops on the battle field of Chickamauga" and provide funding for the research associated with this activity. This act created the Ohio Chickamauga and Chattanooga National Park Commission and appointed eight men to lead it. The original group made its first visit to the battlefield on 25 November 1891 and met with the park commissioners to adopt "plans for the prosecution of the work." A smaller group returned in April 1892 to start the process of surveying the ground and marking the positions of Ohio units, but they decided not to make any binding decisions without some help from the veterans themselves.[11]

Beginning in September 1892, members of the Ohio Commission and forty-five Chickamauga and Chattanooga veterans walked the woods and hills of the battlefields in an attempt to locate the positions of their units and the appropriate places for the monuments. This turned out to be a tedious and somewhat unsatisfactory exercise for all parties involved. Part of the problem seemed to be Captain Kellogg, who was reluctant to approve many of the locations the veterans pointed out without further investigation. In his diary covering 16, 17, and 18 November 1892, Kellogg simply noted that some sites had been "located but not accepted" during the September visit and that another tour with members of both the Ohio Commission and his fellow park commissioners had produced some consensus regarding a few regiments. He noted that "it was agreed by both commissions to accept the location made for the 18th Ohio Infantry as placed in September, the monument to be located in rear of the point where the right of the regiment stood." The commissioners also accepted the locations of the 2nd, 33rd, and 94th Ohio infantries where they had been originally located by their veterans, but "with Commissioner Kellogg dissenting." Although all the location issues were not resolved at this time, this session did clarify (at least to the commissioners' satisfaction) several controversies involving some Ohio cavalry units and one particular infantry regiment.[12]

The 1st, 3rd, and 4th Ohio Cavalry regiments discovered a problem with the location of their monuments because they did most of their fighting on land that was not within the boundaries of the park. During the busy September of 1892, 1st Ohio Cavalry veteran W. L. Curry and several of his comrades, accompanied by some former Confederates, endured a jostling wagon ride to find the spot where their regiment's commander, Lt. Col. Valentine Cupp, had been mortally wounded on 20 September 1863. Curry wrote that they "had no difficulty in locating the grounds and satisfied ourselves beyond a doubt as to the exact location of the Chicago Board of Trade Battery." Once they had confirmed that their battle positions were outside the boundary, they went immediately into the park to find an alternative monument location.

As they debated where to position the three regimental monuments, Curry noted that "everywhere we would see groups of officers and soldiers earnestly discussing the situation and marking the lines of Regiments and Brigades." He and a group of veterans representing the 2nd Brigade consulted with the park commissioners and after some discussion decided to put the 1st, 3rd, and 4th Ohio monuments within the park on the Widow Weather's land. This was eventually slightly adjusted by all of the parties to a spot within a few hundred yards of the Widow Glenn's house, which had served as Rosecrans's headquarters on 20 September. Curry reported that "the point selected is a prominent place and will be visited by all persons who visit the battlefield" since it was within a half mile of the railroad depot and dominated by the imposing Wilder Tower (which was under construction at the time). The three granite Ohio cavalry monuments were made by two different firms at a cost of $1,470 each and were placed in the chosen location by the State of Ohio in September 1894.[13]

Another debate on monument location that was resolved "with adjustments" in November 1892 involved the 21st Ohio Infantry. On 20 September 1863, during the chaotic last hours on Horseshoe Ridge, the 21st Ohio was involved in one of the most controversial moments of the battle. It was part of the 3rd Brigade in Maj. Gen. James Negley's XIV Corps's 2nd Division. The regiment ended up as part of the makeshift defensive line formed by parts of John Brannan's, Charles Harker's, and John Beatty's commands on Horseshoe Ridge after Negley and much of the rest of the division had left the field following Longstreet's breakthrough. Armed with Colt repeating rifles, the 21st made up a formidable part of the defense that held the Confederates at bay until late in the afternoon. As Thomas pulled back his men from their original line in the Kelly field, some units, like Van Derveer's 3rd Brigade of the 3rd Division came up in support of the line on Horseshoe Ridge. They, along with Steedmen's reinforcements, held this position until Thomas ordered a general retreat.

The controversy occurred when some regiments, including the 21st Ohio and Boynton's own 35th Ohio, did not get specific orders to withdraw along with Granger's men and the rest of the defenders on the ridge. The 21st claimed that it had run completely out of ammunition and was still holding the right of Brannan's line when it was ordered by some unknown officer, possibly Van

Derveer, to make a bayonet charge. When other troops pulled out around them, they, the 22nd Michigan, and the 89th Ohio, who had also been ordered forward in the counterattack, were surrounded and many men, including the 21st Ohio's commander, Maj. Arnold McMahan, were captured.[14]

That a few members of the 21st escaped was thanks in part to Lieutenant Colonel Boynton, the 35th Ohio, and the 9th Indiana, who returned to line in the gloom only to stumble into the advancing Confederates. In a flurry of mistaken identities and the sporadic exchange of fire that followed, some of the captured men got away and found their way back to Union lines, while the 35th Ohio and 9th Indiana covered the rest of the Union forces' withdrawal from the ridge.[15] The trouble with all of these facts is that they had been disputed by various participants from the time they happened until the point at which the Ohio Commission was attempting to place the monuments to the regiments involved. The first key element in the ongoing debate was Boynton's refusal to accept the 21st's claim that his commander and friend Van Derveer had given the fatal order to the Ohio and Michigan troops, thus leading to their capture. The second was his insistence that the 35th had more or less single-handedly defended the critical flank where the 21st had done its hardest fighting after the other regiments (21st Ohio, 89th Ohio, and 22nd Michigan) had allegedly collapsed and left it unguarded.

Of course, Boynton had a huge advantage when it came to putting forth his version of events. He wrote the more compelling report after the battle (McMahan was in Libby Prison for a year and had a difficult time getting his version into the *Official Records*) and had numerous chances to repeat his story to his readers of the *Gazette and* the *National Tribune,* the members of the Society of the Army of the Cumberland, and various audiences around the country. Boynton was an influential newspaperman pushing a popular message of reunion, patriotism, and the courage of the American fighting man to a public that was happy to hear such things. He was also the founder and major representative of the nation's first National Military Park, which was dedicated to those values and had a vested interest in its success. As a direct participant in the fighting on 20 September, he was motivated to glorify (or defend) the actions of his division (Brannan) and brigade (Van Derveer) commanders and uphold the reputation and contributions of the regiment that he commanded on the field. On top of all that, he was a stubborn man who rarely admitted when he was wrong.[16]

James Kaser uses this incident to frame a discussion of the importance of perspective in the construction of collective memory and offers a compelling explanation for its ultimate outcome in favor of Boynton's claims. According to Kaser, there were three levels of memory at work in the creation of the

FIG. 19: The prominent location of his own 35th Ohio Infantry monument on Snodgrass Hill reflects Boynton's influence as a park commissioner. Note the base of the viewing tower—which no longer stands—in the background. Courtesy of the Chattanooga–Hamilton County Bicentennial Library.

Chickamauga park. The first was based on Van Horne's *History of the Army of the Cumberland,* which sought to elevate both George Thomas and his army to the level of greatness achieved by the eastern armies. The second is Boynton's extension of this view, which attempts to vindicate Rosecrans, glorify Thomas, and portray Chickamauga as a Union victory. Boynton added the theme of reunion to this construction by exalting the courage and hard fighting of both Union and Confederate soldiers in this battle. The third level of memory is the self-interest of individuals and regiments who wanted their own roles remembered and accurately recorded for the historical record. This is where Boynton may be guilty of a conflict of interest. He claimed to want to get the history right but sacrificed it to uphold the larger glory, both his own and that of his army, corps, division, and brigade.[17]

Kaser believes that Boynton erred when he created the park as both a commemorative and an educational landscape, since collective memories and historical facts do not always agree. He uses the efforts of Arnold McMahan and the survivors of the 21st Ohio to set the record straight as an example of how collective memories can be altered by the adoption of different perspectives.

Ultimately, the scattered and contradictory accounts provided by the 21st Ohio veterans are no match for the more compelling memories being pushed by Boynton and the park commissioners. Although McMahan manages to collect some witnesses that place his men on the right of Brannan's line all day and fighting until their ammunition was gone, a member of the 21st, Wilson Vance, ended up supporting Boynton's version by blaming the commander of the 22nd Michigan for ordering the charge and later claiming they were captured after mistaking the flanking Confederates for Steedmen's men.

The war of words went on for several years, but McMahan was at a clear disadvantage. In an unpublished draft of his report written while still a captive, McMahan states "that I cannot close this report without expressing my conviction that our capture was due to the neglect of the brigade commander [Brannan] in abandoning us without giving us any orders . . . and the neglect of Col. Vandervere [sic] in not ordering us to retire in time to avoid the greatly superior number of the enemy." He repeats in several places that "we were left without orders" and plaintively says "Why we were not ordered to withdraw from this isolated position before dark I am unable to state." Clearly, McMahan's frustration and confusion predated Boynton's claims and explain why he fought so hard to get at the truth.[18]

As a final point of contention, it is worth examining a statement from each man regarding the close of the combat on Snodgrass Hill. In his diary, McMahan states that "I have the honor to report that my regiment did the last firing upon and offered the latest resistance to the advance of the enemy which . . . checked his advance & ended the battle of Chickamauga." Contrast that statement with Boynton's 1888 version: "The volley [from the 35th] had scattered the enemy on the ridge, and the force in the rear had withdrawn. These were the last shots on the right" and, therefore, the last of the battle. When confronted with such contradictory evidence, both the Ohio commissioners and the park commissioners took a decidedly middle position. As Kaser points out, the 21st Ohio's surviving eyewitnesses gave vague and contradictory accounts that did not provide enough evidence to go against the one being pushed by the park. McMahan's single-minded crusade to get the details right ran up against one that "incorporated established heroes . . . and played on National themes." The description of the 21st Ohio monument in the Ohio Commission's published report simply states: "In the dusk of the evening a superior force of the enemy, gaining its rear, surprised and captured 131 of its officers and men." The monument was finally located "at the point where the surprise and capture occurred," and, as Kellogg noted, this was "accepted by all the Commissioners, with slight alterations to the right or left of positions as originally designated [by] the Ohio Commissioners."[19]

If the placement of monuments was not enough of a headache for both state and national commissioners, the designs and inscriptions on the monuments provided more aggravation. An article in *Century Illustrated* questioned "whether sufficient consideration has been given to the service that art may render on the battlefield in perpetuating the fame of brave men." Noting that the creation of the battle lines was important from a historical point of view, the writer pointed out that "it is art in some form . . . that appeal must be made to posterity in realization of the idea of heroism associated with hallowed ground." After pointing out that "there are not but four good pieces of sculpture on the battlefield at Gettysburg," the magazine suggested that the commissioners at Chickamauga consider several ways to improve the artistic value of the park. In addition to hiring professional landscape architects and sculptors and using modest stone markers for the battle lines, the writer proposed limiting unit monuments to the corps level to assure artistic quality and avoid the clutter and excesses of the regimental monuments that mar the Gettysburg landscape. Unfortunately, most states, including Ohio, had already committed funds and awarded contracts to sculpting firms for regimental monuments, thus rendering this suggestion impractical.[20]

If Ohio had been able to limit regimental monuments, it might have avoided the embarrassing case of the 26th Ohio Infantry, whose public and private complaints about the park's handling of its design went all the way to the Secretary of War. The monument committee of the 26th Ohio Infantry was led by John T. Raper, editor of the *Ohio Soldier and National Picket Guard,* a Chillicothe-based newsletter for local veterans. He complained that both the Ohio and National Park commissions had rejected their monument design, which featured, among other things, a statue of a woodchuck (the unit mascot) and a Bible verse that read "He will speak Peace unto his people; let them not turn again to folly." The monument's descriptive text stated that "here the tide of battle was stayed by the blood of 213 comrades of the 26th Ohio Volunteer Infantry." Raper and his comrades could not understand why these had been rejected and "resolved that the committee be continued, and be instructed to appeal to the Secretary of War for a revocation of the objectionable rule . . . to secure the restoration of our regimental monument." A letter stating these demands went to Commissioner Fullerton, was read and passed along by numerous War Department functionaries, and ended up in the hands of Aquila Wiley, a member of the Ohio Commission.[21]

Wiley's letter to the secretary of war was a model of efficiency and decorum, which barely cloaked his exasperation that this even had to be addressed. He stated clearly that he supported all of the changes made to the monument by the commission and made no apologies for doing so. He observed that "the

Ground Hog is an animal that was never known to fight except upon compulsion and in the last extremity, and I considered it in execrable taste to adopt it as an emblem for a fighting regiment." He concluded that "in voting to strike from the design . . . the effigy of this ignoble beast . . . I was doing an act to relieve a gallant and meritorious regiment from undeserved ridicule." The inscriptions failed to meet the park's standards, which required them to be "purely historical" and related directly to the battle or campaign. He pointed out that the Psalm in question had nothing to do with either war or peace; that the term "peace" in this context was in reference to "a mental state or condition" brought on by the Jew's faith in God. He was equally unimpressed with the other text, since it bore no relation to the regiment's actual conduct on the field; he supported its replacement with a simple description of the unit's movements on the two days of the battle.

The chairman of the Ohio Commission, John Beatty, endorsed Wiley's letter and reminded the secretary that "the design of the monument, after much delay and much needless whiffling [sic], on the part of Captain Raper, was prepared under his own supervision." He also pointed out that "the only thing the Commission did with respect to it was to abate the woodchuck and make the inscriptions conform to the rules." The chairman added for good measure, "It should be known that Captain John T. Raper is the only persistent pestiferous bore the Ohio Commission has encountered while in the discharge of its official duties." In the end, Ohio placed fifty-five individual regimental monuments on the battlefield prior to the dedication in 1895, which represented the largest number of units and troops from one state on either side in the battle.[22]

A well-rounded description of the trials and tribulations of the Ohio Commission would not be complete without an example of its members being pitted against the Chickamauga and Chattanooga Park commissioners. The controversy in question stems from some of the errors made by Commissioner Kellogg during his tenure and involves an exchange of letters between Aquila Wiley, other members of his commission, and Henry Boynton regarding the placement of monuments at the scene of action on 19 September 1863. At the root of this conflict is the time that various regiments of John Palmer and Absalom Baird's divisions arrived on the field and the concern on the part of the Ohioans that the wrong times would appear on the monuments. After receiving the first letter from Wiley, Boynton answered, saying, "If we differ in any respect, it is only because of our judging from different lights, and in the end, I doubt not that we shall fully agree because we are only intended in finding the truth and are not engaged in establishing theories." Responding to a request from Commissioner McElroy concerning some of the monument locations, Wiley sent another letter reminding Boynton that "I have no doubt that

FIG.20: The 26th Ohio Infantry monument as it stands today minus the groundhog and flowery language that the Ohio and national commissions deleted prior to its placement in the park. Photo by author.

the battle was fought on Saturday on the left where you have located it . . . the point at which I differ with you is as to the *time* at which it was fought." He concluded by pointing out that his previous letter was "purely personal and not intended for the commission" and confessed that he has "the utmost faith in your indulgent nature and *love for free discussion.*"[23]

As the former commander of a regiment in Palmer's XXI Corps division, Wiley had an interest in this part of the field that kept him engaged in this exchange. When Boynton responded to Wiley's letter of 4 December, he assured him that "I read and study all your letters not only with interest but much profit" and promised "that we shall be able to go over this ground before long." But Wiley was being spurred by pressure from Ohio veterans to get some of these problems corrected. One group made it clear that "if we are not going to have the right position, then we would rather not have a monument at all, for it would simply be a permanent lie if placed otherwise." Wiley responded by urging these Ohioans to file an affidavit requesting a change in the monuments, but admitted that "I have no doubt that the finding of the Commission would be against you." Wiley continued to push the belief that the misplacement of the markers (based in part on General Baird's erroneous reports that exaggerate his own contributions) did a disservice to other regiments, including his own. Whatever Wiley said in his subsequent correspondence to Boynton is mostly lost, but Boynton's responses indicated that he hit a nerve. On 16 January 1895, he began a typed communiqué with "you have written me a letter which I am sorry to say is of an exceedingly unpleasant character." He defended himself from Wiley's charge that he was inflexible by stating that "I have always been ready to change any conclusion I had reached upon the presentation of what seemed to be satisfactory evidence."[24]

The headstrong Wiley apparently did not take the hint to tone down his rhetoric. His next letter elicited the following response: "I began your second letter . . . with much satisfaction, because the opening paragraph gave promise of a letter of more pleasant tone than the first. But I soon found out that while the former was unpleasant, this was offensive." Boynton went as far as to imply that he would not even have responded to the second letter except that he felt obligated to address Wiley's "very thinly disguised by its form of words . . . claim that, while my intentions are good, my work is that of an idiot." The incensed Boynton spent another half-dozen pages analyzing and criticizing Wiley's many arguments regarding the position of troops on 19 September and summarily dismissed nearly all of them. He concluded by criticizing Wiley's tendency to claim that so many official reports were incorrect by insisting that "where they say one thing they mean something else, and always something that will fit your battle, which for this part of the field is not the battle of Chickamauga." The hard-headed Ohio commissioner had clearly met his match in the equally stubborn Henry Boynton.[25]

In addition to the unit and battle markers, the commissioners placed fourteen "square-based" stacks of cannon balls at the sites of headquarters and eight triangular-based pyramids where brigade commanders had been killed or mortally wounded on the Chickamauga field. Although they avoided the mounted statues of generals that were so pervasive in Washington and at Gettysburg, they did allow state memorials that honored all of the state's participants at once. The first of these was the New Jersey Monument on Missionary Ridge that recognized the participation of the 13th and 33rd New Jersey Infantry regiments. The Confederates occasionally approached the Commission with requests as well. One notable example was the desire of the 60th North Carolina Infantry to be recognized as "having reached the furthest point attained by Confederate troops in that famous charge." With dozens of commissions, thousands of veterans, and hundreds of monument placements to deal with, it was truly amazing that the Chickamauga Park commissioners had the place in an acceptable state of readiness for the grand dedication set for 18, 19, and 20 September 1895.[26]

The last necessary step in the sanctification of a sacred landscape is a public ritual of dedication that reinforces the purpose of the site, the values it upheld, and the ways it is to be used by the community. For the founders and commissioners of the Chickamauga and Chattanooga National Military Park, the official dedication was a validation of all of their work and a chance to put their efforts, both in 1863 and the present, back into the public spotlight. By 1895, the park at Gettysburg was on the verge of getting its own congressional charter and being taken over by the War Department. The battlefield at Shiloh was being developed in much the same way as the Chickamauga park had been. Just as Boynton had hoped, the Chickamauga battlefield was a model for the creation of other parks like it; the dedication ceremonies would need to make clear that theirs was the first, the biggest, and the most significant.

Although the public was invited to attend the dedication, they were not the most important constituency represented that day. People had been visiting the park since its inception, in spite of the early lack of facilities and the overall ramshackle state of the grounds. By 1892, the secretary of war saw fit to authorize the use of paid guides for visitors touring the park, while local businesses rented horses, carriages, and other conveyances to park users. The Society of the Army of the Cumberland Reunion brought a surge of visitors to all parts of the park in 1892 as its veterans worked to mark and memorialize their sites. While the commissioners, with the exception of A. P. Stewart, operated out of an office at the War Department, the park's operation was in the hands of a paid staff consisting of a superintendent, rangers, a book-keeper, and a clerk. Thus, the big ceremony was less of a "grand opening" for the public and more of a "grand recognition" directed toward Congress, the states, the War Department, and the veterans themselves who had created and supported the park.[27]

The dedication, above all else, was a celebratory event honoring a commemorative landscape. On the first day of the weekend-long event, many of the states dedicated their own monuments in separate ceremonies. These proceedings generally recognized the value of the park, the sacrifice of the states' soldiers, the appeal of reunion, and the efforts on the part of the various state legislatures and commissions to get the monuments in place. Ohio's dedication was perhaps larger than most, but typical in its content and emphasis. In his speech, Ohio commissioner John Beatty reminded listeners that "we come here today ... with no reproaches for the living, and no lamentations for the dead" but to celebrate the greatness of the American people. Charles Grosvenor gave credit to Gen. Henry V. Boynton for creating the park and bringing it to life. The former governor, James E. Campbell, paid tribute to the late General Van Derveer, and poor Captain McElroy was stuck with the task of making the financial report. The job of recounting the battle and the heroism of Ohio's troops was given to Aquila Wiley, who reminded the listeners that "we are not here to indulge in melancholy reflections or vain regrets for the past, but to rejoice in the realities of the present and the grand possibilities of the future."[28]

The evening of the first day was given over to the large gathering of veterans from both armies. Nearly 10,000 people attended the annual meeting of the Society of the Army of the Cumberland, whose numbers were swelled by members of both Union and Confederate organizations, including the United Confederate Veterans and the Society of the Army of the Tennessee, whose commander, Grenville Dodge, gave one of the orations. Other speakers included Chattanooga mayor Adolph Ochs, Boynton, and Commanding General of the Army John Schofield, whose speech hammered at the reunion theme: "By your justice and generosity in the hour of victory, and in your constant brotherly conduct in extending the right hand of fellowship to your southern brethren, you have finally won the greatest victory of which man is capable." Gen. Joseph Wheeler represented the Confederate view of reconciliation, saying "[we] are here to view the spectacle of soldiers who once fought each other in deadly battle now one people, with one interest, one flag, one country, and one ambition." Perhaps the oddest and most inappropriate speech of the night was given by Gen. Willard Warner, who rambled on about utopian ideas, religious issues, "clerical ostracism," and other topics that must have had the delegates squirming in their seats.[29]

The big event on 19 September was held on Snodgrass Hill and drew a crowd of 40,000 people, who listened to another slate of speakers invoke reunion and the courage of the American people. Vice President Adlai Stevenson spoke first, after which he turned things over to the two main speakers, John Palmer for the North, and John B. Gordon representing the South. Palmer recounted the history of both the war and the battle, concluding with thanks to God that "we are permitted to see an established Union." Gordon picked up the reunion theme, crying out "what an hour . . . is this, wherein once warring heroes meet to lay in mutual confidence and respect their joint trophies on the common alter . . . to dedicate by joint action Chickamauga's field to common memories and the immortal honor of all." Other speeches echoed similar themes, while giving praise to the veterans, the states, the commissioners, the park, the city of Chattanooga, and everyone else involved. It was a "love feast" between North and South that put an exclamation point on the process of reunion, the greatness of America, and the prospects for the future.[30]

Although there had not been a dynamic speech equal to Abraham Lincoln's address at Gettysburg, the dedication ceremonies in September 1895 succeeded in sanctifying the battlefield at Chickamauga. As many of the Dedication Day speakers had acknowledged, the park paid tribute to the soldiers on both sides, in general, and to George Thomas and the Army of the Cumberland, in particular. At the same time, it promoted the ideals of reunion and patriotism for all Americans. The next phase in the life of the Chickamauga and Chattanooga National Military Park was to demonstrate its practical uses to both the Chattanooga community and the War Department by promoting tourism and economic development to the former and offering the park as a training ground to the latter. While these uses might seem incompatible with the battlefield's status as a commemorative landscape, the park commissioners set out to span the gap between the secular and sacred. On the one hand, they promoted the park as a learning environment for present-day soldiers and citizens and as a source of revenue for the local community; on the other, they emphasized the moral lessons conveyed by the sacrifice, redemption, and reunion of both northern and southern heroes.

Although they could not know it then, all of these factors would play a part in the growth and expansion of the United States into an industrial giant at home and a world power overseas. The very values being celebrated by the participants at the dedication ceremonies would be tested, and then reinforced, by the events of 1898. As America ventured into the uncertain waters of foreign involvement and expansionism, the patriotic rhetoric of reunion and the sacred terrain of the Civil War battlefield at Chickamauga would play a remarkable and dramatic role.

SEVEN

"A Maker of Glorious History"

The creation and dedication of the Chickamauga and Chattanooga National Military Park represented a significant accomplishment for the veterans, the Chattanooga community, the War Department, and the nation as a whole. For the soldiers on both sides who had fought in the fields and hills around Chattanooga, the park's monuments and markers recognized their courage and sacrifice in 1863, while at the same time validating their contributions to society since the war. The veterans of the Union and Confederate armies were able to build the battlefield and construct common memories by downplaying the issues of victory and defeat and embracing their mutual courage in combat. The Society of the Army of the Cumberland saw the project move from idea to fruition in a fairly short time and basked in the national spotlight for the first time since it had dedicated statues in Washington, D.C., to former comrades George Thomas and James Garfield.

For the City of Chattanooga, the establishment of the park was another large step in its emergence from the wartime, postwar, and reconstruction eras. The involvement of Adolph Ochs and Union veteran John Wilder as mayors, businessmen, and original park committee members ensured that the community supported the project from start to finish. The influx of visitors during the establishment of the park grew steadily and culminated in the huge turnout for the dedication in September 1895. The spirit of reconciliation that provided the underpinnings for the creation of the park also filtered into the community around the battlefields. Although there was some resentment among a few landowners and a little bit of price gouging during the acquisition of the park lands, many local businessmen recognized the potential economic benefits that the park might provide. Railroad companies in particular stood to profit from the increase in tourism that resulted from the creation of the park and other attractions.

In addition to its use as a commemorative landscape, the founders of the Chickamauga and Chattanooga National Military Park also emphasized the battlefield's value as an educational tool. The tactical challenges that faced the regimental, brigade, and division commanders at Chickamauga provided models for future generations of military officers that could be studied on the battlefield itself. The care taken by the state and national commissioners to properly "mark the lines" reflected the veterans' belief that the park's instructional use was as important as its commemorative one. As a reflection of the original enabling legislation, Congress authorized the periodic use of the park as a military training ground by both Regular Army and state National Guard troops. This provided another layer in the process of memory construction by supplementing the ritual and ceremonial activities, such as monument dedications and reunions, with occasional military exercises that connected the landscape's past to the present.

A dramatic conjunction of these elements occurred before, during, and after the Spanish-American War in 1898. The overlapping messages of courage, sacrifice, and national reunion combined to encourage patriotism and public enthusiasm for military action in Cuba. The memories and images of Civil War manhood allowed the veterans to participate in a variety of ways, including actual military service under one flag. Once the war began, the War Department added another element to the connection between the Civil War and the War with Spain by utilizing the Chickamauga park as a primary training ground for troops mobilizing for the invasion of Cuba. The subsequent influx of men, material, and public attention had a dramatic effect on the City of Chattanooga. The presence of thousands of young men, particularly of state volunteers, ushered in some short-term problems, but in the long run, reinforced the impression that the park and its many uses were a benefit to the community. When confronted by questions and controversy regarding the operation in the park of Camp Thomas, the veterans, community, and park officials joined ranks to defend its value and importance to the nation.

Like many towns and cities throughout the south, Chattanooga was undergoing a transition in the decades after 1865. Having overcome the hardships of war, the city occasionally was forced to deal with the ravages of nature, as the Tennessee River overflowed and caused devastating floods in 1867, 1875, and 1886. The community also endured a yellow fever outbreak in 1878 that left much of the region shaken by the number of lives it claimed. On top of that, a huge fire in 1888 consumed several blocks of businesses in the downtown area. However, Chattanooga was a resilient city whose ideal location utilized both river and railroad transportation to potentially make it "a leading manufacturing and business center" in the emerging New South. One observer noted that "there is hardly a county in Eastern Tennessee where the resources destined to make Chattanooga one of the commercial centers of the country do not abound." Not only did the city make use of the human and natural resources from the surrounding region, but it drew on the help provided by former Yankees like John Wilder and Henry Boynton, who brought energy, capital, and vision into the community.

Although it never reached the manufacturing level of Birmingham, Alabama, Chattanooga did take advantage of the nearby availability of coal, coke, and iron ore to add to the production of pig iron and steel that had begun with the Southwestern Iron Company and continued with the Roane iron works in the 1870s. By 1885, there were "nine furnaces and seventeen foundries and machine shops" operating in the city. Hiram Chamberlain, a veteran of the 1st Ohio Cavalry, who had come to Chattanooga to manage the Roane Foundry for his old commander, eventually started his own Citico Furnace Company in 1884 and numbered among the city's handful of millionaires by 1890. Another Union veteran, George Washington Wheland of Pennsylvania, came south to learn the machinist's trade from an uncle. He moved to Chattanooga in 1873 and started the extremely successful Wheland Foundry, which is still in existence today. In addition to the iron and steel businesses, Chattanooga contained several breweries, a textile mill, and numerous tanneries. In 1879, Union veteran Zeboim Patten founded the Chattanooga Medicine Company, which produced and distributed potions like "Black Draught" and "Wine of Cardui" to customers throughout the region.[1]

Among the keys to Chattanooga's success were the railroad lines that connected it to major cities in both the North and South. Part of Chattanooga's wartime railroad legacy included the Great Locomotive Chase of 1862 when a handful of Union soldiers stole a train on the Western and Atlantic line between Chattanooga and Atlanta. Several of the men captured in the raid were confined in the "Negro prison" in Chattanooga, while eight of the soldiers executed by the Confederates ended up being buried in the Chattanooga National Cemetery. After the war, the Western and Atlantic continued to serve the city until 1890, when it was leased by the Nashville, St. Louis, and Chattanooga Railroad. The Cincinnati Southern Railroad opened in 1880 and spanned the 335 miles between Cincinnati and Chattanooga and joined the Southern Railroad Company as the Western and Atlantic's competition. An 1895 advertisement touted the climate and "charming mountain towns" of the region and noted that "the Queen & Crescent carries the tourist into the midst of the scenes, once the seat of battle's din and bloodshed." This particular advertisement mentioned that "the great battlefields are being preserved and beautified by our government"

FIG. 21: A group of "notables" that most likely included several Army of the Cumberland veterans posed on Lookout Mountain while attending the great meeting and barbeque on 20 September 1889. Many returned six years later for the dedication of the Chickamauga and Chattanooga National Military Park. Courtesy of the Chattanooga–Hamilton County Bicentennial Library.

and noted that the "Chickamauga National Military Park has been established so quietly that the country at large just begins to comprehend the magnitude of the project."[2]

Tourism was certainly one of the ways that southern cities like Chattanooga could draw both visitors and potential businesses during the last decades of the nineteenth century. The stunning natural wonder of Lookout Mountain provided a marvelous starting point for the area's tourist trade and acted as the centerpiece for nearly all of the attractions in the area. The prominent knob on the mountain known as Sunset Rock, along with Lover's Leap, the Old Man rock, and the Natural Bridge drew numerous visitors to the top of the mountain, which led several private entrepreneurs to attempt to fence in the area that became known as Point Park and charge an entrance fee.

To reach these lofty heights, enterprising developers built a broad-gauge rail line around the mountain and constructed an incline that traversed the one mile at a seventy-seven degree angle to the top. After the yellow fever epidemic, numerous hotels and spas were built along the crest of the mountain to take advantage of the cool breezes and "healthier" air and to accommodate the growing number of visitors to the area. By the 1890s, a second incline joined the first and eventually put that one out of business. A narrow-gauge railroad supplanted the older line, which was replaced by an electric trolley. Eventually, Point Park ended up as a part of the National Military Park, thanks to the efforts of Mayor Ochs and others. All of this was both good and bad for the battlefields around the city. On the one hand, some sites were much more accessible to the public; on the other, most of the land was privately owned and open to development with little regard to its historical context.[3]

The dedication of the Chickamauga and Chattanooga National Military Park represented another huge step for the community in its quest to become a more vital and economically diverse city. In his welcoming address to the veterans and dignitaries attending the park dedication, Mayor Ochs "pledge[d] for this city, this State, and for all the people of the South, a hearty cooperation in the task you have undertaken" and exclaimed that "the City of Chattanooga . . . is indeed proud that history will again be emblazoned with its renown as the scene of this apotheosis of a reunited country." While the mayor eloquently recognized the battlefield as "a token proclaiming that civil discord is forever at an end," other citizens of the area took a more practical approach to the dedication festivities and the visitors that accompanied them.

A national periodical reported that since many of the battle's actual relics had already been gathered by "industrious gleaners" for sale to collectors, there was a booming trade in the creation of "curious bric-a-brac" disguised as "original battle souvenirs." Using scuffing, staining, marking, and creative manufacturing processes, these enterprising cheaters turned out fake shell fragments, minié balls, buckles, firearms, canteens, bullet-pocked tree limbs, walking sticks, and leather goods that could be sold to unwitting out-of-town visitors. In spite of the copious commemorative rhetoric, the presence of these hucksters indicated that the park represented different things to different people in the area.[4]

As the community adjusted to the park and its supporting attractions, the park commissioners continued building roads, placing markers, and overseeing the continued construction of unit and state monuments. Commissioner Alexander Stewart was the only member of the commission who actually lived near the park. He was primarily responsible for overseeing the staff, sorting out difficulties with local landowners, meeting with veterans and dignitaries, and keeping things moving forward. Stewart was particularly active in encouraging fellow Southerners to support the construction of state memorials on the battlefield that equally honored all the soldiers who fought there from a particular state. He spoke at the 1898 dedication of the Tennessee monument and proclaimed that the reason the Confederacy had lost the war "was that Almighty God had need of this Union." The redoubtable Stewart overcame serious illness and the death of his beloved wife to serve longer than any of the original park commissioners. He had not officially relinquished his role with the park at the time of his death in 1908. Alexander Stewart put a friendly, energetic, and largely non-controversial southern face on the park that partially mitigated the occasional controversies generated by Boynton and the other commissioners.[5]

One interesting development that generated mixed effects on the Chickamauga park was the creation of several other national military parks during the 1890s. In the East, a battlefield park commemorating the Battle of Antietam grew around its National Cemetery and came under the War Department's jurisdiction soon after the Chickamauga Park was created in 1890. Congress overcame concerns that there were too many parks being created and gave the Shiloh National Military Park its official recognition in 1894. The Gettysburg park joined the War Department's collection of battlefields in 1895 after its early years as a semi-public park under the leadership of the Gettysburg Memorial Battlefield Preservation Association and the Grand Army of the Republic. A park commemorating the Union triumph at Vicksburg rounded out the first five in 1899. All of these parks began under similar circumstances with the same general set of intentions. They all had national cemeteries nearby, most enjoyed dynamic leadership from groups and individuals, and they often split their focus between commemorative, practical, and educational goals.[6]

The presence of a single dynamic individual in the life of these parks is an interesting parallel between them. Henry Boynton was the dominant personality in the story of the Chickamauga park, just as John Bachelder provided the initial guiding force behind the early Gettysburg battlefield. At Shiloh, Army of the Tennessee veteran David Reed served as the park's first historian and became the primary source for several dominant interpretations of the battle. The first was the focus on the Hornet's Nest as the key moment of the first day's action; the second was the idea that the arrival of Don Carlos Buell's Army of the Ohio late in the afternoon and evening on 6 April 1862 did not really affect the outcome of the battle the following day. This interpretation drew the ire of Boynton and the Society of the Army of the Cumberland, since many units from that organization had served under Buell in the Army of the Ohio. Boynton was outraged that the interpretation of the park focused mostly on the first day and thus overlooked the contributions of Buell's troops on the second day of the fighting. When combined with his already contentious opinions of Grant and Sherman, whose mistakes nearly lost the battle of Shiloh, Boynton's defense of his own army fueled his growing feud with the Army of the Tennessee. As historian Tim Smith points out, Reed's thesis survived this challenge and not only affected the historiography of the battle, but continues to be the interpretation that dominates the signs, markers, and park literature on the battlefield to this day.[7]

Likewise, the Vicksburg National Military Park benefited from Commissioner William T. Rigby's participation as its energetic patron and planner and Medal of Honor recipient John S. Kountz as its historian. At Antietam, Union veteran George B. Davis took the reins at the behest of the secretary of war to bring direction to that project. In each case, these men had a profound influence on the placement and content of historical markers that interpreted the action on the fields to the public and future students of the battles. Eventually, all five of the original park commissions had Confederate members, and in many cases, commissioners from one park assisted in the creation and organization of other parks.[8]

Making the battlefield a source of information as well as inspiration was certainly in the minds of Boynton and the Chickamauga park commissioners from the very beginning. In one of his many speeches leading up to the creation of the park, Boynton repeated his description of the "deadliest battle of modern times" and reiterated his belief that "the ground of such fighting deserves to be preserved for pilgrimages and historic study." He hammered home his point with a comparison to another famous field:

> We propose to take a very important, very necessary, and eminently practical step beyond the far-famed Gettysburg Memorial Association, and ascertain and permanently designate all the lines of both armies, and set up tablets to mark the lines of advance and extreme points reached by each squadron, battery, or regiment, be it Union or Confederate, and state their strength and losses, to the end that the ordinary visitor or military student shall be able, one and all, to understand our great object lesson of American prowess on the field of battle.

As has already been described in this study, the process of accurately interpreting the battle's many facets and clearly marking every unit position was far more difficult than the participants and commissioners imagined. Nonetheless, the park commissioners' intent to use the carefully preserved battlefield as an instructional tool was firmly entrenched.[9]

The War Department made this mission official with an act of Congress in May 1896, stating that "national military parks . . . and their approaches are hereby declared to be national fields for military maneuvers for the Regular Army . . . and the National Guard or Militia of the States." It specifically allowed the secretary of war to "designate . . . such portions of the military forces of the United States as he may think best, to receive military instruction there." This rule was not limited to the Chickamauga park; it applied to all the military parks, present and future, and could be broadly interpreted by the War Department in a variety of ways. Overall, the intent was to give as many military personnel as possible an opportunity to study the great battles on the ground where they actually took place. While this certainly fit in with the veterans' desire to have their deeds recognized and remembered, it also promoted a potential conflict with the preservation of the landscape itself and the commemorative purposes of the monuments they had placed there. As the law was written, it gave the secretary of war a great deal of discretion in determining the circumstances under which the parks could be utilized. For example, stationing troops from New Orleans to escape an 1897 yellow fever epidemic seems to have been an example of the War Department simply exercising its right to use the park any way it saw fit.[10]

This military use provision had both short- and long-term implications for the new national military parks at Chickamauga, Gettysburg, Antietam, and Shiloh. It led to the construction of observation towers at key points on the battlefields that could be used by both the public and military personnel to see how and where the battle lines moved at specific points in the conflict. There was also an even greater responsibility on the part of the park commissioners to get the facts and locations of each unit's participation in the battle "fixed beyond dispute" so that students of the battle would come away with an accurate account of events. Although the parks differed in the style and placement of the descriptive signage, they all put a huge emphasis on the details of the battle and the actions of specific units. In some ways, the focus on military tactics also led to the emphasis on defining key moments and places on the battlefields as part of the park's interpretation of the battle. This led to a focus on the units engaged on Cemetery Ridge and Little Round Top at Gettysburg, the Hornet's Nest at Shiloh, Burnside's Bridge and the Sunken Road at Antietam, Snodgrass Hill (a.k.a. Horseshoe Ridge) at Chickamauga, and Orchard Knob and Lookout Mountain at Chattanooga.[11]

More importantly, the "maneuver law" also raised the issue of practicality as a primary reason for creating, funding, and maintaining national military parks. Commissioner Fullerton articulated the belief among the veterans that

Chickamauga is the pioneer park, as a historical memorial; and its example is, we believe, being followed, at a long distance, by those who have control at Gettysburg. Our park has been the model for the preservation of other historic fields of the Civil War. The law out of which the Chickamauga and Chattanooga National Military Park materialized has been a maker of glorious history on the bloody field at Shiloh, at

Antietam . . . and the good work will go on until the last one of the sites of our great struggles will be the property of our nation, held in trust for the instruction of generations to come.

However, there were those who thought otherwise. A skeptical congressman objecting to the creation of yet another military park at Shiloh argued that one battlefield from the East and one from the West was sufficient. He went on to observe that "The [proposed] Shiloh field is very inaccessible . . . [and] for this reason is less convenient than Chattanooga, for example, for purpose of instruction. It is a flat, uninteresting field, without any striking natural features. Antietam and Gettysburg in the East and Chickamauga in the West would answer all the needs of technical military instruction at the time, and would also meet the needs of the War College." Although the notion that all of these battlefields were primarily sacred commemorative ground was still present among many veterans, their families, and the public, the pressure to make these fields *useful* made an impression on the various park commissions. What initially seemed to be a minor provision in the War Department's management of the parks became an important issue as the United States drifted closer and closer to war with Spain.[12]

The multiple missions of the Chickamauga park and its brethren were destined to collide with one another during the tumultuous year of 1898. As tensions between the United States and Spain regarding Cuba escalated, the role of the Civil War veterans as models of manhood and patriotic sacrifice became a key element in the nation's march to war. The theme of reconciliation so prominent at the park dedication also took center stage as the prospect of a reunited country at war with a foreign foe found much appeal among the press and public. Finally, the War Department's use of its national military parks as training grounds brought the memories and images of the Civil War and the Battle of Chickamauga into the foreground. By making an active contribution to the war effort, the veterans and their park served as more than just symbols to much of the nation during its first meaningful overseas war.

EIGHT

"To Cement Forever the Bonds of Sectional Reunion"

The causes of America's War with Spain can be divided into several major categories. The diplomatic reasons generally have to do with Spain's presence in the western hemisphere in direct violation of the Monroe Doctrine. Its apparently despotic rule over Cuba a mere ninety miles from the United States seemed contrary to both the sanctity of our hemisphere and the cause of liberty among the oppressed Cuban people. The role of the American press and its use of "yellow journalism" are well known to historians to the extent that it constituted a "cause" of the war in and of itself. Public reaction to the sinking of the *Maine* in Havana harbor was stimulated in part by its understanding of the situation based on the press's exaggerated reports of Spanish atrocities leading up to that tragedy. Finally, the degree to which sectional reunion and the desire to rekindle the nation's patriotic fire influenced "war fever" in 1898 cannot be underestimated. If part of the catalyst for remembering the Civil War was a desire to recapture the essence of American manhood, then the connection between the glories of the past war and the possible benefits of a new conflict made a great deal of sense.

The United States at the end of the century was a nation nearly bursting at the seams with industrial progress and national pride. The decades after the Civil War had been filled with unprecedented economic growth that had only been recently tarnished by unemployment and labor problems resulting from the Panic of 1894. Industrial giants like John D. Rockefeller and Andrew Carnegie presided over massive corporations, built around oil and steel, that generated great wealth for their owners and shareholders. Increasing numbers of immigrants from eastern and southern Europe were entering the industrial workforce as a source of low-paid, unskilled, and exploitable labor. At the same time, the western frontier, once the bellwether of American expansion and Manifest Destiny, had finally been conquered by the forces of civilization.

Politically, a Republican administration led by Civil War veteran William McKinley had overcome the disruptive forces of Populism in 1896 by appealing

to traditional social values, sectional reconciliation, and economic conserva-
tism. America was in the midst of dramatic changes that foretold great promise,
while at the same time prompting a certain amount of apprehension among
its citizens. When confronted by such changes, Americans sought reassurance that their values, goals, and interests could be preserved and promoted
in spite of this chaos. They found those reassurances in the dual euphoria of
sectional reunion and the prospects of territorial expansion and a righteous
foreign war.[1]

The Spanish-controlled islands of Cuba and Puerto Rico represented one
of the last bastions of the Old World that infringed on U.S. territorial sovereignty as spelled out by the 1823 Monroe Doctrine. During the early 1890s, a
Cuban revolutionary movement began to orchestrate armed resistance against
the Spanish on parts of the island. This insurgency brought forth a Spanish
military response that included a harsh, scorched-earth policy on the offending districts. Aside from the influential pro-Cuban blocks in several American
cities, the activities in Cuba might have had a minimal impact in the United
States if it were not for the remarkable influence of aggressive expansionists
like Theodore Roosevelt and Henry Cabot Lodge and the role played by the
nation's popular press.[2]

Along with the boom in industrial production, the late nineteenth century
experienced a similar rise in newspapers and periodicals capable of reaching
large numbers of readers. The New York papers, in particular, commanded
a great deal of influence. Joseph Pulitzer had recently purchased the *World*
from Jay Gould and molded it into a sensationalistic tabloid along the lines of
the San Francisco-based chain of papers owned by William Randolph Hearst.
The use of sensational, lurid headlines and speculative reporting predated the
Spanish-American War itself, but the situation in Cuba lent itself to the types
of stories that required few verifiable facts but lots of gory, and often entirely
fabricated, details. The "yellow press" enjoyed two main sources of information
on the situation in Cuba. One was the Cuban contingent in New York, whose
"unrivalled propaganda bureau" was happy to regularly supply the papers
with stories of Spanish outrages and insurrectionist successes. Walter Millis
observes that "whatever may have been their prowess in war, the Cuban patriots seemed to be the first of modern peoples fully to grasp the military value
of propaganda." Misled by carefully crafted accounts alleged to be from "the
front," the American public "began to picture the Cuban war in the dramatic
(though wholly unwarranted) terms of formal military operations, sieges, and
pitched battles" rather than the real, but far less glamorous, guerrilla struggle.
As effective as the "junta" was in supplying the press with information, the
emergence of field reporters was even more likely to produce titillating "firsthand" stories from the scene of the action.[3]

The competition for dramatic information from the conflict in Cuba inspired the major papers, particularly the *Journal* and the *World*, to send correspondents to the island to ferret out the gritty details. The quality and professionalism of these individuals varied widely, as did the accuracy of the events on which they reported. Not only were they inclined to tell the story the readers wanted to hear, but they were at the mercy of Cuban interpreters who fed them plenty of pro-insurrectionist fodder. Richard Harding Davis was one of the more competent correspondents, who eventually covered the war itself and published a book based on his many adventures. Even though a great many of the accounts forwarded by these reporters were "wild, self-contradictory, and impossible of credence," many people in the United States, including politicians from both parties, embraced them as truth.

Often the most compelling (and thus prone to exaggeration) accounts were those involving crimes perpetrated by the Spanish against Cuban women. Amid the trumped-up reports of rape and pillage, a few real examples actually emerged to fuel the propaganda machine. The plight of Evangelina Cisneros, who was imprisoned by the Spanish for attempting to rescue her insurrectionist father from jail, made headlines in the Hearst papers and inspired a passionate "free Evangelina" campaign across the country. Another lurid account involving Spanish violations against women on the American ship *Olivette* spurred even more outrage. Whether true or not, the image of women in peril stimulated a powerful impulse within the public psyche that reinforced the American desire to restore its individual and collective manhood.[4]

The plight of Cuban women stimulated what Kristen Hoganson calls the "chivalric impulse" in American men. The social changes of the late century, including the rise of a viable women's rights movement, caused many Americans to question whether American males still possessed the manly qualities that had been exhibited by their Civil War ancestors. The stirring, if overstated, exploits of Cuban patriots seemed to exemplify acts of chivalry that had long since faded in the rapidly urbanizing United States. The strength and growing independence of American women made it more difficult for men to exercise those manly qualities, so the focus soon shifted to protecting the "noble" women of Cuba from the "bestial" Spanish oppressors. Hoganson argues convincingly that the jingoistic impulse that swept the United States on the eve of the Spanish-American War was heavily influenced by the nation's desire to restore its sense of manhood. This was particularly important for southern men, who had failed to uphold the honor of southern women during the Civil War and had taken much of their frustration out on black men in the form of lynch mobs. With a foreign foe threatening the honor of womanhood, both northern and southern men could embrace the martial values that their grandfathers and fathers had shown in the War between the States.[5]

The concept of manhood was not limited to its social and cultural impact on American males. It also served as an anchor for a foreign policy that encouraged national vigor and strength on the world stage. The late nineteenth century was an era of ambitious colonialism and imperialism on the part of the major European powers in all parts of the world. Unwilling to stand by and let the Old World dominate this process, the United States took control of the Hawaiian Islands in 1893 with an eye toward acquiring a larger economic and diplomatic role in the Pacific. In the minds of many statesmen, notably Henry Cabot Lodge and Theodore Roosevelt, the United States must flex its muscle and exert its national energies or be left behind in the race for international dominance. The so-called "jingoists" used the military theories of Alfred Mahan, which advocated the construction and utilization of a strong navy, to encourage the expansion of America's "Manifest Destiny" beyond the boundaries of the continental United States. A war against Spain for the liberation of Cuba and the possible annexation of other Spanish colonial holdings in the Caribbean and Pacific were appealing ways to give the nation a sense of empowerment.[6]

For Theodore Roosevelt and those who agreed with him, war served as a way for both individual males and the collective society to embrace the ennobling values of courage, patriotism, endurance, and sacrifice. Roosevelt was so convinced that the experience of combat would improve his own individual character that he vowed to resign his position as assistant secretary of the navy and go to the scene of action as soon as war was declared. He also understood and promoted the model that the Civil War veterans provided for the current generation of young Americans who had never been tested by the trials and rigors of combat. In one essay, he wrote that "none of our heroes of peace, save a few great constructive statesmen, can rank with our heroes of war." For a man with aspirations to high public office, this belief was more than rhetoric. To serve his nation in the field of battle would fill a gap in his personal development that he had felt strongly since his own father's failure to take a military role in the Civil War. In a sense, it would make him the complete man that he had set out to be since his early days as a spindly, asthmatic boy. But more than his personal honor, Roosevelt truly believed that "all the great masterful races have been fighting races." In his mind, a war with Spain was the best thing that could happen to the United States.[7]

If Cuba could be perceived as a fair maiden in distress and Spain the swarthy bully, then the United States was a white knight in shining armor. The misconception that the Cubans were light skinned was due largely to distortions attributed to the yellow press and helped alleviate the misgivings that some Americans might have in supporting a dark race over a European one. Since the Cubans were certainly not of Anglo-Saxon origin, there were some disagreements among interventionists regarding their ability to sustain independence. The paternalistic notion that the United States ultimately knew what was good for these people reflected the perception of the "white man's burden" that was shared by the industrial nations toward those seen as underdeveloped. Oddly, many Americans saw Spain as an obstacle to capitalist development in the Caribbean and a representation of a decadent, backward culture rather than a peer among industrial nations. Given the lack of real knowledge that most Americans, particularly those in the Midwest, had of Cubans or Spaniards, it was easy to see the issues surrounding Cuba in these simple terms.[8]

Things were not as simple for President McKinley, who had to balance the public's clamor for war with the need for a more moderate diplomatic approach. When he took office in March 1897, McKinley was hopeful that a political shift in the Spanish government would lead to some sort of compromise on the Cuban issue. The American attaché in Havana was Robert E. Lee's nephew, Fitzhugh Lee, who had been appointed by former President Grover Cleveland. In response to Lee's urgent requests for support following riots in Havana early in 1898, McKinley sent the battleship *Maine* to the city on a combined diplomatic and security mission. In return, Spanish naval ships visited New York harbor as a gesture of good will. All these good intentions vanished when the *Maine* exploded in February 1898, killing over 200 American sailors. McKinley resisted the hysterical calls for war, while a joint U.S. and Spanish investigation attempted to find the cause of the catastrophe. The results were inconclusive, but the board of inquiry implied that a mine or some other form of explosive was responsible. When the Spanish government failed to respond to the administration's ultimatum to abandon its colonial interests in the Caribbean, McKinley gave in to public pressure and allowed Congress to pass a resolution to use force on 19 April, which led to a formal declaration of war on 25 April.[9]

Historian Lewis Gould proclaims that "in order to end a bloody conflict, the United States, under the leadership of William McKinley, went to war in 1898 against a foe that had resisted all attempts at peaceful compromise." While this is a satisfactory interpretation of the president's reasoning, it does not tell the whole story of McKinley's dilemma. As a Civil War veteran, the president carried the responsibility of representing that generation while leading the nation through the current crisis. He had been able to defeat William Jennings Bryan in 1896 precisely because of his decorated military career and his association with the increasingly heroic and sentimentalized Civil War period. His reluctance to commit the country to war led some of his Republican supporters, including Roosevelt, and many of his Democratic critics to question his courage and manhood. Suddenly, it was not enough for the president to have served nobly in the past war. It became more important that he prove his ability to lead the nation by living up to an updated, more aggressive version of the manly ideal. In the context of the late-century definition of manhood, actions spoke louder than words; failure to take action was seen as a lack of courage to do so. As Kristen Hoganson puts it, "his decision to join the jingoes was less a reflection of his courage or cowardice, strength or weakness, than an acknowledgement that the political system he operated in would not permit any other course of action."[10]

The nation's declaration of war against a foreign country for the first time in fifty years was a giant step in the ongoing process of sectional reconciliation. The common prospect of military service succeeded in bonding Northerners and Southerners, putting them on roughly equal social and political footing. In fact, Nina Silber argues that "the Spanish-American War made northerners of different ideological persuasions recognize and accept the manliness and martial heroism of southern white men" and that both sides "understood their patriotic reconciliation as the cohesion of the Anglo-Saxon race." David Blight agrees and notes that "without the war with Spain, and the South's embrace of the cause . . . reconciliation would not have matured so readily." He goes on to observe that the "deepening radicalization of American patriotism, the growing alliance between white supremacy and imperialism, had profound consequences for race relations and the nation's historical memory." Within days after the declaration of war, the giddy nation enthusiastically launched itself into a conflict that "seemed to cement forever the bonds of sectional reunion and . . . bury the bitterness which had been festering for thirty years."[11]

The broad social implications of this reunion spirit were not apparent to most people in 1898. Most were swept up in the outburst of patriotism, and as one postwar writer observed, "there was something exhilarating, and at the same time pathetic in the promptitude with which party distinctions were dropped . . . whilst such terms as Republican, Democrat, and Populist were unheard" following the president's call to arms. President McKinley added to the spirit of unity by appointing former Confederate cavalry commander "Fightin' Joe" Wheeler to active command as a brigadier general of volunteers in the upcoming invasion. Noting that former Union and Confederate soldiers served together alongside the sons of both former friends and foes, the same writer waxed eloquently on the meaning of it all:

The world was to witness at last what this union truly means. It was to see arise from the ashes of the old, and dead and buried controversies, a power undreamed of by itself before; a vast world power, with which henceforth the nations of the earth must reckon. The swaddling clothes of national babyhood were gone. The giant stood forth in the pride of his manhood, armed . . . and arrayed on the side of humanity and liberty, ready, willing, and able to give battle to all comers who might challenge his supremacy, wherever he might plant the Star-Spangled Banner or set up the standards of free government.

Such language reflected the view that manhood, reunion, and a victory in this war had broader implications for the future of the nation than the mere liberation of Cuba. The Civil War, its memory, its veterans, and its battlefields were more than symbols in this drama; they were vital and active participants.[12]

In spite of the enthusiasm with which much of Congress and the public hurled the country into war, the U.S. military was only marginally prepared to take the offensive against the Spanish. In the aftermath of the *Maine* disaster, Congress appropriated $50 million for "national defense" six weeks before the actual outbreak of hostilities, but the effects of those funds were negligible at the start of the conflict. The reality was that thirty years of peacetime stagnation and a traditional hostility on the part of the American public toward large and expensive standing armed forces had left the United States lagging behind in its military development.

When the war began, the navy was far ahead of the ground forces in terms of both equipment and command structure. Although it only had four modern battleships divided between the Pacific and Atlantic fleets, there were several more under construction, and the supporting ships and crews were solid. While not the best navy of the period, the United States' fleet was considerably stronger than its Spanish counterpart. The widely held perception that the enemy fleet was more effective than it actually was helped give American naval strategy a sense of urgency that quickly produced decisive and positive results. Spurred by Assistant Secretary Roosevelt's prewar instructions, the Asiatic Squadron under George Dewey launched an early strike at the Spanish Squadron in the Philippines and won a major victory at Manila Bay. Dewey's decisive thrashing of the Spanish fleet boosted American confidence, freed up forces for the upcoming Cuban operations, and produced the war's first great hero. Eventually, the navy would help finish the job by destroying the second Spanish fleet at Santiago, but not before taking on the monumental task of shepherding troops and supplies for the army's invasion of Cuba.[13]

The U.S. Army was far less prepared than its naval brethren for an ambitious offensive campaign in Cuba or anywhere else. As one historian cleverly put it "if the U.S. Navy was just emerging from the dark ages of the [eighteen] sixties and seventies, the Army, unhappily, was still wearing animal skins and painting its collective face blue." The Regular Army forces numbered fewer than 30,000 men in all branches, who were scattered around the country in outposts, forts, and garrisons of various types. Although it had recently adopted a new training manual, acquired breech-loading rifles and cannons, and improved the system for the promotion of officers, there was still no unified command or logistical structure for mobilizing the Regulars for a major war. In spite of the urgings of Gen. Emory Upton for major reforms that would have created a functional reserve system, the War Department had not adopted most of them. In 1898, there was still no centralized command structure, no general staff, and a relatively minuscule Quartermaster Department that was undermanned, underfunded, and lacked the materiel necessary to outfit the field army of 60,000 troops that would be required to invade Cuba. As one contemporary writer put it, "the mobilization of troops is really the act of making many mobs into one big mob," with the only difference being the "system and discipline" of military command. This view would be put to the test by several elements that undermined the army's overall structure and complicated the process.

To augment the Regulars, the War Department theoretically had over 100,000 state National Guard troops available for short-term mobilization. The quality of these troops varied from unit to unit and state to state. In many cases, they existed more as social clubs than trained military organizations. The biggest problem was that "no one, including its own members, knew for sure what the Guard's relationship to the Federal government was." The provisions by which the president could summon these individual state "armies" into national service did not include offensive operations in foreign territory. The Hull bill, which attempted to redefine this arrangement, ran into opposition from the states, who felt that it increased the size of the Regular Army too much and eliminated the ability of the states to raise their own volunteer forces in time of war. On top of the organizational problems, many of these National Guard units had to depend on indifferent state governments for their arms and equipment; this meant that they were nearly all using outdated, and often worn out, uniforms and munitions. The shortcomings of this unwieldy structure should not have come as a surprise to anyone by 1898. As early as 1877, a writer in a popular magazine had exclaimed, "it is indeed a marvelous fact that the Government, recognizing as it does the necessity for an army . . . should exhibit such an utter indifference to everything pertaining to its efficiency and welfare." As a result of these factors, the War Department was forced to take dramatic measures to quickly put an army in the field.[14]

The secretary of war, Russell Alger, and the commanding general of the army, Nelson Miles, were both Civil War veterans who knew that winning the war would not be as easy as the public thought. On the other hand, they believed that a properly organized and supported expedition consisting of roughly 50,000

Regular Army troops could successfully capture Cuba. As soon as Congress authorized general mobilization in April, they ordered as many units of the Regular Army as possible to concentrate in the South for a proposed invasion aimed at Santiago. General Miles, on the advice of the surgeon general, suggested waiting until the fall to avoid the yellow fever season. However, as one historian pointed out, "Americans were not used to procrastination once their bile was up," so the administration decided that such a delay in an offensive movement was inadvisable.

The other major development affecting the army was the pressure put forth by state governors to include both National Guard regiments and batteries in the active-duty force. The original plan proposed increasing the Regular Army to 60,000 men with volunteers and calling up 50,000 guard troops to man the coastal forts. However, after Congress declared war, President McKinley quickly increased the number of state troops to 125,000 as the volunteers came forth in waves to answer the patriotic call to arms and fill under-strength state guard units. Such a rapid deployment called for the establishment of rendezvous points and camps of instruction that could funnel invasion troops to the departure points in Florida.[15]

Even before the outbreak of hostilities, the War Department had chosen the Chickamauga and Chattanooga National Military Park as one of the main camps for the concentration of Regular Army units being gathered in preparation for war. Not surprisingly, Henry Boynton (now one of the park commissioners) was directly involved in this decision. From his office within the War Department he had close contact with Secretary Russell Alger, who had been one of the original board members during the creation of the park. The order to mobilize the Regulars came on 15 April, which gave park officials only a few days to prepare for the arrival of an estimated 7,300 cavalry, infantry, and artillery forces, along with roughly 8,300 horses and 6,700 mules. Chickamauga Park was an excellent choice for a number of reasons. First, it was already War Department property, with all the necessary legislative permission in place for its use as a training ground. Second, it had two railroad lines, the Western and Atlantic, and the Chattanooga, Rome, and Southern, that would effectively serve to shepherd troops and supplies in and out of the camp. Third, it had a good water supply and a favorable "conditioning" climate for soldiers headed to the tropics. And finally, it had space; the Chickamauga section contained over 7,000 acres of mostly rolling and often open ground that was available for camps, drills, and field maneuvers.[16]

There was an interesting delegation of authority in the early administrative structure of the camp. Colonel Q. C. Lee, chief quartermaster of the army, "assumed the responsibility of activating an army post on the park," while at

FIG. 22: Maj. Gen. John H. Brooke (center) and Gen. M. V. Sheridan (on left) posed for a photograph at Camp Thomas in April 1898. Brooke was the camp's first commander while Sheridan was the son of Army of the Cumberland veteran, Phillip Sheridan. Courtesy of the Chattanooga History Center.

roughly the same time Boynton was given a commission as brigadier general of volunteers and ordered to ready the park for military use. Within days of the original mobilization order, Maj. Gen. John R. Brooke, a Civil War veteran who had served in the Army of the Potomac, was at the park to assume command of the arriving troops. It was Brooke who chose to name the facility "Camp George H. Thomas" in honor of the Army of the Cumberland's revered commander. This was done with Boynton's approval and encouragement, thus suggesting that the camp name had received the de facto support of the Society of the Army of the Cumberland. The War Department's utilization of the park and its designation as Camp Thomas certainly fit the parameters that the veterans set forth when they created the park in the first place. The message of sectional reunion symbolized both the spirit behind the park and the current war. Using the park land for drill and training satisfied the oft-stated practical, educational goals. At the same time, the new camp's acknowledgement of Thomas and the Army of the Cumberland appealed to the sense of vernacular, collective memory that the battlefield represented.[17]

The explosion of activity on the park grounds during those weeks in April was unprecedented; there had not been that much bustle and din since the battle itself. A railroad spur was constructed off of the nearby Chattanooga, Rome, and Southern line that ran along the western edge of the park, creating what became known as Lytle Station. Workers stripped the nearby rise known as Lytle Hill of vegetation so they could unload supplies and build corrals, the quartermaster depot, and a bakery. Within days, "the area took on the appearance of a permanent camp." Boynton, well aware that water would be a key issue, ordered a number of wells dug to supplement the five natural springs on the property. Because the Regulars would report to camp with their own baggage and equipment, there was no urgency on the part of the camp and park officials to accumulate a great deal of camp equipage. Since much of this early work was in progress prior to the president's call for volunteers, the assumption among the camp organizers was that the army's stay would be of short duration en route to more permanent assignments. With the exception of wood and water, the Regular Army units were essentially in self-sustaining field mode and thus required little in the way of logistical care.[18]

The first Regular regiment to arrive was the 25th U.S. Infantry, an all-black unit from Montana on its way to Tampa. It camped in the open field just east and south of the Wilder Tower monument and drilled for several days as other units arrived and joined the growing camp. The 10th U.S. Cavalry, known as the Buffalo Soldiers from their service fighting Indians on the Great Plains, arrived soon afterward and were joined by other African American units, the 9th U.S. Cavalry and 24th U.S. Infantry. Over the next few weeks, the rest of the Regular Army units arrived in large numbers, creating "a great crush of soldiers at Chickamauga." Nearly 6,000 arrived on 23 April alone, causing the railroad company to cancel the civilian excursions into the park that they had been selling. Because they had set out prior to the declaration of war, nearly all of the regular units originally assigned to Camp Thomas were in the park by 27 April, a mere two days after war had been declared. Although their stay was temporary, the Regulars left a powerful impression on the park officials, citizens, and local press that would be long remembered as the source of great pride and excitement.[19]

Among the army's preparations was giving vaccinations to the Regulars as a "necessary sanitary precaution." The troops spent much of their time drilling in all kinds of weather conditions. The camps were spread over a wide area of the park, so there was enough room for everyone and opportunity to wander around and visit other units during off-duty hours. The Regulars were remarkably healthy in spite of the shift from cooler northern climates to the hot, humid southern one. At one point, the only person in the hospital was a soldier who was accidentally wounded in the leg by a comrade who dropped a pistol at drill. After several weeks of training, re-equipping, and getting in shape, many of the units left the camp on their way to Tampa and other points

FIG. 23: Black Regular Army troops training at Camp Thomas in April 1898.
Courtesy of the 6th Cavalry Museum, Fort Oglethorpe, Ga.

to the south. By 14 May, all of them had moved on to their next posts and the campground was virtually empty except for the headquarters staff and provost guard. Overall, the Regular units had been well supplied, disciplined, and easily cared for, making the initial weeks of Camp Thomas's existence "a complete success" according to General Boynton.[20]

However, the experiences of the black troops at Chickamauga demonstrated the many conflicting impulses that the public, the soldiers, and the nation were experiencing during the first month of the war crisis. The four African American regiments that ended up at Camp Thomas "were finely officered, well drilled, . . . well experienced in camp and field . . . [and] . . . well fitted to take their place in that selected host of fighting men which afterwards became the Fifth Army Corps." As they made their way from St. Paul to Chattanooga in mid-April, "they were greeted by enthusiastic crowds" who mistakenly thought the war had started and cheered the troops accordingly. When they passed through Chattanooga, they received a great reception, with "the band blowing and hammering away at 'Dixie' in a manner sufficient to stir the life blood of a wooden Indian."

As the first unit to arrive at Chickamauga, the 25th Infantry was assigned a campground by Boynton himself and lay claim to "being the first camp of the war." They enthusiastically named their encampment "Camp Boynton" in honor of the park's founder. A local paper reported that "the colored 'dough boys' are a fine drilled body of men," and the historian for the 25th Infantry reported that, "it was pleasing to see the fraternity that prevailed between the black and white regulars." In spite of the trouble-free status of the Regulars in the camp, the presence of black soldiers caused some problems in the community that revealed the lingering issues of race that remained unresolved.[21]

As one modern historian put it, in spite of the local enthusiasm for the camp, "the presence of hundreds of Black men with weapons alarmed white Southerners and led to a tense situation for a few days." Although thousands of people, including "nearly the entire colored population of Chattanooga and the country around" came into the camps to gawk and buy Navajo blankets from the Buffalo Soldiers, the white citizens of Chattanooga were less comfortable when the soldiers came into the city on leave and mixed with the population. On 24 April, the Chattanooga *Times* reported an incident of "drunken rowdyism [sic] and riotous conduct" involving members of the 10th Cavalry that resulted in "great indignation . . . in the city over the conduct of the lawless colored troopers." Apparently, the heavily armed soldiers attempted to free two local blacks, who were being loaded into a police wagon, by shooting indiscriminately at both the police and the prisoners. The two prisoners were wounded, several offending soldiers were arrested, and General Brooke was compelled "to issue stern orders prohibiting troops from leaving camp with weapons."[22]

Although not referring directly to this report, the 25th Infantry's chaplain and historian noted that "Southern newspapers indulged in considerable malicious abuse of colored soldiers" and that "certain newspapers of Chattanooga [gave] expression to their dislike of Negro troops in general and those in their proximity especially." While such a hostile attitude among some southern whites might be expected, the fear and distrust ran both ways. Another writer, who also followed the fortunes of black troops in the war, explained that "as only a few of them [black soldiers] have been in the south before, they have exaggerated ideas of how southerners treat Negroes. They imagine they are hated, and they resent this hatred by making things uncomfortable for helpless whites." Clearly, the presence of African American soldiers upset the balance of things in the area, and notwithstanding their status as protectors of the Union they were the object of mixed feelings.[23]

Although the overall view that the Regulars' time in camp was a great success, the effects on the nearby communities were mixed. On the positive side, the locals gave most of the arriving units rousing welcomes as they passed through Nashville, Knoxville, and Chattanooga on their way to the camp. A local paper reported that, "cavalry and artillery pouring into Chattanooga were met at the depot by pretty southern girls who fairly smothered them with fragrant flowers" and that some Rhode Island troops received "an enthusiastic welcome" while passing through Knoxville. To the delight of the Chattanooga breweries, the soldiers had a great liking for beer. A newspaper report noted "soldiers, many of them, if they are good fellows, will drink beer, and since they have been at Chattanooga, the brewery . . . has been kept busy brewing for the boys in blue." The men also kept a colorful array of mascots, including an eagle, a monkey, a coyote, a parrot, and "a little homeless wanderer, a boy of twelve years," which kept both soldiers and visitors amused.[24]

Many of the soldiers had appreciated the historical meaning of the park. In spite of their role in temporarily naming their camp for Boynton, the 25th-Infantry historian reflected on the role that the Rock of Chickamauga had played in saving the Union and wrote: "In honor of this stubborn valor, and in recognition of this high expression of American tenacity, the camp established . . . by the assembling army was called Camp George H. Thomas." The same writer noted that "monuments, judiciously placed, speak with mute eloquence . . . and point to the valor displayed" by the men who fought there, concluding that "the whole park is a monument." Another writer described the initial establishment of the 25th Infantry's bivouac on Snodgrass Hill by exclaiming: "Thus among the monuments was formed the nucleus of Camp Thomas, named in remembrance of the general who . . . led the boys in blue over that same . . . hill to victory on the field of Chickamauga." If nothing else, such pronouncements validated Boynton's persistent efforts to recognize Thomas as the hero and the battle as a Union victory.[25]

There were a few negative effects to the mass influx of troops as well. The soldiers did not always interact in positive ways with the citizens. In one incident, a black member of the 25th U.S., who was being harassed, "hit the restaurant man so hard that he lost all interest in his immediate surroundings." Some ornery soldiers in Knoxville were arrested after "they caught a country man and pretended to conscript him. The fellow was scared out of his wits and went into a fit." The sheer volume of soldiers, civilians, and other traffic often overwhelmed the local railroad facilities. At one point, railroad officials considered building a spur of the Western and Atlantic to accommodate the comings and goings of all the troops. Regardless of their reasonably strict Regular Army discipline, the troops foraged the area for food, cut down trees and took fences for firewood, and turned green fields into "all brown earth" where "dust flies in clouds." Although it had expected around 7,300 men, the camp at Chickamauga Park contained between 12,000 and 25,000 during the mass movement of Regular units to the south in the weeks after war was declared. While there were no major problems, largely due to the short duration

FIG. 24: Civilians visited Chickamauga Park throughout the army's occupation of Camp Thomas. The food concession wagon and soldiers languishing in the background indicate the degree to which the public had access to the camp and its soldiers. Courtesy of the Chattanooga History Center.

of their stay, this huge influx of men foretold the problems resulting from the impending arrival of the volunteers in May.[26]

As of 14 May, the War Department's prewar mass mobilization and concentration of Regular units at Chickamauga Park was a resounding success. In spite of its organizational and logistical shortcomings, the government had successfully transported nearly its entire standing army, made up of all its branches, to one location, equipped and drilled it, and sent it on its way in good order. Contrary to concerns that "many troops have come from higher altitudes or essentially different climates," there was no outbreak of disease among the disciplined Regulars, who judiciously followed military procedures regarding water and sanitation. Commissioner Boynton and his engineer, Edward E. Betts, had worked well with General Brooke and his staff on the placement of camps, roads, and facilities, so that the needs of the troops were more than adequately met. Not only had the army used the park, but the public and the press had visited it in droves, bringing massive amounts of business to the City of Chattanooga, the railroads, and countless entrepreneurs, hoteliers, tavern owners, and tour guides who took full advantage of the mass of potential customers. The city, the park, and the veterans were in the spotlight once again as the symbol of reunion, martial power, and patriotic pride.[27]

The situation was about to become more complicated with the arrival of the National Guard and volunteer units that had been organized after the declaration of war. The numbers and overall makeup of these units would be far different than the commanders had experienced with the Regulars. The volunteers would bring with them a different set of expectations, far less preparation, and an entirely new set of needs for the park commissioners and military leaders to deal with. In the process, the reputation of the park, the city, the region, and the memories of the veterans of the Battle of Chickamauga would be challenged and threatened from a variety of sources.

NINE

"It Is Terrible That Man Is Such a Brute"

The patriotism, reunion spirit, and martial enthusiasm that accompanied the outbreak of war in April 1898 corresponded with the interests and memories of the nation's aging Civil War veterans. The popular public image of a reunited nation rescuing oppressed people by facing down a foreign foe was enhanced by the promotion of former Confederates like Joe Wheeler to command positions in the rapidly emerging volunteer army. Concerns about the state of America's collective and individual manhood led to an increasing focus on the accomplishments and model behavior of the Civil War's veterans from both the North and South. More importantly, the War Department's choice of Chickamauga and Chattanooga National Military Park as its primary concentration point for much of the army put the Civil War, the Battle of Chickamauga, and the battle's veterans back into the public spotlight.

For many of the men who volunteered to take part in the Spanish-American War, the parallels between their experiences and those of their Civil War predecessors were immediate and unmistakable. The process of memory construction initiated by the Civil War veterans in the latter part of the century through their writings, reunions, monuments, and the creation of the battlefield parks seemed to be coming to fruition with the outbreak of the War with Spain. The use of the park enhanced the sense of continuity between generations that had been missing in much of modern life and encouraged the younger soldiers' sense of patriotism and commitment. The myth of the war experience—the journey from civilian to hero via duty and sacrifice on the battlefield—was within their grasp and only needed training, combat, and victory to achieve it. However, what happened at Chickamauga Park would complicate this formula, making the struggle more dramatic and painful—and the rewards more elusive—than most of the soldiers and the public anticipated.

The creation of Camp George H. Thomas on the main battlefield at Chickamauga presented some formidable challenges to the park commissioners and staff. By giving Henry Boynton both military rank and the primary responsibility for overseeing the park's transformation into a training camp, the War Department legitimized his status as the de facto spokesman and representative of the park. His presence at the park during its occupation by the Regulars helped facilitate the relatively positive experience that the soldiers (both black and white) and park officials reported and ultimately remembered. Aside for some minor damage to the landscape from both soldiers and spectators and a notable loss of trees and wooden fences, the park weathered the arrival; camp life; military maneuvers; and rapid departure of thousands of men, horses, wagons, and mules reasonably well.

Yet, in spite of the camp's successful first month, the commanders and park officials felt some uneasiness regarding the arrival of dozens of volunteer units from around the country in mid-May. The influx of even larger numbers of men would put more stress on the park's landscape, foliage, and water supply. The knowledge that many of these troops would be under-equipped meant that there would be higher demand for shelter, uniforms, camp equipage, and other items that had not been a problem for the Regulars. Ultimately, the issues that sparked the most controversy involved the glaring inexperience of the enthusiastic, impatient, and green recruits who filled the camp during the hot summer months of 1898. Not only did their physical needs tax the War Department and camp commander's logistical resources, but their lack of discipline and careless behavior threatened the park, the community, and the health of the men themselves. In the process of meeting these challenges, Boynton and his comrades would be compelled to defend their park and their honor in order to uphold the memories that went with them.

If the War Department's decision to use large numbers of volunteers was controversial, the plan to quickly transport the volunteer units to Camp Thomas and other large camps at Falls Church, Virginia (Camp Alger, near the Manassas battlefield); St. Petersburg, Florida; Mobile, Alabama; and San Francisco, California, was a debatable one as well. If General Miles had his way, the volunteers would have remained in local and state camps until they were properly uniformed, armed, and equipped. The additional time training as individual regiments might have made the transition into the brigade, division, and corps level easier for everyone involved and left most of the fighting to the Regulars. However, as the Regulars were en route to the invasion staging area at Tampa, public pressure to see their volunteers "on to Havana!" compelled Secretary Alger and the War Department to transfer the rapidly organized, often poorly outfitted, regiments directly to the large "reserve" camps in May.

Among the unforeseen results of the modified volunteer bill were a lack of recruits for Regular units and a loss of officers, who accepted promotions in both volunteer and guard units. The *Knoxville Tribune* observed in April that "there is not much in the man who is satisfied to be a private in the regular army," but was sure that "in the case of actual war, however, there will be no lack of volunteer soldiers." The War Department got off to a good start with its early mobilization of the Regulars, but public pressure and congressional meddling soon led to difficulties. According to historian Graham Cosmas, the War Department's deviation from its original plan and the inclusion of a massive volunteer contingent sowed the seeds of disaster. These factors, combined with the army's supply problems and its "unremedied organizational weakness . . . accounted for most of the mistakes and misfortunes that ensued."[1]

As if there were not enough complications with this plan, not all volunteer units were created equally. In addition to mobilizing National Guard units and enlisting volunteers in the states, the War Department decided to "organize companies, troops, battalions, or regiments, possessing special qualifications." What it had in mind were the frontiersmen, Indians, and cowboys of the West, whose "special qualifications" were those of "horsemen and marksmen." This led to the creation of three hand-picked U.S. volunteer cavalry regiments that theoretically would enjoy a slightly higher level of experienced officers, modern equipment, and quality training than those organized at the state level. Among these was the 1st U.S. Cavalry "Rough Riders" commanded by former Regular Leonard Wood and mostly recruited by his enthusiastic second-in-command, Lt. Col. Theodore Roosevelt.

As he formed this unit, Roosevelt made a point of recruiting frontiersmen, believing that "in all the world there could be no better material for soldiers than afforded by these grim hunters of the mountains, these wild rough riders of the plains." Yet, to prove that these traits could be learned and mastered by any American male, he also gathered students from eastern universities who "possessed the common traits of hardihood and thirst for adventure" as their western counterparts. Throughout the short history of the regiment, Roosevelt made a particular effort to separate his unit from the other volunteers by pointing out that in the areas of drill, discipline, and camp deportment, "they were as good as . . . any Regular regiment." Although such distinctions seemed trivial and self-serving at first, they would become increasingly important in both Camp Thomas and Cuba during the war's grueling summer months.[2]

As thousands of volunteers began to pour into Camp Thomas, the first challenge for the camp commanders was to get the new troops located in bivouacs throughout the park, immediately followed by seeing that they were properly equipped with uniforms, weapons, and accouterments. The next task would be assuring that all of the men were regularly supplied with adequate rations and water. Another key priority was to institute a regular routine of drill, guard

mounts, fatigue duties, and other aspects of military life to keep the men occupied and morale high. While they were grappling with the first three issues,
the newly created corps, division, brigade, and regimental commanders had
to turn these raw regiments into combat troops capable of joining the invasion
forces that were already on their way to Cuba. On top of these strictly military
concerns, there were problems accompanying the interactions between soldiers
and civilians both inside and outside of the park. While some issues could be
quickly addressed, others would intensify with the rising heat of the summer
and the diminishing prospects of getting all of these units into the war.

The first volunteer regiments to arrive at Camp Thomas on 15 May were
the 3rd Wisconsin Infantry, the 1st Ohio Cavalry, and the 1st Ohio Infantry. Between that date and mid-June, they were joined by dozens of infantry
regiments, cavalry units, and artillery batteries from numerous northern and
southern states. A U.S. Army Signal Corps unit stayed near headquarters,
while a small, single company of Regulars made up the provost guard for the
camp. The entire contingent was arranged much like a Civil War army under
the overall command of General Brooke. It consisted of two army corps (designated I and III) divided into two or three divisions each. The infantry divisions contained three brigades; each brigade was made up of three regiments
of twelve companies apiece.[3]

The influx of between 45,000 and 60,000 troops in such a short period of
time forced the camp to expand beyond its original areas into the more thickly
wooded, lower-lying eastern part of the park. Many of the volunteer regiments
were placed between Lafayette Road and Chickamauga Creek, "where they
can be most conveniently accommodated . . . and contiguous to the best water
supply." Because the regiments were grouped according to their division and
brigade assignments, camping areas along the main park roads needed to be
cleared and expanded accordingly. To keep the large open fields clear for drill,
the camps were located in the woods (as the Regular's camps had been), which
led to a great deal of cutting and trimming to make room for tents and company streets. Forested areas that had once been thick with underbrush were
converted into open woodlots with spaces wide enough for a wagon road running among and between the camps. A soldier of the 9th Pennsylvania wrote
that his camp in the woods "seemed an ideal spot and a beautiful shelter from
the sun" adding that "the natural beauty of the place enchanted us." A corporal of the 1st New Hampshire, unhappy with his campsite, complained that he
"knew of no other spot on the earth more thickly covered with rocks except
John Symond's pasture." Yet, General Brooke was pleased with these early arrivals, exclaiming that he "has never seen a finer set of young men." He could
only hope that all the volunteers would prove to be as easy to work with.[4]

FIG. 25: Unidentified volunteers in front of their tents at Camp Thomas, Georgia, 1898. Note the proximity of the camp to the tree line, the blue wool uniforms, and the stacked rifles. Courtesy of the Chattanooga History Center.

Many of the regiments had interesting trips from their state camps on the way to the train station at Lytle and ultimately to Camp Thomas. Members of the 9th Pennsylvania, having heard that Kentucky was known for bluegrass, fine race horses, and beautiful women, noted that "after we had passed through the state and seen no blue grass [*sic*], no race horses, we were somewhat skeptical as to the existence of the beautiful women," but admitted that the reception they received at most stops was warm and enthusiastic. Unfortunately, a fire on the train destroyed much of the officers' baggage and delayed the whole regiment's arrival. A soldier in the 52nd Iowa wrote home to his local paper that it was the "same thing all along, crowds at depots, ugly and pretty girls and foolish women, whose husband's [*sic*] wasn't there all asking for buttons in return for sweet smiles and hat pins." He described Indiana as being "as flat as a cooking school cake" and exclaimed that the mountains of Kentucky were "large enough to grow moonshine whiskey and lanky people." According to the local papers, as the 1st New Hampshire passed through Knoxville, some of "the boys . . . got a little bit fresh" with a few of the local girls, who reportedly "were insulted at some of the soldiers' remarks and actions." A young recruit arriving in late June wrote that "on the train here most of the soldiers were terribly drunk and the entire train smelled of whiskey." For many of the small-town boys from the Midwest, even the journey to war was a great adventure.[5]

This massive influx of humanity and equipment did not take place without incident. A *Knoxville Tribune* headline for 20 May reported that the "Railroads were blocked by volunteer arrivals," and the story indicated that "officials of the various roads have been working together harmoniously to relieve the congestion." A crash involving a troop train and a passenger train claimed the life of a soldier from the 1st Missouri, injured several others and resulted in the arrest of the engineer and fireman of the passenger train. The 1st New Hampshire reached Chattanooga on a Friday night, sat in sweltering cars for the day, and bivouacked under the stars in the evening before hiking to its camp in the park. The march in the hot sun from the drop-off points to the camp sites was difficult for the unseasoned troops. While men in some units simply "dropped out" from the exertion, others suffered a worse fate, like a private from the 12th New York who died of heart failure during the trek.[6]

The first weeks following the arrival of the bulk of the volunteer regiments were particularly chaotic due to the equipment shortages among the new regiments. The distribution of material among the units varied from state to state, regiment to regiment. The 1st Ohio Cavalry arrived at their campsite on 15 May without uniforms or equipment, prompting one observer to note that "they did not, therefore present a very formidable appearance." An equally unimpressed member of the regiment's Troop G reported that when they arrived at the Lytle depot near Chickamauga Park, "all you could see was Negroes and flies." The fully outfitted 1st Ohio Infantry arrived a few hours later but could not be unloaded in the darkness and got stuck sleeping on the train. The 9th Pennsylvania also endured a twenty-six-hour wait on their train before they could disembark and march the three miles to their campsite. The commander of the 52nd Iowa refused to send his men into camp without tents, so they "spent a very comfortable night in the [Pullman] sleeping cars" before entering camp the next morning.[7]

The 3rd U.S. Cavalry, in spite of its cowboy origins and special status, had only a third of its men in uniform and was totally without weapons. Likewise, the 1st Illinois Cavalry and the 160th Indiana Infantry arrived in camp without uniforms, while a Kentucky regiment showed up carrying few provisions but with a supply of the distilled spirits their state was known for. A captain in the 1st Vermont remarked that the men "were in a deplorable condition" and often resorted to "drilling barefoot with sticks on their shoulders . . . [wearing] only the shirt and trousers or overalls they had worn from the farm or shop." Not only did many of the soldiers lack essential items, but to make things more complicated, they did not lack the same items. Therefore, the camp quartermaster had to procure large amounts of virtually everything to meet the needs of the massed recruits.[8]

FIG. 26: Colonel Melvin Grigsby and staff at Camp Thomas, 1898. Grigsby's "Cowboys" later became the 3rd U.S. Volunteer Cavalry, but, unlike Roosevelt's Rough Riders, the regiment never saw service outside of the United States. Courtesy of the Chattanooga–Hamilton County Bicentennial Library.

The supply problem existed at all levels, from manufacturing and requisition to distribution and delivery. At the manufacturing level, there were certain items that could not be procured in substantial amounts when the war started. Secretary of War Alger reported that "there was no khaki cloth in the United States and no establishment familiar with its manufacture." Thus, most troops started the war in heavy blue wool uniforms. Likewise, high-quality duck canvas required for tents was in short supply, to the extent that the War Department was forced "to secure the aid of the force in the National Post Office Department mail-bag repair shop." The Quartermaster Department was swamped by the sheer quantities of goods required to sustain the army. Alger estimated that the fifty-seven-man department received requests for roughly 4,000 shoes a day between April and August, and furnished some 50,000 articles of various types a day during this stretch. Although the army had recently switched to the .30 caliber, five-shot Krag-Jorgensen rifle, there were only about 53,000 available and not enough smokeless cartridges, cartridge belts, and accouterments to outfit more than 20,000 men. As a result of this shortage, most of the National Guard troops were destined to be armed with the outdated black-powder, single-shot, breech-loading .45-70 caliber Spring-field rifle. Caught flat-footed by the sudden increase in the number of troops being mobilized, the War Department scrambled to requisition the necessary items from private manufacturers across the country.[9]

Getting the needed material to the troops at Camp Thomas was also a monumental challenge for the camp quartermaster and his staff. The single rail line running through Lytle was overwhelmed by the arrival of both sol-diers and supplies. The existing depot and warehouse facilities that had been constructed early in the occupation were insufficient for the massive volume of goods flowing into the camp. Eventually, the quartermaster procured space in warehouses in Chattanooga and "managed to co-opt almost all the avail-able rolling stock on the railroads to transport the incoming supplies to Camp Thomas." As a result of this inadequate system of distribution, some units re-ceived plenty, while others went without. Even units that drew supplies did not get them all at once. Okey Dillon of the 1st Ohio Cavalry reported getting "two blue shirts, two pair of drawers, a pair of heavy campaign shoes, a pair of leggings, two pair of socks and a campaign hat," but only "some of the boys got pants." He reported optimistically that "the rest of our uniforms we will get soon." Items like eating utensils, cookware, canteens, and other personal equipment were in short supply and frequently had to be shared with others by the men fortunate enough to have them.[10]

Even when the uniforms and equipment arrived, the soldiers' reactions were mixed. Trooper Dillon declared that "the boys are all proud of their suits" and with the addition of the rest of his gear, proclaimed that "our uniforms are *out of sight.*" He happily sent his civilian vest and coat back home, but reported that since "the rest are not worth sending, I gave them to a Negro." However, a member of the 52nd Iowa was less impressed, writing later that "it would be hard for people to believe that a country would actually equip soldiers for combat duty with such obsolete firearms and clothing." Upon receiving his uniform on 30 June, an impatient soldier from a unit that had arrived only a week earlier complained that "it's about time . . . we have waited long enough."[11]

The impracticality of the blue wool uniforms in the hot summer was relieved somewhat with the issue of khaki uniforms to some of the regiments. The ir-repressible "Duffy" from the 52nd Iowa noted that this change in colors "was surely a new thing for the boys in blue. They will be boys in brown, 'brownies' in fact." A member of the 3rd Wisconsin explained in a letter home that "the canvas trousers are for work and battalion drills, the blue trousers and blouse for dress uniform." By early June, the supply situation had improved enough for the band master of the 160th Indiana to receive "sample cornet parts of our latest and best military band music" in the mail from a Chattanooga musical instrument company.[12]

FIG. 27: Two unidentified soldiers pose at Camp Thomas, 1898. The uniforms and older-style rifles indicate that these are most likely volunteers. The small howitzer is not the same type as those used for display in the Chickamauga park, which suggests that it is a Spanish-American War period gun. Courtesy of the Chattanooga–Hamilton County Bicentennial Library.

When it came to food at Camp Thomas, the problem was not so much one of quantity as quality. After the initial shock of the first couple of weeks, the Commissary Department, under the leadership of Lt. Col. H. G. Sharpe, began to produce enough of the basics—meat, potatoes, sugar, coffee, canned vegetables, and hardtack—to keep the men fed. Once the bakeries were fully operational, the entire army regularly received fresh bread. The problem was that the fresh pork, beef, and potatoes spoiled quickly if they were not consumed. Even with careful instructions on food storage and preparation, a great deal of food went to waste. Charles Remington wrote that "we get fresh bread and meat for dinner," and noted on 1 June that "the Gov't issues green coffee, rice, and oatmeal now." The easily pleased Dillon reported that "we had fried potatoes, a piece of beef, two hard tacks, and a cup of coffee for breakfast" and a selection of "mutton . . . peas and busquits [sic] for dinner."

A disgruntled member of the 31st Michigan noted in his diary that his plans for "Hamburg steak" fell through because "the ___ cook made and cooked it yesterday and didn't take care of it and it spoiled and all we had was coffee and H.T. [hardtack]." One soldier who had been in camp less than a week complained that "we are recently getting very bad food and very little of it." Another lamented that he "could not make a meal out of bacon and a piece of hardtack with coffee whose odor sickens me" and described loaves of bread "tossed around as they would wood." Responding to complaints about inadequate food supplies, Henry Boynton felt compelled to testify that "there was more food left over in that army at Camp Thomas every day . . . than the Army of the Cumberland had to eat during the entire siege of Chattanooga."[13]

Water was an ongoing concern throughout the camp and continued to be a source of controversy well after the war was over and the camp was closed. The system of wells, pipes, and hydrants that had supplied the Regulars was not sufficient for the amount of water needed in the volunteer camps, so other means had to be employed. Chickamauga Creek and the nearby Crawfish and Blue Springs were obvious sources, but the fact that they were some distance away and, in the case of the springs, on private property, made using them difficult. Hauling water in barrels from the creek allowed for a great deal of spillage and did not produce the most palatable drinking water. One member of an Iowa regiment remembered "water pipes were laid on the ground and water was pumped from a creek . . . we had to use small hand filters to get the sand out of the water." Eventually, the army posted guards at all the nearby springs to prevent damage to the property or the water supply. One enterprising guard detail from the 3rd Wisconsin enjoyed all kinds of provisions, including "ginger snaps . . . cheese . . . and a dozen cookies" because "every wagon that comes near the spring has to pay their tole [sic]" adding parenthetically "not by military regulations, but by ours." When people came to the springs, the soldiers dipped the water out for them, for which they received "a nickel cigar, drink, or something of the sort."[14]

Water would become a major issue when health concerns overwhelmed the camp, its occupants, the park officials, and the public during the months of July and August. In the short term, however, the business of the camp commanders was turning the "mob" that they had inherited into a functioning military organization. Getting the men into tents, uniforms, and equipment was the first step; drilling them in the arts of soldiering was the next task. Even Colonel Daugherty of the 9th Pennsylvania, who believed that the officers in charge of the camp "seemed entirely devoid of administrative and executive ability," conceded that their Regular Army experience "equipped [them] with splendid technical ability." As long as there was a chance that these troops would be sent into combat, they needed to be trained to confront the realities of battle. At the same time, trying to bring discipline to young men stuck in a hot, crowded camp was an uphill battle that was destined to spread from the camp to the community before the summer was over.[15]

Once they were armed and uniformed like soldiers, the men began to fall into the routine of army life. For most of the camp, reveille was at 5:00 A.M., followed by roll call, mess call, and a period of company drill. After a guard mount and lunch, there were regimental drills and school of the soldier, an evening mess, and a dress parade. The final roll call and tattoo came at around 9:00 P.M.; "Taps" was sounded at 9:15. The men did not so much complain about the drills themselves as they did about doing them in the heat of the day. William Mitchell of the 1st New Hampshire wrote in his journal that drill "has been almost evil to my mind in this hot sun." On one occasion, he recorded that after a surprise arms inspection "they chased us over the field at squad drill, forward double time, lie down upon halting, etc. It is all well but in the heat it is pretty hard." Others found some things more aggravating than others. A member of a Michigan unit wrote in his diary "in place of ordinary Co. drill this morning we stacked tents. Orders confused and some roll tents out, others rubber blankets out. All had to have tents out as some fool who has the say about it thinks rubber will crack in the sun." After falling in and falling out again without marching, the exasperated soldier declared "we have had our drill for today."[16]

The usual routines were frequently punctuated by target practice, impressive large-scale dress parades, and mock battles. One lucky cavalry trooper proudly wrote to his mother, "you aught [sic] to see the gun I have. It shoots six times without loading." Most of the infantry soldiers discovered that the older-model Springfield rifled muskets they were issued did not guarantee accurate shooting. Earle Clock of the 52nd Iowa noted in his diary after an eight-mile evening march in the pouring rain to the shooting range that "the score was rather poor on the 200 yd. range" the next day. Private "Duffy" Wands confessed that "the boys . . . did not cover themselves in glory as [he] expected them to." Even the "top sergeant" of the company "could not hit a flock of barns." Like the others, the trip to the range involved a temporary bivouac on a rainy night where "everything was flooded and the little pup tents leaked like sieves."[17]

Even if their shooting did not give them much to brag about, their participation in large unit maneuvers and the sight of masses of troops drawn up in formation impressed the new soldiers. One wrote that after a great cloud of dust had settled on the drill ground "there was the whole division in battalion formation stretched out for a quarter of a mile across the field," adding "it was a great sight and I would have give [sic] a quarter to see the rest." A private in the 3rd Wisconsin recorded later that the unit's first dress parade on the Kelly Field at Chickamauga "was grand, with its memories of other days, and gave us a feeling of exaltation which was inspiring." A giant review of both corps in early July drew 25,000 spectators, including thousands transported to camp on special excursion trains.[18]

If the dress parades were inspiring, the mock battles were downright exhilarating and provided many of the soldiers with their only taste of combat. These "sham" battles, several of which involved "long marches" outside the park boundaries, consisted of tactical situations that required commanders to maneuver their troops, capture enemy positions, and engage in battle using blank powder charges. There were supposedly strict rules for these engagements, but several of these actions became so heated that they had to be called off by the officers for safety reasons.

On one occasion, a captain in the 16th Pennsylvania led a charge against the 1st Ohio and took a powder charge in the face at close range, "inflicting painful and serious injuries." Not surprisingly, "bad blood was engendered by the incident and the men rushed together. It was only by the coolness and presence of mind of officers that bloodshed was averted." The 4th Ohio Infantry also had an encounter with some Pennsylvania troops that resulted in one Ohio sergeant who was "nearly thrust with an artillery saber" before the incident was defused. Some incidents were less intense and more amusing. A member of the 3rd Wisconsin reported that "during a sham battle Captain Newton killed a quail with his sword and brought it back," adding that it "tasted better than anything [he] had ever eaten." For many of these men the mock battles conducted directly on the sacred ground of the Chickamauga battlefield would be as close to the combat experience as they would get.[19]

In general, the first phase of the volunteer mobilization had been reasonably successful. All, however, was not well at Camp Thomas. As a few new regiments and bunches of recruits continued to arrive, no one seemed to be leaving for the front. The stress on the camp's logistics continued to increase, as did the impatience of the soldiers who now felt ready to move on to the next phase of their experience. In the second phase, a combination of elements would create a breakdown in camp discipline leading to tragic consequences for everyone involved. In the process, the memory of the camp, the park, and the battlefield would be profoundly affected.

Beyond the strictly military aspects of their experience, the volunteers at Camp Thomas had the opportunity to engage in a variety of interesting activities during their stay. Some grappled with the strange creatures, the environment, and the local farmers, while others appreciated the battlefield and visited other attractions in the area in their spare time. They enjoyed a host of entertainments, including hazing new recruits, collecting mascots, playing games in camp, and drinking beer. They found themselves the objects of aggressive marketing by merchants, souvenir peddlers, and a variety of wheelers and dealers in an area known as "the Midway" and were eventually drawn toward the bars, brothels, and businesses of nearby Chattanooga. The volunteers

FIG. 28: An infantry regiment conducts maneuvers at Camp Thomas while mule-drawn wagons pass by in the foreground. Courtesy of the Chattanooga History Center.

endured the rigors of the camp and the weather while engaged in numerous distractions. News of U.S. military victories on both land and sea were met with mixed responses. On the one hand, victory was cause for celebration; on the other, it meant that the likelihood of being sent to active duty diminished. This uncertainty proved to be the catalyst for a variety of tribulations leading to the camp's major crisis.

The men at Camp Thomas obsessed about finding ways to entertain themselves in the midst of their hot, crowded camps. They got to experience all kinds of things that they may not have encountered back home. One of these was the army mule. A pamphlet entitled "The Army Mule: A Chronic Kicker" made the rounds at Camp Thomas and celebrated the unique critter in some tongue-in-cheek photo captions as a "comrade in arms," the "angel of the regiment," and "backbone of the republic." In a practical sense, they were the primary means of transportation for food, water, and baggage throughout the park, so that many men had contact with them in one way or another. Several soldiers detailed to the ambulance service got a chance to deal with mules, leading one regimental doctor to complain that "my father didn't send me to college for four years to learn to drive mules."

Handling mules was delicate business and injuries were not uncommon, particularly with both inexperienced mules and handlers. While an expert claimed that "even a stubborn mule will learn to obey a kind master" the prevailing view about the "orn'ry [sic]" creature was "ther' [sic] won't no kindness melt him when he's hitched to army stuff." After getting a mule "out of a snarl" one soldier sarcastically described them as "wonderful animals." Another, apparently driven to his wit's end, ended up in the guardhouse for "sticking a mule with a bayonet."[20]

Like any group of mostly young men kept under military discipline, the soldiers at Camp Thomas took advantage of any opportunity to stretch their legs and see the surrounding area. Private Mitchell was an eager observer of the countryside, noting that in "this hot and often dry climate there is no sense of dampness" as one would find back home. While guarding a small bridge somewhere between Reed's and Alexander Bridges, he learned about the local farming practices from Mr. Reed. He observed that there was "profit" in the small amounts of wheat, corn, fruits, cotton, and vegetables being grown using the simple local methods, and concluded that "an intelligent farmer with industry and a little means might do well here." Overall, the private "enjoyed this experience and learned much from it." Members of the 3rd Wisconsin picked blackberries outside of the camp and on one occasion, two different men appeared before their captain, each with half a pig that some cavalry soldiers had allegedly killed and offered to split with them. Noting that "between them they had the whole pig" an observer concluded "[it] was evident that the cavalry didn't have much to do with the killing." Such forays led to more restrictive rules regarding the men's activities and at least two soldiers were shot by farmers for trying to steal livestock.[21]

The memory of the Civil War and the Battle of Chickamauga was evident all through the camps and in the surrounding countryside as well. The most remarkable sources of memory were the members of various units who had fought in the war on both sides and treated the men to "firsthand accounts" of their experiences in battle. Private Rossiter of the 3rd Wisconsin noted that "it was intensely interesting to get an ex-confederate who had taken part in the fight to go over the ground, point out where he was, and where the 'Yanks' were" and found it reassuring "to know that Colonel Moore had fought on the Northern and Colonel Castleman of the First Kentucky had fought on the Southern side, and here we were brigaded together and the best of friends." Some members of the 4th Ohio who had been in the original battle "would pick out the positions of their regiments in the great battle and relate their experiences . . . to their younger comrades." While on guard duty at the bridge, Private Mitchell noted that Mr. Reed had been a Confederate veteran and that since his own comrades in the 1st New Hampshire "knew little of the history and conditions" surrounding the late war, "their questions were al-most as ludicrous as his answers."[22]

Another way that the soldiers got in touch with the past history of their battlefield camp was searching for relics in and around the park. This was one case where the park officials completely ignored the normal restrictions on removing materials from government property as the men scoured the area for items to send home as mementoes that connected their service to the events of the past. While indicating that "in every part of the park could be picked up parts of rifles, bayonets, pieces of shell, bullets, canon [sic] balls . . . and even human bones," a member of the 4th Ohio added "the trees themselves bore evidence of the fierce struggle . . . which had been played out . . . less than a half century before." Private Wands of the 52nd Iowa reported in a letter to his hometown paper that "the boys put in all their spare time looking for relics." Noting that the best conditions for finding bullets were "after a heavy rain," another soldier reported that "it seemed like a dream to find them." While on an expedition to the shooting ranges outside the park, a member of the 31st Michigan found "a 12 lb. cannon ball and two smaller balls." Within days of ar-riving at the park, Trooper Dillon of the 1st Ohio Cavalry reported that he had found "a piece off [sic] an old bayonett [sic] shield," his buddies had "found two bullets apiece," and exclaimed in his letter that "we are going out after dinner to hunt for more relicks [sic]."[23]

The soldiers found the battlefield's commemorative landscape interesting and spent quite a bit of time examining the "beautiful monuments" throughout the park. Reading about the movements and heroics of the units during the battle led one man to remark that "many a time we thanked a kind fate that we didn't have to fight such men" and that they were "supremely grateful that we are united as we never were before." Photographs illustrating the memoirs of the Spanish-American War 3rd Wisconsin show members of the regiment posed next to the monument of the Civil War 10th Wisconsin with a caption "Wisconsin—then and now." Another shows one of the stacked cannonball monuments with the caption "'The Blue and the Gray.' Where a brave Confed-erate Officer fell," while yet another has a mounted officer posing next to the monument to the 18th U.S. Infantry. Numerous other monuments appear in the background of photographs in this book and in other souvenir booklets published for purchase by both soldier and visitors. One such volume pur-porting to "give nearest a correct idea of what the life of a soldier in camp is made up of" touted the inclusion of photographs of "the most expensive and uniquely designed monuments . . . to be found in no other locality."[24]

The memory connections between the Civil War soldiers and the men at Camp Thomas were emphasized by the physical presence of the monuments, artifacts, and veterans of the battle in and around the park. Their gradual mastery

FIG. 29: A soldier with bugle and drum poses next to a Civil War artillery piece in the Chickamauga and Chattanooga National Military Park. Although labeled "Camp Thomas, 1898," this photo may be postwar, since the soldier seems to be wearing a Spanish-American War service medal. Photo courtesy of the Chattanooga History Center and the 6th Cavalry Museum, Fort Oglethorpe, Ga.

of training, marching, shooting, and skirmishing gave the men in Camp Thomas a sense of accomplishment and enabled them to feel a strong kinship with the men who had fought before them. Following President McKinley's call for an additional 75,000 volunteers on May 26, many units sent officers and men back to their home states to fill out companies and regiments with new men. In addition to bringing in more warm bodies, the recruiters and the rookies provided the men in camp with up-to-date news and packages from home. Interestingly, the process of integrating the recruits into existing regiments gave the newly minted "veterans" a chance to compare themselves with a batch of "rookies" as green as they had been just a month or two before. It also gave them a chance to amuse themselves at the expense of the clueless newcomers.

Not surprisingly, the rookies were hapless foils for the pranks of their new comrades. Ernest "Duffy" Wands of the 52nd Iowa described the ordeal in a speech given shortly after he returned from the war. He details how the rookie's visions of military glory fizzled when he discovered that to his jaded comrades "he was a handy man to have around to do police duty and run errands as he hearkens to the bogus tips given him by a host of willing advisors." Instead of "laying [sic] around the camp fire talking of the glorious deeds to be performed," his evenings were consumed listening to his comrades tell their own brand of horror stories. These consisted of tales "about a captain of another regiment shooting a rookie for not standing up when addressed" or how the rookies would have to care for the fever patients "because it would be better to lose the green men and save the trained ones." After he received his uniform and found that none of his clothes fit, his shoes were too big, and the army would rather adjust his feet to fit the shoes than the other way around, the rookie reluctantly confessed that having endured all of this and "learned to smoke cigarettes and has got a gun . . . now he is a soldier."[25]

It was not only the new men who had to endure a seemingly endless cycle of work that fell under the general categories of "fatigue, police, and kitchen duty." Along with the rookies, men who failed to answer roll call or "violated the thousand one other rules of the camp" frequently ended up on one of these work squads. These details gave the men a chance to "practice shoveling gravel or carrying water or wood," along with being ordered to "dig trenches, clean the officer's streets, police the camp, and do all manner of dirty work." By far the toughest and most odious of these duties was "digging sinks" for latrines or the disposal of other garbage. A soldier in the 4th Ohio observed that "there were sinks from four to seven feet deep for all imaginable purposes and many a hard day's task was required to complete them." Other tasks included routine policing of the camps by picking up trash, trimming brush, or arranging "large piles of stones around trees." Some of the hazards of such work included sunstroke,

FIG. 30: The band of the 1st Pennsylvania Volunteers was one of many regimental bands that tried to keep up morale among the troops at Camp Thomas. Courtesy of the Chattanooga–Hamilton County Bicentennial Library.

poison ivy, and general exhaustion. Not surprisingly, this kind of mundane labor in the hot sun, along with drills, guard duty, and other required activities left many men annoyed and disgruntled. Without the prospect of combat to buoy them, the volunteers chafed under the repetition and monotony of camp life.[26]

There were some wholesome and pleasant activities to keep the men busy. Church services were held regularly under a variety of conditions to meet the spiritual needs of the men. A member of the 31st Michigan reported that "our church tomorrow is to consist of prayer and preaching by our guns." Another soldier attended church on a Sunday in June, followed by "a walk in the country near Crawfish Springs." The Army Christian Commission not only set up tents for worship services, but supplied the men with writing tools and even fishing poles. Correspondents for Christian periodicals reported not only good regular attendance at services, but a "revival" in some units, where scores of men "came forward and declared their acceptance of Christ." There was plenty of secular socializing between the men of both North and South. A member of the 1st Illinois Cavalry wrote "the boys out here are kind to one another," while the diarist from a Michigan regiment spent time at the Young Men's Christian Association (YMCA) tent and described his status as "fat and lazy." In another letter, the Illinois cavalryman wrote home and instructed his friend to "tell Shorty that I enjoy myself and if I was in Chicago, I would smoke his cigars."[27]

Over the course of the summer, the men acquired a variety of mascots and discovered a number of other ways to keep themselves amused. The mascots varied from the usual canines to a goat that "follows his master around like a dog." However, by far the most unusual were the black men and boys that at least one unit "adopted" along the way and kept as mascots throughout its service. The veteran historian of the 3rd Wisconsin recorded matter-of-factly that "'Rastus' our colored mascot joined us at Chickamauga. . . . He simply appeared on the scene as though he had been waiting for us all his life." When the 3rd left Camp Thomas for the Puerto Rican expedition, it was reported that Rastus "went through the whole campaign, and came home with us."

Oddly enough, another soldier from the same unit told of a black "charater [sic]" named "Frank" that they "picked up in Atlanta" on their way to Puerto Rico. In spite of orders to get rid of all mascots before embarking, the men smuggled Frank onto the ship and took him to Puerto Rico, where he served as the regimental scrounger, water fetcher, and hospital aide during the campaign. While the former soldier admitted that taking Frank "was not up to regulations," he rationalized it saying, "we were only 35 years from the Civil War and

FIG. 31: The Camp Thomas theater was owned by local businessmen and located at the intersection of the Lafayette and Brotherton-Lytle roads. It could seat 2,000 people for various programs and performances. Courtesy of the Chattanooga–Hamilton County Bicentennial Library.

Negroes were still chattel." Still, he claimed that all the officers "adored" the man and that after they returned to New York, the unit "collected a substantial bonus for him, gave him a banjo and a bootblack outfit" and set him tearfully out on his own.[28]

Sometimes the men just played. They tossed each other on blankets, visited each other's camps, traded uniform buttons, played baseball, and generally goofed off as much as any young men would in such a situation. They also engaged in games of chance among themselves, the favorite being poker. One soldier noted that there was "quite a little gambling at the guard house" and explained that although the men in the company indulged quite a bit "the stakes [were] in proportion to the government paycheck." One rainy evening found members of the 1st New Hampshire playing "hearts" by the light of "a dimly burning candle," with all of the requisite banter, critiquing, and kibitzing that one would find in any game. The Kentuckians were fond of "craps" and after every payday, "could be found in little groups all over the grounds intensely interested in winning and losing." Had the soldiers been isolated and left to their own devices, they probably would not have gotten into much trouble. However, temptations existed both inside and outside of the camp that would contribute to the overall air of disorder that began to infiltrate the troops.[29]

Visitors were in the camp all the time. Friends and family arrived regularly to visit regiments, companies, and individuals. Although they delivered treats, packages, and news from home, they also made many of the men homesick and unintentionally contributed to the gradual erosion of military decorum in the camp. When there were young ladies involved, the men went out of their way to be attentive. One soldier's efforts to strike up a conversation with a "very pretty dark-eyed girl" involved repeated trips to bring water to her horse. After the soldier was rewarded with a smile and a thank you, an observer concluded "that perseverance is a great thing, and is sure to win . . . although the horse did not really care for that last pailful [sic]" of water. Many of the men kept up "extensive correspondence with the fairer sex" whom they had met en route to camp. In addition to soldiers' families and the locals from Chattanooga who came to watch the drills and dress parades, the visitors included foreign military observers from England, France, Germany, Russia, and even China. In between the familiar faces from home and the distinguished visitors from overseas, there were many exotic things nearby to tempt bored and impressionable young soldiers.[30]

The least detrimental, but still controversial, sources of amusement for many soldiers were the numerous regimental "canteens" that were scattered throughout the camps. Essentially a cross between a sutler's store and an enlisted man's club (and the forerunner of the modern Post Exchange or PX), the canteens offered miscellaneous goods, a variety of nonissue food (sometimes a fully cooked meal), periodicals and newspapers, and occasionally beer. The original idea behind these establishments was to drive the type of unscrupulous, independent merchants who had followed the armies during the Civil War out of the picture and replace them with an internal, unit-run cooperative store. In this way, the soldiers would be less likely to run up large bills, the quality and price of goods could be regulated, and the money would go back into the regimental coffers for a variety of uses. These establishments strictly prohibited gambling, rowdiness, or drunkenness on the premises, and because they were part of the military structure, could be regulated by the camp commander or provost. The soldiers saw the canteens as a blessing; some outside observers considered them a curse.

To the men of the 3rd Wisconsin, the canteen "was a pleasure and a help, where excess was not permitted" and the beer was always cold and refreshing. Another member of the unit used the canteen to get fresh meat, vegetables, and canned food, and agreed that having beer in the canteens was "no problem." Fed up with "raw potatoes and green coffee," Private Remington headed for the Illinois canteen to get a lunch, writing home "that cost me 25 [cents] before I got enough to phase me at all." One of the canteens was housed in a "big circus tent" and claimed to be the largest such establishment in the army. Although the 52nd Iowa had no canteen, one soldier recalled that the boys were able to get beer at the 1st Maine's Canteen and "wine called Mountain Dewdrops" at the canteen run by the 3rd Tennessee, noting "that seemed to be plenty to satisfy all their needs." The 4th Ohio's canteen helped raise funds to pay off the debt from the creation of the regiment's band. The canteens filled a necessary recreational need among the soldiers, and in spite of the presence of low-powered alcohol, these establishments did not lead to a great breakdown in either morale or discipline.[31]

A far more likely culprit was the morass of tents, booths, stands, and businesses that evolved along the Lytle spur and was known as "the Midway" due to its resemblance to the similarly named stretch at fairs and carnivals. Much of the Midway's infamy was the result of its location near the only train depot leading directly into the park. It was virtually the first thing that soldiers and civilians encountered upon their arrival. Before the camp was created, there had been only a modest little depot and few buildings, including a combination grocery and post office, on the site. The army quickly built a large unloading platform, warehouses, and a giant corral as part of its operation. From there, the once quiet area grew into "a very metropolitan, but temporary little city." There were plenty of legitimate businesses set up at Lytle, including "newspaper branch offices, telegraph and express companies, military supply stores,

FIG. 32: The 2nd Nebraska canteen was typical of the regimental sutlers that operated at Camp Thomas. Although less sordid than the merchants on the Midway, the canteens came under attack from reformers for allegedly selling unhealthy food and alcohol to the troops. Courtesy of the Chattanooga History Center.

photographers," a theater, and booths representing local hotels and restaurants. Many of these facilities met some clear and legitimate needs among both the soldiers and civilians, but like many other cities, the flotsam that grew up around them was a far more dubious addition to the camp community.[32]

Along with the legitimate businesses and services came a colorful flock of hucksters, "gambling dens, and all the catch penny-schemes known to the fakir's art." The opportunity to sell to both soldiers and civilians was too much to resist for the purveyors of sweet treats, alcohol, souvenirs, carnival cons, prostitutes, and other such indulgences. Like a frontier town in the western territories, Lytle's Midway grew without much structure, regulation, or management. The result was a wild and wooly place that alternately attracted and horrified the soldiers who encountered it. The always observant Corporal Mitchell gives this account of his trip to Lytle:

It is impossible to describe the impressions that I got there. I have seen a new side of army life, one which I previously knew of but which I had not seen. Men recently paid off crowded around booths where drinks, etc. were for sale. The odor of whiskey was everywhere prevalent; cursing and swearing was the language used. They conversed, those who could, of their debaucheries of whiskey and lewd women. Several were unable to walk. One fellow stood with arms and legs sprawled and waving, drooling from the corners of his mouth, and kept up a continuous flow of words to the edification of his comrades who rejoiced in this noble presence of their . . . friend! . . . It is terrible that man is such a brute. But it is the same old story. To what depth of immorality, vice and aims will wine and women not lead?

Big business did its part. On the Fourth of July, the Pabst Brewing Company sent an entire train car full of beer to the siding at Lytle. Not only had the situation in and around the camp begun to slip, but the aura of disorganization threatened to spread into the nearby city of Chattanooga and to the public beyond.[33]

Many of the men took advantage of General Brooke's initially liberal pass policy to visit the attractions around Chattanooga. They enjoyed "the most magnificent view in the world" while visiting Lookout, Umbrella, and Sunset rocks, along with the Natural Bridge and other wonders. Corporal Mitchell enjoyed the view and his ride in the cable car to the top of the mountain, which cost a total of forty-five cents. Mitchell was impressed with the cleanliness of the city, the quality of its houses, and the politeness of its people, concluding that "I think this section of the country has a future." Unfortunately, not all the soldiers appreciated the finer things in life and looked to the city for more basic entertainment and an escape from army life. More typical were three noncommissioned officers of the 3rd Wisconsin's Company I who went to Chattanooga and "enjoyed their holiday like school boys" but tried to extend their six o'clock deadline to well after midnight. Missing a surprise roll call at evening dress parade led to the discovery of their ruse and resulted in the loss of passes for all three.[34]

Overstaying passes was the least of the problems generated by the soldiers in Chattanooga. As early as 23 May, the local newspaper reported that a provost guard had to be posted in the city because of "the disorderly conduct of many of the young soldiers, who have been guilty of many lapses of discipline, [and] in a number of cases, to violence and insulting language in the streets." Not surprisingly, the men occasionally ran amuck in town, drinking heavily, visiting brothels, and indulging in other bad behavior. In one oft-repeated incident, an officer staying in town woke up one morning to find thirteen drunken soldiers asleep in the street beneath his window. Doctors in the camp hospital found themselves treating increasingly large numbers of venereal disease cases as the summer wore on. When the army attempted to curb the number of men in town by limiting them to two passes a day per company, Chattanooga mayor Edward Watkins protested and urged a more liberal visitation policy, since the soldiers were putting between $15,000 and $20,000 a day into the local economy.

Knowing that the soldiers' stay was temporary certainly must have helped the city fathers decide that the income was well worth the inconvenience.[35]

The balance at Camp Thomas between patriotism, camaraderie, and duty, on the one hand, and boredom, misery, and chaos, on the other, was shifting precariously back and forth by the early days of July 1898. While many regiments and individual soldiers carried out their duties with few problems, a growing number of men found the heat, tedium, and pointless discipline increasingly aggravating. Most of the men found the first month in camp to be an exciting adventure, reinforced by friendly crowds, warm receptions, and the inspiring atmosphere of the Chickamauga battlefield. The memory of the Civil War was all around them, as was the awareness that they were following in the footsteps of brave men from both the North and the South. The spirit of reconciliation that had been a key element in the creation of the park was alive and well among the volunteers in the camp. The soldiers drilled, marched, labored, languished, and kept their morale high based on the hope of being sent to the scene of action.

Ironically, two pieces of good news would serve as the catalyst for more drama in the camp. The first was the American victory at Santiago in early July; the other was the announcement that General Brooke and much of the I Corps would be leaving to participate in operations in Puerto Rico by the middle of the month. For the troops called to active duty, the remaining days at Camp Thomas were filled with activity and anticipation. For the remaining soldiers, the knowledge that the campaign in Cuba was nearly over and their prospects of seeing action were becoming less likely served to undermine their already fragile morale. While the temptations and excesses of town and the Midway continued to corrupt its share of young men, other negative elements entered the picture, thrusting the camp and the park into the public eye once again. The twin demons of disease and death struck the vulnerable army at Chattanooga and added another layer to the complex construction of memory surrounding both wars.

TEN

"What They Will Do with Us Now Is a Mystery"

As June rolled into July 1898, the situation at Camp George H. Thomas could still be viewed by the War Department as a success. In less than three months, it had transported, housed, equipped, fed, and trained over 75,000 regular and volunteer soldiers from all three branches of the army. With the help of Henry Boynton and the park commissioners, the military had converted the commemorative landscape of the Chickamauga and Chattanooga National Military Park into a functional camp and training facility. Although this massive occupation by men, animals, and equipment put stress on the landscape itself, it still fulfilled several of the park's original goals. The thousands of soldiers and civilians who flocked to the camp enthusiastically noted and appreciated the monuments, markers, cannons, and scenic beauty of the preserved battlefield. They posed for photographs, purchased souvenir albums, and wrote about the park to friends and family back home. In addition, many of the soldiers in the park drew inspiration from the enlistment, travel, and training experiences that bonded them to the men of the previous generation who had done many of the same things in the 1860s. The actual presence of Civil War veterans in many of the regiments reinforced this connection and helped construct another layer of memory around the battle and the landscape.

Just as importantly for the veterans, the park, and the soldiers was the knowledge that they were making a valuable contribution to America's war effort. The influence and participation of Civil War veterans from President McKinley, Secretary of War Russell Alger, and Commander of the Army Nelson Miles, on down to the rank and file was direct and visible. The active participation of both Union and Confederate veterans left little doubt that they were playing an important role in the development of both reunion and patriotism. The immediate utilization of Chickamauga Park as the army's main concentration point validated both its symbolic and practical purposes. The arrival of trainloads of troops, cheering crowds, martial music, acres of tents, and the

spectacles of drills and mock battles on the old battlefield were inspiring reminders of the nation's vitality and military tradition. To have the battlefield
resonate once again with the sounds and sights of troops marching under one
flag was gratifying to everyone involved with the park's creation. The Regulars
who had trained in the park early in the war were playing an important role
in the campaign in Cuba. If at least some of the volunteers managed to make
it to the front, the War Department and the commanders of the camp would
have fulfilled their mission and demonstrated the park's value and usefulness.

Unfortunately, the bonds of memory and experience that united the Civil
War veterans and the Spanish-American War volunteers would not withstand
the sequence of events that began to unfold in July 1898. The United States was
winning the war, and doing it more quickly than anyone could have imagined.
While this was undoubtedly good news for the nation, it meant that the troops
training at Chickamauga and other camps like it might be left out of the action.
As a portion of the camp's population shipped out for Puerto Rico, disease, the
scourge of armies throughout history, struck the remaining troops at Camp
Thomas. The health crisis grew within a few weeks from a few isolated cases
to a full-scale epidemic, and led to anger, recriminations, and debate that extended well beyond the confines of the camp. When the victorious army that
conquered Cuba experienced a similar health crisis, the situation at Camp
Thomas became part of a larger debate over the War Department's effectiveness in providing for the well-being of the troops. Ultimately, all of these factors
would come together to produce a set of mixed and contradictory memories
of the Spanish-American War.

The ground campaign in Cuba had proceeded quickly following the landing of American forces under the overall command of Gen. William Shafter at
Daiquiri on 22 June. After establishing a beachhead and supply base at nearby
Siboney, the army marched inland toward Santiago. The army's dismounted
cavalry, under the command of Joe Wheeler (and including Roosevelt's Rough
Riders), fought its first battle at Las Guasimas on 24 June, and the Americans
quickly pushed the Spanish back to the outer defenses of Santiago. A week
later, the army launched a series of attacks on strong Spanish fortifications
on Kettle Hill, San Juan Hill, and the village of El Caney. After fierce fighting,
the Americans, spearheaded by the Rough Riders and the Regulars, captured
these key positions. In spite of this victory, the U.S. position was tenuous. The
troops were ill and exhausted, supplies were short, and rumors of Spanish reinforcements were in the wind. In spite of their success so far, the possibility
of an extended battle or siege was an alarming prospect to the American commanders in Cuba.

The issue was decided within days by the U.S. Navy, albeit much to everyone's surprise. On the morning of 3 July, while the fleet's commander,

William Sampson, was ashore conferring with General Shafter, the Spanish naval squadron that had been bottled up in Santiago harbor made a run for it. In a battle even more one-sided than Dewey's victory at Manila, the American ships reduced their slower, under-gunned Spanish counterparts into shattered, flaming hulks within a few hours. By the time Admiral Sampson returned to his flagship, his second-in-command, Commodore Winfield Scott Schley, was already in the process of mopping up the remnants of the once-vaunted Spanish Atlantic armada. The rest of the day saw much of the American fleet engaged in the rescue of hundreds of Spanish survivors, saving many of them from drowning, being eaten by sharks, or falling victim to Cuban sharpshooters. Drawing on a bit of hyperbole, historian Frank Freidel described the overwhelming naval triumph as "one of the most momentous days in the history of the United States."[1]

News of the navy's victory reached most of the nation on 4 July, and its conjunction with the celebration of Independence Day triggered frenzied demonstrations across the country. The loss of their fleet virtually assured the fall of Santiago, which in turn meant that the Spanish no longer had the ability to hold Cuba. In other words, the war's end was already in sight. Prior to the news of the navy's great accomplishment, the men at Camp Thomas had already spent the night of 2–3 July celebrating the army's triumph at San Juan Hill. Local newspapers reported "twenty-thousand men out in their nighties . . . struggling along the road singing national airs and cheering." The spirit of sectional harmony was duly noted as "northern bands played southern airs and southern bands returned the compliment" while the commanders of various units embraced and gave "rousing speeches." The report concluded by exclaiming that "the whole camp was wild for a time."[2]

When word of the destruction of the enemy's navy arrived at Chickamauga Park two days later, it led many soldiers to believe that they would soon be relieved of their military obligations. Earle Clock noted in his diary on 5 July that "[t]he news of [Sampson's] victory reached us and the boys are happy and talk of going home at once." On 6 July, another soldier wrote, "I hope Sampson's great victory is the beginning of the end of this war," and added cryptically "what they will do with us now is a mystery." For many of the men waiting in the wings at Camp Thomas, the stunning sequence of events in Cuba left them wondering if they would have any role at all in what was rapidly evolving into a great national triumph.[3]

However, a significant number of soldiers in the camp were going to get their chance to contribute, whether they liked it or not. As early as 25 June, it became known that some 15,000 men from Camp Thomas would be mobilized and transported during the next few weeks to either reinforce Shafter or participate in an expedition to Puerto Rico. This opportunity arose chiefly because General Shafter reported that the forces currently in Cuba were in no shape to take on another operation, thus allowing the War Department to call on its volunteer reserve for this mission. Another important development regarding this movement was Secretary of War Alger's decision to transport troops by rail to New York City; Newport News, Virginia; or Charleston, South Carolina, before shipping them out to reinforce Shafter or head to Puerto Rico. The reason for this move was based largely on the problems experienced by the original Cuban invasion force with the port of Tampa. The city was served by only one railroad line, which had caused massive delays as troops and supplies were caught in the bottleneck leading into the port. The move to more northern ports would also allow the War Department to gather and upgrade additional transport ships, while preventing the waiting troops from suffering in the tropical Florida heat any longer than necessary.

Another factor affecting the troops at Camp Thomas was the War Department's decision to forward the Puerto Rican expedition forces to their respective ports a brigade at a time. This meant that there would be no mass exodus from Camp Thomas. Instead, the selected units would depart gradually, thus avoiding the chaos that accompanied their arrival two months earlier. It also meant that they would not have to wait at the ports for more than a few days before boarding the newly outfitted transports and heading to their destinations. However, this system caused the inevitable "hurry up and wait" element that plagued the soldiers for days and weeks prior to their actual departure. On 5 July, orders that would have sent the six "best-equipped" regiments to the front were apparently "rescinded" by the War Department in spite of the fact that the trains were ready to be loaded on the siding at Lytle.[4]

Between the first inklings of the move at the end of June and the big transfer of most of the I Corps in late July, there were many false alarms, premature preparations, and an endless number of rumors floating around the park. All of this added to the air of anxiety within the already active and excitable camps. The anticipation was further heightened when news of the surrender of Santiago reached the men on 17 July. One soldier reported that "the receipt of this great news was the occasion of great demonstrations in Chickamauga Park" in the form of impromptu parades, serenades, speeches, and plenty of cheering. He also noted that "after all had quieted down, the men went to their tents to drown their sorrow at not being able to help." As it turned out, he was one of the lucky ones. After a seemingly endless pattern of "issuing and immediately revoking orders," his regiment, the 4th Ohio, was "directed to proceed through Lexington, Kentucky, to Newport News, Virginia, where transportation would be waiting to take the regiment to Porto Rico [sic]." When it was finally clear that they were really going, the soldier wrote, "no one was to be left behind on this expedition and everybody was happy."[5]

Although the transfer of significant numbers of troops to points of departure for the front was an exciting development, it did not change the reality of the situation at Camp Thomas. It was clear from the start that at best, only the I Corps was slated to make this move. A few volunteer units had left the camp for Cuba prior to this recent mobilization, but once General Brooke and the I Corps' 1st and 2nd Divisions—fifteen regiments in all—were dispatched to Puerto Rico, no one expected another major transfer to take place.[6] Even within the I Corps, there was "great apprehension . . . that portions of it may be left behind," and if that were the case, "the disappointment would almost be crushing." With the war rapidly coming to an end and the prospects of duty at the front dwindling, the remaining soldiers "were tired of the routine of camp life and longing for some more thrilling incidents." Many were simply ready to go home. The conditions that they had endured up to this point had been made tolerable by the excitement, novelty, and heroic expectations that the mostly young volunteers had carried with them on the trains into Chickamauga Park. Those elements were no longer able to counter the boredom, discouragement, and sickness that began to sweep through the camp. The only thing keeping morale in the camp afloat was the prospect of deployment to the front, and that possibility was sinking rapidly with each passing day.[7]

For some of those fortunate enough to go, the Puerto Rico experience rekindled their sense of accomplishment and gave meaning to their time in the service. It was not easy, but at least it was better than languishing, and perhaps dying, in a stateside camp. The 3rd Wisconsin, one of the earliest units to leave Camp Thomas, experienced a hot, tedious, two-week layover in "glorious, hospitable Charleston" waiting for transports before being sent to Puerto Rico. They arrived on 27 July, along with 1st Division commander James Wilson, and participated in several skirmishes during the brief, successful campaign. One member of the regiment "came down with malaria the second day after . . . landing" and reported that "we had dysentery all the time we was in [sic] the island." Since they arrived ahead of the hospital ship, he reported that "the boys set up a tent and shifted for themselves" and that "all we had for medicine was whiskey." In spite of the onset of "malaria, typhoid, and yellow jack," he stated, "we got goat milk and hardtack and all pulled through."[8]

After a short delay awaiting transports, the 4th Ohio departed Newport News on the *St. Paul* and, after a voyage marked by much seasickness, arrived in Puerto Rico on 3 August. The regiment took a prominent role in an assault on Spanish positions at Guayama, which led to the capture of the town of Coamo. After the cease-fire on 13 August, the regiment occupied a "miserable" camp at Guayama and endured a considerable amount of sickness caused by "the absence of proper food, the change in climate, homesickness, and the indulgence in the use of native fruits and pastry." The 4th remained in Puerto Rico

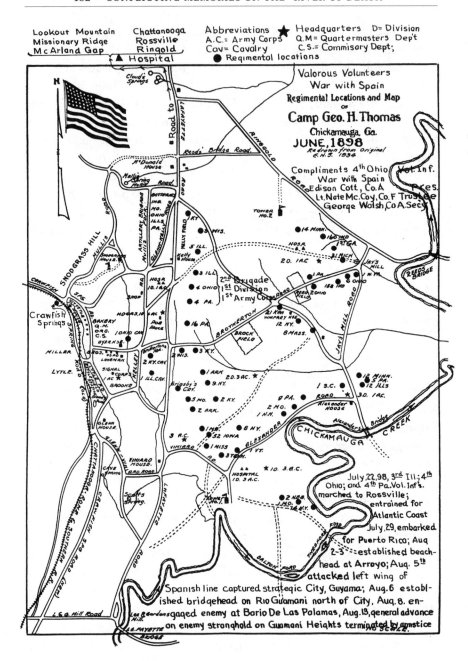

FIG. 33: A copy of a map of Camp Thomas showing regimental positions, with details of the 4th Ohio Infantry's service added. Most of the camps were located on the heavily wooded eastern section of the park where the fighting took place on 19 September 1863. The more open second day's field was used for support units and drill. From the author's collection.

as part of an occupation force and established several different camps until early October, when it was sent home following the disbandment of the 2nd Brigade. In reference to the regiment's performance in the campaign, one veteran proudly noted that its brigade commander "had watched the Fourth Ohio all through its training at Chickamauga Park . . . and had learned to know that they were made of the stuff that goes where duty calls." He went on to claim that following their baptism of fire at Guayama, the general "freely announced that he could trust any officer or man in the regiment with any duty which falls to the lot of a soldier."[9]

Not all the volunteers who departed for the front exulted in the opportunity. After a "prosperous" voyage from Newport News to the islands on the transport *Massachusetts*, Corporal Mitchell, who had been transferred to the 1st Division Ambulance Reserve, had nothing good to say about the rest of the experience. On 4 August, their ship had been "foolishly" run aground on a reef just short of its destination. After spending twenty-four hours unsuccessfully trying to free it, those in charge finally allowed the men to unload. Mitchell lamented the "incompetency [*sic*] in management from head to foot, from major to steward" that had characterized "our whole trip from Chickamauga." The members of the ambulance corps also stayed in Puerto Rico as part of the occupation force and were still there "as orderlies to the civilian drivers" on 3 November, when the corporal expressed his frustration: "It is an exact repetition of our life at Chickamauga. No system, no organization, no place for clothing or to sleep, little and poor food, and much misery. . . . If it were the beginning of the war I could understand it; but if they are not organized and settled by this time, when will they be? It would be a great pleasure to know definitely when we are to go home or what is to be done with us. No one seems to know yet where we are needed." As the war came to an end, the organizational problems encountered by the soldiers both in the camps and overseas gradually generated an increasing amount of controversy. The debate surrounding these issues eventually challenged the notion that it had indeed been a "splendid" war for all the men in the ranks.[10]

Even as the war wound down, there was still hope that other state units might be needed or used in the Caribbean. Throughout the month of July, recently organized companies of the 4th Tennessee and 6th U.S. Volunteer Infantry regiments had been training and preparing for future service at Camp Bob Taylor and Camp Wilder near Knoxville. Many at Camp Thomas grumbled that there was "discrimination" in the choices of regiments sent to active duty. In an attempt to pacify the governors of various states who wanted to see their troops take part in the war overseas, the War Department authorized the creation of a special division made up of units from several camps whose states were not represented. The plan was to use these troops to reinforce General Miles in Puerto Rico, and it included several regiments, from states such as Maine and Indiana, that were currently stationed at Camp Thomas. Unfortunately, General Miles notified the War Department on 10 August that no more troops would be required for this operation; thus none of these troops got much beyond the camps located near the various stateside ports, if they got that far.[11]

General Miles's suspension of further troop deployments predated a general armistice with Spain by less than a week. Barring a breakdown in the treaty negotiations, the war in the Caribbean was essentially over on 13 August 1898. If the remaining 45,000 men in Camp Thomas retained any hopes of seeing action, they were now clearly out of luck. Not only were the remaining regiments and batteries not going to the front, they were not leaving Camp Thomas immediately, either. Since there might be a need for replacements or occupation troops during the period following the cease-fire, the War Department was understandably reluctant to prematurely demobilize its entire volunteer reserve. Thus, the men at Camp Thomas faced the worst possible scenario. The war was essentially over, they were no longer needed at the front, and their camps were being overrun by sickness at an alarming rate. Unfortunately for everyone involved, the events of the next few weeks would serve to taint the nation's victory and soil the reputation of the camp, its commanders, the War Department, and the park.[12]

Sickness and death were not unusual in the lives of armies and soldiers. After all, more men had died of disease in the Civil War than had been killed by bullets and shells. A few illnesses, accidents, and deaths seemed a perfectly natural consequence of taking thousands of men from their homes and environments, transporting them hundreds of miles, cramming them together in camps, and compelling them to march, drill, sleep, and live in all kinds of weather. Although any noncombat losses were regrettable, what most military commanders really feared was the widespread outbreak of diseases like influenza, malaria, smallpox, dysentery, typhoid, or yellow fever that physically and mentally crippled soldiers, regiments, and armies. Although medical technology had improved quite a bit since the Civil War, the threat of epidemics still hung heavily over every army that took the field.[13]

There were plenty of everyday sicknesses and injuries floating around Camp Thomas prior to the mid-summer health crisis. Earle Clock recorded in his diary on 3 June that "three men [were] overcome by heat . . . yesterday and one man had his head peeled back by a horse." Corporal Mitchell suffered from what he called "the Frenchman trots" shortly after arriving at Camp Thomas; this bout of diarrhea knocked him out of the ranks for several days and took a week to clear up. A member of a Michigan regiment wrote in his diary that his "heel was so badly blistered" he could not drill or even stand in formation. Members of a company in the 52nd Iowa enjoyed general good health other than a few cases of measles and the ever-present diarrhea, which was shrugged off as nothing more than "the usual complaint." One divisional surgeon reported that most of the illnesses were minor and caused by poor food preparation and catching chills in the evening after working up a sweat during the day. He felt that as the men became more accustomed to the work and demands of military life, their health would improve if they adopted the proper diet and modified their behavior. Notwithstanding the minor aches and pains, he felt that "this camp is a thoroughly healthy place."[14]

The unexpected deaths of soldiers in camp obviously attracted far more attention than injuries and illnesses, but if isolated and few in number were rarely cause for alarm. In addition to the previously mentioned fatalities caused by a train accident and a heart attack, there were other deaths in the camp prior to the onset of serious disease problems. Within a week of arriving, three northern volunteers died at Camp Thomas. Two young men expired from pneumonia contracted before they came to Chattanooga; the third, a member of the 5th Illinois, died of blood poisoning. A soldier writing in June reported that "six deaths have been the result of drowning" but that there had been fewer than three a week from other causes. A soldier in the 1st South Carolina died after drinking moonshine that allegedly had "eaten holes in the unfortunate man's stomach." In July, another member of the 5th Illinois died suddenly from "peritonitis caused by eating unripe fruit." While this last death could possibly be connected to camp food issues, the others were largely circumstantial to the victim's military service. For much of the early summer, the health problems in the camp were described by the camp surgeons as "inconsequential."[15]

The army attempted to head off some disease problems by weeding out the unfit recruits and inoculating all the volunteers against smallpox after they arrived at Camp Thomas. Most of the preliminary physical exams were conducted in the state camps before the units departed for their assignments. In the 52nd Iowa, twenty-three men out of one company of seventy-two were rejected before leaving "Camp McKinley" in their home state. The regiment's unofficial commentator, "Duffy," reported that there were some tense moments among the officers during their physicals; their tall, thin, middle-aged major failed his exam in spite of drinking extra water to gain weight and "humping his shoulders so as to be shorter." During the recruiting process in Knoxville for the local Tennessee regiments, many people expressed concern that the exams were "too rigid," resulting in a 30 to 40 percent rejection rate. This meant that some "able-bodied men" who had been members of National

Guard companies could not serve and had to be replaced with "fresh fish." A few local Civil War veterans weighed in by claiming that their medical exams back in 1861 had been far less stringent but they turned out fine once they had gotten accustomed to life in the field.[16]

Although most saw the necessity of the mandatory inoculations, few soldiers found the experience very reassuring. Following their vaccinations, some members of the 3rd Wisconsin complained of "a great variety of aches and pains," including one man "having [such] a terrible time" with the side effects that he had to spend time in the hospital. The 52nd Iowa received its vaccinations in mid-June, and not surprisingly, Private Wands found humor in the experience, especially when it concerned the new recruits. As the poor, put-upon "rookie" was about to receive his vaccination "he hears of seven men who died from blood poisoning and about the fellows in the cow boy [sic] cavalry who lost their arms . . . [and] if a man was not careful, the maggots would get in the sore and he would die of lockjaw." His greatest fear was "that he will faint, and that will be pleasing to all his admirers for it will be something new to guy [sic] him about." Duffy's lighthearted observations notwithstanding, the government's attempts to protect the men from epidemic diseases were sincere and ongoing. First Division surgeon John Woodbury indicated that although there were short-term side effects among some of the men, "the virus used [for the vaccinations] was entirely bovine and of the best quality."[17]

The onset of serious health problems at Camp Thomas did not happen overnight. Like most situations involving disease, the rate of sickness increased proportionally to the number of people involved and the length of time they spent in close proximity to one another. As has already been noted, some of the units that left the camp in July were already suffering from some sicknesses that surfaced once they arrived in Puerto Rico and continued throughout their tour of duty. But the men at Camp Thomas who suffered the most from the escalation of debilitating illnesses were those left behind in the stifling August heat and humidity. While it is difficult to pinpoint exactly, the correlation between the soldiers' morale, behavior, and the spread and severity of sickness was apparent to many contemporary observers and generated a great deal of controversy. It is also important to note that similar sicknesses infected American troops in other training camps, in Cuba, the Philippines, and Puerto Rico; thus, Camp Thomas was not an isolated incident, but part of a larger, national problem.[18]

The typhoid fever outbreak in Camp Thomas challenged the endurance of the troops and the War Department's responsibility to respond to the crisis. The public perception that the soldiers were victims of the government's malfeasance raised serious doubts about the value of the war and the costs and

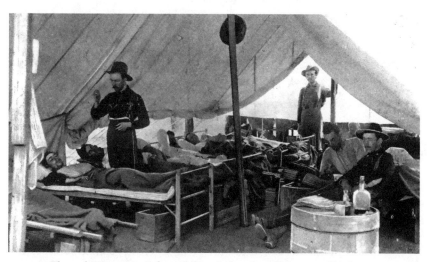

FIG. 34: The 3rd Wisconsin Infantry's hospital at Camp Thomas, Chickamauga Park, 1898. The crowded, primitive conditions were typical of the regimental hospitals, which often were staffed with only one "surgeon" and a variety of concerned, but mostly unskilled, comrades. Courtesy of the Chattanooga History Center.

benefits of victory. The health crisis that swept the American military both stateside and in the Caribbean undermined the heroic rhetoric of victory and partially repudiated the Victorian notions of manhood and the "good" death. Once the volunteers, press, and public got over the giddy euphoria of victory, they were left with a growing sense that the war had been something less than the glorious experience they had imagined and bore little resemblance to memories of the legendary Civil War past.

ELEVEN

"Ground Unfit for Men to Live On"

Death is an inevitable consequence of war and the key element in the construction of war memories. Unlike the Civil War, where the combined casualties from wounds, combat, and disease accumulated over a four-year period, the War with Spain produced a disproportionate number of fatalities due to sickness in a very short stretch of time. To make matters worse, many soldiers suffered and died in the stateside camps like the one at Chickamauga, where supplies, medical care, and government oversight might have reduced or prevented the catastrophe. While the malaria-related tribulations of the army in Cuba might have been tolerated in light of the quick victory, the squalor and misery at Camp Thomas contradicted the established ideals of heroic suffering and the popular notion of a "good death." The way that the disease scandal unfolded during the summer of 1898 and the responses it brought forth from the troops, press, public, veterans, and War Department served to shatter the connection between the memories of the Civil War and those constructed during the War with Spain.

Although there were a number of deaths from other causes, the number one killer of soldiers in the Spanish-American War was typhoid fever. Of the 1,832 soldiers who died of disease in the war, 1,590 of those deaths were attributed to typhoid fever. The shocking 761 deaths from this disease at Camp Thomas amounted to the highest single total among all the major army concentrations and nearly half the overall number of typhoid deaths during the whole war. Ironically, the identification of this particular fever and its causes was one of the most important medical discoveries that took place after the Civil War. Not only had scientists identified typhus as being similar to other fevers and poxes in its mode of transmission, they had also determined its connection to sanitary conditions, particularly those having to do with human waste. The War Department had anticipated the problem of typhoid fever prior to the outbreak of the conflict with Spain and had taken steps to prevent it from infecting and killing large numbers of soldiers in the camps. The apparent failure of this policy led to a great deal of public controversy and finger-pointing after the war, much of it surrounding the specific conditions at Camp Thomas. Although there ended up being a strong consensus as to the ultimate reason the epidemic erupted at Chickamauga, the circuitous route the debate traveled had a powerful effect on the memory of both the war and the camp for many people.[1]

When it came to attaching blame for this catastrophic turn of events, there were essentially three schools of thought. The one put forth by Christian groups, the Red Cross, some military officials, and other civilian organizations placed the blame on the Army canteens and Midway vendors for providing beer, tobacco, and other unhealthy food to the troops. While the army tended to agree that the products peddled on the Midway were detrimental, it defended the canteens and expanded the list of forbidden foods to include the "care packages" sent from home. The second major theory put the burden on the War Department, blaming it for issuing poor food, supplying impure water, crowding the troops into an "unhealthy" environment (including the geological landscape itself), and providing inadequate medical care at Camp Thomas. Not only did the War Department strongly disagree that these were the sources of the problems, it countered this charge by blaming the volunteers themselves. According to this line of thinking, the volunteers carelessly violated the Army's specific sanitation rules and by doing so spawned disease and death in a filthy environment of their own making. Ultimately, the report issued by Dr. Walter Reed and his team of medical experts upheld parts of the latter two theories but added a few twists of its own.

The attack on the canteens tied the problem of disease to the moral decline caused by alcohol, gambling, and overall decadence in and around the camp. The scientific basis for this connection was dubious at best, but in the atmosphere of outrage that accompanied the scandal, it made for a compelling case. For the Christian clergy and missionaries who visited the camp, the government's tacit sponsorship of alcohol, tobacco, and the accompanying evils in the canteens was inexcusable. Several postwar articles claimed that there were fifty canteens at Camp Thomas plying beverages and debauchery. In their minds, the ready availability of alcohol had "a demoralizing influence" on the soldiers and served as "an unmitigated curse to the army." According to canteen opponents, the presence of alcohol caused them to "dawdle in their duties . . . resent the severities of discipline, and often to pay the penalty for their debauch in the guardhouse." The canteens contributed to disease by eroding their physical well-being and depriving them of "athletic conditions that fit men to 'endure hardiness as good soldiers.'"[2]

The exaggeration of the number of canteens most likely stemmed from the presence of non-canteen "refreshment" booths on the Midway at Lytle. One writer claimed that some canteens were run by the brewers, but it is unlikely that these were operated by military personnel. Well-meaning missionaries hoped to dissuade men from drinking in these establishments by offering ice water, lemonade, and religious revivals as alternatives. One article claimed that after "great spiritual work" one regimental canteen's beer revenue dropped from $180 to $125 per day "and has since closed entirely." One anti-canteen advocate had to admit that the regulated sale of beer by canteens was preferable to "a vile compound known as 'boot leg moonshine'" that some soldiers turned to for recreation. Yet, pressure from organizations like the Women's Christian Temperance Union to restrict or close the canteens mounted as the summer went on. On 13 July, General Brooke sent out a press release that reiterated the positive role that regimental canteens played and the small amounts of beer, cigars, and tobacco they dispensed. He promised to supervise them, but would not close them. One member of the 3rd Wisconsin reported that "our company was allowed a canteen . . . but a lady organization got to Sect. of War Alger and it was cancelled."[3]

In spite of its appeal to certain civilian organizations, the canteen issue was a "red herring" that had very little to do with the spread of typhoid fever and the deaths that resulted from it. It did, however, stem from the desire on the part of many people to do something about the overall conditions of the camp. The military authorities got caught up in this impulse with their attempts to control the flow of food and drink coming to the soldiers from both the Midway and in "care packages" from home. For the army, it was all about quality control. Soldiers' complaints about the army food notwithstanding, the general consensus among most military personnel was that it was sufficient for the maintenance of general good health. On the other hand, the unregulated fruits, pies, "pop," booze, and other substances being peddled by "the dirty fringe of fly-by-night saloons, greasy restaurants, gambling dens, and bordellos" on the Midway were seen as a menace to both good order and the digestive tracts of the men. Attempts to control the flow of goods passing through the shops at Lytle were only partially successful. One soldier detailed to "search the sutlers" ended up procuring some of the confiscated goodies for himself; he noted that, more often than not, "that bulge in the coat pocket was overlooked."

The same applied to the "care packages" sent from home or delivered by well-intentioned visitors. Upon hearing that the boys were "starving" in camp, the folks at home sent sweets and treats that the army considered unhealthy. As a result of this policy, "as fast as the express wagons would deliver the loads of boxes of pies, cakes, and pastry, the regimental surgeons would dump it into a sink dug expressly for that purpose." One soldier came to the conclusion that, as unappealing as army food was, "the addition of desserts promiscuously selected [was] not conducive to the best results of a military camp." Another sol-

FIG. 35: The notorious Midway at Lytle Station, Camp Thomas, 1898. Note how close the Midway was to the train tracks and the variety of legitimate businesses catering to the troops, including M. C. Lilley & Company, Aunt Jemima's Pancake Kitchen, Jacob Reed's Sons, and the Chattanooga Restaurant. Courtesy of the Chattanooga–Hamilton County Bicentennial Library.

dier agreed, writing that "it would really be better for the boys if their friends would stop sending them pastries and knickknacks, for we have observed that when a box comes from home sickness is more prevalent among those who receive it." Even basic staples like milk were the subjects of controversy. The army did not supply it as part of its ration, so the men sought it elsewhere. One soldier purchased milk from a merchant that was so "thin and bitter" that he "downed half and threw the rest away." Others bought it as a treat and found it satisfactory. The Red Cross, in its ongoing effort to improve the lot of the soldiers, particularly those in the hospitals, worked "to get a sufficient quantity of good, pure milk and deliver it [to Camp Thomas] . . . in good condition."[4]

Putting the blame on army food was just another element that clouded the true causes of the disease epidemics. The soldiers' complaints about the quality of the food and the methods of preparation have already been noted in a previous chapter. What changed in the months after the epidemic were the connections made between the poor food, the corresponding weakened condition of the men, and the spread of disease throughout the army. As will be seen, it seems pretty clear that aside from sanitary issues that affected food preparation, the rations at Camp Thomas were not a major cause of disease among the troops. In all likelihood, the lingering memory of bad food at Chickamauga

FIG. 36: One of the many sutlers located on the Midway at Camp Thomas, 1898. These merchants peddled food and alcohol along with offering other forms of entertainment to the troops. Courtesy of the Chattanooga History Center.

was tied to the "beef scandal" that swirled around the press, Congress, and War Department in the months after the war. At the center of the controversy was the "canned fresh roast beef" that was issued to the troops in the field during much of the war. The debate over this product, which was not a staple at Camp Thomas, will be discussed in the next chapter, but suffice it to say, it influenced the pervasive memory of poor-quality food that found its way into the Camp Thomas disease narrative.

For the most part, claims by soldiers, church groups, and civic organizations that alcohol, debauchery, climate, and bad food had helped foster the diseases that ravaged Camp Thomas were unfounded. Yet, the false causation would not go away. During the government's investigation of the health problems at Camp Thomas, the camp's chief quartermaster reinforced this theory by stating that "the contiguity of Chattanooga, with its saloons, and the freedom with which the selling of pies, cake and beer in the camp was permitted was a far more prolific cause of disease . . . [than] any other cause that has been suggested." His statements were quoted in a Christian publication and seemed to support the view that the army's laxity in moral and behavioral issues was at the center of the problem. Notwithstanding the scientific evidence to the contrary, the image of an epidemic sweeping through an out-of-control camp had a significant effect on the collective memories of many Americans.[5]

Although it is fairly easy to dismiss claims that food and boozing were responsible for the typhoid epidemic, the theory that the camp's supply of drinking water had something to do with it hits much closer to the mark. There had been concerns about both the quantity and quality of the park's water since the beginning of the army's occupation. Park officials had augmented the regular water supply by digging additional wells prior to the arrival of the regulars. When the volunteers filled the camp, the camp's administrators added more wells and installed a pumping system that drew water from Chickamauga Creek through a series of aboveground pipes leading to various parts of the camp. In addition, water was hauled in barrels or drawn directly from the creek or nearby springs at Jay's Mill, Blue Spring, and Crawfish Spring by the units that were camped closest to those sources.

Although the heat and dust were a constant source of discomfort to those in the camp during May and early June, there was plenty of rain later in the month and into July that more or less remedied the drought-like conditions. Thus, the creeks and springs ran at normal capacity and were never in danger of drying up during the course of the army's occupation. Unlike the situation in September 1863, Chickamauga Creek was not isolated behind enemy lines or under hostile fire, which had made fresh water virtually inaccessible to most of the men on both sides. Indeed, the early choice of Chickamauga Park for the camp's location included an adequate water supply as one of its positive attributes. Thus, there was not an overall lack of water available to the camp; rather, there was a consistent shortage of *potable* water that could be safely consumed by the men. Narrowing the water issue down to a question of quality rather than quantity actually complicated the process of attaching responsibility for the disease situation in the camp.[6]

Once again, there were multiple ways to look at the role of water in the deadly outbreak of typhoid fever at Camp Thomas. One line of thinking blamed both the water and landscape for causing the problem by implying that the water in the creek, the wells, and the surrounding low ground was inherently impure. The significant offshoot of this theory was that the whole park and area surrounding it was "unhealthy" and should never have been used in the first place. A second variation on this approach argued that even if the water was not bad at the source, the army's methods of distributing it to the men were flawed and thus led to the outbreak of disease. The most compelling and ultimately convincing theory was that the waste from the numerous camps polluted the water supply and perpetuated the spread of disease. One interesting consequence of this theory was the realization that the soldiers, not the landscape, the park, or the army, may have caused much of the problem.

In the months after the war, veterans of several New England regiments responded to a survey by the Massachusetts Reform Committee that asked specific questions about rations, clothing, water, supplies, and any specific "conditions of hardship" that existed in the camps they had occupied. Several replied to these questions with specific remarks about the water. A company officer in the 1st New Hampshire reported that "when we first arrived in Chickamauga, [we] were obliged to dig shallow wells to get drinking water," which was later supplemented by water "hauled from springs outside the park." He described his men eventually filtering and drinking the creek water and concluded that "it was impure water that was the cause of much sickness." He also added a bit of ammunition to the notion that the men's needs had not been adequately met by claiming that "many times we were without water for a whole day, and [it] caused much suffering."

A staff officer from the same regiment reported that when they arrived at the park "nothing was said as to the condition of the drinking water" so "the officers and men drank from the creeks" without hesitation. He speculated that because the water was "saturated with lime, it immediately produced a bad effect on systems accustomed to pure New England water." According to another report, this led to "acute diarrhea" among many men from "drinking filthy surface water." He charged that the army did nothing to improve the quality of the drinking water "until it was suspected that typhoid germs might be in it." The subsequent policy that required the men to boil water that was hauled from the creek in barrels led to shortages and days where the men "suffered for the want of water." While he acknowledged that the men may have wasted some water at times "and drank from streams from which orders were given that no man should drink," he still shifted most of the blame to the officers in charge. Noting that there was no enforcement of the boiling mandate, he concluded that "the order practically amounted to nothing." The 1st New Hampshire's regimental surgeon concurred, noting that the order was "nearly impossible to carry out" until they were issued enough boilers and barrels.[7]

Another regiment hit hard by disease in Camp Thomas was the 1st Vermont Infantry. According to its historian, this unit's "indescribable miseries" were due in general to "the Nation's neglect," and more specifically to "heat, poor water, typhoid fever, dysentery, [and] disgusting food." According to numerous reports from officers of this unit, "water mains were not laid into camp until well into the summer," which limited each company to one barrel of creek water a day. Although the water eventually provided by the pipes was deemed "sufficient," it "was most unwholesome, if not actually polluted, rendering the tedious processes of filtering and boiling necessary." A captain of the regiment recalled the men hauling water for miles, which forced them to "drink any water they could get." Yet another company officer confirmed the long distances required to fetch water both before and after the laying of the pipeline and reported that "after July 1, water was boiled." Other testimony echoed the overall impression that both the limited availability of good water and "indiscreet use of poor water" were key factors in the regiment's health problems.[8]

Those who blamed the water were only partially right. Water contributed to the disease problem at Camp Thomas, but was not the cause of it. The Army's belated attempt to stem the tide of sickness by mandating that drinking water be boiled seemed to be damning evidence that the problem rested with the water supply. Yet, like its attempts to control alcohol or regulate the quality of food, the army was trying to do something in the face of a growing situation that it had already (unsuccessfully) done a great deal to try to prevent. The army was well aware that drinking ground water from random and unregulated creeks, puddles, and springs was a bad idea; its elaborate system for hauling water to the camps from pure sources bears this out. The poor taste and appearance of the piped-in water was not an indication of its un-healthfulness; nor was the coldness or clarity of water a sign that it was safe. One perceptive soldier noted that after a long hot march to Crawfish Springs, the men eagerly drank from the "cool, pure" gurgling spring. However, he noted that "it did not seem good to drink one's fill of water without a thought of the disease germs it contained." The inability of the officers to compel their men to boil water even after the threat of disease was imminent was an indication of the real problem confronting the camp: making volunteer soldiers to do what they were told.[9]

After considerable investigation, the Reed Commission report determined that "infected water was not an important factor in the spread of typhoid fever," thus effectively neutralizing the argument that the camp did not supply safe water. The report did concede that "some of the local water supplies at Chickamauga became specifically contaminated" with the typhoid *bacillus*, but only after the disease had been transmitted to the men by other means. Troops that drew water from sources that were easily contaminated, like "wet weather springs" (essentially puddles) and from the creek, after it had been exposed to fecal runoff, were undoubtedly drinking contaminated water. But studies of the wells in the park conducted by the park staff and the Reed Commission's own scientists in the months after the camp was abandoned found very little contamination. In addition, troops moved to other camps continued to get sick, in spite of the clean water in those locations. It was also clear that the lack of typhoid fever among civilians who regularly used these sources of water before and after occupation meant that the disease was being spread in a specific way within a specific constituency—not simply by drinking "bad" water.[10]

The subtle distinction between causes and catalysts was one that got lost in the construction of memory regarding the typhoid epidemic at Camp Thomas. Once the men who suffered through the heat, the unpleasant food, "the filthy drinking and cooking water," and the seemingly heartless rigors of military life decided that the army, the park, and the government were to blame, there was not much that would change their minds. From a strictly scientific standpoint, neither food nor water caused the typhoid epidemic, although both were somewhat responsible for its rapid dissemination throughout the camp once it was infected. As the scientists investigating the problem discovered, the nature of the typhoid *bacillus* was such that it was able to contaminate unprotected food, water, and soil, regardless of their original qualities. Thus, rather than being a product of Camp Thomas itself, typhoid fever was a by-product of military mobilization that infected any and all camps, regardless of their specific conditions. The root cause was found in the specific concentrations of human waste most often associated with army camps. From there, circumstances like soil, water, camp location, and the effectiveness of diagnosis and treatment dictated how much damage the disease would do to the military population it infected.[11]

The document submitted by Dr. Walter Reed and his colleagues in 1904 entitled *Report of the Origin and Spread of Typhoid Fever in United States Military Camps during the Spanish War of 1898* was a massive tome by any standards. One volume contained nearly 700 pages of evidence and in-depth analysis covering every sickness, every hospital case, and every major or minor incident of typhoid fever that surfaced in all regular or volunteer regiments in the United States Army during the War with Spain. It described in great detail the nature of the typhoid *bacillus*, the method of infection it used, the time it took to incubate, and the way it spread throughout a human population. It offered studies, case histories, experimental data, regimental reports, surgeons' statements, and a host of other evidence to support its findings.

The report came to three major conclusions about the typhoid epidemic that had plagued Camp Thomas and other camps like it. First, the disease originated in the state camps of instruction and arrived with the soldiers; second, the improper disposal of human waste, along with the crowded conditions inherent in a military camp, allowed the disease to get out of control; and third, although the outbreak of the disease was almost inevitable, mistakes made by camp commanders, company and regimental officers, hospital administrators, and the soldiers themselves added to the problem and probably led to more deaths than were necessary. The report's introduction stated that "our sole endeavor has been to get as near the absolute truth as possible." If ever there was a document that should have laid much of the controversy to rest, this was it. Of course, it did not do anything of the sort.

In spite of the publication of its findings in an abstract in 1899, the Reed report came too late to head off the controversy, finger-pointing, and conflicting memory construction that began before the camps even closed. In fact, the preliminary findings suggested that some of the theories that had been suggested as causes—like the location of, and overcrowding in, the regimental camps—might still have merit. More importantly, the report's claim that many of the troops who arrived at Camp Thomas were already infected was largely buried by other issues. Debates over the purity of the water, the extent and cause of the fecal filth, and the quality of care for the sick received far more attention from the press and public. On top of that, the actions taken by the War Department during the month of August, including bringing in a new camp commander, moving camp locations within the park, and transferring regiments to new camps far from Chickamauga Creek, seemed to indicate that the landscape itself might still be at fault.[12]

Simply put, the typhoid fever germ generates oozing pustules (similar to smallpox blisters) in the intestines of the infected individual, who passes it into the outside environment in the form of tainted fecal matter. It spreads when the typhoid-infected feces come in contact with hands, food, clothing, soil, dust, or air, which are in turn eaten, drunk, absorbed, or inhaled by people. Because of the unique concentrations of both men and excreta in army camps, this disease was likely to appear any time large numbers of men assembled in one place and remained as a group for a significant length of time. More importantly, it did not require very many infected individuals or particularly large camps to quickly spread the disease throughout individual companies and regiments. What also became apparent to the researchers was that typhoid fever generally began to show up from six to eight weeks after the unit had first been assembled in its state camp. By combining the known incubation rate of the disease, the time frame that most units arrived at Chickamauga Park, and the first appearance of typhoid fever in the earliest arriving units, the commission concluded that "it is quite certain that most, if not all, of the regiments . . . reached Chickamauga with one or more men infected."[13]

This statement, which appears early in both versions of the report, seems to exonerate the park from the primary responsibility for the appearance of this deadly epidemic among the soldiers stationed there. If it was indeed true that one in four recruits in a typical volunteer regiment was already infected with the disease at the beginning of their service, then the general circumstances of military life would allow them to pass the disease to their comrades within a matter of days or weeks. With this knowledge already established in prewar scientific literature, military doctors generally realized that "typhoid could never be entirely eliminated from camp life." Recent studies indicate that as many as "sixty-two infected regiments from twenty-nine state camps imported typhoid into the national encampments" during the war. Given these statistics, it is now safe to say that the War Department's plan to group the volunteers into big, permanent camps was a recipe for disaster, since the concentration of men and filth "supercharged" the spread of a disease that essentially could not be prevented.[14]

As will be seen shortly, the War Department eventually took plenty of heat for the health problems of the troops during the war, but the fact remains that it did actively try to prevent the epidemic spread of typhoid fever in its camps. The key to prevention was cleanliness, particularly in the latrines, where the men were most likely to come into contact with the typhoid germs. On the date that the orders for mobilization went out to the state volunteers, Surgeon General George M. Sternberg issued "Circular No. 1," which gave specific instructions regarding the disposal of waste, the layout of camps, and the basic rules of camp hygiene. Reports from Camp Thomas near the end of the Regular's occupation testified that these rules were being carefully followed by the officers and men. The most important of these were the creation and maintenance of proper latrines, or "sinks," in the individual regimental camps. From the War Department's perspective, the epidemic that erupted during the volunteers' stay at the park "indicates that the sanitary recommendations made in this circular have not been carried out."[15]

A description of the health-related precautions being taken by the Regular Army troops published in May 1898 summarized the key elements of the Sternberg policy: "Sinks, suitably sheltered, are dug for each company, and a layer of fresh dirt is thrown on the fecal evacuations twice daily. When the contents of the pit are within eighteen inches of the surface it is filled up, marked, and a new one dug. All organic refuse and liquid slops are placed in tight barrels and removed daily . . . other refuse is collected in piles and burned." In addition to these precautions, the company streets were "ditched and drained," then coated in gravel, while the soldier's beds were lined with straw and elevated, if possible. In addition, they raised the sides of the tents and exposed the blankets and straw "to the sun and air for at least two hours" every day. Medical officers inspected the food and reported any problems "to the proper authority." As the surgeon making this report pointed out, "every opportunity is taken to impress upon officers and men the purpose and importance of sanitary regulations." That was how it was supposed to be done; unfortunately, topography, inexperience, stubbornness, and the sheer numbers of volunteers in the camps combined to undermine these practices.[16]

Among the reasons that several of the volunteer officers gave for the failure of their latrines to contain the waste from their regiments was the topography and geology of the park. An officer from the 1st Vermont noted that the sinks "could be dug on an average of only about two feet deep without blasting the strata of rock which laid . . . under our camp." Another concurred and added that "the soil was so hard that nothing would sink into it" and "that it was impossible to keep [the latrines] in proper condition for the length of time we remained there." Members of the 1st New Hampshire echoed the claim that "it was impossible to dig a sink more than three feet deep, and we had to dig them wherever we could." While a lieutenant admitted that the sinks were sometimes "too near the kitchen, and others, too far from the company," a staff officer insisted "it is hard to lay blame anywhere regarding the sinks." Although their close proximity to the camps and kitchens was one problem, the most oft-repeated complaint about these shallow sinks and rocky ground was that they overflowed when it rained.[17]

A private from the 8th Massachusetts told his state's relief commission that "the sinks were at the highest part of the camp" so that "when it rained, the sinks overflowed; and the contents washed down towards the kitchen." This complaint was repeated by members of several regiments who were apparently camped on either high or rocky ground. A field officer from New Hampshire who acted as the "division officer of the day" for the I Corps, 3rd Division, found that nearly all the sinks among the nine regiments he inspected were "in a very filthy condition." He repeated the claim that following any sort of rain "the contents would be washed about the camp." A member of the 52nd Iowa explained the consequence of this phenomenon to the townsfolk back home following a downpour in mid-June:

> [I]n a short time the small creeks, rivulets, and gulches were pouring a perfect torrent of water towards the Chickamauga River so that the stream was swollen far above its normal condition. All the refuse and excrement in and around that part of the park sloping toward the river was washed into the stream, so that its water (none the best at any time) was made turgid with the filth and debris that had been gathering for weeks. The stream of course is the water supply of the southern part of Camp Thomas and its waters were rendered so dirty and nauseous that none would venture to drink it or even to use it for cooking purposes.

Having identified one of the catalysts for the spread of the disease, the writer oddly contradicts himself by adding that the rain "had warded off some malignant disease" by "wash[ing] the camp clean of filth which would have been sure to breed some such disease as typhoid fever." His first observation was far more accurate than the second. The pollution of the water supply by fecal waste was precisely the type of disaster the camp commander feared. The actions of humans had once again made Chickamauga Creek "the River of Death."[18]

The shocking overflow of waste from poorly built latrines was not the whole story. The rushing rain waters also gathered "surface waste" from the areas around the camps. Surface waste consisted of organic garbage of various types (most often uneaten food, rotten fruit, dirty clothing, animal droppings, and other unpleasant substances) that careless soldiers failed to dispose of properly. In addition, "fecal matter was deposited on the surface about the camps at Chickamauga . . . especially where there were strips of woods" by soldiers too ill or too lazy to go to the sinks. According to regulations, none of this waste should have been above ground, but in practice, it had accumulated in and around camps where discipline was lax or where sickness prevented men from cleaning up after one another. Prior to being washed into the water supply, this filth created a nasty stench and drew swarms of flies as it festered in the mid-summer heat. As morale deteriorated during those early days of August, the atmosphere in the camps was both literally and figuratively stifling.[19]

In early August, the I Corps' 1st Division surgeon published an article in which he proposed a new latrine design that would curtail the problems he witnessed at Camp Thomas. In the process, he summarized what he believed to be the reasons for the "filthy condition and carelessness in policing" that he encountered during his inspections. He declared that the problem arose "from the lack of knowledge of the regimental surgeons as to the proper methods of [latrine] construction, the ignorance of the line officers as to the necessity of absolute cleanliness, and prevailing carelessness of the men themselves, who, imagining that they would be ordered to the front at once, and ignorant of the fact that they were in a semi-permanent camp, let go [of] every thought for the morrow, and became indescribably filthy in these matters." He believed that a comfortable and functional latrine, along with the rigorous process of "covering the dejecta [sic] of the men to the depth of four inches every six hours with earth" would encourage cleanliness and ward off disease. More significantly, the emphasis he put on the men's role for the disaster at Camp Thomas echoed what other army officers and medical personnel were saying in defense of the camp and the park, namely, that if the volunteers had followed regulations, there would not have been an epidemic.[20]

The soldiers voiced one complaint that was at least partially upheld by the army and the Reed Commission, which was that the regiments had stayed in the same camping locations too long. Theoretically, a well-maintained, semi-permanent camp should be able to be occupied indefinitely by a well-supplied, disciplined body of men. However, the volunteer camps at Camp Thomas were not particularly well maintained, the supplies were barely adequate, and the soldiers were far from being highly disciplined. By the first week of August, the ground occupied by the tents, company streets, kitchens, latrines, corrals, and drill spaces belonging to the dozens of regiments that remained was completely denuded of grass and foliage. Some of the volunteer regiments were camped on spots that had been previously occupied by Regulars back in April, which violated "an axiom of military hygiene . . . that one command should not be located on a site recently vacated by another." During the intervening weeks, the soil around the tents had been alternately churned to mud and stirred into great clouds of dust. Many soldiers echoed the suggestion that "all troops should be frequently moved, if only a short distance . . . before the camp becomes fever stricken."[21]

The 1st Maine Infantry was a regiment particularly hard hit by disease. By the time it mustered out in September, it had suffered 188 cases of typhoid fever, which had caused all of the unit's forty-five deaths during its tenure in the service. One member of this regiment upon arriving home compared the crowded, filthy conditions at Camp Thomas to those that had plagued Union prisoners at the notorious Andersonville stockade during the Civil War. In a less heated, but nonetheless critical commentary, a lieutenant from this regiment gave a good representation of what he thought were the problems at Chickamauga: "I believe that the principle cause of the suffering of our regiment was from there being so many regiments in the park. All of these men staying

FIG. 37: This photo is labeled "3rd Tennessee Infantry troops in Camp Thomas . . . during the Spanish-American War." The lack of trees, the wearing of overcoats, and what appear to be clean, wooden latrines suggests that it was taken shortly before the regiment's departure on 5 September 1898. Paul A. Heiner Collection, Chattanooga–Hamilton County Bicentennial Library.

there so long, with no sewerage, brought on a terrible condition." He went on to state his belief that "the character of the ground [was] unfit for men to live on in large or small numbers." After pointing out that the clay soil and "bed-rock" surface caused excessive runoff, " heavy mud," and excessive dampness, he concluded that "the fever was a natural result of the overcrowded condition of the park and occupying of the place for so long a time."[22]

In their general conclusions, the authors of the *Typhoid Fever Report* concurred with some of the men's complaints about the location of camp sites. They agreed that some camps were "unwisely located," noting that "some regiments at Chickamauga . . . were so located that they received the drainage of other regimental camps." They also confirmed that some units were crowded together so that sinks from one regimental camp were placed only a few yards from the kitchens of another. In light of the space available at Chickamauga Park, they concluded that "there was certainly no sufficient excuse for this." Although they did not state it explicitly, their comments suggested that leaving regiments in the same camp for the entire duration of their stay was not a good thing. They noted that the 5th Pennsylvania was originally placed on low ground that created mud, overflowing sinks, and "washings from other camps," but was not allowed to move to higher ground until 12 August. They also conceded that the clay ground at Chickamauga "made it quite impossible to keep the contents of these sinks properly covered," but insisted that "line officers were to some extent responsible for the condition of the camps under their command."[23]

On 2 August, the War Department sent Maj. Gen. Joseph Breckinridge to replace General Wade as commander of Camp Thomas. Breckinridge ordered the camps moved out of the woods, where General Brooke had originally placed them, to "air out" the soldiers' tents, bedding, and living spaces. The thinking behind this movement was that the shaded areas "held in" the bad air and contributed to the sickness. Moving the troops out into the sun exposed them more to the heat, but did get them away from some of the accumulated debris around their old campsites. Along with this movement, Breckinridge ordered the healthier regiments to take extended marches out of the camp as a way to re-invigorate the men. He also suspended the more rigorous military drills in favor of athletic games, individual competitions, and excursions to local points of interest. While this may have temporarily raised morale, it also reminded the men that the need for strict military decorum had become less urgent. For volunteers who had expected to be either at the front or back at home, having leisure time in and around Camp Thomas provided little comfort or satisfaction.[24]

Getting the men entirely out of Camp Thomas was the other option that its new commander actively pursued. If the problems stemmed from the polluted environment at Chickamauga, then moving the men away from it should improve their health and morale. The first troops to be transferred out were the moderately sick soldiers in various units, most of whom were sent home or to hospitals on furlough until they could eventually be discharged with their regiments. As a result of inspections by state, local, and private agencies responding to bad publicity about the camp, a number of slackers and malingerers may have found their way onto the sick rolls in time to take advantage of this process. General Boynton remarked that following a visit from its state inspector general, the 8th New York filled the division hospital with "a great many cases [where] it was difficult to tell that anything was the matter with them."

On 8 August, Secretary of War Alger followed the advice of his surgeon general and ordered the gradual dispersal of all the troops at Camp Thomas to other locations prior to their mustering out. Some, like the 1st Maine, were sent directly home. Others, like regiments from the unassigned portions of the I and III Corps, spent time in Lexington, Kentucky, and nearby Knoxville before returning to their respective states to be disbanded. While these movements helped curtail the misery of the soldiers and reduced the accumulation of trash in the camp, they did not immediately stop the spread of typhoid fever.[25]

The prospect of moving troops from the well-worn confines of Camp Thomas was certainly appealing, and nowhere was it more enthusiastically received than in neighboring Knoxville. Since the City of Knoxville had organized several

FIG. 38: This panoramic view of the training camp at Knoxville during the Spanish-American War shows the open rolling terrain and a line of wooden latrines some distance from the tents. Touted as a healthy alternative to the disease-ridden Camp Thomas, the Knoxville camps hosted two regiments of "immunes," who were thought to be resistant to tropical diseases. From the author's collection.

regiments and housed them in local camps, its citizens were proud of their contribution to the war effort. As the situation at Camp Thomas worsened, the local paper noted that some of the sickness there "grew out of local causes from which Knoxville is entirely exempt." In the same article, the writer noted that there "was not a sick man in the hospitals" in camps Taylor and Wilder and claimed that "Knoxville [is] known as one of the healthiest cities in the United States." In the process of praising its preferred location, the writer addressed what many people thought were the main problems down the road at Chickamauga. Describing Knoxville's "fresh mountain air, with the purest of water, and fine drainage," the writer suggested that these qualities made their area "an ideal camp ground," implying, not so subtly, that Chickamauga was far from it.[26]

For all of the concerns voiced from various parties (many of them legitimate) about the soil, water, air, and healthfulness of the camps, the fact remained that moving the men to another location did not get rid of typhoid fever. Just as they had brought the infection with them from their state camps, members of the regiments sent to new camps in clean, uninfected areas took the disease with them. The Reed report pointed out that "the spread of the typhoid fever continued after the regiments had been moved to Knoxville . . . where the water supply was above suspicion," the sinks were properly dug, and the ground was "ideal" for a camp. The report also made it clear that "notwithstanding all these favorable conditions, typhoid fever continued, and instead of showing the slightest abatement increased in prevalence." Even if the tents, clothing, and equipment of an infected unit were properly disinfected, the disease was still present in men who did not yet show signs of infection and therefore kept reappearing within the camps. Escaping from Camp Thomas did not necessarily mean that the soldiers had eluded the deadly disease.[27]

Of all the charges leveled at the camp by the soldiers and outside critics, the most disquieting was the accusation that the epidemic worsened because of improper care for sick soldiers. Part of the problem stemmed from the usual practice of leaving men in individual regiments under the care of their own surgeons. Under normal circumstances, this system worked well, but in the midst of an outbreak of diseases like malaria, yellow fever, or typhoid fever, the lack of consistency in diagnosis and care from one regiment to another often compounded the problem. Conversely, the eventual grouping of typhoid cases into larger hospital facilities removed the ill men from the care of their friends and compounded the shock that accompanied their untimely and often unexpected deaths. Complaints about medical care ranged from moderate to extreme. On one end of the spectrum was the likelihood that

FIG. 39: This homey photo of Lt. Col. Hannah, Co. C, 4th Tennessee Volunteer Infantry, and his dog taken by "Chaney, the Soldier's Photographer," in Camp Poland, reinforces the contrast between Knoxville's comfortable, healthy camps and the alleged squalor at Chickamauga park. Courtesy of the McClung Historical Collection, Knoxville (SPC 2003.001).

many inexperienced regimental doctors misdiagnosed their patients and inadvertently allowed typhoid to spread. At the opposite extreme were charges of gross incompetence leading to the horrific neglect of patients. Somewhere in the middle lay the more predictable problems of inexperience, carelessness, and misguided good intentions.

The inability of many regimental doctors to anticipate and recognize the symptoms of typhoid fever had a distinctive impact on the eventual spread of the disease. At the root of this problem was the mistaken belief that the disease evolved from fecal matter and other types of filth. As a result, they did not realize that the men were infected prior to the onset of diarrhea and the accumulation of excrement in the latrines. The onset of the various bowel disturbances due to diet, water, and other causes served to mask the fact that typhoid was present; therefore, the process of treatment was often delayed by days or even weeks. Former division surgeon Victor Vaughn confirmed that "the early symptoms of typhoid fever are often confounded with those of simple gastro-intestinal catarrh." Another problem stemmed from the tendency to lump typhoid fever together with malaria and yellow fever. These two diseases were most often associated with humid, tropical locales and therefore drew a disproportionate amount of attention from doctors concerned about exposing northern soldiers to an inhospitable southern climate. According to Vaughn, not only was "typhoid . . . frequently reported as malarial fever," but by seeking "fresh mountain air" and other climate and location changes as cures, the doctors were missing the real causes and treatments of the disease responsible for most of the deaths.

These were honest mistakes made by men of limited ability in a difficult situation, so it is not entirely fair to charge them with neglecting their duties during the spread of the epidemic. Another problem was the shortage of doctors, rather than their quality. One common observation made by officers and men in several regiments concerned the army's practice of detailing regimental surgeons to division hospitals, headquarters units, and the ambulance corps. This left the regiments shorthanded, with only one "assistant surgeon" delegated "to vaccinate, inspect, make reports, and attend all sick calls." The idea that distributing medical men throughout the division would help serve the general good of the camp was understandable, but proved ineffective when it came to combating a disease like typhoid fever. Even when available, some soldiers "had no confidence in certain . . . regimental surgeons, whom they did not think qualified." The Reed report determined that the disease spread quickly from company to company within the same regiment before jumping into the larger camp population; stripping regiments of their most competent surgeons weakened the first line of defense against the epidemic.[28]

FIG. 40: Dr. Charles Greenleaf and his staff appear to be far more military than medical as they investigate the conditions at Camp Thomas. Courtesy of the Chattanooga–Hamilton County Bicentennial Library.

At the very least, the quality of care that soldiers received in the hospitals at Camp Thomas left something to be desired. Very few outside the higher ranks praised it, and while most found it merely adequate, though rife with problems, many condemned it,. Among the most common grievances were the incompetence and insensitivity of the aides, stewards, and male nurses who cared for the men. One surgeon reported that "the nurses were inefficient; they did not pretend to be anything else" and charged, "it seemed to be the idea of some superior medical officers that any man was competent to nurse the sick." Most described the attendants as "inexperienced," "overworked," and occasionally, "an untrained, careless, and shiftless lot of men." A New Hampshire staff officer classified the orderlies as being part of "the class that were too lazy to drill, and thought that they might find it a little easier in the hospital." A member of the 1st Maine testified that "those who had charge of the hospitals . . . were inexperienced . . . clumsy fellows detailed from the ranks, ignorant and without habits of personal cleanliness."[29]

This lack of qualified hospital workers not only led to some "rough handling" of patients, but posed a genuine threat to the overall health of the camp. As they came into contact with infected clothing, bedpans, foods, and patients, they often failed to practice basic personal or medical hygiene. There were numerous accounts of orderlies from one shift emptying bedpans onto the ground outside of the tents and being reprimanded for it, only to have their replacements in the next shift repeat the mistake. In the Reed report, the doctors "specifically condemned the method . . . of detailing men from the ranks as orderlies at the hospitals." The report also described numerous incidents in which orderlies ate, handled food, and returned to their regimental camps without washing their hands after treating typhoid patients.[30]

Medical historian Vincent Cirillo sees the problems of lack of cleanliness, hospital staffing, and the overall health of the camp stemming from the "tension between line and medical officers." On the one hand, military officers had little use for medical dictums that they viewed as "unrealistic and unnecessary fads." The experienced officers believed that some hardship was a valid way to harden men for combat; the inexperienced volunteers simply ignored directions as a matter of course. As a result, regimental commanders deliberately detailed their slackers, dullards, and troublemakers as hospital aides, while at the same time ignoring the strict rules regarding cleanliness handed down from the medical experts. When it came to making decisions for the whole camp, "the army doctor had little power other than the power of persuasion" and "was reduced to an advisor" rather than a policy maker. Part of the problem was that line officers saw the role of medical officers strictly as caretakers for the sick; "therefore, any attempts . . . to interfere with the daily activities of healthy soldiers—to prevent illness—came dangerously close, in the line officer's eyes, to usurping their command." In spite of the lessons of the Civil War, the wide gap between old military habits and modern civilian and medical ideas resulted in the tragic loss of lives among the common soldiers.[31]

Whether it was the dispersal of the medical professionals, the inexperience of the orderlies, or, as many people insisted, the shortage of supplies, the fact was that there were many people who thought that the medical care at Camp Thomas was not only terrible, it bordered on criminal. Even those who were willing to give the doctors and staffs the benefit of the doubt found fault with the organization of the camp's medical facilities. The indecision among the camp's commanders regarding the care of typhoid victims was a perfect example of the conflicts between army officers, medical professionals, and state and private relief agencies. While the hospital surgeons were technically under the command of their division commanders, some claimed that "they were a sort [sic] of do-as-you-please fellows under nobodies [sic] command." When the stripped-down regimental hospitals were thought to be unable to deal with the influx of sick men, the camp's chief surgeon, Col. Rand Huidekoper, ordered that all the sick be sent to division hospitals so he could "keep them under his personal supervision." This policy was gradually reversed in order to allow the men to convalesce among their comrades. Eventually, the army built the 750-bed Sternberg Hospital on the site to care for the worst patients.[32]

This confusion led to obvious and unfortunate consequences when it came to supplying medicine and medical equipment to the various hospitals. Aside from being caught shockingly flat-footed by the sudden increase in the number and severity of illnesses, the surgeons at Camp Thomas found out that getting supplies to either regimental or division hospitals was extremely difficult. The chain of command from regiment to division to quartermaster did not accommodate medical requests very efficiently, and, as a result, there were shortages of everything from beds and linens to bedpans and thermometers. The result was a period of time where conditions in the hospitals were horrible. Men lay in filth without proper bedding, clean water, or competent care. Rather than get the very specific care that typhoid patients required, the unfortunate victims of the disease at Chickamauga received just the opposite. The squalor in the hospitals corresponded with the awful condition in the camps, leading members of the 52nd Iowa to plead "that we be removed from here immediately."

The case of the 52nd Iowa was typical of many regiments in Camp Thomas. They had arrived at Chickamauga Park on 31 May at half strength only a week after being mustered in back in Iowa. By the time they augmented their numbers with recruits, the first cases of typhoid fever had already appeared in the regiment. Earl Clock documented the typhoid death of one member of his company on 9 July. Early in August, he reported that his brother Ned was "very sick" and deteriorating rapidly. His comrades treated him with "quinine and brandy" and had a hard time keeping the delirious patient in bed as he ranted about cyclones and pigs. Several relatives arrived from Iowa, and they eventually moved the furloughed man to the Soldier's Rest in Chattanooga, then to the Knights of Pythias Hospital, where he died on 5 August. The hometown newspaper reported that "there is a widespread feeling here that our boys are not getting the care they should have at Chickamauga." This impression was heightened when a group of men from the regiment wrote the "River of Death" letter, stating that "death and sickness are attacking our regiment," and begged to be sent home.[33]

Another member of the 52nd Iowa was sick three times during his service at Camp Thomas and managed to endure two stays in camp hospitals. Oscar Blood of Company E experienced his first bout of illness when his arm swelled up on 22 June "from the effects of vaccination working inwardly." On 12 July he noted in his diary that he was "sick of stomach trouble" and then spent the next seventeen days in what he referred to as the "Co [company] hospital" before moving back to his tent on 29 July. During his last bout of illness, which began with a "terrible head-ache" and a temperature of 105 degrees, he explained that the Company H cook tent doubled as the company's hospital. When the regiment moved its camp, he was transferred on 18 August to the division hospital, where he remained until the whole unit embarked for home on 24 August. Although he reported not feeling well throughout his various ordeals, he never complained about his care or feared for his life.[34]

When reports of sickness, squalor, and neglect reached the home states of regiments at Camp Thomas, there was a flood of response from across the nation. The first impulse was to send help. The Red Cross, Knights of Pythias, Young Men's Christian Association (YMCA), Daughters of the American Revolution (DAR), Women's National War Relief Association, various Christian organizations, and state aid groups poured into the camp, bringing supplies, nurses, and transportation for men being furloughed. Both the city of Philadelphia and the state of Pennsylvania dispatched aid for their regiments at Camp Thomas. A report from the Chattanooga branch of the National Relief Commission described the process of procuring supplies, caring for the sick, and improving conditions in the hospitals as "a labor of love and duty." The War Department finally overcame the traditional resistance to female orderlies and allowed trained nurses to work in its hospitals. Although the nurses did not make a real impact until after the war ended, their professionalism, understanding of "the importance of scrupulous cleanliness, the use of disinfectants, and the safe handling of infectious excreta" made them invaluable to the recovery of thousands of men. Their attention to detail kept them from contracting the disease themselves, which in turn made them more effective caregivers.[35]

Part of the credit for encouraging female participation and increasing the quality of care in the camps can be attributed to the American Red Cross. Led by its founder and Civil War nursing pioneer, Clara Barton, the Red Cross mobilized both funds and personnel for use during the war. Unhampered by military red tape and spurred on by the desire to contribute to the well-being of the soldiers, the Red Cross was able to provide relief to the men in the hospitals at Camp Thomas well ahead of the War Department. In addition to acquiring supplies of milk and ice, the Red Cross at Camp Thomas was able to fill 340 requisitions for all types of food, clothing, hospital gear, and medicines including "opium, paregoric, laudanum, salol, sub-gallate bismuth, calomel and soda, sulfonal, trional, and many others." They also worked "harmoniously" with the military doctors to establish the Sternberg Hospital and not only supplied 160 female nurses, but built the dormitories to house them. Even after Camp Thomas closed, the Red Cross actively assisted "some charitable ladies in Chattanooga" with the creation and staffing of Epworth Hospital, which was created "with the object of caring for sick soldiers en route for their homes."[36]

A number of Catholic orders, including the Daughters of Charity from Emmitsburg, Maryland, and Sisters of Mercy out of Baltimore answered the call for nurses issued by the DAR. Both groups sent contingents to Camp Thomas to assist in the treatment of the typhoid patients. The women experienced the same hardships as the soldiers due to heat, rain, flies, a shortage of materials, the lack of staff help, and innumerable other inconveniences. Several became ill and many reported that the degree of filth and neglect was higher than it should have been in the camp hospital. When Camp Thomas emptied out, many of the sisters continued to serve in other camp hospitals, including the ones in Knoxville, where many of the men from Chickamauga Park ended up. While their efforts were noble and their contributions of immeasurable value, their accounts of the squalor and "primitive" conditions at Camp Thomas added fuel to the controversies surrounding the care of the sick.[37]

The contributions of the Red Cross and the sisters and the successful creation of a female army nurse corps were some of the few bright spots to come out of the typhoid epidemic that ravaged most of the major camps in the United States during the war. By the time the Typhoid Board had completed its inspection and the last troops had left Camp Thomas in late August and early September, the conditions in the camps and hospitals had improved considerably. With the shifting of camp sites and the departure of most of the soldiers, the sanitation issues that had plagued the camp had largely been solved. Most of the typhoid sufferers had either departed the camp (taking the disease with them) or were being well cared for by the doctors and nurses in Sternberg Hospital. By the time the Sternberg facility closed its doors on 4 November, it held only a handful of patients, who were sent to other locations. The chill of fall eventually killed any typhoid germs that may have remained in the camp debris, signaling that the epidemic was over.[38]

Unfortunately, the fallout from the mess at Camp Thomas did not go away with the men or the disease. By all accounts, the volunteer experience at Chickamauga Park had ranged from mildly aggravating to downright catastrophic. Worse yet, the disaster had not gone unnoticed by Congress, the press, or the American public. As if the scandals surrounding the training camps were not enough to taint the memory of the war, other issues involving the health of the American Army in Cuba and Puerto Rico were also drawing negative attention to the War Department and its beleaguered secretary, Russell Alger. Controversies surrounding the quality of food, equipment, and medical care led to the creation of investigating boards, commissions, and inquiries that served to erode the luster from America's quick victory over Spain. On top

FIG. 41: This photo was originally captioned as "tents at Camp Thomas" but the flag indicates that this collection of shelters may have served as a hospital or R&R facility operated by the civilian Red Cross. Courtesy of the Chattanooga–Hamilton County Bicentennial Library.

of all that, people who opposed what they considered to be the McKinley administration's imperialistic ambitions called both the war and the treaty with Spain into question.

The memories of Camp Thomas were partially forged out of the experiences of the volunteers who spent several exciting, frustrating, uncomfortable, and frequently miserable months there. Much of the rest of its legacy would be influenced by the scandals that wracked the War Department and the nation in the months after the war. With the reputation of their commemorative landscape and their memories at risk, Henry Boynton and the Civil War veterans forcefully defended the integrity of their park and the memories of the Battle of Chickamauga that they had worked so hard to construct and preserve. Ironically, after spending time, money, and effort repairing and reconstructing their sacred battlefield, the veterans compromised their memories to accommodate the needs of the Chattanooga community. Rather than isolate their commemorative landscape, the park commissioners allowed the Army to construct a permanent military installation on the edge of the park. The construction of memory around "the River of Death" was rarely simple and almost always controversial.

TWELVE

"One Huge Pest House"

By September 1898 the only troops left at Camp Thomas were the two regiments of "immunes" that had originally trained in Knoxville and a handful of typhoid patients at Sternberg Hospital. The rest of the volunteers who filled the grounds of the Chickamauga and Chattanooga National Military Park between May and August were either still occupying Puerto Rico, recuperating in other camps, or on their way back to their home states for discharge. In their wake, the thousands of volunteers generated some compelling questions about the nation's preparedness and the overall conduct of the war. Not only had the War Department apparently failed to adequately feed, supply, and care for the men, but some observers suggested that the soldiers themselves had not lived up to the traditions passed down to them by the previous generation of veterans. The implication of these deficiencies, combined with charges of neglect, incompetence, and corruption within President William McKinley's administration, created a muddled and contradictory environment for the construction of memories of the war.

The merger of health, organizational, and discipline problems that surfaced at Camp Thomas was not an isolated incident. The dismantling of the camp at Chickamauga coincided with the American press and public casting a critical eye toward the performance of the War Department in the short and stunningly successful war against Spain. Along with the typhoid epidemic that had ravaged the stateside camps, the army in Cuba had been so badly weakened by outbreaks of yellow fever and malaria that some of its officers had demanded its immediate evacuation from the island following the cease-fire on 13 August 1898. This crisis was followed by an investigation of the War Department by a presidential commission, which heard testimony on all aspects of the War Department's performance, including its handling of the Camp Thomas fiasco. The commission issued mixed findings, which added yet another layer to the complex construction of memory regarding the war.

The bitter public debate over annexation and imperialism and a bloody ongoing war against insurrectionists in the Philippines further sullied the nation's victory over Spain. With the exception of Theodore Roosevelt, who managed to ride his war-hero status all the way to the White House, the notion that the conflict with Spain had ennobled American manhood fell rather quickly out of favor with many Americans. As a result of all this uncertainty about the value and meaning of their war, the Spanish-American War volunteers acquired a unique and somewhat negative perspective regarding their services to the nation. Having been largely badly supplied, underutilized, and exposed to a host of deadly diseases by their War Department, some Spanish War veterans argued that the country had let them down. Rather than heroes, the shell-shocked, disease-wracked, and unappreciated volunteers felt like they were victims of the nation's indifference and neglect.

All of these issues had a profound effect on the Chickamauga battlefield and the memories that it represented. At the onset of the conflict with Spain, Henry Boynton and the park commissioners had enthusiastically embraced the War Department's plan to use their commemorative landscape as a major concentration point for its army. The resulting training camp brought thousands of people and a great deal of attention to the park; it also fit the veterans' desire to see the battlefield used to promote the martial spirit that they had so proudly upheld during the Civil War. Unfortunately, much of the reunion spirit, patriotism, and mutual respect between the Civil War veterans and the volunteers wilted in the fetid summer heat of July and August 1898. Not only had the careless, rowdy soldiers done a huge amount of physical damage to the park, they had inadvertently defiled the Army of the Cumberland's sacred ground and sullied the name of its most beloved commander. To mend the damage, the Civil War veterans would have to repair the park's grounds and restore the integrity of its commemorative landscape.

The issues specifically connected to the park, combined with the national questions about the conduct and meaning of the war, produced an atmosphere that was ideal for the construction of competing memories. While the Spanish-American War volunteers recalled the poor ground, undrinkable water, and callous inefficiency of Camp Thomas, the park commissioners and War Department remembered a mob of disrespectful, undisciplined, careless recruits who nearly ruined their park. The resulting struggle between these two groups left a lasting mark on the interpretation of both the Civil War battlefield and the War with Spain.

The typhoid fever epidemic that ravaged the stateside training camps and killed hundreds of men at Camp Thomas was not the only problem facing the War Department in the fall of 1898. The victorious army that captured Santiago was far from the fresh, strapping, cocky force that had landed on the Cuban shore back in the spring. It had been weakened by disease, not just the typhoid that had run rampant in the crowded training camps, but the more traditionally feared tropical maladies of malaria and yellow fever. Not only had tropical diseases taken their toll, but many of the soldiers were still suffering from a lack of food, medicines, and proper equipment after nearly three months in the field. The logistics of supplying an invading army and the rapidly growing training camps had swamped the undermanned War Department quartermasters and created shortages everywhere. When it became apparent to the press and the public that the War Department might have failed to properly take care of its troops both at home and abroad, the criticism from state governors, reform groups, disgruntled soldiers, and the administration's political opponents was immediate and vociferous.

Ironically, there had been a significant amount of debate in the McKinley administration at the outset of the war regarding the threat that tropical diseases posed to the armies invading both Cuba and the Philippines. Surgeon General George Sternberg and Commanding General Nelson Miles both cautioned against launching an offensive during the humid summer months due to the increased prevalence of malaria and yellow fever at that time of year. They were overruled based on the then current, but mistaken, theory that, like typhoid fever, malaria and yellow fever were caused by a lack of cleanliness, not climate. The notion that these diseases could be prevented convinced President McKinley and Secretary of War Russell Alger that if the army kept clean camps and proper sanitation, they could avoid serious epidemics. The problem with this assumption, aside from it being based on faulty science, was that it required extraordinary measures on the part of the troops to maintain camp and personal cleanliness at the front. This proved to be impossible not only due to the conditions that the troops faced, but also because the War Department was unable to supply the equipment and materials necessary to accomplish it. Thus, the War Department left itself open to criticism for both the flawed plan and its shoddy execution.[1]

Of the handful of diseases that were most likely to cripple an army or a civilian population, yellow fever was perhaps the most feared and misunderstood. Like malaria, it was a malady most often associated with the heat and humidity of summer and occurred more often in regions closer to the southern hemisphere. The scourge of yellow fever had haunted the southern United States since colonial times and had most recently appeared in New Orleans in 1897, triggering fears throughout the South that those escaping from the city would spread the disease to other areas. In a recently published article, historian Mariola Espinosa argues that one of the motivations for the War with Spain was to capture Havana, which was suspected by some medical professionals of being one of the primary sources of yellow fever, and remedy the conditions that might be spawning the disease. In any case, there was a clearly developed sense of urgency among both military and medical personnel regarding the threat of yellow fever to the troops being sent to the tropics.[2]

Unfortunately, this fear did not manifest itself in effective prevention, and, as a result, many soldiers were threatened with some form of this awful disease. Apart from the disastrous misunderstanding of its causes and methods of dissemination, the army was hampered by the same problems that stoked the typhoid epidemic in the stateside camps. There were a shortage of qualified doctors, inadequate stockpiles of medicine and equipment, and a bureaucracy that did not function well under pressure. The McKinley administration can also be criticized for calling up far more soldiers than it needed or could logistically support. One historian described this error as "the undo [sic] priority of manpower mobilization over materiel mobilization." Regardless of the specificity of the problem, the onus of failure fell on Secretary Alger and the War Department. Considering the known threats of both yellow and typhoid fevers and the concerns voiced prior to the conflict regarding them, it is inconceivable that one of the undersupplied branches would have been the Medical Department.

The problems in the Medical Department ranged from top to bottom, starting with Dr. Sternberg, a kindhearted researcher with few organizational skills, who "devoted his time and energy to small details and delegated many important tasks to his subordinates." Sternberg was well aware of the threat posed by infectious diseases and, as already noted, took steps to prevent them from crippling the forces both in the field and the training camps. The problems of enforcement notwithstanding, his efforts to save the troops from malaria and yellow fever were misdirected and doomed to failure. By attempting to control these diseases by strict sanitary procedures, disinfectants, a regulated diet, change of camp location, and exposure to fresh air, he and his staff were at least partly responsible for the hardships that befell the V Corps in Cuba. While adherence to these doctrines might have kept typhoid fever at bay and improved the overall health of the troops, they could not effectively have controlled the spread of yellow fever or malaria.[3]

Even if Sternberg had possessed a workable plan, he did not have the men or materiel to carry it out during the war's short duration. At the start of the conflict, the Army Medical Department had 190 medical officers, of whom only about 100 were available for active duty. This shortage compelled Dr. Sternberg to hire hundreds of civilian surgeons. Needless to say, the range of experience, knowledge, and understanding of the newest medical ideas among these doctors was incomplete and inconsistent. As a result, not every unit in the field or the camps received anything like quality treatment for the most serious diseases. The Medical Department also paid the price for sticking to the system of hospital organization that had emerged during the Civil War, relegating regimental medical staffs to the status of field aide workers and assigning the bulk of their surgeons and patients to larger division hospitals. This had backfired at Camp Thomas by raising the rate of infection among patients and inexperienced hospital corpsmen and was not resolved until after the arrival of adequate supplies and experienced nurses. Unfortunately, the system failed in Cuba and in the relief camps back home for many of the same reasons.

The problems with organization and experience were exacerbated by the "ignorance, friction, and consequent lack of co-operation" between line officers and medical personnel. While the lack of medical supplies available in Cuba during the invasion can be attributed to many logistical factors, the unwillingness of line officers to heed medical advice, as well as the reluctance of doctors to listen to regimental officers, contributed to the situation. At the most basic level, the army's decision to put guns, ammunition, and other supplies ashore, instead of hospital units, rested with officers who should have known better. The threat of diseases was real, yet the means for treating them often remained on the transport ships, or worse yet, back in Tampa. Whether it was requisitioning supplies, moving camps to healthier locations, or coming to a consensus on the nature of the men's ailments, there was constant friction between medical men and line officers of all ranks, which slowed the process of caring for sick men.[4]

In spite of all these drawbacks, the Medical Department went into the conflict with some dramatic advantages over the previous war. For soldiers who were wounded in combat, the level of care beyond the aide station was excellent. A state of the art hospital ship, complete with X-ray equipment and operating rooms, accompanied the expedition to Cuba and did an admirable job of treating men wounded in the fighting at El Caney and San Juan Hill. This floating hospital was joined by another fully equipped vessel operated by the Red Cross and staffed with well-trained, well-provisioned doctors and female nurses. Their strict standards of cleanliness made them ideal for the treatment of typhoid patients, and their distance from shore protected them from the malaria- and yellow fever–carrying mosquitoes as well. Unfortunately, there were not enough of these facilities to accommodate all the fever and malaria sufferers who swamped the system in late July. Plus, the fear that yellow fever could be spread from human to human kept many patients suspected of having this disease from being transferred onto these ships.

Unlike Camp Thomas, where there was an extended period of deceptively good health, the troops who landed in Cuba showed signs of disease within a couple of weeks of their arrival. While the greatest fear revolved around yellow fever, the more common camp illnesses, such as dysentery, also took their toll on the men. Unlike the stateside troops who languished in camps waiting for disease to overtake them, the Regular and volunteer regiments of the V Corps were in action almost from the day they landed until the fall of Santiago on 17 July. Although they initially avoided the filthy camp conditions that usually spawned typhoid fever, the humid tropical air, frequent rains, poor food, and inadequate supplies quickly took their toll. By the time the army settled into its camps outside of Santiago following the armistice, "Shafter's troops [had] degenerated into a mob of shambling scarecrows." The city of Santiago itself was awash in filth, disease, and death. Although the first cases of yellow fever had appeared as early as 6 July, the Medical Department was still largely unprepared for a major epidemic of any of the threatening tropical diseases.[5]

Ultimately, the army's response to the disease crisis was hampered by its obsession with yellow fever as the main threat to the health of the troops. Unfortunately, the weakened condition of the force surrounding Santiago in late July was largely due to the debilitating effects of malaria, not yellow fever. Although rarely fatal by itself, the sickness lasted for days or even weeks. Worse yet, its long-term effects might linger for months or years. Factored in with dysentery, some typhoid fever, exhaustion, and the effects of poor food and water, the crippling malarial symptoms posed a serious threat to both the health and effectiveness of the V Corps.

The commanders and field officers were equally handcuffed by the mistaken belief that a change in the location of regimental camps to higher, more healthful ground would stop the spread of both malaria and yellow fever and restore the troops to fighting trim. For several critical weeks, General Shafter and his division commanders waffled about what to do with their army. They tried to contain the yellow fever by burning infected villages, relocating troops to better ground, and quarantining units diagnosed with the disease. At the same time, regimental commanders were attempting to declare their units free of the fever to clear them for further service in the Puerto Rican campaign. All the while, Shafter hoped to keep the authorities in Washington in the dark regarding the actual situation until he could get it remedied.[6]

One of the few volunteer regiments to make it into the Santiago campaign was the 8th Ohio Volunteer Infantry. Mobilized as one of Ohio's National Guard regiments and known as "McKinley's Own" because of its Stark County origins, it spent a short time at Camp Alger, Virginia, before shipping out to Santiago as reinforcements on 5 July. The unit arrived on or about 13 July and occupied a camp on very poor ground that they nicknamed "Camp Mud." After only a few days the regiment's commander, Col. Curtis V. Hard, made a personal entreaty to General Shafter requesting that he be allowed to move his men to higher ground, only to be rudely turned down. Eventually, General Miles personally approved the move, which was made immediately, but Colonel Hard remained bitter. He wrote later, "there is not the slightest doubt that the seeds of disease were sown in that camp on the banks of the river, which afterward developed into the epidemic that took hold of us on the hill." Twenty-five of the regiment's men died in Cuba; nearly twice that many died after leaving the islands for the United States. Several seem to have perished of typhoid fever, but most of the others died from the effects of yellow fever, malaria, and various other undetermined causes.[7]

Eventually, the army commanders in Cuba made several decisions regarding the health of the troops, none of which served to stave off the effects of disease. The first, still based on the clean-camp theory, was to move the entire army away from the camps around Santiago and locate it on the higher ground further inland. This would be accompanied by an order that regimental camps be moved every few days. This plan was destined to fail for two main reasons. One, the mosquitoes that were carrying the disease were just as numerous in the new camps as the old; and two, the stress of the move did more harm than good to the already weakened soldiers. As noted in the examples from Camp Thomas, changing camp locations did not wipe out typhoid fever once the men had been infected, nor did it help suppress the spread or the symptoms of malaria or yellow fever. There were attempts to quarantine units that were suspected of having yellow fever in the new locations, but men continued to get sick. With the mosquito acting as the heretofore unknown vector, the move to new camps only had an effect if it reduced the men's exposure to this insect.

As it turned out, the order to move the camps had a profound effect on the army that its unnerved and indecisive commander, General Shafter, had not anticipated. First, since the men who were most ill were left behind in the division hospitals, it served to separate these sick men from their concerned comrades. Second, those able to make the move found the process exhausting, frustrating, and ultimately more trouble than it was worth. For men weakened by malaria, diarrhea, heat prostration, and the rigors of combat, the strenuous process of moving tents and baggage, often without wagons, nearly did them in. By the time the army was settling into its new camps, it was in even worse shape than it had been before headquarters issued the order to move.[8]

No one was more aware of the condition of the troops than the regimental commanders, who watched as their men collapsed around them. Colonel Hard observed that the shocking physical deterioration of many of his men was accompanied by "dementia of varying degrees," which in turn led to "not a few sad cases of extreme insanity." Already miffed at the high command's apparent disregard for the well-being of their soldiers, some of these officers took a drastic and unprecedented step to "save the army."[9]

One of the catalysts for this action was none other than Theodore Roosevelt, whose Rough Riders had played such a dramatic role in the victory at Santiago. Like many other officers, he was shocked at the condition of his men in the weeks after the cease-fire. He ridiculed the army's plans to rotate the camps, move the men to higher ground or to the interior of the island as recipes for "the early destruction of the army." The bombastic young volunteer colonel described the potential outcome of such solutions as "simple butchery." Until early August, the widespread fear that the army was infected with yellow fever had prevented it from being moved out of Cuba; now the situation was critical and required immediate action. At about the same time that General Shafter wired Washington with an urgent appeal to withdraw his army from the island, some of his subordinates drafted the infamous "round robin" letter that reiterated that request in even stronger language.

The impetuous Colonel Roosevelt was not convinced that the meeting between General Shafter and his officers on 3 August had produced a decisive enough result. In a letter written to the commanding general, he stressed the danger of leaving the army in Cuba any longer and argued that none of the army's plans would preserve its health. He pointed out that malarial fevers were the greatest threat, making the men "ripe for dying like rotten sheep." He concluded by assuring the general that "I write only because I cannot see our men, who have fought so bravely and endured extreme hardship and danger so uncomplainingly, go to destruction without striving so far as lies in me to avert a doom as fearful as it is unnecessary and undeserved." Roosevelt was prepared to submit this presumptuous missive to the general single-handedly, but discovered that other officers had already come to the same conclusion.[10]

The "round robin" letter was essentially a reaffirmation of the points that Roosevelt had made in his document. Restating that the current threat of yellow fever was minimal and posed no danger to the population in the United States, the officers insisted that "the army must be moved at once, or perish" from the epidemic they foresaw happening in a few weeks. Even more ominously, they added "the persons responsible for preventing such a move will be responsible for the loss of many thousands of lives." In addition to Colonel Roosevelt, the letter was signed by seven general officers, including Leonard Wood and Civil War veteran Adelbert Ames. The 8th Ohio's Colonel Hard approved of the letter's contents, but noted that "it was an act that crowded closely upon insubordination." He was entirely correct, however, in stating that "it produced results." Within days, the army was in transit for home.[11]

There were unforeseen and decidedly negative consequences generated by the letters that Roosevelt and his comrades sent to the War Department. These startling documents, in which the army's principal officers talk openly of catastrophe, went directly into the nation's newspapers via the Associated Press. This generated a public outcry that resonated clear into the halls of the White House, which was apparently unaware of the extent of the problem and thus blindsided by the letter and its consequences. Correspondents who had little to do after the fall of Santiago had a story once again and were eager to tell it. While there was some criticism directed toward Roosevelt and the other officers for their apparent insubordination, there was far more hostility aimed at General Shafter, Secretary Alger, and the administration. At about the same time, stories describing the mess at Camp Thomas were also beginning to filter throughout the country. The horrifying vision of an army struck down by disease both at home and abroad galvanized both the public and the administration. As questions about the War Department's performance began to appear in papers all over the country, the government was frantically working to extract the ailing army out of harm's way.[12]

It is ironic that the single most outspoken proponent of war's ennobling effect on manhood should also become a whistleblower against the very army that had provided him with the opportunity to experience the glory of combat. Roosevelt's actions validated two contradictory sets of memories. One held to the official version of the "splendid little war" that boosted America's power and prestige; the other portrayed the soldiers as victims of an inefficient and unresponsive military bureaucracy. Roosevelt had claimed the honors at San Juan Hill for himself at the expense of the Regulars, which aggravated the very men he hoped to emulate. By bucking the chain of command and going to the press with news of the army's dire condition, the ambitious colonel had risked destroying the very memories he had worked so hard to promote. However, this would be his only slip. By the time he returned to the states, he was back to touting the splendid performance of his Rough Riders and the positive benefits of the war. Amazingly, Roosevelt could claim that he had not only led the army to victory, he had also saved it from disaster. Hence, he served as the ideal example for the construction of memory and provided a key factor in the process of making heroes and presidents.[13]

In response to earlier suggestions that the army be sent to a cool, East Coast location to demobilize, on 1 August the War Department began construction of a camp at Montauk Point, on the eastern end of New York's Long Island. The sudden revelations regarding the V Corps' poor condition and the rapidity of the War Department's response meant that the troops from Cuba would be arriving much sooner than anticipated. This turned out to be unfortunate for a number of reasons. In the haste to get them out of Cuba, the troops had been loaded onto transports hurriedly and subsequently suffered numerous hardships on the trip. When they arrived, they found a camp that was not prepared to receive them. Even worse from the government's perspective was the press coverage given to the arrival of the returning regiments. As a result of the public's intense interest, the ragged condition of the troops and the army's shocking lack of preparation were immediately obvious to "scores of newspapermen and hundreds of relief workers and ordinary citizens." What should have been a triumphant homecoming quickly degenerated into a national scandal.[14]

There was no getting around the fact that the logistics for transporting thousands of sick men over hundreds of miles of ocean were going to be difficult and costly. Spurred on by visions of epidemics and public outrage, the War Department tried to do too much too soon; as a result, its actions brought on more criticism. The experience of the 8th Ohio provides an effective example of the process from start to finish. They were ordered to report to the wharf in Santiago for transport for the six-day trip on 16 August, but when they arrived, their ship was unfit for boarding. They tried to procure native labor to clean it up, but ended up doing it themselves so that they could finally set sail on the seventeenth. Once on board, they discovered that fresh water and food were in short supply. Colonel Hard also realized that since there were technically no ill soldiers on board (according to orders, only those deemed healthy were allowed to make the trip) they had no "sick rations" for the two-hundred or more men suffering from malaria and other maladies.[15]

In spite of all of this, only two men died on the *Mohawk* while in transit from Santiago to Montauk. Therefore, Colonel Hard was understandably surprised when he reached New York and read reports in the "yellow journals" that his men had suffered, starved, and died during their journey. While admitting that "the government transport service . . . was somewhat defective" and conditions on the ship less than ideal, he was certain that the genesis of the sensational story was more than likely "the creature of some enterprising newspaper reporter's vivid imagination." However, the scandal-hungry press would not be dissuaded by the truth, and the colonel had to repeatedly reassure visitors and reporters that his regiment's voyage had not been one of unmitigated death and suffering. He also recounted that both his sick and healthy men were reasonably well fed and cared for by both civilian and military organizations when they arrived at Montauk on 24 August. The men of the 8th Ohio had benefited from effective leadership and good timing on their journey; not all regiments were as fortunate.[16]

Camp Wikoff (the name given to the camp at Montauk) was caught unprepared for the influx of men that began arriving on 14 August. While it was true that the earliest arrivals were forced to sleep on the ground while the buildings were being constructed, within a week the facility began to operate more efficiently. One witness observed that during the major influx of troops "everything at Camp Wikoff was at white heat." The camp was hampered by a congested railroad siding and the usual bureaucratic snafus, but eventually food, medicine, and trained medical personnel arrived and went to work. Once the president appointed Gen. Joseph Wheeler to take command of the camp things began to improve due to his no-nonsense approach to getting things done. Both Secretary of War Alger and President McKinley visited Camp Wikoff during the 8th Ohio's stay and hurried the process of untangling red tape and promoting efficiency. As a member of the Red Cross later recounted, "according to the 'yellow journals' Camp Wikoff was one huge pest house . . . according to General Wheeler's testimony . . . it was the Garden of Eden. The truth lies, as it usually does, between these two extremes."[17]

Regardless of the truth, from the standpoint of memory, the negative images far outweighed the positive outcomes of the camp at Montauk Point. The government's failure to construct adequate hospitals led to multiple problems. In addition to the noise and disruption of the ongoing construction, the constant shortage of beds made it necessary to move one group of patients to make way for the next. As a result, men whose malaria symptoms were in remission "were compelled to leave the hospital because of the lack of space," and as a result "collapsed at the railway station, in the cars, in Long Island City, in the streets of New York, and on the way to their homes." This, noted the writer, "caus[ed] a great deal of deserved criticism, not only in the newspapers, but among thoughtful men." The shortage of beds was predictably accompanied by the temporary lack of qualified hospital workers. This was eventually remedied by sending sick soldiers to nearby civilian hospitals and procuring the services of trained, female, Red Cross nurses for the Camp Wikoff facilities.[18]

For all of its efforts and in spite of the help it received from the Red Cross, the War Department could not escape the inevitable backlash from its actions. As one historian put it, "through a mixture of scientific ignorance, misunderstanding between the field commander and his superiors in Washington, and poor distribution of responsibility, the War Department had bungled the return of Shafter's troops to the United States." Notwithstanding the frequently irresponsible and often malicious reporting of the yellow press that exaggerated the problem, the public could see the army's mismanagement everywhere as exhausted, sickly, crippled, and disheartened soldiers returned to their homes across the country. Even the proud, reasonably well-disciplined 8th Ohio showed signs of its disgruntlement as it sat for eleven days in Wooster, the county seat of Wayne County, Ohio, awaiting its final pay and discharge. After some minor incidents that stretched the limits of the small town's hospitality, the regiment departed with "its reputation in Wooster perhaps a bit tarnished." Likewise, the reputations of the secretary of war and several of his subordinates were put to the test during the fall and winter of 1898.[19]

Amazingly, the War Department's ordeal was far from over. The health crisis in the training camps and the shocking condition of the army returning from Cuba merged into one big public relations catastrophe for the McKinley administration. As Walter Millis observed, "the Republicans had annexed the war; unfortunately, it meant that it had annexed the warriors as well." As the scandal intensified, the "fiercely sentimental public" had little patience with the "mass of statements, counter-statements, apologies, and controversies in which the responsible officials sought to exculpate themselves." As Millis observed, "slowly the many blasts of criticism drew together and focused on the devoted head of Mr. Alger, the convenient and obvious target." Just when the pressure from the press and public couldn't get any worse, the War Department was blindsided by none other than its commander of the army, Gen. Nelson Miles.[20]

General Miles had not been happy with his superiors in Washington since the beginning of the war. He resented having his mobilization plans overruled and chafed at not being put in command of the Santiago expedition. Although his operations in Puerto Rico had been successful and relatively free of major disease problems, he returned to the United States with an ax to grind. He found a willing audience for his claims of War Department malfeasance among the administration's political opponents, the always-willing yellow press, a horrified public, and thousands of disgruntled soldiers. He also found a forum for his charges in the special commission set up by President McKinley to examine the performance and conduct of his War Department.

The president charged the commission established on 8 September with the task of unraveling the many threads of responsibility that made up the tangled postwar mess. He appointed Gen. Grenville Dodge, a Civil War veteran and successful railroad executive, as the chair of this commission. Although a member of the Republican Party, Dodge was widely respected for his integrity and took the task of uncovering the truth seriously. The Dodge Commission heard testimony from hundreds of witnesses, collected data from experts like those on Walter Reed's Typhoid Fever Board, and sifted through thousands of documents. Before it could make any determination on the conditions in the training and recovery camps, the Dodge Commission had to deal with General Miles's accusation that the beef the War Department supplied to the troops was impure, inedible, and in the case of the refrigerated and fresh beef, "embalmed." In his opinion, the issuance of these poor-quality products instead of "beef on the hoof" was "one of the serious causes of so much sickness and distress on the part of the troops."[21]

There was little doubt that the soldiers were not thrilled with the beef ration. A member of the 4th Ohio vilified the mislabeled "Prime Roast Beef" as "the lowest grade of beef," which after months of shipment and storage was often "absolutely sickening to look at." Members of several Massachusetts regiments described the canned product as "the residue of beef." One soldier proclaimed that it was "more like a box of axle grease than prime roast," while another Bay Stater complained that "one can which I opened was simply carrion of the most rotten variety." Yet another exclaimed that "the beef would not keep over night without becoming so bad that one could not approach it." Essentially, the complaints about the canned meat were grouped into two major categories: the meat was bland, greasy, and tasteless; worse yet, when the air temperature was hot, the product's consistency deteriorated into a sort of sludge.[22]

As bad as the canned product was, Miles used the term "embalmed" to criticize the preserved "fresh" beef that he suspected as having been doctored with dangerous chemicals to enhance its shelf life. Such an accusation suggested that the War Department was "experimenting" on the soldiers with new technologies. This particularly offended Commissary General Charles Patrick Eagan, who had authorized the army's purchase and use of these products. Several days after Miles's bombastic testimony, Eagan counterattacked and shocked the commission by calling the commanding general of the army a liar. Although many may have agreed with him, Eagan's outburst violated all manner of military protocol, and he was subsequently dismissed from the service. The Dodge Commission ultimately ruled that although the various beef products were not very tasty and were ill-suited for the tropics, there was nothing inherently unhealthy about them. Miles insisted on having yet another board review his claims, and it was not until April 1899 that the findings of the "Beef Board" put these accusations to rest.[23]

The Dodge Commission's ruling on the quality of the beef mirrored its findings regarding many of the War Department's problems. It found the army at fault for a variety of details such as overcrowding in camps, inefficiency in the medical department, poor choices of warm-weather rations, inadequate transportation to and from the front, and some questionable decision-making at many levels. However, it dismissed the notion that the War Department was guilty of the kind of malfeasance that Miles and the yellow press were accusing it of. It based most of its findings regarding the spread of disease on the reports of Walter Reed and other medical experts, who reinforced the fact that the major diseases, particularly typhoid fever, had not been caused by poor food, embalmed or otherwise. Indeed, one of the salient facts that emerged from the hearings was that the failure of volunteer officers and men to maintain the appropriate levels of cleanliness in the stateside camps was one of the catalysts for the typhoid epidemic. This observation had been expressed often during the commission's testimony and turned out to be an important element in the construction of memories about Camp Thomas and its place in the history of Chickamauga Park.[24]

The public's reaction toward government hearings on the War Department's conduct during the War with Spain split much of the nation into two points of view. Those holding the most negative perspectives consisted of Democrats already hostile to the McKinley administration, some governors, various relief organizations, other outspoken critics of the War Department, and the anti-imperialists, who believed that the United States should not accept territory as a result of the war. Added to this core constituency were members of the public influenced by the yellow press and willing to believe the worst about Secretary Alger, Adjutant General Henry Corbin, General Shafter, and the rest of the army high command—minus General Miles, who positioned himself as the people's champion.

Disgruntled volunteer soldiers from state units that had served in the various camps, along with their hometown supporters, also joined the chorus of criticism directed at the government. The voices of those who felt they had been neglected at Camp Thomas were joined by men who had allegedly had horrible experiences on board the transports or at Camp Wikoff. In addition, there were a significant number of soldiers who held General Miles in high regard and saw his beef crusade as a sign of his genuine solicitude on their behalf. Within this range of perspectives was an underlying sense of victimization that hinged on the belief that the volunteers, their families, the Cubans and Filipinos, General Miles's career ambitions, and perhaps the nation as a whole had been helpless pawns of the incompetent Russell Alger and his War Department.[25]

Those who rose to the defense of Secretary Alger, Adjutant General Corbin, Surgeon General Sternberg, and the War Department were motivated by both principle and self-preservation. From their perspective, "the tremendous burdens of the Spanish War were bravely and successfully borne" by the administration, as evidenced by the fact that the war was won in such a short time. For them, "the victory was marvelous [and] overwhelming; the results incalculable; the glory immeasurable." The only failures, particularly in regard to the health of the troops, were largely due to the inability of volunteer army officers from the corps level on down to enforce the Surgeon General's well-established standards of deportment, diet, and sanitation.

To the defenders of the administration, members of the yellow press, the complaining volunteers, and the self-aggrandizing General Miles were "contemptible pessimists of American soil [who] rob the epoch of its splendor by assailing the organization that made it possible." For the most part, the War Department's partisans consisted of loyal Republicans and a great many Civil War veterans, including Chickamauga Park commissioner Henry Van Ness Boynton. However, not all Republicans took a firm position. According to one historian, the man who had played such a prominent role in both glorifying the war and exposing the army's weaknesses stood firmly on middle ground by supporting the president but distancing himself from the others. As "the Administration itself shook beneath the responsibility for Mr. Alger," Theodore Roosevelt, who disliked both Miles and Alger, "damn[ed] the War Department and its head in the happy confidence that his own official career was associated with the Navy."[26]

If collective memory is often the product of social conflict, then the polarizing debates between these factions after the Spanish-American War provided the ideal conditions for the construction of contentious and contradictory memories. The battle for memory was played out on the national stage during the Dodge Commission hearings and in Congress as its members debated the annexation provisions of the treaty. On the slightly less visible arena of the Chickamauga and Chattanooga National Military Park, the struggle over the memory of Camp Thomas took a somewhat different route to accomplish the same goals. In the months after the war, the McKinley administration worked to restore its credibility and take possession of the Philippines, Guam, Puerto Rico, and Cuba as the fruits of victory. At the same time, the park commissioners endeavored to wipe away the stain of Camp Thomas by restoring the commemorative landscape that had been violated by carelessness, filth, and disease.

Before the Spanish-American War could fade into the realm of memory, the McKinley administration had to tie up the loose ends left over from its successful campaign against Spain. The Dodge Commission and Beef Board dispensed with the most damaging charges against the War Department, but there was not much that could protect Secretary of War Alger's job. He managed to save face by pursuing a Michigan senate seat after his dismissal in July 1899, but his departure came as no surprise to anyone, including his supporters. General Miles remained as the commanding general of the army and eventually regained much of his former respect among veterans and peers by supporting and implementing Secretary of War Elihu Root's reforms. He continued to be a lightening rod for controversy before and after his retirement in 1903. McKinley's reelection and untimely death in 1901 helped to dilute much of the direct criticism of his administration's conduct of the war. However, two of the issues that occupied the attention of the new president, Theodore Roosevelt, were the ongoing war in the Philippines and the related debate over America's expansionism as a result of the war.[27]

What made these two issues relevant for collective memory of the war is that they had both a political and a moral element. The debate over the annexation of the territories ceded to the United States by Spain spilled over into larger questions of America's role in the world, its attitude toward people of other races, and whether the annexation of a few islands constituted a policy of imperialism. In spite of the altruistic motives put forth for the "rescue" of Cuba in April 1898, the realities tempered much of this misplaced enthusiasm, replacing it with indifference or outright hostility. The Cubans had not proved to be particularly useful or enthusiastic allies during the fighting and many American officials came away doubting that they could run the country themselves. This added yet another element to the divisive debate in Congress over the island's annexation. Relations between the inhabitants of Puerto Rico and the American forces occupying the island were far more positive, but the status of this territory was also a controversial subject.[28]

The reason for this debate rested in a small but influential wing of the Democratic Party that was against annexation of any territory as a result of the war and sought to block ratification of the treaty. Led by Nebraska Democrat William Jennings Bryan and seventy-two-year-old Republican Senator George F. Hoar and consisting of a diverse mix of philanthropists, businessmen, pacifists, suffragettes, and nativists, the anti-imperialists challenged the McKinley administration's acquisition of the former Spanish territory using a mixture of moral and economic arguments. Although they were ultimately unsuccessful in blocking passage of the treaty, their objections added another layer of doubt to the notion that the outcome of the war had been the best thing for both the United States and the non-white peoples it had "conquered" and annexed. Nowhere was the question of America's intentions more controversial and uncertain than in the Philippine Islands, where the United States was embroiled in a brutal war against Filipino rebels.[29]

The problems in the Philippines had begun almost immediately after George Dewey's victory at Manila Bay. The ground war to capture the city had gone fairly well during the months that followed, but the American commanders were distrustful of the Filipino army, led by Emilio Aguinaldo, that hovered on the outskirts of the city. Once Spain was defeated, the Filipinos directed their hostility toward the American occupation forces. Beginning in February 1899 with a fierce battle for Manila, a long, bitter struggle between the American forces and Aguinaldo's Army of Liberation for control of the islands began. During the course of this three-year-long conflict, a mix of U.S. Regulars, state volunteer regiments, and U.S. volunteer units struggled to defeat a determined opponent on his own territory. Eventually, the American commanders were forced to resort to some fairly heavy-handed methods in order to counter the hit-and-run guerrilla tactics favored by the Filipinos. Three years and 4,200 American deaths (and many thousands more Filipinos) later, the rebellion was finally suppressed and the islands secured in the hands of the United States.[30]

These territorial acquisitions, along with the necessary reforms in the War Department's organization, medical department, and command structure ushered the United States into its new status as a world power. The election of the hero of San Juan Hill to the governorship of New York in 1899 and the vice-presidency of the United States in 1900 seemed to uphold the heroic image of the war that he promoted during his campaigns. Yet, all was not quite settled in the memory of the War with Spain. The lingering specter of the Philippines was a reminder that American soldiers were still in harm's way and suffering the hardships of both combat and tropical diseases. There was not much that was heroic in the Philippine War, nor had the stain of the army's hardships at its stateside training and recovery camps entirely disappeared. Among the casualties of the Spanish War and Philippine conflict was the widespread belief that the experience of war was a way for the current generation to connect with the Civil War ideals of manhood.

Kristen Hoganson makes a convincing case that although such advocates of expansion, imperialism, and the "strenuous life" as Roosevelt and Henry Cabot Lodge maintained their position in American society, a growing number of people questioned this aggressive point of view. Among the ranks of the anti-imperialists were increasing numbers of women who were not persuaded by the aggressive and warlike definition of manhood. Many of these women had been involved in relief efforts at camps Thomas and Wikoff and had encountered the "good old boy" mentality that permeated the Army's medical corps and kept the nurses and caretakers from being as effective as they could have been. To these women, the manly notion that war, hardship, suffering, and exposure to more decadent cultures enhanced the development of young men was not only absurd, but downright harmful. In addition to the diseases that ravaged the troops, their exposure to alcohol, prostitutes, tobacco, and other vices in stateside canteens, big cities, and foreign countries was harmful to the perpetuation of proper Christian, American manhood. Rather than successfully spreading American virtues to inferior peoples, the brutality of the warfare that U.S. soldiers had encountered and carried out in the Philippines served to desensitize them and potentially render them as savage as the people they were fighting.

There were glaring contradictions between the war's confusing moral out-come and the originally chivalric motives of liberating the helpless Cubans, bringing liberty to an oppressed people, and upholding American manhood. These provided the prime ingredients for the construction of conflicting memo-ries of the war. Both the Cubans and the Filipinos largely repudiated the United States' self-appointed role as their liberators. The Cubans demanded indepen-dence (which they received only with strings attached), while the Filipinos took up arms against the American occupation forces in an attempt to win their au-tonomy. Neither the volunteer soldiers who remained in the service nor many people around the nation as a whole were prepared for another three years of separation, combat, atrocities, and hardship on some far-off Pacific island. The expansionists argued that it was necessary to subdue the Filipinos to give them the benefits of American culture, while the anti-imperialists argued that such a war of subjugation undermined the United States both at home and abroad.[31]

In the midst of these varied points of view lay the equally dichotomous meanings and memories of the Spanish-American War. On the one hand, it could be remembered as a symbol of national reunion, an example of martial might, and the catalyst for the nation's emergence as a great world power. This, by John Bodnar's definition, would constitute the *official* memory put forth by both the McKinley and Roosevelt administrations and adopted by most historians of the period. Conversely, there were those who believed that the war had been reckless and misguided from the start and was merely an ex-pansionist exercise carried out at the expense of the people both at home and abroad. This set of vernacular memories saw the War Department's inefficiency as a conspiracy and the nation's victory as the first steps toward imperialism. Theodore Roosevelt's aggressive presidency and jingoistic policies may have suppressed this second set of memories, but they did not go away entirely.

The one place that many negative memories regarding the War with Spain lingered was among some of its veterans. Their experiences at camps Thomas, Alger, and Wikoff left many of them frustrated and bitter. Their criticism of the War Department and its facilities provided a centerpiece for their claims that they had been misused and abandoned by the country. Those expressions contravened the ones held by the founders, caretakers, and commissioners of the Chickamauga and Chattanooga National Military Park, who felt that the army's troops had been well-served by their facility and had little room for complaint. Thus, in the midst of these wider postwar controversies, the status of the park, the legacy of the camp, and the reclamation of landscape and memory at Chickamauga would be largely determined by the men whose memories created the park in the first place, the veterans of the Civil War.

THIRTEEN

"A Lunacy Worthy of France"

The public and political fallout from the army's health issues, the beef scandal, anti-imperialist opposition to the treaty ending the war with Spain, and the lingering bloodshed of the Philippine insurrection made the construction of memories much more complicated in the years immediately following the War with Spain. Although the Republican administration survived the scandals and successfully retained power in subsequent elections, there were still many unresolved issues resulting from the war's conduct and outcome. As is the general pattern with memory construction, the seeds are planted at the time of the event, but the real meaning often does not surface until many years later. For a number of reasons, the roots of scandal and dissent failed to take hold in the American psyche in the decades after the war. In spite of the high-profile controversies surrounding the War Department's flawed performance, the official version of the conflict with Spain, characterizing it as "a splendid little war" that succeeded in strengthening America's position in the world, lingered on as the prevailing, though weakened, national memory.

This was possible because many of the key issues raised during the war were fairly quickly resolved and occasionally inspired significant reforms. The publicity surrounding the yellow-fever scare and outbreak of sickness that had forced the V Corps' evacuation from Cuba led to further research on the spread of both yellow fever and malaria. Within a remarkably short time, Dr. Walter Reed and his colleagues identified the mosquito as the primary means of transmission, which led directly to more effective forms of prevention. This in turn allowed the United States to continue its involvement in Latin America, most notably during the construction of the Panama Canal.

On the other hand, the prevailing opinion regarding typhoid fever in the army camps emphasized that the spread of the disease would have been entirely preventable if everyone in the military had done his job. According to one expert, in the event of another war, the army should "freely demand the services of [its] medical officers in their capacity of sanitary experts, and [expect] full and effective cooperation on the part of the line [officers] in the teachings, suggestions, and recommendations of the sanitary service." As part of its effort to implement such changes, the Army's much-maligned Medical Department underwent needed modifications, including the permanent addition of a female nurse corps.[1]

To improve the efficiency of the War Department, the new secretary, Elihu Root, took steps to increase the size of the Regular Army, create a permanent general staff, and clarify the role of the National Guard as a functional part of the military structure. In spite of the efforts of the anti-imperialists to block passage of the treaty, the United States annexed Guam, Puerto Rico, Hawaii, a few small islands in the Pacific, and the Philippines as colonial territories. The occupation of Cuba proved troublesome for General Brooke (former commander at Camp Thomas), who struggled with tropical diseases, sullen and resentful Cubans, and a makeshift army made up of unruly "immunes" and inexperienced U.S. volunteers. Eventually and reluctantly, the United States granted Cuba its conditional independence, retaining only a military base at Guantanamo Bay and some diplomatic concessions for its efforts. In 1900, the United States sent troops to suppress the Boxer Rebellion in China as part of its new role as a world power.[2]

Just as it had in the Civil War, military service in the Spanish-American War opened the door to political careers for many participants. Theodore Roosevelt's meteoric rise to the presidency was in many ways "a continuation of his military campaigns" and reinforced traditional heroic images of manhood. Even William Jennings Bryan, who led the anti-imperialists, tried to exploit his commission as a volunteer officer in spite of the fact that he never commanded troops or left the United States. Joe Wheeler, who supported both the war and expansionism, also enjoyed a brief flurry of consideration as a candidate for higher office before trading his Democratic seat in Congress for a stint in the Philippines and a commission in the Regular Army. Another veteran who ran on his "war record" was John Lind, who served as quartermaster of the 12th Minnesota while it was stationed at Camp Thomas. In spite of his rear-echelon status in a controversial stateside camp, Democrat Lind was elected to the governorship of a largely Republican state.[3]

In light of its stunning successes at Manila Bay and Santiago, one would think that the Navy would have emerged from the war unscathed by scandal. However, it could not escape the public embarrassment of an internal squabble between two of its highest-ranking officers. Admirals William Sampson and Winfield Scott Schley disagreed over who should receive credit for the defeat of the Spanish force at Santiago. When President McKinley promoted Sampson, who was absent from the actual battle, to a higher rank, the popular Schley took his case to the press and the people, but to no avail. On the other hand, the remaining untarnished naval hero, Admiral George Dewey, enjoyed so much popular acclaim that many thought he could win the presidency if he wanted to; oddly enough, he did not want the job. Richard Hobson, the young officer who sank a barge in Santiago harbor to block the Spanish fleet, also won a seat in Congress and the reputation as "the most kissed man in America" based on his heroic exploits.[4]

For every hero of the war, there were thousands more men who saw their service in a far less idealized context. Spurred on by their own misery and encouraged by the negative press aimed at the War Department, many volunteer veterans had joined the national chorus of criticism and victimization directed toward Alger and his staff at the War Department. Ironically, with the conclusions established by the Dodge Commission, the ouster of the unpopular Alger, and the resolve of the new secretary of war to correct the logistical and organizational problems, many of the soldiers' complaints disappeared from the public eye by early in the new century. In the long run, the aggrieved volunteers lost the battle for memory regarding their tainted service in the war. Many of those who saw action in Cuba, Puerto Rico, and the Philippines rested on their laurels; a few even took time to commemorate their service in the years after the war. However, for the thousands who were stuck at camps Thomas and Alger and suffered the indignities of disease and boredom, the battle for memory proved to be an uphill struggle. Nowhere is this more apparent than on the once-consecrated, recently violated, soon to be restored battlefield at Chickamauga.[5]

Throughout the many controversies, disputes, hearings, and debates, Henry Boynton stood firmly on the side of Russell Alger and the War Department. As a loyal Republican and Washington insider, Boynton did not hesitate to defend his friends and comrades in the administration from their political enemies and the yellow press. He described the attacks on Alger as "cruel, baseless, and infamous" and the actions of the press "journalistic diabolism." During the beef scandal, Boynton denounced Miles for his unpatriotic, self-serving attacks on the administration and was annoyed by the commanding general's "brazen and defiant" attempts to advance his career at the expense of the government and the nation. It was not just party or personal loyalty that put Boynton on the side of the War Department during the postwar controversies. He was even more motivated by his deep commitment to the integrity of the Chickamauga and Chattanooga National Military Park that he had helped create and promote.[6]

There is little doubt that Boynton understood the value of memory. He and his comrades had dedicated much of their postwar lives to honoring and remembering the accomplishments of their regiments, brigades, and divisions in the Army of the Cumberland. The battlefield at Chickamauga was this army's primary commemorative landscape. Boynton, the state and national commissioners, and the former soldiers from both armies had designed monuments, interpreted the battle lines, and dedicated the park for the express purpose of honoring their mutual valor and manhood. Even the park's secondary use as a training ground was meant to connect the current generation of soldiers with the deeds and accomplishments of the Civil War generation. As the park's founder, Henry Boynton acted as its pitch man, designer, administrator, and advocate. When the troops began arriving in the spring of 1898, he personally took charge in order to assure that the landscape would be used effectively. When things went wrong, he took it very much to heart and fought back vigorously.

To restore the integrity of the park and reconstruct the appropriate forum for the maintenance of Civil War memory, Boynton had to accomplish three distinct, but overlapping and seemingly contradictory, tasks. First, he had to answer the charges leveled at the park by soldiers and the press regarding its food and water supply, overcrowding, care for the sick, and general unhealthfulness. At least part of this process invited comparisons between the Spanish War soldiers and their Civil War counterparts; the other involved blaming the Spanish-American War volunteers for creating the mess themselves. Second, he and the government needed to repair the damage to the park and restore the commemorative landscape to its former status. In doing so, the commissioners would obliterate virtually all signs of Camp Thomas and most of the memories associated with it. And third, he would try to uphold the park's continued usefulness as a training ground for the War Department and the Chattanooga community by focusing exclusively on the positive aspects of the Camp Thomas experience.

It must have been a source of extreme discomfort for Boynton to have his park vilified from so many directions in the months during and after its occupation by the volunteers. Hearing soldiers describe the camp as a "Hell on Earth" comparable to Andersonville Prison must certainly have rankled Boynton and many of his veteran comrades. What had started out as a model training facility had been "in the crazed language of the time . . . held up to the country as a 'pest hole'" that was deemed "incurably infected" and unsuitable for habitation. While some simply exclaimed that "everything about the camp was badly managed," others singled out "filthy drinking and cooking water and poor sanitation" as the primary causes of disease and death.[7]

Critics also highlighted the allegedly poor care given to the sick as the camp's most egregious problem. One outraged writer denounced the health care at the camps as "a disgrace to civilization" and ranted that the soldiers were "being murdered by this wretched system." He challenged his readers to picture the worst types of wartime atrocities imaginable, "but for God's sake don't imagine that anything can be more terrible than any destruction of our volunteer army under the miserable hospital system." Such sensationalistic language helped draw clear and distinct battle lines over what would constitute the legacy and memory of Camp Thomas. Regardless of the degree to which these accusations were true or false, they demanded a firm and uncompromising rebuttal.[8]

Boynton was not an unbiased observer; he was an active participant in the events of April through August 1898 and had a vested interest in the defense of the War Department, the camp, and the park. He was also a man unaccustomed to being criticized or told he was wrong about things that he felt were within his realm of expertise. Boynton eagerly flew to the defense of Camp Thomas during his testimony before the Dodge Commission. He continued his crusade in letters, reports, and speeches to interested parties, particularly Civil War veterans. In general, his counterattack against the critics hinged on three main points: the park was well-suited for a camp, with no inherent flaws in the soil, water, or climate; that given the short period it had to work with, the War Department did a remarkable job in supplying and maintaining the camp and its hospitals; and finally, the fault for much of the sickness and bad publicity lay with the careless and duplicitous behavior of the volunteers themselves.

It comes as no surprise that Boynton approached the camp's critics from his own perspective as a veteran "who for four years saw war waged on a tremendous scale, with battle after battle whose casualty lists exceeded the previous records of the modern world." The plucky general could not resist comparing the "boys of 98" with the clearly superior "boys of 61–65" by suggesting that the elder veterans might have the advantage of "knowing beans . . . about . . . camp life, sanitation, and the care of rations and men." It was an understandable, but not entirely valid basis for comparison. The well-established memories that had already been constructed by the Civil War veterans revolved around the battles, marches, and hardships they had experienced at the peak of their service, not at their awkward beginnings. At Chickamauga, the members of the Army of the Cumberland had "marched the whole night before the battle opened . . . and fought through the day without food or water till night," then engaged in another full day of marching and fighting. By then, however, they were "iron veterans" with nearly two full years of service under their belts.

Although he was reluctant to measure his comrades' own period of clumsy adjustment to military life against that of the current soldiers, Boynton was quick to praise the efforts of the Regulars and volunteers who engaged in combat and produced "marvelous results" in the War with Spain. He praised the Regulars he observed at Camp Thomas for their "completeness of organization

... physical development ... perfection of discipline and drill ... intelligence and deportment of [the] rank and file, and the professional attainment of [their] officers." He also made clear that "the comparatively small numbers" of troops who faced the enemy in Cuba, Puerto Rico, and the Philippines "bore themselves as American soldiers always do, to the lasting credit of their country and themselves." However, he had little use for the "grumblers" at Camp Thomas who claimed that they had suffered great hardships on the same ground where he and his comrades had "marched two nights and fought two days with scarcely anything to eat or drink, and until every third man engaged was killed or wounded." In the struggle to redefine a sacred landscape, the outcome was already tilted toward those who held the most compelling memories.[9]

In his "Report upon the Sanitary Conditions of Camp George H. Thomas," Boynton emphasized the quality of the park's landscape and its suitability for a large-scale camp. He included Inspector General Joseph Breckinridge's observations that the rolling nature of the terrain, "with its surrounding hills and ridges, and cool bracing air, is most delightful." He also noted that Breckinridge's praise came after "he had full knowledge ... of all the sensational reports to the discredit of the park." The report also pointed out that there had been no disease problems among workers or troops camped at the park during its construction and dedication. Assistant Adjutant General Nicholas Senn was quoted as saying that "Chickamauga Park is admirably adapted for a large camp" due to the "vastness of the ground," which allowed regiments to camp a reasonable distance from one another. As for those who criticized General Brooke's original placement of camps in the woods, Boynton responded by pointing out that "the 5,000 acres of forest in which the volunteers were camped ... are not so thickly shaded, as has been persistently represented, as to deprive the camps of sunlight, and render them damp and unhealthy."[10]

The public complaints about poor equipment and food drew a sharp response from Boynton, which reflected his comparative view of the issues. In his report, he stated unequivocally that "the work of the Quartermaster and Commissary Departments [at Camp Thomas] was beyond praise, and the quality, quantity, and variety of material furnished exceeded anything that the veterans of the Civil War ever saw or dreamed of." In a speech to his comrades in the 35th Ohio, he reminded them of their night on the battlefield in 1863 "with only a few crackers and scraps of bacon and pork which could not be cooked" because the hostile lines were so close together. In contrast, he pointed out that the Camp Thomas bakery produced bread daily for "every soldier and civilian employee of that army" and added that 5,100,000 pounds of fresh beef had been issued "without the loss of a pound, except where some of it fell into the hands of ... men who did not know how to care for fresh meat in hot weather."

He also explained that the men got "good" bacon and "three vegetable rations," yet, "the country was made to believe that the men were given spoiled food, and short rations even of that."

The general also expected that his comrades would have little sympathy for modern soldiers who had been transported by the War Department to and from their training camps in modern passenger cars instead of the "box, cattle, and platform cars in which you rode the very few times you were favored with railroad transportation." In short, it seemed that the Spanish War soldiers had enjoyed a certain degree of luxury when it came to transportation and food compared to the experiences of the Civil War veterans. He stressed that these conveniences were "fair indications of the splendid management [by the War Department] throughout all the great camps" and that in spite of some understandable missteps, "its main results were wonderful, and commendable, beyond any similar efforts in military history." The problem, it seemed, was that the current generation of soldiers could not face their hardships "without filling the land with baby-talk and groaning because they were not daily served with pies as their mothers used to make."[11]

Interestingly, Boynton did take a slight detour from his comparative bashing of the volunteer soldiers to attack one of the straw men of Camp Thomas, the canteens and the Midway. He blamed the canteens for promoting sickness by serving beer in hot weather, but reserved his most scathing condemnation for the Midway "pest hole" and its "filthy dens" of temptation. As noted earlier in this study, he and the camp commanders tried to regulate the sale of "indigestible pies, green fruits, pop, manufactured milk, and slop of every name and every deleterious nature" as a way of slowing the spread of sickness. Boynton also noted that a liberal pass policy, particularly after General Brooke's departure, allowed more volunteers into Chattanooga, which "thronged with soldiers and all the saloons and viler places were abundantly patronized day and night." This line of argument favored Boynton's overall defense because it implied that outside forces had caused the problem, not his friend Brooke's management of the camp. While he may have overstated the case by claiming that "a large percentage of the sick list at any one time was directly attributable to the debauchery in Chattanooga," such a statement suggested that the soldiers lacked self-control and brought some of the problems on themselves.[12]

Perhaps no subject aroused more passion among both the camp's detractors and its defenders than the purity of the water supply in Chickamauga Park. The alleged lack of good drinking water was a factor in both the overall comfort and health of the volunteers and as a suspected vector for the spread of typhoid fever. This was a particularly sensitive issue to Boynton and the other park officials because questions about the inherent purity of the water supply could jeopardize the long-term use of the facility as a training ground. Boynton noted in his October 1898 report that a plan to keep troops stationed there after the war had failed because "such a howl was raised in reference to the unhealthy conditions of the park." Boynton tried to counter such claims by stating that "there is no more healthful region in the United States than the two mountain counties of north Georgia in which Camp Thomas lies." General Alger concurred, insisting that "these unhealthy conditions are not chargeable to the site or fitness of Camp Thomas for assembling a large body of soldiers." Notwithstanding such general claims, Boynton knew that if the future of the park depended, in part, on its continued usefulness as a training ground, then the issue of its water would have to be put to rest.

In his sanitation report, Boynton quoted Inspector General Breckinridge, who upheld the quality of the water supply and remarked that "the impure water talk, in my opinion, is simply nonsense of the worse type." Boynton suggested that "the first outcries against the water in the camp" may have been "started by the agents of several filter firms who came . . . for the purpose of securing the use of their filters." The agents tried to stir up business by citing bogus scientific reports claiming that the water was bad and fomenting fears of an epidemic. Boynton condemned such tactics, but conceded that it was "probably the most successful advertising device brought to the attention of those in command during the history of the camp." Despite having found a chemist in Knoxville who attested to the purity of the camp's wells and springs, Boynton complained that "the press of that city had been engaged in a bitter and prolonged attack upon the character of the water supply at Chickamauga."[13]

Further clarification of the state of the water supply can be found in a report filed in October 1898 by park engineer Edward E. Betts. Betts addressed many of the complaints about the water and described the steps that the park officials took to remedy the problems. At various times, they replaced pipes and pumps; dug a trench to bypass the garbage washed into creek near the intake pipe; placed a stone dike nearby, which "scoured the bottom to rock and kept the intake pipes free"; and placed guards over the springs to prevent further pollution. Based on these efforts and the conclusions of several scientific studies, Betts could confidently say that "it is just and right to state here that the water supply of Camp Thomas has always been pure, full, convenient, and complete for men and animals for all purposes." Given that knowledge, the reports "by ill-informed and careless writers about the water supply at Camp Thomas, charging scarcity and contamination" were false, and "undoubtedly inspired by interested parties."[14]

Of course, the outbreak of typhoid fever raised everyone's concerns about the water supply to new levels. There were two very different ways of explaining the role of the water in the epidemic. One report published in September 1898 surmised that the epidemic that had ravaged the camp "had the water supply for the main if not the exclusive cause." However, to support this statement, the article went on to mention how the existing water sources were tainted by runoff from the camps and that drinking water was mishandled during transport. As the preliminary Reed Report clarified a few months later, water was neither the cause nor the primary means of infection during the outbreak of typhoid fever (flies played a much larger role). Although some water was polluted by the poor placement of specific regimental camps and the careless disposal of waste, preventive measures like filtering and boiling water would not have slowed the spread of the typhoid *bacilli* as long as other sanitary precautions were being violated.[15]

In a moment of inspired rhetoric before his comrades in October 1899, Henry Boynton stated that "there was no such thing as polluted water at Chickamauga, any more than there was such a thing as embalmed beef." Aside from the cheap shot at General Miles's discredited claims regarding meat, Boynton actually misstated his case. What he really meant to say was that there was no problem with the water supply that was not caused by outside factors, namely the poor sanitary habits of the volunteers. As several other witnesses would suggest, the normally healthy soil and water in the park had been *temporarily* polluted by the careless disposal of waste in direct violation of orders from the camp commanders. As proof of this, Boynton referred to the occupation of the camp by Regular troops both before and after the epidemic. He was particularly anxious to point out that among the properly disciplined and well-officered 6th and 8th U.S. volunteers, who "camped in the same section of the park where the departing troops had been, not a case of fever developed in either of these forces."[16]

The intrepid Boynton did not settle for a passive defense; he had more and bigger fish to fry. His sanitation report contained detailed accounts of specific regiments that were guilty of promoting filthy conditions in their camps, either through ignorance or defiant malice. First, he identified those who had contributed to the so-called "water crisis" by creating circumstances that fouled the available supply. For example, the 1st Mississippi, 3rd Tennessee, 8th New York, and 1st Vermont allegedly polluted an otherwise clear stream by washing clothes in an area of the creek outside of the park. According to the report, the 1st South Carolina, 9th Pennsylvania, and 5th Missouri trenched their camps and created a mud hole on the lower ground. This puddle was then used by horses, which in turn exposed the men who used this water to all manner of diseases, including typhoid. It is important to note that some of the camp's loudest and most persistent complainers were among the regiments Boynton singled out for criticism.

Not only was Boynton sure that these units had contributed to the fouling of the camp's otherwise pure water supply, he was also convinced that "the widespread attacks upon the wholesomeness of the water supply of the park have been largely directed by various officers of the troops encamped here and by the sensational press of the country." From his point of view, the croakers and complainers were not motivated by concern for their men; rather, they were trying to cover up their own incompetence and culpability. Boynton clearly spelled out his belief that the accusations of "unhealthfulness [sic] and polluted water . . . were excuses behind which many officers who had neglected sanitary orders sought to shield themselves from the consequences of their own neglect." Henry Boynton's experiences in the military, newspapers, and politics had taught him that in the battle for credibility and memory, nothing is gained by holding back. In his mind, the public attacks on his park had been wild and irresponsible; thus, there was no reason to refrain from firing back with all the weapons at his disposal.[17]

General Boynton reserved a special dose of vitriol for the 8th New York, a regiment he felt was guilty of a multitude of sins. In a report to the secretary of war, he used the published criticism of the camp by New York's surgeon general to illustrate how easily the truth was being distorted by these self-interested volunteers. The state official had publicly complained that "the camp was in bad sanitary condition . . . [and] situated in an open field in the hot sun with no water to be found within five miles." Boynton countered this claim by pointing out that the regiment's officers had moved the camp out of the woods ten days prior to this visit because they thought it would help contain sickness. The new camp was located on "clean ground" that had never been occupied by other troops and was within two miles of an adequate and unadulterated water source. Thus, New York surgeon general's critical observations were of a camp that "had been transformed within this period by the troops of the 8th New York into a place filthier and dirtier than the slums of New York." Boynton also accused this regiment of blatantly padding its sick list and added that it operated "one of the filthiest and most disgusting canteens to be found in the entire army."[18]

If the 8th New York was the most infamous violator, there was more proof for Boynton's charges of laxity and neglect in the condition of various regimental camps after the troops pulled out of them. Boynton claims that "it was a notorious fact that . . . the sinks of the 12th Minnesota, the 5th Pennsylvania, the 12th New York, and the 9th Pennsylvania, were in exceedingly filthy condition, and remained so up to the time that their first camps were abandoned." In spite of specific orders requiring that the troops clean up after themselves, several of these regiments left behind open, overflowing latrines and other filth when they moved or departed for home. In addition to the actions of these specific offenders, the entire facility showed signs of having been trashed by the volunteers. In the park commission's widely publicized 1899 report to the secretary of war, Boynton explained that "the park was left in a most filthy and deplorable condition by the outgoing troops, so far as unfilled sinks . . . and unburned refuse of various kinds could defile it." This was clearly more than mere carelessness; it was an affront to the park's sacred ground.[19]

Boynton made it clear that he considered these offenses acts of deliberate defilement by including accounts of the most blatant and disgusting violations of camp policy. He described the ground around the camp of the 1st Maine as "exceedingly filthy, owing to the fact that many of the men did not use the sinks." Although the camp was next to the brigade commander's headquarters, workmen in the quarry 150 yards away complained about the sight and smell of soldiers doing their sanitary business on the ground and "found it difficult to prosecute their work on account of these indecencies." There were also problems with the "dumping of camp refuse and manure in the woods [and] . . . causing a great nuisance and very serious menace to health." The horrific state of things going on in the camps in direct violation of military orders led Boynton to surmise that "the most salubrious place in the world, watered by fountains of perpetual youth, would have bred sickness under the conditions as were created by these officers."[20]

Not surprisingly, Boynton considered the complaints registered against the camp's hospitals as simply variations of the same pattern, and he responded to them in kind. During one his speeches, he insisted that "representing . . . the hospitals as in terrible condition, was the quickest way and the shortest way which the diabolical journals of sensationalism found to the hearts of the people." Boynton appealed to his fellow veterans, saying "that those hospitals which received the severest press denunciations . . . were better and more fully supplied than any we saw during the Civil War." He repeated his contention that the sources of most of the complaints were from officers covering up their own neglect by attacking the camp administrators and the hospitals. He admitted that there had been some problems, such as overcrowding, a lack of nurses, and some disorganization, but assured his audience that "there was no lack of supplies or care or excellent attention, beyond what was inseparable from the rapid organization of a great camp."[21]

In response to the public outcry that the care for the sick had been rife with incompetence and neglect, Boynton wrote that "so far from believing . . . that medical officers have been heartless or negligent, I believe that these officers and hospital attendants . . . have exerted themselves to discharge their duties faithfully." As proof of this assertion, he pointed out that "they have worked unceasingly until a quarter of the whole force has itself been stricken by disease resulting from their exhausting labors." He asserted that "the death rate at Camp Thomas is the best test of all the sensational stories with which the country was deceived, enraged, and driven well-nigh crazy." Contrary to frantic claims that "the soldiers there died off like sheep," Boynton estimated that the number of deaths at the camp from its opening to its close was a minute percentage of its total population. As far as the general was concerned, the accusations against the medical department were motivated by the biases and self interest of dishonest men and therefore were as baseless as all the others.[22]

A few soldiers took their complaints about the medical care far enough to reach high-ranking authorities within the military hierarchy. A soldier named Gibson, from the 1st Mississippi, claimed that he had received poor treatment from an incompetent surgeon in the Second Division hospital, where he was being treated for typhoid fever and pneumonia. He also complained that when he passed around a petition regarding his dilemma, he was arrested by camp authorities. The soldier's case unraveled when Boynton could find no record of his pneumonia, determined that the doctor was in fact "a physician in excellent standing," and got the man to admit that he had not really been arrested. Yet, as Boynton pointed out, the newspapers in the soldier's hometown back in Mississippi had picked up on the story, which contributed to the growing public hostility toward the hospital conditions in the camp.[23]

Henry Boynton had spearheaded the counterattack against the War Department's critics, reserving his sharpest words for the state volunteers who had described Camp Thomas in the harshest, most negative terms. Although the complainers and newspapers who leveled the charges against the administration had skillfully utilized the shocking, unstable situation in 1898, their momentum had faded by late 1899. The more experienced Boynton took advantage of both timing and perspective as he formulated his indictment of those who mislead the nation with "horrible tales . . . that finally caused the honest people of this land to believe that inhumanity in every form to their boys and failure and neglect at every branch of military duty were the rule without exception at Camp Thomas." Boynton had done more than systematically dissect these tales; he had challenged the manhood of the soldiers who made the complaints.[24]

In the speeches he gave to his comrades Boynton made it abundantly clear that with the possible exception of the men who had seen combat, many of the Spanish-American War volunteers did not measure up to the standards set by veterans of the Civil War. Writing a year before his death, Boynton explained that once a soldier had volunteered to serve, his primary responsibility in time of war was "faithfully and efficiently executing all orders, whether on the battlefield or elsewhere under the flag." While the volunteers had rallied with enough enthusiasm, many of them had failed miserably at the task of becoming soldiers.

Reminding the reader that "once enrolled, and subject to orders, it is not in the power of any soldier to control his career," he emphasized the fact that "the humblest private places his life at the disposal of the government." Clearly, the complaints that resonated from Camp Thomas and the other stateside camps contradicted the established standards of soldierly duty.[25]

Boynton and his comrades realized that the torch needed to be passed from their generation of veterans to the next. He declared that the Civil War was "a memory of great days of the Republic that will always live and grow brighter as the years pass—but its leaders are either at rest or nearing the limit of life." While Spanish War veterans like Theodore Roosevelt had lived up to the mantle they inherited, others had not. In Boynton's mind, the performance of the War Department, made up of many Civil War veterans, had been "wonderful and credible to a degree that language can scarcely express." Those who complained about the inevitable shortages and mistakes that were part of war's hardships had failed to comprehend what "every true soldier" should have understood: "The quartermaster's and commissary's departments could not supply cradles and trundle-beds and Mother Winslow's Soothing Syrup on the spur of the moment, and so it was impossible to check the squalling of the few who imagined they were going on a summer encampment, and found themselves in war camps instead. And the sensational journals became the willing organs in all this baby business." Not only had these malcontents attacked their own War Department during a decisive military victory, but they had compromised their own status as men and veterans in the process. It was a mistake that would cost them dearly in the battle for memory and result in their exclusion from the sacred landscape at Chickamauga Park.[26]

During the course of his defense of the War Department and his vilification of those who attacked it, Boynton drew on images of manhood, duty, and patriotism that his fellow veterans would understand. The memory presented by the veterans was of a nation that had achieved a victory against a formidable foe in spite of its notable lack of military preparedness. It had liberated oppressed people, shown great humanity to its defeated enemies, and acquired territories that served to usher in its status as a world power. Yet there had been a rash of incomprehensible complaints about the government's conduct of the war that threatened the memory and meaning of the victory.

Boynton saw this struggle as a moral conflict and insisted that once people understood the truth about the camps, the facts would "supplant the wild craze founded, in every material element, upon abominable falsehood" that in his opinion had "swept the nation into a lunacy worthy of France." He singled out the politically motivated opposition, "including the Copperheads of Boston and the Reform Club of Massachusetts," whom he accused of "investigating war management by means of perfumed correspondence from its luxurious offices, and pronouncing it bad." Boynton could not understand how so many people could have been taken in by "cruel, baseless, false, and damnable accusations," which had threatened the honor of the nation's military establishment and watered down the fruits of victory. Such a condemnation suggested that if the protesters were not guilty of treasonous insanity, they were at least culpable for their effeminate delusions and belonged with "the wildest of their fellow lunatics in France."[27]

Worse yet, the misguided volunteers who precipitated this malicious attack on the War Department had used the sacred ground of the Chickamauga and Chattanooga National Military Park as one of their key platforms. By doing so, they had violated both the battlefield landscape and the memories it contained. The volunteers had created filth but complained about how dirty the camp was. Their careless behavior caused disease, which in turn led to more fussing about the care they received. Instead of taking responsibility for their mistakes, the officers of the offending regiments had tried to shift the blame to the park's soil, water, and climate. Boynton described the mess they made in classical and biblical terms, speculating that "if the Elysian Fields could have been invaded by some of the regiments of our National Guard . . . these fair fields of fable would have been known, instead, in mythological history, as a veritable Golgotha." Given the value of the battlefield's commemorative landscape, it was the singular task of the Civil War veterans and the park commissioners to make sure that such a fate did not await the Chickamauga Park.[28]

The immediate task facing the park commissioners in the fall of 1898 was to clean up the mess left by the volunteers. The work began before the last troops had gone and continued throughout the next year as "more than 3,000 sinks were disinfected and filled, buildings dismantled, refuse burned, ditches obliterated, and manure from the corrals used to check erosion." The volunteers left a great deal of trash behind, in spite of specific orders to the contrary, and it required a large crew of laborers to perform these tasks. Several buildings had been damaged, and one had been completely dismantled by soldiers for use as flooring for tents and firewood, notwithstanding the fact that "all lumber for legitimate uses was furnished by the Quartermaster Department on application." Another building that the army had used to store munitions was completely destroyed by a mysterious explosion, which may have been caused by members of an artillery unit camped nearby. According to Engineer Betts, the time and materials necessary to correct what the volunteers failed to clean up themselves cost the park $10,000 more than it normally would have spent.[29]

Some of the most glaring and costly damage caused by the occupying forces was to the trees and foliage of the park. In August 1898, Boynton complained to Inspector General Breckinridge that "the serious damage to the forests in important historical portions of the Park has been very great" due to "careless disregard of positive and most specific orders upon the subject." He singled out the 3rd U.S. Volunteer Cavalry for inflicting "general and serious destruction" on a twenty-acre tract of trees surrounding its camp and lamented the devastation caused by both horses and men on other areas. Not only was he concerned about the value of the trees themselves, but he pointed out that much of the area in danger of being ravaged "is historically one of the most important tracts of the battlefield." Boynton condemned the "utter uselessness" of the destruction and attributed much of it to the lack of obedience to orders and an overall "carelessness and neglect" by both officers and enlisted men. To the distraught commissioner, the carnage to the forests throughout the park had been "painful to contemplate."[30]

By the fall of 1899, Boynton was able to report to his comrades that "you will be glad to know that this use [by the War Department] of the Park has not in any way defaced it, and you would not be able to tell . . . that it had been occupied at all." The few remaining buildings and the railroad siding at Lytle would be an asset to the army's future use of the grounds "without in any way interfering with the interests of the park." Other than an abundance of "excellent grass" that had grown prolifically where horses or mules had been pastured, nearly all physical signs of the camp had been obliterated by the cleanup effort. This obliteration was not just a maintenance issue; it was part of the process of reclaiming the commemorative landscape. The struggle to reclaim the park's rightful memory from the stain of scandal was also being won in other ways far from the actual battlefield. Boynton reported that in spite of all the negative publicity surrounding the park, Congress "passed the full appropriation asked for . . . without objection, or a formal vote."[31]

General Boynton had wasted little time getting back to the business of running the park, and his efforts certainly contributed to its rapid recovery. As early as 15 August 1898, he was lobbying to have orders drawn up by the War Department that would free him of his other duties with the army and give him the authority to begin the cleanup process. Citing his concerns over the continued "cutting and barking of timber" and the garbage accumulating in the camps, Boynton expressed his wish "to be enabled to fully discharge my duty to the Secretary in protecting the park." During the Dodge hearings in November, he urged Engineer Betts to complete work on a contour map of Camp Thomas, showing troop positions and water supplies. Boynton felt that a map illustrating "the very great area of the Park which was unoccupied" would serve as "a very effective object lesson for this Army Commission."[32]

While concerns about trees, buildings, and the natural landscape within the park filled a great deal of the staff's time and effort, reports of damage done by the soldiers to private property also required some attention. In two separate inquiries, a member of the Spanish War Claims Board contacted Engineer Betts asking for information on claims by local citizens against the park. A farmer named Gordon claimed that soldiers of the 5th Pennsylvania and 12th Minnesota cut timber worth $200 on his land without permission and that others damaged a substantial portion of his crops. He eventually filed a claim for damages to fencing, crops, trees, and other property that amounted to over $2,500; however, the Claims Board eventually disallowed most of it. Another local businessman argued that the regular watering of army teams above his mill cut off the water supply for 117 days. He estimated his financial loss as being ten dollars per day. Many of the cases considered by the Congressional Claims Board required that Boynton, Betts, A. P. Stewart, and other military and park personnel investigate their validity before it allocated any money. Some of these tales were distressing; others were clearly bogus attempts to get money from the government. Unfortunately, all of them warranted time and attention.

A claim filed by Mrs. F. M. Osborne, a widow with eight children who lived near the park and owned a small orchard, alleged that on numerous occasions, soldiers from the camp "carried away all the apples, tramped down and ruined all of the peas growing in said orchard, thereby incurring a total loss to her." Various witnesses swore that the depredations took place "under [her] continuous and persistent protests, which were wholly disregarded by the soldiers." They apparently also stole her chickens "and oftentimes would curse and abuse" the family when they complained about the thefts. Her total claim for the apples, peas, and chickens amounted to $195. A store owner named Berger made his claim based on a "raid" made on his store by members of the 4th Pennsylvania and 5th Illinois, who "tore down his stock of goods and threw goods on the floor, tramped upon them, and thereby injuring them and damaging them very greatly." Like Mrs. Osborne, he also reported being insulted and abused by the men as they ransacked his place of business. His claim was for the modest amount of $106.[33]

While it is likely that some of these claims were generated by opportunistic lawyers taking advantage of the publicity surrounding the camp and park, others supported Boynton's contention that the camp's soldiers were out of control much of the time. The common thread running through many of these accounts was the lack of discipline among the men, the absence of officers during the incidents, and the disrespect the volunteers expressed toward both people and property. Even if half the claims were dismissed because there was no evidence or they had taken place off of national park property, it was clear that some soldiers behaved like they were foraging in enemy country. The theft of food and crops seemed particularly unnecessary because of the relative abundance of food in and around the camps. Notwithstanding the variety of details, the volunteers had again failed to live up to the standards of respect, discipline, and honor that were expected of them by their elders.

Although the young soldiers had shown considerable disrespect for the soil, water, trees, and neighbors, they did manage to avoid doing substantial damage to the monuments, markers, cannons, and other objects directly related to the battle. In his October 1898 report, Engineer Betts indicated that "the damage to the monuments, markers, and other works by the soldiers has been comparatively little" next to the carnage left behind on the rest of the landscape. There was some damage to a couple of gun carriages due to reckless driving and three fifty-five pound, eight-inch shells had been stolen off of the stacks "and probably shipped home as relics." The three monuments that were "slightly disfigured" were quickly repaired, and "in two of these cases, the culprit was discovered and punished." There was other minor damage to monuments early in the occupation as a result of horses and mules rubbing against them; the park responded by placing barbed wire around some of them and requiring that all livestock be kept at a safe distance.[34]

Boynton and the park commissioners successfully countered many of the negative effects of the Camp Thomas experience in the months after the war by answering their critics and restoring the damaged landscape. In the process, they reinforced their collective belief that the Civil War experience was the bar by which American manhood and martial skill should be measured. As a consequence of their complaints and criticisms of the army and Camp Thomas, many of the Spanish-American War volunteers had fallen short of their forefathers' expectations. Confronting the physical damage to the park reinforced these unfavorable opinions and encouraged a quick and efficient restoration of the commemorative landscape. There was more at stake for the park's supporters than just a return to more appropriate uses for the landscape. To prove that the charges against the park were unfounded, Boynton and his comrades threw their support to a local effort to secure a permanent military installation in the vicinity. To accomplish this, they could not completely obliterate the Camp Thomas experience; they simply had to reconfigure the memory of that sultry, sickly summer.

FOURTEEN

"Where American Valor Met American Valor"

enry Boynton's defense of the park and the criticisms he leveled at General
Miles and the soldiers who complained about their service in the War with
Spain were the latest in a long series of efforts by the Army of the Cumberland's veterans to uphold the honor and memory of their Civil War service.
The battlefield was sacred ground that the veterans had willingly offered to the
nation as a camp for its volunteers. Naming it Camp George H. Thomas was
meant to honor the general who best represented the Army of the Cumberland's toughness, perseverance, and heroic devotion to duty. The disaster that
overwhelmed the park in 1898 was a shocking slap in the face to their good
intentions and threatened their carefully constructed commemorative landscape. Having stifled their most egregious critics, Boynton and the other commissioners worked to restore, repair, and re-sanctify their sacred landscape.
Not content to return to the status quo, they then proceeded to push for even
more recognition by advocating the creation of a permanent military installation on the edge of the park.

A key step in the rehabilitation of the park and the reconstruction of
Civil War memory was the continuation of commemorative rituals on the
battlefield. The placement of state and unit monuments, along with the requisite dedication ceremonies, went a long way toward reestablishing the
park's primary purpose. During the park's occupation, at least two monument dedications took place amid the military hoopla. Betts reported that
on 12 May 1898, "the Tennessee state commissioners dedicated their monuments in Chickamauga Park and Snodgrass Hill," and on 9 July the Wisconsin commissioners held a dedication on Orchard Knob in Chattanooga. In
each case, "arrangements were made for the public's comfort" by providing
seating platforms or chairs.[1]

During the following year, additional state monuments and markers went
up in the park as the landscape returned to normal. Indiana dedicated a total of thirty-seven monuments and seventy-five unit markers, including the

FIG. 42: The Georgia monument was one of many state monuments placed through-out the Chickamauga and Chattanooga National Military Park in the decade fol-lowing the Spanish-American War. Dignitaries at the monument's 1899 dedication included Gov. Allen Chandler and General Longstreet and his wife. Paul A Hiener Collection, Chattanooga–Hamilton County Bicentennial Library.

impressive Wilder (Brigade Monument) Tower, on 23 September 1900. The event drew a crowd of over 1,000 that included the state's governor, commis-sioners, and a host of its veterans. During this ceremony, General Boynton took the time to recognize the former Confederates, whose attendance "lifts today in your honor a lofty edifice of patriotism." Speaking on behalf of the secretary of war, he intoned that "this monument of grand proportions to a splendid brigade, thus dedicated by North and South, is received, with a due sense of honor conferred into the perpetual care and keeping of our restored, indissoluble, and mighty Union."

The state of Illinois constructed "two state monuments of large dimensions and artistic design," which were scheduled to be dedicated by its commission in January 1901. New York, whose troops had done most of their fighting around Chattanooga, placed the venerable Daniel Sickles at the head of its monument commission, which, according to Boynton, "promises to place New York at the head of all state efforts at the various battlefield parks." He also noted that the state had a large sum of money available for the shaft of a monument on

Lookout Mountain and "a liberal appropriation for a colossal bronze group at the summit." He predicted that New York's effort "will place it far in advance of any monument on any military field in the country, not excepting New York on the Gettysburg field."[2]

Kentucky and Georgia both dedicated "imposing state monuments" on 4 May 1899, in concurrent ceremonies. The Kentucky activities drew most of the press's attention due to the presence of the state governor, W. O. Bradley, and former Confederate general James Longstreet. The newspaper article noted that the governor's previous visit to the park had been "to alleviate the suffering of soldiers from Kentucky who had volunteered to fight under the old flag against Spain." On this occasion, however, his task "was to present to the national government a monument emblazoning in letters upon bronze for future generations the deeds of those Kentucky regiments who wore the blue and those who wore the gray." The coverage also indicated that when the speakers mentioned General Longstreet in their remarks, "there was always applause." In addition to adding to the ambiance of the battlefield, Kentucky's monument reemphasized the reunion spirit that had characterized the park since its inception.[3]

In a report to his fellow Army of the Cumberland veterans, Henry Boynton described the Georgia monument "as the finest one in Chickamauga Park." However, as he elaborated, the compliment became more convoluted. The monument "stands eighty-seven feet high, and while height and other large dimensions are not necessarily evidence of artistic beauty," he expounded that "this is in every respect what it should be for a monument of those imposing proportions." Regardless of what he thought of the individual designs, the placement of dedication of monuments served to reinforce the commemorative use of the landscape and re-sanctify the ground that had been violated by the excesses of the camp. By 1900, Boynton could report that commissions in South Carolina, Pennsylvania, Michigan, Ohio, Indiana, Minnesota, Mississippi, Louisiana, and Virginia were all planning to construct state memorials at various locations in the park.[4]

The park commission also took another definitive step toward reestablishing the primacy of Civil War memory on the landscape by inviting members of Congress, state governors, and the veterans of both the Union and Confederate armies to return to the park in October 1900 "to secure an inspection . . . of all historical work thus far completed on the park with a view to the correction of such errors as may have been made in inscriptions upon tablets or monuments and locations of battle lines." Although there was a small risk of re-igniting controversies between various units and leaders, the benefits of this invitation far outweighed the risks. As the War Department circular pointed out, "the ranks of the veterans of these fields have sorrowfully diminished, [yet] enough remain to inspect and intelligently correct all errors, and thus insist . . . on assuring historical accuracy in the restoration of [these] notable fields." More importantly, such an effort served to reintroduce the veterans to their sacred ground and reinvigorate the construction of memory that was interrupted by Camp Thomas.[5]

The veterans, including the former Confederates, responded enthusiastically to this request. Gen. John B. Gordon, president of the United Confederate Veterans, urged all southern veterans and citizens to consider this request "so that they can see the impartiality and fairness which has actuated this splendid commission and see the praiseworthy and strenuous efforts now made by the patriotic Union soldier and his associates to render full and exact justice to both sides." In his appeal, Gordon urged "the remnant of those heroic survivors" to gather "not in battle array, nor in anger . . . but, in amity . . . fraternity and brotherhood" in order to reaffirm their accomplishments. He was certain that by locating the "exact spots where American valor met American valor in deadly conflict . . . future generations can visit these battlefields . . . and there gather inspiration for renewed devotion to [our] love for our common country." Gordon had identified nearly all the values that had inspired the military park in the first place, while glaringly ignoring the role of the recent War with Spain in keeping those values alive.

The inspection visits also corresponded with the Society of the Army of the Cumberland's annual meeting, thus giving that organization a needed boost in membership and attendance from other organizations. In an informal invitation to its own members, the society wrote, "it is expected that one of the attractions of this Reunion will be the opportunity afforded to meet, as friends, many of the survivors of the gallant men who followed Bragg and Longstreet." It also invited members to bring their families and friends "and renew . . . those sentiments of patriotism and valor which have won glory and renown for . . . American soldiers." The organizers of this grand event also reminded the invitees that the railroads were offering reduced fares, a trolley service would convey them to the edge of the park, there were plenty of accommodations in the city, and that the weather in the region was particularly pleasant during that time of year.[6]

The results of the inspection tour were satisfying, but not all that dramatic. Although they were issued a carefully worded card that gave them the opportunity to correct specific mistakes, the veterans only reported a handful of location and inscription errors. Although not mentioned specifically in the report, one of those may have been registered by the Survivor's Association of the 8th Indiana Cavalry and 39th Indiana (Mounted Infantry) Volunteers, who submitted an impassioned grievance to the park commissioners in August 1901, claiming that other units had been given credit for their actions on 20 September 1863. They challenged the park's language on the interpretive markers, which "do great injustice and are in contravention of the very purposes for which the Chickamauga National Park was created—the establishment and perpetuation of the truths of history." Their complaint was not that their monument was incorrectly located, but that the state and national commissioners had "surrounded the monument with false battle markers and inscriptions on monuments of other regiments," which served as "false witnesses" to claims that they had occupied the Glenn Hill before the 39th had arrived and after it had been forced to withdraw. The survivors of that regiment disputed these facts and implored the commissioners to "chisel out" the misleading texts, so that "the memory of our noble dead must not be coupled with a lie."[7]

Notwithstanding the occasional conflict, the park commissioners and Civil War veterans had successfully regained control of their battlefield landscape. The large gathering of Union and Confederate veterans in 1900 had shown the park to be totally repaired and fully recommitted to telling the story of the battles of Chickamauga and Chattanooga. Individuals and groups of veterans returned with their families over the next few years to revisit the sites of their great accomplishments. The veterans' age and increasing infirmities made visiting the battlefield more difficult. During a meeting of the Society of the Army of the Cumberland, General Wilder suggested building a trolley line through the park to alleviate the high cost of renting a horse and buggy. Other members reacted with horror at the prospect, with one stating that "I would just as soon grant a charter build an electric road . . . to run a line of cars over my mother's grave as to build it through Chickamauga Park."

The objections raised against this suggestion revealed the depth of feelings for the sacredness of the site and the old soldiers' reactions to the modern world. Col. D. M. Steward, who made the above remark, clarified his opinion, stating "it seems to me that this is a hallowed ground; . . . the blood of our fathers and brothers and friends . . . as well as the blood of the Confederates . . . flowed on that ground." He made it clear that those who wanted access to the park would have to do it "without desecrating it by railroads and overhead trolley wires and all the other indications of this gross commercialism to which our country had been driven." He also reminded his comrades that attempts to get rid of a trolley line at Gettysburg Park "had cost the Government $30,000 . . . and they are not through with it yet." Once the others assured him that the rates for hack rentals had been fixed by the government and that price gouging was already forbidden, Wilder withdrew his suggestion. The combination of desecration, commercialism, and costs had touched a raw nerve among the veterans, who wanted to maintain their battlefield's integrity in the face of change.[8]

However, the park commissioners and the veterans were not entirely afraid of commercialism and change; nor were they merely content to rest on their laurels. Having denounced the naysayers, cleaned up the damage, and obscured the presence of the offending Camp Thomas, those who had built and maintained the park needed to reestablish not just its commemorative status, but its usefulness to the community and the nation. Their efforts to those ends made up the final steps in the reconstruction of memory for the veterans and the park and required that they allow a small portion of Camp Thomas to creep back into the spotlight.

The park's primary purpose had always been to uphold the memory of the veterans of the battles of Chickamauga and Chattanooga, and by 1900 the park commissioners had achieved that goal to the best of their ability. One of the ways that the park's founders had envisioned the perpetuation of that goal was to make the landscape useful to the people of the United States. Certainly, its status as a shrine to American heroism and valor served that purpose, as did the development of the grounds as an accurate chronicle of the events that took place between September and November 1863. It also had value to the Chattanooga community, which gained revenue from the presence of the national park in a variety of ways, including its use by the War Department as a military installation. As a parting gesture to the people of Chattanooga, the aging veterans who operated the park at the turn of the century set out to ensure that the government would continue to use it as a place to train troops. To accomplish that task, both the community and the veterans would have to come to some resolution regarding the memory of Camp Thomas.

While perhaps not the most important element in the process, the proposal put forth by members of the Society of the Army of the Cumberland to make Chattanooga the permanent site for its annual reunions was a step in the right direction. Col. M. D. Wickersham made the first suggestion that Chattanooga be the "permanent annual meeting place for the Society of the Army of the Cumberland" during the annual meeting at Chattanooga in 1900. In supporting this suggestion, General Wilder reminded his comrades of the importance of the city to the memory of the army and added, "there is no place which can stir patriotic memories or do as much to perpetuate patriotic pride in American citizenship as Chattanooga." He concluded his statement by urging the members to think about it, "and when the time comes, for God's sake adopt it." Others who spoke in support described the battlefield as an "object lesson" for the nation and a place to "meet and perpetuate [the] memory" of General Thomas, "the hero who stands over every hero of the Civil War."[9]

The motion was referred to the executive committee, and after annual meetings in St. Paul, Minnesota (1902), and Washington, D.C. (1903), the society considered the permanent move to Chattanooga at its 1904 meeting in Indianapolis. Letters and resolutions from the Chattanooga mayor and the chamber of commerce extended "a most cordial invitation" to the society, while the local Grand Army Post spoke on behalf of both its own members and the local Confederate veterans in support of the idea. Communications also arrived from the Chattanooga Builders Exchange; the Nashville, Chattanooga & St. Louis Railroad; and the Cincinnati, New Orleans & Texas Pacific Railway Company, "all expressing the usual interest in the matter" and extending a variety of welcomes. The speaker, George W. Patten, also pointed out that "we have a larger percentage of Union soldiers who were members of the Army of the Cumberland living in Chattanooga than in any other city in the country" and that "the large industries, almost without exception, are controlled by Army of the Cumberland men."

This led to the introduction of General Wilder as a man "who manufactures more gas tips, [and] more electric insulators than are manufactured in any other establishment in the world." Wilder spoke affectionately of the city and its citizens and gushed "that a bigger hearted and more generous people do not live on God's earth than inhabit Chattanooga." He reminded his comrades that "the Society of Confederate Veterans . . . came in uniform, and made speeches in our favor" during the dedication of the Wilder Brigade monument and that "even the Daughters of the Confederacy have captured our men." Several other speakers followed, extolling the virtues of the monuments, the park, and a local community where "Southerners feel that they have not been dishonored by being whipped by men of equal courage." As one member intoned, "let us go to this historic ground and go soon, for the time is not far distant when there will be but few left to assemble anywhere."[10]

The last to speak was Henry Boynton, who unbeknownst to himself or anyone else, was presiding over his last reunion. He recalled the days prior to the big dedication in 1895 when the citizens of Chattanooga opened up their homes "to every veteran without inquiry as to position in life, rank in life, or whether Union or Confederate." He talked about Chattanooga as the "cosmopolitan city of the South," which regardless of whether they were Republicans or Democrats, Northerners or Southerners, "extends hospitality towards any association that makes an appearance in that city." Just before introducing the resolution to accept Chattanooga as the society's permanent home, its leader suggested that "it seems to me there is nothing better we can do as soldiers than go once a year if possible and drink in the inspiration of those scenes, which are stronger, brighter, better with every visit." He confessed that his last visit to the city "awoke memories which are in all your hearts even more vividly, as the day when I saw the great Army go up those heights." The resolution carried unanimously.[11]

The final step in the process of securing the lasting connection between the battle, the veterans, the park, and the community was the creation of a permanent Regular Army military garrison on or near the battlefield. This idea seems to have been in the minds of civic leaders and park officials from very early in the park's history. In September 1895, just prior to the park's official dedication, the Chattanooga Chamber of Commerce passed a resolution that suggested approaching the secretary of war during his visit for the dedication and urging him to give "favorable consideration of the establishment of a garrison and camp of instruction for United States troops at Chattanooga." Hiram S. Chamberlain, H. Clay Evans, and Adolph Ochs were all members of the first committee charged with pursuing this idea. Although it did not result in the creation of such a camp right away, this request helped produce the congressional legislation authorizing the military use of the park that passed in 1896.

The community did not wait long before trying to take advantage of the new law and bring this vision to life. An undated newspaper clipping from 1897 revealed a plan by a committee of business leaders led by Robert S. Sharp to persuade the War Department to consider Chattanooga for a permanent post. In the meantime, Secretary Alger and Henry Boynton had apparently put in motion a proposal to gather "that part of the United States Army in the south, as well as western regiments, to mobilize in the park for spring and summer maneuvers." There were high hopes among all the interested parties that such a gathering might take place sometime after January 1898 and be an annual event leading eventually to the construction of a permanent camp.[12]

There was great enthusiasm for this early plan. Some people pointed out that by having summer-long maneuvers at Chattanooga, the federal and state governments could save a great deal of money that would otherwise have been spent transporting and housing troops elsewhere. Although the article's author expressed minor annoyance at the prospect of nearby state National Guards "adding four or five thousand men to the mobilization without extra expense," the benefits were far greater than the inconvenience. In fact, the article predicted that "thousands would be drawn here as spectators to witness the evolutions" and that "if four thousand troops came here for a three months stay, it would be the equivalent of a crowd of three-hundred and sixty thousand people for one day." The economic possibilities for the Chattanooga community seemed endless, leading the scribe to reflect that "an army of ten thousand men at Chickamauga Park next summer would make a spectacle worthy of contemplation from many points of view."[13]

Of course, what they got was an army six or seven times that number, and, as predicted, it served as a huge boost to the local economy. Aside from the run-ins with intoxicated soldiers and the complaints lodged by a few local farmers, the concentration of the Regulars and volunteers at Camp Thomas was everything the business leaders and park officials envisioned. The scandals and concerns about disease proved to be only a temporary setback, thanks to the efforts of General Boynton and others to reassure the community that the fault lay not with the park or the presence of troops there, but with the behavior of these particular men and officers. Shortly after the troops departed from Camp Thomas, the *Chattanooga Times* quoted Maj. Emmett Giffen, "one of the most distinguished and best equipped scientists in the Army" as stating, "in my opinion, Chickamauga Park is one of the healthiest locations in the entire country, that possibly could have been chosen for a great military encampment." He presaged the findings of the Dodge Commission and others by blaming disease on the carelessness of the troops, noting finally that "the blame has been placed where it belongs."[14]

The combination of an intervening year and the park's continued clean bill of health revived the army post plan by late 1899 and early 1900. A special committee representing the community and the park went to Washington to lay out its case for a permanent garrison at Chattanooga. Among the twenty benefits they listed were its central location, variety of topography, good water, an abundance of cheap building material and labor, low price of land, number of railroads, inexpensive food and forage, nearness to seaports (yet safe distance from the coast), and a navigable river. In addition, the commissioners added that "the proximity of so many great battlefields must inspire enthusiasm in the troops being trained there" and suggested that "soldiers could guard monuments and government property at the park without extra cost for the work." The delegation's final reason states simply, "because the establishment of an army post in the vicinity of Chattanooga is most earnestly desired by more than 100,000 people." In addition to all these good reasons, the proponents of the idea enjoyed the advantage of having Henry Boynton on their side.[15]

In a combination of seriousness and good fun, the *Chattanooga Times* sponsored an essay contest that encouraged citizens to compose reasons why the post should be located near the city. Some were practical, citing the quality of the terrain for maneuvers, engineering, and signaling exercises; another described it as "an ante room in which to temper the soldiers going and coming from the blasts of the north or to the blistering sun of the tropics." Charles R.

Evans, son of a prominent citizen and former officer in the 6th U.S. "Immunes," repeated most of the already stated arguments but added the appeal of Chattanooga as a "convention city" and its "social influences" including "the best of schools." Others pointed out its "cosmopolitan nature," and one writer added "a tender and lofty sentiment shared alike by all sections for the soldiers of all sections who fought here and here the ashes of their dead repose in the National cemetery and other beautiful cities of the dead."

Virtually all the writers included the Chickamauga and Chattanooga National Military Park as part of the area's appeal. In doing so, they cited the park's practical use as an instructional ground and its inspirational appeal as the site of great heroism and sacrifice. One author quoted from a speech given by one of the region's politicians in which the intangible elements of post and park combined. Describing the battlefield as a "veritable holy land . . . rendered sacred by the blood of our heroes slain in battle . . . and consecrated anew . . . by the hearts and hands of the surviving heroes of that mighty struggle" the speaker went on to make the obvious connection between the past and present in his crowning remarks. He hoped that "when American citizens of the future come here to read the eloquent story carved on metal and marble of how on these fields American soldiers fought and fell" they would be moved "at sight of brave young blue coated boys of the Chattanooga army post, who, having drawn inspiration from the surroundings, will be as ready to carry the old flag into hell of battle as were their fathers of old." Although it is not known who won the ten-dollar prize, the combination of essays, special committees, and the park commissioners' actions eventually secured the desired post.[16]

Boynton and the War Department were also in favor of the army post idea and took steps to bring it to fruition. The biggest concern was maintaining the integrity of the park's commemorative landscape while simultaneously developing and operating a useful, long-term military installation. Boynton and E. E. Betts found the solution to this problem in the government's purchase of a several-hundred-acre tract of land on the northern boundary of the park, which would serve as the location of the actual post. This allowed the construction of barracks and buildings without damaging the ambiance of the battlefield or its historical context. In the meantime, the park lands would still be used for drill, large-scale maneuvers, and temporary National Guard encampments, but for the most part their status as sacred ground would not be permanently violated.

Having purchased the space, the War Department's establishment of the actual post was a foregone conclusion. Without any apparent controversy or special legislation, an army board approved the creation of the post in February 1902, and the government began construction of temporary wooden barracks and other structures during the summer of that year. Although Fort Oglethorpe did not become the official home of a twelve-company cavalry regiment until the completion of permanent buildings and the 1904 dedication, military activities involving both Regular and National Guard units took place on park grounds during those intervening years. There is little documentation of the process by which the new post came to be named "Fort Oglethorpe," after Georgia's first governor, James Oglethorpe. While it is not surprising that the sullied name of George H. Thomas was not revived as the permanent name for the post, it seems odd that no military personnel from either the Civil War or Spanish-American War seem to have received consideration. That no one in the Society of the Army of the Cumberland pushed the idea of a "Fort Henry V. Boynton" also seems inconsistent with its tendency to honor one of its own.[17]

The guardians of the battlefield were quick to assure the secretary of war that "there is no reason why the work of the park establishment and the use of the park for field practice of every nature should interfere with each other." Although the temporary structures used to house Regular Army troops returning from occupation duty in Cuba blocked the public's view of several of the monuments on that part of the battlefield, the new post would remedy that problem. Boynton reported that "eight veteran organizations, whose monuments have been obscured by the [temporary] camp buildings, have manifested much restiveness under the present conditions." These issues were solved by the creation of the permanent structures on the land occupied by Fort Oglethorpe, the dismantling of the temporary buildings, and the "restoration of former conditions" on the actual battlefield. In all cases where troops utilized the park, the commissioners worked to assure that the park lands would be protected and restored.[18]

Of course, the irony in the successful creation of Fort Oglethorpe was the need on the part of its local proponents to view Camp Thomas in a positive light. Throughout the essays submitted to the newspaper, several of the writers referred to the concentration of troops in the park during the War with Spain as proof of its utility. Most were quick to cite the soldiers' carelessness as the cause of disease before continuing with the business of praising the landscape's adaptability. Charles Evans, whose 6th Immunes had occupied the park without suffering any notable sickness, added his endorsement to the positive aura that many of Chattanooga's citizens created around the memory of the camp. Nearly all the missives saw the fate of both Chattanooga and the park as inseparable. As one essayist looked to the future military needs of the nation, he envisioned a "post . . . located here [Chattanooga] or at Chickamauga as the nucleus for the creation of a permanent maneuvering and mobilization camp of the United States Army at the latter place."[19]

Putting the Camp Thomas Spanish-American War experience in the proper light also required some ceremonial acknowledgment of the men who died there. In May 1899, the local Civil War and Spanish-American War veterans conducted "joint Memorial Day ceremonies" to honor the dead buried in the national cemetery in Chattanooga. The ceremonies were planned and carried out by a committee made up of members of Chattanooga's GAR post and its Women's Auxiliary and the Spanish-American War veterans (who at this point had no formal organization), led by Maj. Charles R. Evans. The young Evans was clearly the central figure representing the veterans of the War with Spain. In addition to heading the committee and planning the events of the day, Evans himself read "the list of the dead of the United States Volunteer army who died at Chickamauga Park last summer." The graves of the Spanish-American War dead "were decorated by former volunteers, assisted by the ladies," while members of the GAR and its auxiliary handled the traditional decoration of Civil War graves.

The message of the day was the value of the War with Spain as the catalyst for the reunion of the sections. Time after time, the newspapers and speakers referred to the war as having "finally and forever closed the breech between north and south." One article noted that "mingling in the audience were those who wore the blue and the gray, and the sons of these who wore only the blue as members of the great army of volunteers which cemented more closely the ties that bind the north and the south—the army that had effaced sectional lines from the continent forever." Noting that "although the graves of the dead of the Spanish American War do not contain those who lost their lives amidst the deadly conflict of shot and shell" they would be given the same measure of respect as "those who fell . . . in any of the . . . battlefields of the past year's conflict." Even on a day partially dedicated to their memory, the Spanish War dead barely earned equal billing with the soldiers from the "big war" forty years previously.[20]

The keynote speaker, Reverend. J. H. Race, whom the newspapers introduced as "president of U. S. Grant University," delivered an oration that "paid an equal measure of sentimental tribute to the heroes of the two wars." He reminded the assembled listeners that the reunion of the two sections "is worth the whole cost of the war." The reverend saw the war as a positive pursuit in which "we buried old sectional strifes [sic] and worked together for the supremacy of American arms." He warned against the return of "the pharisaical spirit" in society and urged his listeners to follow the example of the sons of the blue and gray "who rushed to the defense of the old flag." For a day at least, the veterans of the Spanish-American War enjoyed their status as the most recent saviors of the nation's honor. However, there were no ceremonies held for them in Chickamauga Park, nor was there any official participation in the day's events by members of the Society of the Army of the Cumberland.[21]

The Civil War veterans were reluctant to pass the torch to a group of veterans who had come dangerously close to betraying their elders' trust. When Henry Boynton expressed his support for Theodore Roosevelt's candidacy for president, he exclaimed that the Civil War was "a memory of the great days of the Republic that will always live and grow brighter as the years pass" but that due to the advancing ages of its veterans, "a grateful nation can no longer select its President from those honored ranks." His basis for holding Roosevelt up to the standards of previous veterans was "that promptly upon the declaration of war, he put behind him high and attractive office . . . and accepted a subordinate regimental position so that he might serve as a soldier under his country's flag." That unquestioning call and adherence to duty were the basis for Boynton's assessment of his fellow veterans. He was willing to bury old animosities among his comrades since they had already met these expectations. In many ways, his negative assessment of those who sullied the memory of Camp Thomas was premised on their failure to reach this standard.[22]

The Civil War had produced great leaders. The Army of the Cumberland alone sent eighty-eight of its members to Congress in the years after the war; two of them, James Garfield and Benjamin Harrison, were elected president. Countless others held important positions in government, from the secretary of war on down. They were leaders of business and industry in both the North and South, with members reaching to the West Coast and beyond. Numbering among the Society of the Army of the Cumberland's great accomplishments was the creation of the Chickamauga and Chattanooga National Military Park, which not only served to commemorate their past accomplishments, but also, "by becoming a practical value to the government," served as a training ground. All of this had been accomplished by the Civil War veterans in spite of the complaints and criticism the park received during the War with Spain. The exclusion of a meaningful amount of Spanish-American War–related memory from the park was due not only to the vigilance of the veterans and the park commissioners, but also to the failure of the Spanish War volunteers to assert a positive reason for doing so.[23]

Unfortunately, many Spanish-American War veterans were unable to reach the heights of accomplishment that the Civil War veterans had, for a variety of reasons. Their numbers were comparatively small in relation to those who had fought in the wars that took place before and after theirs. With fewer than 500,000 military personnel of all branches to draw from, the collective impact of this block of veterans on the nation was fairly light. Considering that a significant percentage of those spent most of the war at Camp Thomas or other training camps, where the experience did little to enhance their sense of accomplishment, one can see how difficult the task of memory construction was likely to be. One piece of literature described the Spanish War veterans as "An American Order of Nobility," since "no new blood can be born into it; there are no growing ranks from which recruits can be drawn." Rather than a group whose memories encompassed those of the nation, the veterans existed on an island inhabited by relatively few.[24]

The United Spanish War Veterans (USWV) became the postwar equivalent of the Civil War's Grand Army of the Republic by merging a variety of post-war veterans' organizations into a national one in 1904. Its women's auxiliary (Auxiliary of the United Spanish War Veterans—AUSWV), actually predated it, having been started by the relief organizations formed during the war. An examination of the "amalgamation agreement" that merged all of these groups into one reveals a lack of philosophical purpose for the new organization. It described itself in the first section as "fraternal, patriotic, and lasting," but did not state any specific purpose that bound it together. Perhaps the memory gap between the heroes of San Juan and Santiago and the sufferers and whiners at Camp Thomas was too wide to bridge. On the other hand, even a stronger organization would have been hard pressed to make a dent on the hold that the Civil War veterans had on the nation's politics, economy, and memory.[25]

Without a clear focus, the ability of the Spanish-American War veterans to construct lasting memories was even more difficult. A document entitled "I am Proud to be a Spanish War Vet" listed thirty reasons why veterans of that war were unique, if not superior to those of other wars. It included many of the elements that made up the official memory of the war such as the "abolition of yellow fever and kindred diseases" and the improvements in the military. The proclamation also touted the "rebirth of a Nation," the acquisition of territory, and the emergence of the United States as a world power as part of the war's major accomplishments. In addition, this manifesto revealed some interesting things about the Spanish-American War veterans' vernacular memories. Included among their reasons for pride are that "we fought the war with poor equipment, poor food, antiquated guns and black powder," and that the conflict "taught the lesson of unpreparedness that claims more lives than war [sic]." Finally, it submitted the odd claim that "the commands preserved their State entity and were responsible for the honor of their State."

Most revealing are the comparisons that the USWV document made with the Civil War. It bragged that its was "the only 100% volunteer army the world has ever known" and that its "losses in deaths from all causes were 4.3% as compared with six tenths of one percent for the Civil War." The document claimed that the combined duration of the Spanish and Philippine wars exceeded the Civil War by two months and that "property was acquired at the value of eight billion [dollars] as compared with none for the Civil War." The inescapable connection between the Civil War and the Spanish and Philippine conflicts is revealed near the end of the list, with the notation that "seventy-three percent of our veterans were the sons of Civil War veterans"; however, it did not admit how many servicemen in "their wars" may have been Civil War veterans themselves. It is difficult to read this list and not feel that there was a lingering sense of resentment among this population of veterans against the longer-lasting and more dynamic memories of the nation's Civil War generation.[26]

Also contained as a part of the USWV literature was an essay entitled "The Hiker" that described the Spanish War veterans in glowing and positive terms. In stark contrast to Boynton's characterizations of the Camp Thomas complainers, the writer touted the "model" veteran as "self-reliant" and stated that "he could and did take care of himself. He wanted no coddling. He cared not for hardships, deprivations, and dangers." Clearly referring more specifically to those who saw action (in spite of the fact that most never did) this description noted that the hiker "was no machine. He wanted to be led, not driven . . . His was a passion for duty . . . he gloried in his manhood and held danger in contempt." Claiming that "his courageous spirit has blessed millions of his fellow men" the essay concluded by proclaiming that "he stands unique, distinctive, one who deserves the admiration of all mankind." "The Hiker" was an attempt by the USWV to construct a "common soldier" symbol of the Spanish-American War, Philippine insurrection, and Boxer Rebellion that would unify their collective memories. However, for all their claims and efforts, the Spanish War veterans could not crack the hold that the Civil War veterans had on memory.[27]

Timing was also a factor in the inability of the Spanish War–era veterans to secure lasting memories of their experiences at Camp Thomas and elsewhere. By the time of the war's twenty-fifth anniversary, when many groups began to finally commemorate their collective memories, the United States had experienced the First World War, which created millions of new veterans and an entirely different set of military images. Those who made an effort to construct permanent memorials, like the 4th Ohio Volunteers, did so in Cuba and Puerto Rico, where they had won a significant amount of respect and rightfully laid claim to positive memories in line with the official memory of the war. The stateside camps were a different story. Several states' attempts to place markers at Chickamauga Park commemorating their regiments' stay there had met with less than satisfactory results. At a time when the Spanish War veterans should have been formulating their own identities, they were still caught between the formidable shadow of the Civil War memories and the grim realities of World War I.[28]

An excellent example of the awkward position occupied by the Spanish-American War veterans can be seen in the proceedings of the USWV Department of New York's annual encampment in 1921. A Civil War veteran representing the

FIG. 43: The 4th Ohio was one of the few Camp Thomas regiments to see action in Puerto Rico. They returned in 1923 to place a marker at the site of their skirmish near Guyana. From the author's collection.

GAR reminded the assemblage that "there were a number of kids in the Civil War . . . that were twenty-one and under, and I happened to be one of those kids." He congratulated the USWV on being "the only organization that was composed absolutely of volunteers" and expressed the rather interesting wish "that the Spanish War Veterans will be eventually consolidated into the Grand Army and . . . take up the work that we have been doing." The next speaker was the commander of the Utica American Legion Post, who highlighted the "bond of fellowship . . . between the Spanish War Veterans and the Veterans of the World War" and insisted that the American Legion "hope[d] to emulate the fine example" set by their predecessors. In spite of the mix of condescending, kind, and hopeful words, it seems clear that the Spanish and Philippine war veterans were still obscured by the legacy of the Civil War and overwhelmed by the sheer numbers of veterans from the recent world war.[29]

Two speeches given by Minnesota veterans illustrate the simmering frustrations resulting from mixed and contradictory Spanish-American War memories. The first was delivered at the 1929 Minnesota USWV banquet by the Hon. Rice W. Means. He began by reminding his audience that "comparisons are odious" and that by serving in any of America's wars "you are entitled to great consideration by the American people." He claimed that "more benefits have flowed to this country from the efforts of the men of '98 than in any war . . . since the day of Independence." Means lamented the high rate of unemployment among aging Spanish War veterans and the unnecessary deaths and disabilities caused by service "in the fever camps or in the tropics." Claiming that these problems were unique to these veterans, he charged that "the Veterans of the World War received much . . . because of the force of their numbers." Since modern industrialism had relegated workers over the age of fifty "to the scrap heap," the speaker urged his audience to demand that the Spanish War veterans get the same "hospitalization, vocational training, and everything" that the world war veterans had allegedly asked for and received from the government.[30]

The second address was delivered to the U.S. House of Representatives four years later by the Hon. Ernest Lundeen, a congressman from Minnesota. In language shockingly reminiscent of the Camp Thomas testimonials, he recounted being stationed in Florida, where he was "bitten by swarms of insects . . . under unspeakable sanitary conditions" and issued food that was "scanty and unwholesome." He went on to claim that "our hospital was little more than a name" where "medicines and supplies [were] almost wholly lacking and medical attention largely a pretense." They were discharged while still "gaunt and fever-stricken" and "bearing the seeds of disease." Once they returned to civilian life, the veterans had seen "small evidence of appreciation of [sic] their sufferings" from their government and fellow citizens. In contrast to the veneration heaped on the fading Civil War generation, the congressman saw himself and his comrades as "forgotten men—discriminated against, dishonored, and disowned by the Government for which they offered their lives." He appealed to his fellow legislators to pass a bill that would provide "a few dollars for our disabled veterans and for our widows and orphans" and declared "that any man who votes against a fair and just compensation for . . . these heroes of 1898, is unpatriotic and un-American."[31]

The Spanish-American War veterans were caught in a conundrum that had a lasting effect on their memories of the war. Their sense of victimization, stemming from the epidemics in the training camps, the tropical miseries of Cuba and the Philippines, and the troubling experience at Montauk, was still evident in their literature. Yet many of these claims were repudiated by the Dodge Commission and had subsequently faded from the public spotlight. What remained was the official and modestly triumphant memory of the Spanish-American War, which obliterated the problems in the camps and downplayed the controversial Philippine War. In many ways, Camp Thomas represented this conflict by serving as the physical site of both sets of memories. In spite of the deaths of numerous "heroes" on the Chickamauga park's property, the volunteers' own behavior and their violation of the Civil War's sacred ground negated any claim they had to the commemorative landscape.

Like their Civil War counterparts, the men who served between 1898 and 1902 suffered long-lasting consequences that affected them for years after their war was out of the public's memory. William Wysong was a member of Company I, 51st Iowa Volunteers, which, unlike its sister unit stuck in Georgia, found itself in California on its way to the Philippines in the late fall of 1898. According to its "Welcome Home" badge, the regiment served in 15 battles and suffered 32 dead before mustering out in November 1899. Unfortunately, William had not made the trip to the Philippines. According to his discharge papers and an affidavit he filed in 1933, Wysong contracted the measles while at the Presidio and after "this sickness infected the heart" he received a medical discharge in November 1898. At the age of 73, William testified to a Veterans Administration official that "this experience has ruined my whole life and now that the years have piled up on me, I am indeed totally disabled in the line of duty." In the letter informing Wysong's wife of his death in March 1934, the chief medical officer of the veterans' home in Kansas reminded her "that he served his country and died honored and respected by all of us." Although there is no reason to doubt the sincerity of this condolence, it belies the fact that the effects of William's service were sadly un-heroic and eminently forgettable.[32]

A final example of the contradictory memories that Camp Thomas conjured up among the Spanish-American War veterans can be found in two poems

FIG. 44: William Wysong of Company I, 51st Iowa was left behind at the Presidio in San Francisco with a heart ailment when his regiment sailed for the Philippines. The resulting disability had a negative impact on his life, and his case reflected the frustrations of many Spanish-American and Philippine war veterans regarding the government's inadequate compensation for their services. From the author's collection.

that appeared years apart in Iowa and Vermont. The untitled Iowa piece was in response to a newspaper article on pensions and was composed "by an Ames minister who was also a Spanish War Vet." It told the story of Camp Thomas from the perspective of those who suffered and spared no details in doing so:

> You'd have a new slant on the matter,
> If you had served in a fever camp
> With bull beef and beans on the platter,
> And everyone suffering cramps
> If you'd served in the sick ward as I did,
> And watched the boys die like flies
> The death tent filled with some mother's kids,
> With coppers over their eyes

He went on to lament:

> They were only boys out for a ride;
> Of cares they knew not a thing
> They should have been securely tied
> To their mother's apron strings.
> With latrines on a hillside
> And soldiers camped below
> Flies over everything;
> Perhaps you didn't know.

He goes on in a similar vein, until later where he states:

> These sturdy boys went to camp;
> Were sent home physical wrecks
> They certainly had the Lord to thank,
> If he had saved their necks

The rest of the poem condemns a pension system that did not want to recognize the effect of camp fevers because "their doctors are dead [so] they can't prove their troubles [are] service connected.[33]

This sharply contrasts with the inspiring piece that appeared in the 1st Vermont's fiftieth anniversary booklet. In spite of the fact that this regiment was extremely critical of the War Department's management of Camp Thomas, the poem, by Laura Brigham Boyce, entitled "At Chickamauga: Memorial Day, 1898," almost entirely expressed the official memory of the experience, which even Boynton would have approved.

Under the sunny Southern sky, the Stars and Stripes are floating high
And standing 'neath the flag today, are sons of men who wore the gray
With sons of men who wore the blue;
And every heart beats staunch and true
> At Chickamauga

On this historic battle ground, an army bivouacs around;
Where hissed the shot and screamed the shell;
And cannons belched the fires of hell
And bayonets gleamed and sabers flashed,
As foemen to the carnage dashed
> At Chickamauga

No more, no more! We're brothers all, who loyal heeded our country's call
Shoulder to shoulder, side by side, our soldiers stand in warlike pride
Sons of the far Green Mountain State, with Tennesseans proudly mate.
> At Chickamauga

Softly and reverently tread, O, soldiers o'er the quiet dead
And as ye march above their clay, cement the bond 'twixt blue and gray.
We're brothers, and no South, no North,
But patriots all from now henceforth
> At Chickamauga

Under the sunny Southern sky
The Stars and Stripes are floating high
Every heart to the flag is true; every soldier wears the blue
Dear to the heart each glowing star, and every stripe as they shout huzza!
> At Chickamauga

Although written shortly after the war, its appearance in conjunction with a regiment whose historians consistently denounced the experience at Camp Thomas is puzzling but indicative of the mixed memories about the war.[34]

Time was working both for and against the Civil War veterans who protected the memories of Chickamauga Park from any threats posed by its more recent occupiers. On the one hand, they were passing away rapidly. On the other, they left a legacy that was firmly established and difficult to challenge. When Henry Boynton died in June 1905, he had only served as president of the Society of the Army of the Cumberland for the prior two years. For most of the rest of its history, he had served in a variety of offices, but none that did justice to his role in the preservation of that organization's interests and memories. One testimonial described him as "truthful, straight, honest, a gentleman always" and praised his "uniform courtesy" in conducting the society's business. Without hesitation, a longtime comrade stated, "to my mind, General Boynton was the nearest to a perfect man of any I ever knew."[35]

Yet their recognition of Boynton's importance or his aura of perfection did not keep the steadfast members of the Society of the Army of the Cumberland from continuing his work. They elected a new president, assigned another member to report on the park, and discussed the big army encampment that had taken place in the summer of 1906. In spite of the disagreements and differences they had experienced with one another over the years, the Civil War veterans stuck together when the time came to protect the memory of their war. In doing so, they left the legacy that continues to dominate our memory of the conflict and is reflected in the commemorative landscape of the national battlefield parks around the country. Chickamauga's uniqueness was due not only to its clouded outcome in 1863, but also to its focus on reconciliation, reunion, and mutual respect, which dominated the creation of its commemorative landscape.[36]

The challenge presented by Camp Thomas served to both strengthen and modify the battle's place in the nation's memory. It had brought attention, prestige, and thousands of soldiers to the park when the War Department named it as its primary camp of instruction in 1898. The scandals surrounding the typhoid outbreak threatened the park's reputation and soiled the sacred landscape. Yet, the efforts by Boynton and his comrades to restore the park's integrity built another layer of memory onto the ones that they had already preserved. They restored the importance and primacy of the Civil War battle and the spirit of reconciliation that helped create the park. At the same time, they allowed the War Department to build its permanent camp on the commemorative landscape in order to please the local community and align the park with the official memories of the War with Spain. Because of the tireless efforts of Henry Boynton, the veterans of the Civil War had succeeded in securing their place in memory.

FIFTEEN

"Through the Most Trying Ordeals"

By 1906, Henry Boynton and his fellow Civil War veterans had successfully forged a functional relationship between the commemorative and practical uses of the Chickamauga and Chattanooga National Military Park. In doing so, they perpetuated memories of the 1898 occupation of the park that matched the official version of the War with Spain, unabashedly celebrating the accomplishments of the nation's navy and War Department despite great logistical obstacles. This interpretation included the government's claims, expressed most eloquently by Boynton himself, that the health problems at Camp George H. Thomas were mostly the fault of the volunteer officers and men. By placing the burden on the volunteers for the deaths of hundreds of their comrades, the park's defenders cast a shadow over the memory of the Spanish-American War that questioned the commitment to duty and manhood of many of its veterans. Based on this hastily constructed memory of the recent past, the park commissioners threw their support behind the construction of a permanent army post on the park's boundary, which would simultaneously benefit the local community and continue the site's usefulness to the nation.

At the same time, however, the veterans in the Society of the Army of the Cumberland and their Confederate counterparts in the United Confederate Veterans were reaffirming their commitment to the historical and commemorative value of the park's Civil War significance. By revisiting the field, repairing the damage done by Camp Thomas, and dedicating a number of new monuments, these aging warriors worked to regain control of the park, its landscape, and the memories associated with it. The reunion theme that had played such a valuable role in the creation and dedication of the park in the first place had also been a key element in the creation of Camp Thomas. As controversial and painful as the Spanish-American War experience had been for many of the parties involved, it still had its place in the overall identity of the Chickamauga and Chattanooga National Military Park as the greatest example of its military utility. Thus, the veterans hoped to straddle the fine line between the battlefield's status as sacred and protected ground and its usefulness to the War Department as a supplemental training field for the soldiers stationed at Fort Oglethorpe.

As confident as the veterans and park commissioners were of this arrangement at its outset, it was not without significant drawbacks. Even if well-trained Regular Army and National Guard troops left few physical signs of their passage on the park during low-impact maneuvers, the movement of horses, mules, and other military equipment naturally produced some damage. Throughout the first decade of the twentieth century, the park's managers attempted to return the landscape to its original state after every military encampment. Conflicts emerged as the army exercised its authority by cutting trees, building cavalry hurdles, dumping manure, and leaving trash around the monuments. Rarely did the battlefield host a large number of troops at any one time prior to 1917, but its ongoing use as a training ground became a regular, increasingly disruptive occurrence.[1]

This element of "practical use" thrust Chickamauga Park back into the national spotlight during the First World War, when the War Department again utilized the park as a training center for troops being mobilized for duty overseas. With Fort Oglethorpe recently established as a brigade-level post, the military authorities had little problem adapting the park to large-scale military occupation. There were three new camps established within the park: Camp Forrest, Camp McLean, and Camp Greenleaf. These involved the most intensive exploitation of the landscape since Camp Thomas, and the resulting encampments had a dramatic effect on the park. The construction of wooden barracks, stables, storage buildings, gun emplacements, trenches, and other facilities on the actual battlefield cluttered the commemorative landscape and did a great deal of damage to the ground itself. The use of tanks and other motorized vehicles caused plenty of wear and tear on roads that had originally been designed for horse and buggy traffic. Off-road maneuvers tore up the soil and foliage, and, depending on the weather, the daily human, animal, and vehicle traffic caused plenty of problems with dust and mud. The extent of the World War I facilities and the length of their use posed a greater threat to Chickamauga's battleground than the five-month occupation by the troops at Camp Thomas ever had.

Although the War Department had issued specific orders for the protection of the park's monuments and natural environment, the sheer size and complexity of the army's facilities meant that the landscape suffered more than it should have. There were cantonments throughout the park, including a medical complex; a nearby prisoner-of-war camp; YMCA, Knights of Columbus, and Red Cross compounds; hundreds of buildings; and thousands of tents. In

FIG. 45: This aerial view of the WWI cantonment shows how much the army's facilities sprawled into the Chickamauga park from nearby Fort Oglethorpe. Although most of the temporary structures were removed after the war, the park grounds suffered extensive damage while being used as a training ground. Courtesy of the Chattanooga–Hamilton County Bicentennial Library.

all, nearly 1,600 semi-permanent structures cluttered the landscape, crowded the monuments and markers, and obscured the details of the commemorative landscape. Only the end of the war in November 1918 prevented further expansion of military operations in the park.[2]

In addition, some of the other negative elements from the Camp Thomas era reappeared during this period. There were reports of drunken soldiers in town; several bordellos appeared near the edge of the camp, and an influenza outbreak caused fears of an epidemic like the one in 1898. In the opinion of the park commissioners (particularly the last remaining Civil War veteran, Joseph Cumming) and the War Department's own inspector, this intrusive military use of the landscape "was in direct conflict with the historical value of the park" and posed a serious threat to its integrity. By the time the army demobilized following the war's end, the unanimity of history, commemoration, and practicality that had been forged by Boynton and the national park's original founders was in serious jeopardy.

During the 1920s, the park superintendent worked to dismantle the various military cantonments and restore the battlefield landscape to its original condition. It was an uphill battle, considering that the military continued to periodically utilize the park's grounds for bivouacs and maneuvers by both Regular Army and state National Guard units. During the 1930s, the utilitarian use of the park expanded to accommodate an airstrip on Wilder Field and included regular summer encampments on the battlefield by the Reserve Officers Training Corps (ROTC), a civilian military training group, and students from the Army War College. Even the government's creation of the National Park Service and the park's separation from the War Department in 1933 failed to curtail the regular use of the park by the troops stationed in and around Fort Oglethorpe. Throughout the early twentieth century, the influence of the military and its interests took precedence over the historical, commemorative, and educational aspects of the park.[3]

During World War II, the battlefield once again accommodated thousands of troops, buildings, equipment, and training exercises of all types. This time the grounds hosted not only a compound for German prisoners, but a large camp for the recently created Women's Auxiliary Army Corps (WAAC), which brought a great deal of positive national attention to the park, including a visit by President Franklin D. Roosevelt in April 1943. Nearly 50,000 women passed through the training facility between 1942 and 1945; in addition, thousands of other servicemen used the extensive facilities, including a golf course, for recreation and rehabilitation as they traveled to and from active duty. The end of the war signaled the end of the military's use of the park, which forced the War Department to reluctantly relinquish its authority to make use of the battlefield whenever it wished. By 1948, Fort Oglethorpe was closed and all of the buildings that had been constructed on the park were gone. The army turned over a small part of the old Fort Oglethorpe to the Park Service for its use; the rest became part of the local civilian community.[4]

During this long stretch between 1900 and 1945, the Army's priorities frequently overwhelmed the interests of the park commissioners and thereby threatened the commemorative uses of the landscape. This process accelerated as the original guardians of the park—its Civil War veterans—retired from their positions of power and gradually passed away. The exigencies of war in both 1917 and 1942 allowed the War Department to extend its authority over the park to a greater extent, much to the detriment of its monuments, markers, and natural landscape. Although Camp Thomas set the precedent for the use of the park during war, the absence of the connection to the Civil War battlefield that the earlier volunteers had possessed made the later occupations ever more dangerous to the commemorative integrity of the landscape. If the national and local memories of the Civil War were somewhat compromised by the two world wars, those of the Spanish-American War were almost, but not completely, obliterated.

The decades from 1900 through 1920 were also the last that saw Civil War veterans dominating the Chickamauga Park Commission. The death of Boynton in 1905 left only Alexander Stewart as the original surviving veteran (Confederate) member. His death in 1908 meant that subsequent commissioners would be appointed by the War Department from the diminishing pool of interested and capable veterans. The last functioning park commission under the old organizational structure consisted of John Wilder and Charles Grosvenor, both of whom were Army of the Cumberland veterans; Joseph Cumming, who represented the Confederates; and Union veteran Wilbur J. Coburn, serving as secretary. The other significant change moved the commission's offices from Washington, D.C., to Chattanooga and reorganized it as a board of commissioners. After a squabble between board members that resulted in Coburn's ouster in 1911, the two members of the park's original charter organization, Wilder and Grosvenor, carried on until their deaths permanently dissolved the commission.[5]

There was a slow, but gradual decline of major commemorative activity in the park leading up to World War I. South Carolina dedicated its state memorial in 1901; numerous other states followed suit with either state or individual unit monuments. Iowa dedicated its three nearly identical monuments in 1906. The long-anticipated New York "Peace" Memorial had its dedication in Point Park in 1910, with Daniel Sickles giving the keynote speech. Florida and Alabama dedicated their state memorials in 1913 in conjunction with a United Confederate Veterans (UCV) reunion, while the completion of a monument to Ohio troops who fought at Lookout Mountain led to ceremonies in October 1917. Although there was a reunion to commemorate the fiftieth anniversary of the battle held on the Chickamauga battlefield in 1913, its size and the attention it garnered from the press was not comparable to the Great Reunion that took place on the Gettysburg landscape in the same year. Elaborate public ceremonies also accompanied the seventieth and seventy-fifth anniversaries of the battle in 1933 and 1938.[6]

Perhaps the most unusual public commemorative activity to take place on the park grounds during this period was the reenactment held on Snodgrass Hill in 1923 to celebrate the sixtieth anniversary of the battle. With members of the UCV, the GAR, and USWV in attendance and a crowd of 10,000 looking on, an odd mixture of "soldiers" recreated a portion of the Battle of Chickamauga. The Union forces were represented by ROTC students from various local schools, who lined up on the crest of Snodgrass Hill and blazed away for some time. After the youngsters "withdrew for safety's sake," the Confederates appeared in the form of a dramatic mounted charge by the 6th U.S. Cavalry. As the troopers rode around the Union forces and "charged them from the rear," the account noted that, due to the rough ground, "several of the men were unhorsed and fell, while some of the horses stumbled and fell, giving the appearance of being shot." The spectacle was followed by a big barbeque that fed 4,500 hungry and enthusiastic souls. The emphasis on entertainment and the corresponding lack of historical accuracy in this spectacle was typical of the mixture of history and heritage that frequently accompanied this type of popularized event.[7]

This spectacle was apparently part of the activities surrounding the National USWV Annual Encampment being held in Chattanooga that same week. For the Spanish-American War veterans to choose the anniversary week of the original Battle of Chickamauga for its meeting could have been seen as presumptuous by the few surviving Civil War veterans. It was, however, apparently well received by the Chattanooga community. If nothing else, the occasion revived the dormant memories of Camp Thomas. One local writer recalled that "the assembling of some 70,000 young men . . . during the spring and summer of 1898 was an invigorating sight and their stay put new life and energy into the people of this community and started a revival in business that has gone on and on. . . ." Noting that "Chattanooga can well claim the credit of being the reunion city of the south," another journalist effused that "we are honored by the Spanish-American war convention as we were by the gathering of the veterans of the War Between the States." In the midst of all the sentimental remembrance, one guest columnist made only passing reference to the health problems at Camp Thomas by stating that the boys "developed into men through the most trying ordeals through which humans can pass and live" and ultimately returned home "with a firm belief of a reunited country and a greater reverence for the flag that stands for freedom not only at home but on the high seas and in every land."[8]

The altered memory of Camp Thomas was apparent in another article in the *Chattanooga Times* that referred to the camp as "a new suburb," which had "added greatly to the temporary residential population" of the city in the summer of 1898. It touted President McKinley's confidence in the location and recalled how the citizens worked to make the soldiers "feel, insofar as possible, really and truly at home." Noting that the city had enjoyed the economic benefits of the camp, the author admonished his readers that viewing the city's warm response to the soldiers as simply "mercenary" would "grossly and grievously wrong her and her people." Speaking for the veterans of Camp Thomas, the writer referred to the "tender memories that have lain fallow in the soldier's mind," which might bring back the pleasure of his time spent there. He concluded by recounting the story of the 9th New York and its emotional farewell to Gen. Joseph Breckinridge, who gave a "grateful and moderately eloquent" speech to the assembled soldiers. Clearly, the span of twenty-five years had allowed the memory of the camp to soften considerably among many of the local people.[9]

Spanish-American War veterans from Iowa and Vermont took advantage of this favorable sentiment by requesting the War Department's permission to erect permanent memorial markers in Chickamauga Park on the sites of their regiments' 1898 camps. The process, which had begun in 1922, was initially delayed when Superintendent Richard Randolph reminded the War Department that the original 1890 legislation specified that all markers and monuments should commemorate the actions of Union and Confederate troops in 1863. It also prohibited the placement of any other monuments not connected with those battles on any of the park grounds. Randolph feared setting a precedent in which "markers and memorials for camp sites would dot the fields and woodlands of Chickamauga Park in such a way as to defeat the object for which the park was created."

In spite of the superintendent's urging that the secretary of war did "not deem it wise to encourage or permit any encroachments on the battlefield at Chickamauga," the Spanish-American War veterans initially got their way. In 1925, Congress and the War Department authorized the placement of memorials to the Spanish-American War regiments on the battlefield landscape. However, by the time plans for the monuments were well under way, Randolph had convinced the War Department that placing the markers at the actual camp sites on the old battlefield would be detrimental to the dominant Civil War interpretation. The compromise was to construct a "memorial circle" at the intersection near the park entrance and place all of the Spanish-American War monuments on that location. The Iowa and Vermont veterans agreed to this and placed their markers in that location in 1927 and 1929, respectively. Neither the circle nor the markers are evident in the park today.[10]

By mid-century, the clouded and often confusing legacy of the much larger and bloodier Philippine War, along with America's participation in two global wars, served to further obscure the national importance of the relatively small contingent of Spanish War veterans. Historian John Pettegrew argues that the virtues of manhood that remained from the War with Spain helped set a standard for the doughboys of 1917, but the slaughter of modern war served to dampen such imagery by 1919. In addition, membership in national veterans' organizations like the Veterans of Foreign Wars and the American Legion after World War I effectively filled the political and social vacuum left by the demise of the Grand Army of the Republic and dwarfed the dwindling numbers in the

USWV. During the 1920s, the USWV and its auxiliary got involved in both pension and "Americanism" issues, which boosted their memberships to the highest levels; but in many ways, this was their last hurrah. Although the Sons of Spanish American War Veterans (SSAWV) continue to keep some memories alive, this group barely makes a ripple in the modern veterans' community.[11]

Even the *Maine,* which had served as one of the catalysts and rallying cries for the war, became more remembered as an "ambiguous and tragic" symbol of the horrors of war than a monument to its glories. In 1905, the War Department, seeking additional evidence that might explain the explosion that destroyed the ship in 1898, raised the hull of the *Maine* from Havana harbor and re-examined it. Before the navy towed the shattered hulk out to sea to be scuttled, it salvaged the mast and many other pieces of the ship's superstructure and sent them back to the United States. The mast ended up in Arlington National Cemetery as a memorial to all to those who lost their lives in the explosion and in many ways serves as the nation's primary memorial to the entire War with Spain. Other sections of the ship ended up in several American cities, including President McKinley's hometown of Canton, Ohio. Over the years, these individual sections frequently turn up in city parks or as parts of veterans' memorials commemorating all wars, thus blending into, but not defining, these commemorative landscapes.[12]

The relative weakness of the Spanish-American War era in the nation's long-term memory helps explain why the site of Camp Thomas does not have a permanent presence in Chickamauga and Chattanooga National Military Park. Even without the negative memories attached to the camp, the overall meaning of the 1898 war and its aftermath are largely obscured by time. The Spanish-American War retains a minor place in the park's collective memory only as a symbol of sectional reunion and national reconciliation. Since those themes dominated the planning, construction, and dedication of the park in the 1890s, they remain an important element in the ongoing story of the park. Thus Camp Thomas, which is rarely mentioned by name in the current park interpretation, survives only in a roundabout way as evidence of the battlefield's importance in the process of "healing the wounds" of the Civil War. The park's creation in 1890 is also presented in its current interpretation as a model for the effective historical preservation of important places and battlefields, a claim that the War Department's forty-year-long use and abuse of the park clearly contradicts.

More importantly, it seems clear that the intrusive and often destructive exploitation of the park by military forces during the Spanish-American War and the first half of the twentieth century have caused significant conflict between the commemorative and practical uses of the landscape. In some ways, this made the Chickamauga and Chattanooga National Military Park unique among national battlefields and historic sites. It seems likely that the amount of non-commemorative activity in this park during its formative years kept it from developing the status of "sacred site" shared by its eastern counterpart at Gettysburg. While there are plenty of examples of historic sites being violated by development *before* being sanctified as commemorative landscapes, there are few that had as much damage or as many alterations made to them *after* their dedication as sacred ground. At the Chickamauga and Chattanooga park, this has manifested itself in several ways that are only marginally related to its military uses.[13]

One element that contributes to the park's unusual status and its uncertain hold on memory is the separation between the Chickamauga and Chattanooga sections of the park. While the much larger Chickamauga portion underwent the trials and tribulations of military occupation, the areas of the park in and around the city of Chattanooga developed in their own ways. As mentioned in the introduction, one important difference between the two wings of the park is the segmented character of the park grounds in Chattanooga. The park owns only isolated "reservations" along the crest of Missionary Ridge, representing the location of Braxton Bragg's headquarters, the position assaulted by William T. Sherman's troops, and several other small areas named for northern states or units. These are connected by "Crest Road," which runs roughly eight miles along the spine of the ridge. The park has an easement on either side of the road that provides space for cannon and markers, but the rest is in private hands. In many cases, artillery pieces point toward nearby houses, giving the scene a decidedly non-historical and certainly un-sacred feel. The other key section of the park is Lookout Mountain, which at various times contained a photography studio and the "Adolph S. Ochs Observatory-Museum," along with a variety of caves, rock formations, and waterfalls. All of these served to draw tourists to the area, but tended to make the Chattanooga portions of the battlefield just another "thing" to see.[14]

In many ways, the Chickamauga and Chattanooga sections seem like two different parks. Their memories intersect at the point where George Thomas and the Army of the Cumberland redeemed themselves for the defeat at Chickamauga by storming the heights and dashing the remnants of the Confederate Army of Tennessee's marginal victory at Chickamauga. Yet, the identities of the Army of the Cumberland veterans and their stalwart commander are still wrapped firmly around the gloomy knoll that came to be known as Snodgrass Hill, where they defied the odds and salvaged a stalemate out of what should have been a catastrophic defeat. In Chattanooga, both Lookout Mountain and Missionary Ridge tower spectacularly over the city and the battlefield.

However, the battlefield's commemorative landscape is scattered throughout the city among its other tourist attractions. The memories associated with famous generals like Ulysses S. Grant and William T. Sherman mix with those of the Great Locomotive Chase, the "battle above the clouds," the Chattanooga Choo-Choo, the National Cemetery, the region's healthful environment, billboards encouraging visitors to "See Rock City," and the gradual commercial rebirth of the city itself.[15]

A dozen miles to the south lies the 7,000-acre Chickamauga battlefield in its preserved, apparently uninterrupted state. The great "military road" that ran from Chattanooga through Rossville and connected the two battlefields in 1895 is now a state highway cluttered with retail development and suburban sprawl. Occasionally, oddly out-of-place monuments and markers stand out from the modern scenery as reminders of the veterans' 1863 and 1890s perspectives of this contested route. A new highway bypass reroutes the through traffic around Chickamauga Park, allowing the visitors to use the old Lafayette Road as part of the tour with less fear of being run over by a speeding commuter or a semi. Traveling south from Chattanooga, the rural, wooded boundary of the park signals a sudden end to the urban environment as visitors enter the commemorative landscape and confront the grand monuments constructed by the Kentuckians, Georgians, and Floridians along the main road. This quiet mix of fields, trees, cannon, and monuments is the battlefield the veterans created; these are the memories they wanted to preserve.[16]

What makes the Chickamauga battlefield unusual is that the threats to its commemorative integrity came from an internal element within its original design, not from the usual external forces, in the forms of development. The use of the park as a military base in 1898, 1917–1919, and 1942–45 was the real test of its commemorative aspect. While the park's founders and managers welcomed the practical use and educational value these occupations provided to the country's military personnel, the physical damage to the park was disruptive to its historical character. Ironically, the open lands and rural environment that effectively protected the park from commercialization and urban sprawl invited the intrusion of cavalry, infantry, and artillery units that needed precisely that kind of terrain for their maneuvers. In 1898, those maneuvers at least resembled the tactics of 1863 and kept the memories of the Civil War in the foreground; the same could not be said for the trenches, tanks, and trappings of modern warfare in the twentieth century.

The Civil War centennial in the first half of the 1960s revived an interest in the war and its battlefields that had waned since the deaths of the conflict's last veterans during the late 1950s. This four-year-long national event allowed Americans to celebrate their patriotic heritage in the midst of the cold war and rekindled the spirit of sectional harmony that had been unhinged by the drama of the civil rights movement. Of course, white Southerners embraced the opportunity to display the symbols of the Lost Cause in a friendly, government-sanctioned environment. African Americans, however, chafed at the general lack of recognition of their role in the war and their exclusion from some commemorative events. While some historians denounced the commercialism and potential politicization of certain state and local celebrations, most accepted the reality that the focus of the centennial would largely revolve around the war's military actions. This placed most of the public's focus on battles, battlefields, and generals rather than on the more complex and controversial social, political, and economic aspects of the war.[17]

The renewal of the reconciliation spirit that accompanied the creation of Chickamauga and Chattanooga National Military Park fit in perfectly with the overall theme of the centennial, yet the park's participation in the celebration was fairly modest. Members of the local centennial commission and the associated Civil War roundtables, with the blessing of the National Park Service, invited all of the states whose soldiers had fought at the battles of Chickamauga and Chattanooga to rededicate their monuments on the battlefield on specific "state days." Numerous states, including Indiana, Louisiana, Tennessee, Alabama, Georgia, Louisiana, Michigan, and South Carolina took advantage of their particular "days" during the summer and fall of 1963 to hold a variety of ceremonies. A few actually were able to hold their commemorative activities on the anniversary of the Battle of Chickamauga in September. Unfortunately, the assassination of President John F. Kennedy in November of that year put a damper on the planned events to commemorate the fighting around Chattanooga and ended the anniversary year with a whimper, rather than a shout.[18]

Oddly enough, the park followed its Civil War anniversary commemoration with a "Post Days" celebration in the fall of 1964, which recognized the events that had taken place at Fort Oglethorpe and in the park during the Spanish-American War and the two world wars. This unusual gesture certainly reflected the final loss of the Civil War veterans in the local community and the ascension to prominence of those from other wars. It also signified the pride that Chattanooga's citizens and civic leaders took in their contributions to the nation's military history since the climactic events of 1863. The town of Fort Oglethorpe kept the memory of the military occupation of the park alive in spite of the absence of any physical reminders of the various camps on the field itself. It seems likely that Post Days was more of a community "heritage" activity celebrating a general sense of the past rather than a true commemorative event, thus maintaining the dominance of Civil War memory on the park itself.[19]

The centennial signaled the beginning of America's obsession with the Civil War and its emergence as a heritage industry. This has been a mixed blessing for battlefield parks, which are caught between their desires to enlighten the public, memorialize the veterans, and increase the number of visitors. Battle reenactments and living history demonstrations often straddled the fence between history and entertainment. During the 1970s and 1980s there were so many non-commemorative concerts, races, picnics, and "heritage days" at Chickamauga that the park's historians remarked that "concerned preservation groups have repeatedly called attention to recent uses of the park for recreational rather than inspirational purposes." Many historians questioned the Park Service's contention that these activities were compatible with "the spirit that led to the founding of the park," given their apparent lack of educational or commemorative content.[20]

Through all of the trials and tribulations that have befallen the park, the interpretation of events that took place in September and November 1863 still belongs to the veterans who built it. A sidebar in the park's own battlefield guide notes that in spite of all the conflicts and disagreements, including those presented by modern historians, most of the historical markers in the park still reflect the version of the battle established by Henry Cist and Henry Boynton. Through perseverance and a solid grasp of what was needed to construct and protect memory, Boynton and his comrades created a permanent commemorative landscape for themselves and their legacy. Fighting off the challenges posed by Camp Thomas and its controversial aftermath served to strengthen those memories. The spirit of national reunion that the park's founders incorporated into their commemorative landscape has served them well. Many modern preservationists, reenactors, and historians invoke the same images and memories in their efforts to honor their Union and Confederate forefathers. Somewhere, Henry Van Ness Boynton might be smiling, or shaking his head—or at least, not complaining.[21]

EPILOGUE

"Close of the Battle—7:30 P.M."

I made my most recent visit to the Chickamauga battlefield on a sweltering day in June 2010. As on my previous excursions, I spent the first few hours tromping around the first-day field, trying to make sense of the chaotic fighting that had raged in the woods and thickets along the "River of Death." I got out of my vehicle to visit isolated batteries, pay homage to Confederate generals Helms, Deshler, and Smith, and stir up the local wildlife. Once I returned to the auto tour route, I encountered another kindred spirit at the 26th Ohio monument, whom I regaled with the story of the ill-fated groundhog and my interest in Camp Thomas. After photographing modern farm equipment cutting and baling hay between the monuments on one of the fields in the park, I returned to the air-conditioned visitor center, where I discussed the difficulty in interpreting the first day with one of the staff and spent money in the book store. During my brief loop through the displays, I sadly noted a new exhibit describing the damage inflicted on monuments by vandals and thieves, which occurs with depressing regularity throughout the park. For the most part, little had changed since my last trip. In fact, my main concern was that I would end up taking pictures of the same monuments that I had already photographed on previous visits.

As the afternoon turned into evening, I found myself drawn to the ground that saw much of the second day's carnage. From the Wilder Tower I could picture the broken remnants of Rosecrans's right wing streaming across the Brotherton field, pursued by columns of howling southern infantry. On the way down the steep spiral staircase, I met a shell-shocked dad trailing several panting children and carrying a toddler. "You're almost there," I lied, wondering whether they would find the view worth the climb. When I looked back from the ground at the delighted children peering over the parapet I recalled my first time up in the tower nearly a decade earlier. I was alone on the battlefield, so when two young men joined me at the top of the Wilder Monument,

I chatted happily about the battle, the view, and my joy at being there. They listened sullenly, and after I returned to the parking lot, I looked back just in time to see them tipping a bottle wrapped in brown paper to their lips. I recall feeling a mix of amusement, alarm, and anger at their blatant violation of this sacred place, but realized that in the eyes of many local residents, this was, after all, their park.

Later in the day, I stood in the lengthening shadows on the edge of the Dyer field, where Union guns and a makeshift line of mixed and shattered infantry regiments had held off the Confederate onslaught for a precious few minutes. "It must have been something to see," I thought to myself. Resisting the urge to follow the path of the rebel advance across the sun-scorched meadow, I drove to the end of the little side road and hiked a trail that traversed the hillside, leading to the crest of Horseshoe Ridge. I could feel the heat and sense the struggle of those veteran Confederates to cover the last few hundred yards, penetrate that blazing Yankee line above them, and maybe change the course of the war—and with it the story of American history. My reverie was interrupted by the sound of orders being shouted in a shrill, female voice. "Keep going!" it shouted, "Keep it up!" I thought about those Confederate officers shouting above the din of battle, urging their weary men to one more effort. Through the trees I caught a glimpse of bright-colored movement, and then the sounds faded up the hill.

Reaching the crest of Snodgrass Hill, where Thomas had made his heroic stand, I passed the straggling column of sweating, spandex-clad runners and their athletic, noisy leader. "What crime did you commit to deserve this misery?" I asked. "The fat crime" responded a wheezing 100-pound waif. "Try it in wool with someone shooting at you," I responded. I left this bedraggled group and hiked purposefully to the point where the battle had climaxed. A bunch of whitetail deer scattered from the edge of the mowed clearing as I reached the 35th Ohio's monument. The heading on the marker at the edge of the woods read: "Close of the Battle, Sept. 20, 1863, 7:30 P.M." I glanced at my watch; it read exactly "7:30." Inspired by this bit of kismet, I waded into the gloom below the 21st Ohio's position, where I could sense their desperate fight for survival against the Tennesseans and Carolinians who assailed them. As I drove out of the park at dusk, I realized how powerful the landscape was and how much I wanted to connect to the men who had fought there in 1863. I also realized that I had thought about Camp Thomas only twice during the whole five hours.

The first time was up in Wilder Tower (which appears in several turn-of-the-century photographs surrounded by drilling militia troops), where I tried to envision the bustling camps and rows of tents belonging to the 1898 multitudes. The other point was when I reached the western edge of the park and encountered the single rail line running the length of the boundary. For a moment, I could almost see the cars, buildings, and crowds of soldiers, horses, hucksters, and harpies on the Lytle Midway during the Camp Thomas era. But as I discovered early on, the evidence of Camp Thomas on the Chickamauga battlefield is not apparent to most visitors, nor is it ever likely to be. What is apparent is the widespread use of the park roads and trails by joggers, hikers, bikers, pet walkers, runners, and other folks engaged in everyday recreational activities. In spite of its multiple uses by the military over the course of 150 years, the dominant activities in the park these days seem to revolve around things that can be seen in any city park in any community.

In spite of their incongruity to the commemorative landscape, the joggers, bicyclists, and the occasional partiers were really not much of a distraction during my tours of the battlefield. Their modern activities and appearance did not undermine the fundamental power and value of the sacred ground any more than do ubiquitous tour buses, nearby fast-food emporiums, and similar activities at Gettysburg. The public's uses of the landscape, while non-commemorative, don't damage it to the extent that the military camps did in 1898, 1918, and 1944, nor do most of these casual users intend to disrespect the park. We have seen that the park's founders wanted their sacred ground to be accessible and useful, which is why they pushed so hard to have Fort Oglethorpe built soon after the Camp Thomas debacle. If the greatest enemy to memory is forgetting, then the joggers and hikers who utilize the park's space and appreciate its tranquility are perpetuating memory whether they know it or not. For all the superficial uses and abuses of the landscape that have come and gone, there seems to be no real threat to the interpretation of the battle that Boynton and his contemporaries put forth when they built the park. Even if the average American does not recognize Chickamauga as the "River of Death" or know that the "Rock of Chickamauga" is not an actual rock, they know that a Civil War battlefield and a national military park both signify something important that they should visit while in the area.

Perhaps Chickamauga is really not much different from Gettysburg, in spite of the latter's vastly more familiar name. As at Gettysburg or Antietam or Shiloh, the Chickamauga battlefield's ability to withstand physical challenges to the landscape can be attributed to the strength and durability of the memories that helped create it. Multiple, non-commemorative uses, like military training, created subordinate memories that were ultimately obliterated by, or absorbed into, the dominant one. No matter how compelling, dramatic, physically destructive, or inappropriate these activities and their legacies might seem, they cannot diminish the power of sanctified ground. As the unfortunate "Boys of

'98" discovered, the lasting memories are not the ones fueled by raw emotions, the howling press, or bitter congressional battles. The memories that endure are built by the participants over time, nurtured by our need to find comfort in the past, and written in stone on sacred landscapes.

APPENDIX A

Order of the Battle
Battles of Chickamauga and Chattanooga

THE BATTLE OF CHICKAMAUGA

<small>UNION: THE ARMY OF THE CUMBERLAND[1]</small>
Major General William S. Rosecrans

Fourteenth (XIV) Army Corps: Major General George H. Thomas
    First Division: Major General Absalom Baird
        First Brigade: Colonel Benjamin F. Scribner
        Second Brigade: Brigadier General John C. Starkweather
        Third Brigade: Brigadier General John H. King

    Second Division: Major General James S. Negley
        First Brigade: Brigadier General John Beatty
        Second Brigade: Colonel Timothy R. Stanley (w);
            Colonel William L. Stoughton
        Third Brigade: Colonel William Sirwell

    Third Division: Brigadier General John M. Brannan
        First Brigade: Colonel John M. Connell
        Second Brigade: Colonel John T. Croxton (w); Colonel William H.
            Hays
        Third Brigade: Colonel Ferdinand Van Derveer

    Fourth Division: Major General Joseph J. Reynolds
        First Brigade: Colonel John T. Wilder (mounted infantry)
        Second Brigade: Colonel Edward A. King (k); Colonel Milton S.
            Robinson
        Third Brigade: Brigadier General John B. Turchin

Twentieth (XX) Army Corps: Major General Alexander McCook
First Division: Major General Jefferson C. Davis
First Brigade: Colonel Sidney P. Post
Second Brigade: Brigadier General William P. Carlin
Third Brigade: Colonel Hans C. Heg (k); Colonel John A. Martin

Second Division: Brigadier General Richard W. Johnson
First Brigade: Brigadier General August Willich
Second Brigade: Colonel Joseph B. Dodge
Third Brigade: Colonel Philemon P. Baldwin (k); Colonel William
W. Berry

Third Division: Major General Philip H. Sheridan
First Brigade: Brigadier General William H. Lytle (k); Colonel Silas
Miller
Second Brigade: Colonel Bernard Laiboldt
Third Brigade: Colonel Luther P. Bradley (w); Colonel Nathan H.
Walworth

Twenty-first (XXI) Army Corps: Major General Thomas L. Crittenden
First Division: Brigadier General Thomas J. Wood
First Brigade: Colonel George P. Buell
Second Brigade: Brigadier General George D. Wagner
Third Brigade: Colonel Charles G. Harker

Second Division: Major General John M. Palmer
First Brigade: Brigadier General Charles Cruft
Second Brigade: Brigadier General William B. Hazen
Third Brigade: Colonel William Grose

Third Division: Brigadier General Horatio H. P. Van Cleve
First Brigade: Brigadier General Samuel Beatty
Second Brigade: Colonel George F. Dick
Third Brigade: Colonel Sidney M. Barnes

Reserve Corps: Major General Gordon Granger
First Division: Brigadier General James B. Steedman
First Brigade: Brigadier General Walter C. Whitaker
Second Brigade: Colonel John B. Mitchell
Detached Brigade: Colonel Daniel McCook

Cavalry Corps: Brigadier General Robert H. Mitchell
    First Division: Colonel Edward M. McCook
        First Brigade: Colonel Archibald P. Campbell
        Second Brigade: Colonel Daniel M. Ray
        Third Brigade: Colonel Lucius D. Watkins

    Second Division: Brigadier General George Crook
        First Brigade: Colonel Robert H. G. Minty
        Second Brigade: Colonel Eli Long

CONFEDERATE: THE ARMY OF TENNESSEE
General Braxton Bragg

RIGHT WING[2]
Lieutenant General Leonidas Polk

Polk's Corps: Lieutenant General Leonidas Polk
    Cheatham's Division: Major General Benjamin F. Cheatham
        Jackson's Brigade: Brigadier General John K. Jackson
        Maney's Brigade: Brigadier General George Maney
        Smith's Brigade: Brigadier General Preston Smith (k); Colonel A. J.
            Vaughn, Jr.
        Wright's Brigade: Brigadier General Marcus Wright
        Strahl's Brigade: Brigadier General O. F. Strahl

    Hindeman's Division (assigned to Left Wing, September 20)

Hill's Corps: Lieutenant General Daniel Harvey Hill
    Cleburne's Division: Major General Patrick Cleburne
        Wood's Brigade: Brigadier General S. A. M. Wood
        Polk's Brigade: Brigadier General Lucius E. Polk
        Deshler's Brigade: Brigadier General James Deshler (k); Colonel
            Roger Q. Mills

    Breckinridge's Division: Major General John C. Breckinridge
        Helm's Brigade: Brigadier General Benjamin H. Helm (k)
        Adams' Brigade: Brigadier General Samuel W. Adams (w) (c);
            Colonel Randall Lee Gibson
        Stovall's Brigade: Brigadier General Marcellus A. Stovall

Walker's Reserve Corps: Major General W. H. T. Walker
  Walker's Division: Brigadier General States Rights Gist
      Gist's Brigade: Colonel P. H. Colquitt (k); Lieutenant Colonel Leroy
          Napier
      Ector's Brigade: Brigadier General Matthew D. Ector
      Wilson's Brigade: Colonel Claudius C. Wilson

  Liddell's Division: Brigadier General St. John R. Liddell
      Liddell's Brigade: Colonel Daniel C. Govan
      Walthall's Brigade: Brigadier General Edward C. Walthall

LEFT WING
Lieutenant General James Longstreet

Buckner's Corps: Major General Simon B. Buckner
  Stewart's Division: Major General Alexander P. Stewart
      Bate's Brigade: Brigadier General William B. Bate
      Clayton's Brigade: Brigadier General Henry D. Clayton
      Brown's Brigade: Brigadier General John C. Brown (w); Colonel
          Edmund C. Cook

  Preston's Division: Brigadier General William Preston
      Gracie's Brigade: Brigadier General Archibald Gracie, Jr.
      Kelly's Brigade: Colonel John C. Kelly
      Trigg's Brigade: Colonel Robert C. Trigg

  Johnson's Division: Brigadier General Bushrod R. Johnson[3]
      Johnson's Brigade: Colonel John S. Fulton
      Gregg's Brigade: Brigadier General John Gregg (w); Colonel
          Cyrus A. Sugg
  McNair's Brigade: Brigadier General Evander McNair (w); Colonel David
      Coleman

  Hindeman's Division (from Polk's Corps): Major General
  Thomas C. Hindeman (w); Brigadier General Patton Anderson
      Anderson's Brigade: Brigadier General Patton Anderson; Colonel
          J. H. Sharp

Deas's Brigade: Brigadier General Zachariah C. Deas
Manigault's Brigade: Brigadier General Arthur M. Manigault

Hood's Corps; Major General John Bell Hood (w)[4]
McLaw's Division: Brigadier General Joseph B. Kershaw
Kershaw's Brigade: Brigadier General Joseph B. Kershaw
Humphreys's Brigade: Brigadier General Benjamin G. Humphreys

Hood's Division: Major General John Bell Hood; Brigadier General
E. McIver Law
Law's Brigade: Colonel James L. Sheffield; Colonel William Oates
Robertson's Brigade: Brigadier General Jerome C. Robertson;
Colonel Van H. Manning
Benning's Brigade: Brigadier General Henry L. Benning

Corps Artillery: Colonel E. Porter Alexander (in transit, so not engaged)[5]

CAVALRY

Wheeler's Corps: Major General Joseph Wheeler
Wharton's Division: Brigadier General John A. Wharton
Crews's Brigade: Colonel C. C. Crews
Harrison's Brigade: Colonel Thomas Harrison

Martin's Division: Brigadier General William T. Martin
Morgan's Brigade: Colonel John T. Morgan
Russell's Brigade: Colonel A. A. Russell
Roddey's Brigade: Brigadier General Phillip D. Roddey

Forrest's Corps: Brigadier General Nathan B. Forrest
Armstrong's Division: Brigadier General Frank C. Armstrong
Armstrong's Brigade: Colonel James T. Wheeler
Forrest's Brigade: Colonel George G. Dibrell

Pegram's Division: Brigadier General John Pegram
Davidson's Brigade: Brigadier General Henry B. Davidson
Scott's Brigade: Colonel John S. Scott

BATTLE OF CHICKAMAUGA TOTALS FOR BOTH ARMIES:[6]

Army	Numbers Engaged	Killed	Wounded	Missing	Total Casualties	%
Union	58,222	1,657	9,756	4,757	16,170	28
Confederate	66,326	2,312	14,674	1,468	18,453	28

BATTLES FOR CHATTANOOGA[7]

UNION ARMY
Major General Ulysses S. Grant

Army of the Cumberland: Major General George H. Thomas
    Fourth (IV) Army Corps: Major General Gordon Granger
        First Division: Brigadier General Charles Cruft
        Second Division: Major General Philip Sheridan
        Third Division: Brigadier General Thomas J. Wood

    Fourteenth (XIV) Army Corps: Major General J. M. Palmer
        First Division: Brigadier General Richard W. Johnson
        Second Division: Brigadier General Jefferson C. Davis
        Third Division: Brigadier General Absalom Baird

    Engineer Troops: Brigadier General William F. Smith

    Artillery Reserve: Brigadier General J. M. Brannan
        First Division: Colonel James Barnett
        Second Division

    Cavalry
        Second Division—Second Brigade: Colonel Eli Long

POST OF CHATTANOOGA: COLONEL JOHN G. PARKHURST

Detachment from the Army of the Potomac: Major General Joseph Hooker[8]
    Eleventh (XI) Army Corps: Major General Oliver O. Howard
        Second Division: Brigadier General Adolph von Steinwehr
        Third Division: Major General Charles Schurtz

Twelfth (XII) Army Corps: Major General Henry Slocum
    Second Division: Brigadier General John W. Geary

Army of the Tennessee: Major General William T. Sherman
    Fifteenth (XV) Corps: Major General Frank P. Blair, Jr.
        First Division: Brigadier General Peter J. Osterhaus
        Second Division: Brigadier General Morgan L. Smith
        Third Division: Brigadier General Hugh Ewing

    Seventeenth (XVII) Army Corps
        Second Division: Brigadier General John E. Smith

CONFEDERATE ARMY OF TENNESSEE[9]

GENERAL BRAXTON BRAGG

Hardee's Corps: Lieutenant General William J. Hardee
    Cheatham's Division: Brigadier General John K. Jackson

    Stevenson's Division: Major General Carter L. Stevenson

    Cleburne's Division: Major General Patrick Cleburne

    Walker's Division: Brigadier General States Rights Gist

Breckinridge's Corps: Major General John C. Breckinridge

    Hindeman's Division: Brigadier General J. Patton Anderson

    Breckinridge's Division: Brigadier General William B. Bate

    Stewart's Division: Major General Ambrose P. Stewart

    Reserve Artillery
        Robertson's Battalion: Captain Felix H. Robertson
        Williams's Battalion: Major S. C. Williams

BATTLES OF CHATTANOOGA, TOTALS FOR BOTH ARMIES:[10]

Army	Numbers Engaged	Killed	Wounded	Missing	Total Casualties	%
Union	56,360	753	4,722	349	5,824	10
Confederate	46,165	361	2,160	4,146 [11]	6,667	14

APPENDIX B

U.S. Troops at Camp George H. Thomas[1]
Major General John R. Brook

FIRST (I) ARMY CORPS: MAJOR GENERAL JOHN R. BROOK
FIRST DIVISION: MAJOR GENERAL JAMES H. WILSON

UNIT[2]	ARRIVED	LEFT	STRENGTH/ DEPARTURE	DEATHS/ DEPARTURE	DEATHS/ DEC. 2
First Brigade					
1st Kentucky	—	July 6	1,318	1	18
3rd Wisconsin	May 16	July 6	1,313	2	30
5th Illinois	May 16	Aug. 3	1,296	11	17
Second Brigade					
4th Ohio	May 16	July 22	1,313	2	29
3rd Illinois	May 16	July 22	1,321	6	37
4th Penn.	May 16	July 23	1,294	6	32
Third Brigade					
16th Penn.	May 17	July 6	865	3	39
2nd Wisconsin	May 23	July 6	1,326	7	27
3rd Kentucky	June 2	July 28	1,293	1	15
I CORPS, FIRST DIVISION TOTALS:			11,339	39	244

Second Division: Brigadier General John S. Poland

UNIT[2]	ARRIVED	LEFT	STRENGTH/ DEPARTURE	DEATHS/ DEPARTURE	DEATHS/ DEC. 2
First Brigade					
31st Michigan	May 17	Aug. 21	1,290	4	9
160th Indiana	May 17	July 28	1,312	2	7
1st Georgia	June 17	Aug. 21	1,212	5	11
Second Brigade					
6th Ohio	May 18	Aug. 27	1,299	3	11
158th Indiana	May 18	Aug. 25	1,288	4	9
1st W. Virginia	May 20	Aug. 26	1,298	3	10
Third Brigade					
2nd Ohio	May 18	Aug. 28	1,297	6	14
1st Penn.	May 18	Aug. 29	1,071	5	12
14th Minn.	—	Aug. 28	1,277	3	4
I CORPS, SECOND DIVISION TOTALS:			11,344	35	87

Third Division: Brigadier General John A. Wiley; Brigadier General J. P. Sanger

UNIT[2]	ARRIVED	LEFT	STRENGTH/ DEPARTURE	DEATHS/ DEPARTURE	DEATHS/ DEC. 2
First Brigade					
1st S. C.	June 7	July 29	1,163	7	18
12th Minn.	May 20	Aug. 23	1,299	9	18
5th Penn.	May 20	Aug. 23	1,291	12	18
Second Brigade					
8th Mass.	May 20	Aug. 23	1,317	8	22
21st Kansas	May 20	Aug. 24	1,264	17	21
12th N.Y.	May 20	Aug. 25	1,302	4	17

Third Brigade

9th Penn.	May 20	Aug. 26	1,291	15	24
2nd Missouri	May 20	Aug. 27	1,269	13	13
1st N. H.	May 22	Aug. 26	1,296	18	29
I CORPS, THIRD DIVISION TOTALS:			11,492	103	180

THIRD (III) ARMY CORPS: MAJOR GENERAL JAMES F. WADE
FIRST DIVISION: BRIGADIER GENERAL FREDERICK D. GRANT

Unit	ARRIVED	LEFT	STRENGTH/ DEPARTURE	DEATHS/ DEPARTURE	DEATHS/ DEC. 2
First Brigade					
14th New York	May 20	Sept. 3	1,277	12	26
1st Missouri	May 21	Sept. 4	1,275	11	17
5th Maryland	May 21	June 2	985	3	19
Second Brigade					
2nd Nebraska	May 22	Aug. 31	1,303	9	25
1st D. C.	May 23	June 1	942	1	22
2nd New York	May 21	June 1	1,014	0	28
Third Brigade					
3rd Tennessee	May 24	Sept. 5	1,293	4	15
1st Vermont	May 24	Aug. 18	996	7	26
8th New York	May 23	Sept. 6	1,301	11	21
III CORPS, FIRST DIVISION TOTALS:			10,386	58	199

SECOND DIVISION: BRIGADIER GENERAL C. F. COMPTON

UNIT	ARRIVED	LEFT	STRENGTH/ DEPARTURE	DEATHS/ DEPARTURE	DEATHS/ DEC. 2
First Brigade					
2nd Kentucky	May 25	Sept. 12	1,332	11	27
9th New York	—	Sept. 13	1,292	19	44
1st Arkansas	May 27	Sept. 9	1,290	14	22

UNIT	ARRIVED	LEFT	STRENGTH/ DEPARTURE	DEATHS/ DEPARTURE	DEATHS/ DEC. 2
Second Brigade					
5th Missouri	May 27	Aug. 27	1,274	7	16
2nd Arkansas	—	Sept. 9	1,291	10	18
69th N.Y.	May 27	June 2	1,026	0	19
Third Brigade					
1st Maine	May 30	Aug. 23	1,286	9	41
52nd Iowa	May 31	Aug. 29	1,304	13	35
1st Mississippi	May 31	Sept. 9	1,029	13	18
III CORPS, SECOND DIVISION TOTALS:			11,124	96	240

OTHER TROOPS
Cavalry Brigade: Colonel Grigsby[3]

UNIT	ARRIVED	LEFT	STRENGTH/ DEPARTURE	DEATHS/ DEPARTURE	DEATHS/ DEC. 2
3rd U.S. V.	May 28	Sept. 10	1 013	10	18
1st Illinois	May 20	Aug. 24	1,219	9	16
1st Ohio	May 15	July 13	833	0	8
2nd Ky.[4]	June 3	Aug. 28	202	0	0
CAVALRY TOTALS:			3,267	19	42

U.S. REGULAR TROOPS[5]

UNIT	ARRIVED	LEFT	STRENGTH/ DEPARTURE	DEATHS/ DEPARTURE	DEATHS/ DEC. 2
6th Cavalry	April 20	July 23	65	0	2
8th Infantry	April 20	—	59	0	0
REGULAR TOTALS:			124	0	2

Light Artillery Brigade

UNIT	ARRIVED	LEFT	STRENGTH/ DEPARTURE	DEATHS/ DEPARTURE	DEATHS/ DEC. 2
Illinois-A[6]	May 21	July 24	175	1	2
27th Indiana	May 16	July 24	173	0	0
28th Indiana	May 16	Sept. 3	177	0	1
Missouri-A	May 18	July 24	171	0	4
Ohio[7]	May 17	Sept. 5	697	3	11
Penn.-B	May 18	Sept. 4	176	0	1
Georgia-A, B	June 8	July 24	324	0	2
ARTILLERY TOTALS:			1,893	4	21
GRAND TOTAL			60,989	354	1,415

APPENDIX C

Selected Legislation Pertaining to the
Establishment and Maintenance of the Park[1]

I. Enabling Legislation, 1890

The Act of Congress Establishing Park,

Be it enacted by the Senate and House of Representatives of the United States of America in Congress Assembled, that for the purpose of preserving and suitably marking for historical and professional military study the fields of some of the most remarkable maneuvers and most brilliant fighting in the war of the rebellion, and upon the ceding of jurisdiction to the United States by the States of Tennessee and Georgia, respectively, and the report of the Attorney-General of the United States that the title to the lands thus ceded is perfect, the following-described highways in those States are hereby declared to be approaches to and parts of the Chickamauga and Chattanooga National Military Park as established by the second section of this act, to wit: First, the Missionary Ridge Crest road from the Sherman Heights at the north end of Missionary Ridge, in Tennessee, where the said road enters upon the ground occupied by the Army of the Tennessee under Major-General William T. Sherman in the military operations of November twenty-fourth and twenty-fifth, eighteen hundred and sixty-three; thence along said road through the positions occupied by the army of General Braxton Bragg on November twenty-fifth, eighteen hundred and sixty-three, and which were assaulted by the Army of the Cumberland under Major-General George H. Thomas on that date, to where the said road crosses the southern boundary of the State of Tennessee, near Rossville Gap, Georgia, upon the ground occupied by the troops of Major-General Joseph Hooker, from the Army of the Potomac, and thence in the State of Georgia to the junction of said road with the Chattanooga and Lafayette or State road at Rossville Gap; second, the Lafayette or State road from Rossville, Georgia, to Lee and Gordon's Mills, Georgia; third, the road from Lee and Gordon's Mills, Georgia, to Crawfish Springs, Georgia; fourth, the road from Crawfish Springs, Georgia, to the crossing of the Chickamauga at Glass's Mill, Georgia; fifth, the Dry Valley road from Rossville, Georgia, to the southern limits of McFarland's Gap in Missionary Ridge; sixth, the Dry Valley and Crawfish Springs road from McFarland's Gap to the intersection of the road from Crawfish Springs to Lee and Gordon's Mills; seventh, the road form Ringgold, Georgia, to Reed's Bridge on the Chickamauga River; eighth, the roads from the crossing of Lookout Creek across the northern slope of Lookout Mountain and thence to the old Summertown Road and to the valley on the east slope of the said mountain, and thence by the route of General Joseph Hooker's troops to Rossville, Georgia, and each and all of these herein-described roads shall, after the passage of this act, remain open and free public highways, and all rights of way now existing through the grounds of said Park and its approaches shall be continued.

SEC. 2. That upon the ceding of jurisdiction by the legislature of the State of Georgia, and the report of the Attorney-General of the United States that perfect title has been secured under the provisions of the act approved August first, eighteen hundred and eighty-eight, entitled "An act to authorize condemnation of land for sites of public buildings and other purposes," the lands and roads embraced in the area bounded as herein described, together with the roads described in section one of this act, are hereby declared to be a national park, to be known as the Chickamauga and Chattanooga National Park; that is to say, the area inclosed by a line beginning on the Lafayette or State road, in Georgia, at a point where the bottom of the ravine next north of the house known on the field of Chickamauga as the Cloud House, and being about six hundred yards north of said house [crosses said road], due east to the Chickamauga River and due west to the intersection of the Dry Valley road at McFarland's Gap; thence along the west side of Dry Valley and Craw-fish Springs roads to the south side of the road from Crawfish Springs to Lee and Gordon's Mills; thence along the south side of the last-named road to Lee and Gordon's Mills; thence along the channel of the Chickamauga River to the line forming the northern boundary of the park, as hereinbefore described, containing seven thousand six hundred acres, more or less.

SEC. 3. That the said Chickamauga and Chattanooga National Park, and the approaches thereto, shall be under the control of the Secretary of War, and it shall be his duty, immediately after the passage of this act, to notify the Attorney-General of the purpose of the United States to acquire title to the roads and lands described in the previous sections of this act under the provisions of the act of August first, eighteen hundred and eighty-eight; and the said Secretary, upon receiving notice from the Attorney-General of the United States that perfect titles have been secured to the said lands and roads, shall at once proceed to establish and substantially mark the boundaries of the said park.

SEC. 4. That the Secretary of War is hereby authorized to enter into agreements, upon such nominal terms as he may prescribe, with such present owners of the land as may desire to remain upon it, to occupy and cultivate their present holdings, upon condition that they will preserve the present buildings and roads, and the present outlines of field and forest, and that they will only cut trees or underbrush under such regulations as the Secretary of War may prescribe, and that they will assist in caring for and protecting all tablets, monuments, or such other artificial works as may from time to time be erected by proper authority.

SEC. 5. That the affairs of the Chickamauga and Chattanooga National Park shall, subject to the supervision and direction of the Secretary of War, be in charge of three Commissioners, each of whom shall have actively participated in the battle of Chickamauga or one of the battles about Chattanooga, two to be appointed from civil life by the Secretary of War, and a third, who shall be detailed by the Secretary of War from among those officers of the Army best acquainted with the details of the battles of Chickamauga and Chattanooga, who shall act as secretary of the Commission. The said Commissioners and secretary shall have an office in the War Department building, and while on actual duty shall be paid such compensation, out of the appropriation provided in this act, as the Secretary of War shall deem reasonable and just.

SEC. 6. That is shall be the duty of the Commissioners named in the preceding section, under the direction of the Secretary of War, to superintend the opening of such roads as may be necessary to the purposes of the Park, and the repair of the roads of the same, and to ascertain and definitely mark the lines of battle of all troops engaged in the battles of Chickamauga and Chattanooga, so far as the same shall fall within the lines of the Park as defined in the previous section of this act, and, for the purpose of assisting them in their duties and in ascertaining these lines, the Secretary of War shall have authority to employ, at such compensation as he may deem reasonable and just, to be paid out of the appropriation made by this act, some person recognized as well informed in regard to the details of the battles of Chickamauga and Chattanooga, and who shall have actively participated in one of those battles, and it shall be the duty of the Secretary of War, from and after the passage of this act, through the Commissioners and their assistant in historical work, and under the act approved August first, eighteen hundred and eighty-eight, regulating the condemnation of land for public uses, to proceed with the preliminary work of establishing the Park and its approaches as the same are defined in this act, and the expenses thus incurred shall be paid out of the appropriation provided by this act.

SEC. 7. That it shall be the duty of the Commissioners, acting under the direction of the Secretary of War, to ascertain and substantially make the locations of the regular troops, both infantry and artillery, within the boundaries of the Park, and to erect monuments upon those positions as Congress may provide the necessary appropriations; and the Secretary of War in the same way may ascertain and mark all lines of battle within the boundaries of the Park and erect plain and substantial historical tablets at such points in the vicinity of the Park and its approaches as he may deem fitting and necessary to clearly designate positions and movements, which, although without the limits of the Park, were directly connected with the battles of Chickamauga and Chattanooga.

SEC. 8. That it shall be lawful for the authorities of any State having troops engaged either at Chattanooga or Chickamauga, and for the officers and directors of the Chickamauga Memorial Association, a corporation chartered under the laws of Georgia, to enter upon the lands and approaches of the Chickamauga and Chattanooga National Park for the purpose of ascertaining and marking the lines of battle of troops engaged therein; provided that before any such lines are permanently designated the position of the lines and the proposed methods of marking them by monuments, tablets, or otherwise shall be submitted to the Secretary of War, and shall first receive the written approval of the Secretary, which approval shall be based upon formal written reports, which must be made to him in each case by the Commissioners of the Park.

SEC. 9. That the Secretary of War, subject to the approval of the President of the United States, shall have the power to make, and shall make, all needed regulations for the care of the Park and for the establishment and marking of the lines of battle and other historical features of the park.

SEC. 10. That if any person shall willfully destroy, mutilate, deface, injure, or remove any monument, column, statues, memorial structure, or work of art that shall be erected or placed upon the grounds of the Park by lawful authority, or shall willfully destroy or remove any fence, railing, inclosure, or other work for the protection or ornament of said park, or any portion thereof, or shall willfully destroy, cut, hack, bark, break down, or otherwise injure any tree, bush, or shrubbery that may be growing upon said Park, or shall cut down or fell or remove any timber, battle relic, tree, or trees growing or being on such Park, except by permission of the Secretary of War, or shall willfully remove or destroy any breastworks, earthworks, walls, or other defenses or shelter, on any part thereof, constructed by the armies formerly engaged in the battles on the lands or approaches to the Park, any person so offending and found guilty thereof before any justice of the peace of the county in which the offense may be committed shall for each and every such offense forfeit and pay a fine, in the discretion of the justice, according to the aggravation of the offense, of not less than five nor more than fifty dollars, one half to the use of the Park and the other half to the informer, to be enforced and recovered, before such justice, in like manner as debts of like nature are now by law recoverable in the several counties where the offense may be committed.

SEC. 11. That to enable the Secretary of War to begin to carry out the purposes of this act, including the condemnation and purchase of the necessary land, marking the boundaries of the Park, opening or repairing necessary roads, maps, and surveys, and the pay and expenses of the Commissioners and their assistant, the sum of one-hundred and twenty-five thousand dollars, or such portion as may be necessary, is hereby appropriated, out of any moneys in the Treasury not otherwise appropriated, and disbursements under this act shall require the approval of the Secretary of War, and he shall make annual report of the same to Congress.

Approved, August 19, 1890.

II. MILITARY USE ACT, 1896[2]

An Act authorizing the Secretary of War to make certain uses of national military parks. Approved, May 18, 1896.

Be it enacted by the Senate and House of Representatives of the United States of America in Congress assembled, that in order to obtain practical benefits of great value to the country from the establishment of national military parks, said parks and their approaches are hereby declared to be national fields for military maneuvers for the Regular Army of the United States or Militia of the States: Provided, that the said parks shall be opened for such purposes only at the direction of the Secretary of War, and under such regulations as he may prescribe.

SEC. 2. That the Secretary of War is hereby authorized, within the limits of appropriations which may from time to time be available for such purpose, to assemble, at his discretion, in camp at such season of the year and for such period as he may designate, as such field of military maneuvers, such portions of the military forces of the United States as he may think best, to receive military instruction there. The Secretary of War is further authorized to make and publish regulations governing the assembling of the National Guard or Militia of the several States upon the maneuvering grounds, and he may detail instructors from the Regular Army for such forces during their exercises.

III. Monument Guidelines

Regulations governing the erection of monuments, tablets, and markers in the Chickamauga and Chattanooga National Park[3]
War Department, Chickamauga and Chattanooga National Park Commission, Washington, D.C., December 14, 1895

In accordance with the act of Congress approved August 19, 1890, establishing the Chickamauga and Chattanooga National Park, the following revised regulations are published for the information and guidance of all interested in the erection of monuments, tablets, or other methods of indicating lines of battle or positions within the limits of the park:

1. Statements of the proposed dimensions, designs, inscriptions upon, and material for all monuments, tablets, or other markers must be submitted, in duplicate, to the Commissioners of the Park, and in the case of monuments, plans, and elevations showing exact measurements, and a close estimate of the weight, must also be submitted. The Park Commissioners will report upon all these to the Secretary of War, and upon his approval such monuments, tablets, or markers may be erected, but not until such has been obtained.

2. Monuments, markers, and other permanent memorials must be constructed of bronze, granite, or such other durable stone, as, after investigation by the Park Commissioners, may be by them recommended to and be approved by the Secretary of War. The number of markers shall be limited to such as, in the judgment of the Secretary of War, may be necessary to designate important positions.

3. Inscriptions must be purely historical, and must relate only to the Chickamauga and Chattanooga campaigns. They must also be based upon and conform to the official reports of these campaigns, and must be submitted to the Secretary of War, through the Park Commissioners, for his approval before being inscribed upon monuments, tablets, or other markers.

4. Regimental monuments shall be placed on brigade lines on ground where the regiments did notable fighting. Provided, however, that in case a regiment concerned became separated from its own brigade and most distinguished itself while alone or attached to another, its monument may be so placed as to show this fact. General memorial monuments erected by states must be located on ground upon which some of the troops of the State erecting the monument were engaged. Where troops fought outside the limits of the Park, their monuments may be placed at such points within the Park as the Commissioners of the Park may designate.

5. The location proposed for each monument, marker, or other permanent memorial must be submitted to the Secretary of War, through the Park Commissioners, for his approval, and none shall be erected until such approval shall have been obtained.

6. The foundations of all State monuments will be constructed, without cost to the States, under the direction of the Park engineer.

7. The hauling of loads over the Park roads and approaches in excess of 5,000 pounds, the weight of the wagon included, must be done in wagons specially adapted to the purpose, the load to be equally distributed and carried on four wheels.[4] It shall be the duty of the engineer of the Park to forbid and prevent the erection of any monument or marker which shall have to be hauled in violation of this regulation, and to report the facts to the Park Commission.

8. No work upon monuments or other marker or tablets within the Park or on its approaches shall be allowed on Sunday.

9. Brigades, divisions, and corps may be designated in the inscriptions by their numbers where that method was used, and also by the names of designation of their respective commanders, as "First Brigade, First Division, Fourteenth Corps," or "Scribner's Brigade, Baird's Division, Thomas's Corps," "Polk's Brigade, Cleburne's Division, Hill's Corps," [or both]. The numerical designations alone would be meaningless to most visitors.[5]

For the Commission: J. S. Fullerton, Chairman

Approved, December 13, 1895

NOTES

INTRODUCTION

1. The four presidents directly involved in this story are Ulysses S. Grant, James Garfield, William McKinley, and Theodore Roosevelt. A fifth, Union veteran Benjamin Harrison, was in office when the park was created. Early histories of the campaign written by Union veterans include Henry Cist, *The Army of the Cumberland, Campaigns of the Civil War* (New York: Scribner's and Sons, 1892) and Thomas Van Horne, *History of the Army of the Cumberland, Its Organization, Campaigns, and Battles,* 2 volumes (Cincinnati, Ohio: Robert Clarke & Co., 1875). Archibald Gracie, *The Truth About Chickamauga* (published by the author, 1911; facsimile reprint, Dayton, Ohio: Morningside Books, 1997) takes on some of the controversies on both sides. Among modern histories, the most useful are Glenn Tucker, *Chickamauga: Bloody Battle in the West* (Bobbs-Merrill Company, 1961; reprint, Dayton, Ohio: Morningside Books, 1992); Steven Woodworth, *Six Armies in Tennessee: The Chickamauga and Chattanooga Campaigns* (Lincoln: University of Nebraska Press, 1998) and, as editor of *The Chickamauga Campaign,* Civil War Campaigns in the Heartland Series, Steven D. Woodworth, series editor (Carbondale: Southern Illinois University Press, 2010); Peter Cozzens, *This Terrible Sound: The Battle of Chickamauga* (Urbana: University of Illinois Press, 1992), which was followed by *The Shipwreck of Their Hopes: The Battles for Chattanooga* (Urbana: University of Illinois Press, 1994).

2. Note that the uses of memory and rituals in non-literate societies often serve as primary sources of information on the past as part of a broadly defined "oral tradition." Maurice Halbwachs, *The Collective Memory,* translated from *La Memoire Collective* (New York: Harper Colophone Books, 1980); Paul Connerton, *How Societies Remember* (Cambridge: Cambridge University Press, 1989); David Lowenthal, *The Past Is a Foreign Country* (Cambridge: Cambridge University Press, 1995), 185–239.

3. For a general discussion of memory and tradition, see Eric Hobsbawm, "Introduction: Inventing Traditions," in *The Invention of Tradition,* ed. Eric Hobsbawm and Terrence Ranger (Cambridge, 1984); W. Fitzhugh Brundage, "No Deed But Memory," in *Where These Memories Grow: History, Memory, and Southern Identity,* ed. W. Fitzhugh Brundage (Chapel Hill: University of North Carolina Press, 2000), 1–28; Anthony Molho and Gordon S. Wood, eds. *Imagined Histories: American Historians Interpret the Past* (Princeton, N.J.: Princeton University Press, 1998), 16–18; David Lowenthal, *Possessed by the Past: The Heritage Crusade and the Spoils of History* (New York: The Free Press, 1996); Pierre Nora, "Between Memory and History: *Les Lieux de Memoire,*" *Representations* 26 (Spring 1989), 8.

4. David Blight, *Beyond the Battlefield: Race, Memory, and the American Civil War* (Amherst: University of Massachusetts Press, 2002); John Bodnar, *Remaking America: Public Memory, Commemoration, and Patriotism in the Twentieth Century* (Princeton, N.J.: Princeton University Press, 1992); Michael Kammen, *Mystic Chords of Memory: The Transformation of Tradition in American Culture* (New York: Alfred A. Knopf, 1991); G. Kurt Piehler, *Remembering War the American Way* (Washington, D.C.: Smithsonian Institution Press, 1995); William Blair, *Cities of the Dead: Contesting the Memory of the Civil War in the South, 1865–1914* (Chapel Hill: University of North Carolina Press, 2004), and Edward Linenthal, *Sacred Ground: Americans and Their Battlefields* (Champaign: University of Illinois Press, 1993).

5. The terms "civic" and "popular" are used by Kammen, *Mystic Chords of Memory*, 4–11; while Bodnar prefers to use "official" and "vernacular" to distinguish between dominant and subordinate memories, *Remaking America*, 13–15.

6. David Blight, *Race and Reunion: The Civil War in American Memory* (Cambridge, Mass.: The Belknap Press of the Harvard University Press, 2001); John R. Neff, *Honoring the Civil War Dead: Commemoration and the Problem of Reconciliation*, Modern War Series (Lawrence: University Press of Kansas, 2005).

7. A well-documented look at Civil War reenacting can be found in R. Lee Hadden, *Reliving the Civil War: A Reenactor's Handbook* (Mechanicsburg, Pa.: Stackpole Books, 1996), and Rory Turner, "Bloodless Battles: The Civil War Reenacted," *TDR* 34, no. 4 (Winter 1990): 123–36, JSTOR; Kris Kristofferson, *Nor Shall Your Glory Be Forgot: An Essay in Photographs* (New York: St. Martin's Press, 1999) examines reenacting through black-and-white photographs made to look somewhat like "period" photography. In addition to several scholarly journals, popular periodicals include *Civil War Times Illustrated, Blue and Gray, North and South,* and *America's Civil War.* The History Channel's *Civil War Combat* used extensive reenactor footage to illustrate generally non-partisan and non-political accounts of battles and leaders. See Geoffrey C. Ward with Ric Burns and Ken Burns, *The Civil War: An Illustrated History* (New York: Alfred A. Knopf, 1999, eighth paperback printing, 2000), which includes documentation and interpretations used in Burns's 1989 film *The Civil War* by historians John C. Fehrenbacher, Barbara Fields, James C. McPherson, and C. Vann Woodward; criticism of Burns's view can be found in Eric Foner, "Ken Burns and the Romance of Reunion," in *Who Owns History? Rethinking the Past in a Changing World* (New York: Hill & Wang, 2002), 189–204; this and other critiques can be found in Robert B. Toplin, ed., *Ken Burns's "The Civil War": Historians Respond* (New York: 1996); the films *Gettysburg* and *Gods and Generals* were based on Michael Shaara's novel, *The Killer Angels* (New York: Ballantine Books, 1974) and his son, Jeff Shaara's, *Gods and Generals* (New York: Ballantine Books, 1996), both of which accept much of the sentimental, "Lost Cause" interpretation of the war. A critical assessment of these and other films can be found in Gary Gallagher, "Hollywood Has It Both Ways: The Rise, Fall, and Reappearance of the Lost Cause in American Film," in Joan Waugh and Gary W. Gallagher, eds., *Wars Within a War: Controversy and Conflict Over the American Civil War* (Chapel Hill: University of North Carolina Press, 2009), 157–83. Tony Horwitz, *Confederates in the Attic: Dispatches from the Unfinished Civil War* (New York: Pantheon Books, 1999) offers a penetrating look at many of these issues from a modern journalistic perspective; for an overview of Confederate symbols, see J. Michael Martinez, William D. Richardson, and Ron McNinch-Su, *Confederate Symbols in the Contemporary South* (Gainesville: University Press of Florida, 2000).

8. Discussions of the importance of place and the various types of historic and commemorative sites can be found in William E. Leuchtenburg, *American Places: Encounters*

With History (New York: Oxford University Press); John Brinckerhoff Jackson, *A Sense of Place, a Sense of Time* (New Haven, Conn.: Yale University Press, 1994); David Lowenthal, "European and English Landscapes as National Symbols," in David Hoosen, ed. *Geography and National Identity* (Oxford, UK: Blackwell Publishers, 1994); at the opposite end of sanctification is "obliteration" wherein the site is covered completely by non-commemorative development or left entirely vacant, see Kenneth E. Foote, *Shadowed Ground: America's Landscapes of Violence and Tragedy* (Austin: University of Texas Press, 1997), 1–9, 33.

9. Quoted from a paper presented as the keynote speech, "Memorializing Memory," delivered by Dennis Frye at the Civil War Preservation Trust Spring Conference, held at the Chattanoogan Hotel, Chattanooga, Tenn., April 28, 2002.

10. An interesting overview of the topic of historical preservation can be found in Georgie and Margie Holder Boge, *Paving Over the Past: A History and Guide to Civil War Battlefield Preservation* (Washington D.C.: Island Press, 1993); see also William Murtagh, *Keeping Time: The History and Theory of Preservation in America* (New York: John Wiley & Sons, 1997) and Diane Barthel, *Historic Preservation: Collective Memory and Historical Identity* (New Brunswick, N.J.: Rutgers University Press, 1996). An insightful discussion of the multiple uses of a potentially sacred piece of ground can be found in Peter Svenson, *Battlefield: Farming a Civil War Battleground* (Boston: Faber & Faber, 1992). Mailings and solicitations by the Civil War Preservation Trust, along with the magazine entitled *Hallowed Ground* that is sent to its members, reflect this attitude toward battlefield preservation. The underlying message in this literature is that corporate, political, and public insensitivity toward the preservation of Civil War sites (even minor and obscure ones) is a sign of a deteriorating sense of history and a loss of values linked to our past. Due to these ongoing threats, virtually all battlefields are considered sacred, even prior to the process of preservation or the rituals of sanctification.

11. Carol Reardon, *Pickett's Charge in History and Memory* (Chapel Hill: University of North Carolina Press, 1997); Edward Tabor Linenthal, *Sacred Ground: Americans and Their Battlefields*, 2nd ed., with a foreword by Robert Utley (Urbana: University of Illinois Press, 1993); Jim Weeks, *Gettysburg: Memory, Market, and an American Shrine* (Princeton, N.J.: Princeton University Press, 2003); Thomas Desjardin, *These Honored Dead: How the Story of Gettysburg Shaped American Memory* (Cambridge, Mass.: De Capo Press, 2003); Barbara Platt, *This Is Holy Ground: A History of the Gettysburg Battlefield* (Harrisburg, Pa.: Huggins Printing, 2001); a featured article by Benjamin Y. Dixon appears as "The Gettysburg Battlefield, One Century Ago," *Adams County History* 6 (2000): 5–54.

12. Timothy B. Smith, *This Great Battlefield of Shiloh: History, Memory, and the Establishment of a Civil War Battlefield Park* (Knoxville: University of Tennessee Press, 2004) and *The Untold Story of Shiloh: The Battle and the Battlefield* (Knoxville: University of Tennessee Press, 2006); idem, *The Golden Age of Battlefield Preservation: The Decade of the 1890s and the Establishment of America's First Five Military Parks* (Knoxville: University of Tennessee Press, 2008), which discusses Shiloh, Chickamauga, Gettysburg, Antietam, and Vicksburg National Military Parks, and *A Chickamauga Memorial: The Establishment of America's First Civil War National Military Park* (Knoxville: University of Tennessee Press, 2009). See also, idem, "Henry Van Ness Boynton and Chickamauga: The Pillars of the Modern Military Park Movement," in Steven Woodworth, ed., *The Chickamauga Campaign*, 165–87. Until Smith's studies, the only other works that dealt directly with the founding of the park were John C. Page and Jerome A. Green, *Administrative History of the Chickamauga and Chattanooga National Military Park* (Denver, Colo.: Denver Service Center, National Park Service, U.S. Department of the Interior, 1983); James A. Kaser, "The Army of the Cumberland and the Battle of Chickamauga: An Exercise in Perspectivist

Historical Research," PhD. diss., Bowling Green State University, 1991, and idem, *At the Bivouac of Memory: History, Politics, and the Battle of Chickamauga*, American University Studies, Series IX (New York: Peter Lang, 1996).

13. Gracie, *Truth about Chickamauga*, vii; H. V. Boynton, *The National Military Park, Chickamauga—Chattanooga: An Historical Guide, with Maps and Illustrations* (Cincinnati: Robert Clarke Company, 1895), 224.

14. Jerry Desmond, "Camp Thomas During the Spanish-American War: A Pictorial History," *Chattanooga Regional Historical Journal* 1, no. 2 (July 1998): 118–40; Gregory Chapman, "Army Life at Camp Thomas, Georgia During the Spanish-American War," *Georgia Historical Quarterly* 70 (1986): 633–56; Richard A. Sauers, "From Hallowed Ground to Training Ground: Chickamauga's Camp Thomas, 1898," *Civil War Regiments: A Journal of the American Civil War* 7, no. 1, *Chickamauga and Chattanooga, Battles for the Confederate Heartland* (2000): 129–43; Graham Cosmas, *An Army for Empire: The United States Army in the Spanish-American War* (Columbia: University of Missouri Press, 1971; 2nd edition, Shippensburg, Pa.: White Mane Publishing, 1994).

1. "THE CONSEQUENCES WILL BE MOMENTOUS"

1. Several versions of the "River of Death" story can be found in Cozzens, *This Terrible Sound*, 90–91; David J. Eicher, *Civil War Battlefields: A Touring Guide* (Dallas, Tex.: Taylor Publishing Co., 1995), 43; Jim Miles, *Paths to Victory: A History and Tour Guide of the Stones River, Chickamauga, Chattanooga, Knoxville, and Nashville Campaigns.* The Civil War Campaign Series (Nashville: Rutledge Press, 1991), 71; and "The Chickamauga Curse: 'River of Death'" in *Civil War Times Illustrated*, 9, no. 1 (October 1991): 52. A local historian, and self-published expert on the Battle of Chickamauga, disputes the commonly repeated "River of Death" story, claiming it "has no basis in fact." Rather, he explains that the Chickamauga were a group of pro-British Cherokee who broke with other bands and settled in northern Georgia, who either named, or took their name from the nearby creek. Thus, one could say that in addition to all the other controversies surrounding this place, its very name is still a topic for debate, E. Raymond Evans, *Chickamauga, Civil War Impact on an Area: Tsikamagi, Crawfish Spring, Snow Hill, and Chickamauga* (Walker County, Ga.: City of Chickamauga, 2002), 11–18.

2. Quoted in Freeman Cleaves, *Rock of Chickamauga: The Life of General George H. Thomas* (Norman: University of Oklahoma Press, 1948), 161–62; further usage of the "River of Death" will be discussed in detail in later chapters, but an interesting description of the battle's landscape and legacy can be found in John Bowers, *Chickamauga and Chattanooga: The Battles that Doomed the Confederacy* (New York: Avon Books, 1994), including the "primeval" quote, 75. Having grown up in the area, Bowers described Chickamauga as "a stupendous, awesome event, in almost living memory" and talked of his grandfather's participation in it "as some sons today proclaim of their fathers' having fought at Normandy or on Iwo Jima," xi, xv. General references to the bloody nature of the combat at Chickamauga can be found in idem, 45 and 74. References can be found throughout Cozzens, *This Terrible Sound*; Miles, "The Chickamauga Curse," 52–54; Miles, *Paths to Victory*, 47–62; and Steven F. Woodworth, *Six Armies in Tennessee*, which contains an aptly titled chapter, "Savagery and Confusion."

3. Brief accounts of the role of veterans in the creation of the park can be found in J. L. Rogers, *The Civil War Battles of Chickamauga and Chattanooga* (J. L. Rogers, 1942), 5; Richard West Sellars, *Pilgrim Places: Civil War Battlefields, Historic Preservation, and*

America's First Military Parks, 1863–1900 (Fort Washington, Pa.: Eastern National, 2005), 16–28; Miles, *Paths to Victory,* 72–77; and William C. Davis, *Civil War Parks: The Story Behind the Scenery* (published in cooperation with the Eastern National Park & Monument Association; KC Publications, 1984. Sixth Printing, 1996, rev. ed.), 46–49.

4. Letter "to the Governor and the people of Iowa, 15 August 1898," Spanish-American War Survey no. 1393, 52nd Iowa Infantry Box, George Wykoff folder, United States Army Military History Institute (USAMHI), Carlisle Barracks, Carlisle, Pa. For a general description of Camp Thomas, see Sauers, "From Hallowed Ground to Training Ground," 129–43.

5. A solid, readable synthesis of the importance of 1863 can be found in Joseph E. Stevens, *1863: The Rebirth of a Nation* (New York: Bantam Books, 1999, paperback, 2000); see also *1863: High Tide of the Civil War,* a special edition from the publisher of *America's Civil War, Civil War Times,* and *Military History* (2003). The best and most recent scholarly treatment of the Army of the Cumberland is Larry J. Daniel, *Days of Glory: The Army of the Cumberland, 1861–1865* (Baton Rouge: Louisiana State University Press, 2004). For excellent accounts of the history of the Confederate force, see Thomas L. Connelly, *Army of the Heartland: The Army of Tennessee, 1861–1862* (Baton Rouge: Louisiana State University Press, 1967: paperback, 2001) and its companion volume, *Autumn of Glory: The Army of Tennessee, 1862–1865* (Baton Rouge: Louisiana State University Press, 1971; paperback, 2001); Stanley Horn, *The Army of Tennessee* (Bobbs Merrill, 1941; paperback: Norman: University of Oklahoma Press, 1993); Richard M. McMurry, *Two Great Rebel Armies: An Essay in Confederate Military History* (Chapel Hill: University of North Carolina Press, 1999).

6. Two excellent studies involving soldiers and combat are Earl Hess, *The Union Soldier in Battle: Enduring the Ordeal of Combat* (Lawrence: University Press of Kansas, 1997) and Gerald Linderman, *Embattled Courage: Experiences of Combat in the American Civil War* (New York: Free Press, 1987).

7. Reardon, *Pickett's Charge,* 1–10; for recent organizational histories of the Army of the Potomac and the Army of Northern Virginia, see Jeffery Wert, *The Sword of Lincoln: The Army of the Potomac* (New York: Simon & Schuster, 2005) and Joseph Glattharr, *General Lee's Army: From Victory to Collapse* (New York: Free Press, 2008).

8. Many postwar books emphasized the experience of "common soldiers" as a main theme. Among them are John D. Billings, *Hardtack and Coffee: The Unwritten Story of Army Life* (Boston: George E. Smith & Co., 1887; reprinted for Time-Life Collectors Library of the Civil War [TLCLCW], 1982); Leander Stillwell, *The Story of a Common Soldier of Army Life in the Civil War, 1861–1865* (Kansas City, Mo.: Franklin Hudson Publishing Co., 1920; reprint of 2nd ed. for TLCLCW, 1983); John Beatty, *The Citizen Soldier or, Memoirs of a Volunteer* (Cincinnati, Ohio: Wilstach, Baldwin & Co., 1879: reprint for TLCLCW, 1983); and on the Confederate side, Carleton McCarthy, *Detailed Minutiae of Solder Life in the Army of Northern Virginia, 1861–1865* (Richmond, Va.: Carleton McCarthy and Company, 1882; reprint for TLCLCW, 1982). Most modern scholars continue to use Bell Irvin Wiley's *Life of Billy Yank* and *Life of Johnny Reb* as models for study of the common soldier experience, while Reid Mitchell, *The Vacant Chair: The Northern Soldier Leaves Home* (New York: Oxford University Press, 1995) offers a closer look at the volunteers' connections to their homes and communities, as does James M. McPherson, *For Cause and Comrades: Why Men Fought in the Civil War* (New York: Oxford University Press, 1998). See also Larry M. Logue, *To Appomattox and Beyond: The Civil War Soldier in War and Peace,* American Ways Series (Chicago: Ivan Dees, 1997); Linderman, *Embattled Courage;* and Hess, *Union Soldier in Battle.*

9. Scholarly histories exist for all of the brigades mentioned here and it was not uncommon for the members of these famous units to include their brigade affiliations when

writing their own memoirs or regimental histories. However, the literature is overwhelmingly dominated by regimental accounts written by both veterans and modern scholars. For examples, see 103rd Ohio Volunteer Infantry, *Personal Reminiscences and Experiences: Campaign Life in the Union Army from 1862 to 1865* (Oberlin, Ohio: News Printing Co., 1900; reprinted by the 103rd O.V.I. Memorial Association, Fred Weidner & Sons, 1984); Jacob Smith, *Camps and Campaigns of the 107th Regiment Ohio Volunteer Infantry from August, 1862 to July, 1865* (reprint of unpublished original, Navarre, Ohio: Indian River Graphics, 2000); Ralsa C. Rice, *Yankee Tigers: Through the Civil War with the 125th Ohio,* Larry A. Baumgartner and Larry M. Strayer, eds. (originally published as "Three Years with the 125th Ohio: Opdyke's Tigers" in 1905; reprint by Huntington, W.Va.: Blue Acorn Press, 2000); William Kepler, *History of the Three Months and Three Years Service from April 16th, 1861 to June 22d, 1864, of the Fourth Regiment Ohio Volunteer Infantry in the War for the Union* (Cleveland, Ohio: Leader Printing Company, 1886; reprint by Blue Acorn Press, 1992); Franklin Sawyer, *A Military History of the 8th Regiment Ohio Volunteer Inf'y; Its Battles, Marches, and Army Movements,* [original], ed. by George A. Groot (Cleveland, Ohio: Fairbanks & Co. Printers, 1881; reprint by Blue Acorn Press, 1994), "Brave Old Regiment," 7. Note that the dust jackets of both the 4th Ohio and 8th Ohio reprints include "Gibraltar Brigade, Army of the Potomac" as a prominent subtitle. Constantin Grebner, *We Were the Ninth: A History of the Ninth Regiment, Ohio Volunteer Infantry, April 17, 1861, to June 7, 1864,* trans. and ed. by Frederic Trautman (Kent, Ohio: Kent State University Press, 1987), 2.

10. For detailed descriptions of Union armies and their histories, see Frank J. Welcher, *The Union Armies, 1861–1862: Organization and Operations,* vol. I: *The Eastern Theater;* vol. II: *The Western Theater* (Bloomington: Indiana University Press, 1993); recent histories of the major armies include Gerald Prokopowcz, *All For the Regiment: The Army of the Ohio, 1861–1862* (Chapel Hill: University of North Carolina Press, 2001); Wert, *The Sword of Lincoln;* Steven E. Woodworth, *Nothing But Victory: The Army of the Tennessee, 1861–1865* (New York: Alfred Knopf, 2005); problems with the Confederate departmental system and issues affecting the Army of Tennessee are discussed in Steven Woodworth, *No Band of Brothers: Problems in the Rebel High Command,* Shades of Blue and Gray Series, Herman Hattaway and Jon L. Wakelyn, eds. (Columbia: University of Missouri Press, 1999), 51–80; the theory that the South lost the war because of the poor performance of armies in the West can be found in Richard McMurry, *The Fourth Battle of Winchester: Toward a New Civil War Paradigm* (Kent, Ohio: Kent State University Press, 2002).

11. Although the promotion of Rosecrans signaled the birth of the Army of the Cumberland, the corps structure and makeup of the army was not finalized until late January 1863, when the War Department created a new Department and Army of the Ohio under the command of Gen. Ambrose Burnside, see Daniel, *Days of Glory,* 183, 227. Details on the early Army of the Ohio, the creation of the Army of the Cumberland, and Burnside's Army of Ohio can be found in Welcher, *The Union Armies,* vol. II, 159–74, 192–213; see also Prokopowcz, *All for the Regiment;* a brief assessment of the Army of the Tennessee's sense of identity can be found in Joan Waugh, *U. S. Grant: American Hero, American Myth,* Civil War America Series, Gary Gallagher, ed. (Chapel Hill: University of North Carolina Press, 2010), 58–59. Union armies tended to be named for rivers, thus the Federal Army of *the* Tennessee; Confederates named theirs for states, as in the Army of Tennessee.

12. An example of this was the 104th Ohio, which began its service in 1862 in Kentucky, joined Burnside's army at Knoxville in 1863, ended up in John M. Schofield's 23rd Corps

(also known as the Army of Ohio) under Sherman during the Atlanta campaign, and fought with Thomas at Franklin and Nashville late in 1864. They were in North Carolina when the war ended; see Bradley S. Keefer, "They Stood to Their Guns: The 104th Ohio Volunteer Infantry in the Civil War," unpublished Master's thesis, Kent State University, 1984.

13. Direct comparisons between the Army of Tennessee and Army of Northern Virginia and the notion that the western army was flawed from the start can be found in Richard M. McMurry, *The Fourth Battle of Winchester: Toward a New Civil War Paradigm* (Kent, Ohio: Kent State University Press, 2002) and *Two Great Rebel Armies;* as the quotes and its title imply, Andrew Haughton, *Training, Tactics, and Leadership in the Confederate Army of Tennessee: Seeds of Failure,* Cass Series: Military History and Policy (London: Frank Cass, 2000), 1–10, attributes the army's lack of success to a combination of factors that includes inadequate training of its officers and men at all levels.

14. William Glenn Robertson, "The Chickamauga Campaign: The Fall of Chattanooga," *Blue and Gray,* 23, no. 4 (Fall 2006), 7–8; a solid assessment of Rosecrans's strengths and weaknesses can be found in W. J. Wood, *Civil War Generalship: The Art of Command* (Westport, Conn.: Praeger, 1997), 95–102; Lincoln's frustration with Rosecrans is described in Woodworth, *Six Armies in Tennessee,* 4–5, 16–19.

15. Robertson, "The Fall of Chattanooga," 8; Daniel, *Days of Glory,* 189–92, describes Crittenden as "mediocre" and blames McCook's incompetence for the near disaster at Stones River; Cozzens, *This Terrible Sound,* 7–10, is somewhat less critical of their abilities, but implies that most of the officers had not lived up to their own egos. Similar assessments can be found in William A. Lamers, *The Edge of Glory: A Biography of General William S. Rosecrans, U.S.A.,* with a new introduction by Larry Daniel (Baton Rouge: Louisiana State University Press, 1999), 183–87. Lamers, Daniel, and Cozzens all repeat John Beatty's assessment of McCook as a "chucklehead" and do not effectively dismiss Colonel Beatty's claims of drinking, swearing, or self-aggrandizement among these officers as recounted in *Citizen Soldier,* 235–36; a detailed assessment of both McCook and Crittenden can be found in Ethan Refuse, "In the Shadow of the Rock: Thomas L. Crittenden, Alexander McCook, and the 1863 Campaigns for Middle and East Tennessee," in Woodworth, *The Chickamauga Campaign,* 5–49; the reputation for drinking in the Army of the Cumberland was reinforced based on an article that recalled that nearly all of the officers, except Garfield and Thomas, were "stiff old drinkers and stiff old fighters as well," Major Ben C. Truman, "In the Convivial Days of Old," *Overland Monthly and Out West Magazine* 55, no. 3 (March 1910): 317, APS online.

16. Assessments of Bragg's career, weakness, and struggles with his subordinates can be found in Robertson, "The Fall of Chattanooga," 13–14, David S. and Jeannie T. Heidler, eds., *Encyclopedia of the American Civil War: A Political, Social, and Military History* (New York: W. W. Norton & Co., 2000), s. v. "Bragg, Braxton, Confederate General" by James H. Meredith; Judith Lee Hallock, *Braxton Bragg and Confederate Defeat,* vol. II (Tuscaloosa: University of Alabama Press, 1991), 1–46; Connelly, *Autumn of Glory,* 70–73; and Wood, *Civil War Generalship,* 116–27. His mixed performances at Shiloh, Perryville, and Stones River are discussed specifically in Larry Daniel, *Shiloh: The Battle That Changed the Civil War* (New York: Simon & Schuster, 1997), 207–14; Kenneth W. Noe, *Perryville: This Grand Havoc of Battle* (Lexington: University Press of Kentucky, 2001), 337–39; and Peter Cozzens, *No Better Place To Die: The Battle of Stones River* (Chicago: University of Illinois Press, 1991), 200–18. Sam Watkins, *Co. Aytch, Maury Grays, First Tennessee Regiment; or a Side Show of the Big Show* (Dayton: Morningside Bookshop, 1992) expressed hatred for Bragg throughout, "tyrannical" quote 41.

17. The importance of the Chattanooga campaign at this point in the war is nicely summarized in Stevens, *1863*, 323–27; quoted in John Jones, *A Rebel War Clerk's Diary*, 2 vols. (Philadelphia: J. B. Lippincott & Co., 1866; reprint TLCLCW, 1982), 2: 49.

2. "THE FATE OF THE ARMY DEPENDED ON THIS CHARGE"

1. William B. Feis, "The Deception of Braxton Bragg: The Tullahoma Campaign, June 23—July 4, 1863," *Blue & Gray* 10, no. 1 (October 1992): 10–21, 46–53; Michael R. Bradley, "Tullahoma Campaign: The Wrongly Forgotten Campaign," *Blue & Gray* 27, no. 1 (2010), 6–25, 40–44, 47–50; David A. Powell and David A. Friedrichs, *The Maps of Chickamauga: An Atlas of the Chickamauga Campaign, Including the Tullahoma Operations, June 22–September 23, 1863* (New York: Savas Beatie, 2009) 2–15; Woodworth, *Six Armies in Tennessee*, 19–44, 47–49; Daniels, *Days of Glory*, 268–97; Cist, *The Army of the Cumberland*, quote, 170; Van Horne, *History of the Army of the Cumberland*, makes a strong point for Rosecrans being forced to move "with inadequate forces . . . under conditions that involved great peril" by the Washington authorities (2:312) and was the first to push the idea that Rosecrans's foot dragging in the early summer was due to his theory that both of the Union armies in the west should not be fighting major battles at the same time (2:299–301). A favorable analysis of Halleck's dealings with Rosecrans can be found in Stephen Ambrose, *Halleck: Lincoln's Chief of Staff* (Baton Rouge: Louisiana State University Press, 1962; paperback, 1990), 103–10, 123–25, 150–56. An even more favorable view appears in Herman Hattaway and Archer Jones, "'Old Brains' Was Brainy After All," in Herman Hattaway and Ethan Refuse, eds. *The Ongoing Civil War: New Versions of Old Stories* (Columbia: University of Missouri Press, 2004), 26–39. A more critical assessment can be found in John F. Marszaleck, *Commander of All Lincoln's Armies: A Life of General Henry W, Halleck* (Cambridge, Mass.: The Belknap Press of Harvard University, 2004).

2. For a detailed analysis of these failures, see Steven E. Woodworth, "In Their Dreams: Braxton Bragg, Thomas Hindeman, and the Abortive Attack at McLemore's Cove," and Alexander Mendoza, "The Censure of D. H. Hill: Daniel Harvey Hill and the Chickamauga Campaign," in Woodworth, ed., *The Chickamauga Campaign*, 50–83; William G. Robertson, "The Chickamauga Campaign—McLemore's Cove: Rosecrans' Gamble, Bragg's Lost Opportunity," *Blue & Gray* 23, no. 6 (Spring 2007), 6–26, 42–50.

3. Most historians agree that Rosecrans was fooled by rumors of Confederate demoralization and that Bragg's subordinates failed to execute the attacks on the isolated elements of the Union army, see Cozzens, *This Terrible Sound*, 61–89; Woodworth, *Six Armies in Tennessee*, 61–78; Bowers, *Chickamauga and Chattanooga*, 40–45; Jerry Korn, *The Fight for Chattanooga: Chickamauga to Missionary Ridge*, The Civil War (Alexandria, Va.: Time-Life Books, 1985), 35–42; Daniel Ward Howe, *The Civil War* (Indianapolis: The Bowen-Merrill Company, 1902) 164–71. A widely quoted contradictory view was provided by Daniel H. Hill, "Chickamauga—The Great Battle of the West," in Robert Underwood Johnson and Clarence Clough Buel, eds., *Battles and Leaders of the Civil War*, 4 vols. (New York: Thomas Yoseloff, reprint, 1956), who claimed that the failures were due to Bragg's "lack of knowledge of the situation . . . [and] lack of personal supervision of the execution of his orders," 3:641; Connelly, *Autumn of Glory*, takes the middle ground by observing that "Bragg's command structure had collapsed," which ultimately led to failure on several levels, 189–90. Horn, *Army of Tennessee*, agrees with Hill that Bragg's distance from the scene led to "a paralysis of inaction," 254. See also Craig L. Symonds, *Stonewall of the*

West: Patrick Cleburne and the Civil War, Modern War Studies (Lawrence: University of Kansas Press, 1997), 142.

4. In addition to book-length accounts of the battle by Cozzens, *This Terrible Sound,* and Tucker, *Chickamauga,* fairly detailed descriptions also appear in Bowers, *Chickamauga and Chattanooga,* 47–164; Korn, *The Fight for Chattanooga,* 44–77; Powell and Friedrichs, *Maps of Chickamauga,* 34–257; and Woodworth, *Six Armies in Tennessee,* 79–128. As expected, both Cist, *The Army of the Cumberland,* 193–229, and Van Horne, *History of the Army of the Cumberland,* 2:310–85, devote considerable space to this pivotal battle. A useful summary of the battle for writing this portion of the chapter was William G. Robertson, *The Battle of Chickamauga,* National Park Civil War Series (Fort Washington, Pa.: Eastern National Park Service Publication, 1995); I have chosen not to cite commonly held facts regarding events of the battle taken from this source. Robertson also contributes a fuller history of the battle in a series of articles on the Chickamauga campaign for multiple issues of *Blue & Gray* magazine beginning with fall 2006 through summer 2008. Other interpretations, quotes, or accounts taken from other sources will be cited accordingly. For a purely tactical view of the battle, see James R. Arnold, *Chickamauga, 1863: The River of Death,* Osprey Military Campaign Series 17 (Oxford, UK: Osprey Publishing Ltd., 1992).

5. Both Horne, in *Army of Tennessee,* 255–57, and Connelly, *Autumn of Glory,* 202–5, are critical of Bragg's failure to locate the actual position of the Union left and his inability to adjust when his original plan fell apart; both Union cavalry units were armed with repeating rifles, which increased their defensive firepower; Colonel Minty gives his version of his men's resistance at Reed's Bridge and makes it clear that they only withdrew when Wilder's men withdrew, see *Remarks of Brevet Major General R. H. G. Minty made September 18, 1895 at the Dedication of the Monument erected to the Fourth Michigan Cavalry at Reed's Bridge, Chickamauga National Park* (Ogden, Utah: Brantley Paper Co., 1896) in the Robert H. G. Minty Papers, 1876–1903, USAMHI Archives.

6. The 69th Ohio was part of Col. Dan McCook's brigade of Granger's Reserve Corps and withdrew according to orders to the North shortly after burning the bridge. A veteran writing on behalf of the 69th years later claimed that they had captured a Confederate band late on the eighteenth and that "the burning of said bridge brought on the battle of Chickamauga" on the nineteenth. He also mistakenly claimed to have isolated Longstreet's artillery by this action, but this was unlikely since it had not yet reached the area, Elliot Chenowith to J. C. McElroy, letter October 30, 1893, Chickamauga Park Commission Papers, Folder 3, Aquila Wiley Papers, MS 2127, Western Reserve Historical Society Library (WRHSL). This incident is used as an example of the "effect of false assumptions" in Glenn Robertson, et al., *Staff Ride Handbook for the Battle of Chickamauga, 18–20 September, 1863* (Fort Leavenworth, Kan.: Combat Studies Institute, 1992), <http:// usacac.army.mil/cac2/cgsc/carl/resources/csi/Robertson3/robertson3.asp>, 62–68. The 105th Ohio was part of the 1st Brigade, 4th Division, XIV Corps; "leap" quote from undated typed manuscript account of the Battle of Chickamauga, Norman Smith Papers, private collection, Geauga County, Ohio.

7. These units made this attack without clear orders from Bragg, who simply told Stewart to go where the fighting was heaviest. The column of brigades provided successive waves of fresh troops, ammunition, and firepower to the same point, unlike the more commonly used en echelon attack. Sam Davis Elliot, *Soldier of Tennessee: General Alexander P. Stewart and the Civil War in the West* (Baton Rouge: Louisiana State University Press, 1999), 122–29; Robertson, *Staff Ride Handbook,* 22–23; Lee White, "A. P. Stewart at Chickamauga," in Woodworth, *The Chickamauga Campaign,* 84–101.

8. This came after a great deal of debate between Lee and Jefferson Davis, and many

believed that Longstreet supported it because he had designs on the western command for himself. Burnside's capture of Knoxville complicated the transport of the two divisions by rail, but they arrived in the nick of time anyway; see Douglas Southall Freeman, *Lee's Lieutenants: A Study in Command*, vol. 3: *Gettysburg to Appomattox* (New York: Charles Scribner's Sons, 1945), 220–30. A more critical account is Judith Lee Hallock, *General James Longstreet in the West: A Monumental Failure*, Civil War Campaigns and Commanders (Abilene, Tex: McWhiney Foundation Press, 1998); William G. Robertson, "'Bull of the Woods?' James Longstreet at Chickamauga," in Woodworth, *The Chickamauga Campaign*, 116–39.

9. Quoted from an account of 93rd Ohio, Capt. R. Lysle to "Dear Father and Mother," 27 September 1863, Hoff Family Correspondence, 1863, the Ohio Historical Society Archives (OHS); White, "Stewart at Chickamauga," in Woodworth, *The Chickamauga Campaign*, 92–98.

10. Symonds, *Stonewall of the West*, 145–46; an eyewitness account of Smith's death can be found in Joseph C. Stiles, "Capt. Thomas E. King, or, A Word to the Army and the Country: Electronic Edition" (Charleston: South Carolina Tract Society, 1864), Documenting the American South, University of North Carolina at Chapel Hill Libraries, <http://docsouth.unc.edu/imls/stiles/stiles.html>, 8. For a detailed description of this action and "one of the most furious" quote, see Cozzens, *This Terrible Sound*, 265–79, 268, and John R. Lundberg, "A Minute Now is Worth an Hour Tomorrow: Cleburne's Night Attack," in Woodworth, *The Chickamauga Campaign*, 102–15, who argues that the attack led to an unnecessary loss of Confederate manpower and alerted Thomas to the threat on his front.

11. Michael Hendrick Fitch, *The Chattanooga Campaign: With Special Reference to Wisconsin's Participation Therein*, Wisconsin History Commission: Original Papers 4 (Wisconsin History Commission, 1911), 90, 149–50; Chickamauga account, Norman Smith Papers. The nature of the fighting on September 19 makes it difficult, if not impossible, for the National Park Service to interpret the first day on its driving tour of the battlefield. Of the eight stops on the tour, only one—the Viniard Field stop no. 5—is clearly associated with day one and emphasizes "one of the battlefield's bloodiest actions," Chickamauga and Chattanooga National Military Park, National Park Service, Department of the Interior (GPO 2009—349–224/80325, reprint 2008).

12. The "pinching cold" quote from James Carnahan, *Personal Recollections of Chickamauga* (Cincinnati: H. C. Sherrick & Co., 1886); "heart-rending" quote from Chickamauga account, Norman Smith Papers; the cold, shortage of water, fires, hazards, and attempts to help the wounded are well described in Cozzens, *This Terrible Sound*, 280–88.

13. The most widely recognized account of the council of war at Gettysburg is John Gibbon, "The Council of War on the Second Day," in *Battles and Leaders*, 3:313–14. The source for the council story at Chickamauga is Charles M. Dana, *Recollections of the Civil War* (New York: Boughmans, 1898), 113–14; his version gained wide readership when published in serial form as "Reminiscences of Men and Events of the Civil War," *McClure's Magazine* 10, no. 4 (February 1898): 347, APS Online. Historical accounts of this meeting include Cozzens, *This Terrible Sound*, 294–99; Lamers, *Edge of Glory*, 333–35; and Freeman Cleaves, *Rock of Chickamauga: The Life of General George H. Thomas* (Norman: University of Oklahoma Press, 1948), 162–64. Both of Thomas's most recent biographers repeat the claim that Thomas napped through both the Stones River and Chickamauga councils, only to awaken and deliver sage advice, Benson Bobrick, *Master of War: The Life of General George H. Thomas* (New York: Simon and Schuster, 2009), 154–55, 180–81,

and Christopher J. Einolf, *George Thomas, Virginian for the Union,* Campaigns and Commanders, Gregory J. W. Urwin, series editor (Norman: University of Oklahoma Press, 2007), 149–50, 167–68.

14. The most oft-repeated accounts of Longstreet's initial encounter with Bragg are in James Longstreet, *From Manassas to Appomattox: Memoirs of the Civil War in America* (Philadelphia: J. B. Lippincott, 1896), 337–40, and G. Moxley Sorrell, *At the Right Hand of Longstreet: Recollections of a Confederate Staff Officer* (Lincoln: University of Nebraska Press, Bison Books, 1999; originally published by New York: Neal Co. 1905) 192–94. Tucker, *Chickamauga,* expands on these accounts as well, 211–17; Connelly, *Autumn of Glory,* 208–20; on Hill's role in the confusion, see Mendoza, "The Censure of Hill," in *The Chickamauga Campaign,* 75–77.

15. A clear description of Rosecrans's deployment can be found in Lamers, *Edge of Glory,* 337–44; Connelly, *Autumn of Glory,* 217–22; W. M. Polk defends his father by blaming the delay on Hill in "General Polk at Chickamauga," in *Battles and Leaders,* 3:662–63.

16. An interesting perspective on the battle and this incident, which notes that "pique, jealousy, and self-importance were not confined to the Confederate army," can be found in William Weir, *Fatal Victories* (Hamdon, Conn.: Archon Press, 1993), 146–51. See also Lamers, *Edge of Glory,* 342–50; Albert Castel, "Victorious Loser: William S. Rosecrans, Part II," *Timeline,* 19, no. 2 (Sept.–October, 2002): 31–32.

17. More than one historian described the location and timing of Longstreet's attack as the result of "sheer luck" rather than planning. Weir, *Fatal Victories,* 149. During his tour of the battlefield during the 2002 CWPT Annual Conference, Mac Wykoff explained that the depth of Longstreet's attack was due to the terrain, not planning, and provided a drawing of "what Longstreet wanted" and "what Longstreet got." Another good account of the attack appears in Arnold Blumberg, "On They Came Like an Angry Flood," *Civil War Battles: Brother vs. Brother,* Special Issue (2006), 42–52; Tucker, *Chickamauga,* gives Bushrod Johnson credit for executing the successful attack and describes Wilder's encounter with Dana, 275–78, 314–16; Wilder's men claimed after the battle that they had repulsed 20,000 enemy troops and would have changed the course of the battle had they been allowed to fight; see Graham Garrison and Parke Peirson, "Lightning at Chickamauga," *America's Civil War* (March 2003), 47–53. This was disputed in a letter by a member of the 92nd Ohio published in the *National Tribune,* "Shafer letter," William Kemper Diary, vol. 2, William Kemper Papers, 836/1/2, Ohio Historical Society Library. A discussion of McCook and Crittenden's roles in the disaster can be found in Ethan Rafuse, "'In the Shadow of the Rock': Thomas Crittenden, Alexander McCook, and the 1863 Campaign for Middle and East Tennessee," in Woodworth, *The Chickamauga Campaign,* 5–49.

18. Connelly, *Autumn of Glory,* 224–25; Robertson, "'Bull of the Woods?'" in Woodworth, *The Chickamauga Campaign,* 116–39.

19. Rosecrans's reaction to the breakthrough and his decision to return to Chattanooga are discussed in detail in Lamers, *Edge of Glory,* 351–61; Tucker, *Chickamauga,* 309–15; Cozzens, *This Terrible Sound,* includes in his account Rosecrans's meeting with survivors of Negley's division, who "told a lurid tale of defeat and despair" that led him to believe that Thomas had been routed as well, 403–5.

20. Quote from Van Horne, *Army of the Cumberland,* 352; Tucker, *Chickamauga,* 329–39; regarding Negley's abandonment of the field, Daniels writes that "Wood and Brannan would never forgive him," *Days of Glory,* 332; an impartial but critical analysis of Negley is in David Powell, "Negley at Horseshoe Ridge, September 20, 1863," in Woodworth, *The Chickamauga Campaign,* 140–61. Horseshoe Ridge is a spur that extends from the slightly

higher ground around the Snodgrass house, from which the hill takes its name. In some accounts the terms are used interchangeably, which adds to an already confusing situation.

21. The "breathing" and "every man" quotes from Isaac C. Doan, *Reminiscences of the Chattanooga Campaign: A Paper Read at the Reunion of Company B, Fortieth Ohio Volunteer Infantry, at Xenia, Ohio, August 22, 1894* (Richmond, Ind.: J. M. Coe's Printery, 1894); the Pennsylvania soldier also noted that "the Battle of Chickamauga was the only one that we had to leave the field because our ammunition run out and we couldn't get any," Memoir, John Eicker Papers, Harrisburg Civil War Roundtable Collection, USAMHI.

22. One of the main eyewitness sources for the dramatic arrival story was newspaperman William Shanks, who was present on Snodgrass Hill after most other reporters had fled the field. J. Cutler Andrews, *The North Reports the Civil War* (Pittsburgh: University of Pittsburgh Press, 1955), 456–57. Writer and veteran Ambrose Bierce also claimed to have been the one to see Granger's bayonets gleaming in the sun while serving as an aide to Thomas; Ambrose Bierce, *Phantoms of a Bloodstained Period: The Civil War Writings of Ambrose Bierce*, Russell Duncan and David Klooster, eds. (Amherst: University of Massachusetts Press, 2002), 198. It eventually became the stuff of legend as seen in Joseph W. Morton, ed, *Sparks from the Campfire: Tales of the Old Veterans* (Philadelphia: Keystone Publishing, 1890), 331–32. Tucker, *Chickamauga*, insists that Granger was following Rosecrans's "discretionary orders" to support Thomas when he moved his division and repeats the dramatic arrival story, 340–46; the "frenzy" quote is from T. J Woods, *Steedman's Men at Chickamauga* (Toledo, Ohio: Blade Printing, 1876), 58–68. This is the most direct source supporting Steedman's claim that he marched on his own initiative and in violation of orders. The version giving credit to Granger is from his chief of staff Joseph Fullerton, "Reinforcing Thomas at Chickamauga," in *Battles and Leaders*, 3:665–67.

23. The claim that Bragg was morose and unaware comes from Longstreet, *From Manassas to Appomattox*, 452–56.

24. The notion that Garfield was the source of information on Rosecrans's rout and that the rebels could have been defeated is most often attributed to Granger and appears in Fitch, *The Chattanooga Campaign*, 188–199, and in Cleaves, *The Rock of Chickamauga*, 174. Ambrose Bierce is the best-known source for the "rebel yell" story, but claims that it occurred after darkness had halted the fighting, Bierce, *Phantoms of a Bloodstained Period*, 199.

25. Cist, *The Army of the Cumberland*, has the line being held until dark (including quotes), 211. Fitch places the time of the withdrawal at 5:30 and attributes the losses to troops staying too long behind the breastworks or taking the wrong direction when pulling back, *The Chattanooga Campaign*, 122–23; the best overall description of the actions on the ridge during the army's withdrawal is Cozzens, *This Terrible Sound*, 497–501; "heroic" quote from Woodworth, *Six Armies in Tennessee*, 128. A more detailed discussion of the controversies involving Henry Boynton, the 21st Ohio, and the positions of their regiments is in Chapter Six.

26. Cozzens, *This Terrible Sound*, 512–21; Hallock, *Braxton Bragg*, contests some of Longstreet's claims that Bragg was out of touch with the army and attributes the lack of an aggressive pursuit to "confusion among units and exhaustion among the soldiers," 77–87.

27. The Army of the Cumberland had 57,000 men at Chickamauga; the Confederates had a total of 71,500, about 49,000 of whom were part of the original Army of Tennessee; "The Opposing Forces at Chickamauga," in *Battles and Leaders*, 3: 672–76; an older battlefield guide uses figures that amount to 28 percent casualties for each army; James R.

Sullivan, *Chickamauga and Chattanooga Battlefields, Chickamauga and Chattanooga National Military Park, Chattanooga, Tennessee,* National Park Service Historical Handbook Series No. 25 (Washington D.C., 1956; reprint 1961), 24.

28. The "tactics" quote is from Luther Bradley, "Recollections of the Civil War," in Luther Bradley Papers, box 6, USAMHI; this veteran was of the opinion that Rosecrans should never have moved out of Chattanooga; then the "useless battle" would have never been fought; Smith Atkins, *Chickamauga: A Useless, Disastrous Battle* (Freeport, Ill.: Journal Printing, 1907), Ohio Historical Society Library.

29. Henry Boynton argued that since Chattanooga was the object and Rosecrans was headed in that direction anyway, the withdrawal from the battlefield was not a "retreat" but an "advance" to occupy the city; "Annual Address by General H. V. Boynton," Society of the Army of the Cumberland, *Twenty-third Reunion, Chickamauga, Georgia, 1892* (Cincinnati: Robert Clark & Company, 1892), 85.

30. Howe, *Civil War Times,* 163.

31. Bowers, *Chickamauga and Chattanooga,* 160

32. One has to be skeptical of Dana's accounts, since he seems to have made a career as a snitch for the administration in the western armies; his presence in Grant's headquarters at Vicksburg mirrors his actions later in Chattanooga, Waugh, *U. S. Grant,* 62–63.

33. Daniel, *Days of Glory,* 338–58; Woodworth, *Six Armies in Tennessee,* 146–49; a solid analysis of the conditions and controversies in both armies after Chickamauga can be found in Wiley Sword, *Mountains Touched by Fire: Chattanooga Besieged, 1863* (New York: St. Martin's Press, 1995), 2–54; Ethan Rafuse believes that McCook deserved to be sacked but Crittenden did not; both were cleared by a court of inquiry, but never regained major commands; "In the Shadow of the Rock," in Woodworth, *The Chickamauga Campaign,* 38–42.

34. In addition to Sword and Woodworth, detailed histories of the operations around Chattanooga can be found in James Lee McDonough, *Chattanooga—A Death Grip on the Confederacy* (Knoxville: University of Tennessee Press, 1985), Cozzens, *The Shipwreck of Their Hopes,* and Richard A. Baumgardner and Larry M. Strayer, *Echoes of Battle: The Struggle for Chattanooga* (Huntington, W.Va.: Blue Acorn Press). Quote from Cist, *The Army of the Cumberland,* 262.

35. The conflicts involving Bragg and his subordinates and the army's subsequent failure at Chattanooga are well documented in Hallock, *Braxton Bragg,* 87–149; and Connelly, *Autumn of Glory,* 235–78. Other works that place the command problems in a larger context include James I. Robertson, Jr. "Braxton Bragg: The Lonely Patriot," in *Leaders of the Lost Cause: New Perspectives on the Confederate High Command,* Gary Gallagher and Joseph Glatthaar, eds. (Mechanicsburg, Pa.: Stackpole Books, 2004), 71–99; and Steven Woodworth, *Jefferson Davis and His Generals: The Failure of Confederate Command in the West* (Lawrence: University Press of Kansas, 1999). The problems between Longstreet and Bragg are addressed in Hallock, *Longstreet in the West;* and Edward Carr Franks, "The Detachment of Longstreet Considered: Braxton Bragg, James Longstreet, and the Chattanooga Campaign," in *Leadership and Command in the American Civil War,* Steven E. Woodworth, ed. (Campbell, Calif.: Savas Woodbury Press, 1995), 29–65. Both suggest that Longstreet's poor performance at Knoxville undermined a viable strategic alternative to maintaining the army's investment of Chattanooga.

3. "THE GRANDEST [CAUSE] THAT EVER ROSE, THE PUREST THAT EVER FELL"

1. Quoted in J. Kurt Piehler, *Remembering War the American Way* (Washington D.C.: Smithsonian Institution Press, 1995), 1–9; Sellars, *Pilgrim Places*, 7–10.

2. Piehler, *Remembering War*, 11–24; even the earliest and most fundamental celebration of 4 July, Independence Day, was a contested holiday among regions and political factions; Bodnar, *Remaking America*, 21–27; Matthew Dennis, *Red, White, and Blue Letter Days: An American Calendar* (Ithaca: Cornell University Press, 2002), 31–46.

3. Piehler, *Remembering War*, 11–24; Linenthal, *Sacred Ground*, 9–23; both Piehler and Linenthal trace the evolution of commemorative activities surrounding Revolutionary War sites over time and confirm Foote's contention that it takes time for communities to create widely recognized memories. Even the Washington Monument was delayed for decades, and his home at Mount Vernon was only preserved in the mid-nineteenth century through the efforts of privately financed, women-run organizations. For more on Mount Vernon, see Patricial West, *Domesticating History: The Political Origins of America's House Museums* (Washington, D.C.: Smithsonian Institution Press, 1999), 1–35; Kirk Savage, *Standing Soldiers, Kneeling Slaves: Race, War, and Monument in Nineteenth-century America* (Princeton N.J.: Princeton University Press, 1997), 166–68; Sellars, *Pilgrim Places*, 7–10.

4. Piehler, *Remembering War*, 24–26, 37–39, 41–43

5. Ibid., 40–41, 44; ironically, the Battle of the Alamo, a single event that preceded the Mexican War by nearly a decade, became the most enduring war memory from the period and continues to be considered one of the nation's most heroic and sacred sites; see Linenthal, *Sacred Ground*, 53–81; Randy Roberts and James S. Olsen, *Line in the Sand: The Alamo in Blood and Memory* (New York: Free Press, 2001); Phillip Tucker, *Exodus from the Alamo: The Anatomy of the Last Stand Myth* (Philadelphia: Casemate, 2010); David Clary, *Eagles and Empire: The United States, Mexico, and the Struggle for a Continent* (New York: Bantam Books, 2009); Wayne, Wei-Siang Hsieh, *West Pointers and the Civil War: The Old Army in War and Peace* (Chapel Hill: University of North Carolina Press, 2009).

6. Piehler, *Remembering War*, 45–46; Linenthal, *Sacred Ground*, 23–26; Anne Sarah Rubin, "Seventy-six and Sixty-one: Confederates Remember the American Revolution," in Brundage, *Where These Memories Grow*, 85–105.

7. Piehler, *Remembering War*, 46–48, 57; since there is such a vast amount of literature on the Civil War available, it might be helpful to examine James M. McPherson and William Cooper Jr., eds., *Writing the Civil War: The Quest to Understand* (Columbia: University of South Carolina Press, 1998), which contains historiographic essays by leading historians on northern and southern strategy, battlefield tactics, the common soldier, the home front, presidential leadership, economics, politics, slavery, and gender. For more on the "Lost Cause" see Gaines Foster, *Ghosts of the Confederacy: Defeat, the Lost Cause, and the Emergence of the New South, 1865–1913* (New York: Oxford University Press, 1987); Gary Gallagher and Alan T. Nolan, eds., *The Myth of the Lost Cause and Civil War History* (Bloomington: Indiana University Press, 2000); William C. Davis, *The Cause Lost: Myths and Realities of the Confederacy* (Lawrence: University Press of Kansas, 1996); Thomas L. Connelly, *The Marble Man: Robert E. Lee and His Image in American Society* (New York: Alfred Knopf, 1977); Connelly and Barbara Bellows, *God and General Longstreet: The Lost Cause and the Southern Mind* (Baton Rouge: Louisiana State University Press, 1982; paperback, 1995); and Charles Reagan Wilson, *Baptized in Blood: The Religion of the Lost Cause, 1865–1920* (Athens: University of Georgia Press, 1980).

8. The effects of the war on soldiers and the home front, including sections on the postwar period, are discussed in Larry P. Logue, *To Appomattox and Beyond: The Civil War Soldier in War and Peace,* The American Ways Series (Chicago: Ivan Dees, 1996); Gerald Linderman, *Embattled Courage: The Experience of Combat in the American Civil War* (New York: Free Press, 1987); Earl J. Hess, *The Union Soldier in Battle: Enduring the Ordeal of Combat* (Lawrence: University Press of Kansas, 1997); Reid Mitchell, *The Vacant Chair: The Northern Soldier Leaves Home* (New York: Oxford University Press, 1993); the conflicting interpretations of these and other works is analyzed in idem, "Not the General but the Soldier: The Study of Civil War Soldiers," in McPherson and Cooper, *Writing the Civil War,* 81–95. The standard work on prisoners of war is William B. Hesseltine, ed., *Civil War Prisons* (Kent, Ohio: Kent State University Press, 1962); another overview and selected photographs of prison camps can be found in Frank L. Byrne, "Prison Pens of Suffering," in William C. Davis, ed., *Fighting for Time: The Image of War, 1861–1865,* vol. 4, A Project of the National Historical Society, (New York: Doubleday & Co., 1983), 396–450; in addition to the other five volumes in the Image of War series, a general overview of period photography can be found in James D. Horan, *Mathew Brady: Historian with a Camera* (New York: Bonanza Books, 1955).

9. Drew Gilpin Faust, "The Civil War Soldier and the Art of Dying," *The Journal of Southern History* 76, no. 1 (February 2001): 1–38 and *This Republic of Suffering: Death and the American Civil War* (New York: Alfred Knopf, 2008); the notion that coping with "mass suffering" was a measure of individual and social virtues is explored in Anne C. Rose, *Victorian America and the Civil War* (Cambridge: Cambridge University Press, 1992), 235–45.

10. Ellen M. Litwicki, *America's Public Holidays, 1865–1920* (Washington, D.C.: Smithsonian Institution Press, 2000), 9–21; J. Michael Martinez and Robert M. Harris, "Graves, Worms, and Epitaphs: Confederate Monuments on Southern Landscapes," in J. Michael Martinez, William D. Richardson, and Ron McNinch-Su, eds. *Confederate Symbols in the Contemporary South* (Gainesville: University Press of Florida, 2000), 135–45, quoted on the first page of the *History of the Confederated Memorial Associations of the South* (published by the Confederated Southern Memorial Association, 1904), which detailed the efforts of dozens of ladies memorial associations to identify and decorate Confederate soldiers' graves across the South; see also Caroline Janney, *Burying the Dead but Not the Past: Ladies Memorial Associations and the Lost Cause* (Chapel Hill: University of North Carolina Press, 2008); Cynthia Mills and Pamela Simpson, eds., *Monuments to the Lost Cause: Women, Art, and the Landscape of Southern Memory* (Knoxville: University of Tennessee Press, 2007), xvi; Wilson, *Baptized in Blood,* identifies the "funeral of a wartime hero" as one of the "rituals" of the Lost Cause religion, 25–28; Leonne M. Hudson, "The Making of a Southern Ritual: Confederate Memorial Day," *Confederate Veteran* 5 (1999): 39–42; proof that the burial and grave decoration rituals are still important in the maintenance of Southern memory can be found in Virginia B. Morton, "Confederate Son Laid to Rest" and Michael J Mitchell, "Special Touches are Added to C.S.A. Cemetery" in *The Civil War Courier* 18, no. 5 (June 2002): 3, 22, 12, 14.

11. Piehler, *Remembering War,* 49–53; Monro MacCloskey, *Hallowed Ground: Our National Cemeteries* (New York: Richards Rosen Press, 1968), 21–37; Robert M. Poole, *On Hallowed Ground: The History of Arlington National Cemetery* (New York: Walker and Company, 2009), 77–79; Gary Willis, *Lincoln at Gettysburg: The Words That Remade America* (New York: Simon & Schuster, 1992) places Lincoln's speech clearly within the existing Victorian "culture of death," 63–89; Litwicki, *America's Public Holidays,* 9–49; Catherine W. Zipf, "Marking Union Victory in the South: The Construction of the National Cemetery System," in Mills and Simpson, *Monuments to the Lost Cause,* 27–45; Smith, *Battlefield Preservation,* 11–22.

12. George Mosse, *Fallen Soldiers: Reshaping the Memory of the World Wars* (New York: Oxford University Press, 1990), 3–11, suggests that the "cult of the dead," combined with the "myth of the war experience," became a model for European nations fifty years later to commemorate the monumental casualties of World War I. Savage, *Standing Soldiers, Kneeling Slaves,* puts a slightly different spin on this idea by suggesting that the initial parallel between military service and a form of "slavery" was heroically recast by veterans and society after the war, 167–75.

13. A short discussion and sample ad for these statues appears in the introduction to Mills and Simpson, *Monuments to the Lost Cause,* xix–xx.

14. Savage, *Standing Soldiers, Kneeling Slaves,* 163–66, notes that virtually all of these types of soldier statues depicted white men, which meant that separate Union and Confederate statues could only be distinguished by minor variations in uniforms and equipment, 177–87; Martinez and Harris identify three types of monuments. Type 1 are "non-symbolic historical markers" on battlefields and sites of past events, Type 2 are "symbolic edifices" located in the vernacular landscapes of cemeteries and burial places, and Type 3 (including unit memorials and soldier statues) are either vernacular or official symbols placed on public landscapes other than cemeteries, "Graves, Worms, and Epitaphs," 160; the momentum generated by these public commemorations led to further recognition of earlier wars, *Remembering War,* 75–77; for a discussion of ladies memorial associations and local commemoration, see Catherine Bishar, "A Strong Force of Ladies: Women, Politics, and Confederate Memorial Associations in Raleigh," in Mills and Simpson, *Monuments to the Lost Cause,* 3–26.

15. An analysis of the creation of the *Official Records* appears in Andre Noah Trudeau, "To Mold the Judgment of History," in *The Ongoing Civil War: New Versions of Old Stories* (Columbia: University of Missouri Press, 2004), 139–54.

16. For a recent overview of postwar issues as they relate to memory, see Blight, *Race and Reunion;* a somewhat dated, but still useful discussion of the effects of "victory" and "defeat" can be found in Paul H. Buck, *The Road to Reunion: 1856–1900* (Boston: Little, Brown, and Company, 1937), 3–43. For scholarly studies of national veterans organizations, see Wallace Davies, *Patriotism on Parade: The Story of Veterans and Hereditary Organizations in the United States, 1783–1900* (Cambridge: Harvard University Press, 1957); and Stuart McConnell, *Glorious Contentment: The Grand Army of the Republic, 1865–1900* (Chapel Hill: University of North Carolina Press, 1992).

17. Descriptions of the Grand Review can be found in McConnell, *Glorious Contentment,* 1–17; and Georg R. Sheets, *The Grand Review: The Civil War Continues to Shape America* (York, Pa.: York, Inc., 2000). By the time of the Grand Review, the XIV Corps (formerly in the AOC) and XX Corps were considered part of the Army of Georgia, which was the unofficial designation for the left wing of Sherman's Army of the Tennessee under Henry Slocum. It marched behind the Army of the Tennessee in the Review under that identity; Welcher, *The Union Armies,* 2:227. The account of the Grand Review in Steven Woodworth, *Nothing but Victory: The Army of the Tennessee, 1862–1865* (New York: Alfred Knopf, 2005) describes how well the army marched, with no mention of the colorful elements noted by other observers, 639–41. Gary Ecelbarger, *Black Jack Logan: An Extraordinary Life in Peace and War* (Guilford, Conn.: Lyons Press, 2005), 228–32; Logan was promoted and given command of the Army of the Tennessee by General Grant several days before the review.

18. Wilson, *Baptized in Blood;* he summarizes his thesis in "The South's Lost Cause," in Sheets, *The Grand Review,* 66–77; see also Hudson, "Confederate Memorial Day," 39–41.

19. The South's reaction to defeat and early methods of coping are well covered in Foster, *Ghosts of the Confederacy*, 12–46; Buck, *The Road to Reunion*, 26–71; and Blight, *Race and Reunion*, 6–95.

20. Eric T. Dean, *Shook All Over Hell: Post Traumatic Stress, Vietnam, and the Civil War* (Cambridge: Harvard University Press, 1997), 46–114; also see Linderman, *Embattled Courage*, 266–97. Quote from Henry King, "The Western Soldier," *Century Illustrated Magazine* 38, no. 1 (May 1889): 148, APS Online.

21. Charles Bracelen Flood, *Lee: The Last Years* (Boston: Houghton Mifflin Company, 1981), 161, 230–47; William C. Davis, *Jefferson Davis: The Man and His Hour* (Harper Collins, 1991), 648–706. Davis's daughter Winnie was widely considered the "first daughter of the Confederacy" by veterans and the public, particularly after his death. The dedication of the Stonewall Jackson monument in Richmond in 1875 is considered one of the most powerful symbols of the Lost Cause; Blight, *Race and Reunion*, 80–84; Foster, *Ghosts of the Confederacy*, 120–23. This 1881 ceremony honored famous leaders and common soldiers at the same time; "Dedication of the Tomb of the Army of Northern Virginia Association and Unveiling the Statue of Stonewall Jackson in New Orleans," *Southern Historical Society Papers*, vol. IX: *January to December, 1881* (Richmond, Va.: Rev. J. William Jones; Millwood, N.Y.: Kraus Reprint Co., 1977) 212–19.

22. See Connelly, *The Marble Man;* and Connelly and Bellows, *God and General Longstreet;* Gary W. Gallagher, "Shaping Public Memory of the Civil War: Jubal Early, Robert E. Lee, and Douglas Southall Freeman," in *The Memory of the Civil War in American Culture*, Alice Fahs and John Waugh, eds. (Chapel Hill: University of North Carolina Press, 2004), 39–63. An overview of the UCV is found in Foster, *Ghosts of the Confederacy*, 104–41; S. A. Cunningham, "The United Confederate Veterans" (n.p., 1912), <www.civilwarhome.com/confederateveterans.htm>; and Richard K.Kolb "Thin Gray Line: Confederate Veterans in the New South," Veterans of Foreign Wars of the United States, <http://vaudc.org/confed_vets.html>, 2000.

23. McConnell, *Glorious Contentment*, 125–204; Blight, *Race and Reunion*, 86–97; Buck, *Road to Reunion*, 236–62; the first quote is from John E. Gilman, "The Grand Army of the Republic" (n.p., 1910), <http://www.civilwarhome/grandarmyofrepublic.htm>; George Morgan, "Bronze Button Heroes: A Study of the G.A.R.," *Lippincott's Monthly Magazine* 64 (September 1899): 381, APS Online, 437. For another contemporary view, see "History of the Grand Army of the Republic," in Joseph Morton, ed. *Sparks from the Campfire or Tales of the Old Veterans* (Philadelphia: Keystone Publishing, 1890), 479–612. The earliest joint activity between Union and Confederate veterans may have been in 1881, when Union veterans visited Luray, Virginia, and the Southerners returned the courtesy with a trip to Carlisle, Pennsylvania. George A. Kilmer, "A Note of Peace: 'Reunions of the Blue and the Gray,'" *Century Illustrated Magazine* 36, no. 3 (July 1888): APS online; for Logan's role, see Ecelbarger, *Black Jack Logan*, 233–51.

24. Buck, *Road to Reunion*, 177–243; Linderman, *Embattled Courage*, 266–74; Frances Sands, "The Loyal Legion and the Civil War," *War Papers, 51–97 MOLLUS, D.C. Commandery* 86 (March 1912): 10; MOLLUS was formed on April 20, 1865, by Union officers who had escorted Lincoln's body to Springfield and was patterned after the Society of Cincinnati. It allowed all officers who had served in volunteer or Regular forces to become members and eventually created state commanderies throughout the North; Richard Girard Carroon, "The Military Order of the Loyal Legion: 135 Years of Service to the Nation," Military Order of the Loyal Legion of the United States: Loyal Legion Vignettes, Sons of Union Veterans website, (February 2000), <http://suvcw.org/mollus/art015.htm>.

4. "STAMP OUT VENERABLE FALSEHOODS"

1. Morton, "History of the Grand Army of the Republic," in *Sparks from the Campfire*, lists the 1863 Third Corps Union as the first such organization, credits the Society of the Army of the Tennessee as being formed "shortly before the disbanding of the army," and does not mention the others at all, 480. *Report of the Proceedings of the Society of the Army of the Tennessee; 38th Meeting* (Cincinnati, Ohio: Chas. O. Ebel Printing Company, 1909), 3–4.

2. Society of the Army of the Cumberland (SAOC), *Report of the First Meeting of the Society of the Army of the Cumberland, 1868* (Cincinnati, Ohio: Robert Clarke & Company, 1868), 1–16; the initial letter referred to the Army of the Tennessee as its "noble twin" and invited General Sherman to take a prominent role in the proceedings. An article was added to the original constitution that expanded membership to enlisted men and members of the XXIII Army Corps, ibid., 18–20.

3. Quoted in SAOC, *First Annual Report,* 46–47.

4. *Official Records,* XXX, Part I, 634–35; quoted in Matt Spruill, ed., *Guide to the Battle of Chickamauga,* U.S. Army War College Guide to Civil War Battles (Lawrence: University Press of Kansas, 1993), 174–75. Cist, *Army of the Cumberland,* 222–24 (the italics are found in the original).

5. Society of the Army of the Cumberland, *The Burial of General Rosecrans, Arlington National Cemetery, May 17, 1902* (Cincinnati, Ohio: Robert Clarke Company, 1903); these quotes appear in copies of correspondence and articles assembled by Henry V. Boynton for a section entitled "The Relief of Rosecrans," 84–102; Cist, *Army of the Cumberland,* 226; J. T. Woods, *Steedmen's Men at Chickamauga* (Toledo, Ohio: Blade Printing, 1876), 74.

6. "The Removal of Rosecrans," *Harper's Weekly,* 31 October 1863, <www.harpweek.com>; Garfield's role in Rosecrans's downfall is discussed in James M. Perry, *Touched with Fire: Five Presidents and the Civil War Battles that Made Them* (New York: Public Affairs, 2003), 125–30.

7. Quoted in SAOC, *Burial of Rosecrans,* 44; Van Horne, *History of the Army of the Cumberland,* I: 317. Donn Piatt, *General George H. Thomas: A Critical Biography, with Concluding Chapters by Henry V. Boynton* (Cincinnati, Ohio: Robert Clarke, 1893), 384. Rosecrans defended himself in W. S. Rosecrans, "The Mistakes of Grant," *The North American Review* 49, no. 349 (December 1885): 580, APS Online; Dana, *Recollections of the Civil War,* 127, 124. "The Removal of Rosecrans," *Harper's Weekly,* 31 October 1863.

8. Thomas had refused to replace Don Carlos Buell as commander of the Army of the Cumberland in the fall of 1862, and some saw this as a reluctance to accept the responsibilities of independent command, Einolf, *George Thomas,* 124; and Bobrick, *Master of War,* 125–26.

9. Burnside never moved in response to these orders and was eventually besieged by Longstreet's corps until relieved by Sherman in early December. Stephen Ambrose, *Halleck, Lincoln's Chief of Staff* (Baton Rouge: Louisiana State University, 1962; paperback, 1990), 152–56. Freeman Cleaves, *Rock of Chickamauga: The Life of General George H. Thomas* (Norman: University of Oklahoma Press, 1948), 182–83; Grant quoted in William T. Sherman, *The Memoirs of General W. T. Sherman, Written by Himself,* 2 vols., 4th ed. (New York: Charles Webster, 1891), I: 390.

10. Cist, *Army of the Cumberland,* 231–39; Wiley Sword, *Mountains Touched with Fire: Chattanooga Besieged, 1863* (New York: St. Martin's Press, 1995), 53–63; James R. Arnold,

The Armies of US Grant (London: Arms and Armour, 1995), 133–37. The debate over Smith's role in the operation that opened the "cracker line" begins with Ulysses S. Grant, "Chattanooga," and carries through William F. Smith, "Comments on Grant's 'Chattanooga,'" that includes a section by Henry Cist in *Battles and Leaders*, 3: 679–711, 714–18. It should be noted that Smith was already on the Army of the Cumberland's staff when Grant arrived, thus crediting Smith and giving him command of the Brown's Ferry operation. Grant's statement that he could not understand why it had not been done before he arrived and Smith's postwar bombast triggered the bitter debate. See William Farrar Smith, *The Re-opening of the Tennessee River near Chattanooga, October 1863* (Wilmington, Del.: Mercantile Printing Co., 1895) and idem, *Brown's Ferry, 1863* (Philadelphia: E. McManus Jr. and Company, 1901); see also Brooks D. Simpson, *Ulysess S. Grant: Triumph Over Adversity, 1822–1865* (Boston: Houghton Mifflin Company, 2000), 228–44.

11. Sword, *Mountains Touched with Fire*, 84–104; Ulysses S. Grant, *Memoirs and Selected Letters* (New York: Literary Classics, 1990), 448–49.

12. Thomas quoted in Society of the Army of the Cumberland, *First Annual Meeting*, 84–85; quoted in Morton, *Sparks from the Campfire*, 447; Grant quoted in Sherman, *Memoirs*, 1: 332; the "burning" and "ugly orphan" quotes in Sword, *Mountains Touched with Fire*, 281, 295. A critical, though non-scholarly modern interpretation of the Grant/Thomas situation can be found in Bob Redmon, "Politics in the Union Army at the Battle of Chattanooga," *Army of the Cumberland website* (2000), <www.aotc.net>; Bobrick's biography bluntly contends that Grant and Sherman deliberately manipulated their accounts of Chattanooga to cast doubt on Thomas's performance and elevate their own; *Master of War*, 198–216.

13. James A. Brisbin, *From the Towpath to the White House: The Early Life and Public Career of James A. Garfield* (Philadelphia: Hubbard Brothers, 1880), 221–22; Phillip Sheridan, *The Personal Memoirs of P. H. Sheridan* (New York: C. L. Webster, 1888; reprint, New York: De Capo Press, 1992), 156. The list of units attached to Thomas at the end of the day and the sequence of dispatches ordering troops to Thomas throughout the morning can be found in Van Horne, *Army of the Cumberland*, 2: 368–72. Rafuse, "In the Shadow of the Rock," in Woodworth, *The Chickamauga Campaign*, 41–42; Boynton claims that Thomas controlled all or part of twelve of McCook and Crittenden's brigades during his defense of Snodgrass Hill; H. V. Boynton, *The National Military Park, Chickamauga—Chattanooga, An Historical Guide* (Cincinnati, Ohio: Robert Clarke Company, 1895), 290–91.

14. Joseph S. Fullerton, "The Army of the Cumberland at Chattanooga," in Johnson and Buel, *Battles and Leaders of the Civil War*, 3:725; Grant, *Memoirs*, 446–47; Grant, "Chattanooga," *Battles and Leaders*, 706–7; Bobrick calls Grant's anger at the unauthorized charge "next to insane"; *Master of War*, 211; Arnold, *The Armies of U. S. Grant*, 143; Thomas quoted from Cist, *Army of the Cumberland*, 262.

15. Sherman, *Memoirs of W. T. Sherman*, 2: 101, 210, and 223.

16. Daniel, *Days of Glory*, 426–34; the quote and a description of Thomas's death from "a stroke of apoplexy" on 28 March 1870, appear in "Gen. George H. Thomas," *Harper's Weekly*, 16 April 1870, <www.harpweek.com>; the theory that John M. Schofield was the author of the critical letters and contributed to Thomas's death from a stroke can be found in Steven F. Hoffman, "One Man Around a Coffin: The Death of Major General George H. Thomas and the Controversy over the Battle of Nashville," independent study in history, December 1978, Dr. David B. Eller, advisor, Bluffton College, Bluffton, Ohio; Bobrick concurs, but also includes Grant as one who contributed to Thomas's death; *Master of War*, 330–32.

17. Sherman, *Memoirs of W. T. Sherman*, 2: 209–16; review quote from "Sherman's Memoirs," *The Galaxy: A Magazine of Entertaining Reading* 20, no. 4 (October 1875): 450, APS Online; Henry V. Boynton, *Was General Thomas Slow at Nashville? With a Description of the Greatest Cavalry Movement of the War and General James H. Wilson's Cavalry Operations in Tennessee, Alabama, and Georgia,* (New York: F. P. Harper, 1896), and more directly in idem, *Sherman's Historical Raid: The Memoirs, in Light of the Record* (Cincinnati, Ohio: Wilstach, Baldwin, & Company, 1875). A reference to Grant's drinking attributed to Joseph Hooker appeared in James Clement Ambrose, "Grant as a Soldier: General Hooker's View," *Potter's American Monthly* 18, no. 121 (January 1882): 82, APS Online; Timothy Smith, "Henry Van Ness Boynton and Chickamauga—The Pillars of the Modern Military Park Idea," in Woodworth, *The Chickamauga Campaign,* 170–72; the Sherman quote is from an 1887 letter and appears in a discussion of Grant's drinking on the website "Major General George H. Thomas—'The Rock of Chickamauga'—"The Sledge of Nashville," <http://home.earthlink.net/~oneplez/majorgeneralgeorgethomasblogsite/id25.html>; "mother" quote from Michael Fellman, *Citizen Sherman; The Life of William Tecumseh Sherman* (New York: Random House, 1995), 327–30.

18. Quoted in Society of the Army of the Cumberland, *Twenty-third Reunion, Chickamauga, Georgia, 1892* (Cincinnati, Ohio: Robert Clarke and Company, 1892), 79–83.

19. Ibid., 85.

20. Sheridan, *Memoirs,* 156; Bob Redman, "Sheridan's Ride at Chickamauga," *Army of the Cumberland and George Thomas Source Page* (2 September 2003), <http://www.aotc.net/Sheridan>, offers detailed criticism of Sheridan's version of events at Chickamauga and concludes that they "do not hold water."

21. The "permission" and "ride" quotes are in Brisbin, *From Towpath to White House,* 221–22; the resentment for Garfield's duplicity is confirmed in Perry, *Touched by Fire,* 120–30; quoted in Bierce, *Phantoms from a Bloodstained Period,* 197; SAOC, *Burial of Rosecrans,* 84–102. Oddly enough, Garfield made this speech to scold Congress for ignoring Rosecrans in a resolution praising General Thomas.

22. McMurry, *Two Rebel Armies,* 129–32.

23. William P. Snow, *Lee and His Generals* (original and reprint, New York: Richardson, 1865, 1867; reprint New York: Fairfax Press, 1982), 347; *Official Records,* XXX, Pt. 2, 34–35, in Matt Spruill, ed., *Guide to the Chickamauga Battlefield,* 234–35; Robert Selph Henry, *The Story of the Confederacy,* revised edition with a forward by Douglas Southall Freeman (originally published, 1931; reprint Konecky & Konecky, n.d.), 314.

24. D. H. Hill, "Chickamauga: Bloody Battle in the West," in *Battles and Leaders,* 3: 661–62; ironically, one account claims that if Rosecrans had come back to the battle with a few troops, the Union would have won the battle; Emerson Opdyke, "Notes on the Chickamauga Campaign," in *Battles and Leaders,* 3: 671; *Official Records,* XXX, Part 4, in Spruill, *Guide to Chickamauga,* 235–36; J. B. Jones, *A Rebel War Clerk's Diary at the Confederate States Capital,* 2 vols. (Philadelphia: J. B. Lippincott & Co., 1866; reprint Time-Life Books, 1982), 2: 66.

25. Longstreet, *From Manassas to Appomattox,* 472.

26. Bromfield L. Ridley, *Battles and Sketches of the Army of Tennessee* (Mexico, Mo.: Missouri Publishing Company, 1906; Dayton, Ohio: Morningside Press, 1978), 224; Hill "Chickamauga," in *Battles and Leaders,* 3:638–39, 662; Henry, *Story of the Confederacy,* 323–24.

27. Van Horne, *Army of the Cumberland,* 2: 365. This author is a firm proponent of the theory that the dual purpose of this Confederate concentration was to destroy Rosecrans's army and recapture Chattanooga. Having failed to accomplish either goal in September 1863 enhanced the idea that Chickamauga constituted a Union victory rather than a defeat.

28. Details on this purge and its effects can be found in Connelly, *Autumn of Glory*, 335–78; James I. Robertson, "Braxton Bragg: The Lonely Patriot," in *Leaders of the Lost Cause: Perspectives on the Confederate High Command*, Gary Gallagher and Joseph Glatthaar, eds. (Mechanicsburg, Pa.: Stackpole Books, 2004), 71–100. Hallock, *Braxton Bragg and Confederate Defeat*, 2: 88–108; Sword, *Mountains Touched With Fire*, 63–80. A critical assessment of Longstreet's performance at Chattanooga and Knoxville is offered in Hallock, *Longstreet in the West*, 38–88; a more favorable analysis can be found in Jeffry Wert, *General James Longstreet: The Confederacy's Most Controversial Soldier—A Biography* (New York: Simon and Schuster, 1993), 323–77.

29. Connelly, *Autumn of Glory*, 326–426.

30. Hood's version of Franklin and Nashville appears in J. B. Hood, "The Invasion of Tennessee," in *Battles and Leaders*, 4: 425–39. Scholarly analysis of Hood's performance in the West can be found in Richard McMurry, *John Bell Hood and the War for Southern Independence* (Lexington: University Press of Kentucky, 1982), 77–191; James Lee McDonough and Thomas L. Connelly, *Five Tragic Hours: The Battle of Franklin* (Knoxville: University of Tennessee Press, 1983); Winston Groom, *Shrouds of Glory, From Atlanta to Nashville: The Last Great Campaign of the Civil War* (New York: Atlantic Monthly Press, 1995).

31. Connelly, *Autumn of Glory*, 517–35.

5. "OFFERING YOUR LIVES . . . IN VINDICATION OF YOUR MANHOOD"

1. Neff, *Honoring the Civil War Dead*, 11; Reardon, *Pickett's Charge in History and Memory*, 177–85; a variety of scholarly views on the Confederate flag controversy can be found in Martinez, Richardson, and McNinch-Su, *Confederate Symbols in the Contemporary South*; and David Goldfield, *Still Fighting the Civil War: The American South and Southern History* (Baton Rouge: Louisiana State University Press, 2002), 298–319. On reenactors, see Turner, "Bloodless Battles: The Civil War Reenacted," 123–36.

2. David Blight, "Decoration Days: The Origins of Memorial Day in North and South," in *The Memory of the Civil War in American Culture*, Alice Fahs and John Waugh, eds., Civil War America (Chapel Hill: University of North Carolina Press, 2004), 94–123 (quote); see also, idem, *Frederick Douglass' Civil War: Keeping Faith with Jubilee* (Baton Rouge: Louisiana State University Press, 1989) and *Race and Reunion*.

3. Several studies deal with the politics surrounding the elections of the 1870s: J. Matthew Gallman, "Is the War Ended? Anna Dickinson and the Election of 1872," in Fahs and Waugh, *The Memory of the Civil War*, 157–79; and Michael Les Benedict, "Southern Democrats in the Crisis of 1876–1877: A Reconsideration of Reunion and Reaction," *The Journal of Southern History* 46, no. 4 (November 1980): 489–524, JSTOR; Blight, *Race and Reunion*, 122–38; Buck, *The Road to Reunion*, 72–113 and 144–69. Solid modern studies of reconstruction include Eric Foner, *Reconstruction: America's Unfinished Revolution 1863–1877* (New York: Harper & Row, 1988); and Kenneth Stampp, *The Era of Reconstruction, 1865–1877* (New York, 1965). Standard works on the New South include C. Vann Woodward, *Origins of the New South, 1877–1913*, A History of the South Series IX (Baton Rouge: Louisiana State University Press, 1951, 1971); and Edward Ayers, *The Promise of the New South: Life After Reconstruction* (New York: Oxford University Press, 1992). A quotation from "Soldier and Citizen," *Century Illustrated Magazine* 34, no. 6 (October 1887): 950, APS Online, stated that "we hold that the man who attempts to revive or trade on the dead issues of war should be regarded as a public enemy," further exclaiming, "that there can be no motive for sectional feeling that is not personal, partisan, or mercenary."

4. Blight, *Race and Reunion*, 264–99; Nina Silber, *The Romance of Reunion: Northerners and the South, 1865–1900*, Civil War America (Chapel Hill: University of North Carolina Press, 1993), 1–12, 127–38.

5. Silber, *The Romance of Reunion*, 9–10, 105–23. Other discussions of southern women and their role in the memory of the war can be found in Catherine Clinton, *Tara Revisited: Women, War, and the Plantation Legend* (New York: Abbeville Press, 1995); Alice Fahs, "The Feminized Civil War: Gender, Northern Popular Literature, and the Memory of the War, 1861–1900," *The Journal of American History* 85, no. 4 (March 1999): 1461–94; Drew Gilpin Faust, *Mothers of Invention: Women in the Slaveholding South during the American Civil War* (Chapel Hill: University of North Carolina Press, 1996), and "Alters of Sacrifice: Confederate Women and the Narratives of War," *The Journal of American History* 76, no. 4 (March 1990): 1200–1228; Goldfield, *Still Fighting the Civil War*, 89–120.

6. Gaines Foster, *Ghosts of the Confederacy*, 115–44; Blight, *Race and Reunion*, 294, 334–37, 344–45; Hudson, "Confederate Memorial Day," 39–40; Matthew Dennis, *Red, White, and Blue Letter Days: An American Calendar* (Ithaca: Cornell University Press, 2002), 221–39. Dennis sees the transition of the celebration of Memorial Day from commemoration to recreation as a product of reconciliation and describes Armistice/Veterans Day as its eventual replacement. See also Ellen Litwicki, *America's Public Holidays, 1865–1920* (Washington, D.C.: Smithsonian Institution Press, 2000), 9–49.

7. Blight, *Race and Reunion*, 291; Foster, *Ghosts of the Confederacy*, 124–25; Buck, *Road to Reunion*, 170–95; and John Pettegrew, "'The Soldier's Faith': Turn-of-the-Century Memory of the Civil War and the Emergence of Modern American Nationalism," *Journal of Contemporary History* 31, no. 1 (January 1996): 49–73, JSTOR.

8. Evan Thomas, *The War Lovers: Roosevelt, Lodge, Hearst, and the Rush to Empire, 1898* (New York: Little, Brown, and Company, 2010), 55; Silber, *Romance of Reunion*, 5–6.

9. Kristen Hoganson, *Fighting for American Manhood: How Gender Politics Provoked the Spanish-American and Philippine-American Wars* (New Haven, Conn.: Yale University Press, 1998), 21–29.

10. Pettegrew, "The Soldier's Faith," 54; many of Roosevelt's biographers agree that Teddy was self-conscious about his father's non-participation in the war, which in turn drove his own desire to prove his personal courage in battle, Thomas, *War Lovers*, 22–23.

11. Michael Kammen, *Mystic Chords of Memory: The Transformation of Tradition in American Culture* (New York: Alfred Knopf, 1991), 105–9; list of reunions quoted in Kilmer "A Note of Peace," 440; Blight makes specific reference to the above article in *Beyond the Battlefield*, 178–79.

12. Chickamauga and Chattanooga National Park Commission, *Dedication of the Chickamauga and Chattanooga National Military Park, September 18–20, 1895; Report of the Joint Committee to Represent the Congress at the Dedication* (Washington, D.C.: Government Printing Office, 1896), 36–37.

13. Kammen, *Mystic Chords of Memory*, 104–9; Linenthal, *Sacred Ground*, 14–54; Ronald Lee, *The Origin and Evolution of the Military Park Idea* (Washington, D.C.: National Park Service, 1973), online at <http://www.cr.innps.gov/history/nmpidea.htm>, nmpidea4 (since there are no page numbers on the online version, citations will be noted by the file/ sections; for example, chapter 1 is nmpidea3); the Society of the Army of the Cumberland helped fund three heroic monuments in Washington, D.C., for Thomas (1879), Garfield (1887), and Sheridan (1908); Kathryn Allamong Jacob, *Testament to Union: Civil War Monuments in Washington, D.C.* (Baltimore: Johns Hopkins University Press, 1998), 3–17.

14. Linenthal, *Sacred Ground*, 1–3, 89; the relative importance of Gettysburg and the details of its creation can be found in Smith, *Golden Age*, 22–29, 145–78.

15. Linenthal, *Sacred Ground*, 89–118; Platt, *This Is Holy Ground*, 2–11, 22; Richard A. Sauers, "John B. Bachelder: Government Historian of the Battle of Gettysburg," *Gettysburg—Historical Articles of Lasting Interest* 3 (July 1990): 115–127; A. J. Meek, *Gettysburg to Vicksburg: The Five Original Battlefield Parks*, Shades of Blue and Gray Series, Herman Hattaway and Jon L. Wakelyn, eds. (Columbia: University of Missouri Press, 2001), 1–48; Lee, *Origin of the Military Park Idea*, nmpidea5c, 5f. William C. Davis, *Gettysburg: the Story behind the Scenery* (Las Vegas, Nev.: KC Publications, 5th printing, 1995), 11–19.

16. Reardon, *Pickett's Charge*, 199–213; Linenthal, *Sacred Ground*, 103; Thomas Desjardin, *Stand Firm Ye Boys from Maine: The 20th Maine and the Gettysburg Campaign* (New York: Oxford University Press, 1995), 136–67; Jeffery Denman, "What Really Happened on Little Round Top?" *Civil War Times* 44, no. 3 (August 2005): 36–40; Gary Kross, "A Cheeky Piece of Work on Both Sides: The Alabamians' Attack on Little Round Top," *Blue and Gray* 13, no. 3 (Winter 1996): 54–61; Richard Pindell, "The True High Water Mark of the Confederacy: Pickett's Charge . . . or Little Round Top?" *Blue and Gray* 5, no. 4 (March 1988): 18–19; Glenn LaFantasie, "Joshua Chamberlain and the American Dream," in *The Gettysburg Nobody Knows*, Gabor S. Boritt, ed. (New York: Oxford University Press, 1997), 40–55.

17. A bitter disagreement between I, III, and XI Corps units over credit for the defense of East Cemetery Hill can be found in Gary Lash, *The Gibraltar Brigade on East Cemetery Hill: Twenty-five Minutes of Fighting, Fifty Years of Controversy, Gettysburg, July 2, 1863* (Baltimore: Butternut & Blue, 1995); William A. Frassanito, *Gettysburg: A Journey in Time* (New York: Charles Scribner's Sons, 1975); he has since followed up with *Gettysburg: Then & Now* (Gettysburg: Thomas Publications, 1997) and *The Gettysburg Then & Now Companion* (Gettysburg: Thomas Pub., 1997). Frassanito's other works include *Early Photography at Gettysburg* (Gettysburg, Pa.: Thomas Pub., 1995), *Antietam: The Photographic Legacy of America's Bloodiest Day* (New York: Charles Scribner's Sons, 1978), *Grant and Lee: The Virginia Campaigns, 1864–1865* (New York: Charles Scribner's Sons, 1983), and, as a consultant, the National Historical Society's *The Image of War, 1861–1865*, 6 vols. (New York: Doubleday & Co., 1981–84). See also Garry E. Adelman, *The Early Gettysburg Battlefield: Selected Photographs from the Gettysburg National Military Park Commission Reports 1895–1904* (Gettysburg, Pa.: Thomas Pub., 2001) and John Huddleson, *Killing Ground: Photographs of the Civil War and the Changing American Landscape* (Baltimore: Johns Hopkins University Press, 2002); Stan Cohen, *Hands Across the Wall: The 50th and 75th Reunions of the Gettysburg Battle* (Charleston, W.Va.: Pictorial Histories Publishing, 1982); Anna Jane Moyer, "Tenting Tonight, Boys! Gettysburg, 1938—Last Reunion of the Blue and Gray," *Blue and Gray* 6, no. 1 (October 1988): 45–49; Diana Loski, "Our Fervent Hope: Echoes of the Last Reunion," *The Gettysburg Experience* (January/February 2012), <http://thegettysburgexperience.com/past_issue_headlines/2010/july2010/hope.html>.

18. Dixon, "The Gettysburg Battlefield One Century Ago," 5–53; Dixon contends that the early park reflected the current trends in cemetery design, which emphasized a peaceful, pastoral, organized landscape. The cemetery was laid out by Scotsman William Saunders, who aimed for "simple grandeur"; Lee, *Origin of the Military Park Idea*, nmpidea5c; Platt, *This Is Holy Ground*, 17–21; the danger of losing meaning is expressed in Weeks, *American Shrine*; Desjardin, *These Honored Dead*; and Davis, *Gettysburg Scenery*, 12.

19. For a philosophical view of the battlefield and its connection to the past, see Kent Gramm, *Gettysburg: A Meditation of War & Values* (Bloomington: Indiana University Press, 1997).

20. Gilbert E. Govan and James Livengood, "Chattanooga under Military Occupation,"

The Journal of Southern History 17, no. 1 (February, 1951): 43–47, JSTOR; Constantine G. Belissary, "The Rise of Industry and Industrial Spirit in Tennessee, 1865–1885," *The Journal of Southern History* 19, no. 2 (May 1953): 198, JSTOR. Zelda Armstrong, *The History of Hamilton County and Chattanooga Tennessee*, vol. 2 (Chattanooga, Tenn.: Lookout Publishing Company, 1940), writes "it is true that the people of Chattanooga, while frankly of northern and southern elements and opinions, assimilated rapidly due to the leadership of some particularly wise and sane veterans of both armies," 61.

21. David S. and Jeanne Heidler, "Wilder, John Thomas," in idem, eds., *Encyclopedia of the American Civil War: A Political, Social, and Military History* (New York: W. W. Norton & Company, 2002), 2108; Timothy P. Ezzell, "Adolph Simon Ochs," in the *Tennessee Encyclopedia of History and Culture* (Knoxville: University of Tennessee Press, 1998), online edition at <http://tennesseeencyclopedia.net>; Jerry R. Desmond, *Chattanooga, Images of America* (Charleston, S.C.: Arcadia Press, 1996), 25–44.

22. Grant quoted in Sword, *Mountains Touched with Fire*, 356; SOAC *Twenty-Third Reunion*, 51.

23. Van Horne, *History of the Army of the Cumberland*, 1: 406; Govan and Livengood, "Chattanooga under Military Occupation," *JSH*, 27; Edwin C. Bearss, "The War for Tennessee," in *The South Besieged*, The Image of War, vol. 5 (National Historical Society, 1983), 15–75; Roger C. Linton, *Chickamauga: A Battlefield History in Images* (Athens: University of Georgia Press, 2004); Desmond, *Chattanooga*, 12, 17, 26–27.

24. Smith, *Golden Age*, 16–17; Thomas Buell, *The Warrior Generals: Combat Leadership in the Civil War* (New York: Three Rivers Press, 1997), 294–95; "History of the Chattanooga Confederate Cemetery," originally published in Zella Armstrong, *The History of Hamilton County and Chattanooga Tennessee*, vol. 1 (Chattanooga: Lookout Publishing Company, 1931), found online at < http://www.scv-nbforrest3.com/confederate%20cemetery.htm>. Most of the Confederates killed at Chickamauga are buried in Marietta, Georgia; a few from the battles around Chattanooga were buried in separate cemeteries in that city; Miles, *Paths to Victory*, 77, 102.

25. For an award-winning analysis of Grant's heroic status after the war, see Waugh, *U. S. Grant*, 156–65.

26. Flood, *Lee: The Last Years*, 194–98; Rosecrans also served two terms in Congress and chaired the Military Appropriations Committee; William Feis, "Rosecrans, William Starke," in *Encyclopedia of the Civil War*, 1677–78; one editorial called this incident "one of the higher comedies of the canvass" and noted that "as a Democratic campaign document, [the letter] is one of the feeblest conceivable"; "General Rosecrans and General Lee," *Harper's Weekly*, 19 September, 1868, <www.harpweek.com>; Society of the Army of the Cumberland, *First Annual Report*, 106; also see Lamers, *Edge of Glory*, 440–50.

27. Einolf, *George Thomas*, 295–325; The medal is described in "The Thomas Medal," *Harper's Weekly*, 22 December 1866 and 16 April, 1870, <www.harpweek.com>; James L. Isseman, "Thomas, George Henry," in *Encyclopedia of the Civil War*, 1943–44; Buell, *Warrior Generals*, 424.

28. For Bobrick, although Sheridan and Schofield are part of the clique, the main culprits were Sherman and Grant "whose deliberate suppression of his fame . . . is a continuing national tragedy," *Master of War*, 343; SAOC, *First Annual Report*, 39.

29. Einolf, *George Thomas*, 336–39; funeral testimonials included tributes by Hooker and McClellan; Bobrick, *Master of War*, 334; Jacob, *Testament of Union*, 85–88.

30. The total cost of the statue was $60,000; as it had for Thomas, Congress provided $30,000 for the statue's base, Jacob, *Testament of Union*, 133–36; Kammen, *Mystic Chords of Memory*, 102

31. Jacob, *Testament of Union*, 135–38; Ward had sculpted the statue of Thomas in Washington that was thought to be "the finest equestrian statue in the world" and considered the Sheridan affair "the one great disappointment of his artistic career," "The First of American Sculptors," *Current Literature* 48, no. 6 (June 1910): 667, APS Online; Gates Thurston to W. H. Taft, 1 November 1907, Society of the Army of the Cumberland, History C, Acc. 5, Box 2, folder 4, Chattanooga–Hamilton County Bicentennial Library.

32. Boynton was born in Massachusetts in 1835, moved to Ohio as a child and attended college in Cincinnati. He served as Major and Lieutenant Colonel with the 35th and was brevetted a Brigadier after he was wounded leading the regiment at Missionary Ridge; he received the Medal of Honor on 15 November 1893 for his actions on 25 November 1863; "Henry Van Ness Boynton, Brigadier General United States Army," *Arlington National Cemetery Website*, <http://www.arlingtoncemetery.net/hvnboynt.htm>; Smith, *A Chickamauga Memorial*, 15–17; Smith, "Boynton and Chickamauga," in *The Chickamauga Campaign*, 166–72; "Biography of Vice President Henry Wilson (1873–1875)," in Mark O. Hatfield, with the Senate Historical Office, *Vice Presidents of the United States, 1789–1993* (Washington, D.C.: Government Printing Office, 1997) 105–116, online at <www.allamericanpatriots.com>; Ari Hoogenboom, "The Disputed Election of 1876," <www.rbhayes.org>; Loren P. Beth, "President Hayes Appoints a Justice," *Supreme Court Historical Society 1989 Yearbook*, <www.supremecourthistory.org>.

33. Quoted in Henry Howe, "Henry Van-Ness Boynton," in *Historical Collections of Ohio in Two Volumes* (Cincinnati, Ohio: C. J. Krehbiel & Co. Printers, 1908), 1: 852; Boynton's efforts and Cleveland's poor track record with veterans and pensions helped get Benjamin Harrison elected president in 1888; Perry, *Touched With Fire*, 296–304. Kaser, *At the Bivouac of Memory*, identifies Boynton as a member of the Western Press Association, which encouraged sectional cooperation and reconciliation, 51–52.

6. "NO PLACE FOR LOVERS TO BIDE TRYST"

1. The story of the carriage ride and initial park idea appears in Smith, "Boynton and Chickamauga," in *The Chickamauga Campaign*, 165; idem, *A Chickamauga Memorial*, 13–14; and John C. Paige and Jerome Green, *Administrative History of the Chickamauga and Chattanooga National Military Park* (Denver, Colo.: Denver Service Center, National Park Service, U.S. Department of the Interior, 1983), online at <http://www.nps.gov/history/history/online_books/chch/adhi1.htm>. As with the Lee online book, citations will be by file identification, using adhi1, adhi2, and so on. Since the chapters are longer, page numbers will be added, as in adhi1:1–2. See also Golden Link, "Chickamauga-Chattanooga National Military Park: Attraction Overview," *About North Georgia* at <http://ngeorgia.com/ang/chickamauga_battlefield>.

2. Henry V. Boynton, *Chattanooga and Chickamauga: Reprint of Henry V. Boynton's Letters to the Cincinnati Commercial Gazette, August 1888*, 2nd ed. with corrections (Washington, D.C.: Geo. R. Gray, Printer, 1891), 5; this edition was distributed to members prior to the society's September reunion on the 25th anniversary of the battle.

3. Paige and Green, *Administrative History*, adhi1:3; "Chickamauga: Attraction Overview," <http://ngeorgia.com>; Jill K. Hanson and Robert W. Blythe, *Chickamauga and Chattanooga National Military Park: Historic Resource Study* (Atlanta, Ga.: Cultural Resources Stewardship, Southeast Regional Office, National Park Service, U.S. Department of the Interior. 1999), online at <www.nps.gov/history/history/online_books/chch/hrs/hrs.htm>, 30–33.

4. Paige and Green, *Administrative History,* adhi1: 3; Hanson and Blythe, *Historic Resource Study,* 31–33; Boynton and Rosecrans quoted in Robertson, *The Battle of Chickamauga,* 27–28; Boynton, *Chickamauga Letters,* 54 and *The National Military Park,* 221–32; both the Park Service and *The Friends of Chickamauga & Chattanooga National Military Park* use the Crawfish Springs gathering as the centerpiece of its Visitor Center introductory film, which stresses "the spirit of peace, reconciliation, and remembrance in which our park was born"; membership letter from Executive Director Kay Parish to Bradley Keefer, 12 January 2006.

5. Paige and Green, *Administrative History,* adhi1:5; Chickamauga and Chattanooga National Park Commission, *Legislation, Congressional and State, Pertaining to the Establishment of the Park* (Washington, D.C.: Government Printing Office, 1897), 7–10; Lee, *Military Park Idea,* nmpidea5f; Hanson and Blythe, *Historic Resource Study,* 32–34.

6. Paige and Green, *Administrative History,* adhi1: 6, adhi1a: 1–4; Kellogg's successor, Maj. Frank Smith, was a Chickamauga veteran; an article in the *Chattanooga Times,* 14 February 1892, noted that "the owners of the land which was selected as the site of the park were averse to disposing of their land without first being tickled with a rather exorbitant acreage," Clipping File, Local History, Chickamauga-Chattanooga National Park folder, Chattanooga-Hamilton County Bicentennial Library; SOAC, *Twenty-third Reunion,* 61; Tim Smith, "A Western Gettysburg: Alexander Peter Stewart and the Founding of Chickamauga and Chattanooga National Military Park," undated and unpublished seminar paper, Mississippi State University, 7 and *A Chickamauga Memorial,* 42–49; Sam Davis Elliot, *Soldier of Tennessee: General Alexander P. Stewart and the Civil War in the West* (Baton Rouge: Louisiana State University Press, 1999), 287–92.

7. The 1893 appropriation for park development (not including land purchase) was $100,000 and in 1894 it was $75,000; Paige and Green, *Administrative History,* adhi1a: 3–4; Smith, "A Western Gettysburg," 5–6.

8. Society of the Army of the Cumberland, *23rd Reunion,* 57; Paige and Green, *Administrative History,* adhi1: 6; Hanson and Blythe, *Historic Resource Study,* 33.

9. Quoted in Smith, "Boynton and Chickamauga," in Woodworth, *Chickamauga Campaign,* 178.

10. Paige and Green, *Administrative History,* adhi1: 6; Smith, "Western Gettysburg," 5; Elliot, *Soldier of Tennessee,* 288.

11. The National Park Commissioners had final say on the placement, design, and language on the monuments and markers and usually required a simple majority among themselves to overrule dissent. Joseph C. McElroy, *Chickamauga: Record of the Ohio Chickamauga and Chattanooga National Park Commission* (Cincinnati, Ohio: Earhart & Richardson, Printers and Engravers, 1896), 135–36. Former colonel James Watson replaced Van Derveer upon the death of the park's co-founder.

12. "Ohio Monument Locations—Kellogg's Diary," Chickamauga and Chattanooga National Military Park Archives (CHCH), 205–3200, "Ohio Monuments, 1904–1917," series II, box 13, folder 209; it was May 1894 before all had been accepted, McElroy, *Chickamauga, Ohio Commission,* 137.

13. W. L. Curry, "A Visit to Chickamauga Twenty Years after the Battle of September 20, 1863," in *Twelfth and Thirteenth Reunions of the First Ohio Volunteer Cavalry, Newark Ohio, September 15, 1891, Galloway Ohio, September 13, 1892* (Columbus, Ohio: Landon Printing and Publishing, 1893), 18–31. There seem to be some odd date discrepancies with this source. The "twenty years" in the title is inaccurate; Curry says later in the paper that it had been twenty-nine years since the battle. All the statements in the article and in the other sources confirm that he was there during the AOC reunion on 15–16 Septem-

ber 1892, which makes it impossible for him to have given this speech at the thirteenth annual reunion in Ohio on the same weekend. It is likely that this "speech" was added before the publication of the reunion report in 1893, which might also explain the mistake in the title. Kellogg notes that the three cavalry units "did not decide" where to put the monuments in September, but that by November all commissioners had approved the location near the Widow Glenn's "as originally designated" by the veterans, Kellogg Diary, CHCH. The decision to place them in the park was made by 20 September and confirmed by the following correspondence: Curry to "the ex-soldiers of the First, Third, and Fourth, O.V.C.," 20 September 1892, Curry to General Eli Long, 15 October 1892, and Curry to General Eli Long, 14 December 1892 in the Eli P. Long Papers, United States Army Military History Institute Archives (USAMHI); Curry's account of this decision is also found in W. L. Curry, *Four Years in the Saddle: History of the First Regiment, Ohio Volunteer Cavalry* (Columbus, Ohio: W. L. Curry, 1898; reprint Jonesboro, Ga.: Freedom Hill Press, 1984) and is cited in Nancy Pape-Findley, *The Invincibles: The Story of the Fourth Ohio Veteran Volunteer Cavalry, 1861–1865* (Tecumseh, Mich.: Blood Road Publishing, 2002), 166–67, n 284. The 1st Ohio was part of the 2nd Brigade, 2nd Division of the Army of the Cumberland Cavalry Corps and consisted of the 1st, 3rd, and 4th Ohio and the 2nd Kentucky; "Opposing Forces at the Battle of Chickamauga," in *Battles and Leaders*, 3: 673. The cost of the monuments was $1,500, minus $30 for the Ohio Seal. The 1st and 3rd were made by E. F. Carr & Co. and the 4th monument by Thomas Fox of Cincinnati; McElroy, *Chickamauga, Ohio Commission*, 108–18, 140–41.

14. The best modern account of the 21st's ordeal is in Cozzens, *This Terrible Sound*, 435–38, 484–87, 503–9; the problem with the Colt's was the need for specific .56 caliber ammunition that did not match the .577 or .58 caliber cartridges used by most of the rest of the infantry troops in either army; had the ordnance sergeant issued seventy rounds to the 21st prior to the battle, giving each man 95 rounds; attempts to use Enfield cartridges resulted in "a good many of our guns bursting," John H. Bolton, Diary, with a description of Chickamauga, vol. 393, Ohio Historical Society Archives, Columbus, Ohio; in an article about the 96th Illinois (part of Steedman's relief column) and the controversy surrounding its performance in the battle, the author claims that his brigade commander, Walter Whittaker, neglected to inform the 21st and others of the order; Dave Powell, "The 96th Illinois and the Battles for Horseshoe Ridge, 1863 and 1895," *North & South*, 8, no. 2 (March 2005), 52–56.

15. Cozzens, *This Terrible Sound*, 503–9.

16. Ibid. Interestingly, Tim Smith uses this in his introduction as an example of Boynton's argumentative nature, but does not elaborate in the text of *Chickamauga Memorial*, xxv; he does, however, refer to Boynton's self-interest regarding the role of the 35th Ohio in *Golden Age*, 78–79 .

17. Kaser, *At the Bivouac of Memory*, 40–52.

18. Ibid., 59–71; "McMahan's Libby Prison Memo Book, 1863–1864," Center for Archival Collections, United States Army, Ohio Infantry Regiment, 21st, MS 562 Transcripts: Box 14, Folder 1, <www.bgsu.edu/colleges/library/cac/ms/trans/page53569.html>. McMahan's point of view is defended and vigorously upheld in Gracie's *The Truth about Chickamauga*, in which he casts much of the blame on Brannan for abandoning the 21st, which had been put under his command by Negley early in the day. He is equally critical of Van Derveer for not passing along the word to retreat and ordering troops to hold a line without ammunition. He provides plenty of evidence to support McMahan's version, including letters and other correspondence in an appendix, 206–26 and 415–37. John Turchin calls the failure to pass withdrawal orders to these regiments "dereliction of

duty" and a "disgraceful occurrence" on the part of Brannan and others, John B. Turchin, *Chickamauga* (Chicago: Fergus Printing Company, 1888), 155.

19. Quoted from McMahan Memo Book, CAC, 53569; Boynton, *Letters to the Cincinnati Commercial*, 49; Kaser, *At the Bivouac of Memory*, 74; McElroy, *Chickamauga, Ohio Commission*, 46–47; the marker placement is verified without comment in the Kellogg Diary, CHCH; the 96th Illinois was also dissatisfied with its monument placement and engaged in a similar battle to correct it during the creation of the park, Powell, "The 96th Illinois," 56–59.

20. Quoted in "Art on the Battlefield," *Century Illustrated Magazine* 50, no. 5 (September 1895): 795, APS Online; an act passed by the Ohio legislature in April 1893 limited the cost per monument to $1,500 and awarded contracts to a half-dozen different firms for specific unit monuments, McElroy, *Chickamauga, Ohio Commission*, 138–45. Specific guidelines for monument designs were spelled out in Chickamauga Park Commission, *Legislation Pertaining to the Park*, 24–26.

21. During the battle, Wiley had been the colonel of the 41st Ohio, 2nd Brigade, 2nd Division, XXI Corps, while the 26th Ohio was 1st Brigade, 1st Division in that corps; "The Opposing Forces at Chickamauga," in *Battles and Leaders*, 3: 673; J. S. Fullerton to the Honorable Secretary of War, 12 October 1894; printed broadside from "The Office of the Ohio Soldier and National Picket Guard"; John T. Raper to Hon. Daniel Lamont, Secretary of War, 9 October 1894.

22. Aquila Wiley to the Honorable Secretary of War, 22 October 1894; John Beatty to the Honorable Secretary of War, 27 October 1894, all from acc. 205–3200, War Department Park Commission, 1890–1933 [Ohio Monuments, Lookout Mountain, correspondence, 1894–1949], Series II, Box 3, Folder 41, CHCH Archives.

23. Wiley to Andrew Jackson, 30 November 1892 and __ December 1892; quoted in Boynton to Wiley, 29 November 1893; McElroy to Wiley, 4 December 1893; quoted in Wiley to "my dear general" Boynton, 4 December 1893 (underlined in the original), all in Aquila Wiley Papers, MS 2127, Chickamauga Park Commission Papers: Correspondence, maps, and histories, 1892–1901, Folder 3, Western Reserve Historical Society Library, Cleveland, Ohio.

24. Baird's 1st Division was part of the XIV Corps, while Boynton was a member of that corps' 3rd Division; "Opposing Forces at Chickamauga," in *Battles and Leaders*, 3: 672; Boynton to Wiley, 6 December 1893 and 22 December 1893; William C. Webber to Wiley, 22 January 1894; Wiley to Webber, 5 February 1894; Boynton to Wiley, 16 January 1895; all in Aquila Wiley Papers, MS 2127, Chickamauga Park Commission Papers, Folder 3, WRHSL.

25. Boynton to Wiley, 24 January 1895, Aquila Wiley Papers, WRHSL.

26. J. L. Rogers, *The Civil War Battles of Chickamauga and Chattanooga* (J. L. Rogers, 1942), 1; Jack Kerr, *Monuments and Markers of the 29 States Engaged at Chickamauga and Chattanooga*, (Collegedale, Tenn.: The College Press, n.d.), The eight brigade commanders killed at Chickamauga were: Col. Hans C. Heg, Col. Philemon Baldwin, Col. Edward King, and Brig. Gen. William Lytle for the Union; Col. Peyton Colquitt, Brig. Gen. Benjamin Helms, Brig. Gen. Preston Smith, and Brig. Gen. James Deshler for the Confederates. James M. Ray to Gen. A. P. Stewart, 15 June 1901, "veterans correspondence," Series II, Box 16, Folder 259, CHCH Archives; Judge A. C. Avery, "Farthest to the Front at Chickamauga," in *Tar Heels: Five Points in the Record of North Carolina in the Great War of 1861–1865*, Patrick Schroeder, ed. (Goldsboro, N.C.: Nash Brothers, 1904; reprinted in Daleville, Va.: Schroeder Publications, 2001); the author determined that the 58th N.C., not the 60th, is the unit that reached the farthest point in Thomas's line on 20 September, 55–56.

27. Paige and Green, *Administrative History*, adhi1a: 3–7; the Chickamauga park dedi-

cation was one of several events going on in the south during that month. Many veterans had recently attended the national GAR reunion in Louisville, Kentucky, that had included many Confederate veterans. There was also a large public exhibition in Atlanta, Georgia, that included veteran participation and is notable for being the site of Booker T. Washington's "Atlanta Compromise" speech, which was given on the same day as the Chickamauga dedication; "The Grand Army at Louisville," and "Three Events in the South," *A Weekly Newsmagazine* 22, no. 2 (November 1895): 218, 220, APS Online; Blight, *Beyond the Battlefield,* 180–81.

28. Beatty acknowledged the former Confederates, saying that "no man can positively deny that those who faced death on this battlefield did so believing they were fighting in an honest cause, and for the best interests of mankind," McElroy, *Chickamauga, Ohio Commission,* 146–86.

29. Paige and Green, *Administrative History,* adhi1a: 6–7; *Dedication of Chickamauga and Chattanooga Park,* 103, 124, and 140–51; Schofield's participation is ironic considering the likely role he played in sabotaging Thomas's reputation and perhaps causing his death.

30. *Dedication of the Chickamauga and Chattanooga Park,* 28–36, 38–40; Kaser, *At the Bivouac of Memory,* 113–121; Paige and Green, *Administrative History,* adhi1a: 6–9.

7. "A MAKER OF GLORIOUS HISTORY"

1. Ayers, *Promise of a New South,* 55–80, 110; quoted in "Southern Mountain Rambles: In Tennessee, Georgia, and South Carolina," *Scribner's Monthly* 8, no.1 (May 1874): 5 APS Online; R. Desmond, *Images of America: Chattanooga* (Charleston, S.C.: Arcadia Press, 1996), 13, 62–70; Donald R. More, "The Industrial Boom Towns of the State [*sic*] of Dade in Georgia," *Chattanooga Regional Historical Journal* 1, no. 2 (July 1998): 141–54. See also Constantine Belissary, "The Rise of Industry and the Industrial Spirit in Tennessee, 1865–1885," *The Journal of Southern History* 19, no. 2 (May 1953): 193–215, JSTOR. Former Confederate general Gustavus Smith tried unsuccessfully to revive the southwestern plant, which was operated by Wilder's Roane works until it closed in 1877; Leonne M. Hudson, *The Odyssey of a Southerner: The Life and Times of Gustavus Woodson Smith* (Macon, Ga.: Mercer University Press, 1998), 192–94.

2. Desmond, *Chattanooga,* 9; William Pittenger, *Daring and Suffering: A History of the Great Railroad Adventure* (Philadelphia: J. W. Daughaday, 1863; reprint Time Life Collector's Library of the Civil War, 1982), editors' comments; Pittenger referred to this jail as "the Black Hole of Calcutta," 127–35. Jim Leeke, "Always Very Daring and Reckless: Private William J. Knight and the Andrews Raid," *Timeline* 20, no. 6 (November–December 2003): 2–17. Advertisement 10, "Southern Summer Resorts," *Current Literature* 17, no. 6 (June 1895): 0_008, APS Online. Bodnar argues that in spite of the railroad companies' attempts to make battlefields tourist destinations, "the underlying purpose served by the original construction of these symbols was the need of ordinary people to express sorrow and honor for the dead," *Remaking America,* 28.

3. Desmond, *Chattanooga,* 9–23; Paige and Greene, *Administrative History,* adhi2e:1; Ochs's influence in the area grew after he bought the *New York Times* and became a nationally known figure. Although he spent most of his time on the New York paper, he still remained active in Chattanooga affairs; Gerald W. Johnson, *An Honorable Titan: A Biographical Study of Adolph S. Ochs* (Westport, Conn.: Greenwood Press, 1970), 65–72, 96–106.

4. Ochs quoted in Boynton, *Dedication of the Park,* 85; "Making Original Battle Souvenirs," *Current Literature* 18, no. 4 (October 1895): 335, APS Online; it is likely that most

of the actual artifacts gathered and sold were picked up prior to the creation of the park, after which it was illegal; Chickamauga and Chattanooga National Park Commission, *Legislation, Congressional and State, Pertaining to the Establishment of the Park*, (Washington, D.C.: U.S. Government Printing Office), 10, 15–16; a metal detector survey of the Union "retreat corridor" carried out by the National Park service in 1992 yielded surprisingly few artifacts, which may be a reflection of the success enjoyed by postwar relic hunters, including the Spanish-American War occupants of the area; John E. Cornelison Jr., "The Archaeology of Retreat: Systematic Metal Detector Survey and Information System Analysis at the Battlefield of Chickamauga, September 1863," in Clarence R. Geier and Stephen R. Potter, eds., *Archaeological Perspectives on the American Civil War* (Gainesville: University Press of Florida, 2000), 289–304.

5. Davis, *Soldier of Tennessee*, 286–300, quoted on 294; Smith, "A Western Gettysburg," 7–9.

6. Smith, *Golden Age*, explains that Antietam was created without enabling legislation and only sections of the battlefield were bought, rather than the whole large chunk as had been done at Chickamauga, 89. During the legislative process, one of the Shiloh park's congressional sponsors admitted that this park responded "to the wishes of the Western Armies"; the senator who suggested there might be too many parks was Joseph Dolph of Oregon, while Senator Francis Cockrell warned that eventually the veterans requesting this money would want to make a park on every battlefield; idem, 122–23; see also Richard West Sellars, *Pilgrim Places: Civil War Battlefields, Historic Preservation, and America's First Military Parks, 1863–1900* (Fort Washington, Pa.: Eastern National, 2005).

7. Meek and Hattaway, *Gettysburg to Vicksburg*, 9–14, 96–100, 119–20, 140–47; the authors make the point that although it was the first park created, the Missionary Ridge portion of the Chickamauga and Chattanooga National Military Park "is by far the most disappointing commemorative site" among all of the parks, xi–xiii, 60–62; Timothy B. Smith, *The Untold Story of Shiloh*, 2–19. See also, idem, and for a detailed overview of all five parks, *The Golden Age of Battlefield Preservation;* members of the Society of the Army of the Cumberland were upset to find that the Army of the Ohio's role in the battle had been minimized in Reed's published volumes on the battle, which they claimed were "crowded with errors, neither of them agreeing with each other or the official records," H. V. Boynton to the officers and members of the executive committee (SOAC), 17 May 1905, Society of the Army of the Cumberland, Correspondence, etc., 25 Feb. 1905–May 1905, Hist C, Acc. 5, Box 2, Folder 3, Chattanooga Hamilton County Bicentennial Library; the matter was discussed at the 1904 meeting of the society, which resolved to submit the matter to the secretary of war, SOAC, *Thirty-Second Reunion, Indianapolis, Indiana, September 20, 21, 1904* (Cincinnati, Ohio: Robert Clarke, 1905), 100–104.

8. Smith, *Golden Age*, 94–110 (Davis), 186–98, at Vicksburg, Confederate Stephen Lee was head of the commission for some time while Ezra Carman served on both the Antietam and Chickamauga commission, 110, 201, and 217.

9. Boynton, *The National Military Park*, 230–31.

10. Park Commission, *Legislation Pertaining to the Park*, 15; Paige and Greene, *Administrative History*, ahdi6:1; a discussion of the 1897 epidemic appears in Mariola Espinosa, "The Threat from Havana: Southern Public Health, Yellow Fever, and the U.S. Intervention in the Cuban Struggle for Independence, 1878–1898," *Journal of Southern History* 72, no. 3 (August 2006): 541–48.

11. Boynton mentions the towers throughout his guided tour sections in *The National Military Park*, 167–218; Smith, *Golden Age*, 214–18.

12. Quoted from the *Chattanooga Times*, in "Chickamauga Military Park Dedication," *A Weekly Newsmagazine* 22, no. 2 (November 1895): 223, APS Online; quoted in Meeks and Hattaway, *Gettysburg to Vicksburg*, 98.

8. "TO CEMENT FOREVER THE BONDS OF SECTIONAL REUNION"

1. Descriptions of American society on the eve of the war with Spain include David Traxel, *1898: The Birth of the American Century* (New York: Vintage Books, 1998), 17–62; and Ivan Musicant, *Empire by Default: The Spanish American War and the Dawn of the American Century* (New York: Henry Holt and Company, 1998), 3–37. Analysis of the effects of the growth of industrial America can be found in Samuel P. Hays, *The Response to Industrialism, 1885–1914* (Chicago: University of Chicago Press, 1957); Ray Ginger, *Age of Excess: The United States from 1877–1914* (New York: MacMillan, 1965); and Robert Weibe, *The Search for Order, 1877–1920* (New York: Hill and Wang, 1967). Standard studies on immigration include Maldwyn Allen Jones, *American Immigration* (Chicago: University of Chicago Press, 1961); Oscar Handlin, *The Uprooted: The Epic Story of the Great Migrations that Made the American People* (Boston: Little, Brown, and Company, 1951; 2nd ed. enlarged, 1973); Maxine Seller, *To Seek America: A History of Ethnic Life in the United States* (Jerome S. Ozer, publisher, 1977). Discussions on the importance of the frontier can be found in George Rogers Taylor, ed., *The Turner Thesis: Concerning the Role of the Frontier in American History*, Problems in American Civilization (Lexington, Mass.: Heath and Company, 3rd ed., 1972). On Populism, see Lawrence Goodwyn, *Democratic Promise: The Populist Moment in America* (New York: Oxford University Press, 1976); for a discussion of the role of Civil War memory in the defeat of Populism, see Patrick J. Kelley, "The Election of 1896 and the Restructuring of Civil War Memory," in Fahs and Waugh, *The Memory of the Civil War*, 180–212.

2. Walter Millis, *The Martial Spirit: A Study of Our War with Spain* (Boston: Houghton Mifflin Company, 1931), 1–37; Musicant, *Empire By Default*, 38–77; Traxel, *1898*, 78–80. Numerous accounts of the war appeared shortly afterward, many of them focused heavily on Spain's oppressive policies toward the Cubans. See John W. Abbot, *Blue Jackets of '98: A History of the Spanish-American War* (New York: Dodd, Mead, & Company, 1904); W. R. Copeland, *A Complete History of the Spanish-American War of 1898* (New York: Mershon Company, 1899); Murat Halstead, *Full Official History of the War with Spain* (New York: W. W. Wilson, 1899); Henry Watterson, *History of the Spanish-American War* (New York: W. W. Wilson, 1898); Thomas, *The War Lovers*, looks at the influence of all three.

3. Millis, *The Martial Spirit*, 32, 41; Traxel, *1898*, 80–86; Hearst eventually purchased the New York *Daily Journal*, while the Ochs-owned *Times* avoided sensational reporting and remained "steady, sensible, and careful—and highly unprofitable," Johnson, *Honorable Titan*, 178–82; Charles H. Brown, *The Correspondent's War: Journalists in the Spanish-American War* (New York: Scribner's and Sons, 1967), 95–102.

4. Millis, *The Martial Spirit*, 41–43, 66–70; Traxel, *1898*, 82–86; Hoganson, *Fighting for American Manhood*, 56–61. The New York newspaper rivalry between Hearst and Pulitzer is described in the context of postwar monuments in Michele H. Bogart, "'Maine Memorial' and 'Pulitzer Fountain': A Study in Patronage and Process," *Winterthur Portfolio* 21, no. 1 (Spring 1986): 41–63, JSTOR. Richard Harding Davis, *The Cuban and Porto Rican Campaigns*

(New York: Charles Scribner's Sons, 1904); Brown, *The Correspondent's War,* 81–83; the contingent of reporters included two women, who practiced the "sob sister journalism" that Hearst had used in San Francisco, 39–40; Thomas, *War Lovers,* 99–107, 179–85.

5. Hoganson, *Fighting for American Manhood,* 43–67; Silber, *The Romance of Reunion,* 159–178.

6. Traxel, *1898,* 87–92; although initially hostile to annexation, Hawaiians supported the U.S. during the war; Thomas Bailey, "The United States and Hawaii During the Spanish-American War," *The American Historical Review* 36, no. 3 (April 1931): 552–60, JSTOR; a historiographic analysis of America's motives for war appears in Thomas G. Paterson, "United States Intervention in Cuba, 1898: Interpretations of the Spanish-American-Cuban-Filipino War," *The History Teacher* 29, no. 3 (May 1996): 341–61, JSTOR; Thomas, *War Lovers,* 70–71, 200.

7. Quoted in Hoganson, *Fighting for American Manhood,* 39; quoted in H. W. Brands, *T.R.: The Last Romantic* (New York: Basic Books, 1997), 316–17; Traxel, *1898,* 89–92; John Milton Cooper, *The Warrior and the Priest: Woodrow Wilson and Theodore Roosevelt* (Cambridge Mass.: Harvard University/Belknap Press, 1983), 38–40; Dale L. Walker, *The Boys of '98: Theodore Roosevelt and the Rough Riders* (New York: Tom Doherty Associates, 1998), 61–83; Thomas, *War Lovers,* 197–98.

8. Hoganson, *Fighting for American Manhood,* 44–55; George W. Auxier, "Middle Western Newspapers and the Spanish-American War, 1895–1898," *The Mississippi Valley Historical Review* 26, no. 4 (March 1940): 523–34, JSTOR.

9. Lewis L. Gould, *The Spanish-American War and President McKinley* (Lawrence: University Press of Kansas, 1982), 19–53.

10. Gould, *McKinley and the War,* 53; Hoganson, *Fighting for American Manhood,* 88–106; see also Margaret Leech, *In the Days of McKinley* (New York: Harper and Brothers, 1959), 144–93. There was also a widespread belief that Republican-dominated business interests opposed going to war for humanitarian reasons; Gerald F. Linderman, *The Mirror of War: American Society and the Spanish-American War* (Ann Arbor: University of Michigan Press, 1974), 6–8. See also H. Wayne Morgan, *America's Road to Empire: The War with Spain and Overseas Expansion* (New York: John Wiley and Sons, 1965).

11. Silber, *The Romance of Reunion,* 178–80; Blight, *Race and Reunion,* 352; Millis, *The Martial Spirit,* 162.

12. Watterson, *History of the Spanish-American War,* 35–36; John P. Dyer, *From Shiloh to San Juan: The Life of "Fightin' Joe" Wheeler* (Baton Rouge: Louisiana State University Press, 1941; revised paperback, 1989), 215–23.

13. Traxel, *1898,* 91; Musicant, *Empire by Default,* 154–60; Frank Freidel, *The Splendid Little War* (Boston: Little, Brown, and Company, 1958), 3–31. An example of Dewey's fame and the impact it had on the nation can be found in Murat Halstead, *The Life and Achievements of Admiral Dewey from Montpelier to Manila* (Chicago: H. L. Barber, 1899).

14. Jack C. Dierks, *A Leap to Arms: The Cuban Campaigns of 1898,* Great Battles of History (Philadelphia: J. B. Lippincott, 1970), 40; "relationship" quote in Graham A. Cosmas, "From Order to Chaos: The War Department, the National Guard, and Military Policy, 1898," *Military Affairs* 29, no. 3 (Autumn 1965): 105–16; a detailed examination of the prewar army can be found in Cosmas, *An Army for Empire: The United States Army in the Spanish-American War* (Columbia: University of Missouri Press, 1971; reprint, White Mane Publishing, 1994), 1–80. "Mob" quoted from Gilsom Willets, *The Triumph of Yankee Doodle* (publisher and date unknown), 24, CHCH Archives, misc. Span-Am Box; see also Stephen Ambrose, *Upton and the Army* (Baton Rouge: Louisiana State University

Press, 1964; paperback, 1994), 113–35. The "efficiency" quote from R. Williams, "Army Organization in the United States," *The Galaxy: A Magazine of Entertaining Reading* 24, no. 5 (November 1877): 594, APS Online.

15. Quoted in Dierks, *A Leap to Arms*, 42; part of the problem was a provision in the watered-down Hull bill that allowed states to send existing guard units into the federal service intact and under their own field officers. This led many states to accept poorly prepared volunteers into under-strength units in order to qualify them for active duty. A second call for 75,000 troops in May was necessary to allow these units to be filled, in spite of the lack of guns, uniforms, and other equipment at all levels; Cosmas, "Military Policy, 1898," 114–21; idem, *An Army for Empire*, 91–94; Peter DeMontravel, *A Hero to His Fighting Men: Nelson A. Miles, 1839–1925* (Kent, Ohio: Kent State University Press, 1998), 232–34.

16. Chapman, "Army Life at Camp Thomas," 635; Sauers, "From Hallowed Ground to Training Ground," 129–30; Ed Tinney, "Chickamauga Battlefield Military Occupation—1898," undated manuscript, Fort Oglethorpe-Camp Thomas Box (misc. Span-Am), 6, CHCH Archives; Paige and Greene, *Administrative History*, adhi6:1.

17. Tinney, "Military Occupation," 6, CHCH; Sauers, "Hallowed Ground to Training Ground", 129–30; the name was approved by the War Department on April 24 at the same time that the troops under Brooke's command were designated as a temporary corps, consisting of one infantry division and a brigade of light artillery; Chapman, *Army Life at Camp Thomas*, 636.

18. Chapman, "Army Life at Camp Thomas," 637–39; Lytle Station and Lytle Hill were named for Brig. Gen. William Lytle, a respected commander and renowned poet from Cincinnati, who was killed on 20 September, Cozzens, *This Terrible Sound*, 385–89; "The Late General Lytle," *Harper's Weekly*, 14 November 1863, H<www.harpweek.com>; Roy Morris Jr., "September 1863: Death of a Warrior Poet," *1863: High Tide*, 73–80.

19. *Knoxville Tribune*, 23 and 24 April 1898. The *Tribune* on 28 April reported that the last unit, the 16th U.S. Infantry, was expected "tomorrow night."

20. The headline "Orders to Stab the Soldiers" announced the vaccination policy; *Knoxville Tribune*, 28 April 1898; Willets, *Triumph of Yankee Doodle*, 22–25, 27; Boynton's "success" statement quoted in Sauers, "Hallowed Ground to Training Ground," 130.

21. The "finely officered" quote from T. G. Steward, *The Colored Regulars in the United States Army* (Philadelphia: A. M. E. Book Concern, 1904; reprint series, The American Negro: His History and Literature, New York: Arno Press, 1969), 91–101; "Dixie" quote from *Knoxville Tribune*, 15 April 1898. According to the newspaper report, Boynton wanted to name it "Camp Rosecrans," but the 25th's colonel was "obdurate" about keeping it "Camp Boynton." As noted previously, Camp Thomas became the official name assigned by the War Department after 24 April. Quote, "fine drilled . . ." from *Knoxville Tribune*, 17 April 1898.

22. Sauers, "Hallowed Ground to Training Ground," 130; "Negro Troopers in Drunken Frenzy Nearly Provoke a Riot," *Chattanooga Times*, 24 November 1898, clipping file, Folder 1, Chattanooga-Hamilton County Bicentennial Library (CHCBL); *Knoxville Tribune*, 27 April 1898, reported that 50,000 people had visited the camp on the previous day; Chapman, "Army Life at Camp Thomas, 637–38; the historian for the 10th Cavalry does not mention this incident, Hershel V. Cashin, *Under Fire with the 10th U.S. Cavalry* (New York: F. Tennyson Neely, 1899; reprint, New York: Arno Press, 1969), 57–62; a version of the "riot" story appears in Willets, *Triumph of Yankee Doodle*, who claims that "a howling band of colored troopers at the point of pistols took forcible possession of the Black Maria in Chattanooga, because the police were arresting a wench," 26.

23. Stewart, *Colored Regulars*, 97, 100; Willets, *Triumph of Yankee Doodle*, 26.

24. *Knoxville Tribune*, 21 April, 24 April, 3 May 1898; Willets, *Triumph of Yankee Doodle*, 27.

25. Stewart, *The Colored Regulars*, 98,100; Willets, *Triumph of Yankee Doodle*, 11–12; interestingly, the first section of Willets's book contains what is most likely an apocryphal story of a little black girl, the granddaughter of a park caretaker, who becomes the "mascot" of the camp. After she is saved from being trampled in a cavalry charge during a mock battle by a soldier of the 10th U.S., General Brooke allegedly refers to her as "the finest pickanniny in all Georgia," 11–19.

26. *Knoxville Tribune*, 15 April, 28 April, 23 April 1898; Willets, *Triumph of Yankee Doodle*, 24–25.

27. *Knoxville Tribune*, 27 April 1898; although there was no serious illness, members of the 24th Infantry "suffered very much from the excessive heat which they had not been exposed to" while previously stationed on the northwestern frontier; Cashin, *Under Fire*, 121.

9. "IT IS TERRIBLE THAT MAN IS SUCH A BRUTE"

1. DeMontravel, *A Hero to His Fighting Men*, 234; Nelson Miles, *Serving the Republic: Memoirs of the Civil War and Military Life* (New York: Harper and Brothers, 1911), 268–73; although no one doubted that they would sign up, local recruits from eastern Tennessee expressed the concern that "when they enlist it will be in the U.S. Army and they will have Army officers put over them," *Knoxville Tribune*, 16 April, 29 April 1898. If Miles really had had his druthers, the volunteer forces would have been a nonfactor; at the very least, the original plan required volunteer units to remain in local camps until they had been issued all their equipment; Cosmas, *Army for Empire*, 90–101. Secretary Alger defended the decision to muster the volunteers and send them to the large camps in order to better supply them, mix them with Regulars and volunteers with other regions, train them in large-scale drill, and get them away from local influences "that tended to retard military discipline"; R. A. Alger, *The Spanish-American War* (New York: Harper and Brothers, 1901), 24–26. See also Ronald J. Barr, *The Progressive Army: US Army Command and Administration, 1870–1914* (New York: St. Martin's Press, 1998), 16–35; Freidel, *Splendid Little War*, 33–34.

2. War Department language quoted in Walker, *Boys of '98*. Ironically, only the 1st U.S. saw actual combat. The other two regiments—the "Rocky Mountain Riders" (2nd) and "Grigsby's Cowboys" (3rd) never got out of training camp. Walker erroneously makes a distinction between "Camp Thomas, Georgia and Chickamauga Park, Tennessee" in describing the locations of those regiments' training and drill, 85–86. Quoted in Theodore Roosevelt, *The Rough Riders* (New York: Scribner's, 1899; republished as part of the Modern Library War Series, New York: Random House, 1996), 11, 13, and 21; other accounts of Roosevelt's military career can be found in Brands, *T.R.*, 323–63 and Edmund Morris, *The Rise of Theodore Roosevelt* (New York: Coward, McCann, & Geoghegan, 1979), 615–61; for a more critical view of his time in the army, see Peggy and Harold Samuels, *Teddy Roosevelt at San Juan: The Making of a President* (College Station: Texas A&M University Press, 1997); Roosevelt's insistence that his troops were equal to Regulars and his high-profile exploits in Cuba led one veteran of the 5th U.S. Cavalry to admit that "relations between Volunteers and Regulars were rather strained" because "the press lavished so much praise on the Volunteer and little or none on the Regular." As far as many Regulars were concerned, the volunteers were seen as "usurpers"; William H. Oliver, *Roughing It with the Regulars* (New York: William F. Parr, Printers, 1901), 67.

3. *Knoxville Tribune*, 16 May 1898; The 1st SC arrived later, on 7 June, the 1st GA on

17 June, and the 1st PA on 29 August; the arrival dates of the 14th Minnesota, 9th NY, and 2nd Arkansas are listed as "unknown" by this source; Tinney, "Chickamauga Occupation," 2–6. After waffling back and forth, both the National Guard and Regular Army infantry regiments adopted the three-battalion, twelve-company formats; Cosmas, *Army for Empire*, 100. Eventually, Maj. Gen. James Wade assumed command of the III Corps; Paige and Greene, *Administrative History*, adhi6: 2. According to orders issued on 15 May, a total of three corps—almost half the volunteers mustered—were to be mobilized at Camp Thomas; Sauers, "Hallowed Ground to Training Ground," 131; note that one of the three corps, the VI, never came together; Alger, *The Spanish-American War*, 25. At some point late in May, Gen. Joe Wheeler passed through Camp Thomas on his way to Tampa; Dyer, *Shiloh to San Juan*, 220.

4. *Knoxville Tribune*, camp location quote, 10 May 1898; "finer set" quote, 17 May 1898; 9th PA quoted in Sauers, "Hallowed Ground to Training Ground," 132. Tinney, "Military Occupation," gives a detailed description of regimental strengths and camp locations in relation to present-day park monuments and facilities, 2–8. William Hugh Mitchell, "Spanish-American War Journal, May—December, 1898, Company E, 1st New Hampshire Volunteer Regiment," transcribed by William E. Clark, 12, Misc. Span-Am, 1898 Box, CHCH Archives (hereafter cited as Mitchell, "Journal," CHCH).

5. Quoted in Richard Sauers, *Pennsylvania in the Spanish-American War: A Commemorative Look Back* (Harrisburg, Pa.: Capitol Preservation Committee, 1998), 14; "Duffy Heard From," in an unknown newspaper clipping dated 6 June 1898, E. E. Wands, 52nd Iowa, Spanish-American War survey file 1320, USAMHI Archives; "fresh" quote from *Knoxville Tribune*, 20 May 1898; "drunk" quote from Paul Dewitz to Dear Papa, 23 June 1898, unknown regiment, typescript translated from the original German, Spanish-American War survey file 213, USAMHI Archives. The Spanish-American War survey, or more formally the "Spanish-American War, Philippine Insurrection, and Boxer Rebellion Veterans Research Project," was conducted by the USAMHI in the late 1960s and early 1970s in an attempt to gather information from the war's remaining veterans. The survey consisted of a standardized "Army Services Experience Questionnaire" that covered a variety of topics and invited the respondent to elaborate beyond the simplest answers. Not all sent back the questionnaires, but many veterans or their relatives supplied additional material that makes up many of the collection's files. In addition to being numbered, the files are grouped by state, then by regiment (if known), then by the individuals within each particular unit.

6. *Knoxville Tribune*, 20, 21, and 22 May 1898; Mitchell, "Journal," 13, CHCH.

7. *Knoxville Tribune*, 16 May 1898; letter from Okey Dillon to Mother, 16 May 1898, "Letters, 1st O.V.C.," Misc. Span-Am Box, Ft. Oglethorpe and Camp Thomas Folder, CHCH Archives; Sauers, "Hallowed Ground to Training Ground," 132; the experiences of the 52nd Iowa are recounted in a series of wartime newspaper clippings published in 1938 as *Camp Life of Company K, Spanish American War 1898: A Souvenir Book Compliments of L. H. Mayne, Emmetsburg*, and reproduced as "A Gift from Tim Laros to People of Palo Alto County," transcribed by Cathy Labath for the *Palo Alto Co., Iowa USGenWeb Project*, <http://www.celticcousins.net/paloalto/kcamplife.htm>, 10 (hereafter cited as Mayne, *Camp Life of Company K*).

8. Chapman, "Army Life at Camp Thomas," 640; both Sauers and Chapman repeat the story of the 3rd U.S. patrolling its camp with wooden clubs for several weeks before the men were issued weapons; clothes and drill quote from Vermont Adjutant and Inspector General's Office, *Vermont in the Spanish-American War* (Montpelier, Vt.: General Assembly, 1929), 39; Sauers, *Pennsylvania in the Spanish-American War*, 14–19.

9. In spite of the early shortages, the secretary proudly listed the massive amounts of all types of material on hand near the end of the war; Alger, *The Spanish-American War*, 24–25; Cosmas, *Army for Empire*, 4–5, 148–57; Sauers, "Hallowed Ground to Training Ground," 137; although Cosmas points out that only Regulars and "connected" volunteers like the Rough Riders were issued the Krag weapons, Roosevelt complained that the Spanish use of smokeless powder and the American troops' lack of similar ammunition gave the enemy a huge advantage in battle, Roosevelt, *Rough Riders*, 51, 54; Teddy also managed to get his men khaki uniforms, noting in a letter to his family that "most of them are in blue, but our rough riders are in brown," H. W. Brand, *The Selected Letters of Theodore Roosevelt* (New York: Cooper Square Press, 2001), 185.

10. Chapman, "Army Life at Camp Thomas," 640–41; quoted in Sauers, "Hallowed Ground to Training Ground," 133–34; Dillon to Mother, 22 May 1898, CHCH Archives.

11. Phrase underlined in typed transcript, Dillon to Mother, 22 May 1898, CHCH Archives; complaint in Howard Schoonover survey questionnaire, Schoonover file, 52nd Iowa, Spanish-American War survey folder 217, USAMHI Archives; trouser quote from Paul Dewitz to Dear Papa, 30 June 1898, USAMHI.

12. "Duffy Heard From," newspaper clipping, 6 June 1898, USMHI. The term "brownies" seems to have been widely used, and appears frequently on stationery and envelopes from Camp Thomas with the phrase, "Where stood our Heroes in Blue and Gray, now stand our Brownies equipped for the fray," Chas to Dear Winsors, 28 May 1898, Charles Remington Papers, 3rd Wisconsin, Spanish-American War survey folder 1048, USAMHI Archives; the first officer to appear in camp in a khaki uniform was called "the yellow kid" by the soldiers; Emanuel Rossiter, *"Right Forward, Four's Right": The Little Story of "Company I" Third Wisconsin Volunteers* (n.p., n.d.), photocopy in Rossiter file, Misc. Span-Am Box, Chickamauga Chattanooga National Military Park Archives (hereafter cited as Rossiter, *Story of Company I*, CHCH); E. A. Marshall to Band Master, 160th Indiana, James Swihart, 160th Indiana folder, Spanish-American War survey 182, USAMHI Archives.

13. Chapman, "Army Life at Camp Thomas," including Boynton quote, 643; Sauers, "From Hallowed Ground to Training Ground," 134–35; "fresh" quote from Chas to Dear Folks, 1 June 1898, Remington Papers, USAMHI; "fried potatoes" quote in Dillon to Dear Folks, 22 May 1898, CHCH; "hamburg" quote in William Kimmel Diary, 31st Michigan, Spanish-American survey file 789, USAMHI; "bad food" in Dewitz to Papa, 30 June 1898; "sickened" quote in Mitchell, "Journal," 14, 16, CHCH.

14. Sauers, "From Hallowed Ground to Training Ground," 134; Chapman, "Army Life at Camp Thomas," 64–142; water system description in H. L. Burbank, 52nd Iowa, Spanish-American War survey questionnaire, USAMHI; Remington described guarding a water hydrant "a snap" in Chas to Dear Folks, 11 June 1898, and reported having a "delightful time" taking in the extra food and treats at the spring in a letter to them on 19 June 1898, USAMHI.

15. Sauers, *Pennsylvania in the Spanish-American War*, 15.

16. Ibid., 16; Mitchell, "Journal" 14, CHCH; Kimmel Diary, 2 July 1898, USAMHI.

17. Six-shooter quote in D. Dillon to Dear Mother, 17 June 1898, CHCH; Earle Clock diary, 52nd Iowa, Spanish-American War survey 1812, USAMHI Archives; Clock's diary is a typed, photocopied transcript that includes some newspaper clippings and other transcribed material. Some of the dates have been cut off the left margin, so I will use the transcript's page numbers to cite the location of items from his source. The eight-mile distance from the park is also mentioned in the Kimmel Diary, 10 July 1898, USAMHI; bad shooting described in "Duffy's Letter," unknown paper, dated 31 July 1898, E. E. Wands, 52nd Iowa, USAMHI; evidence of the location of target ranges appeared during the 1992

archaeological study of the Union retreat route, when metal detectors discovered large numbers of .45-70 caliber bullets "confined to one hill location"; Cornelison, "The Archaeology of Retreat," *Archaeological Perspectives,* 296.

18. Review described in Chas to Dear Folks, 11 June 1898, USAMHI; Rossiter, *Story of Company I,* CHCH.

19. Mock battles described in Chapman, "Army Life at Camp Thomas," 648; Sauers, "Hallowed Ground to Training Ground," 138; idem, *Pennsylvania in the Spanish-American War,* 16; *Knoxville Tribune,* 26 May 1898; melee and saber quote from Charles E. Creager, *The Fourteenth Ohio National Guard—The Fourth Ohio Volunteer Infantry* (Columbus, Ohio: Landon Printing and Publishing, 1899), 106–8; quail story in Rossiter, "Company I," CHCH; rules of engagement in Paige and Green, *Administrative History,* adhi6:2. It is striking to note the similarities between these mock battles and the Civil War reenactments that I have participated in over the years, including the accidents caused by close combat and over-exuberance on the part of the participants.

20. Marion Franklin Ham, *The Army Mule: A Chronic Kicker, Camp Thomas, July 4th, 1898* (Marion F. Ham, 1898); Sauers, *Pennsylvania in the Spanish-American War,* 16; Arbel C. Cantley, "Pack Service in the United States Army," *A Weekly Newsmagazine* 27, no. 6 (September 1898): 591, APS Online; Rossiter, *Story of Company I,* CHCH; "wonderful" quote in Mitchell, "Journal," 22, CHCH; bayonet quote in Clock Diary, 2, USAMHI.

21. Mitchell, "Journal," CHCH, 17, 18; Rossiter, *Story of Company I,* CHCH; Sauers, "Hallowed Ground to Training Ground," 137; members of the 52nd Iowa on a blackberry picking expedition encountered a farmer who threatened to shoot them because he had been previously raided and robbed; Mayne, *Camp Life of Company K,* 16.

22. Chapman, "Army Life at Camp Thomas," 647; Rossiter, *Story of Company I,* CHCH; Creager, *Fourth Ohio,* 103; Mitchell, "Journal," 17, CHCH; references to Civil War veterans and their recollections appear several times in Mayne, *Camp Life of Company K,* 12, 16.

23. Creager, *Fourth Ohio,* 102; "Duffy Heard From," 6 June 1898, Wands survey file, USAMHI; "heavy rain" in Rossiter, *Story of Company I,* CHCH; cannonball quote Kimmel Diary, 10 July 1898, USAMHI; O. D. Dillon to Dear Mother, 22 May 1898, CHCH; Corporal Clock and his comrades in the 52nd Iowa also found relics, Clock Diary, 2, USAMHI.

24. Rossiter, *Story of Company I,* CHCH; the exact identification of the monuments in the photographs was provided in a "Memorandum from Mark Barnes, Archaeologist to James Ogden, Historian, 10 February 1998: 3rd Wisconsin Span-Am Images" in the Rossiter File, 3rd Wisconsin, Misc. Span-Am Box, 1898, CHCH Archives; A. W. Sidebottom, *The "Boys" in Camp Thomas, Chickamauga-Chattanooga National Military Park, Georgia* (Chattanooga, Tenn.: Sidebottom & Kerr, 1898); see also Stan Cohen, *Images of the Spanish-American War, April—August, 1898* (Missoula, Mont.: Pictorial Histories Publishing, 1997), 140–47.

25. Chapman, "Army Life at Camp Thomas," 647; Ernest Eugene Wands, "Response to the Toast 'Lo the Poor Rookie,' October 30, 1899," in E. E. Wands file, 52nd Iowa, Spanish-American War survey 1320, USAMHI Archives; Wands gave a preview of his "rookie" material in a "Duffy Still on Earth" letter to his hometown paper, 27 June 1898, where he included "you'll make a good looking corpse" to his list of not-so-welcoming phrases; reference to the harassment of rookies also in Mayne, *Camp Life of Company K,* 15–16.

26. Wands, "Lo the Poor Rookie," USAMHI; a list of transgressions and jobs can be found in a letter from the 1st Vermont dated 13 June in "War History in Private Letters: A New Recruit to a Veteran," *Outlook* 59, no. 16 (30 August 1898): 968, APS Online; Creager, *Fourth Ohio,* 109; letter from 1st Illinois Cavalry in "War History in Private Letters," *Outlook* 59, no. 15 (13 August 1898), 919, APS Online; Corporal Clock got poison ivy on two separate occasions in June and July, Clock Diary, 2, 4.

27. "Church" and "fat and lazy" quoted in Kimmel Diary, 9 July 1898, USAMHI; "Religious Work in Military Camps," *Christian Advocate* 73, no. 26 (30 June 1898): 1048, APS Online; "Emergency in the Army Camp," *New York Observer and Chronicle* 76, no. 26 (30 June 1898): 911, APS Online; "The Revival in the Army Camps," *Christian Advocate* 73, no. 29 (21 July 1898): 1198, APS Online; the "walk," "kind," and "cigar" quotes from Henry Malone to Jacob Best, 15 and 17 July 1898, Henry Malone Letters, Fort Oglethorpe [Camp Thomas] 1898 folder, Chattanooga Regional History Museum Archives (CRHMA), Chattanooga, Tenn.; the popularity of the YMCA canteen is noted in Mayne, *Camp Life of Company K*, 13–14.

28. In addition to dogs and the goat, the writer wondered if the "grey-backs" (lice) that some of the boys had accumulated could be considered "pets" rather than pests; "Duffy Still on Earth," letter to unknown newspaper, 27 June 1898, E. E. Wards, 52nd Iowa, USAMHI. It seems unlikely that the same unit would have two such mascots. Rossiter's story of Rastus in "Company I" is pretty vague; the story of Frank appears in Evander Noble's Spanish-American War survey questionnaire, USAMHI, and while written many years after the fact, contains enough details to make it credible. Rastus and Frank may very well have been the same person recalled differently in two postwar accounts.

29. Rossiter, *Story of Company I*, CHCH; Noble survey questionnaire, USAMHI; Mitchell, "Journal," 22, CHCH.

30. Quotes from Rossiter, *Story of Company I, CHCH*; Creager, *Fourth Ohio*, 104; the writer suspects the company cook quit performing that task so he could maintain his letter writing to the girls, Mayne, *Camp Life of Company K*, 15.

31. Maj. Louis Livingston Seaman, "Why the Army Canteen Should Be Restored," *The North American Review* 176, no. 44 (January 1903): 80, APS Online; Rossiter, "Company I"; Chas (Remington) to Dear Folks, 11 June 1898, USAMHI; Noble survey questionnaire, USAMHI; Schoonover survey questionnaire, 52nd Iowa, UASMHI; Creager, *Fourth Ohio*, 102. A member of the 52nd Iowa reported that the beer at the Maine canteen was "stale and hot" so when the YMCA tent opened, the men shifted their business to it—in spite of its lack of beer—and created a "sort of rivalry" between the two establishments, Mayne, *Camp Life of Company K*, 14.

32. The legitimate attractions of the Midway are described in Creager, *Fourth Ohio*, 98, 102; Chapman, "Army Life at Camp Thomas," 643.

33. Creager, *Fourth Ohio*, 102; Sauers, "Hallowed Ground to Training Ground," 135; long quote from Mitchell, "Journal," 23, CHCH; beer delivery noted in Noble survey questionnaire, USAMHI.

34. Clock Diary, 2, USAMHI; during this trip, Mitchell and his comrades "did justice" to a thirty-five-cent dinner consisting of "chicken soup, beef, chicken, lamb, beef's tongue, new potatoes, tomatoes, cucumbers, beans, corn, turnips, two kinds of pie, two of pudding, ice cream, bananas, oranges, watermelon, corn cake, bread, buttermilk, iced tea, coffee, and milk," and the corporal observed that the meal they had "was surely a seventy-five-cent dinner as prices are in New England"; Mitchell, "Journal," 19, CHCH; AWOL story in Rossiter, *Story of Company I*, CHCH.

35. *Knoxville Tribune*, 23 May 1898; Sauers, "Hallowed Ground to Training Ground," 137; Chapman, "Army Life at Camp Thomas," 644; a few men sold their chance to get passes in a company drawing for fifty cents; Mayne, *Story of Company K*, 11.

10. "WHAT THEY WILL DO WITH US NOW IS A MYSTERY"

1. Freidel, *Splendid Little War,* 88–291, quote, 193; the contrast between Shafter's gloomy assessment of the situation following the land battle and the results of the shocking naval victory on 3 July are particularly noted in Musicant, *Empire by Default,* 351–466; Cosmas, *Army for Empire,* 202–26.

2. *Knoxville Journal & Tribune,* 3 July, 5 July 1898. The paper noted that many southern cities celebrated the 4 July holiday in "grand style" for the first time in many years. I can find no explanation for the paper's name change, which seemed to coincide with the beginning of July.

3. Clock "Diary," 4, USAMHI; Mitchell, "Journal," 23, CHCH.

4. Cosmas, *Army for Empire,* 222–24; Alger, *The Spanish-American War,* 298–303; *Knoxville Journal & Tribune,* 5 July 1898. According to the papers, the regiments slated to go were the 2nd and 3rd Wisconsin, 16th and 4th Pennsylvania, 4th Ohio, and 3rd Illinois; as the papers noted, all were part of the 1st Division, but were not all in the same brigades within the division; Sauers, *Pennsylvania in the Spanish-American War,* 19–20n; this delay was most likely the result of the change in policies regarding the ports of departure, since the original order, issued on 26 June, specified that all forces would rendezvous in Tampa for the expedition. In his *Story of Company I,* CHCH, Private Rossiter of the 3rd Wisconsin cites 5 July as the departure date from camp, "after many heartbreaking recalls," a date confirmed in Walter Reed, Victor C. Vaughn, and Edward O. Shakespeare, *Report of the Spread of Typhoid Fever in U.S. Military Camps during the Spanish War of 1898,* vol. I (Washington, D.C.: Government Printing Office, 1904), 16 (hereafter cited as Reed, *Typhoid Fever Report*).

5. Since it took nearly a week to finalize negotiations with the Spanish at Santiago prior to the official surrender on 17 July, rumors and reports of its impending fall reached the camp in bits and pieces, Freidel, *Splendid Little War,* 253–59; Creager, *History of the Fourth Ohio,* 110–11; Reed, *Typhoid Fever Report* cites 22 July as the departure date for regiments in the 2nd Brigade, including the 4th Ohio, 22.

6. There is some confusion among historians of the camp regarding the departure times of troops prior to the July call-up. In Sauers, "Hallowed Ground to Training Ground," 138, 142–43n, he reports that "on May 30, four regiments—3rd Pennsylvania, 157th Indiana, 1st Ohio, and 1st Illinois—boarded trains and headed for Tampa and the expedition assigned to attack Cuba." He cites his own *Pennsylvania in the Spanish-American War,* 18, 20n, in the article's endnotes; however, in that book, he gives 2 June as the date that these units departed. In both cases, the primary source seems to be General Brooke's report in *Annual Report of the Major-General Commanding the Army to the Secretary of War, 1898* (Washington, D.C.: Government Printing Office, 1898), 138; the matter is further complicated because he shortens this citation to "Brooke's Report" in the Camp Thomas article and "1898 Report" in his book, and provides no page number in the book's endnote (which may be an unfortunate editorial error, since a comma dutifully follows the shortened title). Charles Remington of the 31st Michigan wrote in a letter to his "folks" dated June 1 that "several regiments are moving out of here today," which confirms Sauers's report; Remington file, USAMHI. Chapman's article predates both of Sauers's publications and is cited heavily in both, but he makes no reference to the late-May, early-June departure of any troops from the camp; "Army Life at Camp Thomas," 649; a report in the *Knoxville Journal & Tribune,* 14 July 1898, has the 1st Ohio departing for Ringgold (Georgia) "in a downpour of rain" on that date. This is certainly a misidentification of the unit, but does

not fit the departure time for the 4th Ohio, either. Further clarification is provided in Reed, *Typhoid Fever Report,* which states that the 1st Ohio arrived at Camp Thomas on 17 May and left on 2 June; the 157th Indiana was only there "for a few days," and arrived in Tampa on 1 June. The 3rd Pennsylvania shipped out from Camp Thomas at the same time and arrived in Tampa on 4 June, where it remained as part of the IV Corps until being moved to Fernandina, Florida, then to Huntsville, Alabama, where it remained until discharged; "Pennsylvania Volunteers in the Spanish-American War, 1898–1899: Third Regiment Soldiers & History," <http://www.paspanishamericanwar.com/thirdregiment>. Oddly, the 1st Illinois is not among the regiments included in Reed's study, which seemed to cover virtually every unit mobilized for the war, 484–91; however, there is a brief reference to the 1st Illinois as a combat unit engaged at San Juan Hill in Cosmas, *Army for Empire,* 147, and an essay on their experiences in Cuba in G. C. Hagerty, "With the First Illinois," *The Chicago Record's War Stories by Staff Correspondents in the Field* (Chicago Record, 1898), 198–201.

7. *Knoxville Journal & Tribune,* 24, 26 July 1898; Sauers, *Pennsylvania in the Spanish-American War,* 19–20n; Chapman, "Army Life at Camp Thomas," 649–50.

8. According to Rossiter, the brigade was originally slated to reinforce the army at Santiago, but fears of yellow fever caused the layover and shifted their mission to Puerto Rico, *Story of Company I,* CHCH; "goat milk" quote in Noble survey questionnaire, US-AMHI; Freidel, *Splendid Little War,* 265; Reed, *Typhoid Fever Report,* confirms a significant number of sick from typhoid, malaria, and "undetermined fevers" after the regiment's arrival in Puerto Rico, 16; James Harrison Wilson, *Under the Old Flag: Recollections of Military Operations in the War for the Union, the Spanish War, the Boxer Rebellion, etc.* 2 vols. (New York: D. Appleton and Company, 1912), 2: 424–59; interestingly, Wilson noted that while they were welcomed as liberators in Puerto Rico, the former rebels of Charleston "were slow to respond" to the presence of "hirelings of a hated government." Although they eventually warmed to one another, he pointed out that "the two weeks of our occupation of Charleston were really the only period in the history of the town when a United States force strong enough to hold it was concentrated in its borders," 259.

9. Creager, *History of the Fourth Ohio,* 112–239, quote, 163; the 4th played an key role in the fighting, losing five wounded in action and two "prostrated by heat." A planned all-out attack on the Spanish defenses did not take place because of the ceasefire, Musicant, *Army for Empire,* 533–40; Freidel, *Splendid Little War,* 271–77.

10. He and his friend Charlie Carr "put in an application for the Hospital Corps" on 27 June and were transferred on 3 July. While they escaped the typhoid epidemic that killed thirty-two members of their old regiment, they had to remain in the service much longer. The rest of the 1st New Hampshire left Camp Thomas on 26 August and ended up in Lexington, Kentucky, before returning home to be discharged in September, Mitchell, "Journal," 22, 40–41, CHCH; Reed, *Typhoid Fever Report,* 158; Mitchell's complaints of chaos and mismanagement echo Teddy Roosevelt's vivid description of the situation at Tampa prior to the Cuban invasion, Brand, *Letters of T.R.,* 185–90.

11. *Knoxville Journal & Tribune,* 12, 16, and 26 July 1898; Musicant, *Empire by Default,* 539–40; the 6th U.S. was one of the regiments designated by the War Department as "Immunes," due to their southern origins and conditioning that would supposedly make them less vulnerable to tropical diseases; Cosmas, *Army for Empire,* 127, 266; Camp Bob Taylor was named for the governor of Tennessee; Camp Wilder was eventually renamed Camp Poland in honor of a local officer who died at Camp Thomas, and was used by regiments escaping the typhoid problem at Chickamauga; William Rule, *Standard History of Knoxville, Tennessee* (Chicago: Lewis Publishing Co., 1900), 188–92.

12. Cosmas, *Army for Empire*, 269; the 4th and 6th U.S infantries ended up as occupation forces in Cuba and Puerto Rico due to their supposed "immune" status. They remained for several months after the state volunteers stationed mustered out, returning in March 1899; Rule, *History of Knoxville*, 189–92.

13. Roosevelt had feared that the men would "die like sheep" from diseases if the start of the war was delayed until summer; Thomas, *War Lovers*, 220.

14. Clock Diary, 3, USAMHI; Mitchell, "Journal," 14–15, CHCH; Kimmel Diary, 3 July 1898, USAMHI; Mayne, *Camp Life of Company K*, 13–16; John McG. Woodbury, "The Advantages of the Camp at Chickamauga—Hard Work for the Recruits—Remarkable Health of the Troops," *Medical News* 73, no. 2 (9 July 1898): 45, APS Online.

15. *Knoxville Tribune*, 30 May 1898; the two pneumonia deaths were members of the 14th Minnesota and 8th Massachusetts infantry regiments; *Knoxville Journal & Tribune*, 18 July 1898; the drowning deaths were mentioned in Mayne, *Camp Life of Company K*, 12; the moonshine was made of "alcohol, wood ashes, pepper, and a few other ingredients," *Knoxville Journal & Tribune*, 20 July 1898.

16. "Another letter from Duffy," clipping from unknown paper, 3 May 1898, E. E. Wands, 52nd Iowa, Spanish-American Survey, USAMHI; the 52nd's Company K did better—only six out of seventy-six failed—but he confirms the efforts on the part of some officers to conform to regulations by drinking water; Mayne, *Camp Life of Company K*, 4–6; Clock Diary, 2–3, USAMHI; *Knoxville Tribune*, 19 May 1898; an opposing view from the surgeon of the 1st Ohio Cavalry regarding the physicals stated, "many men were allowed to enlist who did not physically comply with the requirements," and claimed that "men who were underweight, some with deformed feet, and some with hernia were accepted," is found in Reed, *Typhoid Fever Report*, 274; a total of 14,764 men were rejected due to various deficiencies, the most common among white troops were eye problems and "imperfect physique"; Vincent Cirillo, *Bullets and Bacilli: The Spanish-American War and Military Medicine* (Brunswick, N.J.: Rutgers University Press, 2004), 11.

17. Rossiter, *Story of Company I*, CHCH; Clock Diary (16 June), 3; "Lo, the Poor Rookie," 3, Wands, 52nd Iowa, USAMHI; some annoying side effects from the inoculations lingered for several days among men in the Iowa regiment and a few actually fainted during the vaccination procedure; Mayne, *Camp Life in Company K*, 13–15; Woodbury, "The Advantages of the Camp," 47.

18. The first statement under the heading "General Statements and Conclusions" in Reed's 700 page *Typhoid Fever Report* reads: "During the Spanish war of 1898, every regiment constituting the First, Second, Third, Fourth, Fifth, and Seventh Army Corps developed typhoid fever." This alone gives an indication of the vast extent of the problem and the intensity of feeling and memory that accompanied it, 666; this statement and a more concise summary of the medical board's findings can be found in Walter Reed, Victor C. Vaughn, and Edward O. Shakespeare, *Abstract of Report on the Origin and Spread of Typhoid Fever in U.S. Military Camps during the Spanish War of 1898* (Washington, D.C.: Government Printing Office, 1900), 167 (hereafter cited as Reed, *Abstract Report*).

11. "GROUND UNFIT FOR MEN TO LIVE ON"

1. Reed, *Typhoid Fever Report*, 675; Vincent J. Cirillo, "'The Patriotic Odor': Sanitation and Typhoid Fever in the National Encampments during the Spanish-American War," *Army History* 49, PB-20-00-2 (Spring 2000): 17–23; this source lists Camp Thomas deaths as 344 from typhoid out of 397 from all diseases in the I Corps and 417 out of

469 total deaths from disease in the III Corps; the same author cites the number of typhoid deaths among all troops (Regulars and volunteers both black and white) as 2,192 out of 2,595 total deaths from disease and compares this with the 224,586 Union deaths from disease in the Civil War, Cirillo, *Bullets and Bacilli*, 32–35; Cirillo's grand total of 866 Camp Thomas deaths is higher than the 752 cited in Chapman, "Army Life at Camp Thomas," 655, and more than twice the 425 figure given in Sauers, "Hallowed Ground to Training Ground," 138. An unpublished document in the CHCH archives lists "Deaths up to departure" and "Deaths to Dec. 2" for every unit in Camp Thomas. According to this list, there were 324 deaths in camp and 1,022 in all the units, but this clearly includes men who died after they left Camp Thomas either for the front or home; "Camp Thomas Troop Roster," Spanish-American War Records, Camp Thomas, Series IV-205#3204. Box 1, Folder 6, CHCH Archives (see Appendix B).

2. "The Fall of the Canteen," and Chaplain Howard Headernon, "The Army Canteen," both in *Christian Advocate* 74, no. 10 (9 March 1899): 364, 369, APS Online; To the editor of the Medical News from D. I. McMillan, M.D., "Correspondence—the Army Canteen," *Medical News* 78, no. 25 (22 June 1899): 997, APS Online.

3. "Revival in the Army Camps," *Christian Advocate* 73, no. 29 (21 June 1898): 1198, APS Online; Albert Gardner Robinson, "A Sunday at Camp Thomas," *Congregationalist* 83, no. 29 (9 June 1898): 838, APS Online; *Knoxville Journal & Tribune*, 13 July 1898; this soldier also stated that "when we had the canteen [drinking] was no problem . . . but when they went to Chattanooga it was more of a problem because they [the men] laid in an extra supply" of alcohol, Noble survey questionnaire, 3, 5, USAMHI; during the heated investigation that followed, even General Boynton was quoted as condemning the "canteen system" as a catalyst for the camp's problems; "Secular News: The War Investigation," *Christian Observer* 86, no. 42 (12 October 1898): 23, APS Online.

4. The "dirty fringe" quote is from Chapman, "Army Life at Camp Thomas," 137; "search" quote in Noble survey questionnaire, 4, USAMHI; "dumping" quote, Creager, *History of the Fourth Ohio*," 105; although written while still at camp in Iowa, the comments about desserts and other sweets reflected the common idea that it was necessary to "bring the men to a strict army diet before entering on active campaign"; Mayne, *Camp Life in Company K*, 4; milk comments in Remington to the Winsors, 29 May 1898, USAMHI; milk for hospitals in *American National Red Cross Relief Committee Reports, May 1898–March 1899* (New York: Knickerbocker Press, 1899), 219–21; the focus on milk was partly due to the fact that some past civilian outbreaks of typhoid had originated in the milk supply, Cirillo, *Bullets and Bacilli*, 65.

5. Quoted in "Secular News: The War Investigation," *Christian Observer* (12 October 1898), 23.

6. A summary of the camp's problems with dust and the water supply can be found in Paige and Greene, *Administrative History*, adhi6:1–3; the dry, dusty conditions and onset of regular rainfall in mid-June is mentioned in Mayne, *Camp Life of Company K*, 12–13.

7. This investigation was initiated in October 1898 and published because "it is thought that this collection of testimony may have historical value" and might lead to reforms "by which the military service of the country may be improved"; *Report of the Committee of the Massachusetts Reform Club Appointed to Collect Testimony in Relation to the Spanish-American War, 1898–1899* (Boston: George H. Ellis, Printer, 1899), 4, 1st NH quotes on 32–33 (hereafter cited as *Massachusetts Reform Report*); Corporal Mitchell was not the only soldier to have the "trots" within days of arriving. The early appearance of diarrhea in the regiment led Dr. Reed and his colleagues to suggest that "they may have been mild cases of typhoid fever" that came into camp with the men. Although thirty of

the thirty-two men from the 1st New Hampshire who died were victims of typhoid, the large numbers of men suffering bowel disorders throughout the regiment's stay did not translate into equally large numbers of typhoid cases, Reed, *Typhoid Fever Report*, 149–54.

8. The relatively low number of typhoid cases and only twenty-six deaths from all causes seems out of proportion to the level of bitterness expressed by Company B's Captain Frank L. Green in his "Foreword" to *Vermont in the Spanish-American War,* 5, which was published nearly thirty years after the fact; Reed, *Typhoid Fever Report,* 186–90; other Vermont quotes from the *Massachusetts Reform Report,* 36–42.

9. This incident took place on or around 13 June, prior to the rain that fell later in the week; Mayne, *Camp Life In Company K,* 11.

10. Reed, *Report Abstract,* 26; Boynton requested that the camp's water be tested in early August; a letter from the "analytical chemist" in Knoxville to a park commission clerk noted that "it is desirable that we receive the water as soon after it is collected as possible." J. W. Slocum to Hugh B. Rowland, 11 August 1898, "Routine Operations to 1900, Camp Thomas Correspondence, 1898," folder 10, Box 1, CHCH Archives.

11. Quoted from the "River of Death" letter, Wyckoff Spanish-American Survey file, 52nd Iowa, USAMHI.

12. The quote and the commission's "General Statements and Conclusions" can be found in Reed, *Typhoid Fever Report,* xviii, 656–76 and idem, *Abstract Report,* 9, 167–93; for information that appears in both, the Abstract will be cited, due to its easier accessibility; see also Victor C. Vaughn, "Conclusions Reached After a Study of Typhoid Fever Among American Soldiers in 1898," *Medical News* 76, no. 23 (9 June 1900): 907, APS Online; Chapman, "Army Life at Camp Thomas, 651–55.

13. A concise explanation of the discovery and behavior of the disease can be found in Cirillo, *Bullets and Bacilli,* 60–68; Reed, *Abstract Report,* 11, 168–73, 194–239; the quote about the pre-infected men specifically refers to regiments in the 1st Division, I Corps, which arrived in Camp Thomas between 15 and 17 May (the 1st and 3rd Kentucky were the exceptions, arriving 11 June and 2 July, respectively); a full list of all units, their muster dates, their arrival at the national camps, the time of first infections, and date that infections appeared can be found in the second set of page references above.

14. Cirillo, *Bullets and Bacilli,* 64–69.

15. George M. Sternberg, *Sanitary Lessons of the War* (Washington, D.C.: Adams Printing, 1912), 8–14; the surgeon general argued his case in idem, "General Sternberg's Answer to his Critics," *Medical News* 73, no. 11 (10 September 1898): 335, APS Online; and "Sanitary Lessons of the War," *Medical News* 74, no. 23, (10 June 1899): 721, APS Online.

16. The ideal procedures carried out by the Regulars are quoted from Charles F. Mason, "Camp Sanitation at Chickamauga Park, Georgia," *Medical News* 72, no. 20 (14 May 1898): 624, APS Online.

17. Quotes from the Vermont, New Hampshire, and Massachusetts testimonies are in *Massachusetts Reform Report,* 31–47.

18. Ibid. The long quote and comments on the effects of flooding are from Mayne, *Camp Life in Company K,* 13.

19. Reed, *Typhoid Fever Report,* 663, 666; this problem was clearly the result of the soldiers' carelessness. An example was the camp of the 3rd U.S. Cavalry, where "it was impossible to walk through the woods near camp without soiling one's feet with fecal matter"; Cirillo, *Bullets and Bacilli,* 76–77.

20. Chapman, "Army Life at Camp Thomas," 653–55; quoted in John McG. Woodbury, "A Newly Devised Camp Sink, or Latrine, for the Use of Permanent or Semi-permanent Camps," *Medical News* 73, no. 6 (6 August 1898): 170, APS Online.

21. Reed, *Typhoid Fever Report*, 250; "axiom" quote, 671

22. Comments on moving the camps, including the 1st Maine quote, are in *Massachusetts Reform Report*, 43, 46; the 1st Maine Andersonville reference appears in Chapman, "Army Life at Camp Thomas," 654; a similar comment comparing Camp Thomas to Andersonville was made by an officer in the 9th New York; Cirillo, *Bullets and Bacilli*, 81. This comparison must have been particularly painful to both Union and Confederate veterans. For the Union, there was the old claim that their government had left the prisoners there to die without working to exchange them; the Confederates, of course, bore the brunt of accusations that they deliberately abused and starved their charges; see William B. Hesseltine, "Introduction," in W. B. Hesseltine, ed., *Civil War Prisons* (Kent, Ohio: Kent State University Press, 1972), 5–8; and Byrne, "Prison Pens of Suffering," *Images of War* 4: 396–409; Benjamin Cloyd, *Haunted by Atrocity: Civil War Prisons in American Memory,* Making the Modern South, David Goldfield, series ed. (Baton Rouge: Louisiana State University Press, 2010).

23. The report also questioned the army's failure to use lime to counter the filth from the latrines; Reed, *Typhoid Fever Report*, 663–65.

24. Several officers repeated the idea that "soldiers should not be in camp in one place over six weeks at one time"; *Massachusetts Reform Report*, 43; Chapman, "Army Life at Camp Thomas," 652–53.

25. Although Boynton voiced suspicions of malingering in the 8th New York and accused them of having a camp "filthier and dirtier than can be found in the slums of New York," the Reed Commission surmised that "the number of malingerers must have been very small" among the men furloughed due to sickness; Chapman, "Army Life at Camp Thomas," 651–54; Reed, *Report Abstract*, 59; letter draft, Boynton to secretary of war, n.d., Camp Thomas Hospital Report, Series VI, Box 1, Folder 4, CHCH Archives; descriptions of regiments arriving from Camp Thomas in Rule, *History of Knoxville*, 189–92.

26. The community got its wish when several regiments arrived from Chickamauga at Camp Poland for rest and recuperation, Rule, *History of Knoxville*, 189–90; the paper reminded its readers several days later that Knoxville was free of disease and "an ideal place for a military camp," *Knoxville Journal & Tribune*, 12, 15 July 1898.

27. Reed, *Typhoid Fever Report*, 669–71.

28. *Massachusetts Reform Report*, 31–47; complaints about the detailing of regimental medical officers appeared in testimony from members of both the 1st New Hampshire and 1st Vermont. A surgeon from the 1st New Hampshire reported that "after leaving his regiment on July 1, [he] did no actual medical service, being occupied at the time in the ambulance corps." Walter Miller Warren, "Malaria in the Mobilization Camps During the Late War," *Medical News* 74, no. 22 (3 June 1899): 700, APS Online, reports that while on duty in the 2nd Division hospital at Chickamauga "I did not observe a single case of malaria, although typhoid raged rampant." He went on to observe that mosquitoes were almost nonexistent at Camp Thomas; correspondingly, the only cases of malaria he treated were in Knoxville, where three men had suffered extensive mosquito bites and came down with the disease. Dr. Vaughn wrote that "malaria was a rare disease among the troops that remained in the United States." Quotes regarding misdiagnosis from a summary of the Reed report in Vaughn, "Conclusions Reached after Typhoid Study," *Medical News*, 907.

29. Quotes regarding the quality of orderlies are from the *Massachusetts Reform Report*, 39–47.

30. Ibid.; the clearly horrified members of the medical board stated "it seems to us that a no more certain method for the dissemination of an infectious disease could hardly have been invented," Reed, *Typhoid Fever Report*, 666; Cirillo, *Bullets and Bacilli*, 86–88.

31. Cirillo, *Bullets and Bacilli,* 82–86.

32. "Responsibility for the Hospital Surgeons and Their Work" and "The Regimental Hospitals Restored at Camp Poland, Lexington, Ky.," in "Echoes and News: Brooklyn Eagle," *Medical News* 73, no. 14 (1 October 1898): 435, APS Online; Cosmas, *Army for Empire,* 272–73.

33. Cosmas, *Army for Empire,* 272–73; Cirillo, *Bullets and Bacilli,* 85–90; Chapman, "Army Life at Camp Thomas," 652–54; quotes regarding Ned and newspaper references to quality of care found in the Clock Diary, 5–6, USAMHI; letter "From Camp on the River of Death" Wyckoff survey file, USAMHI. The 52nd arrived on 31 May with 572 men and left with twice that many on 28 August; the regiment lost thirty-seven men, with all but one dying of typhoid fever, Reed, *Typhoid Fever Report,* 256–57.

34. Oscar Farrin Blood, "Co. E, 52nd Regiment Iowa Volunteer Infantry 1898 Spanish-American War Diary," Lane-Blood Genealogy, 8, 10–11, 13 (hereafter cited as Blood, "Diary") <http://freepages.genealogy.rootsweb.ancestry.com/~laneblood/spamwadiary.html>.

35. Sauers, "Hallowed Ground to Training Ground," 139–40; Cosmas, *Army for Empire,* 273; Cirillo, *Bullets and Bacilli,* 87–90; although twenty-two male hospital workers died of typhoid at Camp Thomas, only two of the twenty-three female nurses discharged due to illness suffered from typhoid fever, and none died; Reed, *Typhoid Fever Report,* 282–83; letter, "Report of the Local Branch, National Relief Commission at Chattanooga," n.d., Chattanooga Regional History Museum Archives (hereafter, National Relief Report, CRHM), Chattanooga, Tenn.; the case for using female nurses was led by Dr. Anita Newcomb McGee, who used the National DAR as a way to offer the services of her nurses to the surgeon general; Cindy Gurney, "Dr. Anita Newcomb McGee (1864–1940)—A Brief Biography," U.S. Army Medical Department Office of Medical History (July 2010), <http://history.amedd.army.mil/ANCWebsite/McGeeWHMSpecial/McGeeBriefBiography.html>.

36. *Red Cross Reports,* 221–24; the agent who made the report was stricken with typhoid fever in September and nursed back to health in Chattanooga by several Red Cross nurses and his wife. The author of the "National Relief" letter noted that "the Red Cross operated entirely through paid agents and nurses, while all our work is voluntarily given"; National Relief Report, CRHM.

37. Mercedes Graf, "Band of Angels: Sister Nurses in the Spanish-American War," *Prologue: The U.S. National Archives and Records Administration* 34, no. 3 (Fall 2002), <www.archives.gov/publications/prologue/2002/fall/band-of-angels-1.html> (accessed, 25 June 2010).

38. Cosmas, *Army for Empire,* 273–76; "Echoes and News: The Sternberg Hospital," *Medical News* 73, no. 22 (26 November 1898): 694, APS Online.

12. "ONE HUGE PEST HOUSE"

1. Cosmas, *Army for Empire,* 247–54; the surgeon who promoted the flawed theory on the causes of tropical diseases was Dr. Juan Guiteras, "a Cuban yellow fever expert" and professor of pathology at the University of Pennsylvania, Cirillo, *Bullets and Bacilli,* 12.

2. Cirillo, *Bullets and Bacilli,* 113; Espinosa, "The Threat from Havana," 541–68; University of Virginia Health System, Health Sciences Library, "Yellow Fever and the Reed Commission, 1898–1901: the Yellow Scourge in Cuba," exhibit, 25 February–28 April 1997, <http://www.hsl.virginia.edu/historical/medical_history/yellow_fever/>.

3. Quote from Cosmas, *Army for Empire,* 254; Cirillo, *Bullets and Bacilli,* 25–28; a biographical sketch "courtesy of the United States Army" can be found at "George Miller

Sternberg, Brigadier General, United States Army," *Arlington National Cemetery Website*, <http://www.arlingtoncemetery.net/gmsternb.htm>.

4. Oliver O. Edwards, "The Sanitary Service in the War," Department of Military Art, Army Staff College Service Schools, 25 May 1911, original papers, 1910–1911, USAMHI Archives; there are two sets of page numbers on this document: a typed sequence, 245–75, and a handwritten one, 2–32, thus the citation 248/5; Cosmas, *Army for Empire*, 247–48; the original 1818 law establishing the Medical Department limited the ability of medical officers to exercise command outside the medical sphere; Cirillo, *Bullets and Bacilli*, 24; Margaret Leech, *In the Days of McKinley* (New York: Harper & Brothers, 1959), 261–62, 300–302.

5. Cosmas, *Army for Empire*, 255, including "scarecrows" quote; remember that most of the Regulars had been mobilized in late April, so that by 1 July, they had been in camp conditions in Chickamauga, Tampa, on board transport ships, and in Cuba for about eight weeks—the standard incubation time established for the outbreak of typhoid fever among troops in this war; Musicant, *Empire by Default*, 508–12; there were still some who believed that the troops' health problems were at least partially due to their transition from northern to southern climates; Fitzhugh Lee and Joseph Wheeler, *Cuba's Struggle against Spain with the Causes for American Intervention and a Full Account of the Spanish-American War, Including Final Peace Negotiations* (New York: American Historical Press, 1899), 556.

6. Cosmas, *Army for Empire*, 255.

7. The president's nephew, James, was a member of the 8th Ohio; Miles was only in Cuba for two days but outranked Shafter, thus enabling him to authorize the regiment's change of location; Leech, *In the Days of McKinley*, 239–40, 267–68, 279; Curtis V. Hard, *Banners in the Air: The Eighth Ohio Volunteers and the Spanish-American War*, Robert H. Ferrell, ed. (Kent, Ohio: Kent State University Press, 1988), 39–51; Colonel Hard has his men landing in Siboney by 12 July at the latest; the 13 July date given in Reed's *Typhoid Fever Report* may be the day they reported to V Corps HQ, rather than the day they landed. Hard's account also supports the belief that General Miles was originally counting on yellow fever–free V Corps units for his Puerto Rican operation. When most of them, including the 8th Ohio, failed to get a clean bill of health, he called up the volunteers from Camp Thomas, who ironically carried the more contagious of the two fevers; the record for the 8th is one of the most incomplete in the entire typhoid report, which credits only nine deaths out of twenty-three cases to typhoid, leaving the rest of the regiment's sixty-two fatalities unaccounted for; Reed, *Typhoid Fever Report*, 323–24.

8. Musicant, *Empire by Default*, 511–12; Cosmas, *Army for Empire*, 258–59.

9. The 8th Ohio was quarantined when it was diagnosed with yellow fever, which the men acquired by going into Santiago without orders; Hard, *Banners in the Air*, 52–54 and 60–61; Roosevelt, *Rough Riders*, 124–27; Leech, *In the Days of McKinley*, 271–72.

10. Roosevelt, *Rough Riders*, 125–28, copies of Roosevelt's note and the "round robin" letter appear as appendices in this edition, 199–202, and in Brands, *Selected Letters*, 208–10; Cosmas, *Army for Empire*, 260; Musicant, *Empire by Default*, 511–13; Brands, *T.R.*, 358–61; Morris, *Rise of Roosevelt*, 659–61; interestingly, Samuels, *Teddy at San Juan*, makes no mention of his controversial and potentially politically damaging role in triggering this scandal.

11. General Ames sent his own cable to the War Department, which read: "This army is incapable, because of sickness, of marching anywhere expect the transports. If it is ever to return to the United States it must do so at once"; Roosevelt, *Rough Riders*, 201–2; Hard, *Banners in the Air*, 59; Leech, *In the Days of McKinley*, 274–77; the letter to Shafter and the round robin version both appear in Brand, *Letters of T.R.*, 208–11.

12. Morris, *The Rise of Roosevelt,* 660; the press had been hinting at the poor health of the troops, but other stories buried this news until the publication of the "round robin"; Brown, *The Correspondent's War,* 428–40; Cirillo, *Bullets and Bacilli,* 91–96; Leech is very critical of Sternberg's performance and suggests that "he had been too inflexible, and in a humane sense, too unimaginative to rise to the demands of war," Leech, *In the Days of McKinley,* 300–304; Millis is critical of both the press and Roosevelt for exaggerating both the danger to and condition of the troops in Cuba; Millis, *The Martial Spirit,* 344–53.

13. Oliver, *Roughing It with the Regulars,* 67; although the focus of this book is on Roosevelt's self-appointed place in the memory of the war and discusses its effect on the Regulars in the battle, it makes no mention of "Teddy's" role in the "round robin" incident; Samuels, *Teddy at San Juan,* 292–305; Teddy effectively goes from disgruntled critic to heroic candidate for New York governor in a matter of weeks, following his return to the states; Thomas, *War Lovers,* 355–60.

14. Cosmas, *Army for Empire,* 262–66; Leech, *In the Days of McKinley,* 306–12.

15. For the most part, their food supply consisted entirely of "hard bread, canned beef, canned beans, canned tomatoes, coffee, and sugar." Colonel Hard also claimed that when the District of Columbia regiment complained about the condition of its transport vessel it was punished by ending up as "one of the last V Corps regiments to leave the island." In another case, a unit that stocked "sick rations" aboard its ship had all of its ill men removed by the Medical Department and taken to the hospital in Santiago instead of going home with the regiment; *Banners in the Air,* 68–76.

16. The stories of death and suffering appeared in the Cleveland and Pittsburgh papers before the regiment even arrived at Montauk, ibid., 77–83; sensational stories of "horror ships" full of sick, neglected soldiers had been appearing in several papers since late July. Transports like the *Seneca* (which arrived in New York on 20 July) set the standard for such stories and illustrated how easy it was to make fictional details about the *Mohawk* believable; Brown, *Correspondent's War,* 433–35; Leech, *In the Days of McKinley,* 274; members of the 2nd Massachusetts, who traveled home on the *Mobile,* were universal in their condemnation of the conditions on their ship; *Massachusetts Reform Reports,* 16–31, 48–51; the Red Cross reported providing milk, food, and medical care to members of the 8th both at Camp Wikoff and at its "Long Island Relief Station"; *Red Cross Reports,* 250, 257.

17. The Red Cross picked up much of the slack for the early deficiencies in the military operation and eventually worked with General Wheeler to bypass the usual red tape and purchase items directly for the army's use; *Red Cross Reports,* 225–234; Dyer, *Shiloh to San Juan,* 244–48; Alger visited on 24 August, the day of the 8th's arrival, while McKinley's visit came shortly before they left on 6 September (the president's visit was on 4 September, according to the Red Cross, idem, 237); Hard, *Banners in the Air,* 83; Cosmas, *Army for Empire,* 263–65; Cirillo, *Bullets and Bacilli,* 96–98. Wheeler's view of the camp included the claim that "in every possible way the solicitude of the Government was shown for the safety and comfort of the soldiers who had been in Santiago"; Lee and Wheeler, *Cuba's Struggle,* 572–74; testimony by members and relatives of the 2nd Massachusetts were extremely critical of the care their sick received in the camp hospital, *Massachusetts Reform Report,* 51–52.

18. *Red Cross Reports,* 228.

19. Cosmas, *Army for Empire,* 265; all the members of the regiment had actually been sent home on furlough before reassembling in Wooster for the muster out, which certainly explains their ill humor at being confined there for ten days; Hard, *Banners in the Air,* 85–86; of the 21,870 men who passed through Camp Wikoff, 357 died (none of yellow fever, but 120 died of typhoid); Cirillo, *Bullets and Bacilli,* 97.

20. Millis, *The Martial Spirit,* 367.

21. For discussions of the Dodge Commission and beef scandals, see Cirillo, *Bullets and Bacilli,* 100–105; Musicant, *Empire by Default,* 633–37; Cosmas, *Army for Empire,* 284–90; Hirshson, *Grenville Dodge,* 234–38; Lewis Gould, *The Spanish-American War and President McKinley* (Lawrence: University Press of Kansas, 1982), 91–95, 121–23; Hearst's *New York Journal* joined the chorus of criticism against the government as well, partly due to Hearst's own frustration at the minor role he had played in the war itself; Thomas, *War Lovers,* 363.

22. Creager, *History of the Fourth Ohio,* 125; *Massachusetts Reform Reports,* 18, 22, 24–25, 27–29.

23. There were four different types of beef issued to the troops: a fairly acceptable canned corned beef, the reviled prime roast beef, refrigerated fresh beef that was good if not spoiled, and the "embalmed beef" that was often declared inedible by men who encountered it; DeMontravel, *Hero to His Fighting Men,* 313–14; Cosmas, *Army for Empire,* 290–95; Cirillo, *Bullets and Bacilli,* 104–10; Leech, *In the Days of McKinley,* 314–22; General Wheeler blamed Commissary Chief Eagan's overly officious behavior for the food problems at Camp Wikoff; Dyer, *Shiloh to San Juan,* 246.

24. Lewis Gould points out that the presidentially appointed Dodge Commission "deflected a formal congressional probe," thus avoiding "that form of legislative scrutiny," which in turn "extricated McKinley from a tight political corner;" *The War and McKinley,* 94–95.

25. Millis, *The Martial Spirit,* 365–70.

26. Bravery, victory, and "contemptible" quotes from an address by Gen. Joseph W. Burke to the Society of the Army of the Cumberland, *Twenty-ninth Reunion, October 1900* (Cincinnati, Ohio: Robert Clarke Company, 1901), 67; Musicant, *Empire by Default,* 651–53; Boynton defended Alger, and former members of the original park committee, but denounced Miles in the strongest terms; Hirshson, *Grenville Dodge,* 237–38; according to the author, this position was consistent with Teddy's skillful use of the press for his own self-preservation and self-promotion; Millis, *The Martial Spirit,* 367–68.

27. Gould, *The War and McKinley,* 121–23; DeMontravel, *Hero to His Fighting Men,* 326–60; Musicant, *Empire by Default,* 652–54.

28. Kristen Hoganson writes: "Begun as a chivalrous crusade to redeem American honor and liberate the Cubans from Spanish oppression, the Spanish-American War ended as a self-aggrandizing war . . . that resulted not only in the temporary occupation of Cuba but also in the annexation of Puerto Rico and Guam." She also describes the Philippine conflict as "ironic," *Fighting for Manhood,* 133.

29. Although a few Republicans joined the anti-imperialist movement, Democrats made it a partisan issue by passing the treaty, then including opposition to expansionism in their 1900 presidential platform, ibid., 156–79; Gould, *The War and McKinley,* 124–25; a description of the anti-imperialists, who included Grover Cleveland, Andrew Carnegie, and Mark Twain, can be found in H. Wayne Morgan, *America's Road to Empire: The War with Spain and Overseas Expansion* (New York: John Wiley and Sons, 1965), 102–5; a full analysis of the anti-imperialist movement can be found in Richard E. Welch Jr., *Response to Imperialism: The United States and the Philippine-American War, 1899–1902* (Chapel Hill: University of North Carolina Press, 1979); many historians see Bryan's gambit as a huge political blunder; Millis, *The Martial Spirit,* 400–403.

30. Gould, *The War and McKinley,* 123–26; a detailed analysis of the U.S. military campaign in the Philippines can be found in Brian McAllister Linn, *The Philippine War,*

1899–1902, Modern War Studies (Lawrence: University Press of Kansas, 2000); and David J. Silbey, *A War of Frontier and Empire: The Philippine-American War, 1899–1902* (New York: Hill and Wang, 2007).

31. There was a tendency on the part of the expansionists to equate anti-imperialism with unmanliness or feminization; Hoganson, *Fighting for Manhood*, 133–99; reports of atrocities by American soldiers generated a great deal of public pressure on the government; Welch, *Response to Imperialism*, 133–49; among the anti-imperialists were Boston intellectuals, led by William James, who increasingly rejected all expansionism; Thomas, *War Lovers*, 386–89.

13. "A LUNACY WORTHY OF FRANCE"

1. Cirillo, *Bullets and Bacilli*, 111–35; the army created the Department of Military Hygiene in 1905 to teach line officers the basics of sanitation and disease prevention; idem, "Patriotic Odor," 21–22; University of Virginia Health System, Health Sciences Library, "Yellow Fever and the Reed Commission: Finding the Vector, New Strategies Work, and The Impact of the Commission," <http://www.hsl.virginia.edu/historical/medical_history/yellow_fever/mosquitoes.cfm>; Espinosa, "Yellow Fever and Cuba," 567–68; quoted in Edwards, "The Sanitary Service," 259/7, USAMHI; by 1909, the U.S. Army had adopted a typhoid vaccine that had been developed and tested by the British military during the Boer War; Stanhope Bayne-Jones, M.D., *The Evolution of Preventative Medicine in the United States Army, 1607–1939* (Washington D.C.: Office of the Surgeon General, 1968), 123–46, Part VII, <http://history.amedd.army.mil/booksdocs/misc/evprev/ch7.htm>.

2. Leech, *In the Days of McKinley*, 379–96, 517–23; Cosmas, *Army for Empire*, 297–326; Lt. Col. James Parker, "The Militia Act of 1903," *North American Review* 177, no. 561 (August 1903): 278, APS Online; General Wilson served in Puerto Rico, assisted in the occupation of Cuba, and ended up in China as part of the relief force during the Boxer Rebellion; Wilson, *Under the Old Flag*, 2: 439–523; Millis points out that in most cases the so-called southern "immunes" were not immune at all; *The Martial Spirit*, 364, 390; Gould, *The War and McKinley*, 121–38; Morgan, *America's Road to Empire*, 106–15; the Platt Amendment contained a provision that Cuba remain sanitary to prevent disease outbreaks that might threaten the health of the region; Espinosa, "Yellow Fever and Cuba," 567–68.

3. Quoted in Hoganson, *Fighting for Manhood*, 110–17; the 12th Minnesota was at Camp Thomas from 19 May to 23 August and suffered eighteen deaths from disease "and one by accident"; Gina Gage, "The History of the 12th Minnesota Infantry," *The Spanish-American War Centennial Website* (27 July 2006), <http://www.spanamwar.com/12thmnhistory.htm>. Wheeler spent several months leading a brigade in the Philippines before returning home to take command of the District of the Great Lakes in June 1900; Dyer, *Shiloh to San Juan*, 250–59; some thought Dewey should challenge McKinley for the Republican nomination; Leech, *In the Days of McKinley*, 410–31; Dewey's heroism and popularity were enhanced by books like Murat Halstead, *The Life and Achievements of Admiral Dewey from Montpelier to Manila* (n.p.: Our Possessions Publishing Company, 1899).

4. Hoganson, *Fighting for Manhood*, 116–17; Millis, *The Martial Spirit*, 269–70.

5. In spite of atrocity rumors, soldiers who fought in the Philippines were regarded by leaders like Roosevelt as particularly patriotic and worthy of emulation; Hoganson, *Fighting for Manhood*, 151–52, 161–62; many volunteers who served in the Philippines received a rousing hero's welcome when they returned home; Leech, *In the Days of McKinley*, 408–9; the 4th Ohio held its twenty-fifth reunion in Guayama, Puerto Rico, where its veterans

dedicated a memorial plaque to their service; 4th Ohio Infantry Association, *Dedication of Memorial Tablet and 25th Reunion, Guayama, Porto Rico, 1923*, souvenir booklet published by the association, in the author's personal collection.

6. Note that Alger was present at the meeting when Boynton spoke in his defense, and General Dodge had been invited to attend in his capacity as president of the Society of the Army of the Tennessee, Society of the Army of the Cumberland, *Twenty-Eighth Reunion, Detroit, Michigan, September 27 and 28, 1899* (Cincinnati, Ohio: Robert Clarke, 1899), 10–12, 30 (cited hereafter as SAOC, *Twenty-eighth Reunion*); as further evidence of the closeness of Boynton and Alger, the secretary of war included in his memoir a speech Boynton gave at the 1900 reunion of the 35th Ohio in which Boynton attacked the press and defended both the secretary and the park; Alger, *The Spanish War*, 419–24; Boynton's opinion of Miles is found in Hirshson, *Grenville Dodge*, 237–38.

7. Millis, *The Martial Spirit*, 366; the "Hell on Earth" quote, attributed to a member of the 8th New York, appears in Chapman, *Army Life at Camp Thomas*, 651, and in the introduction to the Camp Thomas section of Stan Cohen, *Images of the Spanish-American War, April-August, 1898* (Missoula, Mont.: Pictorial Histories Publishing, 1997); the food and water quote is from the 52nd Iowa's "River of Death" letter, 15 August 1898, Wyckoff folder, USAMHI; the "pest hole" quote is found in Boynton, "The Third Toast: The War with Spain," SAOC, *Twenty-eighth Reunion*, 124.

8. Cohen, *Images of the War*; for the most part, Cohen accepts the most critical account of the camp and includes this undocumented hospital quote in his limited text, 140–47; the comparisons to Andersonville must have rankled a Republican veteran like Boynton, who recognized how the memory of an atrocity could influence the nation's ability to reunite; see Cloyd, *Haunted by Atrocity*, 1–3.

9. The sentiments and quotes above are drawn from two Boynton speeches. One is quoted in Alger, *The Spanish War*, 419; the other is in "the War with Spain" speech, SAOC, *Twenty-eighth Reunion*, 119–22; a typescript of the reunion speech can also be found in "Speech by H. V. Boynton, Third Toast the War with Spain," Veteran's correspondence: Camp Thomas Report and Speech, 1898–99, Series VI, 205–3204, Box 2, Folder 20, Chickamauga and Chattanooga National Battlefield Park Archives; a discussion of the early Civil War volunteer experience can be found in Reid Mitchell, "From Volunteer to Soldier: The Psychology of Service," in Michael Barton and Larry Logue, eds., *The Civil War Soldier: A Historical Reader* (New York: New York University Press, 2002), 354–85.

10. Henry V. Boynton, "Report Upon the Sanitary Condition of Camp George H. Thomas, from the Beginning of Its Occupation until Vacated, October, 1898," War Department Park Commission, 1890–1933: Routine Operations to 1900, Series VI, 205–3204, Box 1, Folder 1, Chickamauga and Chattanooga National Military Park Archives (hereafter cited as Boynton, "Sanitary Conditions," CHCH), 2–6.

11. Quartermaster quote from Boynton, "Sanitary Conditions," 47–48, CHCH; train and food quotes in Alger, *The Spanish War*, 420–22; others from Boynton, "The War with Spain," SAOC, *Twenty-eighth Reunion*, 122–24.

12. Boynton claimed that 373 carloads of beer—187 carrying bottled beer and 186 with one-quarter-gallon (or one-quarter-keg?) barrels—for a total of 566,800 gallons, were shipped into the canteens; the number of passes into the city increased from two per company to six after 1 July; Boynton, "Sanitary Conditions," 26–27, 29–31, 39, CHCH; once again, Boynton's perspective does not include memories of the excesses of his own generation's time in the service, where alcohol, prostitution, gambling, and other vices were widely practiced; see Thomas P. Lowry, *The Story the Soldiers Wouldn't Tell: Sex in the Civil War* (Mechanicsburg, Pa.: Stackpole Books, 1994); and James I. Robertson Jr.,

"Fun, Frolics, and Firewater," in Barton and Logue, *Civil War Soldier,* 122–40; the friendship between Boynton and Brooke is apparent during the latter's appearance at a meeting of the Society of the Army of the Cumberland, *Thirty-first Reunion, Washington, D.C., October, 1903* (Cincinnati, Ohio: Robert Clarke and Company, 1904), 109–12.

13. Quoted in Boynton, "Sanitary Conditions," 5, 15–19, CHCH; the "healthful region" quote is from his "War with Spain" speech, SAOC, *Twenty-eighth Reunion,* 124; Alger, *The Spanish War,* 417; Boynton's reference to hostile studies may be directed at a Mr. P. A. Maignan, whose study (supposedly commissioned by Dr. Sternberg) found that the water in the park was tainted by the presence of "magnesium limestone" that caused it to be "hard" and have "an injurious effect on nutrition." However, the report concluded by saying that if the proper precautions are taken, "there is no reason why the National Park at some future time . . . should not be a first rate camping ground"; see "The Water Supply at Camp Thomas," *Scientific American* 76, no. 12 (17 September 1898): 178, APS Online.

14. Edward Betts, "Annual Report, Office of the Engineer, 10 October 1898," in Series I 205–3199, Box 1, Folder 4, Chickamauga and Chattanooga National Military Park Archives (hereafter cited as "Betts Report, 1898," CHCH), 15–18.

15. This report suggested that the nature of the camp's water made it more susceptible to pollution; "Water Supply at Camp Thomas," *Medical News;* Reed, *Abstract Report,* 179–84.

16. Boynton, "The War with Spain," SAOC, *Twenty-eighth Reunion,* 124; Breckinridge was quoted in 1898 as stating, "in my opinion the sickness in the park was brought here by the troops," a view later sustained by the Reed Report; Boynton, "Sanitary Conditions," 6, CHCH; the surgeon general put forth a detailed argument supporting this theory in a detailed letter to the editor of a national periodical; George M. Sternberg, "General Sternberg's Answer to His Critics," *Medical News* 73, no. 11 (10 September 1898): 335, APS Online; the former secretary of war cites both Sternberg and Boynton and states that "the existence of camp fevers there is due to neglect of camp sanitation"; Alger, *The Spanish War,* 412–19; Boynton points out that 8th U.S. was made up of black soldiers and "not a death occurred from any cause in this regiment"; Chickamauga and Chattanooga National Military Park Commission, *Annual Report to the Secretary of War, 1899* (Washington, D.C.: Government Printing Office, 1899), 3–7; this report was published in its entirety in the *Chattanooga Times* on 25 December 1899, as found in Clipping file–Historical section: Chattanooga—parks—national—Chickamauga and Chattanooga National Military Park, folder 1, Chattanooga-Hamilton County Bicentennial Library.

17. The bulk of these charges are contained in Boynton, "Sanitary Conditions," 12, 15, 20, and 24, CHCH; as has been documented in previous chapters, the 1st Vermont and 9th Pennsylvania were both vocal in their criticisms of the park; see quotes in Sauers, *Pennsylvania in the Spanish-American War,* 15–19; and Greene's introduction in *Vermont in the Spanish-American War;* "Unhealthfulness" quote from Boynton's speech in Alger, *The Spanish War,* 423.

18. He included an account of the 8th's inflated sick call in Alger, *The Spanish War,* 423; the reference to the "slums" was in reference to the New York surgeon general's original statement, which made a similar comparison; Boynton, "Camp Thomas Hospital Report," 21–23, CHCH.

19. The 160th Indiana and 1st Georgia were also guilty of leaving their camps in bad shape; Boynton, "Sanitary Conditions," 41–42, CHCH; Park Commission, *Annual Report, 1899,* 3.

20. Boynton, "Sanitary Conditions," 41–42, CHCH.

21. Alger, *The Spanish War,* 422–23.

22. Boynton, "Hospital Report," 21, CHCH.

23. This complaint had passed through at least three different hands before it ended up on Boynton's lap, "H. V. Boynton to Adjutant General H. C. Corbin, 8 September 1898," Fort Oglethorpe and Camp Thomas: Camp Thomas Soldier Mistreatment Report, 1898, Series , 205–3204, Box 1, Folder 7, Chickamauga and Chattanooga National Military Park Archives.

24. Quoted in Alger, *The Spanish War,* 41.

25. Henry V. Boynton, *Roosevelt's Military Record,* unidentified, undated (1904?) pamphlet, Western Reserve Historical Society Research Library, Cleveland, Ohio, 5.

26. Ibid., 4; Alger, *The Spanish War,* 424.

27. Boynton, "The War with Spain," SAOC, *Twenty-eighth Reunion,* 124–25.

28. A speech in 1904 by Col. John McCook extolled the virtues of "duty and obligation" and the willingness to "endure hardship," using the Civil War as the example with no mention of the Spanish-American War. Another speaker at the same banquet cited America's humanity during the Spanish War, but avoided any mention of dissent or the war's volunteers; Society of the Army of the Cumberland, *Thirty-second Reunion, September, 1904* (Cincinnati, Ohio: Robert Clarke, 1905), 108–16, 128–29; the Elysian fields were a paradise for slain warriors or "a place of ideal happiness"; *The American Heritage Dictionary of the English Language* (New York: Delta Edition, 1977), while Golgotha refers to the hill on which Christ was crucified, *Britannica Online Encyclopedia,* <http://www.britannica.com/EBchecked/topic/238060/Golgotha>.

29. Paige and Greene, *Administrative History,* adhi6: 4; lumber quote is in the "Betts Report, 1898," 2, 28, CHCH; Boynton, "Park Report," SAOC, *Twenty-eighth Reunion,* 28.

30. "H. V. Boynton to J. C. Breckinridge, Camp Thomas, Ga. 5 August 1898," Veteran's Correspondence: Camp Thomas Report and Speech, 1898–99, Series VI, 205–3204, Box 2, Folder 20, Chickamauga and Chattanooga National Military Park Archives (hereafter cited as "Boynton to Breckinridge, August 1898," CHCH); this writer believed that the soldiers were taught to use anything they wanted in any way they desired, which led to the wholesale abuse of the forest cover; Tinney, "Military Occupation," 13–14; some of the damage was from "horses gnawing the bark," "Betts Report, 1898," 28, CHCH.

31. Boynton, "Park Report," SAOC, *Twenty-eighth Reunion,* 28–29; although the grass was an unexpected benefit, this source confirms that damage from horses and mules had been extensive during the occupation of the park, Tinney, "Military Occupation," 12–14, CHCH.

32. "H. V. Boynton to Dear Mr. Evans, 15 August 1898," Fort Oglethorpe and Camp Thomas: Camp Thomas Infractions and Correspondence, 1898, Series VI, 205–3 204, Box 1, Folder 8, Chickamauga and Chattanooga National Military Park Archives (hereafter cited as "Boynton to Evans, 1898," CHCH); "H. V. Boynton to My Dear Mr. Betts, 9 November 1898," Boynton 1898–1902, Camp Thomas Correspondence, 1898–1900, Series VI, Box 2, Folder 12, Chickamauga and Chattanooga National Military Park Archives (hereafter cited as "Boynton to Mr. Betts, 9 November 1898," CHCH).

33. "Frank Smith to E. E. Bates, 13 November 1900," and "Smith to Betts, 19 December 1900," Camp Thomas Spanish War Claims Board, Correspondence, 1900: Smith, 1896–1900, Series VI, 205–3204, Box 2, Folder 13, Chickamauga and Chattanooga National Military Park Archives (cited as "Smith to Betts, date, CHCH); House of Representatives, U.S. Congress, 56th Congress, First Session, *Spanish-American War Claims: Damages by Troops to Private Property, Spanish-American War Document No. 460, Part I, 26 February, 1900,* 371–88; Gordon's claims were excessive and many were discounted because he did not own much of the property he claimed to have lost, *Spanish-American War Claims,* 387–89.

34. "Betts Report, 1898," 36, CHCH; the reference to barbed wire is in Tinney, "Military Occupation," 12–14, CHCH.

14. "WHERE AMERICAN VALOR MET AMERICAN VALOR"

1. "Betts Report, 1898," 31, CHCH.

2. Park Commission, *Annual Report*, 1899, 4–5; Boynton, "Park Report," SAOC, *Twenty-eighth Reunion*, 26; "Gen. H. V. Boynton at Dedication of Wilder Brigade Monument," Wilder Brigade Monument Correspondence, 1892–1899, Series II, 205–3200, Box 5, Folder 73, Chickamauga and Chattanooga National Military Park Archives; Sickles's role expanded from being responsible for New York's monuments at Gettysburg to acting as chair of the overall commission at around this time; Thomas Keneally, *American Scoundrel: The Life of the Notorious Civil War General Dan Sickles* (New York: Nan A. Talese, Doubleday, 2002), 340–45; General Sickles attended the society's meeting in 1900 and, along with President Roosevelt, spoke briefly in remembrance of W. T. Sherman as an honored guest at the Society of the Army of the Cumberland, *Thirty-first Reunion, Washington, D.C., October 1903* (Cincinnati, Ohio: Robert Clarke, 1904), 138–39.

3. Park Commission, *Annual Report*, 1899, 5; ceremonies described in "Dedication of Handsome Kentucky State Monument," *Chattanooga Times*, 4 May 1899, Clipping File, Chattanooga Parks—National—Chickamauga and Chattanooga National Battlefield Park, Folder 1, Chattanooga-Hamilton County Bicentennial Library.

4. Description of Georgia monument in Boynton, "Park Report," SAOC, *Twenty-eighth Reunion*, 29; Chickamauga and Chattanooga National Park Commission, *Annual Report to the Secretary of War, 1900* (Washington, D.C.: Government Printing Office, 1900), 5.

5. Park Commission, *Annual Report*, 1900, 5–8.

6. Gordon's response was quoted in its entirety in Park Commission, *Annual Report, 1900*, 5–8; compliment to Confederates and invitation to wives in SAOC, *Twenty-ninth Reunion*, 4.

7. Park Commission, *Annual Reports*, 1900, 10–11; General Wilder, whose 17th and 72nd Indiana Mounted Infantry were among the units that had staked their claims to the action on Glenn Hill, was named as one of the individuals guilty of perpetuating these mistakes; Orlando B. Somers, *A Protest Against and Appeal from the Action of the Indiana-Chickamauga Park Commission, and Others to the Commissioners of the National Military Park, Chickamauga, Georgia . . . by the Survivors Association of the 8th Indiana Cavalry, 39th Regiment Indiana Volunteers* (Kokomo, Ind.: Tribune Printing, 1901), 5–10, 57–59; a discussion among members of the society, including Somers, regarding the unfinished work of correction errors occurs at the Society of the Army of the Cumberland, *Thirty-third Reunion, Chattanooga, Tennessee, September 18, 19, 20, 1905* (Cincinnati, Ohio: Robert Clarke Company, 1906) 25–33.

8. Society of the Army of the Cumberland, *Thirty-fourth Reunion, Chattanooga, Tennessee, October 17 & 18, 1906* (Chattanooga, Tenn.: McGowan-Cooke Printing Co., 1907), 31–38.

9. SAOC, *Twenty-ninth Reunion*, 90–92.

10. Ibid., 93–97.

11. Ibid.

12. A summary of these early efforts appears under "History of Movement" in a larger article, "Permanent Barracks to Be Built at Once," *Chattanooga Times*, 20 July 1902, in clipping file, Chattanooga Parks—National—Chickamauga and Chattanooga National Battlefield Park, Chattanooga–Hamilton County Bicentennial Library (hereafter cited as "Permanent Barracks" *Times* clipping, 1902, CHCBL); "Rendezvous: Chickamauga Park to Be Occupied for Summer Maneuvers," unidentified undated clipping, H. Clay Evens scrapbook, Vol. 21, 1898, History C, Acc. 108, Box 9, Chattanooga–Hamilton County Bicentennial Library.

13. A clipping with the subheading "Splendid Prospect" was on a different page in the scrapbook, but is most likely an extension of the same article, "Permanent Barracks" *Times* clipping, 1902, CHCBL.

14. Clipping headed "Let the Truth Be Known," from *Chattanooga Times*, 18 September 1898, Evens scrapbook, CHCBL.

15. Quoted in "Permanent Barracks," *Times* clipping, 1902, CHCBL; a bill that proposed such a post failed in 1899, partly due to lingering concerns about the healthfulness of the park; Paige and Greene, *Administrative History*, adhi6–4.

16. "The Army Post Competition" heads a collection of clippings from the *Chattanooga Times* dated between 21 and 31 December 1899 and 1 January 1900, in Charles Roundtree Evans Scrapbook, History C, Acc. 13, Box 2, Vol. 4, 1897–1900, Chattanooga–Hamilton County Bicentennial Library; Charles was the son of H. Clay Evans, who had been a member of the chamber's original "post committee" back in 1895. The elder Evans had been involved in a pension scandal that tainted his career, but his son successfully used his status as "war hero" to advance his own status in the community; notes taken from Charles Evans Scrapbook, op. cit.; by 1905, Henry Clay Evans had been granted honorary membership in the Society of the Army of the Cumberland, where he responded to a toast to President Roosevelt at its banquet, SOAC, *Thirty-third Reunion*, 115–17.

17. An appropriation of $450,000 accompanied the construction of the buildings, which were located on a purported 475-acre tract; "Permanent Barracks," *Times* clipping, 1902, CHCBL; by 1903, Boynton reported the amount of land purchased as being 793 acres and the total cost of the facility (excluding the land) as about $1 million; Henry V. Boynton, "Chickamauga-Chattanooga National Military Park," *Chattanooga Times*, 1 July 1903, clipping file, Chattanooga—Parks—National—Chickamauga and Chattanooga National Military Park, Chattanooga–Hamilton County Bicentennial Library (hereafter cited as Boynton, "Park Report, 1903," *Times* clipping, CHCBL); this source lists the tract as being 813 acres; Paige and Greene, *Administrative History,* adhi6:4; no detailed explanation for the post's name is given in Vincent S. Gannon, "Fort Oglethorpe: The Story of Conflict and Cooperation between the Army and the Chickamauga Park Commission," unpublished manuscript dated August 1964, Fort Oglethorpe and Camp Thomas, misc. Spanish-American Box, Chickamauga and Chattanooga National Military Park Archives (hereafter cited as Gannon "Fort Oglethorpe," CHCH), 1–2; an undated booklet by the Nashville, Chattanooga & St. Louis Railway described the construction of a "model army post" in the park and erroneously reported that it would be named Camp George H. Thomas; *Southern Battlefields: A List of Battlefields On or Near the Lines of the Nashville, Chattanooga & St. Louis Railway and Western Atlantic Railroad* (Nashville, Chattanooga & St. Louis Railway, n.d.), 39.

18. The troops serving as a seasonal, semipermanent force at the pre-Oglethorpe encampment were the 7th Cavalry and the 3rd U.S. Battery, who had been there since returning from Cuba; Park Commission, *Annual Report of the Chickamauga and Chattanooga National Military Park Commission, 1902* (Washington, D.C.: Government Printing Office, 1902), 5; quoted in Park Commission, *Annual Report of the Chickamauga and Chattanooga National Military Park Commission, 1904* (Washington, D.C.: Government Printing Office, 1904), 3.

19. Charles Evans Scrapbook, Vol. 4, CHCBL, unknown date.

20. Ibid.

21. Ibid. Unfortunately, the exact dates and origins of all the newspaper articles in the scrapbook were not recorded or did not come through on my photocopies. Nearly all the individual testimonials to the park as the site for the army post are dated December 1899, and several related articles are dated January 1900; the Memorial Day articles make ref-

erence to "last year's war" so they are clearly from late May or early June 1899. The reference to "U. S. Grant University" may have been an honest mistake by the newspaper or
an attempt to add to the reputation of the speaker, since I can find no such institution in
the historical record.

22. Boynton, *Roosevelt's Military Record*, 3–4, WRHSL; a photograph in the nearby 6th
U.S. Cavalry Museum at Fort Oglethorpe shows Roosevelt in September 1902 about to
embark on a tour of the park led by Henry Boynton (who is not in the photo). This photo
appears in Gerry Depken and Julie Powell, *Images of America: Fort Oglethorpe* (Charleston, S.C.: Arcadia Publishing, 2009), 14.

23. The list of those who served in Congress is found in SOAC, *Thirty-second Reunion*,
15–18; the "practical use" quote is in Park Commission, *Annual Report*, 1902, 5.

24. "American Order of Nobility," in Vermont Historical Society, United Spanish War
Veterans, *Fiftieth Anniversary Mustering in First Vermont Regiment [and] Admiral Dewey's
Victory at Manila Bay, 1898, May 1948* (program booklet), E. H. Prouty file, 1st Vermont,
Spanish-American War survey, USAMHI; one piece of Spanish War veterans' literature
cites 458,000 as the number who served in the combined Spanish, Philippine, and Boxer
operations and cites the motto as "Freedom, Patriotism, and Humanity," in "I Am Proud
to Be a Spanish War Veteran," H. V. Schoonover file, 52nd Iowa, Spanish-American War
survey, USAMHI.

25. The 1904 amalgamation agreement appears in United Spanish War Veterans,
*Proceedings of the Stated Convention of the 81st National Convention, Indianapolis, Indi-
ana, September 8–13, 1979* (Washington, D.C.: Government Printing Office, 1980), 1–10;
Angela K. O'Neal, "Remembering the Maine: Memory Ritual, and Women's Roles in the
United Spanish War Veterans Auxiliary of Elyria, Ohio, 1922–1966," honors thesis, Kent
State University, 1998, 38–41; a newspaper clipping from the *National Tribune* on 1 May
1941 reports that the USWV numbers peaked at 90,000 in 1927 (it makes no mention of
whether this figure included the AUSWV); "Editorial: Spanish War Veterans," Charles H.
Fowler folder, Earnest Beckl file, 12th New York, Spanish-American War survey N65,
United States Army Military History Institute Archives.

26. "Proud to Be a Veteran," Schoonover file, USAMHI. Interestingly, they did not
include freeing the slaves as one of the things that the Civil War accomplished, in spite
of their claims to having liberated oppressed people in other countries.

27. "The Hiker" is attributed to Rice W. Means, editor of the *National Tribune* and
former national commander of the USWV and appears in a pamphlet entitled "The Flag
of Destiny: United Spanish War Veterans, Department of Iowa," rubber-stamped with
"H. V. C. Schoonover, P. D. C.[Past District Commander], United Spanish War Veterans," in Schoonover File, USAMHI; statues and plaques with "the Hiker" are scattered
across the midwestern United States and offer misleading facts and images of both the
War with Spain and the Philippine insurrection, including the figure of a kneeling native
woman, whose chains were apparently being broken by the U.S. military; Loewen, *Lies
Across America*, 136–43, 462.

28. This memorial booklet barely makes mention of Camp Thomas, and members of
the regiment did not make a stop at Chickamauga on their way to Puerto Rico; "Dedication of Memorial," *4th Ohio Twenty-fifth Reunion booklet;* both Vermont and Iowa worked
on memorial projects during the 1920s (see Chapter 15 for details), "Spanish War Memorials," War Department Park Commission, Correspondence, 1922–1927, Series VI, Box 2,
Folder 14, Chickamauga and Chattanooga National Military Park Archives.

29. State of New York, *Proceedings of the United Spanish War Veteran, Department of
New York, for the Year 1921, the Eighteenth Annual Encampment held at Utica, N.Y., July 17th,
18th, 19th, and 20th, 1921* (Albany, N.Y.: J. B. Lyon Company, Printers, 1923), 21.

30. The Spanish War Veterans, "An address delivered by Hon. Rice W. Means at the State-wide Banquet of the United Spanish War Veterans, Department of Minnesota, Minneapolis, Minnesota, May 11th, 1929," Lane-Blood Genealogy, 3–7, <http:/freepages. genealogy.rootsweb.ancestry.com/~laneblood/spamwaaddress.html>.

31. Congressional Record, 73rd Congress, First Session, "'The Veterans of 1898,' extension of remarks of Hon. Ernest Lundeen of Minnesota in the House of Representatives, Saturday, June 10, 1933," Lane-Blood Genealogy, 1–3, <http:/freepages.genealogy.rootsweb.ancestry.com/~laneblood/spamwacongrec.html>.

32. "Welcome Home Fifty-first Iowa U.S.V", County of Leavenworth, State of Kansas, affidavit, 8 May 1933; "To All Whom It May Concern," Discharge Certificate, 10 November 1898; and W. E. Chambers to Mrs. Martha Wysong, 12 March 1934, in Wysong Papers, author's collection.

33. The undated typewritten transcript of the full poem is found in the William B. Durrell file, 52nd Iowa, Spanish-American War survey file 1195, United States Military History Institute Archives. This fear of being denied can be seen in the last line of William Wysong's 1933 V.A. affidavit, where he specifically states that "the records of the hospital at the Presidio will bear me out as to [the] service connection" of his disability, Wysong Papers.

34. Vermont, *Fiftieth Anniversary Booklet,* 25–26, Prouty file, Spanish-American War survey, USAMHI.

35. SOAC, *Thirty-third Annual Reunion,* 107.

36. Gates Thurston was the new president in 1905; SOAC, *Thirty-third Reunion,* 62, 85; see the "business meeting" section for examples of society work; SOAC, *Thirty-fourth Reunion,* 57–71; see "It Is Camp Chickamauga, Lively Times Again at Old Lytle Station," *Chattanooga Times,* 10 July 1906, in clipping file, Chattanooga—Parks—National—CCNMP, CHCBL.

15. "THROUGH THE MOST TRYING ORDEALS"

1. Paige and Greene, *Administrative History,* adhi6:5; in 1908, the park's engineer complained that the cavalry's horses had gotten loose and stampeded through the battlefield, posing a threat to visitors and facilities, since "a stampeded animal is no respecter of persons, objects, or barriers"; quoted in Gannon, "Fort Oglethorpe," 2, CHCH; restoration of the grounds noted in Chickamauga and Chattanooga National Military Park Commission, *Annual Report to the Secretary of War, 1907, 1908, 1909* (Washington, D.C.: Government Printing office, 1907, 1908, 1909); a storm in April 1908 caused quite a bit of destruction to trees and buildings, but all was repaired "in time for July encampment and maneuver," 6 (page numbers are the same in all three reports); Fort Oglethorpe also served as part of a training experiment conducted in 1913 by Gen. Leonard Wood; Robert D. Ward, "A Note on General Leonard Wood's Experimental Companies," *Military Affairs* 35, no. 3 (October 1971): 92–93, JSTOR; see also Stephen L. Ossad, "The Frustrations of Leonard Wood," *Association of the United States Army: Army Magazine* (1 September 2003), <http://www3.ausa.org/webint/DeptArmyMagazine.nsf/byid/CCRN-6CCSAG?>.

2. The local business community lobbied aggressively for the expansion of Fort Oglethorpe into a brigade post; Chamber of Commerce, Chattanooga, Tenn., *Fort Oglethorpe: With Some Views of Proposed Brigade Post and Maneuver Grounds* (Chattanooga, Tenn.: Chamber of Commerce, 1913), USAMHI Library; Paige and Greene, *Administrative History,* adhi6a:1–4; Gannon, "Fort Oglethorpe," 12–15, CHCH; the proposed brigade

post expansion noted in Chickamauga and Chattanooga National Park Commission, *Annual Report to the Secretary of War, 1912* (Washington, D.C.: Government Printing Office, 1912), 6; local businesses cooperated with the military during this period, including offering homes for the boarding of troops and selling goods at lower prices than elsewhere; Office of the Constructing Quartermaster, "Completion Report Covering Cantonment Construction in Chickamauga Park, GA., Fort Oglethorpe, Camp Greenleaf, Camp Forrest, Gen. Hospital No. 14, and Prison Barracks #2, 1919," 7, 21–23, USAMHI; the Army conducted psychological tests on recruits both coming and going from the war at the park's medical facilities; Robert M. Yerkes, "Measuring the Mental Strength of an Army," *Proceedings of the National Academy of Sciences of the United States of America* 4, no. 10 (15 October 1918): 295–97, JSTOR; a report on the park's use as a prisoner-of-war camp can be found in William B. Glidden, "Internment Camps in America, 1917–1920," *Military Affairs* 37, no. 4 (December 1973): 137–41, JSTOR.

3. Gannon, "Fort Oglethorpe," 16–17; quoted in Paige and Greene, *Administrative History,* adhi6a:5–6; even though it was now under the jurisdiction of the Department of the Interior, the original enabling legislation, including the park's use by the military, remained in place, adhi2:6. The National Park Service was created in 1916, but did not get jurisdiction over certain national "shrines" and parks administered by the War Department until 1933; Dwight Rettie, *Our National Park System: Caring for America's Greatest Natural and Historic Treasures* (Urbana: University of Illinois Press, 1995), 46–47.

4. Paige and Greene, *Administrative History,* adhi6a: 5–7 and adhi7: 2–3; Gannon, "Fort Oglethorpe," 17–19, CHCH; the 6th U.S. Cavalry Museum, located just north of the park boundary, tells some of Fort Oglethorpe's story but spends more time tracking the unit's history from the Civil War to the present. There is an untapped collection of scrapbooks, papers, and photographs waiting to be utilized in this little museum, which now has its first full-time, non-veteran curator and is open to the public for a small entry fee.

5. Information on the commissioners found in Paige and Greene, *Administrative History,* adhi2:4–6 and (Appendix E) adhiae: 1; the War Department did not replace Wilder and Grosvenor when they died, choosing instead to dissolve the Board of Commissioners upon the death of its last member, Joseph Cumming, in 1922; Paige and Greene, *Administrative History,* adhi2:5 and adhi5:4–5; details on the Coburn affair can be found in two undated clippings from the *Chattanooga Daily Times* in Miscellaneous file, Personnel, Coburn affair, newspaper clippings, 1911, Series I, Box 5, folder 119; and a pamphlet entitled "To the President," dated November 1911 in Donation, Coburn Affair, Photocopies, 1911–1991, Series I, Box 5, Folder 120, both in Chickamauga and Chattanooga National Military Park Archives. Part of the argument was over the placement and wording of markers for Turchin's brigade on Missionary Ridge; see Albert Parry, "John B. Turchin: Russian General in the American Civil War," *Russian Review* 1, no. 2 (April 1942): 44–60, JSTOR.

6. Paige and Greene, *Administrative History,* adhi4: 5–7; the UCV and GAR held separate reunions, with the Union veterans meeting on the actual anniversary of the battle, but including Confederate veterans in the public ceremonies; Paige and Greene, *Administrative History,* adhi7: 1–2; Kerr, *Monuments and Markers,* "Iowa"; the New York monument and its dedication are featured on the front and inside covers of a guidebook by J. L. Rogers, *The Civil War Battles of Chickamauga and Chattanooga* (Chattanooga, Tenn.: J. L. Rogers, 1942); note that many of the Union veterans of the battles around Chattanooga (those in the old XI and XII Corps) were also connected to the battle of Gettysburg and would most likely have chosen to attend that reunion in July 1913 rather than one farther south in September.

7. In spite of the lack of any mounted cavalry action on 20 September 1863, the article was entitled "Famous Charge at Battle of Chickamauga Re-Enacted," *Chattanooga*

Times, 19 September 1923, in clipping file, Parks—National—CCNMP, folder 1, CHCBL; Bodnar suggests that such large-scale public events were part of a national movement to celebrate "Americanism" during the 1920s; Bodnar, *Remaking America,* 171–73.

8. An Ohioan, Albert D. Alcorn, was national commander in 1923; for a list of all the USWV annual encampments, see "National Encampments United Spanish War Veterans, Elected Commander in Chiefs, 1904–1998," <http://freepages.military.rootsweb.ancestry.com/~sunnyann/uswvnatlencampments.html>; articles by local newspapers and authors on the local activities surrounding the encampment were included in a special edition of a Chattanooga periodical, *The Lookout* 30, no. 21 (14 July 1923), in U.S.—History—Spanish-American War veterans folder, McClung Historical Collection, East Tennessee Historical Society, Knoxville, Tenn.

9. The article, marked *Times,* 19 September 1923, has no heading and can be found in clipping file, Parks—National—CCNMP, Chattanooga–Hamilton County Bicentennial Library.

10. Quoted in Richard B. Randolph to Col. J. P. McAdams, 22 December 1922; Randolph to Quartermaster General, Subject: Erection of Monuments to mark camp sites of Spanish-American War camps, 12 November 1925, in "Spanish War Memorials: Correspondence 1922–1927" folder, CHCH. Paige and Green, *Administrative History,* adhi4: 6–7; the Iowans were informed of the decision to place their marker in the circle and were assured that is was "the most conspicuous location that could be chosen"; Randolph to Almon S. Reed, Commander, Dept. of Iowa, USWV, 28 January 1927; this required a change in the inscription and further approval from the assistant secretary of war, as noted in H. F. Rethers to Assistant Secretary of War, Subject: Spanish War Memorial, 7 July 1927; correspondence regarding the Vermont monument, including a sketch of the circle, the location of both Iowa and Vermont's markers, and the text of the markers are in Randolph to F. R. Scheles, Commander, Dept. of Iowa, USWV, 30 October 1928, all in "Spanish War Memorials: Correspondence 1922–1927" folder, CHCH.

11. As has been previously established in this study, the Spanish-American War soldiers inherited many of these heroic images from the Civil War veterans; see John Pettegrew, "The Soldier's Faith," 60–69, JSTOR; O'Neal, "Remembering the Maine," 37, 44–51; one thing these organizations shared with the USWV was the emphasis on the volunteers and National Guard troops who responded to the nation's call; Jennifer D. Keene, *Doughboys, the Great War, and the Remaking of America* (Baltimore: Johns Hopkins University Press, 2001), 154–58. The New York USWV created a plaque "Dedicated to the Americanism of Theodore Roosevelt" made out of metal from old battleships. In the accompanying speech, the post commander asked rhetorically "why should it be necessary for me . . . to talk about 100 percent Americanism to you people . . . why is it necessary to speak of it at all in this Great Nation?" from *New York UWSV Eighteenth Annual Encampment, 1921.* The last Spanish-American War veteran, Nathan E. Cook, died in 1992, several days before the 94th National Encampment; "Nathan E. Cook (1885–1992)—Last Veteran of the Spanish American War," at <http://freepages.military.rootsweb.com/~sunnyann/cooknathan.html>; the SSAWV and the AUSWV held encampments until 1998, "National Encampments," <http://freepages.military.rootsweb.ancestry.com/~sunnyann/uswvnatlencampments.html >; the first chapter of the SSAWV formed in 1927 and was nationally chartered by the USWV in 1937; Arthur Lou, "A Brief History of the Sons of Spanish-American War Veterans" Sons of Spanish-American War Veterans, <http://freepages.military.rootsweb.ancestry.com/~sunnyann/namilesbriefhistory.html>; and Peihler, *Remembering War,* 86–91.

12. Quoted in Peihler, *Remembering War,* 91; 223 sailors who died on the *Maine* are buried near the memorial in Arlington Cemetery, which was designed by sculptor Andrew Wyeth

and dedicated in 1913; "The USS Maine Memorial, Arlington National Cemetery," *Arlington National Cemetery Website*, <http://www.arlingtoncemetery.net/ussmaine.htm>; see also Ronald W. Johnson and Mary E. Franza, "A Splendid Little War: Does Anyone Remember in 1998?" *Cultural Resource Manangement* 21, no. 2 (1998): 5–8. In Canton, the "base of the conning tower of the USS Maine" rests on a new marble pedestal in a recently constructed "Westbrook Park," which itself is small section of a larger recreational park located on 13th Street, N.W., near Mercy Hospital; the other Spanish-American War–related monument in the same park is a cannon that sits on a marble base, listing all of the Stark County men who died in the war; author's visit, August 2003, and Gary Brown, "Vets Memorial's Signs Link Past to Present, Distant to Stark," *Canton Repository*, 29 May 2000, C-1; the New York City *Maine* memorial that was dedicated in 1913 was built with funds raised by William R. Hearst and constructed partially from metal from the original battleship; Bogart, "'Maine Memorial' and 'Pulitzer Fountain,'" 47–54.

13. The Park Service account of the park's origins can be found in its publication, *The Battle of Chickamauga*, which is one of the National Park's Civil War Series booklets that cover all of its battlefield parks, 27–28. The Chickamauga Visitor Center featured a display in its lobby that recounted the founding of the park and highlighted "reconciliation and re-unions" and "the birth of historic-site preservation" among the prominent captions; notes and photographs taken during the author's visit, April 2002; in both its literature and the film, "The Battle of Chickamauga: A Historical Dramatization," which it produced for the park's visitor center, the Friends of the Chickamauga and Chattanooga National Military Park stresses "the healing" and "the Blue & Gray Barbeque of 1889" as the key points in the history of the park, with Camp Thomas mentioned in passing during the film only as evidence of this process; per the current membership pamphlet, "Arise Ye Sons and Daughters: Enlist," Friends of the Chickamauga and Chattanooga National Military Park.

14. James R. Sullivan, *Chickamauga and Chattanooga Battlefields, Chickamauga and Chattanooga National Military Park, Chattanooga, Tennessee*, National Park Service Historical Handbook Series 25 (Washington D.C., 1956; reprint 1961), 52–56; Hanson and Blythe, *Historic Resource Study*, 34–37. Desmond, *Chattanooga*, 17; according to this source, J. H. Gaston preceded Linn as the proprietor of the photo gallery in 1899 while the Ochs Memorial was constructed with the full support of the park commission; Paige and Greene, *Administrative History*, adhi2a: 1–4, adhi2e:1–2, and adhi3a: 1–2.

15. Advertisements for railroad tours of southern battlefields included pictures of Grant and Lee (who was never at Chattanooga), as well as a variety of other attractions in their sales pitch, Nashville, Chattanooga & St. Louis Railway and Western & Atlantic Railroad, *Battlefields in Dixie Land and Chickamauga National Military Park* (Chicago: Poole Brothers, 1928), 3–63; an article on the Civil War Preservation Trust list-serve discussed the conflict between the tourist-friendly, historical, and sacred elements of the Chickamauga and Chattanooga park; Giovanna Dell'Orto, "Keeping History Alive in the First National Park," Associated Press/*Pittsburgh Post-Gazette*, 11 May 2006, <http://www.post-gazette.com/pg/06131/688451–37.stm>, in *Civil War News Roundup* (12 May 2006), <jcampi@civilwar.org>.

16. Some of the monuments along Route 27 had to be moved when the road was widened; the Park Service's attempts to re-route the highway around the western edge of the park began in the 1950s, with hearings, resolutions, and surveys continuing until the early 1980s, when only action by the secretary of the interior in 1982 kept the thoroughfare from being widened rather than moved. The bypass was finally completed in 2001, much to the annoyance of some local citizens, who are now forced to obey a 35-MPH speed limit on the old two-lane stretch of road that runs through the park; "Roundabout a Glorious Success," *Chick-Chatt* (Winter 2001); and "Park Service and Planning Bodies

Conduct Battlefield Transportation Studies," *Chick-Chatt* (Fall 2003): 3; Paige and Greene, *Administrative History*, adhi3c:1–2.

17. A contemporary overview of the centennial commission's work, which admitted its shortcomings regarding race and the military perspective, was prepared by its chairman, Allen Nevins, *The Civil War Centennial: A Report to Congress* (Washington, D.C.: U.S. Civil War Centennial Commission, 1968), 3–6; the military focus can be seen in a "semi-official" booklet by a Civil War "buff"; William H. Price, *The Civil War Centennial Handbook*, A Civil War Research Associates Series (Arlington, Va.: Prince Lithograph, 1st ed., 1961); for comments on the commercial, racial, and memory implications of the centennial, see Bodnar, *Remaking America*, 206–226, and Kammen, *Mystic Chords of Memory*, 591–610; a reflection on the racial issues can be found in John Hope Franklin, "A Century of Civil War Observance," *Journal of Negro History* 47, no. 2 (April 1962): 97–107, JSTOR; see also Robert J. Cook, *Troubled Commemoration: The American Civil War Centennial, 1961–1965* (Baton Rouge: Louisiana State University Press, 2007).

18. The make-up of state commissions, the origins of roundtables, and some of the activities at Chickamauga are in Nevins, *Centennial Commission Report*, 42–43, 51–60; activities at the park are mentioned in Bodnar, *Remaking America*, 222; Paige and Greene, *Administrative History*, adhi7:3–4; Cook, *Troubled Commemoration*, 201.

19. Paige and Green, *Administrative History*, adhi7:4–5.

20. The issue of reenacting is mentioned in Bodnar, *Remaking America*, 213; Kammen, *Mystic Chords of Memory*, 605–6; Nevins, *Centennial Report*, 44–45; the use of living history interpreters and reenactors in the park is in Paige and Greene, *Administrative History*, adhi5a:4–6; and quoted at adhi8: 2–4. During the past ten years, historians and preservation groups have worked to separate commercial and recreational activities from the commemorative landscapes in order to preserve more of the authentic battlefield that the veterans envisioned. Most national battlefields have committed to this plan, which is explained by Gettysburg National Park Superintendent John Larschar, "From the Park," *Friends of the National Parks at Gettysburg* (Spring 2003): 3.

21. National Park Service, *Battle of Chickamauga*, 45; the current official park brochure and driving tour map also features a section on the founding of the park and credits Boynton and Van Derveer with planning the park for both historical and educational purposes, National Park Service, U.S. Department of the Interior, *Chickamauga and Chattanooga: Official Map and Guide*.

APPENDIX A

1. Adapted from the order of battle in Tucker, *Chickamauga*, unmarked pages (394–96).

2. Ibid. The Confederate order of battle reflects Bragg's adjustments on the night of 19–20 September, which created two wings out of five corps; see also Sullivan, *Chickamauga and Chattanooga Battlefields*, 17.

3. Ibid. Tucker lists Johnson's Division under Hood's Corps, while Sullivan shows him under Buckner's Corps, where he was originally located. Although under Hood's command at times on both days, Johnson was still a part of Buckner's Corps, which was also in the Left Wing.

4. This was two-thirds of Longstreet's Corps in the Army of Northern Virginia; when he was assigned the wing command early on 20 September, he turned the corps over to Hood. When Hood was wounded later that day, no one formally assumed corps command for the remainder of the battle.

5. Sullivan, *Chickamauga and Chattanooga Battlefield*, 17.

6. Ibid., 24.

7. For our purposes, the Battles for Chattanooga include all operations, skirmishes, and battles that occurred from October through November 1863, including Brown's Ferry, Lookout Mountain, Orchard Knob, and Missionary Ridge. Since the narrative of these battles is less detailed, I have only shown the armies at the corps and division levels, which reflect the changes, losses, and new additions to both armies since Chickamauga; Sullivan, *Chickamauga and Chattanooga Battlefield*, 33–42.

8. Like Longstreet's Confederates, all of these troops had been heavily engaged at the Battle of Gettysburg in July prior to their transfer to the West. Unlike Longstreet's men, who rejoined the Army of Northern Virginia in the spring of 1864, these units never returned to the Army of the Potomac. Note that Union division and brigade numbers remain consistent in all cases, even when all divisions or brigades are not present.

9. This order of battle reflects the changes in the Confederate high command and reflects Bragg's detachment of Wheeler, Forrest, Longstreet, and Buckner's commands to various operations away from Chattanooga; Sullivan, *Chickamauga and Chattanooga Battlefield*, 32–35.

10. Ibid., 42.

11. This large number includes those taken prisoner by Union forces during the route of the Confederate army from Missionary Ridge, and thus should be counted as "missing or captured."

APPENDIX B

1. Taken from "Spanish-American War Records at Camp Thomas: Camp Thomas Troop Roster," Series IV, Box 1, Folder 6, CHCH.

2. All units are infantry regiments unless otherwise designated.

3. Attached to the I Corps.

4. Troops A and B only.

5. The portion of the 6th U.S. was Company H, and the 8th U.S. was Company F; both acted mostly as provost and headquarters guards.

6. Letter designations indicate individual batteries.

7. Batteries A, C, G, and H.

APPENDIX C

1. Chickamauga and Chattanooga National Park Commission, *Legislation, Congressional and State, Pertaining to the Establishment of the Park; Regulations, Original and Amended, Governing the Erection of Monuments, Markers, and other Memorials* (Washington, D.C.: Government Printing Office, 1897), 7–10. I have maintained the format of the original as much as possible, including abbreviations, punctuation and spelling.

2. Ibid., 15.

3. Ibid., 26–27; I have included the revised 1895 regulations rather than the original 1893 version on pages 24–25. See exceptions below.

4. Details on specific weight and tire measurements have been omitted.

5. I used the language of the original legislation, which included the examples; the phrase in brackets replaces those examples in the revised regulations, ibid., 25.

BIBLIOGRAPHY

PRIMARY SOURCES AND MANUSCRIPTS

Material in the United States Army Military History Institute Archives, Carlisle Barracks, Carlisle, Pennsylvania (USAMHI)
Edwards, Oliver O. "The Sanitary Service in the War." The Army Staff College Service Schools, 25 May 1911.
Chamber of Commerce, Chattanooga, Tennessee. *Fort Oglethorpe: With Some Views of Proposed Brigade Post and Maneuver Grounds.* Published by the author, 1913.
Office of Constructing Quartermaster. "Completion Report Covering Cantonment Construction in Chickamauga Park, Georgia, 1919."

Spanish-American War veterans survey files:
Bassett, Russell. 5th Ohio.
Beckl, Earnest, 12th New York.
Berris, Brian. 3rd Ohio.
Burbank, H. L. 52nd Iowa, USWV.
Clock, Earl. 52nd Iowa.
Dewitz, Paul. Unit unknown.
Durrell, William B. 52nd Iowa, USWV.
Fowler, Charles, 12th New York, USWV.
Kimmel, William. Diary, 31st Michigan.
Noble, Evander. 3rd Wisconsin.
Prouty, E. A. 1st Vermont, USWV.
Remington, Charles. 3rd Wisconsin.
Schoonover, Howard. 52nd Iowa, USWV.
Swihart, James. 160th Indiana.
Wands, E. E. 52nd Iowa.
Wyckoff, George. 52nd Iowa.

Civil War and other manuscript collections:
Luther Bradley papers.
John Eicker papers.
Eli P. Long papers.
Robert H. G. Minty papers.

Material in the Chickamauga-Chattanooga National Military Park Archives, Fort Oglethorpe, Georgia (CHCH)

Betts, Edward E. "Annual Report, Office of the Engineer, 10 October 1898."

Boynton, Henry V. "Report on the Sanitary Conditions at Camp George H. Thomas, from the Beginning of Its Occupation until Vacated, October 1898."

———. "Camp Thomas Hospital Report."

———. "Speech by H. V. Boynton: The Third Toast, the War with Spain."

Camp Thomas Infractions and Correspondence. Fort Oglethorpe and Camp Thomas.

Camp Thomas Report and Speech, 1898–99. Veteran's correspondence.

Camp Thomas Soldier Mistreatment Report, 1898. Fort Oglethorpe and Camp Thomas.

Camp Thomas Troop Roster.

Camp Thomas War Claims Board, correspondence, 1900.

Coburn Affair. Miscellaneous file.

Dillon, Okey. 1st Ohio Cavalry, Spanish-American War.

Gannon, Vincent. "Fort Oglethorpe: A Story of Conflict and Cooperation between the Army and the Chickamauga Park Commission." Unpublished manuscript, 1964.

Kellogg diary, Ohio monuments, 1904–1917.

Mitchell, William Hugh. "Spanish-American War Journal, May-December 1898."

Rossiter, Emanuel. *"Right Forward, Four's Right": The Little Story of "Company I" Third Wisconsin Volunteers.* No date or publisher. Rossiter file.

Routine Operations to 1900, Camp Thomas correspondence, 1898.

Spanish War Memorials. War Department Park Commission correspondence, 1922–1927.

Tinney, Ed. "Chickamauga Battlefield Military Occupation—1898." Fort Thomas, Camp Oglethorpe box.

War Department Park Commission file, 1890–1933.

Willets, Gilsom. *The Triumph of Yankee Doodle.* Publisher and date unknown.

Material in the Chattanooga–Hamilton County Bicentennial Library, Chattanooga, Tennessee (CHCBL)

Chattanooga—Parks—National—Chickamauga and Chattanooga National Military Park. Clipping files.

Charles Roundtree Evans, clipping file.

Henry Clay Evans, clipping file.

Society of the Army of the Cumberland, correspondence, etc., 25 Feb 1905–May 1905.

Gates Thurston papers, Society of the Army of the Cumberland.

Material in the Chattanooga History Center, formerly the Chattanooga Regional History Museum, Chattanooga, Tennessee (CRHM)

Henry Malone, letters. Fort Thomas [Camp Oglethorpe] folder.

"Report of the Local Branch, National Relief Commission at Chattanooga." Undated letter, (1898?).

Material in the McClung Historical Collection, East Tennessee Historical Society Library, Knoxville, Tennessee (ETHS)

The Lookout 30, no. 21 (14 July 1923). U.S.—History—Spanish-American War Veteran's folder.

Material in the Ohio Historical Society Library and Archives, Columbus, Ohio (OHS)
John H. Bolton diary, 1861, and 19, 20 September 1863. 21st Ohio.
Hoff family correspondence, 1863. 93rd Ohio.
William H. Kemper papers, 1861–1925. 17th Indiana, Wilder's Brigade.

Material in the Western Reserve Historical Society Research Library, Cleveland, Ohio (WRHSRL)
Aquila Wiley papers, MS 2127.
Boynton, Henry. *Roosevelt's Military Record.* Undated pamphlet (1904?).
Chickamauga Park Commission Papers, 1892–1901

Private Collections
Fourth Ohio Infantry Association. *Dedication of Memorial Tablet and 25th Reunion, Guayana, Porto Rico, 1923.* Published by the Association. In author's collection.
Norman Smith papers, 105th Ohio Infantry. Anonymous private collection, Geauga County, Ohio.
William H. Wysong, 51st Iowa Volunteer Infantry, Spanish-American War. Papers and miscellaneous materials in author's collection.

NEWSPAPERS

Canton *Repository* (2000)
Charleston *Mercury* (1863, 1866)
Chattanooga *Times* (clippings, 1890–1910)
Knoxville *Journal and Tribune* (after July 1898)
Knoxville *Tribune* (1890 to July 1898)

PERIODICALS AND PERIODICAL DATABASES

American Periodical Series Online, 1740–1900. A database that contains scanned original articles, editorials, letters, and illustrations. This study utilized the following periodicals, which are designated by "APS Online" at the end of each note citation. <http://proquest.umi.com>.
Advocate of Peace
A Weekly News Magazine
Century Illustrated Magazine
Christian Advocate
Christian Observer
Congregationalist
The Galaxy: A Magazine of Entertaining Reading
Lippencott's
McClure's
Medical News
Monthly Review of Current Literature
New York Observer and Chronicle
North American Review

Outlook

Overland Monthly and *Out West Magazine*

Potter's American Monthly

Scientific American

Harper's Weekly. This database contains online transcriptions and scans of the weekly newspaper during the 1860s and 1870s. <http://app.harpweek.com>.

JSTOR is an online archive of important scholarly journals that contains scanned images of the original journal issues and pages. Articles used in this study will appear in notes and the bibliography as normal citations with the addition of JSTOR following the page number. <http://www.jstor.org>.

Newsletters from Battlefield Preservation Groups:

Chick-Chatt. Friends of the Chickamauga and Chattanooga National Military Park. Friends of the National Park at Gettysburg.

Hallowed Ground. Civil War Preservation Trust, CWPT; formerly the Association for Preservation of Civil War Sites and the Civil War Trust.

The Landscape. Civil War Trust (CWT).

ONLINE BOOKS AND ARTICLES

Bayne-Jones, Stanhope. *The Evolution of Preventative Medicine in the United States Army, 1607–1939.* Washington, D.C.: Office of the Surgeon General, 1968. <http://history.amedd.army.mil/booksdocs/misc/evprev/ch7.htm>.

Beth, Loren P. "President Hayes Appoints a Justice." *Supreme Court Historical Society 1989 Yearbook.* <http://www.supremecourthistory.org>.

Blog site. Major General George H. Thomas—"The Rock of Chickamauga"—"The Sledge of Nashville." <http://home.earthlink.net/~oneplez/majorgeneralgeorgehthomas-blogsite>.

Blood, Oscar Farrin. "Co. E, 52nd Regiment Iowa Volunteer Infantry 1898 Spanish American War Diary." Lane-Blood Genealogy. <http://freepages.genealogy.rootsweb.ancestry.com/~laneblood/spamwadiary.html>.

Carroon, Richard Girard. "The Military Order of the Loyal Legion: 135 Years of Service to the Nation." Military Order of the Loyal Legion of the United States: Loyal Legion Vignettes, *Sons of Union Veterans Website* (February 2000). <http://suvcw.org/mollus/art015.htm>.

Congressional Record, 73rd Congress, First Session. "'The Veterans of 1898': Extension of Remarks of Hon. Ernest Lundeen of Minnesota in the House of Representatives, Saturday, June 10, 1933." Lane-Blood Genealogy.
<http://freepages.genealogy.rootsweb.ancestry.com/~laneblood/spamwacongrec.html>.

Cunningham, S. A. "The United Confederate Veterans." Unknown publisher, 1912. <http://www.civilwarhome.com/confederateveterans.htm>.

Dell'Orto, Giovanna. "Civil War: Keeping History Alive in the First National Park." Associated Press/Pittsburgh Post-Gazette, 11 May 2006.
<http://www.post-gazette.com/pg/06131/688451–37.stm>. Civil War News Roundup. <jacampi@civilwar.org>.

Ezzell, Timothy P. "Adolph Simon Ochs." *Tennessee Encyclopedia of History and Culture*. Knoxville: University of Tennessee Press, 1998. <http://tennesseeencyclopedia.net>.

Gage, Gina. "History of the 12th Minnesota Infantry." *The Spanish-American War Centennial Website*. <http://www.spanamwar.com/12thmnhistory.htm>.

Gilman, John E. "The Grand Army of the Republic." Unknown publisher, 1910. <http://civilwarhome.com/grandarmyofrepublic.htm>.

Golden Link. "Chickamauga and Chattanooga National Military Park: Attraction Overview." *About North Georgia*. <http://ngeorgia.com/attractions/chickamauga.html>.

Graf, Mercedes. "Band of Angels: Sister Nurses in the Spanish-American War." *Prologue: The U.S. National Archives Records Administration* 34, no. 3 (Fall 2002). <www.archives.gov/publications/prologue/2002/fall/band-of-angels-1.html>.

Hanson, Jill K., and Robert W. Blythe. *Chickamauga and Chattanooga National Military Park: Historical Resource Study*. Atlanta, Ga.: Cultural Resources Stewardship, Southeast Regional Office, National Park Service, U.S. Department of the Interior, 1999. <http://www.nps.gov/history/history/online_books/chch/hrs/hrs.htm>.

Hatfield, Mark O., with the Senate Historical Office. "Biography of Vice-President Henry Wilson." *Vice Presidents of the United States, 1789–1993*. Washington D.C.: U.S. Government Printing Office, 1997. <http://www.allamericanpatriots.com/american_vice_presidents_biography_vice_president_henry_wilson_1873_1875>.

Hoogenboom, Ari. "The Disputed Election of 1876." Hayes Presidential Center. <http://www.rbhayes.org/hayes/president/display.asp?id=512&subj=president>.

Kolb, Richard K. "The Thin Gray Line: Confederate Veterans in the New South." *Veterans of Foreign Wars of the United States* (2000). <http://vaudc.org/confed_vets.html>.

Lee, Ronald. *The Origin and Evolution of the Military Park Idea*. Washington, D.C.: National Park Service, 1973. <http://www.cr.nps.gov/history/online_books/history_military/nmpidea1.htm>.

Loski, Diane. "Our Fervent Hope: Echoes of the Last Reunion," *The Gettysburg Experience* (January/February 2012), <http://thegettysburgexperience.com/past_issue_headlines/2010/july2010/hope.html>.

Lou, Arthur. "A Brief History of the Sons of Spanish-American War Veterans" Sons of Spanish-American War Veterans, <http://freepages.military.rootsweb.ancestry.com/~sunnyann/namilesbriefhistory.html>.

———. "The History of the Sons of the Spanish-American War Veterans: A National Organization." *The Spanish-American War Centennial Website*. <http://www.spanamwar.com/SSAWVhistory.htm>.

Mayne, L. H. *Camp Life of Company K, Spanish-American War 1898: A Souvenir Book Compliments of L. H. Mayne*, Emmetsburg, and reproduced in a "A Gift from Tim Laros to People of Palo Alto County," transcribed by Cathy Labath for the *Palo Alto Co. IA USGenWeb Project*. <http://www.celticcousins.net/paloalto/kcamplife.htm>.

McMahan, Arnold. "McMahan's Libby Prison Memo Book, 1863–1864." Center for Archival Collections, United States Army, Ohio Infantry Regiment, 21st, MS 562 transcripts. <http://www.bgsu.edu/colleges/library/cac/ms/trans/page53569.html>.

Means, Hon. Rice W. "The Spanish War Veterans: An address delivered by Hon. Rice W. Means at the State-wide Banquet of the United Spanish War Veterans, Department of

Minnesota, Minneapolis, Minnesota, May 11th, 1929." Lane-Blood Genealogy. <http:/ freepages.genealogy.rootsweb.ancestry.com/~laneblood/spamwaaddress.html>.

No author. "Henry Van Ness Boynton, Brigadier General United States Army." *Arlington National Cemetery Website.* <http://www.arlingtoncemetery.net/hvnboynt.htm>.

No author. "George Miller Sternberg, Brigadier General, United States Army." *Arlington National Cemetery Website.* <http://www.arlingtoncemetery.net/gmsternb.htm>.

No author. "Nathan E. Cook (1885–1992)—Last Member of the United Spanish War Veterans." <http://freepages.military.rootsweb.ancestry.com/~sunnyann/cooknathan.html>.

No author. "National Encampments United Spanish-War Veterans, Elected Commander-in-Chiefs, 1904–1998." <http://freepages.military.rootsweb.ancestry.com/~sunnyann/uswvnatlencampments.html>.

Ossad, Steven L. "The Frustrations of Leonard Wood." *Association of the United States Army: Army Magazine* (1 September 2003). <http://www.ausa.org/publications/armymagazine/archive/2003/9/Documents/Ossad_0903.pdf>.

Paige, John C., and Jerome A. Greene. *Administrative History of the Chickamauga and Chattanooga National Military Park.* Denver Colo.: Denver Service Center, National Park Service, U.S. Department of the Interior, 1983. <http://www.nps.gov/history/history/online_books/chch/adhit.htm>.

Price, Virginia. "The U.S.S. Maine Memorial, Arlington National Cemetery," and Vogel, Steve. "In Remembrance of the USS Maine; Observance Marks Anniversary of the Sinking." (16 February 1998). *Arlington National Cemetery Website.* <http:/www.arlingtoncemetery.net/ussmaine.htm>.

Redman, Bob. "Politics in the Union Army at the Battle of Chattanooga." *The Army of the Cumberland and George Thomas Source Page* (2000). <www.aotc.net/article1.htm>.

———. "Sheridan's Ride at Chickamauga." *The Army of the Cumberland and George Thomas Source Page* (2 September 2003): <http://www.aotc.net/Sheridan.htm>.

Robertson, Glenn, et al. *Staff Ride Handbook for the Battle of Chickamauga, 18–20 September, 1963.* Fort Leavenworth, Kan.: Combat Studies Institute, 1992. <http://www.cgsc.edu/carl/resources/csi/robertson3/robertson3.asp>.

Stiles, Joseph C. "Capt. Thomas E. King, or, A Word to the Army and the Country: Electronic Edition." Charleston, S.C.: South Carolina Tract Society, 1864 (Atlanta, Ga.: Franklin Printing House). Documenting the American South, University of North Carolina at Chapel Hill Libraries. <http://docsouth.unc.edu/imls/stiles/menu.html>.

University of Virginia Health System, Health Sciences Library. "Yellow Fever and the Reed Commission, 1898–1901: The Yellow Scourge in Cuba; Finding the Vector; New Strategies Work; The Impact of the Commission." Exhibit, 25 February to 28 April 1997. < http://www.hsl.virginia.edu/historical/medical_history/yellow_fever/>.

ARTICLES, BOOKS, AND THESES

Abbot, John Willis. *Blue Jackets of '98: A History of the Spanish-American War.* New York: Dodd, Mead & Company, 1904.

Adelman, Garry E. *The Early Gettysburg Battlefield: Selected Photographs from the Gettysburg National Park Commission Reports, 1895–1904.* Gettysburg, Pa.: Thomas Publications, 2001.

Alger, R. A. *The Spanish-American War.* New York: Harper & Brothers, 1901.

Ambrose, Stephen E. *Halleck: Lincoln's Chief of Staff.* Baton Rouge: Louisiana State University Press, 1961; paperback edition, 1990.

———. *Upton and the Army.* Baton Rouge: Louisiana State University Press, 1992.

American Red Cross National Relief Committee. *Reports: May 1898—March, 1899.* New York: Knickerbocker Press, 1900.

Andrews, J. Cutler. *The North Reports the Civil War.* Pittsburgh: University of Pittsburgh Press, 1955.

Armstrong, Zella. *The History of Hamilton County and Chattanooga, Tennessee.* Vol. 2. Chattanooga: Lookout Publishing Co., 1940.

Arnold, James R. *Chickamauga 1863: The River of Death.* Osprey Military Campaign Series 17. Oxford, UK: Osprey Books, 1992.

———. *The Armies of U. S. Grant.* London: Arms and Armour Press. 1995.

Atkins, Smith. *Chickamauga: A Useless, Disastrous Battle. Talk by Smith D. Atkins, Opera House, Mendota, Illinois, February 22, 1907, at invitation of Women's Relief Corps, G.A.R.* Freeport, Ill.: Journal Printing Company, 1907.

Auxier, George W. "Middle Western Newspapers and the Spanish-American War, 1895–1898." *The Mississippi Valley Historical Review* 26, no. 4 (March 1940): 523–34, JSTOR.

Ayers, Edward L. *The Promise of the New South: Life after Reconstruction.* New York: Oxford University Press, 1992.

Bailey, Thomas. "The United States and Hawaii During the Spanish-American War." *The American Historical Review* 36, no. 3 (April 1931): 552–60, JSTOR.

Barr, Ronald J. *The Progressive Army: U.S. Army Command and Administration, 1870–1914.* New York: St. Martin's Press, 1998.

Barthel, Diane. *Historic Preservation: Collective Memory and Historical Identity.* New Brunswick, N.J.: Rutgers University Press, 1996.

Barton, Michael, and Larry Logue, eds. *The Civil War Soldier: A Historical Reader.* New York: New York University Press, 2002.

Baumgardner, Richard, and Larry Strayer. *Echoes of Battle: The Struggle for Chattanooga.* Huntington, W.Va.: Blue Acorn Press, 1996.

Beatty, John. *The Citizen Soldier; or, Memoirs of a Volunteer.* Cincinnati, Ohio: Wilstach, Baldwin & Co., 1879; reprint Time-Life Collectors Library of the Civil War, 1982.

Belissary, Constantine. "The Rise of Industry and the Industrial Spirit in Tennessee, 1865–1885." *The Journal of Southern History* 19, no. 2 (May 1953): 193–215.

Belknap, Charles E. *History of the Michigan Organizations at Chickamauga, Chattanooga, and Missionary Ridge, 1863.* 2nd ed. Lansing, Mich.: Robert Smith Printing Company, 1899.

Benedict, Michael Les. "Southern Democrats in the Crisis of 1876–1877: A Reconsideration of Reunion and Reaction." *Journal of Southern History* 46, no. 4 (November 1980): 489–524, JSTOR.

Bierce, Ambrose. *Phantoms of a Bloodstained Period: The Civil War Writings of Ambrose Bierce.* Edited by Russell Duncan and David Klooster. Amherst: University of Massachusetts Press, 2002.

Billings, John D. *Hardtack and Coffee: The Unwritten Story of Army Life.* Boston: George E. Smith, 1887; reprint, Time-Life Collectors Library of the Civil War, 1982.

Blair, William. *Cities of the Dead: Contesting the Memory of the Civil War in the South, 1865–1914.* Chapel Hill: University of North Carolina Press, 2004.

Blatt, Martin H., Thomas J. Brown, and Donald Yacovone, eds. *Hope and Glory: Essays on the Legacy of the Fifty-Fourth Massachusetts Regiment.* Amherst: University of Massachusetts Press, 2001.

Blight, David. *Frederick Douglass' Civil War: Keeping Faith In Jubilee.* Baton Rouge: Louisiana State University Press, 1989.

———. *Race and Reunion: The Civil War and American Memory.* Cambridge, Mass.: Harvard University Press, 2001.

———. *Beyond the Battlefield: Race, Memory, and the American Civil War.* Amherst: University of Massachusetts Press, 2002.

Blight, David, and Brooks Simpson, eds. *Union and Emancipation: Essays on Politics and Race in the Civil War Era.* Kent, Ohio: Kent State University Press. 1997.

Blumberg, Arnold. "On They Came Like an Angry Flood." *Civil War Battles: Brother vs. Brother* (2006): 43–50.

Bobrick, Benson. *Master of War: The Life of General George H. Thomas.* New York: Simon and Schuster, 2009.

Bodnar, John. *Remaking America: Public Memory, Commemoration, and Patriotism in the Twentieth Century.* Princeton, N.J.: Princeton University Press, 1992.

———. "Pierre Nora, National Memory, and Democracy: A Review." *The Journal of American History* 87, no. 3 (December 2000): 951–63.

Bogart, Michele H. "'Maine Memorial' and 'Pulitzer Fountain': A Study in Patronage and Progress." *Winterthur Portfolio* 21, no. 1 (Spring 1986): 41–63, JSTOR.

Boge, Georgie, and Margie Holder Boge. *Paving Over the Past: A History and Guide to Battlefield Preservation.* Washington D.C.: Island Press, 1993.

Boreman, S. D., and P. J. Fitzgerald, eds. *Ashland Boys at the Front in the Spanish-American War: A Record of the Experiences of Company L, 2nd Wisconsin Volunteer Infantry.* Ashland, Wis.: The Daily Press, 1899.

Boritt, Gabor, ed. *The Gettysburg Nobody Knows.* New York: Oxford University Press, 1997.

Bowers, John. *Chickamauga and Chattanooga: The Battles That Doomed the Confederacy.* New York: Avon Books, 1994.

Boynton, Henry V. N. *Sherman's Historical Raid: The Memoirs in the Light of the Records.* Cincinnati, Ohio: Wilstach, Baldwin & Co., 1875.

———. *Chattanooga and Chickamauga: Reprint of Henry V. Boynton's Letters to the Cincinnati Commercial Gazette, August 1888.* 2nd ed., with corrections. Washington D.C.: Geo. R. Gray, Printer, 1891.

———. *Was Thomas Slow at Nashville? With a Description of the Greatest Cavalry Movement of the War and General James H. Wilson's Cavalry Operations in Tennessee, Alabama, and Georgia.* New York: F. P. Harper, 1896.

———. *Dedication of the Chickamauga and Chattanooga National Military Park, September 18–20, 1895.* Washington D.C.: U.S. Government Printing Office, 1896.

———. *The National Military Park: Chickamauga—Chattanooga; an Historical Guide.* Cincinnati, Ohio: Robert Clarke Company, 1895.

———. *The Battles of Chickamauga and Chattanooga and the Organizations Engaged,* with a new introduction by Timothy B. Smith. Knoxville: University of Tennessee Press, 2010.

Brands, H. W. *T. R.: The Last Romantic.* New York: Basic Books, 1997.

———, ed. *The Selected Letters of Theodore Roosevelt.* New York: Cooper Square Press, 2001.

Brisbin, James S. *From the Towpath to the White House: The Early Life and Public Career of James A. Garfield.* Philadelphia, Pa.: Hubbard Brothers, 1880.

Brown, Charles H. *The Correspondent's War: Journalists in the Spanish-American War.* New York: Scribner's & Sons, 1967.

Browne, Ray, ed. *Rituals and Ceremonies in Popular Culture.* Bowling Green, Ohio: Bowling Green State University Popular Press. 1980.

Brundage, W. Fitzhugh, ed. *Where These Memories Grow: History, Memory, and Southern Identity.* Chapel Hill: University of North Carolina Press, 2000.

———. *The Southern Past: A Clash of Race and Memory.* Cambridge, Mass.: Harvard University Press, 2005.

Buck, Paul. *The Road to Reunion: 1865–1900.* Boston: Little, Brown, and Company, 1937.

Buell, Thomas B. *The Warrior Generals: Combat Leadership in the Civil War.* New York: Three Rivers Press, 1997.

Cammann, William. *History of Troop A, New York Cavalry U. S. V., from May 2 to November 28, 1898 in the Spanish-American War.* New York, R. H. Russell, 1899.

Carnahan, James. *Personal Recollections of Chickamauga: A Paper Read before the Ohio Commandery of Military Order of the Loyal Legion of the U.S., January 6, 1886.* Cincinnati, Ohio: H. C. Sherrick & Co., 1886.

Cashin, Hershel V. *Under Fire with the Tenth U.S. Cavalry.* New York: F. Tennyson Neely, 1899; reprint, New York: Arno Press, 1969.

Castel, Albert. "Glorious Loser: William S. Rosecrans, Part II." *Timeline* 19, no. 2 (September-October, 2002): 31.

Chapman, Gregory D. "Army Life at Camp Thomas, Georgia During the Spanish-American War." *Georgia Historical Quarterly* 70, no. 4 (1986): 633–56.

———. "Casualties of Peace: The United States Army and Camp Thomas, Georgia, 1898." Honors paper in History, Mary Washington College, 1983.

Chicago Record. *The Chicago Record's War Stories by Staff Correspondents in the Field.* Chicago: Chicago Record, 1898.

Chickamauga and Chattanooga National Park Commission. *Dedication of the Chickamauga and Chattanooga National Military Park, September 18–20, 1895; Report of the Joint Committee to Represent Congress at the Dedication of the . . . Park.* Washington, D.C.: U.S. Government Printing Office, 1896.

———. *Legislation, Congressional and State, Pertaining to the Establishment of the Park.* Washington, D.C.: U.S. Government Printing Office, 1897.

———. *Annual Reports of the Chickamauga and Chattanooga National Military Park Commission to the Secretary of War.* Washington D.C.: U.S. Government Printing Office, 1899–1912.

Cirillo, Vincent J. "The Patriotic Odor: Sanitation and Typhoid Fever in the National Encampments during the Spanish-American War." *Army History* PB-20–00–2, no. 49 (Spring 2000): 17–23.

———. *Bullets and Bacilli: The Spanish-American War and Military Medicine.* New Brunswick: Rutgers University Press, 2004.

Cist, Henry M. *The Army of the Cumberland.* Campaigns of the Civil War Series. New York: Charles Scribner's Sons, 1882.

Clary, David A. *Eagles and Empire: The United States, Mexico, and the Struggle for a Continent*. New York: Bantam Books, 2009.

Cleaves, Freeman. *Rock of Chickamauga: The Life of General George H. Thomas*. Norman: University of Oklahoma Press, 1948.

Clinton, Catherine. *Tara Revisited: Women, War, and the Plantation Legend*. New York: Abbeville Press, 1995.

Cloyd, Benjamin G. *Haunted by Atrocity: Civil War Prisons in American Memory*. Making the Modern South, David Goldfield, series editor. Baton Rouge: Louisiana State University Press, 2010.

Cohen, Stan. *Hands Across the Wall: The 50th and 75th Reunions of the Gettysburg Battle*. Charleston, W.Va.: Pictorial Histories Publishing, 1982.

———. *Images of the Spanish-American War, April–August, 1898*. Missoula, Mont.: Pictorial Histories Publishing Co., 1997.

Confederated Southern Memorial Association. *History of the Confederated Memorial Associations of the South*. Published by the author, 1904.

Connelly, Thomas L. *The Marble Man: Robert E. Lee and His Image in American Society*. New York: Alfred Knopf, 1977.

———. *Army of the Heartland: The Army of Tennessee, 1861–1862*. Baton Rouge: Louisiana State University Press, 1967; paperback edition, 2001.

———. *Autumn of Glory: The Army of Tennessee, 1862–1865*. Baton Rouge: Louisiana State University Press, 1971; paperback edition, 2001.

Connelly, Thomas L., and Barbara Bellows. *God and General Longstreet: The Lost Cause and the Southern Mind*. Baton Rouge: Louisiana State University Press, 1982.

Connerton, Paul. *How Societies Remember*. Cambridge, Mass.: Cambridge University Press, 1989.

Connolly, James A. *Three Years in the Army of the Cumberland: The Letters and Diary of Major James A. Connolly*. Edited by Paul M. Angle. Bloomington: Indiana University Press, 1959.

Cook, Robert, J. *Troubled Commemoration: The American Civil War Centennial, 1961–1965*. Baton Rouge: Louisiana State University Press, 2007.

Cooper, John Milton. *The Warrior and the Priest: Woodrow and Theodore Roosevelt*. Cambridge, Mass.: Harvard University/Belknap Press, 1983.

Copeland, W. R. *A Complete History of the Spanish-American War of 1898*. New York: Mershon Company, 1899.

Cosmas, Graham. "From Order to Chaos: The War Department, the National Guard, and Military Policy, 1898." *Military Affairs* 29, no. 3 (Autumn 1965): 105–16.

———. *An Army For Empire: The United States Army in the Spanish-American War*. Columbia: University of Missouri Press, 1971; 2nd ed., Shippensburg, Pa.: White Mane Publishing, 1994.

Cozzens, Peter. *No Better Place to Die: The Battle of Stones River*. Urbana: University of Illinois Press, 1990; Illini Books edition, 1991.

———. *This Terrible Sound: The Battle of Chickamauga*. Urbana: University of Illinois Press, 1992.

———. *The Shipwreck of Their Hopes: The Battles for Chattanooga*. Urbana: University of Illinois Press, 1994.

Creager, Charles. *The Fourteenth Ohio National Guard—The Fourth Ohio Infantry*. Columbus, Ohio: Landon Printing and Publishing, 1899.

Curry, W. L. "A Visit to Chickamauga Twenty Years after the Battle of September 20, 1863." *Twelfth and Thirteenth Reunions of the First Ohio Volunteer Cavalry, Newark, Ohio, September 15, 1891, Galloway, Ohio, September 13, 1892.* Columbus, Ohio: Landon Printing and Publishing, 1893.

———. *Four Years in the Saddle: History of the First Regiment, Ohio Volunteer Cavalry.* Columbus, Ohio: by the author, 1898; reprint, Jonesboro, Ga.: Freedom Press, 1984

Dana, Charles. *Recollections of the Civil War.* New York: Boughman's, 1898.

Daniel, Larry J. *Shiloh: The Battle That Changed the Civil War.* New York: Simon & Schuster, 1997.

———. *Days of Glory: The Army of the Cumberland, 1861–1865.* Baton Rouge: Louisiana State University Press, 2004.

Davies, Wallace. *Patriotism on Parade: The Story of Veterans and Hereditary Organizations in the United States, 1783–1900.* Cambridge, Mass.: Harvard University Press, 1957.

Davis, Richard Harding. *The Cuban and Porto Rican Campaigns.* New York: Charles Scribner's & Sons, 1904.

Davis, William C., ed. *The Image of War, 1861–1865.* A Project of the National Historical Society. 6 vols. New York: Doubleday & Company, 1983.

———. *Civil War Parks: The Story Behind the Scenery.* Eastern National Park and Monument Association. Wickenburg, Az.: KC Publications, 1984; sixth printing, 1996.

———. *Jefferson Davis: The Man and His Hour.* New York: Harper Collins, 1991.

———. *Gettysburg: The Story Behind the Scenery.* Wickenburg, Ariz.: KC Publications, 5th printing, 1995.

———. *The Cause Lost: Myths and Realities of the Confederacy.* Lawrence: University Press of Kansas, 1996.

Day, Maie. *The Blended Flags.* Danville, Va.: Dance Brothers Company, 1898.

Dean, Eric T. *Shook All Over Hell: Post Traumatic Stress, Vietnam, and the Civil War.* Cambridge, Mass.: Harvard University Press, 1997.

DeMontravel, Peter. D. *A Hero to His Fighting Men: Nelson A. Miles, 1839–1925.* Kent, Ohio: Kent State University Press, 1998.

Denk, Danielle. "Collective Memory: Expressed and Interpreted." Honors thesis, School of Architecture, Kent State University, 1998.

Denman, Jeffery. "What Really Happened on Little Round Top?" *Civil War Times Illustrated* 44, no. 3 (August 2005): 36–40.

Dennis, Matthew. *Red, White, and Blue Letter Days: An American Calendar.* Ithaca: Cornell University Press, 2002.

Depken, Gerry, and Julie Powell. *Images of America: Fort Oglethorpe.* Charleston, S.C.: Arcadia Press, 2009.

Desjardin, Thomas A. *Stand Firm Ye Boys from Maine: The 20th Maine and the Gettysburg Campaign.* New York: Oxford University Press, 1995.

———. *These Honored Dead: How the Story of Gettysburg Shaped American Memory.* New York: De Capo Press, 2003.

Desmond, Jerry R. *Images of America: Chattanooga.* Charleston, S.C.: Arcadia Press, 1996.

———. "Camp Thomas during the Spanish-American War: A Pictorial History." *Chattanooga Regional Historical Journal* 1, no. 2 (July 1998): 118–40.

Dierks, Jack C. *A Leap to Arms: The Cuban Campaign of 1898.* Great Battles of History. Philadelphia, Pa.: J. B. Lippincott, 1970.

Dixon, Benjamin Y. "The Gettysburg Battlefield, One Century Ago." *Adams County History* 6 (2000): 5–54.

Doan, Isaac. *Reminiscences of the Chattanooga Campaign: A Paper Read at the Reunion of Company B, Fortieth Ohio Volunteer Infantry, at Xenia, O., August 22, 1894*. Richmond, Ind.: J. M. Coe's Printery, 1894.

Duncan, James, and David Ley, eds. *Place/Culture/Representation*. New York: Routledge Press, 1993.

Duncan, Russell, and Klooster, David J., eds. *Phantoms of a Bloodstained Field: The Complete Civil War Writings of Ambrose Bierce*. Boston: University of Massachusetts Press, 2002.

Durkheim, Emile. *The Elementary Forms of Religious Life*. Translated by Karen E. Fields. New York: Free Press, 1995.

Dyer, John P. *From Shiloh to San Juan: The Life of Fightin' Joe Wheeler*. Baton Rouge: Louisiana State University Press, 1989.

Ecelbarger, Gary. *Black Jack Logan: An Extraordinary Life in Peace and War*. Guilford, Conn.: Lyons Press, 2005.

Eicher, David J. *Civil War Battlefields: A Touring Guide*. Dallas, Tex.: Taylor Publishing Co., 1995.

———. *Mystic Chords of Memory: Civil War Battlefields and Historic Sites Recaptured*. Baton Rouge: Louisiana State University Press, 1998.

Einolf, Christopher, J. *George Thomas: Virginian for the Union*. Campaigns and Commanders, vol. 13. Gregory C. W. Urwin, series editor. Norman: University of Oklahoma Press, 2007.

Elliott, Sam Davis. *Soldier of Tennessee: General Alexander P. Stewart and the Civil War in the West*. Baton Rouge: Louisiana State University Press, 1999.

———, ed. *Doctor Quintard, Chaplain, C.S.A. and Second Bishop of Tennessee: The Memoir and Civil War Diary of Charles Todd Quintard*. Baton Rouge: Louisiana State University Press, 2003.

Elmendorf, John E., ed. *The 71st Regiment New York Volunteers in Cuba*. New York: n.p., 1898.

Engelhardt, Tom. *The End of Victory Culture: Cold War America and the Disillusioning of a Generation*. New York: Basic Books, 1995.

Espinosa, Mariola. "The Threat from Havana: Southern Public Health, Yellow Fever, and the U.S. Intervention in the Cuban Struggle for Independence, 1878–1898." *The Journal of Southern History* 72, no. 3 (August 2006): 541–48.

Evans, Raymond. *Chickamauga, Civil War Impact on an Area: Tsikamagi, Crawfish Springs, Snow Hill, and Chickamauga*. LaFayette, Ga.: Walker County Commission, n.d.

Fahs, Alice. "The Feminized Civil War: Gender, Northern Popular Literature, and the Memory of the War, 1861–1900." *The Journal of American History* 85, no. 4 (March 1999): 1461–94.

Fahs, Alice, and Joan Waugh, eds. *The Memory of the Civil War in American Culture*. Chapel Hill: University of North Carolina Press, 2004.

Faust, Drew Gilpin. "Alters of Sacrifice: Confederate Women and the Narratives of the War." *The Journal of American History* 76, no. 4 (March 1990): 1200–1228.

———. "The Civil War Soldier and the Art of Dying." *The Journal of Southern History* 76, no. 1 (February 2001): 1–38.

———. *Mothers of Invention: Women in the Slaveholding South during the American Civil War.* Chapel Hill: University of North Carolina Press, 1996.

———. *This Republic of Suffering: Death and the American Civil War.* New York: Alfred A. Knopf, 2008.

Fellman, Michael. *Citizen Sherman: A Life of William Tecumseh Sherman.* New York: Random House, 1995.

Fentress, James, and Chris Wickham. *Social Memory.* New Perspectives on the Past. R. I. Moore, series editor. Cambridge, Mass.: Blackwell Publishers, 1992.

Fies, William B. "The Deception of Braxton Bragg: The Tullahoma Campaign, June 23–July 4, 1863." *Blue and Gray* 10, no. 1 (October 1992): 10–21.

Fitch, Michael Hendrick. *The Chattanooga Campaign: With Especial Reference to Wisconsin's Participation Therein.* Wisconsin History Commission: Original Papers 4. Wisconsin History Commission, 1911.

Flood, Charles Bracelen. *Lee: The Last Years.* Boston: Houghton Mifflin, 1981.

Foner, Eric. *Reconstruction: America's Unfinished Revolution, 1863–1877.* New York: Harper & Row, 1986.

———. *Who Owns History? Rethinking the Past in a Changing World.* New York: Hill and Wang, 2002.

Foote, Kenneth E. *Shadowed Ground: America's Landscapes of Violence and Tragedy.* Austin: University of Texas Press, 1997.

Foster, Gaines, M. *Ghosts of the Confederacy: Defeat, the Lost Cause, and the Emergence of the New South, 1865 to 1913.* New York: Oxford University Press, 1987.

Franklin, John Hope. "A Century of Civil War Observance." *Journal of Negro History* 47, no. 2 (April 1962): 97–107, JSTOR.

Frassanito, William A. *Gettysburg: A Journey in Time.* New York: Charles Scribner's Sons, 1975.

———. *Antietam: The Photographic Legacy of America's Bloodiest Day.* New York: Charles Scribner's Sons, 1978.

———. *Grant and Lee: The Virginia Campaigns, 1864–1865.* New York: Charles Scribner's Sons, 1983.

———. *Early Photography at Gettysburg.* Gettysburg, Pa.: Thomas Publications, 1995.

———. *Gettysburg, Then and Now.* Gettysburg, Pa.: Thomas Publications, 1997.

———. *Gettysburg Then and Now Companion.* Gettysburg, Pa.: Thomas Publications, 1997.

Freeman, Douglas Southall. *Lee's Lieutenants: A Study in Command.* 3 vols. New York: Charles Scribner's Sons, 1945.

Freidel, Frank. *The Splendid Little War.* Boston: Brown, Little & Company, 1958.

Frye, James A. *The First Regiment Massachusetts Heavy Artillery: United States Volunteers in the Spanish-American War of 1898.* Boston: Colonial Company, 1899.

Fulton, Robert I., and Thomas Trueblood. *Patriotic Eloquence Relating to the Spanish-American War and Its Issues.* New York: Charles Scribner's Sons, 1900.

Fussell, Paul. *The Great War in Modern Memory.* New York: Oxford University Press, 1975.

Fussell, Paul, and Alan T. Nolan, eds. *The Myth of the Lost Cause and Civil War History.* Bloomington: Indiana University Press, 2000.

Fussell, Paul, and Joseph Glaathaar, eds. *Leaders of the Lost Cause: New Perspectives on the Confederate High Command.* Mechanicsburg, Pa.: Stackpole Books, 2004.

Gallagher, Gary. *Lee and His Generals in War and Memory.* Baton Rouge: Louisiana State University Press, 2004.

Garrison, Graham, and Parke Pierson. "Lightning at Chickamauga," *America's Civil War* (March 2003): 47–53.

Geier, Clarence R., and Stephen R. Potter, eds. *Archaeological Perspectives on the American Civil War.* Gainesville: University Press of Florida, 2000.

Gillis, John R., ed. *Commemorations: The Politics of National Identity.* Princeton, N.J.: Princeton University Press, 1994.

Glassberg, David. *Sense of History: The Place of the Past in American Life.* Amherst: University of Massachusetts Press, 2001.

Glatthaar, Joseph T. *General Lee's Army: From Victory to Collapse.* New York: Free Press, 2008.

Glidden, William B. "Internment Camps in America, 1917–1920." *Military Affairs* 37, no. 4 (December 1973): 137–41, JSTOR.

Goldfield, David. *Still Fighting the Civil War: The American South and Southern History.* Baton Rouge: Louisiana State University Press, 2002.

Gordon, John B. *Reminiscences of the Civil War.* New York: Charles Scribner's Sons, 1903; reprint Time Life Collectors Library of the Civil War, 1981.

Gould, Lewis L. *The Spanish-American War and President McKinley.* Lawrence: University Press of Kansas, 1982.

Govan, Gilbert E., and James Livengood. "Chattanooga Under Military Occupation." *The Journal of Southern History* 17, no. 1 (February 1951): 43–47, JSTOR.

Gracie, Archibald. *The Truth about Chickamauga.* Published by the author, 1911; facsimile reprint, Dayton, Ohio: Morningside Books, 1997.

Gramm, Kent. *Gettysburg: A Meditation on War and Values.* Bloomington: Indiana University Press, 1994.

Grant, Ulysses S. *Memoirs and Selected Letters.* Edited by Mary D. McFeely and William McFeely. New York: Library of America, 2nd ed., 1990.

Grebner, Constantine. *We Were the Ninth: A History of the Ninth Regiment, Ohio Volunteer Infantry April 17, 1861, to June 7, 1864.* Edited and translated by Frederic Trautmann. Kent, Ohio: Kent State University Press, 1987.

Groom, Winston. *Shrouds of Glory, from Atlanta to Nashville: The Last Great Campaign of the Civil War.* New York: Atlantic Monthly Press, 1995.

Haddon, R. Lee. *Reliving the Civil War: A Reenactor's Handbook.* Mechanicsburg, Pa.: Stackpole Books, 1996.

Halbwachs, Maurice. *The Collective Memory.* Translated from *La mémoire collective.* New York: Harper Colophon Books, 1980.

Hallock, Judith Lee. *Braxton Bragg and Confederate Defeat.* Vol. 2. Tuscaloosa: University of Alabama Press, 1991.

———. *General James Longstreet in the West: A Monumental Failure.* Civil War Campaigns and Commanders. Abilene, Tex.: McWhiney Foundation Press, 1998.

Halstead, Murat. *Full Official History of the War with Spain.* New York: W. W. Wilson, 1899.

———. *The Life and Achievements of Admiral Dewey from Montpelier to Manila.* Chicago: H. L. Barber, 1899.

Ham, Marion Franklin. *The Army Mule: A Chronic Kicker, Camp Thomas, July 4th, 1898.* Published by the author, 1898.

Hannaford, Lieutenant E. *The Handy War Book: Containing Authentic Information and Statistics of Subjects Relating to the War.* . . . Springfield, Ohio: Mast, Crowell, and Kirkpatrick, 1898.

Hard, Curtis. *Banners in the Air: The Eighth Ohio Volunteers and the Spanish-American War.* Edited by Robert H. Ferrell. Kent, Ohio: Kent State University Press, 1988.

Harden, Henry O. *History of the 90th Ohio Volunteer Infantry in the War of the Great Rebellion in the United States, 1861 to 1865.* Edited by Scott Cameron. Kent, Ohio: Kent State University Press, 2006.

Harris, Harry L., and John H. Hilton, eds. *A History of the Second Regiment NJNG, Second New Jersey Volunteers (Spanish War), Fifth New Jersey Infantry.* Patterson, N.J.: Call Printing and Publishing Company, 1908.

Hattaway, Herman, and Ethan Rafuse, eds. *The Ongoing Civil War: New Versions of Old Stories.* Columbia: University of Missouri Press, 2004.

Haughton, Andrew. *Training, Tactics, and Leadership in the Confederate Army of Tennessee: Seeds of Failure.* Military History and Policy. London: Frank Cass, 2000.

Heidler, David S., and Jeanne T. *Encyclopedia of the American Civil War: A Political, Social, and Military History.* New York: W. W. Norton & Company, 2000.

Henry, Robert Selph. *The Story of the Confederacy.* Revised edition with a foreword by Douglas Southall Freeman. Indianapolis, Ind.: Bobbs-Merrill, 1931; reprint, Cambridge, Mass.: Da Capo Press, 1989.

Herman, Daniel Justin. *Hunting and the American Imagination.* Washington, D.C.: Smithsonian Institution Press, 2001.

Hess, Earl. *The Union Soldier in Battle: Enduring the Ordeal of Combat.* Lawrence: University Press of Kansas, 1997.

Hesseltine, William B. *Civil War Prisons.* Kent, Ohio: Kent State University Press, 1962.

Hessler, James A. *Sickles at Gettysburg: The Controversial Civil War General Who Committed Murder, Abandoned Little Round Top, and Declared Himself the Hero of Gettysburg.* New York: Savas Beatie, 2009.

Hirshson, Stanley P. *Grenville M. Dodge: Soldier, Politician, Railroad Pioneer.* Bloomington: Indiana University Press, 1967.

Hobsbawm, Eric, and Terrence Ranger, eds. *The Invention of Tradition.* Cambridge, UK: Cambridge University Press, 1986.

Hoffman, Steven F. "One Man Around a Coffin: The Death of Major General George H. Thomas and the Controversy over the Battle of Nashville." Unpublished seminar paper in History, December 1978. Bluffton College, Ohio.

Hoganson, Kristen. *Fighting for American Manhood: How Gender Politics Provoked the Spanish-American and Philippine-American Wars.* New Haven, Conn.: Yale University Press, 1998.

Hoobler, James A. *Historic Photos of Chickamauga-Chattanooga.* Nashville, Tenn.: Turner Publishing Company, 2007.

Hoosen, David, ed. *Geography and National Identity.* Oxford, UK: Blackwell Publishers, 1994.

Horan, James D. *Mathew Brady: Historian with a Camera.* New York: Bonanza Books. 1955.

Horn, Stanley. *The Army of Tennessee.* Indianapolis: Bobbs-Merrill, 1941; paperback edition, Norman, Okla.: University of Oklahoma Press, 1993.

Horwitz, Tony. *Confederates in the Attic: Dispatches from the Unfinished Civil War.* New York: Pantheon Books, 1999.

Howard, L. W. *6th Ohio Volunteer Infantry War Album: Historical Events, Reminiscences, and Views of the Spanish-American War, 1898–99.* Toledo, Ohio: L. W. Howard, 1899.

Howe, Daniel Wait. *Civil War Times.* Bowen-Merrill Company, 1902.

Howe, Henry. *Historical Collections of Ohio: An Encyclopedia of the State in Two Volumes.* Published by the State of Ohio; Cincinnati: C. J. Krehbiel & Co. Printers and Binders, 1908.

Huddleson, John. *Killing Ground: Photographs of the Civil War and the Changing American Landscape.* Baltimore: Johns Hopkins University Press, 2002.

Hudson, Leonne M. *The Odyssey of a Southerner: The Life and Times of Gustavus Woodson Smith.* Macon, Ga.: Mercer University Press, 1998.

———. "The Making of a Southern Ritual: Confederate Memorial Day." *Confederate Veteran* 5 (1999): 39–40.

Hughes, Nathaniel Cheairs, and Gordon D. Whitney. *Jefferson Davis in Blue: The Life of Sherman's Relentless Warrior.* Baton Rouge: Louisiana State University Press, 2002.

Jackson, John Brinkerhoff. *A Sense of Place, a Sense of Time.* New Haven, Conn.: Yale University Press, 1994.

Jacob, Kathryn Allamong. *Testament to Union: Civil War Monuments in Washington, D.C.* Baltimore: Johns Hopkins University Press, 1998.

Janney, Caroline. *Burying the Dead but Not the Past: Ladies Memorial Associations and the Lost Cause.* Chapel Hill: University of North Carolina Press, 2008.

Johnson, Edward A. *History of Negro Soldiers in the Spanish-American War and Other Items of Interest.* Raleigh, N.C.: Capital Printing Company, 1899; New York: Johnson Reprint Company, 1970.

Johnson, Gerald White. *An Honorable Titan: A Biographical Study of Adolph S. Ochs.* Westwood, Conn.: Greenwood Press, 1970.

Johnson, Robert Underwood, and Clarence Clough Buel, eds. *Battles and Leaders of the Civil War.* 4 vols. Century Magazine, 1900; reprint, New York: Thomas Yoseloff, 1956.

Johnson, Ronald W., and Mary E. Franza. "A Splendid Little War: Does Anybody Remember in 1998?" *CRM* 18, no. 2 (1998): 5–8.

Jones, John. *A Rebel War Clerk's Diary at the Confederate States Capital.* 2 vols. Philadelphia: J. B. Lippincott & Co., 1866; reprint Time-Life Collector's Library of the Civil War, 1982.

Kammen, Michael. *In the Past Lane: Historical Perspectives of American Culture.* New York: Oxford University Press, 1997.

———. *Mystic Chords of Memory: The Transformation of Tradition in American Society.* New York: Alfred A. Knopf, 1991.

Kaser, James. A. "The Army of the Cumberland and the Battle of Chickamauga: An Exercise in Perspectivist Historical Research." Ph.D. diss., Bowling Green State University, 1991.

———. *At The Bivouac of Memory: History, Politics, and the Battle of Chickamauga.* American University Studies IX, vol. 179. New York: Peter Lang, 1996.

Kasson, Joy S. *Buffalo Bill's Wild West: Celebrity, Memory, and Popular History.* New York: Hill and Wang, 2000.

Keefer, Bradley S. "They Stood to Their Guns: The 104th Ohio Volunteer Infantry in the Civil War." Master's thesis, Kent State University, 1984.

Keene, Jennifer. *Doughboys, the Great War, and the Remaking of America.* Baltimore: Johns Hopkins University Press, 2001.

Keneally, Thomas. *American Scoundrel: The Life of the Notorious Civil War General Dan Sickles.* New York: Nan A. Talese/Doubleday, 2002.

Kepler, William. *History of the Three Months and Three Years Service from April 16, 1861 to June 22, 1864, of the Fourth Regiment Ohio Volunteer Infantry in the War for the Union.* Cleveland, Ohio: Leader Printing, 1886; reprint by Blue Acorn Press, 2000.

Kerr, Jack. *Monuments and Markers of the 29 States Engaged at Chickamauga and Chattanooga.* Produced by the author. Collegedale, Tenn.: The Collegiate Press, 1990.

Korn, Jerry. *The Fight for Chattanooga: Chickamauga to Missionary Ridge.* The Civil War. Alexandria, Va.: Time-Life Books, 1985.

Kristofferson, Kris. *Nor Shall Your Glory Be Forgot: An Essay in Photographs.* New York: St. Martin's Press, 1999.

Kross, Gary. "A Cheeky Piece of Work on Both Sides: The Alabamians Attack on Little Round Top." *Blue and Gray* 13, no. 3 (Winter 1996): 54–61.

Lamers, William M. *The Edge of Glory: A Biography of William S. Rosecrans, U.S.A.* With a new introduction by Larry J. Daniel. Baton Rouge: Louisiana State University Press, 1999.

Lash, Gary. *The Gibraltar Brigade on East Cemetery Hill: Twenty-five Minutes of Fighting, Fifty Years of Controversy, July 2, 1863.* Baltimore: Butternut and Blue, 1995.

Larner, Jesse. *Mount Rushmore: An Icon Reconsidered.* New York: Thunder's Mouth Press/Nation Books, 2002.

Lears T. J. Jackson. *No Place of Grace: Antimodernism and the Transformation of American Culture 1880–1920.* New York: Pantheon Books, 1981.

Lee, Fitzhugh, and Joseph Wheeler. *Cuba's Struggle Against Spain with the Causes for American Intervention and a Full Account of the Spanish-American War, Including Final Peace Negotiations.* New York: American Historical Press, 1899.

Leech, Margaret. *In the Days of McKinley.* New York: Harper and Brothers, 1959.

Leuchtenburg, William E., ed. *American Places: Encounters with History.* New York: Oxford University Press, 2000.

Levinson, Sanford. *Written in Stone: Public Monuments in a Changing Society.* Durham, N.C.: Duke University Press. 1998.

Linenthal, Edward, T. *Changing Images of the Warrior Hero in America: A History of Popular Symbolism.* Studies in American Religion 6. New York: Edwin Mellon Press, 1982.

———. *Sacred Ground: Americans and Their Battlefields.* Urbana, Ill.: University of Chicago Press, 1991.

Linenthal, Edward, T., and Tom Englehardt, eds. *History Wars: The Enola Gay and Other Battles for the American Past.* New York: Henry Holt, 1996.

Linderman, Gerald. *The Mirror of War: American Society and the Spanish-American War.* Ann Arbor: University of Michigan Press, 1974.

———. *Embattled Courage: Experiences of Combat in the American Civil War.* New York: Free Press, 1987.

Lindsey, T. J. *Ohio at Shiloh: Report of the Commission.* Cincinnati, Ohio: C. J. Krehbiel & Co., 1903.

Linn, Brian McAllister. *The Philippine War, 1899–1902.* Modern War Studies. Lawrence: University Press of Kansas, 2000.

Linton, Roger C. *Chickamauga: A Battlefield History in Images.* Athens: University of Georgia Press, 2004.

Litwicki, Ellen M. *America's Public Holidays, 1865–1920.* Washington, D.C.: Smithsonian Institution Press, 2000.

Loewen, James W. *Lies Across America: What Our Historical Sites Get Wrong.* New York: New Press, 1999.

Logue, Larry. *To Appomattox and Beyond: The Civil War Soldier in War and Peace.* The American Way. Chicago: Ivan Lee, 1996.

Longstreet, James. *From Manassas to Appomattox: Memoirs of the Civil War in America.* Philadelphia: J. B. Lippincott and Company, 1896.

Lowenthal, David. *The Past Is a Foreign Country.* Cambridge, UK: Cambridge University Press, 1995.

———. *Possessed by the Past: The Heritage Crusade and the Spoils of History.* New York: Free Press, 1996.

Lowry, Thomas P. *The Story the Soldiers Wouldn't Tell: Sex in the Civil War.* Mechanicsburg, Pa.: Stackpole Books, 1994.

MacCloskey, Monro. *Hallowed Ground: Our National Cemeteries.* New York: Richard Rosen Press, 1968.

Marszaleck, John F. *Commander of All Lincoln's Armies: A Life of General Henry W. Halleck.* Cambridge, Mass.: Belknap Press of Harvard University, 2004.

Martinez, J. Michael, William D. Richardson, and Ron McNinch-Su. *Confederate Symbols in the Contemporary South.* Gainesville: University Press of Florida, 2000.

Massachusetts Reform Club. *Report of the Committee of the Massachusetts Reform Club Appointed to Collect Testimony in Relation to the Spanish-American War, 1898–1899.* Boston: Geo. H. Ellis, Printer, 1899.

McCarthy, Carleton. *Detailed Minutiae of Soldier Life in the Army of Northern Virginia, 1861–1865.* Richmond, Va.: Carleton McCarthy and Company, 1882; reprint Time-Life Collector's Library of the Civil War, 1982.

McConnell, Stuart. *Glorious Contentment: The Grand Army of the Republic, 1865–1900.* Chapel Hill: University of North Carolina Press, 1992.

McDaniel, Anthonette L. "Just Watch Us Make Things Hum: Chattanooga, Adolph S. Ochs, and the Memorialization of the Civil War." *East Tennessee Historical Society's Publications* 61 (1989): 3–15.

McDonough, James Lee. *Chattanooga: Death Grip on the Confederacy.* Knoxville: University of Tennessee Press, 1985.

McDonough, James Lee, and Thomas L. Connelly. *Five Tragic Hours: The Battle of Franklin.* Knoxville: University of Tennessee Press, 1983.

McElroy, Joseph C. *Chickamauga: Record of the Chickamauga and Chattanooga National Park Commission.* Cincinnati, Ohio: Earhart & Richardson, Printers and Engravers, 1896.

McMurry, Richard. *John Bell Hood and the War for Southern Independence.* Lexington: University Press of Kentucky, 1982.

———. *The Two Great Rebel Armies: An Essay in Confederate Military History.* Chapel Hill: University of North Carolina Press, 1999.

———. *The Fourth Battle of Winchester: Toward a New Civil War Paradigm.* Kent, Ohio: Kent State University Press, 2002.

McPherson, James M., and William Cooper Jr., eds. *Writing the Civil War: The Quest to Understand.* Columbia: University of South Carolina Press, 1998.

———. *Drawn with the Sword: Reflections on the American Civil War.* New York: Oxford University Press, 1996.

Meek, A. J., and Herman Hattaway. *Gettysburg to Vicksburg: The Five Original Civil War Battlefield Parks.* Shades of Blue and Gray. Columbia: University of Missouri Press, 2001.

Mendoza, Alexander. *Confederate Struggle for Command: General James Longstreet and the First Corps in the West.* College Station: Texas A&M University Press, 2008.

Miles, Jim. *Paths to Victory: A History and Tour Guide of the Stone's River, Chickamauga, Chattanooga, Knoxville, and Nashville Campaigns.* The Civil War Campaign. Nashville, Tenn.: Rutledge Hill Press, 1991.

Miles, Nelson A. *Serving the Republic: Memoirs of the Civil War and Military Life.* New York: Harper & Brothers, 1911

Millis, Walter. *The Martial Spirit: A Study of Our War with Spain.* Boston: Houghton Mifflin Company, 1931.

Mills, Cynthia, and Pamela H. Simpson, eds. *Monuments to the Lost Cause: Women, Art, and the Landscapes of Southern Memory.* Knoxville: University of Tennessee Press, 2003.

Mitchell, Michael J. "Special Touches Added to C.S.A. Cemetery." *Civil War Courier* 18, no. 5 (June 2002): 12.

Mitchell, Reid. *The Vacant Chair: The Northern Soldier Leaves Home.* New York: Oxford University Press, 1993.

Molho, Anthony, and Gordon S. Wood, eds. *Imagined Histories: American Historians Interpret the Past.* Princeton, N.J.: Princeton University Press, 1998.

More, Donald R. "The Industrial Boom Towns of the State of Dade in Georgia." *Chattanooga Regional Historical Journal* 1, no. 2 (July 1998): 141–54.

Morgan, Wayne. *America's Road to Empire: The War with Spain and Overseas Expansion.* New York: John Wiley, 1965.

Morris, Edmund. *The Rise of Theodore Roosevelt.* New York: Coward, McCann, and Geoghegan, 1979.

Morris, Roy, Jr. "September 1863: Death of a Warrior Poet." *1863: High Tide of the Civil War.* Special 140th Anniversary Issue (2003): 72–80.

Morton, Joseph W. *Sparks from the Campfire or Tales of the Old Veterans.* Philadelphia: Keystone Publishing Company, 1890.

Morton, Virginia B. "Confederate Son Laid to Rest." *Civil War Courier* 18, no. 5 (June 2002): 3.

Mosse, George. *Fallen Soldiers: Reshaping the Memory of the World Wars.* New York: Oxford University Press, 1990.

Moyer, Anna Jane. "Tenting Tonight Boys! Gettysburg 1938—Last Reunion of the Blue and Gray." *Blue and Gray* 6, no. 1 (October 1988): 45–49.

Murtagh, William J. *Keeping Time: The History and Theory of Preservation in America.* New York: J. Wiley & Sons, 1997.

Musicant, Ivan. *Empire by Default: The Spanish-American War and the Dawn of the American Century.* New York: Henry Holt, 1998.

Nashville, Chattanooga & St. Louis Railway. *Southern Battlefields: A List of Battlefields on or Near the Lines of the Nashville, Chattanooga & St. Louis Railway and Western Atlantic Railroad.* Published by the authors, n.d.

———. *Battlefields in Dixie Land and Chickamauga National Military Park.* Chicago: Poole Brothers, 1928.

Neff, John R. *Honoring the Civil War Dead: Commemoration and Problem of Reconciliation.* Modern War Studies. Series editor, Theodore Wilson. Lawrence: University Press of Kansas, 2005.

Nevins, Allen. *The Civil War Centennial: A Report to Congress.* Washington, D.C.: Civil War Centennial Commission, 1968.

New York, State of. *Proceedings of the United Spanish War Veterans, Department of New York for the Year 1921; the Eighteen Annual Encampment Held at Utica, N.Y., July 17th, 18th, 19th, and 20th, 1921.* Albany, N.Y.: J. B. Lyon Company, Printers, 1923.

Nobile, Philip, ed. *The Bombing of Hiroshima and Nagasaki—Judgment at the Smithsonian: The Uncensored Script of the Smithsonian's 50th Anniversary of the Enola Gay.* New York: Marlowe and Company, 1995.

Noe, Kenneth W. *Perryville: The Grand Havoc of Battle.* Lexington: University Press of Kentucky, 2001.

Nora, Pierre. "Between Memory and History: *Les Lieux de Memoire.*" *Representations* 26 (Spring 1989): 8.

Oates, William C. *The War Between the Union and the Confederacy and Its Lost Opportunities.* Originally published 1905; reprint, Dayton, Ohio: Morningside Press, 1974.

Official History of the Ohio National Guard and Ohio Volunteers: A Complete Description and Chronological Record. Cleveland, Ohio: Plain Dealer Publishing Company, 1901.

Oliver, William H. *Roughing It with the Regulars.* New York: William F. Parr, 1901.

O'Neal, Angela. "Remembering *The Maine:* Memory, Ritual, and Women's Roles in the United Spanish War Veterans of Elyria, Ohio." Honors thesis, Kent State University, 1998.

One-hundred and Third Ohio Volunteer Infantry. *Personal Reminiscences and Experiences: Campaign Life in the Union Army from 1862–1865.* Oberlin, Ohio: News Printing Co. 1903; reprint by the 103rd OVI Memorial Association, Fred Weidner & Sons, 1984.

O'Toole, G. J. A. *The Spanish War: An American Epic—1898.* New York: Norton, 1984.

Pape-Findlay, Nancy. *The Invincibles: The Story of the Fourth Ohio Volunteer Cavalry, 1861–1865.* Tecumseh, Mich.: Blood Road Publishing, 2002.

Parry, Albert. "John B. Turchin: Russian General in the American Civil War." *Russian Review* 1, no. 2 (April 1942): 44–60, JSTOR.

Paterson, Thomas G. "United States Intervention in Cuba, 1898: Interpretations of the Spanish-American-Cuban-Filipino War." *The History Teacher* 29, no. 3 (May 1996): 341–61, JSTOR

Payne, Phillip. "Mixed Memories: The Warren G. Harding Memorial Association and President's Hometown Legacy." *The Historian* 64, no. 2 (Winter 2002): 257–74.

Perry, James M. *Touched by Fire: Five Presidents and Civil War Battles That Made Them.* New York: Public Affairs, 2005.

Peterson, Merrill D. *Lincoln in American Memory.* New York: Oxford University Press, 1994.

Pettegrew, John. "The Soldier's Faith: Turn-of-the-century Memory of the Civil War and the Emergence of Modern American Nationalism." *Journal of Contemporary History* 31, no. 1 (January 1996): 49–73, JSTOR.

Piatt, Donn. *General George H. Thomas: A Critical Biography*, with concluding chapters by Henry V. Boynton. Cincinnati, Ohio: Robert Clarke, 1893.

Piehler, G. Kurt. *Remembering War the American Way*. Washington, D.C.: Smithsonian Institution Press, 1995.

Pindell, Richard. "The True High Water Mark of the Confederacy: Pickett's Charge . . . or Little Round Top?" *Blue and Gray* 5, no. 4 (March 1988): 18–19.

Pittenger, William. *Daring and Suffering: A History of the Great Railroad Adventure*. Philadelphia: J. W. Daughaday Publishers, 1863; reprint Time-Life Collectors Library of the Civil War, 1982.

Platt, Barbara. *This Is Holy Ground: A History of the Gettysburg Battlefield*. Harrisburg, Pa.: Huggins Press, 2001.

Poole, Robert M. *On Hallowed Ground: The Story of Arlington National Cemetery*. New York: Walker and Company, 2009.

Powell, Dave. "The 96th Illinois and the Battles for Horseshoe Ridge, 1863 and 1895." *North & South* 8, no. 2 (March 2005): 51–59.

Powell, David A., and David A. Friedrichs. *The Maps of Chickamauga: An Atlas of the Chickamauga Campaign, Including the Tullahoma Operations, June 22—September 23, 1863*. New York: Savas Beatie, 2009.

Price, William H. *The Civil War Centennial Handbook*. Civil War Associates Research. Arlington, Va.: Prince Lithograph, 1st ed., 1961.

Prokopowicz, Gerald J. *All for the Regiment: The Army of the Ohio, 1861–1862*. Chapel Hill: University of North Carolina Press, 2001.

Reardon, Carol. *Pickett's Charge in History and Memory*. Chapel Hill: University of North Carolina Press, 1997.

Reed, Walter, Victor C. Vaughn, and Edward O. Shakespeare. *Report on the Origin and Spread of Typhoid Fever in U.S. Military Camps During the Spanish War of 1898*. Washington, D.C.: U.S. Government Printing Office, 1904.

———. *Abstract of Report on the Spread of Typhoid Fever in U.S. Military Camps during the Spanish War of 1898*. Washington, D.C.: U.S. Government Printing Office, 1900.

Rettie, Dwight. *Our National Park System: Caring for America's Greatest Natural and Historic Treasures*. Urbana: University of Illinois Press, 1995.

Rice, Ralsa. *Yankee Tigers: Through the War with the 125th Ohio*. Edited by Richard A. Baumgartner and Larry M. Strayer. Huntington, W.Va.: Blue Acorn Press, 1982.

Ridley, Bromfield L. *Battles and Sketches of the Army of the Tennessee*. Mexico, Mo.: Missouri Printing and Publishing Co., 1906; reprint Dayton, Ohio: Morningside Press, 1978.

Roberts, Randy, and James S. Olsen. *A Line in the Sand: The Alamo in Blood and Memory*. New York: Free Press, 2001.

Robertson, William G. "The Chickamauga Campaign: The Fall of Chattanooga." *Blue & Gray* 23, no. 4 (Fall 2006): 6–28, 43–50.

———. "The Chickamauga Campaign: McLemore's Cove—Rosecrans' Gamble, Bragg's Lost Opportunity." *Blue & Gray* 23, no. 6 (Spring 2007): 6–26, 41–50.

———. "The Chickamauga Campaign: The Armies Collide—Bragg Forces His Way Across Chickamauga Creek." *Blue & Gray* 24, no. 3 (Fall 2007): 6–28, 39–50.

———. "The Chickamauga Campaign: The Battle of Chickamauga—Day 1, September 19, 1863." *Blue & Gray* 24, no 6 (Spring 2008): 6–29, 40–52.

———. "The Chickamauga Campaign: The Battle of Chickamauga—Day 2, September 20, 1863." *Blue & Gray* 25, no. 2 (Summer 2008): 6–30, 40–50.

Rogers, J. L. *The Civil War Battles of Chickamauga and Chattanooga.* J. L Rogers, 1942.

Rose, Anne C. *Victorian America and the Civil War.* Cambridge, UK: Cambridge University Press, 1992.

Rosenberg, R. B. *Living Monuments: Confederate Soldier's Homes in the New South.* Chapel Hill: University of North Carolina Press, 1993.

Rudd, Robin A. *Signed with Their Honor: A Photographic Essay Celebrating 100 Years of the Chickamauga and Chattanooga National Military Park.* Published by the Friends of the Chickamauga and Chattanooga National Military Park, 1995.

Rule, William. *Standard History of Knoxville, Tennessee.* Chicago: Lewis Publishing Company, 1900.

Ryan, Daniel J. *Ohio in Four Wars: A Military History.* Columbus, Ohio: Heer Publishing, 1917.

Samuels, Peggy, and Harold Samuels. *Teddy Roosevelt at San Juan: The Making of a President.* College Station: Texas A&M University Press, 1997.

Sands, Francis. "The Loyal Legion and the Civil War." *War Papers, Military Order of the Loyal Legion of the United States, D.C. Commandery* 86 (March 1912): 10.

Sauers, Richard. A. "John B. Bachelder: Government Historian of the Battle of Gettysburg." *Gettysburg—Historical Articles of Lasting Interest* 3 (July 1990): 115–27.

———. *Pennsylvania in the Spanish-American War: A Commemorative Look Back.* Harrisburg, Pa.: Pennsylvania Capitol Preservation Committee, 1998.

———. "From Hallowed Ground to Training Ground: Chickamauga's Camp Thomas, 1898." *Civil War Regiments: A Journal of the American Civil War* 7, no. 1 (Spring, 2000).

Savage, Kirk. *Standing Soldiers, Kneeling Slaves: Race, War, and Monument in Nineteenth-Century America.* Princeton, N.J.: Princeton University Press. 1997.

Sawyer, Franklin. *A Military History of the 8th Regiment Ohio Volunteer Infantry; its Battles, Marches, and Army Movements.* Original edited by George Groot. Cleveland, Ohio: Fairbanks & Company, 1881; reprint Huntington, W.Va.: Blue Acorn Press, 1994.

Schacter, Daniel L., ed. *Memory Distortion: How Minds, Brains, and Societies Construct the Past.* Cambridge, Mass.: Harvard University Press, 1995.

Schroeder, Patrick, ed. *Tar Heels: Five Points in the Record of North Carolina in the Great War of 1861–5.* Goldsboro, N.C.: Nash Brothers, 1904; reprint Daleville, Va.: Schroeder Publications, 2001.

Sellars, Richard West. *Pilgrim Places: Civil War Battlefields, Historic Preservation, and America's First National Military Parks, 1863–1900.* Fort Washington, Pa.: Eastern National, 2005.

Seymour, Digby Gordon. *Divided Loyalties: Fort Sanders and the Civil War in East Tennessee.* 3rd ed., rev. Knoxville: East Tennessee Historical Society, 2002.

Shaffer, Marguerite. *See America First: Tourism and National Identity, 1880–1940.* Washington, D.C.: Smithsonian Institution Press, 2000.

Sheets, Georg R. *The Grand Review: The Civil War Continues to Shape America.* York, Pa.: York, Inc. 2000.

Sheridan, Phillip H. *Personal Memoirs of P. H. Sheridan*. New York: C. L. Webster, 1888; reprinted by De Capo Press, with a new introduction by Jeffery Wert, 1992.

Sherman, William T. *The Memoirs of General William T. Sherman, Written by Himself.* 2 vols. 4th ed. New York: Charles Webster, 1891.

———. *The Capture of Atlanta and the March to the Sea: From Sherman's Memoirs.* Mineola, N.Y.: Dover Publications, 2007.

Sidebottom, A. W. *The "Boys" in Camp Thomas, Chickamauga-Chattanooga National Battlefield Park, GA.* Chattanooga, Tenn.: Sidebottom & Kerr, 1898.

Silber, Nina. *The Romance of Reunion: Northerners and the South 1865–1900.* Chapel Hill: University of North Carolina Press, 1993.

Silbey, David J. *A War of Frontier and Empire: The Philippine-American War, 1899–1902.* New York: Hill and Wang, 2007.

Simpson, Brooks D. *Ulysses S. Grant: Triumph over Adversity, 1822–1865.* Boston: Houghton Mifflin Company, 2000.

Smith, Jacob. *Camps and Campaigns of the 107th Ohio Volunteer Infantry from August 1862 to July 1865.* Reprint of undated, unpublished original. Navarre, Ohio: Indian River Graphics, 2000.

Smith, Timothy. "A Western Gettysburg: Alexander Peter Stewart and the Founding of Chickamauga and Chattanooga National Military Park." Unpublished seminar paper, Mississippi State University, n.d.

———. *This Great Battlefield of Shiloh: History, Memory, and the Establishment of a Civil War National Military Park.* Knoxville: University of Tennessee Press, 2004.

———. *The Untold Story of Shiloh: The Battle and the Battlefield.* Knoxville: University of Tennessee Press, 2006.

———. *The Golden Age of Battlefield Preservation: The Decade of the 1890s and the Establishment of America's First Five Military Parks.* Knoxville: University of Tennessee Press, 2008.

———. *A Chickamauga Memorial: The Establishment of America's First Civil War National Military Park.* Knoxville: University of Tennessee Press, 2009.

Smith, William Farrar. *The Re-opening of the Tennessee River near Chattanooga, October 1863.* Wilmington, Del.: Mercantile Printing Co., 1895.

———. *Brown's Ferry, 1863.* Philadelphia: E. McManus Jr. and Company, 1901.

Snow, William P. *Lee and His Generals.* New York: Richardson, 1865, 1867; reprint, New York: Fairfax Press, 1982.

Society of the Army of the Cumberland. *Report of the First Meeting.* Cincinnati, Ohio: Robert Clarke & Co., 1868.

———. *Twenty-Third Reunion, Chickamauga, Georgia, 1892.* Cincinnati, Ohio: Robert Clarke & Co., 1892.

———. *Twenty-Eighth Reunion, Detroit, Michigan, September 27 and 28, 1899.* Cincinnati, Ohio: Robert Clarke & Co., 1899.

———. *Twenty-Ninth Reunion, October 1900.* Cincinnati, Ohio: Robert Clarke & Co., 1901.

———. *Thirty-First Reunion, Washington, D.C., October, 1903.* Cincinnati, Ohio: Robert Clarke & Co., 1904.

———. *Thirty-Second Reunion, September, Indianapolis, Indiana, September, 1904.* Cincinnati, Ohio: Robert Clarke & Co., 1905.

———. *Thirty-Third Reunion, Chattanooga, Tennessee, September 18, 19, 20, 1905.* Cincinnati, Ohio: Robert Clarke & Co., 1906.

———. *Thirty-Fourth Reunion, Chattanooga, Tennessee, October 17 and 18, 1906.* Chattanooga, Tenn.: McGowan-Cooke Printing Co., 1907.

———. *Burial of General Rosecrans, Arlington National Cemetery, May 17, 1902.* Cincinnati, Ohio: Robert Clarke & Co., 1903.

Society of the Army of the Tennessee. *Report of the Proceedings of the Society of the Army of the Tennessee's 38th Meeting.* Cincinnati, Ohio: Chas. O Ebel Printing Co., 1909.

Somers, Orlando. *A Protest Against and Appeal from the Action of the Indiana-Chickamauga Park Commission, and Others to the Commissioners of the National Military Park, Chickamauga, Georgia . . . by the Survivor's Association of the 8th Indiana Cavalry, 39th Regiment, Indiana Volunteers.* Kokomo, Ind.: Tribune Printing, 1901.

Sorrell, G. Moxey. *At the Right Hand of Longstreet: Recollections of a Confederate Staff Officer.* New York: Neal Co., 1905; reprint, Omaha: University of Nebraska Press, Bison Books paperback, 1999.

Spruill, Matt. *Guide to the Battle of Chickamauga.* U.S. Army War College Guide to Civil War Battles. Lawrence: University Press of Kansas, 1996.

Steelman, Joseph. *North Carolina's Role in the Spanish-American War.* Raleigh: North Carolina Department of Cultural Resource, Division of Archives and History, 1975.

Stevens, Joseph, E. *1863: The Rebirth of a Nation.* New York: Bantam Books, 1999.

Sternberg, George M. *Sanitary Lessons of the War.* Washington, D.C.: Adams, 1912.

Steward, T. G. *The Colored Regulars in the United States Army.* Philadelphia: A.M.E. Book Concern, 1904; reprint series, The American Negro; His History and Literature, New York: Arno Press, 1969.

Stillwell, Leander. *The Story of a Common Soldier of Army Life in the Civil War, 1861–1865.* Kansas City, Mo.: Franklin Hudson Publishing, 1920; reprint of the 2nd edition, Time-Life Collector's Library of the Civil War, 1983.

Sturken, Marita. *Tangled Memories: The Vietnam War, the AIDS Epidemic, and the Politics of Remembering.* Berkeley: University of California Press, 1997.

Sullivan, James R. *Chickamauga and Chattanooga Battlefields: Chickamauga and Chattanooga National Battlefield Park, Georgia-Tennessee.* National Park Service Historical Handbook 25. Washington, D.C.: National Park Service, 1956.

Svenson, Peter. *Battlefield: Farming a Civil War Battleground.* Boston: Faber & Faber, 1992.

Sword, Wiley. *Mountains Touched with Fire: Chattanooga Besieged, 1863.* New York: St. Martin's Press, 1995.

Symonds, Craig L. *Stonewall of the West: Patrick Cleburne and the Civil War.* Modern War Studies. Lawrence: University Press of Kansas, 1997.

Thackery, David T. *A Light and Uncertain Hold: A History of the Sixty-sixth Ohio Volunteer Infantry.* Kent, Ohio: Kent State University Press, 1999.

Thelen, David. "Memory in American History," *Journal of American History* 75, no. 4 (March 1989): 1127.

———. "History after the Enola Gay Controversy: An Introduction," *Journal of American History* 82, no. 3 (December 1995): 1029–35.

Titherington, Richard H. *A History of the Spanish-American War of 1898.* New York: D. Appleton and Company, 1900.

Thomas, Emory. *Travels to Hallowed Ground: A Historian's Journey to the American Civil War.* Columbia: University of South Carolina Press, 1897.

Thomas, Evan. *The War Lovers: Roosevelt, Lodge, Hearst, and the Rush to Empire, 1898.* New York: Little, Brown, and Company, 2010.

Toplin, Robert B., ed. *Ken Burns' "The Civil War": Historians Respond.* New York: 1996.

Traxel David. *1898: The Birth of the American Century.* New York: Vintage Books, 1998.

Trudeau, Noah Andre. *Southern Storm: Sherman's March to the Sea.* New York: Harper Collins, 2008.

Tucker, Glenn. *Chickamauga: Bloody Battle in the West.* Indianapolis, Ind.: Bobbs-Merrill, 1961; reprint, Dayton, Ohio: Morningside Books, 1992.

Tucker, Phillip Thomas. *Exodus from the Alamo: The Anatomy of the Last Stand Myth.* Philadelphia: Casemate Publishers, 2010.

Turchin, John B. *Chickamauga.* Chicago: Fergus Printing Co., 1888.

Turner, Rory. "Bloodless Battles: The Civil War Reenacted." *TDR* 34, no. 4 (Winter 1990): 123–36, JSTOR.

United Spanish War Veterans. *Proceedings of the State Convention of the 81st National Convention, Indianapolis, Indiana, September 8–13, 1979.* Washington, D.C.: U.S. Government Printing Office, 1980.

U.S. Civil War Centennial Commission. *The Civil War Centennial: A Report to Congress.* Washington, D.C., 1968.

U.S. Senate. *Report of the Commission to Investigate the Conduct of the War Department in the War with Spain.* 8 vols. Washington, D.C.: U.S. Government Printing Office, 1900.

U.S. War Department. *The War of the Rebellion: A Compilation of the Official Records of the Union and Confederate Armies.* Washington, D.C.: U.S. Government Printing Office, 1880–1901; reprint Pasadena, Calif.: Historical Times/Broadfoot Publishing, 1985.

Unknown author. *The Green Mountain Boys at Chickamauga (Georgia).* Mexico, Mo.: Head Brothers, 1898.

Van Horne, Thomas. *History of the Army of the Cumberland, Its Organization, Campaigns, and Battles.* 2 vols. Cincinnati, Ohio: Robert Clarke & Co., 1875.

———. *The Life of Major General George H. Thomas.* New York: Charles Scribner's Sons, 1882.

Vermont Adjutant and Inspector General's Office. *Vermont in the Spanish-American War, 1898.* Montpelier, Vt.: General Assembly, 1929.

Walker, Dale. *The Boys of '98: Theodore Roosevelt and the Rough Riders.* New York: Tom Doherty Associates, 1998.

Ward, Geoffrey C., with Ken Burns and Ric Burns. *The Civil War: An Illustrated History.* New York: Alfred Knopf, 1999; eighth paperback printing, 2000.

Ward, Robert D. "A Note of General Leonard Wood's Experimental Companies." *Military Affairs* 35, no. 3 (October 1971): 92–93 JSTOR.

Watkins, Sam. *1861 vs. 1862. Co. Aytch, Maury Grays, First Tennessee Regiment; or, a Side Show of the Big Show.* Reprint of original, Dayton, Ohio: Morningside Books, 1992.

Watterson, Henry. *History of the Spanish-American War.* New York: W. W. Wilson, 1898.

Waugh, Joan. *U. S. Grant: American Hero, American Myth.* Chapel Hill: University of North Carolina Press, 2010.

Waugh, Joan, and Gary M. Gallagher, eds. *Wars within a War: Controversy and Conflict over the American Civil War.* Chapel Hill: University of North Carolina Press, 2009.

Weeks, Jim. *Gettysburg: Memory, Market, and an American Shrine.* Princeton, N.J.: Princeton University Press, 2003.

Weir, William. *Fatal Victories.* Hamden, Conn.: Archon Press, 1993.

Wei-Sang Hsieh, Wayne. *West Pointers and the Civil War: The Old Army in War and Peace.* Civil War America. Series edited by Gary Gallagher. Chapel Hill: University of North Carolina Press, 2009.

Welch, Richard E. *Response to Imperialism: The United States and the Philippine-American War, 1899–1902.* Chapel Hill: University of North Carolina Press, 1979.

Welcher, Frank J. *The Union Army 1861–1865: Organization and Operations.* Vol. II: *The Western Theater.* Bloomington: Indiana University Press, 1993.

Werstein, Irvin. *Turning Point for America: The Story of the Spanish-American War.* New York: Messner, 1964.

Wert, Jeffery D. *General James Longstreet: The Confederacy's Most Controversial Soldier, a Biography.* New York: Simon and Schuster, 1993.

———. *The Sword of Lincoln: The Army of the Potomac.* New York: Simon and Schuster, 2005.

West, Patricia. *Domesticating History: The Political Origins of America's House Museums.* Washington, D.C.: Smithsonian Institution Press, 1999.

Wiggins, David N. *Images of America: Georgia's Confederate Monuments and Cemeteries.* Charleston, S.C.: Arcadia Press, 2006.

Wilkerson, Marcus. *Public Opinion and the Spanish-American War: A Study in War Propaganda.* New York: Russell & Russell, 1932; reissued, 1967.

Willis, Gary. *Lincoln at Gettysburg: The Words That Remade America.* New York: Simon & Schuster, 1992.

Wilson, Charles Reagan. *Baptized in Blood: The Religion of the Lost Cause, 1865–1920.* Athens: University of Georgia Press, 1980.

Wilson, James H. *Under the Old Flag: Recollections of Military Operations in the War for the Union, the Spanish War, the Boxer Rebellion, Etc.* New York: D. Appleton and Company, 1907.

Witelic, Janet, ed. *Native North American Literary Companion.* Detroit, Mich.: Visible Ink Press, 1998.

Women's National Relief Association Organized for the Emergency of the Spanish American War. *Report: March 1898 to January 1899.* New York: Board of Directors, 1899.

Wood, W. J. *Civil War Generalship: The Art of Command.* Westport, Conn.: Praeger, 1997.

Woodward, C. Vann. *The Origins of the New South, 1877–1913.* A History of the South IX. Baton Rouge: Louisiana State University Press, 1951, 1971.

Woodworth, Steven E., ed. *Leadership and Command in the American Civil War.* Campbell, Calif.: Savas Woodbury Publishers, 1995.

———. *Six Armies in Tennessee: The Chickamauga and Chattanooga Campaigns.* Lincoln: University of Nebraska Press, 1998.

———. *Chickamauga: A Battlefield Guide with a Section on Chattanooga.* This Hallowed Ground: Guides to Civil War Battlefields. Lincoln: University of Nebraska Press. 1999.

———. *Jefferson Davis and His Generals: The Failure of Confederate Command in the West.* Lawrence: University Press of Kansas, 1999.

———. *No Band of Brothers: Problems in the Rebel High Command.* Shades of Blue and Gray. Columbia: University of Missouri Press, 1999.

————. *Nothing but Victory: The Army of the Tennessee, 1861–1865.* New York: Alfred A. Knopf, 2005.

————, ed. *The Chickamauga Campaign.* Civil War Campaigns in the Heartland. Series edited by Steven D. Woodworth. Carbondale: Southern Illinois University Press, 2010.

Wooster, Robert. *Nelson A. Miles and the Twilight of the Frontier Army.* Lincoln: University of Nebraska Press, 1993.

Yerkes, Robert M. "Measuring the Mental Strength of an Army." *Proceedings of the National Academy of Sciences of the United States of America* 4, no. 10 (15 October 1918): 295–97, JSTOR.

INDEX